# The Australian
# Wine
# Annual
# 2005

## The Essential Guide to Australian Wine

This best-selling guide
has just become even better…

■ Many more wines and wineries than ever before

■ New: Australia's best under-$20 wines

■ Tasting notes for every new release

■ Simplified layout and key

Published and designed in Australia.

Jeremy Oliver Pty Ltd trading as OnWine Publications
565 Burwood Rd Hawthorn, Victoria, 3122 Australia
Tel: 61 3 9819 4400    Fax: 61 3 9819 5322

| | |
|---|---|
| Printed by | KHL Printing Co Pte Ltd, Singapore |
| Design and Layout by | Artifishal Studios, Melbourne, Victoria, Australia |
| Cover photograph by | Stocksouth |
| Background photograph by | Peter Russell |
| Distributed to book retailers in Australia by | Pan Macmillan Free call 1800 684 459 Free fax 1800 241 310 |
| Distributed to wine retailers in Australia by | Tucker Seabrook Tel:    02 9666 0000 Fax    02 9666 0011 |

Copyright © Jeremy Oliver 2004

ISBN 0-9581032-3-2

# Contents

# Introduction

A new year, a new format. This edition of *The Australian Wine Annual* mightn't look it from the outside, but it's a helluva lot bigger than any of its predecessors. Why? My designers had the bright idea that this book needed a revamp, so they roughed out a format that included tasting notes for each current vintage. Since, to be perfectly frank, I had never been entirely comfortable publishing scores without tasting notes, I jumped at the change.

And now, with a scrambled mind now programmed into communicating about anything and everything in wine-tasting-note-speak (eg: 'What a marvellous car that new BMW M3 is — a terrific shape and a tightly knit package that seamlessly integrates power, structure and style, with a lingering high-octane finish of polycarbon-scented exhaust') that is driving those around me close to distraction, I'm still glad I did it.

Oddly enough, while many wine drinkers rate me as a pretty hard-nosed marker who only grudgingly acknowledges quality when I have absolutely no choice but to, many in the wine industry see me as soft. I'm not unhappy at that, and I firmly believe that a good critic uses as wide a range of scores as possible. The inclusion of tasting notes now gives the reader a chance at least to follow the rationale of why I allocated the score I did, while then of course being perfectly free to agree or disagree with my assessment.

The other big change is the move to marking wine out of 100 points, which I discuss in some detail later on. I also explain later in the book why I have chosen the conversion I have, but the major considerations were to move to a system that facilitates as wide a spread of scores as I can, as well as to adopt a system that was not out of synch with other writers I respect. There is a popular tendency amongst critics to push scores out of 100 so high that one wonders if they are not really marking out of 110. A score of 96, for instance, should genuinely mean that the marker is convinced that only four quality levels could possibly exist above it. As for 100 points, by simple definition that score implies a wine that cannot be improved upon, and one that has no peer, anywhere or anytime. I still haven't tasted a wine like that, but that's possibly simply because I believe there's always going to be a better wine, now or in the future.

So, now that this book has become the equivalent of two rolled into one, I'm not about to waste my annual chance to step up and onto the soapbox. So here goes.

Anyone with any level of contact with Australian wine will be aware that there is currently more of it than ever before. And, despite an astonishing growth in the penetration of export markets, Australia is presently making more wine than it is selling. This, of course, is not the first time it has happened, although for many financial journalists, it is the first time in their conscious understanding of wine.

Spend five minutes reading the business pages of most papers and you could be forgiven for thinking that the top end of Australian wine was about to close shop. Nothing, of course, could be farther from the truth. By and large, the financial markets still expect wine industries to change direction like an antelope on the run, forgetting that wine takes about four years to move from an idea around a discussion table and into a bottle. In my opinion, Australia's largest wine producers, regularly pilloried in the business press, are making a much better fist of their opportunities than they are being given credit for.

Those who aren't doing it as well are the many small producers still finding it tough to get their wares to market. The Winemakers Federation of Australia had a significant win in this year's Federal Budget, achieving an exemption on the first A$1 million of domestic sales from the so-called Wine Equalisation Tax (WET), which will exempt more than 1,700 Australian wineries from this 29% wholesale impost above the 10% GST. It's a galling reflection of the straits in which some producers find themselves that they are seriously contemplating passing the benefit onto their customers and the trade, instead of doing what the wine industry and Government were hoping for, and pocketing it. Many wineries will not only look the gift horse in the mouth, but give it to someone else.

Australia desperately needs to be taken more seriously as a maker of top-end wine. Everyone knows we can make oceans of affordable and quaffable shiraz and chardonnay. And despite the best efforts of many journalists around the world, these are still enjoyed for what they are by countless thousands of people every day. Australia does make world-class top quality wine, but not enough of it. Not enough to fill the shelves and restaurant lists, should the rest of the world ever get really serious about it. I firmly believe that Australia can make more top shelf stuff, and that it would then find secure markets overseas. Not without some work and not without some expense, but the returns would be worth it.

Much of what has been criticised domestically and internationally as Australian makers taking their eyes collectively off the quality ball can fairly be blamed on a succession of tough vintages. We have yet to see a quality, all-round national vintage since 1998. The effects of the largely dry, hot vintages have been cumulative. 2002 popped up as a cool summer, but didn't bring much moisture and stress relief for a country that went straight back onto the frypan in 2003 and 2004. And the wine industry, which while being imperfect remains a significantly more efficient and responsible user of scarce inland water than certain other agricultural industries, has much to do if it is to avoid the looming danger represented by the increasing scarcity and salinity of this critical resource.

As the scores in this book indicate, 2002 provided its share of highlights, especially in the Barossa Valley, McLaren Vale and the Adelaide Hills. I have however been horrified at the number of South Australian wines (from these and other regions) made in this vintage from what appear to have been seriously stressed fruit — and this from the coolest season ever recorded in this State. That doesn't say much for the present state of Australian viticulture.

To finish on a more positive note, just open a bottle of 2003 Eden Valley Riesling.

Cheers.

## Acknowledgements

This book would not have been created without the dedicated assistance provided by a number of people. Thanks to Toby Hines, Stephen O'Connor and Frank Ameneiro of Artifishal Studios for their help in creating and implementing this new design format. Thanks also to the team from my office that has included Michael Wollan, Robyn Lee, Jane Morgan, Peter Bessey, Ian Daubney and my father, Rodney Oliver. It's a finicky and time-consuming process, but a worthwhile one! Thanks also to my wife, Jennifer, and son, Benjamin, who have virtually learned to live without me over the last few months.

Jeremy Oliver, July 2004.

# How to use this book

## Finding the wine or winery

It's dead easy to find the wine you're after in *The Australian Wine Annual*. Each winery or brand of wine is presented in alphabetic order. Under the winery heading, each of its wines or labels is then listed alphabetically. To find the tasting note and ratings for Rosemount Estate Roxburgh Chardonnay, for example, simply search for the start of Rosemount Estate's entries, which begin on page 241 then turn alphabetically through the pages to the Roxburgh Chardonnay, which appears on page 243.

## Winery information

Wherever possible, the actual address of each winery is listed in this book — not its head office or marketing office — plus its region, telephone number, fax number and web site and e-mail address if appropriate. On those occasions where the entries refer to a vineyard whose wines are made elsewhere, the address usually supplied is for the vineyard itself. So, if you're thinking of visiting a vineyard and wish to be sure whether or not it is open for public inspection, I suggest you telephone the company using the number provided.

Each winery included is accompanied by a listing of its winemaker, viticulturist and chief executive, plus brief details concerning any recent changes of ownership or direction, key wines and recent developments of interest.

## The Wine Ranking

*The Australian Wine Annual* provides the only Australian classification of nearly all major Australian wine brands determined on the most important aspect of all: quality. Unlike the very worthwhile Langtons' Classification of Distinguished Australian Wine, which presents a more limited overview of the super-premium market and which is largely based on resale price and performance at auction, the Wine Rankings in this book are not influenced in any way by price or other secondary factors. Being a secondary market, the auction market is usually slow to respond to the emergence of new quality wines, while in some cases, for example the plethora of so-called 'cult' shirazes from the Barossa and McLaren Vale, it can produce excessive prices grossly disproportionate to genuine wine quality.

The Wine Ranking is your easiest and most convenient guide to wine quality. This book allocates to the best wines in Australia a Wine Ranking from 1 to 5, based on the scores they constantly receive in my tastings, which are printed adjacent to each entry. Unless I have good reason to do otherwise, such as opening a bottle spoiled for some reason, the scores printed in this edition relate to the most recent occasion on which I have tasted each wine. Any wine to be allocated a Wine Ranking at all must have scored consistently well in my tastings. So, even if its Ranking is a lowly 5, the wine might still represent excellent value for money.

To provide a rough basis for comparison, a Wine Ranking of 1 is broadly equivalent to a First Growth classification in France. A large number of wines included in this book are not given Wine Rankings, since the minimum requirement for a ranking of 5 is still pretty steep.

Here is a rough guide to the way Wine Rankings relate to scores out of 100, and how they compare to different medal standards used in the Australian wine show system:

| Wine Ranking | Regular Score in Jeremy Oliver's Tastings | Approximate Medal Equivalent |
|---|---|---|
| RANKING **1** | 96+ | Top gold medal |
| RANKING **2** | 94–95 | Regular gold medal |
| RANKING **3** | 92–93 | Top silver medal |
| RANKING **4** | 90–91 | Regular silver medal |
| RANKING **5** | 87–89 | Top bronze medal |

See the flap on the inside front cover for further information.

As far as this book is concerned, if a brand of wine improves over time, so will its Wine Ranking. Similarly, if its standard declines, so will its ranking. Since Wine Rankings are largely a reflection of each label's performance over the last four years, they are unlikely to change immediately as a result of a single especially poor or exceptionally good year.

# Why I don't print meaningless wine prices

It is meaningless to print a current price for each vintage of every wine included in this book. Retail prices vary so dramatically from store to store that there is no such thing as a standard recommended retail price, even for current release wines. Price guides become even less meaningful for older releases, since too many factors come into play. Was the wine bought by a retailer at auction for resale? In what condition is the bottle? How has it been stored? How keen is the buyer and how desperate is the vendor? What margin does the retailer (or restaurateur) wish to apply and for how long have they had the stock? Since no system has yet been invented which even vaguely approximates the price of older wines and which takes into account all of the factors above, I don't use one. I see little value in providing worthless information.

# Current Price Range

All the wines listed are allocated a price range within which you can usually expect to find their latest releases.

# When to drink each wine

To the right hand side of the wine listings is a column that features the suggested drinking range for every vintage of each wine included, within which I would expect each wine to reach its peak. If a '+' sign appears after a range of years, it is quite possible that well-cellared bottles may happily endure after the later year of the specified range.

These drinking windows are my estimations alone, since it's apparent that different people enjoy their wines at different stages of development. Some of us prefer the primary flavours of young wine, while others would rather the virtually decayed qualities of extremely old bottles. However, it's a day-to-day tragedy how few top Australian cellaring wines of all types and persuasions are actually opened at or even close to their prime.

For quick and easy reference, a broad indication of each vintage's maturity is provided with a simple colour background. The chart inside the front cover explains how the colours indicate whether a wine is drinking at its best now, will improve further if left alone, or if it is likely to be past its best.

# Current Trends in Australian Wine

## Cabernet might be doing it tough...

Twenty years ago, when I began writing about wine in Australia, the undisputed king of the red grape varieties was cabernet sauvignon. Shiraz was the perpetual bridesmaid, treated with less respect in the vineyard, the cellar and the market. Grenache and mataro, as it was then exclusively called, were Third World; pinot noir little more than an opportunistic dream.

Clearly, things are not what they were. With an industry, a local market and an export market equally obsessed by Australian shiraz, cabernet has not only slipped down the totem pole of fashion, but is in dire danger of becoming yesterday's look. It's becoming hard to sell in the marketplace, and cabernet grapes are becoming hard to sell to wineries. The 2004 vintage saw a not insignificant quantity of uncontracted cool-climate cabernet from places like the Yarra Valley and Coonawarra sell on the spot market for as little as $200 per tonne. Two years ago similar fruit would fetch $1500–$1800 per tonne.

Cabernet has an image problem. Warm climate cabernet is being made to taste as rich and round as warm climate shiraz. I've never seen so many ultra-ripe, sweet and oaky cabernets as I have in tasting the wines for this edition.

The public doesn't trust the grape like they used to, and it's not their fault. Much of the very large new cabernet plantings in Australia either should have been developed more thoughtfully or never planted at all. Much of the reason why Australians have forsaken cabernet for shiraz has to do with the deluge of skinny, weedy greenish cabernets that have been produced by the truckload from cooler regions in the south-eastern corner of the country comprising Victoria, South Australia and Tasmania, plus the cooler regions of Western Australia and the inland areas of New South Wales like Cowra and Orange. Regrettably, the Australian market is to some extent awash with over-cropped skinny green cabernet that reflects neither site nor variety that nobody wants to drink. Cabernet's profile has undoubtedly suffered as a result.

Funnily, given the recent growth of Australian wine, it's quite probable there is more top and medium-level cabernet being made here than ever before. But the bulk of the product is making life tough for the worthy makers here whose cabernet and blends consistently offer excellent value across the entire spectrum of price-points, from budget to top-shelf.

## ... but Riesling is strutting its stuff

If riesling is your white wine of choice, it's a very good time to be an Australian. The unprecedented but entirely justifiable popularity of the 2002 Clare Valley riesling vintage has been followed by one of equal merit in the Eden Valley's 2003 crop. The best examples of each of these outstanding seasons offer the length and brightness, piercing flavours, sculpted structure and razor-sharp austerity associated with the finest dry European expressions of this variety, which is again being treated with its customary nobility in Australia.

There's also plenty of evidence from makers outside these regions that riesling is again receiving the attention it's worthy of. I am now regularly tasting high-class rieslings from regions like the Adelaide Hills (SA), Great Southern (WA), Mansfield and Great Western (Victoria), as well as from both winemaking extremities of Tasmania. Winemakers are taking a more active role in the process than ever before, experimenting with a range of traditional European techniques like oxidative handling with low sulphur levels (often followed by a decent shot of sulphur dioxide at bottling) and a pre-fermentation cold soak to encourage the development of rounder textures and secondary flavours. There's much evidence these days of extended lees contact after fermentation, while some makers are experimenting with 'indigenous' yeasts for the primary fermentation, as well as using large old oak vats for maturation.

Australian rieslings now reveal more interesting aspects of structure, texture and flavour in their youth than they ever have before. As much as I already enjoy it, I'm sure the breed is about to get better, and that we're just beginning what might turn into a very interesting journey indeed.

# Would you buy it if…

It didn't tell you who made it? Australia is in the grip of a faddish offshoot of its present wine surplus, known as the 'cleanskin' market. This is the Wild West of wine retail, a lucky dip mainly conducted by no-name retailers, several of which are already part of franchises, who have appeared out of the woodwork to offer a surprisingly naïve and unsuspecting market a variety of alternative wines whose labels — if indeed they have them — are typically long in prose but short in detail. They will usually reveal (or claim) a regional origin, a varietal mix and a vintage year, but leave secret the most important factor of all — who made them.

The myths associated with the cleanskin market are legion. Believe all you are told and you will be convinced that such stores are packed to the rafters with great wines from the industry's unsung heroes who for reasons beyond their control are unable to distribute their wine through more conventional means. Or that some of Australia's blue-chip makers habitually made more wine than they believe they can sell, so they then cull off any surplus and sell it on a no-name basis to preserve the integrity of their brand. Or that Australia is simply awash with too much great wine for it all to be sold through conventional retail. Or that an incredible proportion of Australia's exports of top-level wines keep on getting returned to their senders, leaving them with little choice but to quit wine that is no longer of current vintage. I feel my nose getting longer just as I write these words. Sure, some of this is true some of the time, but…

There are of course excellent wines to be bought as cleanskins, but they've very few and far between. Reputable retailers I know who sell their own carefully chosen cleanskins typically say that about one in twenty-five samples they taste comes up to scratch. I wonder where the wines they reject finish up? I hope you're not buying them!

Right now I am anything but convinced that even if their quality was of a par with the conventional market, that the cleanskin specialists offer an advantage in price. Sure, they're the opportunistic outcome of the wine surplus, but no more than the dirt-cheap prices you'll see right now in traditional wine stores for conventionally labelled wine.

I am also deeply concerned about the integrity of the claims made on the labels of so-called cleanskin wines. Who is policing and regulating the names of regions, varieties and vintages? Who can assure me that the self-labelled wine of Retailer X is actually a Coonawarra Shiraz (or within the requisite 85% of each)? Nobody. How is it possible that one can still walk out of a wine store having bought a single bottle of wine with absolutely NO LABEL AT ALL? Aren't there health regulations that are meant to cover this sort of thing? Yet, I could have done exactly that, just yesterday in Melbourne.

The cleanskin market is nothing more than a lucky dip. My advice before buying any wine in this fashion is only to shop at a knowledgeable retailer that you can trust, and to try the wine first. And then think twice.

# The Best Australian Wines Under $20

There has never been a better time to buy Australian wine under $20. Winemakers large and small are competing fiercely in this market, occasionally offering quality well beyond expectations. Here is a list of the best Australian wines I have tasted over the past year under $20. Each of these wines has achieved a score of 90-plus, and in my estimation qualify for at least Silver Medal status.

Not surprisingly, riesling is the strongest variety by some margin. While the prices of the better rieslings are slowly but surely on the rise, there is still plenty of undeniably spectacular value with this variety, for around $15 and even below.

## Cabernet Sauvignon

| | |
|---|---|
| Peter Lehmann The Barossa | |
| Cabernet Sauvignon 2002 | 91 |
| Preece Cabernet Sauvignon 2002 | 90 |

## Chardonnay

| | |
|---|---|
| Blue Pyrenees Chardonnay 2003 | 90 |
| Jacob's Creek Reserve Chardonnay 2002 | 90 |
| Montrose Stony Creek Chardonnay 2002 | 90 |

## Gewürztraminer

| | |
|---|---|
| Lillydale Gewürztraminer 2003 | 90 |

## Marsanne

| | |
|---|---|
| Tahbilk Marsanne | 92 |

## Merlot

| | |
|---|---|
| Preece Merlot 2002 | 90 |

## Riesling

| | |
|---|---|
| Leasingham Bin 7 Riesling 2003 | 95 |
| Castle Rock Estate Riesling 2003 | 94 |
| Knappstein Riesling 2003 | 94 |
| Leo Buring Clare Valley Riesling 2003 | 94 |
| Pikes Riesling 2003 | 94 |
| Alkoomi Riesling 2003 | 93 |
| Goundrey Reserve Riesling 2003 | 93 |
| Jacob's Creek Reserve Riesling 2003 | 93 |
| Mitchelton Blackwood Park Riesling 2004 | 93 |
| Pewsey Vale Riesling 2003 | 93 |
| Rockford Hand Picked Riesling 2001 | 93 |
| Heggies Eden Valley Riesling 2003 | 92 |
| St Hallet Eden Valley Riesling 2003 | 92 |
| Tim Adams Riesling 2004 | 92 |
| Wolf Blass Gold Label Riesling 2003 | 92 |
| Hewitson The Garden Riesling 2003 | 91 |
| McWilliams Eden Valley Riesling 2003 | 91 |
| The Wilson Vineyard Gallery Series | |
| Riesling 2003 | 91 |
| Bethany Eden Valley Riesling 2003 | 90 |
| Capel Vale Riesling 2003 | 90 |
| d'Arenberg The Dry Dam Riesling 2003 | 90 |

| | |
|---|---|
| Grant Burge Thorn Riesling 2003 | 90 |
| Orlando St Helga Riesling 2003 | 90 |
| Peter Lehmann The Barossa Riesling 2003 | 90 |
| Wynns Coonawarra Riesling 2002 | 90 |

## Rhône Blend

| | |
|---|---|
| d'Arenberg d'Arry's Original | |
| Shiraz Grenache 2002 | 90 |

## Sauvignon Blanc

| | |
|---|---|
| Smithbrook Sauvignon Blanc 2003 | 93 |
| Starvedog Lane Sauvignon Blanc 2003 | 93 |
| Shadowfax Sauvignon Blanc 2003 | 92 |
| Omrah Sauvignon Blanc 2003 | 91 |
| Hill Smith Estate Sauvignon Blanc 2003 | 90 |
| Stoney Vineyard Sauvignon Blanc 2003 | 90 |

## Semillon

| | |
|---|---|
| Mount Pleasant Elizabeth 2002 | 95 |
| Grant Burge Zerk Semillon 2002 | 92 |
| Mitchell The Growers Semillon 2002 | 92 |
| Peter Lehmann The Barossa Semillon 2003 | 92 |
| Margan Semillon 2003 | 90 |
| Tim Adams Semillon 2002 | 90 |

## Shiraz

| | |
|---|---|
| Bremerton Selkirk Shiraz 2000 | 92 |
| Seppelt Victorian Premium Reserve | |
| Shiraz 2002 | 92 |
| Water Wheel Shiraz 2002 | 92 |
| Baileys Shiraz 2003 | 90 |
| Blue Pyrenees Shiraz 2001 | 90 |
| Moculta Shiraz 2001 | 90 |
| Morris Shiraz 2001 | 90 |
| Peter Lehmann The Barossa Shiraz 2002 | 90 |

## Verdelho

| | |
|---|---|
| Fox Creek Verdelho 2003 | 90 |
| Sandalford Verdelho 2004 | 90 |

## Viognier

| | |
|---|---|
| Yalumba Eden Valley Viognier 2003 | 90 |

# Scoring Wine out of 100 Points

With some misgivings, it must be said, I have changed the publication of my scores on wine to the 100-point system. Or perhaps to phrase that more accurately, to a 100-point system, since after some fairly detailed research into the subject, there is no universal system by which critics apply scores out of 100 to wine. I believe this was necessary for people to be able to compare and contrast my scores to those of other critics, most of whom today use a 100-point scale.

Having made the decision to change, it then became a matter of choosing some basis on which to make the conversion. After more research into this, it became starkly obvious that while theories abound concerning the conversion from the 20 scale to the 100 scale, most are patently nonsensical. To backtrack a little, in 2002 and 2003 I contributed the annual Australian section to the monthly newsletter of the highly respected American wine critic, Steve Tanzer. Steve, naturally enough, uses a 100-point scale. Since I was writing in his publication, he and I attempted to create a conversion from my scores out of 20 to his scores out of 100, based on his view of the 100-point scale and where we collectively believed our scores intersected. While we both tried to accommodate ourselves, I wasn't entirely satisfied that we had got it right. Without wishing to question Steve in any way, I didn't feel absolutely comfortable in picking up this same conversion again.

It was critical to me to make the change in a way that would enable my readers to compare my scores in a meaningful way with my contemporaries, none of whom I have more respect for than James Halliday, who has been scoring wines out of 100 for some time. It made — and still makes — no sense to me not to follow his lead. Fortunately James agreed. Neither of us are worried if our marks happen to differ on individual wines, and our readers' task is made easier if they know we are comparing apples with apples.

So, with only a couple of marginal adaptions, here is the basis on which I have allocated my scores out of 100. I have drawn a little from James' descriptions and it goes without saying that I am grateful indeed to him for his positive and friendly cooperation.

| | |
|---|---|
| **95+** | Outstanding wines of exceptional quality; either classic representations of their style or variety, or cutting-edge wines at the very sharp end of wine innovation. Roughly equivalent to Gold Medal (18.5) and above. |
| **90–94** | Highly recommended. Wines of genuine class and character. Pretty well covers the gamut of Silver Medal (17.0 to 18.4). |
| **87–89** | Recommended. Certainly above average quality, without faults that interfere beyond a base level of enhancing complexity, able to make a quality statement about variety, technique or region. Solid Bronze Medal (16.0 to 16.9). |
| **84–86** | Reasonably good wine, but lacking genuine distinction and class. Should be free of technical faults. Relatively uncomplicated and straightforward, comprising the better examples of cheap wine (sub $12). Just above and below Bronze Medal status (15.3 to 15.9) |
| **80–83** | Everyday wines, possibly with some technical deficiency, hopefully at the cheaper end of the pricing scale. |
| **75–79** | Something went wrong. Possessing a significant flaw, often through a viticultural or winemaking misfortune. |

I believe this system gives me sufficient flexibility, as well has having enough in common with the 100-point scales used by others. It is worth noting that wines scoring an average of 15.5 out of 20 in Australian wine shows are awarded a Bronze Medal; those that score 17 are awarded Silver Medals; and those that score 18.5 are awarded Gold Medals.

# Australia's Perfect 1s

Of the thousands of table wines made in Australia today, I have allocated a highest possible Wine Ranking of 1 to a mere sixteen. These are the wines that time and again perform to the highest standard. Each has its particular stamp, its special quality and personal identity. To a major degree, each wine reflects the character of the individual or company whose name it carries. Each certainly reflects vintage variation from year to year, usually without compromising the special qualities associated with the label.

I believe these are the modern benchmarks, the wines against which others can be measured. As a group they are continually improving, but together they define the limits of contemporary Australian wine.

### Bannockburn Serré Pinot Noir

An astonishingly deep, ethereal and complex wine from a close-planted vineyard within Bannockburn's vineyard near Geelong, made to Gary Farr's own interpretation of the Burgundian ideal with obvious whole bunch fermentation influences that need significant time to integrate. Recent vintages show even more finesse.

### Bass Phillip Reserve Pinot Noir

Australia's best and longest-living pinot noir: a frustratingly rare, full orchestra wine capable of stunning evolution and expression of briary, meaty complexity and layered structure. From Gippsland, by Phillip Jones.

### Clonakilla Shiraz Viognier

Tim Kirk is succeeding in his ambition to create an exotically perfumed, deeply scented and powerfully flavoured shiraz viognier blend in a style faithful to the best from the northern Rhône Valley. Poles apart from mainstream Australian shiraz, this savoury, firm and fine-grained red has spawned a generation of imitators.

### Cullen Diana Madeline Cabernet Sauvignon Merlot

An essay in concentration, elegance and refinement from Margaret River, but not without its power and presence. The piercing intensity, classically refined structure and enormous potential of Vanya Cullen's premier wine leaves little to the imagination.

### Giaconda Chardonnay

My pick as Australia's finest chardonnay; extraordinarily structured, meaty, savoury and complete, expressing a heritage more Burgundian than Australian. From Rick Kinzbrunner at Beechworth in Victoria.

### Grosset Polish Hill

A modern icon in Australian wine, Jeffrey Grosset's standout Clare Valley Riesling stretches the limits of what this most traditional of Australian varieties is able to achieve.

## Henschke Hill of Grace

In a country full of spectacular single vineyard shiraz wines, Steven Henschke's signature wine from this individual Eden Valley vineyard marries firmness with uniqely velvet-like fineness; vitality with longevity.

## Leeuwin Estate Chardonnay

At the forefront of Australian chardonnay since its first vintage in 1980, this luscious and long-living Margaret River wine has been for many palates the real 'white Grange'.

## Leo Buring Leonay Eden Valley Riesling

A classic and traditional Australian label, whose most recent releases — erratic as their appearance has indeed been — have invariably been spectacular. The cellaring potential of these wines is simply legendary.

## Mount Mary Cabernet 'Quintet'

An inspiration by John Middleton in Victoria's Yarra Valley. The nearest Australian wine to a premier Bordeaux red and a global standard in its own right. Recent vintages are downright brilliant.

## Penfolds Bin 707 Cabernet Sauvignon

Penfolds' most eloquent expression of cabernet sauvignon. A multi-regional blend representing the pick of Penfolds' entire South Australian cabernet crop and matured in new American oak.

## Penfolds Grange

Australia's definitive red wine, a model of style and consistency ever since 1951. Based on Barossa shiraz, with contributions from other regions and small amounts of cabernet sauvignon.

## Petaluma Coonawarra

Petaluma's premier red is a highly protected and handsomely oaked blend of cabernet sauvignon and merlot that takes a considerable time to drink at its best. It has been the most consistent red wine throughout Coonawarra's last and most successful decade.

## Petaluma Tiers Chardonnay

A single-vineyard chardonnay, sourced from the mature block immediately above Petaluma winery. Very fine and restrained, exceptionally long and mineral, it reveals a surprisingly concentrated core of explosive fruit.

## Pierro Chardonnay

The role model for so many of Australia's more opulent and hedonistically proportioned chardonnays, this stunning expression of Margaret River chardonnay by Mike Peterkin is now becoming more elegant.

## Wolf Blass Platinum Label Shiraz

Proof positive that Australia's largest winemakers are working as hard as ever before to make the country's leading wine. Sourced from a collection of small vineyards in the Eden Valley, Barossa floor and Adelaide Hills, it is consistently complex and musky, delivering intensely pure and vibrant shiraz flavour.

# Jeremy Oliver's Wine of the Year

This edition marks the sixth naming of Jeremy Oliver's Wine of the Year. In sequence, the previous winners have been Rosemount Estate's 1996 Mountain Blue Shiraz Cabernet Sauvignon, Cullen's 1998 Cabernet Sauvignon Merlot 1998, Hardy's Eileen Hardy Shiraz 1998, Mount Mary Quintet 2000 and Lake's Folly's Cabernet Blend from 2001. The finalists for this award are the ten best current release Australian wines I have tasted throughout the previous year.

While quality clearly remains paramount in this choice, the winning wine must be commercially available around or shortly after the time of publication and represent some special characteristic of individuality, innovation, maturity or longevity. Wines selected must make a positive statement about style, terroir and winemaking direction.

Here are the finalists for Jeremy Oliver's 2004 Wine of the Year, including the winner itself.

## Wine of the Year
### Wolf Blass Platinum Label Shiraz 2001 (97)

Winemaker Caroline Dunn heads the team responsible for this modern Australian classic. Now in its fourth release, the Platinum Label has established a place amongst the most intensely flavoured and refined of this country's shiraz. The debut vintage was 1998, comprising a finely balanced, velvet-smooth and spicy wine entirely sourced from the Hutton Vale vineyard in Eden Valley. Since then, the Platinum Label Shiraz has managed to deliver exceptional quality and consistency of style through some of the most challenging and diverse vintages in South Australian history through a combination of judicious vineyard sourcing, some very talented winemaking and a very clear focus on style.

The 1999 vintage was 60% sourced from Hutton Vale, but received some Barossa floor fruit to give weight and intensity to its middle palate. To counteract the heat and super-ripeness of Barossa fruit in 2000, the wine was sourced from the Adelaide Hills, largely from a small site near Tea Tree Gully.

The best wine of the series released to date, the 2001 vintage shares the brightness and elegance of the 1998 wine, but its musky, exotic spiciness and extraordinarily pristine fruit are pure Adelaide Hills, from a single dryland vineyard near Oakbank.

According to Dunn, the Platinum Label will vary its sourcing from year to year, as she balances her way between the cooler Adelaide Hills sites, the warmer

Eden Valley and the still warmer Barossa floor sites to maintain what she and her team have identified as the Platinum style. Purity of fruit is the key, and she wants to avoid for this wine the jammier qualities typical of the Barossa region as well as the thin, weedy characters often present in cool climate shiraz from cooler seasons.

To the credit of all involved in this decision, most of the Platinum Label is also bottled under a screwcap seal.

# Finalists

### Bindi Quartz
### Chardonnay 2002 (96)

Bindi burst onto the scene in the mid 1990s with some astonishingly pure and mineral chardonnays as well as several pinot noirs of rare intensity and spicy varietal expression. With the 2002 Quartz Chardonnay, the finest white yet to emerge from this low-yielding vineyard, it returns to absolute top form. As its name suggests, it is selected from a part of the vineyard whose topsoil has a very high quartz content. Typically concentrated and elegant, its characteristic hallmark is its lingering mineral finish.

### Giaconda
### Cabernet Sauvignon 2002 (97)

Rick Kinzbrunner is now using thinner-staved oak to impart a superior quality of oak-derived character to his Cabernet Sauvignon in a shorter period of time. Recent vintages have been bottled slightly earlier than in the past, leaving a greater emphasis of pristine violet and cassis-like fruit. This is a superbly balanced and integrated wine; an assertive and long-term cellaring prospect.

### Giaconda
### Chardonnay 2002 (97)

Sourced from cool south-facing sites, the 2002 vintage of one of Australia's genuine wine icons is a return to the standard of the exceptional 1996 vintage. Like most modern Giaconda Chardonnays, this is a sumptuous, savoury and especially complex wine with its customary cellaring potential.

### Giaconda
### Shiraz 2002 (97)

When tasting the Giaconda releases it never occurred to me that I would be including three in this particular list. When I discovered that they had all arrived here on merit, I admit I then rechecked everything to make absolutely certain that all was in order. It was. This wine in particular carries more than just a single hallmark of greatness. Irrespective of its other wines, Giaconda could soon be making Australia's finest shiraz.

## Leasingham Classic Clare Riesling 2002 (96)

The Clare Valley's signature 2002 vintage for riesling has expressed itself in a number of first-rate wine, of which this Classic Clare was one of the last to be released. For decades, the Leasingham label has been associated with riesling of high quality, but this finely sculpted long-term expression is the best I have ever tasted.

## Leeuwin Estate Art Series Chardonnay 2001 (96)

The regular presence of Leeuwin Estate's icon wine amongst various Australian 'best of' lists is a constant reinforcement of its undisputed status as a definitive, ground-breaking New World wine. The 2001 edition is typically seamless and luxuriant.

## Leo Buring Leonay Eden Valley Riesling 2003 (97)

The most recent of an important lineage in Australian riesling that began with the superlative efforts made by the legendary John Vickery. A more evolved and complex young wine than its predecessors, this pristine, shapely and mineral riesling puts Leo Buring right at the forefront of our best contemporary makers.

## Moss Wood Cabernet Sauvignon 2001 (97)

An amazing wine, in my opinion the best Moss Wood ever made. Keith Mugford has fashioned a typically sumptuous and silky cabernet with layers of flavour and a near-perfect structure. It also represents a welcome step backwards from the higher alcoholic strengths of recent vintages. Simply outstanding.

## Petaluma Merlot 2001 (96)

A very convincing merlot of depth and structure, but most importantly the elusive palate sweetness, generously round texture and fine-grained astringency sought after in vain by so many makers of this variety. It's no shrinking violet, and will develop for many years.

# Cellaring wine

## If you're going to cellar wine

Keep your wine upside down. While some scientists suggest that the partial pressure of water between the wine's surface and the cork in an upright bottle is enough to keep the cork sufficiently moist, I'm not prepared to take the risk. If corks dry out, air gets it. This is ruinous. An added advantage of the growing number of white wines packaged with screwcap seals for longevity and to guard against cork taint is that you can actually cellar them upright without concern. I have been amazed at the ability of both whites and reds to mature with these seals.

Keep your wine in the dark. Ultra-violet light can penetrate most glass bottles to some degree (especially the clear ones) and oxidise the wine inside. This is why so many cellars are dimly lit. If you haven't the space for a dark cellar, keep your bottles in their boxes or else behind a heavy curtain.

Keep your wine still and undisturbed. Regular vibrations accelerate the ageing process with wine. Furthermore, there's no need to turn your bottles every morning, as some people regularly do. This habit began when English gentlemen needed an unobtrusive means of checking that their household staff hadn't secreted any away from their premises, so they actually did this to count their stock.

Temperature should be both constant and low. There is debate about the ideal cellaring temperature. In my experience, if wine is cellared above 18 degrees Celsius it ages too quickly. If it is cellared at around 10–12 degrees, it ages very slowly, perhaps too slowly for some of us. Around 14 degrees is probably ideal, which means that in most parts of Australia, you will need some temperature control. Most importantly, changes in temperature from day to night and from season to season must be avoided if wine is to be kept for even a few months. So keep wine well away from windows and external walls, unless they're very thick.

Think about humidity. If a cellar is too humid then labels and racks may go mouldy. It's unlikely that the wines themselves will be adversely affected, but it's not worth the risk with rare and expensive wines. If there's not enough humidity in the cellar, the outward ends of wine corks may shrink and reduce their ability to impart a seal. This can considerably shorten a bottle's longevity. If there's too much humidity, a small fan can help to keep air moving.

If there's not enough, a bowl of water, or even water tipped onto a gravel floor, can help.

## To make the most of your cellar...

Start by keeping good records. Book-keeping is essential unless you can readily remember the name and age of every wine you own. There's nothing worse than finding a good wine left beyond its peak, so a record-keeping system is crucial. Do it on the computer. There are several cellar management systems available to choose from. Use one that enables you to customise its logic to suit your own cellar. There's another big advantage if your cellar is computerised: you don't have to worry about the bin size or having to construct single bottle slots. All you do is search for a wine by name in your database and its location will automatically appear. Furthermore, in the unfortunate event of fire or flood, your records will at least give you a sporting chance when you make an insurance claim for your cellar contents.

Think about your buying and drinking habits. If you regularly buy wine by the dozen, you'll need bins for twelve bottles, bins for half-dozens and perhaps single bottle slots. That way you can put a new dozen straight into the system, move it along when you're half way through, and then insert the remaining bottles into their own slots. If you're designing a cellar this way, keep between 40–50% for single bottles.

Try to buy by the dozen. Most of us miss wine at its peak by purchasing a small amount and drinking it too soon. With a dozen bottles it has more of a chance and besides, some of us can only summon sufficient resistance with the sight of an unopened box. But if you've bought a dozen, don't rest on your laurels for a decade or more without taking a peep at the wine. Sometimes it's possible to wait too long. Sample a bottle about four years before the wine is expected to peak and then, all being well, about two years before. Your expectations will then be confirmed, or you should alter your approach towards the wine in question. Then, once you expect the time is near, try a bottle every six months or so. That way you should not only have enjoyed watching the wine develop, but have about six or seven bottles left to experience at their best.

## So if your dream home wasn't built with a cellar…

Think about a temperature and humidity-controlled wine cabinet. Then you won't have a worry in the world about the health of your wine or your ability to access it. Some of these units are particularly impressive. Factors you might take into account if considering this option include your ability to change temperature settings, the ease of access to the wines inside, possible temperature zoning within the unit to provide different compartments for 'drink now' wines, whether or not fresh air circulates throughout the unit, that the inside of the unit is dark, that it is lockable, that any glass doors are UV-treated, and that the degree of vibration caused by motor units is minimal.

Find yourself a commercial cellaring facility. When choosing which cellaring facility to go with, ask about the temperature and humidity issues, find out about their data keeping facilities, how much and on what basis you will be charged, the security against theft, flood and fire and what sort of pick-up and delivery service you're offered. Will you be told when a wine is nearing its peak? Will you have the ability to buy from and trade with other customers? Some of these operations are equipped with professional standard tasting rooms and commercial kitchens and even offer club-style memberships to their customers, including newsletters, tastings and dinners. Other leading operations of this kind are networked over the entire country, so you can keep wine in different cities, depending on where you bought it.

# Investing in Australian wine

It's funny how your perspective can change. For years, I'd deliver a stock-standard response to anyone telling me they wanted to invest in buying Australian wine. 'Forget it,' I'd say. 'Don't try to profit from it; just buy what you're going to drink, or else going to enjoy owning. That way you'll keep your lifestyle, your health, some of your wealth and much of your sanity. And if all else fails, you should always be able to find something at least half-decent to drink.'

Despite the fact that many of the superannuation funds which ill advisedly invested in wine portfolios have recently quit stock at embarrassingly low prices, wine investment is still the latest fad. There has been a plethora of investment schemes in buying and storing bottled wines, most of which are unlikely to deliver on their promises. Right now, there are still warehouses of second-rate wine owned by investors living in the misguided belief that they will reap a first-rate return.

## Can you make money from wine?

The golden time for investment in Australian wine has well and truly passed. While another cycle may well occur in the future, the time for a kill occurred around a decade ago, before the rest of the world had awoken to the value and quality of the wines made in this country. If you were there at the right place at the right time, you might have made a small fortune. I have never met anyone who has made a large fortune buying and selling Australian wine.

Nevertheless, the secondary market for Australian wine has expanded dramatically, with the favourable outcome that there is more mature Australian wine available for sale than ever before. You can buy it at auction, from cellaring facilities which market the collections they house, or you can buy it from the large number of retail liquor licenses that now hover over the deceased estates of wine collectors the way that tow-trucks used to prey over the vehicular victims of road accidents.

## Choosing the right stuff

There are some basic rules to follow when buying investment wine, namely:

- Stick with established brands, large and small.
- Avoid poor or ordinary vintages like they're carrying a communicable disease.
- If you buy in dozens, unopened boxes are best.
- The market, especially the overseas component, is spending big on older vintages of top labels and good years.
- Just because a currently available wine may be expensive, it doesn't mean that (a) it is any good, and (b) that it will appreciate in value.
- Right now, shiraz is king, and it's unlikely that the overseas buyers who are currently driving up prices will switch their tastes to other varieties with which Australia doesn't have as quite as distinct an advantage.
- Magnums cost more than they should in Australia, but do appreciate quickly.
- Before you buy or sell, check not only the track record of the agent or auction house, but also the selling and buying commissions applicable.
- Buy at or before release if you can, for the lowest possible price.

The best Australian investment wines fall into two entirely separate categories, cult and classic. Led by Grange, the classic investment wines are those like Henschke's Hill of Grace and Mount Mary Cabernets — wines that, over the years, have developed a proven track record for quality and investment return. Langton's Classification of Distinguished Wine, a catalogue of such wines developed and maintained by Australia's largest and most influential auction house, is as thorough a listing of these wines as you can get.

On the other hand, recent years have seen the emergence of a number of small wineries whose tiny productions — typically of old-vine shiraz — now sell at stratospheric prices. American wine critic Robert Parker jnr simply needs to allocate a wine a single score above 95 to catapult an unheard of wine into the pricing stratosphere. Wines from makers like Torbreck, Wild Duck Creek, Three Rivers, Greenock Creek, Veritas, Noon's and the Burge Family have become the hottest-performing wines on the Australian auction market, before they are quickly shipped off to the US for resale. It would also appear that a relationship exists between the health of the Dow Jones index and the cost people are willing to pay for the most sought-after Australian wines in the US.

## Don't buy just any old bottle

Irrespective of its reputation or price, wine is a perishable thing that is only as good as the way it has been kept or transported. While nobody could seriously deny that many of the wines traded on the secondary market will never actually be opened until well after their earning and drinking peak has passed, the issue of provenance is the dormant volcano beneath the secondary wine market.

A huge and unknown proportion of the wines sold through the various secondary market channels in Australia — by auction, through clubs, private cellars and commercial cellaring operations — are absolutely stuffed, to phrase it as politely as possible. Better customers from virtually all Australia's auction houses have been warned from buying certain lots, or have else been told after discovering that a batch tasted very prematurely aged, that 'Oh yes, we weren't too sure about that lot.' While credits are typically given, it's interesting to contemplate the retrospective nature of much of this advice.

## All that glitters...

Recently we sat back and watched the hysteria surrounding the release of the highly-touted 1998 Penfolds Grange. If you were one of the lucky able to buy at $300 and sell at $800, you might think that wine investment was easy. If you were one of those who bought at $800, I want to know what you were thinking. The last time a Grange was released to such a reaction was the 1990 vintage, which rapidly shot from under $200 to around $600. This great vintage of Australia's flagship red now fetches around $450, significantly less than it did five years ago.

## The big picture

Keep your expectations realistic. Those who make a killing on the stock exchange don't usually do it by accident. With wine, it's no different. You will need to research your purchases thoroughly, learn the system, the margins, the prices and the rules; the good advice and the poor advice. You will have to know how to get hold of the stock you want, which will usually be the stock that everyone else wants. You will need to spend big on cellaring — either for yourself or through a commercial facility.

You might also end up doing exactly what a friend of mine did. He built, and then filled, a very impressive climate-controlled investment wine cellar. Then he rediscovered his love for wine. So he drank it instead.

# Seasonal Variation and Quality

It's clear just by glancing through this book that the same grapes from the same vineyard invariably produce very different wines from year to year. Traditionally, vintage variation in Australia has been considered merely a fraction of that encountered in most European wine regions of any quality, but the last five years have proven it to be a very significant variable that demands consideration when buying wine.

Even if all other variables were consistent from year to year, which they certainly are not, weather provides the greatest single influence in wine quality and style from season to season. Weather can influence wine in an infinite number of ways, from determining whether conditions at flowering are favourable or not, all the way through to whether final ripening and harvest occur in the warmth of sunshine or through the midst of damaging rains. If viticulturists were to turn pagan, it would be to a god of weather that they would build their first shrine.

Weather-influenced variation is nearly always more pronounced and more frequent in the cooler, more marginal viticultural regions. While Australia is principally a warm to hot wine producing nation, a significant proportion of the country's premium wine now comes from cooler regions in the southwestern and southeastern corners of the continent. The spectrum of diverse weather encountered in these regions far exceeds that of the traditional Australian wine growing areas like the Barossa Valley, McLaren Vale, central Victoria and the Clare Valley. Paradoxically, the best years in cool climates are typically the warmer seasons that accelerate the ripening period, creating a finer acid balance, superior sugar levels, flavours and better-defined colours.

Variety by variety, this is how Australia's premium wine grapes are affected by seasonal conditions:

## White wines

### Chardonnay.

Cool years cause chardonnay and most white varieties to accumulate higher levels of mineral acids, resulting in lean, tight wines with potential longevity, provided they have sufficient intensity of fruit. Cool year chardonnays can display greenish, herbal and green cashew flavours, and can resemble grapefruit and other citrus fruit, especially lemon. Warmer year wines become richer and rounder, with fruit flavours more suggestive of apple, pear, quince and cumquat. In hot seasons, chardonnays become flabbier, faster-maturing wines with flavours of peach, green olive, melon and tobacco.

### Riesling.

Although riesling does not need to ripen to the sugar levels necessary for a premium chardonnay, cool-season riesling tends to be lean and tight with hard steely acids, possibly lacking in length and persistence of flavour. Better rieslings from superior years have succulent youthful primary fruit flavours of lime juice, ripe pears and apples, with musky, citrus rind undertones. Significantly broader and less complex than wines from better seasons, warmer year rieslings tend to mature faster, occasionally becoming broad and fat on the palate after a short time.

### Sauvignon Blanc.

Cool season sauvignon blancs tend to be hard-edged wines with steely acids, with over-exaggerated and undesirable herbaceous flavours suggestive of asparagus and 'cat pee', a description for which I have yet to find a polite alternative even half as succinct. The warmer the season the riper the fruit becomes and the less grassy and vegetal the aroma. The downside is often a reduction in the intensity of the wine's primary fruit flavours. Expect sweet blackcurrants, gooseberries and passionfruit from sauvignon blancs in good seasons, with at least a light capsicum note. Warmer seasons create broader, occasionally oily and less grassy wines, with more emphasis on passionfruit, lychee and tropical fruit flavours.

## Semillon.

Semillon tends to react to cooler seasons by creating very tight, lean wines with more obvious grassy influences, but perhaps lacking in primary fruit character. On occasions, these rather one-dimensional young wines can develop stunning flavours in the bottle over many years, as classically unwooded Hunter semillon proves time and again. The best cellaring examples need length on the palate and an absence of green characters while young.

# Red wines

## Cabernet Sauvignon.

A late-ripening grape variety which reacts very poorly to cool, late seasons, cabernet sauvignon has traditionally and wisely been blended with varieties like merlot (in Bordeaux) and shiraz (commonly, until recently in Australia). Cool season cabernet sauvignon makes the classic doughnut wine: intense cassis/raspberry fruit at the front of the palate with greenish, extractive tannin at the back and a hole in the middle. Under-ripe cabernet sauvignon reveals less colour and a thin, bitter finish. Its tannins are often greenish and under-ripe, tasting sappy or metallic, while its flavour can be dominated by greenish snow pea influences more suggestive of cool-climate sauvignon blanc.

Warmer seasons create much better cabernet, with genuinely ripe cassis/plum flavours, a superior middle palate and fine-grained, fully-ripened tannins, although a slight capsicum note can still be evident. In really hot years, the wines tend to become jammy and porty, suggestive of stewed, dehydrated prune and currant-like fruit flavours and lacking in any real definition and fineness of tannin.

## Pinot Noir.

Pinot noir does not react well to very cool seasons, becoming herbal and leafy, with a brackish, greenish palate and simple sweet raspberry confection fruit. Warmer seasons produce the more sought-after primary characters of sweet cherries and plums, fine-grained tannins and spicy, fleshy middle palate. Too warm a season and the wine turns out to be undefined, simple and fast maturing, often with unbalanced and hard-edged tannins.

## Shiraz.

Thin and often quite greenish — but rarely to the same extent as cabernet sauvignon — cool-season shiraz often acquires leafy white pepper characters, with spicy, herby influences plus metallic, sappy and green-edged tannins. Provided there's sufficient fruit, which may not be the case in cool seasons, it can still be a worthwhile wine, although not one likely to mature for long in the bottle. Warmer years create shiraz with characteristic richness and sweetness, with riper plum, cassis and chocolate flavours and fully-ripened tannins. Hot year shiraz is often typified by earthy flavours suggestive of bitumen and leather, with dehydrated prune juice and meaty characters.

# 2004 Australian vintage report

It was nearly Australia's first top-class national vintage since 1998, and it may yet assume the title of the best vintage since 1998, but 2004 has indeed failed to live up to its early expectations. At 1.86 million tonnes, it's certainly a big season; the largest vintage ever recorded in this country. It is 40% higher than its immediate predecessor — the drought-affected 2003 crop — and it was 23% above the previous record of 1.51 million tonnes in 2002. Only as the harvest came in did the industry realise that due to a significant increase in bunch weight over previous years that it was substantially bigger than all estimates. Large as it was, there was however still plenty of high-quality fruit left on the vine.

Red winegrape production increased by 38% to 1.07 million tonnes, hitting 1 million tonnes for the first time, while white winegrape production increased by 43% to 794,000 tonnes. Shiraz increased its production by 133,000 tonnes to 442,000 tonnes, so it now accounts for 24% of Australia's total production. The presently unfashionable variety of cabernet sauvignon (in Australia at least) increased in production by 92,000 tonnes to 317,000 tonnes, accounting for 17% of total production.

The white harvest was dominated by chardonnay, which recorded an increase of 95,000 tonnes or 41% to 329,000 tonnes compared to 2003. Riesling intake increased by 26% to 37,000 tonnes, but was overtaken by sauvignon blanc, which doubled to 43,000 tonnes.

Whether or not the 2004 season delivered the quality anticipated after a perfect start was largely determined by how individual vineyards dealt with scorching temperatures experienced across the southeast of the nation in mid-February. The rest of the ripening season was generally fine, mild and even, without significant threat of rain or disease, except in Tasmania. Prior to the growing season, the winter did deliver decent rainfalls in many regions.

## New South Wales

A terrific white Hunter vintage with some exceptional early-harvest semillon immediately preceded a very ordinary red vintage, troubled again by rain. Mudgee, on the other hand, enjoyed a good late, dry season that should produce some fine reds, especially from cabernet sauvignon. By and large, the vintage experienced by Mudgee and the other New South Wales regions west of the Great Divide was too cool for whites. The Riverina, however, experienced a good vintage for all its table wine varieties with the exception of shiraz, which copped the brunt of the severe February heat. Some excellent whites and cabernets should result.

# South Australia

More than any other State, South Australia's season was particularly affected by the searingly hot spell in mid-February. While the later regions were less affected, opinion on the vintage for Barossa shiraz, for instance, varies between 'good' to 'patchy'. It was actually a cabernet vintage in the Barossa and McLaren Vale (whose shiraz could be very promising), while another early region, the Clare Valley, was also affected by the heat.

Since fruit development was several weeks behind in the cooler Eden Valley region, this area looks to have been less troubled and should produce some fine red wines, while Langhorne Creek has experienced a signature vintage. Other later regions like the Adelaide Hills and Coonawarra performed well, especially with reds. The best wines, many of which will be cabernets, will come from lower-yielding premium vineyards fully able to ripen fruit in the mild, later Indian summer. Higher-cropping Limestone Coast vineyards are likely to have experienced difficulties in fully ripening their fruit.

# Tasmania

Whether or not a particular vineyard made quality Tasmanian wine in 2004 depended as much as anything else on the approach taken towards its viticultural management. If owners got greedy and missed some pretty obvious signs, they got burned. Fruit set was huge, following massive inflorescences, but January was unseasonably cold. The cold spell lasted until mid-February, but many growers unwisely left their potential record crops (which in were not uncommonly around three times normal yield) hanging on their vines. Some heat in later February and March got the lower-cropping vineyards through to full ripeness, but rain and poor weather began again in late March, well before most fruit was picked. Botrytis was a significant issue, and several hundred tonnes of grapes were left hanging. Some were still harvesting in June. Hmmm.

# Victoria

Central and northern Victoria produced some impressively flavoursome red wines, while heat and the ongoing drought have prevented all but the best and more mature vineyards in the Yarra Valley and Mornington Peninsula from enjoying good seasons. Generally speaking, it should be a white wine vintage in the cooler Victorian regions. Rains in January helped Heathcote to enjoy a better season than the immediately preceding drought-affected vintages, and if given the chance, its vineyard could have produced reds of more elegance and balance. The northern regions of the state should have produced some good, if possibly heat-affected reds.

# Western Australia

One State can actually lay claim to a classic vintage, and that State is Western Australia. It enjoyed its first good winter in several years, partially replenishing depleted soil moisture levels. The summer was warm to cool and long, and missed out on the serious heat that affected the east of the continent in February. Reds should be good, whites fine and elegant. Highlights include first-rate reds from the Great Southern region of Western Australia, from Frankland River down to Mount Barker. Despite a slightly humid season, Margaret River cabernets are fine and elegant, à la 2000 vintage, while it has produced some excellent shiraz, chardonnay and sauvignon blanc. With only a little rain, the Great Southern enjoyed a long Indian summer, ripening all varieties perfectly. Pemberton's red wine vintage might be affected by some poor weather near harvest.

# Alkoomi

Wingeballup Road, Frankland WA 6396. Tel: (08) 9855 2229. Fax: (08) 9855 2284.
Website: www.alkoomiwines.com.au Email: alkoomi@wn.com.au
Region: **Frankland River** Winemakers: **Michael Staniford, Rod Hallett** Viticulturist: **Wayne Lange**
Chief Executive: **Merv Lange**

Alkoomi was one of the first serious players in the Great Southern region. Its benchmark wines are its aromatic, spicy Riesling and its long-living red wines, particularly Cabernet Sauvignon. Alkoomi's trademark is the concentrated expression of intense berry flavours in its reds, supported by firm, tight astringency. Its 'Reserve' level Blackbutt blend of red Bordeaux varieties and Jarrah Shiraz offer most complexity and definition of fruit.

## BLACKBUTT RED BLEND

RANKING **3**

**Frankland River** $50+
**Current vintage: 2001** 93

Firm and well structured, with an earthy, cedary bouquet of slightly cooked cassis, dark plum and mulberry aromas. There are underlying nuances of chocolate and crushed bullant. Its powerful, long and fine-grained palate harmoniously delivers intense and well-ripened dark berry and plum fruit tightly knit with cedary oak.

| | | | |
|---|---|---|---|
| 2001 | 93 | 2013 | 2021 |
| 1999 | 88 | 2004 | 2007 |
| 1998 | 92 | 2006 | 2010+ |

## CABERNET SAUVIGNON

RANKING **4**

**Frankland River** $20–$29
**Current vintage: 2002** 86

Earthy, meaty aromas of sweet red and black berries, lightly varnishy oak and menthol precede a smooth, soft and creamy palate whose lightly soupy fruit reveals some underlying herbal notes and a slightly hard and greenish finish.

| | | | |
|---|---|---|---|
| 2002 | 86 | 2007 | 2010 |
| 2001 | 89 | 2009 | 2013 |
| 1999 | 92 | 2011 | 2019 |
| 1998 | 92 | 2010 | 2018 |
| 1996 | 81 | 2001 | 2004 |
| 1995 | 82 | 2003 | 2007 |
| 1994 | 89 | 2002 | 2006 |
| 1993 | 88 | 1998 | 2001 |
| 1992 | 88 | 1997 | 2000 |
| 1991 | 89 | 2003 | 2011 |
| 1990 | 90 | 2002 | 2010 |
| 1989 | 88 | 2001 | 2009 |
| 1988 | 87 | 2000 | 2005 |

## CHARDONNAY

RANKING **5**

**Frankland River** $20–$29
**Current vintage: 2002** 93

Shapely, elegant chardonnay with a delicate, smoky and earthy, appealingly reductive and lightly cheesy bouquet of grapefruit, melon and pineapple flavours over hints of toffee apple. Round, soft and elegant, it's long and savoury, earthy and nutty, with an excellent core of vibrant citrus and tropical fruit, finishing with crisp, lemony acids.

| | | | |
|---|---|---|---|
| 2002 | 93 | 2007 | 2010 |
| 2001 | 89 | 2003 | 2006+ |
| 2000 | 88 | 2002 | 2005 |
| 1998 | 87 | 2000 | 2003 |
| 1997 | 92 | 2002 | 2005 |
| 1996 | 88 | 1998 | 2001 |

## JARRAH SHIRAZ

RANKING **3**

**Frankland River** $30–$49
**Current vintage: 2001** 89

Ultra-ripe aromas of slightly stressed and shrivelled black fruits with pencil-shavings wood and some meaty, horse-hair influences. Spicy, earthy and meaty, with a long and moderately full palate of concentrated dark fruits, chocolate and treacle, polished cedar/vanilla oak and licorice-like undertones. Dries out at the finish, but should make good shorter term drinking.

| | | | |
|---|---|---|---|
| 2001 | 89 | 2006 | 2009 |
| 2000 | 86 | 2005 | 2008 |
| 1999 | 93 | 2007 | 2011+ |

A
B
C
D
E
F
G
H
I
J
K
L
M
N
O
P
Q
R
S
T
U
V
W
X
Y
Z

## RIESLING

**Frankland River** $12–$19
**Current vintage: 2003** 93

Tangy cellar-style riesling whose delicate musky aromas of apple, pear and stonefruit precede a pristine, succulent and brightly flavoured palate whose lime and nectarine flavours culminate in a refreshing, dry and lemony finish.

| | | | |
|---|---|---|---|
| 2003 | 93 | 2011 | 2015+ |
| 2002 | 89 | 2004 | 2007 |
| 2001 | 93 | 2009 | 2013 |
| 1999 | 88 | 2001 | 2004+ |
| 1998 | 90 | 2006 | 2010 |
| 1997 | 91 | 2005 | 2009 |
| 1996 | 91 | 2004 | 2008 |
| 1995 | 91 | 2000 | 2003+ |
| 1994 | 94 | 2002 | 2006 |
| 1993 | 87 | 1998 | 2001 |

## SAUVIGNON BLANC

**Frankland River** $20–$29
**Current vintage: 2003** 87

Simple grassy varietal sauvignon blanc whose light passionfruit and gooseberry aromas and easy-drinking, juicy and clean-finishing palate are typically herbaceous and refreshing.

| | | | |
|---|---|---|---|
| 2003 | 87 | 2003 | 2004 |
| 2002 | 82 | 2003 | 2004 |
| 2001 | 89 | 2002 | 2003 |
| 2000 | 93 | 2001 | 2002 |
| 1999 | 87 | 2001 | 2004 |
| 1998 | 88 | 2000 | 2003 |
| 1997 | 90 | 1998 | 1999 |

### SHIRAZ (Shiraz Viognier from 2002)

**Frankland River** $20–$29
**Current vintage: 2002** 91

Smooth, restrained and refined northern Rhône blend with a spicy perfume of obvious viognier floral influence over sweet red and black berry shiraz aromas. Deeply flavoured with vibrant dark plums and cassis, it's been given some assertive cedary oak and a fine-grained spine of drying tannins. Very drinkable now and later.

| | | | |
|---|---|---|---|
| 2002 | 91 | 2007 | 2010+ |
| 2001 | 87 | 2003 | 2006+ |
| 2000 | 81 | 2002 | 2005 |
| 1999 | 89 | 2007 | 2011 |
| 1998 | 86 | 2003 | 2006 |
| 1997 | 87 | 1999 | 2002 |

# All Saints Estate

All Saints Road, Wahgunyah Vic 3687. Tel: (02) 6035 2222. Fax: (02) 6035 2200.
Website: www.allsaintswine.com.au Email: wine@allsaintswine.com.au

Region: **Rutherglen** Winemaker: **Dan Crane** Viticulturist: **Tim Trimble** Chief Executive: **Peter Brown**

All Saints Estate is known for its bold, robust and rather oaky red wines. Recent years have seen its reds push the envelope into ultra-ripe territory, achieving impressive concentration, but at the expense of vitality and freshness. Their typically ashtray-like oak tends to dominate their prune and currant fruit flavours.

## CABERNET SAUVIGNON

**Rutherglen** $20–$29
**Current vintage: 2002** 80

Rather cooked, pruney and prematurely ageing red with some forward dehydrated fruit and substantial extract. Lacks vitality and freshness.

| | | | |
|---|---|---|---|
| 2002 | 80 | 2004 | 2007 |
| 2000 | 89 | 2008 | 2012 |
| 1999 | 86 | 2004 | 2007 |
| 1998 | 83 | 2003 | 2006 |
| 1997 | 87 | 2002 | 2005 |
| 1996 | 83 | 1998 | 2001 |
| 1995 | 88 | 2003 | 2007 |
| 1994 | 89 | 2002 | 2006 |
| 1993 | 82 | 1998 | 2001 |
| 1992 | 90 | 2004 | 2012 |
| 1991 | 88 | 1999 | 2003 |

## CARLYLE SHIRAZ (Formerly St Leonards)

| Rutherglen | $30–$49 |
|---|---|
| **Current vintage: 1999** | 83 |

Very ripe, very oaky red whose jammy blackcurrant and plum-like aromas reveal suggestions of mocha, treacle and currants. Rather porty, its over-ripened palate marries stressed fruit characters with ashtray-like oak.

| | | | |
|---|---|---|---|
| 1999 | 83 | 2001 | 2004 |
| 1998 | 77 | 2000 | 2003 |
| 1997 | 91 | 2005 | 2009 |
| 1996 | 89 | 1998 | 2001 |
| 1995 | 86 | 2000 | 2003 |
| 1994 | 91 | 2004 | 2008 |

## MERLOT

| Rutherglen | $20–$29 |
|---|---|
| **Current vintage: 2002** | 79 |

Meaty, pruney and tarry aromas of raisins and mocha with spirity and leathery undertones. Forward, very extracted and stewed prune-like fruit finishes hard-edged and bitter, with a lingering impression of stale oak.

| | | | |
|---|---|---|---|
| 2002 | 79 | 2004 | 2007 |
| 2000 | 88 | 2005 | 2008 |
| 1999 | 82 | 2001 | 2004 |
| 1998 | 89 | 2003 | 2006 |
| 1997 | 82 | 1999 | 2002 |
| 1996 | 88 | 2001 | 2004 |
| 1995 | 86 | 1997 | 2000 |
| 1994 | 79 | 1996 | 1999 |

## SHIRAZ

| Rutherglen | $20–$29 |
|---|---|
| **Current vintage: 2002** | 85 |

Earthy, meaty aromas of prunes, currants and confection-like red berries with a spicy background of leather and cedar, chocolate and cloves. Forward and ripe, then rather more hollow in the mid-palate, it finishes with drying, slightly metallic tannins. More fruit than other current releases from All Saints, but sharing their stressed qualities.

| | | | |
|---|---|---|---|
| 2002 | 85 | 2007 | 2010 |
| 2000 | 87 | 2005 | 2008 |
| 1999 | 88 | 2004 | 2007 |
| 1998 | 87 | 2003 | 2006 |
| 1997 | 88 | 2002 | 2005 |
| 1996 | 87 | 1998 | 2001 |
| 1994 | 92 | 2002 | 2006+ |
| 1993 | 90 | 2001 | 2005 |
| 1992 | 88 | 2000 | 2004 |
| 1989 | 88 | 1997 | 2003 |

# Allandale

Lovedale Road, Pokolbin NSW 2320. Tel: (02) 4990 4526. Fax: (02) 4990 1714.
Website: www.allandalewinery.com.au  Email: wines@allandalewinery.com.au
Region: **Lower Hunter Valley** Winemakers: **Bill Sneddon, Rod Russell** Viticulturist: **Bill Sneddon**
Chief Executive: **Wally Atallah**

Allandale makes reliable and affordable traditional Hunter Valley white wines, but sources its Cabernet Sauvignon from Mudgee and the Hilltops region of New South Wales. From a hot vintage, the 2003 vintage whites are forward, vibrant and juicy wines for early enjoyment.

## CHARDONNAY

| Lower Hunter Valley | $12–$19 |
|---|---|
| **Current vintage: 2003** | 87 |

Smooth, soft and approachable chardonnay whose lightly tobaccoey aromas of melon and lemon are lifted by restrained oak influences. Its palate reveals some lively nectarine and peach flavours.

| | | | |
|---|---|---|---|
| 2003 | 87 | 2004 | 2005+ |
| 2002 | 86 | 2003 | 2004 |
| 2001 | 87 | 2002 | 2003+ |
| 2000 | 90 | 2002 | 2005 |
| 1999 | 89 | 2004 | 2007 |
| 1998 | 80 | 1999 | 2000 |

| Lower Hunter Valley | $12–$19 |
| :--- | ---: |
| **Current vintage: 2003** | **87** |

Juicy, honest and regional Hunter semillon with rather an oily texture. Its delicate floral perfume of melon and peach precedes a vibrant, tangy palate whose melon/lemon flavours finish just slightly hot and confectionary. Give it a year or so.

| | | | |
| --- | --- | --- | --- |
| 2003 | 87 | 2005 | 2008 |
| 2002 | 88 | 2007 | 2010 |
| 2001 | 90 | 2006 | 2009 |
| 2000 | 93 | 2005 | 2008+ |
| 1998 | 86 | 2000 | 2003+ |
| 1997 | 89 | 2002 | 2005 |
| 1996 | 92 | 2004 | 2008 |
| 1995 | 90 | 2000 | 2003 |
| 1993 | 94 | 2001 | 2005 |

# Amberley

Thornton Road, Yallingup WA 6282. Tel: (08) 9755 2288. Fax: (08) 9755 2171.
Website: www1.amberleyestate.com.au  Email: amberley@amberley-estate.com.au
Region: **Margaret River** Winemakers: **Eddie Price, Paul Dunnewyk** Viticulturist: **Philip Smith**
Chief Executive: **Eddie Price**

Now owned by the large Canadian wine producer and distributor, Vincor (which also owns another significant Western Australian producer in Goundrey), Amberley is a maker of are typically fresh, juicy and generous white wines, and earthy, rather herbaceous reds. The best value offered by Amberley tends to be found in its in its 'standard' and First Selection labels.

## CABERNET MERLOT
RANKING

| Margaret River | $20–$29 |
| :--- | ---: |
| **Current vintage: 2001** | **86** |

Shorter-term red blend showing both under and over-ripe characters. Its earthy, slightly sweaty and meaty aromas of dark plums and berries herald a rich, chewy mouthful of ripe plummy fruit. Its tannins are slightly herbal and sappy.

| | | | |
| --- | --- | --- | --- |
| 2001 | 86 | 2003 | 2006+ |
| 2000 | 91 | 2005 | 2008+ |
| 1999 | 87 | 2004 | 2007 |
| 1998 | 84 | 2003 | 2006 |
| 1997 | 93 | 2005 | 2009 |
| 1996 | 90 | 2004 | 2008 |
| 1995 | 86 | 2000 | 2003 |
| 1994 | 87 | 2006 | 2014 |
| 1993 | 91 | 2001 | 2005 |
| 1992 | 91 | 2000 | 2004+ |

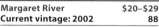

## FIRST SELECTION SHIRAZ
RANKING

| Margaret River | $20–$29 |
| :--- | ---: |
| **Current vintage: 2002** | **88** |

Earthy aromas of dark plums, chocolate and cassis over peppery suggestions of cloves and cinnamon. Fine, long and vibrant, the palate has some structure, presenting lively dark berry and plum flavours bound by soft, approachable tannins and fresh acids.

| | | | |
| --- | --- | --- | --- |
| 2002 | 88 | 2004 | 2007+ |
| 2001 | 82 | 2003 | 2006 |
| 2000 | 86 | 2002 | 2005+ |
| 1999 | 88 | 2004 | 2007 |
| 1998 | 81 | 2000 | 2003 |
| 1997 | 89 | 2002 | 2005 |

## RESERVE CABERNET SAUVIGNON
RANKING

| Margaret River | $30–$49 |
| :--- | ---: |
| **Current vintage: 1997** | **87** |

Very developed, leathery and chocolatey cabernet with meaty, earthy and greenish undertones. It's rustic and charming, but while there's plenty of richness and generosity, there is a capsicum-like thread of flavour and a herbal edge to its tannins.

| | | | |
| --- | --- | --- | --- |
| 1997 | 87 | 2005 | 2009 |
| 1996 | 88 | 2008 | 2016 |
| 1995 | 91 | 2007 | 2015 |
| 1993 | 85 | 2001 | 2005 |
| 1992 | 87 | 2000 | 2004+ |

## SEMILLON SAUVIGNON BLANC

| Margaret River | $20–$29 | 2003 | 84 | 2004 | 2005 |
|---|---|---|---|---|---|
| Current vintage: 2003 | 84 | 2002 | 87 | 2003 | 2004+ |
| | | 2001 | 83 | 2001 | 2002 |
| Slippery, viscous and rather broad-natured | | 2000 | 86 | 2002 | 2005 |
| sauvignon blanc with a dusty, herbal aroma of | | 1999 | 90 | 2004 | 2007 |
| capsicum and asparagus. There's some sweet vanilla | | 1998 | 90 | 2001 | 2004 |
| oak and rather a hot, cloying finish of soft acids. | | 1997 | 88 | 1998 | 1999 |
| Lacks great length and fruit intensity. | | 1996 | 94 | 1998 | 2001 |

# Annie's Lane

Quelltaler Estate, Quelltaler Road, Watervale SA 5452. Tel: (08) 8843 0003. Fax: (08) 8843 0096.
Website: www.annieslane.com.au  Email: cellardoor@annieslane.com.au

Region: **Clare Valley** Winemaker: **Mark Robertson** Viticulturist: **Peter Pawelski** Chief Executive: **Jamie Odell**

Sadly, recent discounting in the marketplace has damaged the image of this excellent Clare Valley label, which has typically been one of the most consistent of Beringer Blass' many performers. The arrival at this winery of the experienced and talented Kiwi winemaker, Mark Robertson, suggests to me that Annie's Lane might still have a positive future. The strong scores given to current red releases underpin the brand's great value.

## CABERNET MERLOT

| Clare Valley | $20–$29 | 2002 | 91 | 2010 | 2014 |
|---|---|---|---|---|---|
| Current vintage: 2002 | 91 | 2001 | 85 | 2003 | 2006 |
| | | 2000 | 87 | 2002 | 2005 |
| Elegant, harmonious blend, medium to full in weight, | | 1999 | 86 | 2001 | 2004 |
| with a sweet earthy perfume of red berries and | | 1998 | 90 | 2003 | 2006 |
| cassis, backed by hints of herbaceousness and | | 1997 | 87 | 2002 | 2005 |
| restrained vanilla oak. Smooth, fine and stylish, pre- | | 1996 | 82 | 1998 | 2001 |
| senting a lively palate of pristine small berry fruit | | 1995 | 94 | 2003 | 2007 |
| supported by oak and fine-grained tannins. | | | | | |
| Great value for the cellar. | | | | | |

## CHARDONNAY

| Clare Valley | $20–$29 | 2003 | 82 | 2003 | 2004 |
|---|---|---|---|---|---|
| Current vintage: 2003 | 82 | 2002 | 87 | 2003 | 2004 |
| | | 2001 | 82 | 2002 | 2003 |
| Dull, rather cooked citrusy and stonefruit aromas | | 2000 | 83 | 2001 | 2002 |
| with assertive butterscotch/toffee undertones. | | 1999 | 89 | 2001 | 2004 |
| Forward and juicy, but dries out to a slightly bitter | | 1998 | 87 | 2000 | 2003 |
| and skinsy finish. Lacks fruit and freshness. | | 1997 | 89 | 1999 | 2001 |
| | | 1996 | 94 | 1998 | 2001 |

## COPPERTRAIL SHIRAZ (formerly The Contour)

| Clare Valley | $50+ | 2000 | 87 | 2002 | 2005+ |
|---|---|---|---|---|---|
| Current vintage: 2000 | 87 | 1999 | 92 | 2007 | 2011 |
| | | 1998 | 93 | 2006 | 2010 |
| Typical 2000 vintage wine whose meaty mulberry, | | 1997 | 93 | 2005 | 2009 |
| cassis and plum-like fruit presents some under | | 1996 | 95 | 2004 | 2008+ |
| and over-ripe influences. Laced with herbal and | | 1995 | 90 | 2003 | 2007 |
| spicy notes of cinnamon and cloves, it's given | | | | | |
| sweetness and length through some fine-grained | | | | | |
| cedar/vanilla oak, before finishing slightly green- | | | | | |
| edged and sappy. | | | | | |

## RIESLING

| Clare Valley | $12–$19 | 2003 | 89 | 2005 | 2008 |
|---|---|---|---|---|---|
| Current vintage: 2003 | 89 | 2002 | 93 | 2007 | 2010+ |
| | | 2001 | 89 | 2006 | 2009 |
| Generous, round and richly flavoured dry riesling | | 2000 | 89 | 2002 | 2005 |
| with a floral and lightly chalky aroma of lemon, | | 1999 | 81 | 2000 | 2001 |
| pear and baby powder. Forward and juicy, it's slightly | | 1998 | 94 | 2003 | 2006+ |
| toasty and developed, but finishes with refresh- | | 1997 | 90 | 2005 | 2009 |
| ing lemony acidity. | | 1996 | 94 | 1998 | 2001 |

## SEMILLON

RANKING 5

**Clare Valley**     $12–$19
**Current vintage: 2002**     **88**

Dusty aromas of lemon, honey and melon are scented with lightly toasty oak. Its round, chewy palate begins with generous lemon detergent and honeydew melon fruit before finishing lean, dry and tight-knit, with lingering vanilla oak and lemony acids.

| | | | |
|---|---|---|---|
| 2002 | 88 | 2004 | 2007+ |
| 2001 | 88 | 2003 | 2006 |
| 2000 | 82 | 2001 | 2002 |
| 1999 | 87 | 2004 | 2007 |
| 1998 | 91 | 2000 | 2003 |
| 1997 | 87 | 1999 | 2002 |
| 1996 | 93 | 2004 | 2008 |

## SHIRAZ

RANKING 4

**Clare Valley**     $20–$29
**Current vintage: 2001**     **90**

A sweet perfume of peppery, spicy raspberries, cherries, redcurrants and violets is neatly underpinned by sweet vanilla and lightly coconut-like oak. Smooth and supple, long and fine-grained, the palate is more restrained than usual for this wine. Intense small berry/plum fruit is tightly integrated with vanilla/chocolate oak and fine, firm tannins.

| | | | |
|---|---|---|---|
| 2001 | 90 | 2006 | 2009 |
| 2000 | 84 | 2002 | 2005 |
| 1999 | 86 | 2001 | 2004 |
| 1998 | 90 | 2003 | 2006 |
| 1997 | 89 | 2002 | 2005 |
| 1996 | 90 | 2001 | 2004 |
| 1995 | 88 | 2000 | 2003 |

# Armstrong

Military Road, Armstrong Vic 3377. Tel: (08) 8277 6073. Fax: (08) 8277 6035.
Email: armstrong@picknowl.com.au

Region: **Grampians, Great Western** Winemaker: **Tony Royal** Viticulturist: **Stan Royal**
Chief Executive: **Tony Royal**

Armstrong is the pet project of experienced winemaker Tony Royal, a long-time senior winemaker for Seppelt. Today he heads the Australian operation for French cooper Seguin-Moreau, whose product receives a decent road-test in the spicy Armstrong reds. As the vineyard gains more maturity, the wines are becoming longer, finer, more elegant and complete, acquiring the typical longevity of Great Western shiraz.

## SHIRAZ

RANKING 3

**Grampians, Great Western**    $30–$49
**Current vintage: 2002**     **92**

An elegant, long-term red with distinctive regional qualities. Its delicate, dusty perfume of blackberries, mulberries and dark plums reveals minty nuances of black pepper and menthol. Tightly interwoven with powder-fine tannins and restrained cedar/vanilla oak, the palate is bright and lively, with a round and succulent middle.

| | | | |
|---|---|---|---|
| 2002 | 92 | 2010 | 2014+ |
| 2001 | 93 | 2009 | 2013 |
| 2000 | 93 | 2008 | 2012 |
| 1999 | 89 | 2007 | 2011 |
| 1998 | 83 | 2000 | 2003 |
| 1996 | 88 | 2001 | 2004+ |

# Arthur's Creek

Strathewen Road, Arthur's Creek Vic 3099. Tel: (03) 9714 8202. Fax: (03) 9714 8202.
Website: www.arthurscreekestate.com Email: tamara2@bigpond.com

Region: **Yarra Valley** Winemaker: **Sergio Carlei** Viticulturist: **Stephen Wood** Chief Executive: **Stephen Wood**

Arthur's Creek has recently changed hands and winemakers, with Sergio Carlei now assuming control of production. Given the considerable age of the current release wines, it will take some time for these changes to become visible in the marketplace. Meantime, the vineyard's traditional reds are minty, robust and menthol-like.

## CABERNET SAUVIGNON

RANKING 4

**Yarra Valley**     $20–$29
**Current vintage: 1997**     **86**

Sinewy, minty and meaty cabernet with extract and astringency. There are greenish aspects to its menthol-like aromas of plums and cassis, while the palate's fruit is rather over-awed by its hard extract. Old fashioned.

| | | | |
|---|---|---|---|
| 1997 | 86 | 2009 | 2017 |
| 1996 | 92 | 2016 | 2026 |
| 1995 | 88 | 2007 | 2015 |

# Arundel Farm

Arundel Road, Keilor Vic 3036. Tel: (03) 9335 3422. Fax: (03) 9335 4912.
Email: arundel.farm@bigpond.com

Region: **Sunbury** Winemaker: **Bianca Conwell** Viticulturist: **Mark Hayes** Chief Executive: **Bianca Conwell**

A tiny vineyard near Keilor, Victoria, Arundel earns its place here on its fine track record of elegant, spicy and peppery Shiraz. They're anything but the biggest of their kind, and neither are they the most Rhône-like in southern Australia. They are however consistently stylish, complex and generous, not to mention relatively affordable for the quality and individuality they represent.

## SHIRAZ

RANKING **3**

| Sunbury | $30–$49 |
|---|---|
| **Current vintage: 2002** | **90** |

| | | | |
|---|---|---|---|
| 2002 | 90 | 2007 | 2010+ |
| 2001 | 92 | 2009 | 2013 |
| 2000 | 93 | 2005 | 2008+ |
| 1999 | 89 | 2001 | 2004+ |
| 1997 | 77 | 1998 | 1999 |

Complex, deeply flavoured southern Victorian shiraz with Cornas-like pretensions. Its wild, spicy aromas of dark plums, berries and undergrowth do reveal some reductive, earthy and herbal complexity, while its slightly rustic and minty palate of medium to full weight is long, savoury and fine-grained. Slightly too herbal for a higher score.

# Ashton Hills Vineyard

Tregarthen Road, Ashton SA 5137. Tel: (08) 8390 1243. Fax: (08) 8390 1243.

Region: **Adelaide Hills** Winemaker: **Stephen George** Viticulturist: **Stephen George**
Chief Executive: **Stephen George**

Ashton Hills is a well-established maker of idiosyncratic wines at the hands of Stephen George, who believes the vintage variation experienced at his cool-climate vineyard site to be the major reason behind the relatively broad spectrum of style and quality it produces. Of the current releases, I am most impressed with the 2002 vintages of the tangy, herbal Chardonnay and longer-living Pinot Noir.

## CHARDONNAY

RANKING **5**

| Adelaide Hills | $20–$29 |
|---|---|
| **Current vintage: 2002** | **92** |

| | | | |
|---|---|---|---|
| 2002 | 92 | 2004 | 2007 |
| 2001 | 88 | 2003 | 2006 |
| 2000 | 89 | 2002 | 2005 |
| 1999 | 83 | 2001 | 2004 |
| 1998 | 85 | 2000 | 2003 |
| 1997 | 82 | 1999 | 2002 |
| 1996 | 84 | 1997 | 1998 |

Tangy, racy chardonnay whose pure, intense fruit qualities are tightly knit with creamy lees and sweet vanilla oak influences. Tropical aromas of pineapple and mango precede a round, almost oily palate richly endowed with apple, pear and tropical flavours, with a lingering note of green olive. It finishes long and refreshing.

## FIVE (formerly Obliqua)

RANKING **4**

| Adelaide Hills | $20–$29 |
|---|---|
| **Current vintage: 2001** | **87** |

| | | | |
|---|---|---|---|
| 2001 | 87 | 2006 | 2009 |
| 2000 | 92 | 2008 | 2012 |
| 1999 | 89 | 2007 | 2011 |
| 1998 | 91 | 2006 | 2010 |
| 1997 | 87 | 2002 | 2005 |
| 1996 | 89 | 2004 | 2008 |
| 1994 | 91 | 1999 | 2002 |
| 1992 | 87 | 1997 | 2000 |
| 1991 | 95 | 1999 | 2003 |
| 1990 | 94 | 1998 | 2002 |

Delicate, almost fragile short to medium term cabernet blend with a dusty, lightly peppery aroma of sweet raspberries and blackcurrants over cedary oak, punctuated by nuances of mint, eucalypt and dried herbs. Lacking great depth, the palate begins with intense forward small berry flavours, then moves through cedar/vanilla oak to a slightly short finish.

## PINOT NOIR

RANKING **4**

| Adelaide Hills | $30–$49 |
|---|---|
| **Current vintage: 2002** | **91** |

| | | | |
|---|---|---|---|
| 2002 | 91 | 2007 | 2010+ |
| 2001 | 87 | 2003 | 2006 |
| 2000 | 89 | 2004 | 2007 |
| 1999 | 89 | 2001 | 2004 |
| 1998 | 89 | 2000 | 2003 |
| 1997 | 96 | 2002 | 2005+ |
| 1996 | 89 | 2001 | 2004 |
| 1995 | 94 | 2000 | 2003 |
| 1994 | 95 | 2002 | 2006 |
| 1993 | 94 | 1998 | 2001 |

Pristine, vibrant pinot fruit with a musky perfume of dark cherries, rose petals and spicy nuances of cloves, cinnamon and forest floor. Long and silky, with exuberant brightness and intensity of small berry/cherry flavours bound by silky tannins. There's a hint of meaty complexity and just a suggestion of herbal, greenish influences beneath.

**Adelaide Hills** $12–$19
**Current vintage: 2003** 89

Round, flavoursome and honest varietal dry riesling. Its delicate aromas of fresh pear, apple and some funky leesy qualities are slightly sweaty, while the palate is unusually oily, but packed with limey apple fruit before a clean and lemony finish.

| | | | |
|------|----|------|-------|
| 2003 | 89 | 2005 | 2008+ |
| 2001 | 95 | 2006 | 2009+ |
| 2000 | 94 | 2005 | 2008+ |
| 1999 | 92 | 2004 | 2007+ |
| 1998 | 93 | 2006 | 2010 |
| 1997 | 94 | 2005 | 2009 |
| 1996 | 90 | 2004 | 2008 |
| 1995 | 82 | 1997 | 2000 |
| 1994 | 94 | 1999 | 2002 |

# Baileys

RMB 4160 Taminick Gap Road, Glenrowan Vic 3675. Tel: (03) 5766 2392. Fax: (03) 5766 2596.
Website: www.beringerblass.com.au  Email: mick.clayton@beringerblass.com.au
Region: **NE Victoria** Winemakers: **Matt Steel, Daniel Bettio** Viticulturist: **Paul Dahlenburg**
Chief Executive: **Jamie Odell**

Baileys is another brand undergoing a healthy resurgence under the ownership of Beringer Blass. It now offers three different shirazes, the more expensive of which are sourced from old vineyards identified by their labels. As a group, they are deeply flavoured and robust without being over-ripened or excessively extractive. In other words, I find them to be balanced, generous and approachable.

## 1904 BLOCK SHIRAZ

RANKING 4

**NE Victoria** $30–$49
**Current vintage: 2000** 90

Sumptuous, well-made shiraz from very ripe fruit, whose spicy and smoky aromas of prunes, currants and leather are handsomely fitted with sweet vanilla and chocolate oak. Very ripe and forward, delivering rich, slightly over-ripened fruit, it's initially velvet-smooth, but finishes rather raw and blocky.

| | | | |
|------|----|------|-------|
| 2000 | 90 | 2005 | 2008 |
| 1999 | 93 | 2011 | 2019+ |
| 1998 | 91 | 2010 | 2018 |

## 1920s BLOCK SHIRAZ

RANKING 4

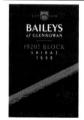

**NE Victoria** $20–$29
**Current vintage: 2001** 87

Ageing, rather dehydrated shiraz whose meaty, tarry aromas of berries, currants and prunes reveal assertive oak and earthy, leathery undertones. Moderately full in weight, it's firm and tannic, with a meaty, up-front palate of concentrated but tiring fruit, drying out towards the finish.

| | | | |
|------|----|------|-------|
| 2001 | 87 | 2003 | 2006 |
| 2000 | 92 | 2005 | 2008+ |
| 1999 | 91 | 2011 | 2019 |
| 1998 | 89 | 2006 | 2010+ |
| 1997 | 87 | 2002 | 2005 |
| 1996 | 88 | 2001 | 2004 |
| 1995 | 86 | 2000 | 2003 |
| 1994 | 93 | 2006 | 2014 |
| 1993 | 87 | 1998 | 2001 |
| 1992 | 90 | 2000 | 2004 |
| 1991 | 94 | 2003 | 2011 |

## SHIRAZ

RANKING 4

**NE Victoria** $12–$19
**Current vintage: 2003** 90

Generous, punchy and flavoursome shiraz with a pungent, spicy and confiture-like aroma of blackberries and raspberries over roasted, bubblegum-like oak. There's volume and brightness aplenty of vibrant blackberry, plum and menthol-like fruit. Framed by fine but firm tannins, it's well set for a little cellaring.

| | | | |
|------|----|------|-------|
| 2003 | 90 | 2008 | 2011 |
| 2002 | 91 | 2010 | 2014+ |
| 2000 | 89 | 2005 | 2008 |
| 1999 | 87 | 2004 | 2007 |

# Balgownie Estate

Hermitage Road, Maiden Gully Vic 3551. Tel: (03) 5449 6222. Fax: (03) 5449 6506.
Website: www.balgownieestate.com.au  Email: info@balgownieestate.com.au

Region: **Bendigo** Winemaker: **Tobias Anstead** Viticulturist: **John Monteath** Chief Executive: **Des Forrester**

The excellent quality of its 2002 reds confirms that Balgownie is right back on track. Extensive remodelling in the vineyard, plus a huge amount of effort in the winery is paying handsome dividends with these two tightly structured and very generously flavoured wines. The Shiraz is a particularly outstanding expression of contemporary Victorian viticulture, revealing meaty, briary complexity and excellent balance.

## CABERNET SAUVIGNON

RANKING **4**

| Bendigo | $20–$29 |
|---|---|
| Current vintage: 2002 | 93 |

Very firm, structured cabernet of refinement and balance. Its earthy fragrance of violets and rose petals, cassis, plums and blackberries overlies tightly integrated cedar/chocolate/vanilla oak and scents of dried herbs. Robust and linear, it delivers piercing, penetrative flavours of dark berries and plums over astringent, bony tannins. Wait for it.

| | | | |
|---|---|---|---|
| 2002 | 93 | 2014 | 2022+ |
| 2001 | 89 | 2013 | 2021 |
| 2000 | 90 | 2012 | 2020 |
| 1999 | 89 | 2004 | 2007 |
| 1998 | 87 | 2006 | 2010+ |
| 1997 | 86 | 2005 | 2009 |
| 1996 | 90 | 2008 | 2016 |
| 1995 | 88 | 2007 | 2015 |
| 1994 | 87 | 2002 | 2006 |
| 1993 | 88 | 2005 | 2013 |
| 1992 | 93 | 2004 | 2012 |
| 1991 | 88 | 2011 | 2021 |
| 1990 | 95 | 2010 | 2020 |

## SHIRAZ

RANKING **3**

| Bendigo | $20–$29 |
|---|---|
| Current vintage: 2002 | 94 |

Excellent central Victorian shiraz with a sneezy black pepper aroma of blackberries and dark plums laced with cinnamon, cloves and tightly knit chocolate/vanilla oak. There's also an earthy and slightly funky meatiness present throughout its sumptuous and intensely flavoured palate of briary and spotlessly clean dark fruit flavours. Framed by velvet-smooth but firm tannins, it's an excellent wine of first-rate balance and integration.

| | | | |
|---|---|---|---|
| 2002 | 94 | 2010 | 2014+ |
| 2001 | 92 | 2009 | 2013 |
| 2000 | 89 | 2005 | 2008 |
| 1999 | 89 | 2004 | 2007 |
| 1998 | 89 | 2003 | 2006+ |
| 1997 | 93 | 2009 | 2017 |
| 1996 | 93 | 2004 | 2008+ |
| 1995 | 94 | 2007 | 2015 |
| 1994 | 90 | 2002 | 2006 |
| 1993 | 93 | 2005 | 2013 |
| 1990 | 94 | 2002 | 2010 |

# Balnaves

Main Road, Coonawarra SA 5263. Tel: (08) 8737 2946. Fax: (08) 8737 2945.
Website: www.balnaves.com.au  Email: kirsty.balnaves@balnaves.com.au

Region: **Coonawarra** Winemaker: **Peter Bissell** Viticulturist: **Peter Balnaves** Chief Executive: **Doug Balnaves**

Balnaves' red wines are typically complex, minty and briary. Compared to most of the reds made by the larger Coonawarra producers, they're rather exotic and gamey, made by a genuine craftsman in Peter Bissell. Its founder, Doug Balnaves, is one of the region's most experienced viticulturists. The Tally Reserve release from 2001 is the company's best-ever wine — a magnificent Coonawarra red of impact and elegance.

## CABERNET SAUVIGNON

RANKING **4**

| Coonawarra | $30–$49 |
|---|---|
| Current vintage: 2002 | 91 |

Tightly knit and focused cabernet with a violet-like fragrance of lightly minty cassis and redcurrant aromas supported by sweet creamy and cedary oak. Austere and fine-grained, its long, briary and brightly lit palate of pristine plum, mulberry and blackcurrant flavours is framed by firm, bony tannins. Although there's a suggestion of wildness, the palate is stylish and elegant.

| | | | |
|---|---|---|---|
| 2002 | 91 | 2010 | 2014+ |
| 2001 | 88 | 2006 | 2009 |
| 2000 | 86 | 2002 | 2005 |
| 1999 | 89 | 2007 | 2011 |
| 1998 | 92 | 2006 | 2010+ |
| 1997 | 87 | 2002 | 2005 |
| 1996 | 90 | 2004 | 2008+ |

## THE TALLY RESERVE CABERNET SAUVIGNON

RANKING **3**

| Coonawarra | $50+ |
|---|---|
| Current vintage: 2001 | 96 |

Meaty, slightly musky layers of deeply concentrated small red and black berry fruits and suggestions of dark olives over cedar and vanilla oak. Sumptuous, powerfully structured palate of pristine small berry and dark plum fruit framed by firm, but velvet-smooth extract. Very long and harmonious, culminating in a silky-fine finish of persistent dark fruit, sweet oak, fresh mint and dried herbs.

| | | | |
|---|---|---|---|
| 2001 | 96 | 2013 | 2021 |
| 2000 | 91 | 2008 | 2012+ |
| 1998 | 93 | 2010 | 2018 |

# Bannockburn

Box 72 Midland Highway, Bannockburn Vic 3331. Tel: (03) 5281 1363. Fax: (03) 5281 1349.
Website: www.bannockburnvineyards.com  Email: info@bannockburnvineyards.com
Region: **Geelong** Winemaker: **Gary Farr** Viticulturist: **Lucas Grigsby** Chief Executive: **Phillip Harrison**

Bannockburn is one of the greatest makers of pinot noir and chardonnay in Australia, and its current mature releases of its icon labels (the Serré and the SRH) are amongst the best of their kind. Winemaker Gary Farr resolutely sticks to making the sort of wines he enjoys drinking, and like many who have discovered them, I'm just one of the lucky ones who appreciates them as well. While the 'standard' Bannockburn releases are also exceptional wines, the Range Shiraz is wonderfully elegant and savoury, a wine with real Rhône-like pretensions.

## CHARDONNAY

RANKING **2**

| Geelong | $30–$49 |
|---|---|
| Current vintage: 2002 | 94 |

Toasty, buttery aromas of sweet quince, melon and tobacco, with underlying slightly charry, fine-grained French oak and oatmeal-like complexity. Succulent and creamy, its juicy palate of candied citrus and melon fruit, tightly integrated spicy oak and refreshing acidity finishes with lingering savoury mineral notes. Uncompromisingly rich and textured, but without the length of fruit from the best vintages.

| | | | |
|---|---|---|---|
| 2002 | 94 | 2007 | 2010+ |
| 2001 | 95 | 2006 | 2009+ |
| 2000 | 95 | 2005 | 2008+ |
| 1999 | 94 | 2004 | 2007 |
| 1998 | 93 | 2006 | 2010 |
| 1997 | 92 | 2005 | 2009 |
| 1996 | 95 | 2001 | 2004 |
| 1995 | 96 | 1997 | 2000 |
| 1994 | 95 | 2002 | 2006 |
| 1993 | 96 | 2001 | 2005 |
| 1992 | 94 | 2000 | 2004 |
| 1991 | 96 | 1999 | 2003 |

## PINOT NOIR

RANKING **2**

| Geelong | $30–$49 |
|---|---|
| Current vintage: 2002 | 91 |

A typically herbal expression of youthful Bannockburn pinot noir whose earthy, meaty fragrance of spices and dill, small red berries and plums reveals a hint of duck fat and some floral perfume. Smooth and supple, its vibrant, dusty palate presents a fleshy core of briary cherry/plum flavours framed by slightly sappy tannins and bound by slightly green-edged acids.

| | | | |
|---|---|---|---|
| 2002 | 91 | 2007 | 2010+ |
| 2001 | 90 | 2006 | 2009 |
| 2000 | 95 | 2008 | 2012 |
| 1999 | 94 | 2007 | 2011 |
| 1998 | 94 | 2003 | 2006 |
| 1997 | 94 | 2005 | 2009 |
| 1996 | 93 | 2004 | 2008+ |
| 1995 | 92 | 2000 | 2003 |
| 1994 | 94 | 2002 | 2006+ |
| 1993 | 88 | 1998 | 2001+ |
| 1992 | 96 | 2004 | 2012 |
| 1991 | 87 | 1996 | 1999 |
| 1990 | 91 | 1998 | 2002 |

## SERRÉ PINOT NOIR

RANKING **1**

| Geelong | $50+ |
|---|---|
| Current vintage: 1999 | 96 |

Wonderfully fragrant, spicy and pristine pinot noir deeply scented with rose petals, sweet maraschino cherries, red berries and plums over a light hint of stalkiness and earthy, cedary undertones. Supremely long, elegant and luscious, perhaps the most deeply fruited wine under this label since the opulent 1994 vintage, with complex, concentrated red berry flavours framed by tight-knit tannins. Excellent structure, length and balance.

| | | | |
|---|---|---|---|
| 1999 | 96 | 2007 | 2011+ |
| 1998 | 96 | 2006 | 2010+ |
| 1997 | 95 | 2005 | 2009 |
| 1996 | 92 | 2004 | 2008+ |
| 1995 | 95 | 2003 | 2007 |
| 1994 | 96 | 2006 | 2014 |
| 1993 | 93 | 2001 | 2005 |
| 1991 | 73 | 1993 | 1996 |
| 1990 | 88 | 1998 | 2002+ |

## SHIRAZ

**Geelong**      $30–$49
**Current vintage: 2002**      88

Restrained, herbal shiraz with vibrant red berry flavours over a smooth, but rather bony under-carriage. Its fragrance of raspberries, red cherries and redcurrants has a little cinnamon/clove complexity against a background of vanilla oak. Silky, almost sappy, the palate reveals pleasing plum and berry-like fruit and restrained oak, culminating in a slightly raw finish of dried herbs.

| | | | |
|---|---|---|---|
| 2002 | 88 | 2007 | 2010+ |
| 2001 | 95 | 2009 | 2013+ |
| 2000 | 96 | 2012 | 2020 |
| 1999 | 89 | 2001 | 2004+ |
| 1998 | 95 | 2006 | 2010 |
| 1997 | 93 | 2005 | 2009 |
| 1996 | 93 | 2004 | 2008 |
| 1995 | 87 | 2000 | 2003 |
| 1994 | 95 | 2002 | 2006 |
| 1993 | 90 | 1998 | 2001 |
| 1992 | 95 | 2000 | 2004 |
| 1991 | 94 | 1999 | 2003+ |
| 1990 | 90 | 1998 | 2002 |

## SRH CHARDONNAY

**Geelong**      $50+
**Current vintage: 1999**      95

Complex, scented, smoky, meaty and cheesy aromas suggest extended lees contact, but bright melon, peach and lanolin-like fruit aromas easily protrude. There's great depth and con-centration of juicy, tobacco-like fruit on the palate, wonderful softness and length, with a clean, lingering mineral finish. Very evolved and savoury;

| | | | |
|---|---|---|---|
| 1999 | 95 | 2004 | 2007 |
| 1995 | 94 | 1997 | 2000 |
| 1994 | 93 | 1996 | 1999 |
| 1993 | 97 | 1998 | 2001 |

# Baptista

139 High Street, Nagambie Vic 3608. Tel: (03) 5794 2514. Fax: (03) 5794 1776. Email: traeger@eck.net.au

Region: **Heathcote** Winemaker: **David Traeger** Viticulturist: **David Traeger** Chief Executive: **David Traeger**

Baptista is the name given by its owner, David Traeger, to the label hosting his very expensive 'The Graytown' Shiraz. Made from ancient, but rejuvenated old vines, its first three releases reflect a positive improvement in concentration and tannin management.

## THE GRAYTOWN SHIRAZ

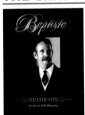

**Heathcote**      $50+
**Current vintage: 1998**      90

Developing, spicy and minty aromas of black and red berries, eucalypt and menthol are offset by assertive new vanilla, chocolate and coconut oak. Firm, smooth and oaky, its minty expression of dark berry fruits is bound by firm, tight tannins and assertive acids. It gives the impression of having needed more aeration, but has more juiciness and texture than the inaugural 1997 vintage.

| | | | |
|---|---|---|---|
| 1999 | 93 | 2011 | 2019 |
| 1998 | 90 | 2006 | 2010+ |
| 1997 | 88 | 2005 | 2009+ |

# Barossa Valley Estate

Seppeltsfield Road, Marananga SA 5355. Tel: (08) 8562 3599. Fax: (08) 8562 4255.
Website: www.bve.com.au  Email: bve@chariot.net.au
Region: **Barossa Valley** Winemaker: **Stuart Bourne** Viticulturist: **Kirsty Waller**
Chief Executive: **Bruce Richardson**

Part-owned by The Hardy Wine Company, Barossa Valley Estate has a couple of first rate strings to its bow in the E&E Black Pepper and Sparkling Shiraz. Its Moculta label is home to many an up-front, fruity and flavoursome Barossa wine, while the mid-priced Ebenezer wines sit a little uneasily between the others.

## E&E BLACK PEPPER SHIRAZ    RANKING 3

| Barossa Valley | | | | $50+ |
| Current vintage: 2000 | | | | 87 |

Earthy, leathery and lightly tarry, jammy aromas of minty raspberries, redcurrants and cassis over some rather greenish bell pepper notes and sweet coconut/vanilla oak. Forward, sweet and slightly vegetal, displaying under and over-ripe fruit influences which some rather charry, sweet coconut oak does its best to smooth over for the short term.

| | | | |
|---|---|---|---|
| 2000 | 87 | 2002 | 2005+ |
| 1999 | 91 | 2004 | 2007+ |
| 1998 | 96 | 2010 | 2018 |
| 1997 | 90 | 2005 | 2009 |
| 1996 | 96 | 2004 | 2008+ |
| 1995 | 93 | 2007 | 2015 |
| 1994 | 93 | 2002 | 2006 |
| 1993 | 93 | 2001 | 2005 |
| 1992 | 91 | 2000 | 2004 |
| 1991 | 95 | 2003 | 2011 |
| 1990 | 90 | 1998 | 2002 |

## E&E SPARKLING SHIRAZ    RANKING 3

| Barossa Valley | | | | $50+ |
| Current vintage: 1999 | | | | 88 |

Varnishy, briary and rather funky sparkling red with a dark, spicy and peppery aroma of plums, small berries and game meats. Its chewy, chocolate and spicecake-like palate is loaded with the flavours of dark wild berries, but culminates in a rather metallic, cedary and crushed ant-like finish.

| | | | |
|---|---|---|---|
| 1999 | 88 | 2007 | 2011+ |
| 1998 | 95 | 2006 | 2010 |
| 1996 | 93 | 2001 | 2004+ |
| 1995 | 91 | 2000 | 2003 |
| 1994 | 94 | 1999 | 2002+ |

## EBENEZER CABERNET MERLOT    RANKING 5

| Barossa Valley | | | | $20–$29 |
| Current vintage: 2001 | | | | 85 |

Earthy, cedary and tobaccoey red whose light berry flavours and creamy oak overlie herbal and vegetal influences. Pleasing enough, but a little short and sappy.

| | | | |
|---|---|---|---|
| 2001 | 85 | 2003 | 2006 |
| 2000 | 85 | 2002 | 2005 |
| 1999 | 90 | 2004 | 2007 |
| 1998 | 87 | 2003 | 2006 |
| 1997 | 80 | 1999 | 2002 |
| 1996 | 91 | 2001 | 2004 |

## EBENEZER SHIRAZ    RANKING 5

| Barossa Valley | | | | $20–$29 |
| Current vintage: 2000 | | | | 83 |

Simple, over-ripe and under-ripe red typical of this difficult vintage. Meaty, pruney fruit and greenish herbal influences finish rather lean and sappy.

| | | | |
|---|---|---|---|
| 2000 | 83 | 2002 | 2005+ |
| 1999 | 88 | 2004 | 2007 |
| 1998 | 90 | 2003 | 2006 |
| 1997 | 88 | 2002 | 2005 |
| 1996 | 88 | 2001 | 2004 |
| 1995 | 92 | 2000 | 2003 |
| 1994 | 91 | 1999 | 2002 |
| 1993 | 86 | 1998 | 2001 |
| 1992 | 87 | 1997 | 2000 |

## MOCULTA CABERNET MERLOT

| Barossa Valley | | | | $12–$19 |
| Current vintage: 2001 | | | | 82 |

Quite a simple, but moderately flavoursome wine with light small red berry and plum-like fruit and cedary oak. Fruity enough, but lacks length and follow-through.

| | | | |
|---|---|---|---|
| 2001 | 82 | 2003 | 2006 |
| 2000 | 88 | 2002 | 2005 |
| 1999 | 82 | 2000 | 2001 |
| 1998 | 80 | 2000 | 2003 |
| 1997 | 88 | 1999 | 2002 |
| 1996 | 82 | 1998 | 2001 |

## MOCULTA CHARDONNAY

Barossa Valley $12–$19
**Current vintage: 2003** 88

| | | | |
|---|---|---|---|
| 2003 | 88 | 2004 | 2005 |
| 2002 | 80 | 2002 | 2003 |
| 2001 | 87 | 2002 | 2003+ |
| 2000 | 89 | 2002 | 2005 |
| 1998 | 87 | 1999 | 2000 |

Flavoursome but lightly oaked chardonnay with a refreshing, clean finish. Lightly dusty aromas of green olives, lemon and melon precede a juicy, tangy palate of sweet peach, apple and citrus flavours. Excellent length for virtually an unoaked style, pleasing balance and harmony.

## MOCULTA SHIRAZ

Barossa Valley $12–$19
**Current vintage: 2001** 90

| | | | |
|---|---|---|---|
| 2001 | 90 | 2003 | 2006+ |
| 2000 | 88 | 2002 | 2005 |
| 1999 | 87 | 2001 | 2004 |
| 1998 | 90 | 2003 | 2006 |
| 1997 | 92 | 1999 | 2002 |
| 1996 | 88 | 1998 | 2001 |
| 1995 | 87 | 2000 | 2003 |

Ripe, rather jammy and slightly tarry Barossa red whose spicy, peppery expression of cassis, blackberry, prune and plum-like fruit integrates well with assertive vanilla/coconut American oak influences. Smooth, velvety and very approachable, it's framed by fine, soft tannins. Uncomplicated, but fun.

# Barwang

Barwang Road, Young NSW 2190. Tel: (02) 6382 3594. Fax: (02) 6382 3594.
Website: www.mcwilliams.com.au  Email: mcwines@mcwilliams.com.au
Region: **Hilltops** Winemaker: **Jim Brayne** Viticulturist: **Murray Pulleine** Chief Executive: **Kevin McLintock**
Barwang has become the flag-bearer for the emerging Hilltops region of New South Wales. While recent releases have been affected by the ongoing drought that has severely restricted access to water and thereby caused a level of fruit stress evident in some recent releases, the Barwang label has established a reliable reputation for its long-living, deeply flavoured and robust red wines.

## CABERNET SAUVIGNON

Hilltops $20–$29
**Current vintage: 2002** 88

| | | | |
|---|---|---|---|
| 2002 | 88 | 2010 | 2014 |
| 2001 | 92 | 2009 | 2013 |
| 2000 | 91 | 2012 | 2020 |
| 1999 | 90 | 2004 | 2007 |
| 1998 | 90 | 2006 | 2010+ |
| 1997 | 94 | 2005 | 2009+ |
| 1996 | 87 | 2001 | 2004 |
| 1995 | 89 | 2003 | 2007 |
| 1994 | 90 | 2002 | 2006 |
| 1993 | 91 | 2001 | 2005 |
| 1992 | 90 | 2000 | 2004 |
| 1991 | 95 | 1999 | 2003 |
| 1990 | 86 | 1998 | 2002+ |

Astringent, firm and minty cabernet, but relatively skilful winemaking is unable to conceal the stressed nature of its fruit. Its briary aromas of small berries, dark olives, menthol and cedary oak precede a rather cooked and grippy palate of plums and chocolate that just lacks sufficient fruit vitality.

## CHARDONNAY

Hilltops $20–$29
**Current vintage: 2002** 87

| | | | |
|---|---|---|---|
| 2002 | 87 | 2004 | 2007 |
| 2001 | 87 | 2003 | 2006 |
| 2000 | 90 | 2002 | 2005 |
| 1999 | 87 | 2001 | 2004 |
| 1998 | 94 | 2003 | 2006 |
| 1997 | 90 | 2002 | 2005 |
| 1996 | 92 | 2001 | 2004 |
| 1995 | 88 | 1997 | 2000 |
| 1994 | 91 | 1996 | 1999 |
| 1993 | 89 | 1995 | 1998 |

Slightly overdone and contrived chardonnay whose creamy, tropical aromas of pineapple and peaches are augmented by nutty oatmeal and vanilla oak influences. Rather forward and angular, its palate lacks sufficient depth and length of fruit to counter its rather assertive measure of smoky vanilla oak.

## MERLOT

### Hilltops $20–$29
**Current vintage: 2002** 91

Powerful, grippy merlot whose sweet aromas of cherries, plums and blackberries, violets, mint and menthol are backed by fragrant, smoky suggestions of vanilla oak. It's rather firm and oaky, with smoky mocha qualities beneath deep, brightly flavoured dark fruits.

| 2002 | 91 | 2010 | 2014 |
|------|----|------|------|
| 2001 | 84 | 2006 | 2009+ |
| 2000 | 87 | 2002 | 2005+ |

## SHIRAZ

### Hilltops $20–$29
**Current vintage: 2002** 88

Meaty, musky and minty aromas of slightly stressed dark berry and plum fruit with vanilla, mocha and chocolate oak. Firm and drying, the palate offers a good length and structure of lightly confected and dehydrated currant, plum and berry flavours over firm tannins.

| 2002 | 88 | 2007 | 2010+ |
|------|----|------|-------|
| 2001 | 93 | 2009 | 2013 |
| 2000 | 89 | 2005 | 2008+ |
| 1999 | 88 | 2004 | 2007 |
| 1998 | 94 | 2006 | 2010 |
| 1997 | 94 | 2005 | 2009 |
| 1996 | 87 | 1998 | 2001 |
| 1995 | 93 | 2003 | 2005 |
| 1994 | 92 | 1999 | 2002 |
| 1993 | 94 | 1998 | 2001 |
| 1992 | 89 | 2000 | 2004 |
| 1991 | 92 | 1999 | 2003 |
| 1990 | 85 | 1998 | 2002 |

# Bass Phillip

Tosch's Road, Leongatha South Vic 3953. Tel: (03) 5664 3341. Fax: (03) 5664 3209.
Email: bpwines@tpg.com.au

Region: **South Gippsland** Winemaker: **Phillip Jones** Viticulturist: **Phillip Jones** Chief Executive: **Phillip Jones**

Finding a Bass Phillip wine to drink has become even harder than ever, thanks to the minuscule yields of the 2002 vintage, from which only a restricted number of different labels were released, each in vanishingly small quantities. Some of the 2003 wines I have tasted, such as The Village, suggest that this might become of this maker's best seasons. Like many Australian tall poppies, Bass Phillip receives its share of criticism, yet as a regular drinker of mature examples of its premier pinot noirs, disappointments for me are very few and far between.

## CROWN PRINCE PINOT NOIR

### South Gippsland $50+
**Current vintage: 2001** 93

A perfumed, floral and exotically fragrant pinot, laced with ethereal, musky aromas of smoked meats and game, with underlying suggestions of slightly cooked cherries, raspberries and red plums. It's silky and creamy, deeply flavoured with wild, briary fruits and musky animal spices. Wrapped in fine-grained tannins, it finishes long and savoury. The best yet under this label.

| 2001 | 93 | 2003 | 2006+ |
|------|----|------|-------|
| 2000 | 91 | 2005 | 2008 |
| 1999 | 93 | 2001 | 2004 |

## ESTATE PINOT NOIR

### South Gippsland $30–$49
**Current vintage: 2002** 93

Silky, stylish pinot with a pungent, smoky and meaty bouquet of red cherries, dark plus, star anise and chocolate, with nuances of prunes and currants. Supple and smooth, it's long and fine-grained, with a generous, vibrant palate of black cherry and berry fruit before a slightly drying, fine-grained finish and lingering meaty farmyard nuances.

| 2002 | 93 | 2010 | 2014+ |
|------|----|------|-------|
| 2001 | 95 | 2006 | 2009 |
| 2000 | 89 | 2005 | 2008 |
| 1999 | 94 | 2004 | 2007 |
| 1998 | 92 | 2003 | 2006 |
| 1997 | 93 | 2002 | 2005 |

## PREMIUM PINOT NOIR

RANKING **2**

BASS PHILLIP

*PREMIUM*

| South Gippsland | $50+ |
|---|---|
| **Current vintage: 2002** | **93** |

Its pungent, spicy bouquet of plums, blackberries, dark cherries and duck fat is opulent and heady, with sweet oak and fivespice undertones. Smooth and succulent, with deep flavours of ripe dark fruits and new oak all along a velvet-smooth palate, finishing with just a suggestion of cooked fruit.

| | | | |
|---|---|---|---|
| 2002 | 93 | 2010 | 2014+ |
| 2001 | 97 | 2009 | 2013 |
| 2000 | 95 | 2005 | 2008 |
| 1999 | 96 | 2007 | 2011 |
| 1998 | 96 | 2006 | 2010 |
| 1997 | 95 | 2002 | 2005+ |
| 1996 | 95 | 2004 | 2008 |
| 1995 | 95 | 2003 | 2007 |
| 1994 | 96 | 2002 | 2006+ |
| 1993 | 95 | 1998 | 2001+ |

## RESERVE PINOT NOIR

RANKING **1**

| South Gippsland | $50+ |
|---|---|
| **Current vintage: 2001** | **97** |

Even more powerful and assertively oaked than the Premium, the Reserve remains an utterly natural and effortless wine of exceptional depth and tightness. While its concentration, smoky meatiness and fattiness, and its voluptuous expression of exotically spicy, tightly focused and almost essence-like fruit are all you'd expect from this label, its fineness and exceptional depth reflect the vineyard's increasing maturity and ability to ripen better and finer tannins. Yes, it's expensive, but pinots so raw yet so polished, so stylish yet so sexy as this is simply don't grow on trees.

| | | | |
|---|---|---|---|
| 2001 | 97 | 2009 | 2013 |
| 2000 | 93 | 2005 | 2008+ |
| 1999 | 96 | 2007 | 2011 |
| 1998 | 96 | 2006 | 2010+ |
| 1997 | 96 | 2005 | 2009 |
| 1996 | 96 | 2004 | 2008+ |
| 1995 | 96 | 2003 | 2007 |
| 1994 | 93 | 2002 | 2006 |
| 1991 | 95 | 2003 | 2011 |
| 1989 | 95 | 1997 | 2001 |

## VILLAGE PINOT NOIR

RANKING **4**

Village

*PINOT NOIR*
*BASS PHILLIP*

| South Gippsland | $30–$49 |
|---|---|
| **Current vintage: 2003** | **95** |

Very silky and intensely flavoured pinot with shape and balance. Its smoky, briary and slightly confectionary aromas of plums, dark cherries and vanilla/cedar oak precede a smooth and vibrant palate bursting with intense fruits. It finishes savoury, with meaty undertones.

| | | | |
|---|---|---|---|
| 2003 | 95 | 2008 | 2011 |
| 2001 | 92 | 2003 | 2006 |
| 1999 | 89 | 2001 | 2004 |

# Batista Estate

Franklin Road, Middlesex WA 6258. Tel: (08) 9772 3530. Fax: (08) 9772 3530.
Region: **Pemberton** Winemaker: **Bob Peruch** Chief Executive: **Bob Peruch**
Batista is one of the leading small vineyards in the Pemberton/Manjimup/Warren Valley region, whose Pinot Noir and Shiraz are deeply flavoured, herbal and spicy.

## PINOT NOIR

RANKING **5**

Batista

PINOT NOIR

WESTERN AUSTRALIA

| Warren Valley | $30–$49 |
|---|---|
| **Current vintage: 2002** | **86** |

Herbal, meaty pinot with a white pepper-like fragrance of slightly tomatoey berry fruit, undergrowth and herbaceous undertones. Fine and supple, its juicy palate of raspberry, plum and tomato-like fruit finishes soft and sappy but slightly hot, with herbal, greenish edges.

| | | | |
|---|---|---|---|
| 2002 | 86 | 2004 | 2007 |
| 2000 | 89 | 2002 | 2005 |
| 1999 | 86 | 2001 | 2004 |
| 1998 | 89 | 2003 | 2006 |
| 1997 | 87 | 2002 | 2005 |

# Best's

Best's Road, Great Western Vic 3377. Tel: (03) 5356 2250. Fax: (03) 5356 2430.
Website: www.bestswines.com  Email: info@bestswines.com
Region: **Grampians, Great Western**  Winemakers: **Viv Thomson, Hamish Seabrook**
Viticulturist: **Ben Thomson**  Chief Executive: **Viv Thomson**

An icon in Australian wine, Best's is an historic winery in western Victoria whose shirazes rate amongst Australia's finest and best. Recent seasons have also seen significant developments with the winery's perfumed and elegant Cabernet Sauvignon and its Riesling, which has become tighter more mineral. The very hot 2001 vintage has produced robust, structured shirazes that lack a little of the vineyard's customary elegance and attitude.

## BIN 'O' SHIRAZ

RANKING **2**

Grampians, Great Western   $30–$49
**Current vintage: 2001**   **92**

A restrained floral fragrance of red cherries and berries, a spicy perfume of white pepper, cloves and cinnamon and a whiff of cedary oak precede a fine, silky-smooth palate whose mulberry and dark plum-like fruit is framed by firm, but supple tannins. It's warmer, slightly riper and more plush than usual, with a hint of the blockiness as well as the slight leafiness that characterises so many 2001 reds.

The 1999 vintage refers to the one-off release of the FHT Shiraz.

| | | | |
|---|---|---|---|
| 2001 | 92 | 2009 | 2013+ |
| 2000 | 93 | 2008 | 2012 |
| 1999 | 95 | 2011 | 2019 |
| 1998 | 95 | 2010 | 2018+ |
| 1997 | 90 | 2005 | 2009 |
| 1996 | 95 | 2004 | 2008 |
| 1995 | 95 | 2007 | 2015 |
| 1994 | 88 | 2006 | 2014+ |
| 1993 | 86 | 1998 | 2001 |
| 1992 | 95 | 2004 | 2012 |
| 1991 | 91 | 1999 | 2003 |
| 1990 | 92 | 1995 | 1998 |
| 1989 | 87 | 1994 | 1997 |
| 1988 | 93 | 1996 | 2000+ |

## CABERNET SAUVIGNON

RANKING **4**

Grampians, Great Western   $20–$29
**Current vintage: 2001**   **91**

A piercing violet-like perfume of cassis and red berries, restrained vanilla oak and delicate herbal notes precedes a supple and silky palate of vibrant small berry flavours. Delightfully ripened, it's long and smooth, bursting with fruit and harmoniously entwined with tight, fine-grained tannins. Restrained but hardly lacking presence or structure, it should develop more elegance and complexity.

| | | | |
|---|---|---|---|
| 2001 | 91 | 2009 | 2013+ |
| 2000 | 87 | 2005 | 2008 |
| 1999 | 91 | 2011 | 2019 |
| 1998 | 91 | 2010 | 2018 |
| 1997 | 90 | 2005 | 2009+ |
| 1996 | 88 | 1998 | 2001 |
| 1995 | 90 | 2007 | 2015 |
| 1993 | 87 | 2001 | 2005 |
| 1992 | 94 | 2004 | 2012 |
| 1991 | 90 | 1999 | 2003+ |
| 1990 | 92 | 1998 | 2002 |
| 1989 | 82 | 1991 | 1994 |

## CHARDONNAY

RANKING **5**

Grampians, Great Western   $20–$29
**Current vintage: 2003**   **87**

Ripe, slightly confected and forward, with a sweet fragrance of peaches and melon, lemon sherbet and green olives, oatmeal and vanilla oak. Tropical, forward and juicy, it should settle back into a finer and more reserved style.

| | | | |
|---|---|---|---|
| 2003 | 87 | 2005 | 2008 |
| 2001 | 92 | 2006 | 2009 |
| 2000 | 84 | 2002 | 2005 |
| 1998 | 86 | 2003 | 2006 |
| 1997 | 88 | 2002 | 2005 |
| 1996 | 89 | 1998 | 2001 |
| 1995 | 93 | 2003 | 2007 |
| 1994 | 94 | 2006 | 2014 |

## PINOT MEUNIER

RANKING **5**

Grampians, Great Western   $20–$29
**Current vintage: 2002**   **87**

Peppery, spicy aromas of fresh basil, minty dark cherries and plums with slightly reductive, leathery and musky undertones. Its lively, flavoursome palate of dark cherries and plums, mint and eucalypt is juicy and vibrant. Supported by sweet vanilla/chocolate oak and modest tannins, it finishes with lingering boiled lolly-like berry fruits.

| | | | |
|---|---|---|---|
| 2002 | 87 | 2007 | 2010+ |
| 2001 | 87 | 2003 | 2006 |
| 1999 | 90 | 2004 | 2007 |
| 1998 | 89 | 2003 | 2006 |
| 1997 | 87 | 2005 | 2009 |
| 1996 | 90 | 2004 | 2008 |
| 1995 | 88 | 2003 | 2007 |
| 1994 | 89 | 2002 | 2006 |

## PINOT NOIR

RANKING **5**

| Grampians, Great Western | $20–$29 |
|---|---|
| Current vintage: 2001 | 88 |

Modestly structured, slightly candied pinot whose sweet red cherry and plum flavours are scented with musky spices and supported by fine, slightly bony tannins. It finishes with bright acidity and undergrowth-like complexity, and should build in the bottle.

| | | | |
|---|---|---|---|
| 2001 | 88 | 2003 | 2006+ |
| 2000 | 87 | 2005 | 2008 |
| 1999 | 87 | 2001 | 2004 |
| 1998 | 89 | 2000 | 2003+ |
| 1997 | 77 | 1998 | 1999 |
| 1996 | 89 | 2001 | 2004 |

## RIESLING

RANKING **4**

| Grampians, Great Western | $20–$29 |
|---|---|
| Current vintage: 2003 | 92 |

Modern, stylish riesling with Austrian-like elements of texture, dryness and tightness. Its delicate floral aromas of lemon and lime, apple and pear precede an elegant, shapely palate whose generous middle fleshy core is bound by a crisp and slightly powdery mineral finish. Some lees-derived flavours and texture contribute to its complexity and charm.

| | | | |
|---|---|---|---|
| 2003 | 92 | 2011 | 2015 |
| 2002 | 93 | 2010 | 2014 |
| 2001 | 88 | 2003 | 2006+ |
| 2000 | 88 | 2005 | 2008 |
| 1999 | 93 | 2007 | 2011 |
| 1998 | 88 | 2003 | 2006 |
| 1997 | 82 | 1999 | 2002 |
| 1996 | 89 | 1998 | 2001 |
| 1995 | 94 | 2003 | 2007 |
| 1994 | 94 | 2006 | 2014 |
| 1993 | 83 | 1995 | 1998 |
| 1992 | 89 | 2000 | 2004 |

## THOMSON FAMILY SHIRAZ

RANKING **2**

| Grampians, Great Western | $50+ |
|---|---|
| Current vintage: 2001 | 93 |

Fragrant aromas of dark cherries, cassis, mulberries and plums are supported by sweet cedar/chocolate oak. There's also plenty of varietal pepper and spice, with an underlying violet-like perfume. Long, very smooth and velvet-like, with a ripe, succulent mouthfeel of berry/plum flavours bordering ever so marginally on the over-cooked. Its length and tight-knit spine of powdery tannins will ensure a strong future.

| | | | |
|---|---|---|---|
| 2001 | 93 | 2013 | 2021 |
| 1998 | 93 | 2006 | 2010 |
| 1997 | 94 | 2005 | 2009+ |
| 1996 | 97 | 2008 | 2016 |
| 1995 | 96 | 2007 | 2015+ |
| 1994 | 93 | 2004 | 2012 |
| 1992 | 96 | 2004 | 2012 |

# Bethany

Bethany Road, Bethany via Tanunda SA 5352. Tel: (08) 8563 2086. Fax: (08) 8563 0046.
Website: www.bethany.com.au  Email: bethany@bethany.com.au
Region: **Barossa Valley**  Winemakers: **Paul Bailey, Geoff & Robert Schrapel**
Viticulturists: **Geoff & Robert Schrapel**  Chief Executives: **Geoff & Robert Schrapel**

A Barossa-based vineyard and winery with a long family tradition in the region, Bethany has struggled to maintain the quality of the red wines that forged its reputation as recent releases have revealed both under and over-ripe influences. Its vibrant and slightly confectionary Rieslings, however, retain their attraction.

## CABERNET MERLOT

RANKING **5**

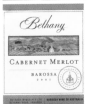

| Barossa Valley | $12–$19 |
|---|---|
| Current vintage: 2001 | 82 |

Herbal, lightly cooked but evolved aromas of plums and cedary oak precede a simple, thick but slightly raw-edged palate framed by aggressive and greenish tannins.

| | | | |
|---|---|---|---|
| 2001 | 82 | 2003 | 2006 |
| 2000 | 88 | 2002 | 2005+ |
| 1999 | 82 | 2001 | 2004 |
| 1998 | 87 | 2003 | 2006 |
| 1997 | 81 | 1999 | 2002 |
| 1996 | 84 | 1998 | 2001 |
| 1995 | 87 | 1997 | 2000 |
| 1994 | 90 | 2002 | 2006 |
| 1993 | 82 | 1995 | 1998 |

## EDEN VALLEY RIESLING

RANKING 5

**Barossa Valley** $12–$19
**Current vintage: 2003** 90

Citrusy, pineapple-like aromas with a suggestion of wet steel. Its restrained but willowy palate of slightly confectionary-like lime, apple and pear flavours is supported by a lightly powdery chalky spine.

| | | | |
|---|---|---|---|
| 2003 | 90 | 2008 | 2011 |
| 2002 | 82 | 2004 | 2007 |
| 2001 | 89 | 2006 | 2009 |
| 2000 | 82 | 2001 | 2002 |
| 1999 | 88 | 2001 | 2004 |
| 1998 | 84 | 2000 | 2003 |
| 1997 | 83 | 1998 | 1999 |
| 1996 | 90 | 2001 | 2004+ |
| 1995 | 87 | 2000 | 2003+ |

## GR RESERVE RED

RANKING 4

**Barossa Valley** $50+
**Current vintage: 1998** 87

Juicy, jammy and floral aromas of slightly cooked currants and prunes over black and red berries, with earthy, herbal undertones. Soft and smooth, the palate begins with lively plum, raspberry, cassis and mulberry flavours and sweet vanilla oak, but finishes with sappy, herbal influences. Lacks genuine shape and definition.

All vintages are Shiraz, except for the 1997 vintage, which is a varietal Cabernet Sauvignon.

| | | | |
|---|---|---|---|
| 1998 | 87 | 2003 | 2006 |
| 1997 | 89 | 2002 | 2005+ |
| 1996 | 90 | 2001 | 2004 |
| 1995 | 86 | 2000 | 2003 |
| 1994 | 92 | 1999 | 2002+ |
| 1992 | 90 | 1997 | 2000 |

## RIESLING

RANKING 5

**Barossa Valley** $12–$19
**Current vintage: 2003** 87

Lemony and slightly oily riesling with a candied, confected aroma of tropical fruit. Vibrant, slightly sweet and lively, its measured palate overlies chalky phenolics, finishing with citrusy fruit.

| | | | |
|---|---|---|---|
| 2003 | 87 | 2004 | 2005+ |
| 2002 | 89 | 2004 | 2007+ |
| 2001 | 87 | 2003 | 2006 |
| 2000 | 87 | 2001 | 2002+ |
| 1999 | 89 | 2001 | 2004 |
| 1998 | 88 | 2000 | 2003 |
| 1997 | 81 | 1999 | 2002 |
| 1996 | 90 | 2001 | 2004 |
| 1995 | 87 | 2000 | 2003 |

## SELECT LATE HARVEST RIESLING

RANKING 4

**Barossa Valley** $20–$29
**Current vintage: 2003** 89

Clean and refreshing, moderately sweet wine with fresh, honeyed and floral aromas of candied lime and a generous, ripe and tangy palate. It's forward and luscious, with up-front fruit flavours, but finishes clean and refreshing, without cloying.

| | | | |
|---|---|---|---|
| 2003 | 89 | 2004 | 2005+ |
| 2002 | 87 | 2003 | 2004+ |
| 1999 | 90 | 2001 | 2004 |
| 1998 | 89 | 2000 | 2003+ |
| 1997 | 90 | 1999 | 2002 |
| 1996 | 91 | 2001 | 2004 |
| 1995 | 87 | 1997 | 2000 |

## SEMILLON

RANKING 5

**Barossa Valley** $12–$19
**Current vintage: 2003** 88

Delicate aromas of green apples, melon and green olives, lightly dusty vanilla oak and hints of lemon rind, before a restrained, but chewy palate. Its reserved apple/melon fruit finishes dry and chalky. It should flesh out well.

| | | | |
|---|---|---|---|
| 2003 | 88 | 2005 | 2008 |
| 2002 | 89 | 2004 | 2007 |
| 2001 | 86 | 2003 | 2006 |
| 2000 | 88 | 2002 | 2005 |
| 1999 | 89 | 2001 | 2004 |
| 1998 | 89 | 2000 | 2003 |

# Bindi

343 Melton Road, Gisborne Vic 3437. Tel: (03) 5428 2564. Fax: (03) 5428 2564.
Region: **Macedon Ranges** Winemakers: **Stuart Anderson, Michael Dhillon** Viticulturist: **Bill Dhillon**
Chief Executive: **Bill Dhillon**

Bindi is a small cool-climate vineyard whose heat-trap site and mineral soils produce low yields of intensely flavoured wines from chardonnay and pinot noir. With the 2002 vintage, it returns to the crackerjack form of the mid 1990s. Poles apart from mainstream Australian styles, the chardonnays reveal remarkable intensity and minerality, while the pinots are deeply perfumed and flavoured, supple and sophisticated.

## CHARDONNAY

RANKING **3**

| Macedon Ranges | $30–$49 |
|---|---|
| **Current vintage: 2002** | **95** |

Harmonious, fine and supple chardonnay with delicacy and focus. Its complex aromas of grapefruit, melon and nectarine reveal spicy cinnamon/clove undertones and creamy, fine-grained vanilla oak. Pristine and brightly flavoured, its refreshing and mineral palate presents clear and lingering stonefruit and citrus flavours tightly interwoven with stony, lemony acids.

| | | | |
|---|---|---|---|
| 2002 | 95 | 2007 | 2010+ |
| 2001 | 89 | 2003 | 2006+ |
| 2000 | 87 | 2002 | 2005+ |
| 1999 | 86 | 2001 | 2004 |
| 1998 | 88 | 2003 | 2006 |
| 1997 | 93 | 2002 | 2005 |
| 1996 | 87 | 1998 | 2001 |
| 1995 | 93 | 2000 | 2003 |
| 1994 | 95 | 2002 | 2006 |

## BLOCK 5 PINOT NOIR

RANKING **2**

| Macedon Ranges | $50+ |
|---|---|
| **Current vintage: 2002** | **95** |

Structured, sophisticated pinot with an earthy perfume of dark cherries, blackberries, dark plums and mocha/chocolate oak over slightly wild, undergrowth-like influences. Pure and vibrant, it reveals a deep, dark core of dark fruit all down its fleshy but supple palate, supported by tightly knit fine tannins and finished with refreshing acidity. Has everything it needs for the long term.

| | | | |
|---|---|---|---|
| 2002 | 96 | 2010 | 2014 |
| 2001 | 94 | 2006 | 2009+ |
| 2000 | 87 | 2002 | 2005+ |
| 1998 | 92 | 2003 | 2006 |
| 1997 | 96 | 2005 | 2009 |

## ORIGINAL VINEYARD PINOT NOIR

RANKING **3**

| Macedon Ranges | $30–$49 |
|---|---|
| **Current vintage: 2002** | **93** |

Silky-fine and elegant pinot whose spicy, lightly dusty floral perfume of maraschino cherries and raspberries, musky meaty complexity and restrained oak influences precedes a tight, fine-grained and savoury palate of suppleness and firmness. Laced with pristine red berry/cherry fruit, it's framed by fine tannins and refreshing acids.

| | | | |
|---|---|---|---|
| 2002 | 93 | 2007 | 2010 |
| 2001 | 90 | 2006 | 2009 |
| 2000 | 87 | 2005 | 2008 |
| 1999 | 86 | 2001 | 2004 |
| 1998 | 91 | 2003 | 2006 |
| 1997 | 95 | 2002 | 2005 |
| 1996 | 95 | 2004 | 2008 |
| 1995 | 94 | 2000 | 2003 |
| 1994 | 94 | 2002 | 2006 |
| 1993 | 93 | 1998 | 2001 |

## QUARTZ CHARDONNAY

RANKING **2**

| Macedon Ranges | $50+ |
|---|---|
| **Current vintage: 2002** | **96** |

Racy, minerally chardonnay of exceptional length, balance and tightness. Its jasmine-like fragrance of honeysuckle, lemon and nutty, spicy oak precedes a tight-knit palate of length and restraint. Its concentrated sweet core of vibrant citrus fruit integrates tightly with restrained oak, before a lingering finish of bracing acidity.

| | | | |
|---|---|---|---|
| 2002 | 97 | 2007 | 2010+ |
| 2001 | 93 | 2006 | 2009 |
| 2000 | 93 | 2005 | 2008+ |
| 1999 | 90 | 2001 | 2004+ |
| 1998 | 95 | 2003 | 2006+ |
| 1995 | 95 | 2000 | 2003 |

# Blackjack

Calder Highway, Harcourt Vic 3453. Tel: (03) 5474 2355. Fax: (03) 5474 2355.
Website: www.blackjackwines.com.au  Email: sales@blackjackwines.com.au
Region: **Bendigo** Winemakers: **Ian McKenzie, Ken Pollock** Viticulturist: **Ian McKenzie**
Chief Executive: **Ian McKenzie**

Blackjack produces small volumes of tightly-focused but deeply flavoured and spicy Shiraz and some robust, earthy central Victorian Cabernet Sauvignon. While the 2002 releases are typically competent and flavoursome, I can't help from wondering how much better off the Shiraz would have been had the Block 6 wine (91, drink 2007–2010) not been separated from it.

## CABERNET MERLOT

RANKING **5**

| | | | | |
|---|---|---|---|---|
| **Bendigo** | **$20–$29** | 2002 | 89 | 2007 | 2010 |
| **Current vintage: 2002** | **89** | 2001 | 90 | 2009 | 2013+ |

Minty, herbal and dusty aromas of small black and red berries, cedar/vanilla oak, over menthol-like undertones. Smooth, soft and integrated, with slightly confectionary blackberry, dark cherry and raspberry fruit overlying nuances of herbs and sweet oak. Good tightness and balance.

| 2002 | 89 | 2007 | 2010 |
|---|---|---|---|
| 2001 | 90 | 2009 | 2013+ |
| 2000 | 89 | 2005 | 2008+ |
| 1999 | 83 | 2001 | 2004 |
| 1998 | 89 | 2003 | 2006 |
| 1997 | 90 | 2005 | 2009 |
| 1996 | 87 | 2001 | 2004 |
| 1995 | 85 | 1997 | 2000 |

## SHIRAZ

RANKING **4**

**Bendigo**    **$20–$29**
**Current vintage: 2002**    **87**

Lacking its customary structure; rather forward and herbal. Perfumed with spicy nuances of violets, red berries and white pepper, with a moderately full and smooth palate whose lively small fruits are framed by rather greenish, herbal edges. Could have used the weight of Block 6 of the same year!

| 2002 | 87 | 2004 | 2007+ |
|---|---|---|---|
| 2001 | 92 | 2006 | 2009+ |
| 2000 | 90 | 2002 | 2005+ |
| 1999 | 88 | 2004 | 2007 |
| 1998 | 89 | 2003 | 2006+ |
| 1997 | 90 | 2002 | 2005 |
| 1996 | 90 | 2001 | 2004 |
| 1995 | 82 | 1997 | 2000 |

# Bleasdale

Wellington Road, Langhorne Creek SA 5255. Tel: (08) 8537 3001. Fax: (08) 8537 3224.
Website: www.bleasdale.com.au  Email: bleasdale@bleasdale.com.au
Region: **Langhorne Creek** Winemakers: **Michael Potts, Renae Hirsch** Viticulturist: **Robert Potts**
Chief Executive: **David Foreman**

Bleasdale is a long-established stalwart of Langhorne Creek, whose wines are typically ripe, generous, approachable and relatively long-living. They're also amongst the most affordable of their kind and quality. To a degree, the current releases reflect some ongoing vine stress in the Langhorne Creek region which, like many others, could use a long, wet winter.

## BREMERVIEW SHIRAZ

RANKING **4**

**Langhorne Creek**    **$12–$19**
**Current vintage: 2002**    **87**

Fragrant, meaty, earthy aromas of cassis, plums and raspberries, backed by dusty hints of white pepper. Quite firm and assertive with a good length of dark berry fruit, but finishes with a salty and slightly metallic note.

| 2002 | 87 | 2007 | 2010+ |
|---|---|---|---|
| 2001 | 89 | 2003 | 2006+ |
| 2000 | 90 | 2008 | 2012 |
| 1999 | 89 | 2004 | 2007 |
| 1998 | 87 | 2003 | 2006 |
| 1997 | 92 | 2005 | 2009 |
| 1996 | 89 | 2001 | 2004 |
| 1995 | 90 | 2000 | 2003 |
| 1993 | 82 | 1995 | 1998 |
| 1992 | 88 | 2000 | 2004 |

## FRANK POTTS CABERNET BLEND

RANKING **4**

**Langhorne Creek**    **$20–$29**
**Current vintage: 2002**    **89**

Richly flavoured and textured but fractionally over-cooked wine whose meaty aromas of small berries, prunes and cedary oak precede a smooth, creamy palate. Its petit verdot accentuates the dark, spicy plum flavours and gives brightness to the riper nuances of currants and raisins.

| 2002 | 89 | 2010 | 2014+ |
|---|---|---|---|
| 2001 | 89 | 2009 | 2013 |
| 2000 | 89 | 2005 | 2008+ |
| 1999 | 93 | 2007 | 2011 |
| 1998 | 90 | 2003 | 2006+ |
| 1997 | 90 | 2005 | 2009 |
| 1996 | 92 | 2004 | 2008+ |
| 1995 | 92 | 2003 | 2007 |
| 1994 | 87 | 1999 | 2002 |
| 1992 | 81 | 1994 | 1997 |

# MALBEC

RANKING **5**

| | Langhorne Creek | $12–$19 |
|---|---|---|
| | **Current vintage: 2002** | **82** |

Rather minty and leafy, with green-edged meaty qualities obscuring its rather simple notes of raspberries and plums. Hollow-centred, finishing herbal and sappy.

| 2002 | 82 | 2004 | 2007 |
|---|---|---|---|
| 2001 | 90 | 2006 | 2009 |
| 2000 | 89 | 2005 | 2008 |
| 1999 | 87 | 2004 | 2007 |
| 1998 | 88 | 2000 | 2003 |
| 1997 | 85 | 1998 | 2001 |
| 1996 | 84 | 1998 | 2001 |
| 1994 | 88 | 1999 | 2003 |
| 1992 | 82 | 1997 | 2000 |

# MULBERRY TREE CABERNET SAUVIGNON

RANKING **5**

| | Langhorne Creek | $12–$19 |
|---|---|---|
| | **Current vintage: 2002** | **87** |

Fractionally sappy and under-ripe, with a delicate minty fragrance of cassis and raspberries over light vanilla oak. Smooth and supple, its delicate, pristine and polished palate of sweet small berries finishes with minty notes and a slightly metallic grip.

| 2002 | 87 | 2010 | 2014 |
|---|---|---|---|
| 2001 | 87 | 2006 | 2009 |
| 2000 | 87 | 2005 | 2008 |
| 1999 | 90 | 2004 | 2007 |
| 1998 | 88 | 2003 | 2006 |
| 1997 | 88 | 2002 | 2005+ |
| 1996 | 89 | 2004 | 2008 |
| 1995 | 82 | 1997 | 2000 |
| 1993 | 87 | 2001 | 2005 |
| 1992 | 89 | 2000 | 2004 |

# Blue Pyrenees

Vinoca Road, Avoca Vic 3467. Tel: (03) 5465 3202. Fax: (03) 5465 3529.
Website: www.bluepyrenees.com.au Email: info@bluepyrenees.com.au
Region: **Pyrenees** Winemaker: **Andrew Koerner** Viticulturist: **Derek Loy** Chief Executive: **John B. Ellis**
A new regime has moved in at Blue Pyrenees Estate, including the very competent ex-Rosemount winemaker Andrew Koerner. While this region has also had some difficulties in recent vintages, including several years of increasingly severe drought, I expect that given a more favourable climate it will again produce wines of finesse and elegance. One of its best and most under-rated wines is its spicy, fine-grained Victoria Shiraz.

## CABERNET SAUVIGNON

RANKING **5**

| | Pyrenees | $12–$19 |
|---|---|---|
| | **Current vintage: 2002** | **84** |

Minty aromas of mulberries, cassis and plums, with herbal undertones and assertively gamey vanilla oak. Smooth and forward, the palate provides a minty expression of plum and blackberry fruit, before becoming hollow and short, with a sappy framework of greenish tannins.

| 2002 | 84 | 2004 | 2007 |
|---|---|---|---|
| 2001 | 88 | 2003 | 2006+ |
| 2000 | 83 | 2002 | 2005 |
| 1999 | 89 | 2001 | 2004 |

## CHARDONNAY

| | Pyrenees | $12–$19 |
|---|---|---|
| | **Current vintage: 2003** | **90** |

Trim, taut and stylish chardonnay with a spicy and slightly varnishy aroma of citrus and melon over undertones of apple. Its smooth, polished palate is fleshy and slightly fatty, but delivers bright flavours and elegance, before a trim, chalky finish of green olives and lemony acids.

| 2003 | 90 | 2005 | 2008 |
|---|---|---|---|
| 2002 | 84 | 2003 | 2004 |
| 2001 | 82 | 2002 | 2003 |
| 2000 | 87 | 2002 | 2005 |

## ESTATE RESERVE CHARDONNAY

RANKING **4**

| | Pyrenees | $30–$49 |
|---|---|---|
| | **Current vintage: 2000** | **86** |

Heavily worked and slightly stale chardonnay with sweet melon fruit beneath layers of nutty, biscuity and creamy oak. Sweet and cloying, it's thickly coated with peach/melon flavours, but finishes marginally short and flat.

| 2000 | 86 | 2001 | 2002+ |
|---|---|---|---|
| 1999 | 93 | 2004 | 2007 |
| 1998 | 88 | 2000 | 2003 |
| 1997 | 93 | 2002 | 2005 |
| 1996 | 91 | 2001 | 2004+ |
| 1995 | 88 | 1997 | 2000 |
| 1994 | 89 | 1999 | 2002 |

## ESTATE RESERVE (Cabernet Blend)  RANKING  3

| Pyrenees | $30–$49 |
| --- | --- |
| Current vintage: 2001 | 87 |

Intense, structured minty central Victorian red whose toothpaste-like aromas of violets, cassis and cedar/mocha new oak reveals some herbaceous undertones. Long and rich, it's fashioned around a firm spine of loose-knit tannins, leaving a minty/menthol impression of plums and small berries. A shade too green for higher points.

| 2001 | 87 | 2009 | 2013+ |
| --- | --- | --- | --- |
| 2000 | 84 | 2005 | 2008 |
| 1999 | 93 | 2007 | 2011+ |
| 1998 | 93 | 2010 | 2018 |
| 1997 | 89 | 2005 | 2009 |
| 1996 | 93 | 2008 | 2016 |
| 1995 | 93 | 2003 | 2007 |
| 1994 | 95 | 2002 | 2006+ |
| 1993 | 94 | 2001 | 2005 |
| 1992 | 92 | 2000 | 2004 |
| 1991 | 94 | 1999 | 2003 |

## SHIRAZ  RANKING  5

| Pyrenees | $12–$19 |
| --- | --- |
| Current vintage: 2001 | 90 |

Intensely minty, meaty and menthol-like aromas of cassis, plums and sweet vanilla oak precede a firm, powdery and structured palate whose slightly cooked plum, currant and pruney fruit delivers length and some leathery charm. Should ease back into a typically meaty, minty style of Victorian red.

| 2001 | 90 | 2006 | 2009 |
| --- | --- | --- | --- |
| 2000 | 90 | 2002 | 2005+ |
| 1999 | 82 | 2001 | 2004 |

# Bowen Estate

Riddoch Highway, Coonawarra SA 5263. Tel: (08) 8737 2229. Fax: (08) 8737 2173.
Website: www.coonawarra.org/wineries/bowen/ Email: bowenest@penola.mtx.net.au
Region: **Coonawarra** Winemaker: **Doug Bowen, Emma Bowen** Viticulturist: **Doug Bowen**
Chief Executive: **Joy Bowen**

Bowen Estate's return to very top form continues with its 2002 reds and 2003 Chardonnay, each of which continue the very impressive run shown by the preceding releases. 2002 was a challenging viticultural year in Coonawarra, which you'd never know by the astonishing depth of flavour delivered by the supremely elegant and finely balanced Shiraz and the long and tightly-crafted Cabernet Sauvignon.

## CABERNET BLEND  RANKING  5

| Coonawarra | $20–$29 |
| --- | --- |
| Current vintage: 2001 | 89 |

Elegant medium to full-bodied Coonawarra red with a light, cedary aroma of delicate small black and red berries and vanilla oak. Framed by dusty, loose-knit tannins, it reveals a smooth and supple palate of pleasing fruit sweetness and refinement.

| 2001 | 89 | 2006 | 2009+ |
| --- | --- | --- | --- |
| 2000 | 89 | 2005 | 2008 |
| 1999 | 86 | 2004 | 2007 |
| 1998 | 82 | 2000 | 2003 |
| 1997 | 87 | 1999 | 2002 |
| 1995 | 86 | 2000 | 2003 |
| 1994 | 82 | 1999 | 2002 |
| 1993 | 88 | 1998 | 2001 |
| 1992 | 93 | 2000 | 2004 |
| 1991 | 92 | 1999 | 2003 |
| 1990 | 93 | 1995 | 1998 |

## CABERNET SAUVIGNON  RANKING  3

| Coonawarra | $30–$49 |
| --- | --- |
| Current vintage: 2002 | 92 |

Classic cooler-season Coonawarra cabernet with wonderfully deep scents of cassis, plums and cedar/chocolate oak over lightly herbal and dusty, leafy nuances. Long, smooth and fine-grained, the palate is stylish and structured, presenting intense, vibrant cassis, mulberry and plum flavours harmoniously balanced with fine-grained oak and tight-knit firm tannins.

| 2002 | 92 | 2010 | 2014 |
| --- | --- | --- | --- |
| 2001 | 94 | 2006 | 2009+ |
| 2000 | 90 | 2005 | 2008 |
| 1999 | 82 | 2001 | 2004 |
| 1998 | 95 | 2010 | 2018 |
| 1997 | 87 | 2005 | 2009 |
| 1996 | 88 | 2008 | 2016+ |
| 1995 | 77 | 1997 | 2000 |
| 1994 | 90 | 2002 | 2006 |
| 1993 | 84 | 1998 | 2001 |
| 1992 | 93 | 2000 | 2004+ |
| 1991 | 93 | 1999 | 2003 |
| 1990 | 94 | 1995 | 1998 |
| 1989 | 91 | 1994 | 1997 |
| 1988 | 87 | 1990 | 1993 |
| 1984 | 95 | 1996 | 2004 |

## SHIRAZ

| Coonawarra | $30–$49 | 2002 | 95 | 2014 | 2020 |
|---|---|---|---|---|---|
| **Current vintage: 2002** | **95** | 2001 | 95 | 2009 | 2013+ |
| | | 2000 | 94 | 2008 | 2012+ |
| | | 1999 | 81 | 2001 | 2004 |
| | | 1998 | 93 | 2010 | 2018 |
| | | 1997 | 88 | 2005 | 2009 |
| | | 1996 | 88 | 2001 | 2004 |
| | | 1995 | 90 | 2003 | 2007 |
| | | 1994 | 93 | 2002 | 2006 |
| | | 1993 | 94 | 2001 | 2005 |
| | | 1992 | 95 | 2000 | 2004 |
| | | 1991 | 94 | 1996 | 1999 |
| | | 1990 | 87 | 1998 | 2002 |

An ethereal perfume of spicy cloves, cinnamon and licorice overlies deep aromas of raspberries, cassis and plums, with undertones of white pepper, rosemary and sweet vanilla/cedar oak. Long, smooth and sumptuous, its deep, pristine fruit, creamy oak and leathery game meat-like complexity culminate in a lingering finish of balance and harmony. Very stylish, very classy.

# Boynton's

6619 Great Alpine Road, Porepunkah Vic 3740. Tel: (03) 5756 2356. Fax: (03) 5756 2610.
Email: boyntons@bright.albury.net.au
Region: **Alpine Valleys** Winemakers: **Kel Boynton, Dennis Clarke** Viticulturist: **Kel Boynton**
Chief Executive: **Kel Boynton**
While it can produce some fine Germanic Rieslings, Boynton's best reds are its varietal merlot, plus its very elegant, tightly focused and harmonious Alluvium blend of red Bordeaux varieties. As one might expect given its alpine location, Boynton's has been faced with rather a severe run of dramatically variable seasons.

## CABERNET SAUVIGNON

| Alpine Valleys | $20–$29 | 2000 | 82 | 2002 | 2005+ |
|---|---|---|---|---|---|
| **Current vintage: 2000** | **82** | 1998 | 89 | 2003 | 2006 |
| | | 1997 | 91 | 2005 | 2009 |
| | | 1996 | 86 | 2005 | 2009 |
| | | 1995 | 75 | 1997 | 2000 |
| | | 1994 | 94 | 2002 | 2006 |
| | | 1993 | 93 | 2001 | 2005+ |
| | | 1992 | 92 | 2000 | 2004 |
| | | 1991 | 87 | 1996 | 1999 |
| | | 1990 | 95 | 1998 | 2002 |

Minty, meaty and oaky red whose green-edged aromas of cassis, mulberries and plums precede a moderately long, but herbaceous expression of small berries and plums, given rather a heavy coating of sweet American oak.

## CHARDONNAY

| Alpine Valleys | $20–$29 | 2000 | 86 | 2002 | 2005+ |
|---|---|---|---|---|---|
| **Current vintage: 2000** | **86** | 1999 | 83 | 2001 | 2004 |
| | | 1998 | 87 | 2000 | 2003 |
| | | 1996 | 84 | 1998 | 2001 |
| | | 1995 | 81 | 1996 | 1997 |
| | | 1994 | 89 | 1999 | 2002 |

Delicate, but rather herbal chardonnay whose greenish aromas of lemon bathpowder, stonefruit, apple and melon herald rather an elegant and restrained palate that finishes with crisp, crackly acidity. Just too herbal throughout.

## MERLOT

| Alpine Valleys | $20–$29 | 2000 | 90 | 2005 | 2008 |
|---|---|---|---|---|---|
| **Current vintage: 2000** | **90** | 1998 | 89 | 2000 | 2003 |
| | | 1997 | 88 | 1999 | 2002+ |
| | | 1996 | 90 | 2001 | 2004 |

A very good wine that could have been even better were it not for some rather raw American oak. Its sweet perfume of dark cherries and coconut-like cedar/chocolate oak has an appealing lift, while its smooth, creamy and moderately full palate presents some delightfully meaty varietal flavour. Its ripe plum and cherry fruit finishes with a dusty hint of tobacco leaf, and its fine-grained tannins are harmoniously integrated.

# RIESLING

**Alpine Valleys**      $12–$19
**Current vintage: 2002**      87

Restrained, marginally under-ripe cool-climate riesling with a limey apple/pear perfume. Tinned tropical and slightly candied apple/pear fruits finish with pleasing length and lively, lemony acids.

| | | | |
|---|---|---|---|
| 2002 | 87 | 2004 | 2007 |
| 2001 | 90 | 2006 | 2009 |
| 2000 | 86 | 2002 | 2005 |
| 1998 | 85 | 2000 | 2003 |

# Brand's

Main Road, Coonawarra SA 5263. Tel: (08) 8736 3260. Fax: (08) 8736 3208.
Website: mcwilliams.com.au Email: brands_office@mcwilliams.com.au
Region: **Coonawarra** Winemakers: **Jim Brayne, Jim Brand** Viticulturist: **Bill Brand**
Chief Executive: **Kevin McLintock**

The challenging Coonawarra seasons of 2000, 2001 and 2002 have taken a little away from the gloss of Brand's red wines, but the past five years have established this maker amongst the forefront of the region's makers of deeply flavoured and finely balanced reds of structure and longevity.

## CABERNET SAUVIGNON

RANKING 4

**Coonawarra**      $20–$29
**Current vintage: 2002**      84

Firm, tight, but herbal and dusty cabernet whose light cassis and mulberry aromas are lifted by a suggestion of violets, dill and cedary oak. Supple and slightly hollow, its green-edged palate is rather reliant on its smoky vanilla oak for sweetness and texture, finishing rather tight and sappy.

| | | | |
|---|---|---|---|
| 2002 | 84 | 2004 | 2007 |
| 2001 | 91 | 2006 | 2009+ |
| 2000 | 91 | 2002 | 2005+ |
| 1999 | 91 | 2004 | 2007+ |
| 1998 | 92 | 2006 | 2010 |
| 1997 | 90 | 2002 | 2005 |
| 1996 | 82 | 1998 | 2001 |
| 1995 | 87 | 2000 | 2003 |
| 1994 | 91 | 1999 | 2002 |
| 1993 | 93 | 1998 | 2001 |

## CHARDONNAY

RANKING 5

**Coonawarra**      $12–$19
**Current vintage: 2003**      88

Honest, flavoursome chardonnay whose fragrant aromas of lemon sherbet, peaches and mango are supported by creamy vanilla oak. Soft and juicy, its gentle palate is quite oaky and viscous, with a toasty, buttery background beneath its peachy fruit. Finishes fresh and clean, with lemony acids.

| | | | |
|---|---|---|---|
| 2003 | 88 | 2004 | 2005+ |
| 2002 | 83 | 2003 | 2004 |
| 2001 | 87 | 2002 | 2003+ |
| 1998 | 87 | 1999 | 2000 |
| 1997 | 88 | 1999 | 2002 |
| 1996 | 86 | 1998 | 2001 |
| 1995 | 88 | 2000 | 2003 |
| 1994 | 87 | 1996 | 1999 |

## MERLOT

RANKING 4

**Coonawarra**      $20–$29
**Current vintage: 2002**      84

Leathery, herbal and simple aromas of confectionary-like berry fruit precede a forward, rather thin and skinny palate deficient in ripeness, length and structure.

| | | | |
|---|---|---|---|
| 2002 | 84 | 2004 | 2007+ |
| 2001 | 93 | 2006 | 2009 |
| 2000 | 90 | 2002 | 2005+ |
| 1999 | 90 | 2001 | 2004 |
| 1997 | 90 | 1999 | 2002 |

## PATRON'S RESERVE RED

RANKING **2**

| Coonawarra | $50+ |
|---|---|
| **Current vintage: 2001** | **90** |

Elegant, finely structured cabernet blend whose lightly smoky, dusty aromas of fragrant small red and black berries, creamy mocha and dark olives reveal a whiff of licorice. Long and restrained, the palate presents some intense cassis, plum and mulberry flavours framed by slightly sappy tannins and lively acids over some meaty, spicy complexity.

| | | | |
|---|---|---|---|
| 2001 | 90 | 2009 | 2013 |
| 2000 | 92 | 2008 | 2012 |
| 1999 | 95 | 2007 | 2011+ |
| 1998 | 94 | 2006 | 2010+ |
| 1997 | 88 | 2002 | 2005+ |
| 1996 | 95 | 2004 | 2008+ |
| 1991 | 92 | 1999 | 2003+ |
| 1990 | 85 | 1995 | 1998 |

## SHIRAZ

RANKING **4**

| Coonawarra | $20–$29 |
|---|---|
| **Current vintage: 2002** | **86** |

Pretty, forward, early-drinking shiraz with a lightly peppery perfume of sweet, spicy raspberries, cassis and smoky vanilla oak. Smooth and supple, its sweet vanilla oak adequately supports its rather herbal expression of forward berry flavours.

| | | | |
|---|---|---|---|
| 2002 | 86 | 2004 | 2007 |
| 2001 | 92 | 2006 | 2009+ |
| 2000 | 87 | 2002 | 2005+ |
| 1999 | 89 | 2001 | 2004 |
| 1998 | 90 | 2000 | 2003+ |
| 1997 | 91 | 2002 | 2005 |
| 1996 | 89 | 1998 | 2001 |
| 1995 | 86 | 1997 | 2000 |
| 1994 | 82 | 1996 | 1999 |

## STENTIFORD'S RESERVE OLD VINES SHIRAZ

RANKING **2**

| Coonawarra | $50+ |
|---|---|
| **Current vintage: 2000** | **89** |

Advancing, old-fashioned expression of chocolatey Coonawarra shiraz whose slightly meaty, leathery and varnishy aroma of plums and prunes, walnuts and hazelnuts precedes a firm, slightly coarse and hard-edged palate. It finishes austere, robust and earthy.

| | | | |
|---|---|---|---|
| 2000 | 89 | 2005 | 2008+ |
| 1999 | 95 | 2007 | 2011+ |
| 1998 | 96 | 2010 | 2018 |
| 1997 | 94 | 2005 | 2009 |
| 1996 | 95 | 2004 | 2008 |
| 1995 | 91 | 2003 | 2007 |
| 1991 | 87 | 1996 | 1999 |
| 1990 | 86 | 1992 | 1995+ |
| 1988 | 87 | 1996 | 2000 |
| 1987 | 79 | 1992 | 1995 |
| 1986 | 91 | 1994 | 1998+ |
| 1985 | 92 | 1997 | 2005 |

# Bremerton

Strathalbyn Road, Langhorne Creek SA 5255. Tel: (08) 8537 3093. Fax: (08) 8537 3109.
Website: www.bremerton.com.au  Email: info@bremerton.com.au
Region: **Langhorne Creek** Winemaker: **Rebecca Willson** Chief Executive: **Craig Willson**
A family affair at Langhorne Creek, Bremerton's steadily improving wines are generously flavoured and substantially oaked, and have shown a tendency to be cropped a little over-ripe. As the Selkirk Shiraz from 2000 ably illustrates, the vineyard is capable of delicious and intensely flavoured fruit of some complexity.

## OLD ADAM SHIRAZ

RANKING **5**

| Langhorne Creek | $30–$49 |
|---|---|
| **Current vintage: 2001** | **89** |

Meaty, almost gamey aromas of plums, prunes and currants, black pepper and spices, mocha and chocolate. Sumptuous and creamy, its vibrant, juicy flavours of cassis, raspberries and plums are evenly matched with sweet chocolate oak, finishing with a firm, but not overly aggressive extract of tannin and a lingering note of mint. There's a hint of dehydration, but the wine is fresh and vibrant.

| | | | |
|---|---|---|---|
| 2001 | 89 | 2006 | 2009 |
| 1999 | 86 | 2001 | 2004+ |
| 1998 | 88 | 2000 | 2003 |
| 1997 | 83 | 2002 | 2005 |
| 1996 | 90 | 2001 | 2004 |

## SELKIRK SHIRAZ

| Langhorne Creek | $12–$19 | | 2000 | 92 | 2005 | 2008+ |
| Current vintage: 2000 | 92 | | 1999 | 86 | 2001 | 2004 |

Flavoursome, fruit-driven shiraz with uncluttered charm and elegance. Its spicy aromas of slightly cooked plums and a hint of prune are exotically scented with cinnamon, cloves and white pepper, with a reserved background of vanilla oak. A pleasingly generous, fleshy and vibrant expression of black fruits plays along the fine-grained palate whose bony tannins provide admirable structure. Finishes with a savoury, peppery note.

| | | 1998 | 85 | 2000 | 2003 |
|---|---|---|---|---|---|
| | | 1997 | 80 | 1999 | 2002 |
| | | 1996 | 89 | 2004 | 2008 |

## WALTER'S CABERNET SAUVIGNON

| Langhorne Creek | $20–$29 | | 2000 | 86 | 2002 | 2005 |
| Current vintage: 2000 | 86 | | 1999 | 88 | 2004 | 2007 |

Ageing, leathery and cedary cabernet with a minty aroma of small berry fruits and a bright, forward palate finishing with slightly sappy, but fine-grained tannins. Quite elegant and competent, but unspectacular.

| | | 1998 | 90 | 2006 | 2010 |
|---|---|---|---|---|---|
| | | 1997 | 86 | 1999 | 2002 |
| | | 1996 | 89 | 2004 | 2008 |

# Brian Barry

Juds Hill Vineyard, Clare SA 5343. Tel: (08) 8363 6211. Fax: (08) 8362 0498. Email: bbwines@senet.com.au

Region: **Clare Valley** Winemaker: **Brian Barry** Viticulturist: **Brian Barry** Chief Executive: **Brian Barry**

Its tightly crafted and elegant 2000 vintage Cabernet Sauvignon arrived as something of a surprise from this notoriously hot and difficult vintage. Brian Barry is perhaps better known for its Juds Hill Riesling, which is typically made in a chalky, talcum powdery style with lemony fragrances.

## JUDS HILL VINEYARD CABERNET SAUVIGNON

| Clare Valley | $20–$29 | | 2000 | 93 | 2008 | 2012 |
| Current vintage: 2000 | 93 | | 1999 | 91 | 2007 | 2011 |

Tightly integrated, deftly balanced and improbably classy cabernet from this difficult vintage. Its delicate bouquet of small berries, cherries and plums has a violet-like perfume and an undercurrent of cedar/mocha-like oak. Its smooth and rather showy palate combines a succulent mouthfeel with a tightly integrated chassis of firm, fine tannins and oak.

| | | 1997 | 81 | 1999 | 2002 |
|---|---|---|---|---|---|
| | | 1996 | 89 | 2008 | 2016 |
| | | 1995 | 88 | 2007 | 2015 |
| | | 1994 | 87 | 2006 | 2014 |
| | | 1993 | 83 | 1995 | 1998 |

## JUDS HILL VINEYARD RIESLING

| Clare Valley | $20–$29 | | 2003 | 88 | 2005 | 2008+ |
| Current vintage: 2003 | 88 | | 2002 | 90 | 2007 | 2010+ |

Floral, talcum powder-like aromas of apple, pear and rose petals, before a generous and even chewy palate of slightly hot, cooked limey lemon fruit with a lingering alcoholic warmth. Good, but a little too spirity.

| | | 2001 | 94 | 2009 | 2013+ |
|---|---|---|---|---|---|
| | | 2000 | 86 | 2002 | 2005 |
| | | 1999 | 80 | 1999 | 2000 |
| | | 1998 | 94 | 2003 | 2006+ |
| | | 1997 | 80 | 1998 | 1999 |
| | | 1996 | 93 | 2001 | 2004+ |
| | | 1995 | 93 | 2003 | 2007 |
| | | 1994 | 95 | 2002 | 2006 |

# Briar Ridge

Mount View Road, Mount View NSW 2325. Tel: (02) 4990 3670. Fax: (02) 4990 7802.
Website: www.briarridge.com.au  Email: indulge@briarridge.com.au
Region: **Lower Hunter Valley** Winemakers: **Steve Dodd, Karl Stockhausen** Viticulturist: **Derek Smith**
Chief Executive: **Cameron McAlpine**

Briar Ridge is one of my favourite small Hunter producers. While the 2003 Chardonnay is clearly affected by the bushfires whose smoke lay over parts of the Hunter Valley during this hot, dry ripening season, the 2002 Shiraz reveals the pleasing charm and elegance I associate with this company's modern wines. Hunter winemaking legend Karl Stockhausen still plays an active role in the making of Briar Ridge wines.

## EARLY HARVEST SEMILLON

RANKING **5**

Lower Hunter Valley $20–$29
**Current vintage: 2003** 86

Rather dull, flat, spicy and estery, lacking this label's customary freshness and focus. Juicy and forward, slightly volatile, simple and short.

| | | | |
|---|---|---|---|
| 2003 | 86 | 2004 | 2005+ |
| 2002 | 87 | 2004 | 2007 |
| 2001 | 88 | 2006 | 2009 |
| 2000 | 84 | 2002 | 2005 |
| 1999 | 92 | 2004 | 2007+ |
| 1998 | 94 | 2003 | 2006+ |
| 1997 | 88 | 1999 | 2002 |
| 1996 | 90 | 1998 | 2001 |

## HAND PICKED CHARDONNAY

RANKING **5**

Lower Hunter Valley $20–$29
**Current vintage: 2003** 76

Cooked melon and tobacco fruit with hints of cumquat dominated by smoky, ashtray-like bushfire smoke influences. Round and forward, but finishes dirty and smoky.

| | | | |
|---|---|---|---|
| 2003 | 76 | 2003 | 2004 |
| 2002 | 87 | 2004 | 2007 |
| 2001 | 90 | 2003 | 2006+ |
| 2000 | 87 | 2002 | 2005 |
| 1999 | 82 | 2001 | 2004 |
| 1998 | 90 | 2000 | 2003+ |
| 1997 | 88 | 1999 | 2002 |
| 1996 | 93 | 2001 | 2004 |

## STOCKHAUSEN SHIRAZ

RANKING **3**

Lower Hunter Valley $20–$29
**Current vintage: 2002** 90

Old-fashioned, restrained and very elegant Hunter burgundy style whose earthy, spicy and leathery bouquet of slightly stewed plum-like fruit, red berries and cherries is lifted by hints of tar and white pepper. Its palate is restrained and almost shy, but offers an excellent length of reserved berry flavours, creamy oak and fine tannins.

| | | | |
|---|---|---|---|
| 2002 | 90 | 2007 | 2010+ |
| 2001 | 89 | 2003 | 2006 |
| 2000 | 85 | 2005 | 2008 |
| 1999 | 95 | 2007 | 2011 |
| 1998 | 95 | 2006 | 2010+ |
| 1997 | 94 | 2005 | 2009 |
| 1996 | 84 | 2001 | 2004 |
| 1995 | 92 | 2007 | 2015 |
| 1994 | 88 | 1999 | 2002 |
| 1993 | 93 | 2001 | 2005 |

# Bridgewater Mill

Mount Barker Road, Bridgewater SA 5155. Tel: (08) 8339 3422. Fax: (08) 8339 5311.
Website: www.petalumalimited.com.au  Email: bridgewatermill@petaluma.com.au
Region: **Various SA** Winemakers: **Brian Croser, Con Moshos** Viticulturist: **Mike Harms**
Chief Executive: **Peter Cowan**

Initially part of Petaluma, and now a label of Lion Nathan's Wine Division, Bridgewater Mill has been allowed to slip in its quality and lose its identity. Its wines do not live up to expectations, and their focus on a 'Three Districts' theme is patently meaningless. Due for a serious makeover.

## CHARDONNAY

RANKING  5

Various, Southern Australia  $20–$29
**Current vintage: 2001**  81

Greenish, toffee-like chardonnay dominated by blown-out malolactic influences. Loads of sweet buttery vanilla oak, but insufficient fruit and freshess. Finishes rather raw.

| | | | |
|---|---|---|---|
| 2001 | 81 | 2002 | 2003 |
| 2000 | 88 | 2002 | 2005 |
| 1999 | 87 | 2001 | 2004 |
| 1998 | 81 | 1999 | 2000 |
| 1997 | 90 | 1999 | 2002 |
| 1996 | 86 | 1998 | 2001 |
| 1995 | 90 | 1997 | 2000 |

## MILLSTONE SHIRAZ

RANKING  5

Various, South Australia  $20–$29
**Current vintage: 2001**  84

Honest, if slightly baked shiraz whose rather stewy plum and berry fruit flavours are matched to creamy and lightly cedary oak but culminate in a blocky finish for a wine of this modest weight. Typical of many 2001s, it just lacks fruit brightness.

| | | | |
|---|---|---|---|
| 2001 | 84 | 2006 | 2009 |
| 2000 | 89 | 2002 | 2005+ |
| 1997 | 86 | 2002 | 2005 |
| 1996 | 90 | 2001 | 2004 |
| 1995 | 88 | 2000 | 2003 |
| 1994 | 91 | 1999 | 2002 |
| 1993 | 92 | 2001 | 2005 |
| 1992 | 93 | 1997 | 2000 |
| 1991 | 88 | 1996 | 1999 |

## SAUVIGNON BLANC

RANKING  5

Various, South Australia  $20–$29
**Current vintage: 2003**  87

Forward and juicy sauvignon with a fresh grassy and nettle-like aroma with nuances of mineral and passionfruit. Slightly oily and confected, with some concentrated tinned pineapple and mandarin-like fruit, but lacks length and tightness at the finish. A shorter term wine.

| | | | |
|---|---|---|---|
| 2003 | 87 | 2003 | 2004 |
| 2002 | 89 | 2002 | 2003 |
| 2001 | 87 | 2001 | 2002 |
| 2000 | 90 | 2001 | 2002 |
| 1999 | 90 | 2000 | 2003 |
| 1998 | 87 | 1998 | 1999 |

# Brokenwood

McDonalds Road, Pokolbin NSW 2320. Tel: (02) 4998 7559. Fax: (02) 4998 7893.
Website: www.brokenwood.com.au  Email: sales@brokenwood.com.au
Region: **Various** Winemaker: **Peter-James Charteris** Viticulturist: **Keith Barry**
Chief Executive: **Iain Riggs**

Brokenwood is an elite Hunter winery that not only produces a small range of regional wines led by the Graveyard (shiraz) and the ILR Reserve Semillon, but also releases an eclectic mix of labels sourced elsewhere, including the popular show pony, the Rayner Vineyard Shiraz. Recent additions to the mix include the Indigo Vineyard Pinot Noir and Viognier from Beechworth in Victoria, plus the Wade Block 2 Shiraz from McLaren Vale.

## CABERNET BLEND

RANKING 4

King Valley  $20–$29
**Current vintage: 2000**  89

Elegant, fine-grained and savoury wine whose meaty, musky perfume of violets and plums does suggest some slightly cooked fruit. Smooth and supple, its restrained but moderately full palate presents a vibrant expression of cassis and plum flavour overlying a gravelly spine of fine, bony tannins.

| | | | |
|---|---|---|---|
| 2000 | 89 | 2005 | 2008 |
| 1999 | 90 | 2004 | 2007+ |
| 1997 | 90 | 2000 | 2005 |
| 1996 | 87 | 2004 | 2008 |
| 1994 | 90 | 2002 | 2006 |
| 1992 | 93 | 2000 | 2004 |
| 1991 | 93 | 1996 | 1999 |
| 1990 | 92 | 1995 | 1998 |

# CHARDONNAY

RANKING 4

**Lower Hunter Valley** $20–$29
**Current vintage: 2003** 85

Unusually sweet, rather oaky, slightly oxidative but flavoursome wine with a spicy aroma of dried flowers, stonefruit, banana and melon. Juicy, round and developed, the palate marries some assertive oak with ripe flavours of peaches, nectarines and figs, with lingering suggestions of grilled nuts. Too sweet for a higher rating.

| | | | |
|---|---|---|---|
| 2003 | 85 | 2004 | 2005 |
| 2001 | 89 | 2003 | 2006 |
| 2000 | 89 | 2002 | 2005 |
| 1998 | 93 | 2000 | 2003+ |
| 1997 | 94 | 2002 | 2005 |
| 1995 | 91 | 2000 | 2003 |

# GRAVEYARD VINEYARD (Shiraz)

RANKING 2

**Lower Hunter Valley** $50+
**Current vintage: 2002** 95

Excellent Hunter Valley shiraz with an already complex, meaty and pungent fragrance of spicy redcurrants, plums and cherries over nuances of undergrowth and polished leather. Its smooth, elegant and savoury palate of full to medium weight is classic Hunter — earthy, leathery and spicy, with a wonderful depth of sweetly ripened fruit framed by fine-grained and silky tannins.

| | | | |
|---|---|---|---|
| 2002 | 95 | 2010 | 2014+ |
| 2001 | 90 | 2009 | 2013 |
| 2000 | 96 | 2012 | 2020 |
| 1999 | 93 | 2004 | 2007 |
| 1998 | 96 | 2010 | 2018+ |
| 1997 | 91 | 2002 | 2005+ |
| 1996 | 93 | 2004 | 2008 |
| 1994 | 95 | 2006 | 2014 |
| 1993 | 88 | 2001 | 2005 |
| 1991 | 95 | 2003 | 2011 |
| 1990 | 90 | 1998 | 2002 |
| 1989 | 94 | 2001 | 2009 |
| 1988 | 94 | 2000 | 2008+ |
| 1987 | 94 | 1995 | 1999 |
| 1986 | 95 | 1998 | 2003 |
| 1985 | 89 | 1990 | 1993 |

# ILR RESERVE SEMILLON

RANKING 3

**Lower Hunter Valley** $30–$49
**Current vintage: 1998** 89

Developing, rather oxidative and spicy aromas of dried flowers, citrus and melon precede a generous, round and evenly textured, smooth palate whose evolved bottle-aged flavours culminate in a lingering nutty and savoury finish. More advanced than previous releases under this label.

| | | | |
|---|---|---|---|
| 1998 | 89 | 2003 | 2006 |
| 1997 | 92 | 2005 | 2009 |
| 1996 | 95 | 2004 | 2008+ |
| 1995 | 93 | 2003 | 2007+ |

# RAYNER VINEYARD SHIRAZ

RANKING 3

**McLaren Vale** $30–$49
**Current vintage: 2002** 94

Very smart, stylish and fully-ripened modern impression of McLaren Vale shiraz with a vibrant aroma of cranberries, red cherries and plums over meaty farm floor undertones, chocolate/vanilla/coconut oak and suggestions of menthol and mint. Smooth, long and luscious, its vibrant, spicy flavours of cassis, dark plums and sour cherries are enhanced by its reductive, charcuterie-like complexity and framed by the finest of tannins. A fraction spirity, but neither over-ripe nor porty.

| | | | |
|---|---|---|---|
| 2002 | 94 | 2010 | 2014+ |
| 2001 | 93 | 2009 | 2013 |
| 2000 | 91 | 2005 | 2008 |
| 1999 | 89 | 2001 | 2004+ |
| 1996 | 93 | 2004 | 2008 |

# SEMILLON

RANKING 4

**Lower Hunter Valley** $20–$29
**Current vintage: 2003** 86

Lightly grassy, with delicate lemon sherbet, bath-powder and melon aromas, this chalky, herbal semillon culminates in a closed, slightly cloying and apparently stressed finish refreshed with lemon detergent-like acids.

| | | | |
|---|---|---|---|
| 2003 | 86 | 2004 | 2005+ |
| 2002 | 90 | 2004 | 2007 |
| 2001 | 91 | 2002 | 2003 |
| 2000 | 91 | 2001 | 2004+ |
| 1998 | 95 | 2003 | 2006+ |
| 1997 | 91 | 2002 | 2005 |
| 1995 | 94 | 2003 | 2007 |
| 1994 | 93 | 2002 | 2006 |
| 1993 | 88 | 2001 | 2005 |
| 1992 | 87 | 2000 | 2004 |

A B C D E F G H I J K L M N O P Q R S T U V W X Y Z

## SHIRAZ

RANKING **4**

| Various | $20–$29 |
| --- | --- |
| **Current vintage: 2001** | **92** |

Rustic, spicy Hunter shiraz with a complex, smoky bouquet of dark berries and plums over musky nuances of cloves and cinnamon, earth and saddlery. Medium in weight, the palate is elegant, soft and supple, delivering attractive and brightly lit cherry/plum flavours and restrained older oak influences against a slightly herbal and tobaccoey background. It finishes fine-grained and savoury.

| 2001 | 92 | 2006 | 2009 |
| --- | --- | --- | --- |
| 2000 | 87 | 2002 | 2005 |
| 1998 | 90 | 2003 | 2006 |
| 1996 | 88 | 2001 | 2004 |

# Brown Brothers

Off main Glenrowan–Myrtleford Road, (Snow Road, )Milawa Vic 3678.
Tel: (03) 5720 5500. Fax: (03) 5720 5511.
Website: www.brown-brothers.com.au  Email: bbmv@brown-brothers.com.au
Region: **NE Victoria**  Winemakers: **Wendy Cameron, Emma Body, Trina Smith**  Viticulturist: **Mark Walpole**
Chief Executive: **Ross Brown**

Through several of its traditional labels such as the Cabernet Shiraz Mondeuse blend and the recently constructed Patricia range of premium wines, there's little doubt that there's a will within the Brown Brothers company to compete at the top end of the market. The company's bread and butter, however is its Victorian and King Valley ranges, which need to do a little more to cut the mustard against some presently stiff opposition.

## CABERNET SHIRAZ MONDEUSE BLEND

RANKING **4**

| NE Victoria | $20–$29 |
| --- | --- |
| **Current vintage: 1998** | **90** |

Deep, dark and chocolatey, with intense aromas of cassis, plums, black olives and fruitcake, plus slightly ashtray-like smoky oak. Powerful and extracted, massively concentrated, with rich, meaty raisin and spicecake qualities supported by smoky oak and a firm, bony spine of robust and presently unyielding tannins.

| 1998 | 90 | 2010 | 2018+ |
| --- | --- | --- | --- |
| 1997 | 90 | 2009 | 2017+ |
| 1996 | 91 | 2008 | 2016 |
| 1995 | 87 | 2007 | 2015 |
| 1992 | 92 | 2004 | 2012 |
| 1990 | 91 | 2002 | 2010 |
| 1989 | 90 | 2001 | 2009 |
| 1988 | 90 | 2000 | 2005 |
| 1987 | 90 | 1999 | 2004 |
| 1986 | 91 | 2006 | 2016 |
| 1985 | 91 | 2015 | 2025 |
| 1984 | 85 | 1992 | 1996 |
| 1983 | 91 | 2003 | 2013 |
| 1982 | 90 | 1994 | 1999 |
| 1981 | 90 | 1993 | 1998 |
| 1980 | 94 | 2010 | 2020 |

## FAMILY RES. CABERNET SAUVIGNON & SHIRAZ

RANKING **5**

| NE Victoria | $50+ |
| --- | --- |
| **Current vintage: 1997** | **88** |

A firm, meaty and astringent red whose earthy, slightly tarry bouquet remains a little closed. Cedary and chocolate-like, it's rich, sumptuous and chewy, delivering a powerful but compact mouthful of minty blackcurrant and plum fruit thickly cloaked with chunky tannin and slightly raw chocolate/mocha oak. Finishing with leathery, savoury complexity, it's a shade extracted for higher marks.

| 1997 | 88 | 2009 | 2017 |
| --- | --- | --- | --- |
| 1994 | 87 | 2002 | 2006 |
| 1992 | 89 | 2000 | 2004+ |
| 1991 | 93 | 2003 | 2011 |
| 1988 | 77 | 2000 | 2008 |
| 1987 | 82 | 1992 | 1995 |

## KING VALLEY BARBERA

RANKING **5**

| Alpine Valleys | $12–$19 |
| --- | --- |
| **Current vintage: 2002** | **87** |

Honest, varietal but slightly greenish barbera with a spicy, confectionary aroma of sweet red cherries and berries, with meaty undertones of diesel oil and nicotine. Smooth and supple, its lively and pristine fruit is supported by fine, tight tannins, before finishing slightly herbal and green-edged.

| 2002 | 87 | 2004 | 2007 |
| --- | --- | --- | --- |
| 2001 | 91 | 2003 | 2006 |
| 1999 | 87 | 2001 | 2004+ |
| 1998 | 81 | 1999 | 2000 |
| 1997 | 85 | 1998 | 1999 |
| 1996 | 88 | 1998 | 2001 |

# KING VALLEY RIESLING
RANKING 5

| King Valley | $12–$19 |
|---|---|
| **Current vintage: 2003** | **87** |

Toasty, developing and rather cooked young riesling whose spicy, musky floral aromas precede a rich, generous and approachable palate of pleasing fruitiness and roundness. Soft, but lacking great length.

| | | | |
|---|---|---|---|
| 2002 | 90 | 2004 | 2007 |
| 2001 | 80 | 2001 | 2002 |
| 2000 | 84 | 2002 | 2005 |
| 1999 | 87 | 2001 | 2004 |
| 1997 | 87 | 1999 | 2002 |
| 1996 | 86 | 1998 | 2001 |
| 1995 | 85 | 2000 | 2003 |
| 1994 | 85 | 1999 | 2002 |
| 1993 | 91 | 1998 | 2001 |

# PATRICIA NOBLE RIESLING
RANKING 5

| NE Victoria | $30–$49 |
|---|---|
| **Current vintage: 2000** | **93** |

Complex, developing dessert style with pleasing fruit and freshness, but without the excessively cloying sweetness of many others. Its toasty aromas of brioche and honey, dried fruit and nuts herald a moderately luscious palate. In addition to its penetrative apple, pear and apricot-like fruit, its nuances of honey, butter and pastry culminate in a lingering lemon meringue finish punctuated by fresh citrusy acids.

| | | | |
|---|---|---|---|
| 1999 | 89 | 2004 | 2007 |
| 1998 | 89 | 2003 | 2006 |
| 1997 | 85 | 1998 | 1999 |
| 1996 | 81 | 1998 | 2001 |
| 1994 | 82 | 1999 | 2002 |
| 1993 | 92 | 1998 | 2001 |

# PATRICIA PINOT CHARDONNAY BRUT
RANKING 3

| King Valley | $30–$49 |
|---|---|
| **Current vintage: 1998** | **94** |

Its meaty, slightly aldehydic bouquet of dried flowers, grilled nuts and creamy, bakery yeast influences heralds an assertive sparking wine of the unashamedly vinous Krug-like ilk. Rich and chewy, it's firmly structured for a fizz, while its pleasing length of fruit finishes with a touch of austerity and a balanced hint of sweetness.

| | | | |
|---|---|---|---|
| 1998 | 94 | 2003 | 2006+ |
| 1997 | 88 | 2002 | 2005 |
| 1996 | 90 | 2001 | 2004 |
| 1995 | 95 | 2000 | 2003+ |
| 1994 | 89 | 1999 | 2002 |
| 1993 | 79 | 1995 | 1998 |

# VICTORIA CABERNET SAUVIGNON
RANKING 5

| Victoria | $20–$29 |
|---|---|
| **Current vintage: 2002** | **87** |

Elegant medium to full-bodied cabernet whose cedary aromas of small red and black berries reveal delicate minty and floral nuances. Smooth and polished, its fine, supple palate presents lively small berry flavours framed by fine, soft tannins, but lacks genuine penetration.

| | | | |
|---|---|---|---|
| 2002 | 87 | 2007 | 2010 |
| 2001 | 89 | 2006 | 2009+ |
| 2000 | 82 | 2002 | 2005 |
| 1999 | 82 | 2001 | 2004 |
| 1998 | 85 | 2000 | 2003 |
| 1997 | 88 | 2002 | 2005 |
| 1996 | 90 | 2001 | 2004 |
| 1994 | 89 | 2002 | 2006 |
| 1993 | 90 | 2005 | 2013 |

# VICTORIA CHARDONNAY

| Victoria | $12–$19 |
|---|---|
| **Current vintage: 2003** | **85** |

Lighter, relatively straightforward chardonnay with an aroma of pineapple, lemon meringue and assertive vanilla oak, but rather a thin palate whose peach, melon and cashew flavours finish with slightly raw-edged oak.

| | | | |
|---|---|---|---|
| 2003 | 85 | 2004 | 2005 |
| 2001 | 83 | 2002 | 2003+ |
| 2000 | 89 | 2002 | 2005 |
| 1999 | 80 | 2000 | 2001 |
| 1998 | 82 | 2000 | 2003 |
| 1997 | 88 | 1999 | 2002 |

# VICTORIA MERLOT

| Victoria | $20–$29 |
|---|---|
| **Current vintage: 2002** | **82** |

Minty aromas of stewed plums, red berry confection, sweet vanilla oak and eucalypt precede a rather forward and cooked palate lacking in mid-palate sweetness and drying out to a hard-edged finish.

| | | | |
|---|---|---|---|
| 2002 | 82 | 2004 | 2007 |
| 2001 | 84 | 2003 | 2006+ |
| 2000 | 81 | 2002 | 2005 |
| 1999 | 89 | 2001 | 2004 |
| 1998 | 90 | 2003 | 2006 |
| 1997 | 81 | 1999 | 2002 |
| 1996 | 84 | 2001 | 2004 |

A B C D E F G H I J K L M N O P Q R S T U V W X Y Z

## VICTORIA SHIRAZ

**Victoria** **$20–$29**
**Current vintage: 2002** **81**

Earthy aromas of spicy black and red berries are partnered by acrid oak, while the moderately full palate of rather transient fruit dries out fairly quickly to a short and lean finish dominated by rather stale and smoky oak influences.

| | | | |
|---|---|---|---|
| 2002 | 81 | 2004 | 2007 |
| 2001 | 87 | 2006 | 2009 |
| 2000 | 86 | 2002 | 2005+ |
| 1999 | 86 | 2001 | 2004 |
| 1998 | 84 | 2003 | 2006 |
| 1997 | 84 | 1999 | 2002 |
| 1996 | 87 | 1998 | 2001 |
| 1995 | 86 | 2000 | 2003 |
| 1994 | 82 | 1999 | 2002 |
| 1992 | 91 | 2000 | 2004+ |

# Burge Family

Barossa Valley Way, Lyndoch SA 5351. Tel: (08) 8524 4644. Fax: (08) 8524 4444.
Website: www.burgefamily.com.au Email: draycott@burgefamily.com.au

Region: **Barossa Valley** Winemaker: **Rick Burge** Viticulturist: **Rick Burge** Chief Executive: **Rick Burge**

Rick Burge is one of those invaluable Barossa Valley characters who are as committed to the region's history and traditions as they are to the essential quality of their own wines. In this case, as in several others, the outcome is a series of wines that continues and enlivens the Barossa's unique heritage of high-class and deeply fruited red wines from Rhône Valley varieties.

## DRAYCOTT SHIRAZ

RANKING 3

**Barossa Valley** **$50+**
**Current vintage: 2001** **93**

A ripe and meaty, but finely crafted Barossa shiraz of surprising elegance and tightness. Its complex smoky, earthy and spicy aromas of dark plums, cassis and red cherries are matched by vanilla and chocolate oak, while the soft, creamy palate of very lightly cooked plum/prune flavours is accentuated by hints of meat and animal hide, tar and spicy, herbal influences. A slight hotness is its only detraction.

| | | | |
|---|---|---|---|
| 2001 | 93 | 2009 | 2013 |
| 2000 | 88 | 2005 | 2008 |
| 1999 | 95 | 2007 | 2011 |

## OLD VINES GARNACHA

RANKING 4

**Barossa Valley** **$30–$49**
**Current vintage: 2001** **92**

Ripe, sweet and almost soupy Barossa grenache with a typically confectionary fragrance of raspberries, cassis and plums laced with spices, pepper and fine-grained chocolate/vanilla oak. Firm and concentrated, the rustic palate has an Old World aspect to its restrained power and firm spine of tight-knit and drying tannins. Rich, ripe and plummy, with lingering chocolate-like flavours, it's bordering on the warm and spirity. I enjoy it and so will many others.

| | | | |
|---|---|---|---|
| 2001 | 92 | 2006 | 2009+ |
| 2000 | 92 | 2005 | 2008 |
| 1999 | 90 | 2003 | 2006+ |

## OLIVE HILL SEMILLON

RANKING 4

**Barossa Valley** **$20–$29**
**Current vintage: 2002** **93**

Tangy Barossa Valley semillon, whose lightly smoky aromas of green melon fruit and fresh vanilla oak precede a juicy, long and citrusy palate of racy freshness before finishing with lingering bathroom powder notes and zesty acidity.

| | | | |
|---|---|---|---|
| 2002 | 93 | 2004 | 2007 |
| 2001 | 87 | 2002 | 2003 |
| 2000 | 86 | 2001 | 2002 |
| 1999 | 90 | 2004 | 2007 |

## OLIVE HILL SHIRAZ GRENACHE MOURVÈDRE

**Barossa Valley** $30–$49
**Current vintage: 2002** 93

Deeply flavoured, savoury and finely balanced blend of Rhône varieties, with a rather closed and introverted meaty aroma of dark plums and exotic spices. Bursting with fruit, its searingly intense palate of concentrated small berry and dark plum flavours finishes long and savoury, with integrated nuances of vanilla oak and fine tannins.

| | | | |
|---|---|---|---|
| 2002 | 93 | 2007 | 2010+ |
| 2001 | 94 | 2006 | 2009+ |
| 2000 | 87 | 2002 | 2005 |
| 1999 | 94 | 2007 | 2011 |
| 1998 | 89 | 2000 | 2003 |

# Burra Burra

Ashton Hills Vineyard, Tregarthen Road, Ashton SA 5137. Tel: (08) 8390 1243. Fax: (08) 8390 1243.
Region: **Burra Burra** Winemaker: **Stephen George** Viticulturist: **Stephen George**
Chief Executive: **Stephen George**
Burra Burra's Lone Star Shiraz is grown and made by Ashton Hills' Stephen George into a deeply ripened, robust and leathery red wine of some longevity. From a very hot season, the 2001 vintage reveals both ripe and under-ripe influences, but should continue to develop in the bottle.

## LONE STAR SHIRAZ

RANKING 4

**Burra Burra** $20–$29
**Current vintage: 2001** 89

Old-fashioned, robust and leathery red whose earthy, meaty bouquet of exotic spices, dried herbs, cinnamon and cloves reveals pleasing red plum, cassis and red berry aromas. The palate is rich, quite concentrated and firm. There are hints of prune and currant, with slightly greenish notes beneath.

| | | | |
|---|---|---|---|
| 2001 | 89 | 2006 | 2009+ |
| 2000 | 90 | 2008 | 2012+ |
| 1999 | 91 | 2011 | 2019 |
| 1998 | 89 | 2006 | 2010+ |
| 1997 | 92 | 2005 | 2009+ |
| 1996 | 84 | 2001 | 2004 |
| 1995 | 89 | 2003 | 2007+ |

# By Farr

Box 72 Midland Highway, Bannockburn, Vic, 3331 Tel: (03) 5281 1363. Fax: (03) 5281 1349.
Region: **Geelong** Winemaker: **Gary Farr** Viticulturist: **Gary Farr** Chief Executive: **Gary Farr**
By Farr is the label owned by Bannockburn's winemaker, Gary Farr, whose fruit is sourced from Farr's own vineyards that lie adjacent to those of Bannockburn itself. While increasing vine age will contribute to the length and structure of the reds, the Chardonnay and Viognier are already rather encouraging.

## CHARDONNAY

RANKING 4

**Geelong** $30–$49
**Current vintage: 2002** 87

Assertive, richly flavoured and meaty chardonnay whose vibrant spicy aromas of quince, cumquat and peaches are complemented by nutty, vanilla oak and creamy lees-derived influences. Its juicy palate of tinned tropical fruits, citrus and melon flavours are forward and full of character, but does not ultimately finish with the same richness and impact.

| | | | |
|---|---|---|---|
| 2002 | 87 | 2004 | 2007+ |
| 2001 | 94 | 2003 | 2006+ |
| 2000 | 91 | 2005 | 2008 |
| 1999 | 90 | 2001 | 2004 |

## PINOT NOIR

RANKING 4

**Geelong** $30–$49
**Current vintage: 2002** 92

Vibrant aromas of red and black cherries, plums and spices overlie stalky herbal nuances, sweet cedar/vanilla oak, undergrowth and meaty, autumnal notes. Fleshy, elegant and sappy, the palate is full-flavoured and assertive, offering a slightly tomatoey expression of red cherry flavours with attractive weight and a chassis of firm, fine tannins. Good length, but finishes slightly herbal.

| | | | |
|---|---|---|---|
| 2002 | 92 | 2007 | 2010 |
| 2001 | 89 | 2003 | 2006+ |
| 2000 | 90 | 2002 | 2005 |
| 1999 | 89 | 2001 | 2004 |

## SHIRAZ

RANKING 5

| Geelong | $30–$49 |
|---|---|
| **Current vintage: 2002** | **90** |

Rustic, meaty farmyard aromas of spicy blackberries, dark cherries and plums, cedar/vanilla oak and stalky herbal undertones. There's also plenty of black pepper and gamey complexity throughout this smooth, savoury shiraz of full to medium weight. Framed by firm fine tannins, it offers plenty of dark berry/plum flavours and rustic, farmyard complexity.

| 2002 | 90 | 2007 | 2010 |
|---|---|---|---|
| 2001 | 88 | 2006 | 2009 |
| 2000 | 89 | 2002 | 2005 |
| 1999 | 88 | 2001 | 2004 |

## VIOGNIER

RANKING 4

| Geelong | $30–$49 |
|---|---|
| **Current vintage: 2001** | **93** |

High-toned and extreme viognier with a pungent and musky bouquet of orange blossom and apricot, with meaty undertones of grilled nuts. Round and oily, it's a punchy, viscous wine for the real viognier addicts, with a creamy, spirity palate that finishes dry and savoury.

| 2001 | 93 | 2003 | 2006 |
|---|---|---|---|
| 2000 | 90 | 2002 | 2005 |
| 1999 | 90 | 2001 | 2004 |

# Campbells

Murray Valley Highway, Rutherglen Vic 3685. Tel: (02) 6032 9458. Fax: (02) 6032 9870.
Website: www.campbellswines.com.au  Email: wine@campbellswines.com.au

Region: **Rutherglen** Winemaker: **Colin Campbell** Viticulturist: **Malcolm Campbell**
Chief Executives: **Colin & Malcolm Campbell**

Campbells is a long-established family winery in Rutherglen, best known for its richly flavoured, but soft and smooth pair of Bobbie Burns Shiraz and The Barkly Durif. A recent tasting provided encouraging evidence that the Bobbie Burns is capable of cellaring for the long term. Its fortifieds are also ripe, soft and generous.

## BOBBIE BURNS SHIRAZ

RANKING 4

| Rutherglen | $20–$29 |
|---|---|
| **Current vintage: 2002** | **87** |

A lighter, more simple and cooler season Rutherglen shiraz, with slightly confection-like raspberry aromas backed by a regional muddy meatiness and a whiff of white pepper. It's long and quite elegant, with attractive bright fruit, an earthy background and fine-grained tannins.

| 2002 | 87 | 2007 | 2010 |
|---|---|---|---|
| 2001 | 90 | 2006 | 2009 |
| 2000 | 90 | 2008 | 2012 |
| 1999 | 89 | 2004 | 2007 |
| 1998 | 90 | 2006 | 2010 |
| 1997 | 89 | 2002 | 2005+ |
| 1996 | 90 | 2008 | 2016 |
| 1995 | 93 | 2003 | 2007+ |
| 1994 | 91 | 2002 | 2006+ |
| 1993 | 88 | 2001 | 2005+ |
| 1992 | 92 | 2000 | 2004+ |

## CHARDONNAY

RANKING 5

| Rutherglen | $12–$19 |
|---|---|
| **Current vintage: 2002** | **87** |

Buttery aromas of peaches and cashews with sweet vanilla oak precede a soft, long and relatively elegant palate for a warm-climate chardonnay. Pleasing roundness and flavour, but drink it soon.

| 2002 | 87 | 2003 | 2004+ |
|---|---|---|---|
| 2001 | 86 | 2002 | 2003 |
| 2000 | 86 | 2002 | 2005 |
| 1999 | 83 | 2001 | 2004 |
| 1998 | 87 | 1999 | 2000 |

# RIESLING

RANKING **5**

| Rutherglen | $12–$19 | | |
|---|---|---|---|
| **Current vintage: 2003** | **79** | | |

Broad, rather flabby and confectionary riesling with some dusty lemon rind fruit, finishing with an impression of sweetness.

| | | | |
|---|---|---|---|
| 2003 | 79 | 2004 | 2005 |
| 2002 | 86 | 2003 | 2004+ |
| 2001 | 87 | 2006 | 2009 |
| 2000 | 87 | 2005 | 2008 |
| 1999 | 87 | 2004 | 2007 |
| 1998 | 86 | 2003 | 2006 |
| 1997 | 83 | 2002 | 2005 |
| 1996 | 88 | 2001 | 2004 |

# THE BARKLY DURIF

RANKING **4**

| Rutherglen | $30–$49 | | |
|---|---|---|---|
| **Current vintage: 2002** | **89** | | |

A lighter, finer durif with spicy, minty aromas of red berries and mulberries, with typical suggestions of meat and confection. Elegant and tightly knit, the palate reveals a pleasing length of briary small berry flavours and gamey nuances supported by a moderately tannic and powdery backbone.

| | | | |
|---|---|---|---|
| 2002 | 89 | 2007 | 2010 |
| 2001 | 90 | 2006 | 2009 |
| 1998 | 89 | 2003 | 2006 |
| 1997 | 89 | 2002 | 2005 |
| 1996 | 91 | 2001 | 2004+ |
| 1995 | 89 | 2000 | 2003 |
| 1994 | 93 | 2002 | 2006 |
| 1993 | 88 | 2001 | 2005 |
| 1992 | 94 | 2000 | 2004+ |
| 1991 | 90 | 1999 | 2003 |
| 1990 | 91 | 2002 | 2010 |

# VINTAGE PORT

RANKING **5**

| Rutherglen | $20–$29 | | |
|---|---|---|---|
| **Current vintage: 1997** | **89** | | |

Elegant, restrained, but long-term port whose tarry, spicy aromas of punchy cassis and plums are a little spirity, raw and stewed. Long and fine-grained, its earthy, savoury palate offers plenty of dark, tarry plum and blackberry fruit before a rather rustic finish of menthol and cough medicine.

| | | | |
|---|---|---|---|
| 1997 | 89 | 2009 | 2017 |
| 1996 | 89 | 2004 | 2008 |
| 1994 | 88 | 2002 | 2006 |
| 1993 | 92 | 2005 | 2013 |
| 1991 | 87 | 1999 | 2003 |
| 1990 | 93 | 2002 | 2010 |
| 1988 | 91 | 2000 | 2005 |
| 1986 | 94 | 1998 | 2003 |
| 1983 | 94 | 1995 | 2000 |

# Cannibal Creek

260 Tynong North Rd, Tynong North Vic 6285. Tel: (03) 5942 8380. Fax: (08) 5942 8202.
Website: www.cannibalcreek.gippslander.com  Email: hardiker@bigpond.com

Region: **Gippsland** Winemaker: **Patrick Hardiker** Viticulturist: **Patrick Hardiker** Chief Executive: **Kath Hardiker**

Cannibal Creek is an emergent small producer of seriously flavoursome and interesting wines from pinot noir, chardonnay and sauvignon blanc. The Pinot Noir is consistently firm and full of character, while the 2003 Sauvignon Blanc is a stylish, lightly grassy and minerally edition with more than a little attitude and class.

## PINOT NOIR

RANKING **4**

| Gippsland | $20–$29 | | |
|---|---|---|---|
| **Current vintage: 2002** | **88** | | |

A fragrant, bony, stony village Burgundy style with a pleasing structure. Its earthy aromas of sweet maraschino cherries reveals nuances of cinnamon and cloves, with lightly herbal undertones. Its juicy, fleshy palate of raspberry and cherry flavours overlies a firmish undercarriage of tight tannins, finishing dry and savoury with lingering sweet fruit.

| | | | |
|---|---|---|---|
| 2002 | 88 | 2004 | 2007 |
| 2001 | 92 | 2006 | 2009 |
| 2000 | 90 | 2005 | 2008 |

# Cape Mentelle

Wallcliffe Road, Margaret River WA 6285. Tel: (08) 9757 3266. Fax: (08) 9757 3233.
Email: info@capementelle.com.au

Region: **Margaret River** Winemaker: **John Durham** Viticulturist: **Brenton Air** Chief Executive: **Tony Jordan**

One of the Margaret River elite, Cape Mentelle continues its astonishingly consistent run of citrusy, minerally Chardonnay and firm and spicy Shiraz in company with dramatic improvement in its oak-matured Walcliffe Reserve white Bordeaux blend, plus a welcome return to form for its Semillon Sauvignon, whose 2003 vintage is a return to the popular and racy style of the late 1990s.

## CABERNET MERLOT 'TRINDERS'

RANKING **5**

| Margaret River | $20–$29 |
| :--- | ---: |
| **Current vintage: 2002** | **86** |

Earthy, dusty bell pepper and cedary aromas, with scents of small red berries and plums precede an elegant and rather polished palate. Its up-front red berry and plum flavours offer reasonable length, but do however finish rather green and sappy.

| | | | |
| --- | --- | --- | --- |
| 2002 | 86 | 2004 | 2007 |
| 2001 | 91 | 2006 | 2009 |
| 2000 | 86 | 2005 | 2008 |
| 1999 | 82 | 2001 | 2004 |
| 1998 | 86 | 2000 | 2003 |
| 1997 | 83 | 1999 | 2002+ |
| 1996 | 90 | 2004 | 2008 |
| 1995 | 90 | 2003 | 2007 |
| 1994 | 90 | 1999 | 2002 |

## CABERNET SAUVIGNON

RANKING **3**

| Margaret River | $50+ |
| :--- | ---: |
| **Current vintage: 2000** | **93** |

Old-fashioned and developed earthy, leathery aromas of dark plums, dark olives and smoky, cedar-like oak, with just a suggestion of currants and capsicum. Lavish, luscious palate whose deep, dark fruit flavours of plums and cassis are presented in a riper, juicier expression of Margaret River cabernet. Not for the super-long term, but both generous and refined.

| | | | |
| --- | --- | --- | --- |
| 2000 | 93 | 2008 | 2012+ |
| 1999 | 93 | 2007 | 2011+ |
| 1998 | 93 | 2010 | 2018 |
| 1996 | 92 | 2004 | 2008+ |
| 1995 | 88 | 2003 | 2007 |
| 1994 | 93 | 2014 | 2024 |
| 1993 | 94 | 2005 | 2013 |
| 1992 | 94 | 2004 | 2012 |
| 1991 | 96 | 2003 | 2011 |
| 1990 | 94 | 1998 | 2002 |
| 1989 | 94 | 1997 | 2001 |
| 1988 | 92 | 2000 | 2008 |
| 1987 | 94 | 2007 | 2017 |
| 1986 | 91 | 1998 | 2006 |
| 1985 | 90 | 1993 | 1997 |
| 1984 | 93 | 1996 | 2001 |
| 1983 | 90 | 1995 | 2003 |
| 1982 | 93 | 1994 | 1999 |

## CHARDONNAY

RANKING **2**

| Margaret River | $30–$49 |
| :--- | ---: |
| **Current vintage: 2002** | **90** |

Generous, heavily worked chardonnay with a regional aroma of tinned pineapples, grapefruit and melon, dusty hessian-like oak and slightly candied buttery, toffee-like malolactic characters. Rich, broad and toasty, its slightly oily palate reveals plenty of vibrant fruit over creamy, leesy complexity, while its slightly sappy but mineral acids just lack a little definition.

| | | | |
| --- | --- | --- | --- |
| 2002 | 90 | 2004 | 2007+ |
| 2001 | 93 | 2003 | 2006 |
| 2000 | 93 | 2005 | 2008 |
| 1999 | 95 | 2004 | 2007+ |
| 1998 | 95 | 2003 | 2006+ |
| 1997 | 90 | 2002 | 2005 |
| 1996 | 95 | 2001 | 2004 |
| 1995 | 96 | 2003 | 2007 |
| 1994 | 94 | 2002 | 2006 |

## SEMILLON SAUVIGNON

RANKING **4**

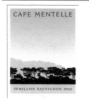

| Margaret River | $20–$29 |
| :--- | ---: |
| **Current vintage: 2003** | **94** |

Right on the style button is this zesty, racy and refreshing Margaret River white blend. Its punchy aromas of passionfruit, lemon and gooseberries present a good measure of grassiness, but not an excessive one. It's smooth, fleshy and textured, with a generous palate finishing with vibrant flavours and acidity, and a measured light dose of slightly smoky oak.

| | | | |
| --- | --- | --- | --- |
| 2003 | 94 | 2004 | 2005+ |
| 2002 | 90 | 2002 | 2003+ |
| 2001 | 87 | 2001 | 2002 |
| 2000 | 88 | 2001 | 2002 |
| 1999 | 88 | 1999 | 2000 |
| 1998 | 95 | 2000 | 2003 |

# SHIRAZ

RANKING 3

| Margaret River | $30–$49 |
|---|---|
| **Current vintage: 2002** | **92** |

Ripe, meaty, spicy and slightly alcoholic shiraz with an earthy, slightly vegetal and spicy bouquet of briary plum and cassis fruit, cinnamon and cloves. A herbal thread lies beneath its smooth, sumptuous palate of dark plum, cassis and currant-like fruit, before a very firm, savoury and tannic finish.

| | | | |
|---|---|---|---|
| 2002 | 92 | 2010 | 2014+ |
| 2001 | 94 | 2009 | 2013+ |
| 2000 | 90 | 2005 | 2008+ |
| 1999 | 93 | 2007 | 2011 |
| 1998 | 93 | 2010 | 2018 |
| 1997 | 94 | 2009 | 2017 |
| 1996 | 93 | 2004 | 2008+ |
| 1995 | 92 | 2007 | 2015 |
| 1994 | 95 | 2006 | 2014 |
| 1993 | 89 | 2001 | 2005 |
| 1992 | 95 | 2004 | 2012+ |

# WALLCLIFFE SAUVIGNON BLANC SEMILLON

RANKING 4

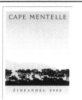

| Margaret River | $30–$49 |
|---|---|
| **Current vintage: 2001** | **95** |

Handsomely the best of the three vintages yet released under Cape Mentelle's flagship white label, this restrained and measured wine has a dusty, herbal aroma of gooseberry fruit, green bean and nutty, lemon and vanilla-like oak. Almost oily, it's long and slippery, with tightly focused fruit partnered by restrained and lightly toasty, biscuity oak, before finishing with refreshing acids.

| | | | |
|---|---|---|---|
| 2001 | 95 | 2003 | 2006 |
| 2000 | 87 | 2001 | 2002 |
| 1999 | 88 | 2001 | 2004 |

# ZINFANDEL

RANKING 3

| Margaret River | $30–$49 |
|---|---|
| **Current vintage: 2002** | **94** |

Uncompromising, but very polished expression of zinfandel with a typically wild and floral perfume of dark, musky, briary, meaty, licorice-like flavours. Sumptuous, warm and smooth, easily carrying its 16% alcohol, its dark, kernel-like fruit reveals a hint of grenache-like confection before a long, firm and chocolatey finish.

| | | | |
|---|---|---|---|
| 2002 | 94 | 2010 | 2014+ |
| 2001 | 87 | 2009 | 2013 |
| 2000 | 92 | 2008 | 2012 |
| 1999 | 93 | 2007 | 2011 |
| 1998 | 95 | 2006 | 2010+ |
| 1997 | 94 | 2005 | 2009+ |
| 1996 | 87 | 2001 | 2004 |
| 1995 | 94 | 2003 | 2007 |
| 1994 | 89 | 2002 | 2006 |
| 1993 | 88 | 1998 | 2001 |
| 1992 | 93 | 1997 | 2000 |
| 1991 | 93 | 2003 | 2011 |
| 1990 | 93 | 1998 | 2002 |

# Capel Vale

Lot 5 Stirling Estate, Mallokup Road, Capel WA 6271. Tel: (08) 9727 1986. Fax: (08) 9727 1904.
Website: www.capelvale.com  Email: winery@capelvale.com

Region: **Geographe, Mount Barker, Pemberton** Winemaker: **Rebecca Catlin**
Viticulturists: **Neil Delroy, Steve Partridge** Chief Executive: **Peter Pratten**

An enigmatic company with vineyards in three major Western Australian regions, Capel Vale is beginning to kick some solid goals with its less-expensive labels, but is still under-achieving with its efforts up town. In my view, its more expensive wines are made from attractive fruit, but need more attention to detail throughout their pre-bottling maturation processes, especially where oak is involved.

# CABERNET SAUVIGNON

RANKING 5

| Various, WA | $20–$29 |
|---|---|
| **Current vintage: 2002** | **90** |

Quite a polished, fine and structured cabernet whose dusty aromas of sweet mulberries, cassis and fresh mint are backed by floral, lightly herbal and capsicum-like complexity. The palate is tight-knit and fine-grained, offering a pleasing length of bright plum, small black and red berry flavours framed by fine tannins. Good balance and integration.

| | | | |
|---|---|---|---|
| 2002 | 90 | 2010 | 2014 |
| 2001 | 88 | 2003 | 2006 |
| 2000 | 86 | 2005 | 2008 |
| 1999 | 84 | 2000 | 2001+ |
| 1998 | 81 | 2000 | 2003 |
| 1997 | 81 | 1999 | 2002 |
| 1996 | 87 | 1998 | 2001 |
| 1995 | 93 | 2003 | 2007 |
| 1994 | 92 | 2002 | 2006 |

A B C D E F G H I J K L M N O P Q R S T U V W X Y Z

## FREDERICK CHARDONNAY

### Capel $30–$49
**Current vintage: 2002** **84**

Dull, cheesy and dusty vanilla oak aromas cloak some light peach, melon and ruby grapefruit. Rather washed out, its palate has developed quickly, revealing dilute, but clear fruit that lacks punch and intensity. There are some pleasing elements of texture and length.

| | | | |
|---|---|---|---|
| 2002 | 84 | 2003 | 2004+ |
| 2000 | 83 | 2001 | 2002+ |
| 1999 | 80 | 2000 | 2001 |
| 1998 | 84 | 2000 | 2003 |
| 1997 | 82 | 1999 | 2002 |
| 1996 | 94 | 1998 | 2001 |
| 1995 | 91 | 1997 | 2000 |
| 1994 | 94 | 1999 | 2002 |

## HOWECROFT MERLOT                          RANKING 5

### Geographe $50+
**Current vintage: 2001** **84**

Big, gritty, oaky merlot with a herbal and varnishy aroma of gamey dark plums, prunes and currants. Richly proportioned, rustic and meaty, it's very firm and thickly coated with oak.

| | | | |
|---|---|---|---|
| 2001 | 84 | 2006 | 2009 |
| 2000 | 87 | 2005 | 2008+ |
| 1999 | 88 | 2004 | 2007 |
| 1998 | 82 | 2003 | 2006 |
| 1997 | 82 | 2002 | 2005 |

## KINNAIRD RESERVE SHIRAZ              RANKING 5

### Mount Barker $50+
**Current vintage: 2002** **89**

Smoky, charcuterie-like aromas of cassis and cooked plums over herbal and Bovril-like nuances. Long, smooth and succulent, it's very briary and meaty, with distinctive smoky, gunpowder-like oak. Very rustic, with a slightly green undercurrent beneath its succulent small berry flavours. A rather wild and meaty effort at a Rhône Valley style.

| | | | |
|---|---|---|---|
| 2002 | 89 | 2007 | 2010 |
| 2001 | 75 | 2003 | 2006 |
| 2000 | 88 | 2002 | 2005 |
| 1998 | 87 | 2003 | 2006 |
| 1997 | 88 | 2002 | 2005 |
| 1996 | 90 | 2001 | 2004 |

## MERLOT                                       RANKING 4

### Capel, Pemberton $12–$19
**Current vintage: 2002** **88**

Early-drinking merlot whose delicate aromas of sweet red cherries, dried herbs and earthy aromas precede a polished, cedary palate whose bright red berry/cherry fruit reveals some tobaccoey and oaky complexity, before a slightly thin and green-edged finish.

| | | | |
|---|---|---|---|
| 2002 | 88 | 2004 | 2007 |
| 2001 | 90 | 2003 | 2006+ |
| 2000 | 91 | 2005 | 2008 |
| 1999 | 89 | 2001 | 2004 |
| 1998 | 76 | 2000 | 2003+ |
| 1997 | 81 | 1999 | 2002 |
| 1996 | 80 | 1997 | 1998 |

## RIESLING                                      RANKING 5

### Various, WA $12–$19
**Current vintage: 2003** **90**

Fresh, floral limey riesling with vibrant lemon rind and apple aromas over a hint of spicy perfume. Lean, fine and delicate, its long, silky palate reveals attractively restrained citrus and stone-fruit flavours neatly wrapped around refreshing acids. Uncomplicated, flavoursome and finely balanced.

| | | | |
|---|---|---|---|
| 2003 | 90 | 2008 | 2011 |
| 2002 | 91 | 2007 | 2010 |
| 2001 | 84 | 2002 | 2003+ |
| 2000 | 87 | 2005 | 2008 |
| 1999 | 77 | 2000 | 2001 |
| 1998 | 87 | 2000 | 2003 |
| 1997 | 80 | 1997 | 1998 |
| 1996 | 87 | 2001 | 2004 |
| 1995 | 89 | 2003 | 2007 |
| 1994 | 90 | 1999 | 2002 |
| 1993 | 94 | 2001 | 2005 |
| 1992 | 87 | 1997 | 2000 |

## SAUVIGNON BLANC SEMILLON              RANKING 5

### Pemberton $12–$19
**Current vintage: 2003** **85**

A little stale and vegetal, with a dusty, asparagus-like aroma of gooseberries and vegetable soup. Broad, juicy and generous, its palate of confection-like gooseberry and melon flavour finishes just a little flat and stale, lacking genuine freshness and bite.

| | | | |
|---|---|---|---|
| 2003 | 85 | 2004 | 2005 |
| 2002 | 87 | 2003 | 2004 |
| 2001 | 83 | 2002 | 2003 |
| 2000 | 90 | 2001 | 2002+ |
| 1999 | 77 | 2000 | 2000 |

## WHISPERING HILL RIESLING

**Mount Barker** $20–$29
**Current vintage: 2002** 86

Spicy, concentrated riesling with a rather spiky lemon/lime aromas and a soft, generous stone-fruit-like palate perhaps reflective of a light presence of botrytis. It finishes juicy, but a little too spicy and herbal.

| | | | |
|---|---|---|---|
| 2002 | 86 | 2004 | 2007 |
| 2001 | 86 | 2003 | 2006 |
| 2000 | 92 | 2008 | 2012 |
| 1998 | 87 | 2000 | 2003+ |
| 1997 | 93 | 2002 | 2005 |
| 1996 | 94 | 2004 | 2008 |

# Carramar Estate

Wakley Road, Yenda NSW 2681. Tel: (02) 6968. 1346 Fax: (02) 6968 1196.
Website: www.casellawine.com.au  Email: info@casellawine.com.au
Region: **Riverina** Winemakers: **Alan Kennet, Phillip Casella** Viticulturist: **Marcello Casella**
Chief Executive: **John Casella**

Carramar Estate is a label owned by the Casella family, owners of the [yellow tail] wine phenomenon. Its leading wine is this typical Griffith-grown late harvest semillon, which John Casella prefers to craft in a finer, more elegant and less syrupy style.

## BOTRYTIS SEMILLON

**Riverina** $20–$29
**Current vintage: 2000** 89

Already at its peak, with a developed marmalade-like nose of candyfloss, treacle and burned butter over intense citrus and melon fruit. Very intense, sweet and syrupy, its luscious, citrusy and rather confectionary palate reveals plenty of flavour but a slightly cooked aspect.

| | | | |
|---|---|---|---|
| 2000 | 89 | 2002 | 2005 |
| 1999 | 92 | 2004 | 2007 |
| 1998 | 86 | 2000 | 2003 |
| 1997 | 83 | 1998 | 1999 |

# Cascabel

Rogers Road, Willunga SA 5172. Tel: (08) 8557 4434. Fax: (08) 8557 4435  Email: cascabel@intertech.net.au
Region: **McLaren Vale** Winemakers: **Susana Fernandez, Duncan Ferguson** Viticulturist: **Robert Ferguson**
Chief Executive: **Duncan Ferguson**

Susana Fernandez' Spanish background imparts a real point of difference at Cascabel, a recent arrival in the McLaren Vale scene. Tempranillo, graciano and mataro were amongst the varieties first planted in 1997. While I am very enthusiastic about what Cascabel is doing to fashion its own point of difference, recent reds have perhaps been given too free a rein to develop complexity by the time of their release.

## GRENACHE et al

CASCABEL

**McLaren Vale** $20–$29
**Current vintage: 2002** 75

Rather cooked, stewy and tarry wine whose level of volatility detracts significantly from some more pleasing aspects.

| | | | |
|---|---|---|---|
| 2002 | 75 | 2004 | 2007 |
| 2001 | 89 | 2003 | 2006 |
| 2000 | 80 | 2001 | 2002 |

## RIESLING

CASCABEL

Riesling
EDEN VALLEY
2002

Made and bottled by Duncan Ferguson and Susana Fernandez
at Cascabel Winery, Rogers Road Willunga SA
12.5% Vol PRODUCE OF AUSTRALIA 750ML

| Eden Valley | $20–$29 |
|---|---|
| **Current vintage: 2003** | **89** |

Rather reductive, probably thanks to the mirror-like qualities of its screwtop seal, this perfumed and fragrant riesling has a honeycomb-like aroma of lime juice and lemon rind. Juicy, spicy and forward, its long and otherwise varietally correct palate is fine and chalky, with lingering citrus fruit bound by bracing, steely acids.

| | | | |
|---|---|---|---|
| 2003 | 89 | 2008 | 2011 |
| 2001 | 83 | 2003 | 2006+ |
| 2000 | 89 | 2008 | 2012 |

## SHIRAZ

CASCABEL

Shiraz
FLEURIEU
2001

Made and bottled by Duncan Ferguson and Susana Fernandez
at Cascabel Winery, Rogers Road Willunga SA
14.0% Vol PRODUCE OF AUSTRALIA 750ML

| Fleurieu | $20–$29 |
|---|---|
| **Current vintage: 2002** | **80** |

Sappy, rather metallic young shiraz whose aromas of raspberry confiture and creamy vanilla oak overlie dusty, herbal undertones with a hint of the forest floor. Forward and quite juicy, but then dries out to a lean, green-edged finish.

| | | | |
|---|---|---|---|
| 2002 | 80 | 2004 | 2007 |
| 2001 | 89 | 2003 | 2006+ |
| 2000 | 83 | 2005 | 2008 |
| 1999 | 83 | 2001 | 2004 |

# Cassegrain

764 Fernbank Creek Road, Port Macquarie NSW 2444. Tel: (02) 6583 7777. Fax: (02) 6584 0354.
Website: www.cassegrainwines.com.au  Email: info@cassegrainwines.com.au
Region: **Hastings River** Winemaker: **John Cassegrain** Viticulturist: **John Cassegrain**
Chief Executive: **John Cassegrain**

More than any other Australian winery, Cassegrain has embraced the hybrid French variety, chambourcin as a cornerstone of its identity, a decision I admire more for its bravery than its wisdom. Its best wine, the Fromenteau Vineyard Chardonnay, is a complex and heavily worked expression of this variety with genuine character, and the 2002 vintage is a top-class effort reminiscent of the excellent wines under this label of a decade ago.

## CHAMBOURCIN

Cassegrain
Chambourcin 2001

| Hastings River | $12–$19 |
|---|---|
| **Current vintage: 2002** | **83** |

Vegetal aromas of confection-like cherries and berries are slightly meaty, with an underlay of vanilla oak. Lacking great length and persistence, the palate's simple raspberry and plum flavours and light oak are bound by sappy and rather greenish tannins.

| | | | |
|---|---|---|---|
| 2002 | 83 | 2003 | 2004+ |
| 2001 | 87 | 2002 | 2003 |
| 1999 | 86 | 2001 | 2004 |
| 1998 | 86 | 1999 | 2000 |
| 1997 | 81 | 1999 | 2002 |
| 1996 | 90 | 1998 | 2001 |
| 1995 | 86 | 1996 | 1997 |
| 1994 | 81 | 1996 | 1999 |

## FROMENTEAU VINEYARD CHARDONNAY

Cassegrain
2002
FROMENTEAU
RESERVE CHARDONNAY

| Hastings River | $20–$29 |
|---|---|
| **Current vintage: 2002** | **93** |

There's some rather pungent reductive complexity about the bouquet of this wine that some will find a little on the cheesy side, but I enjoy the creamy, nutty and smoky, almost meaty background beneath its deep aromas of honeydew melon. Long and savoury, richly textured and seamless, it reveals a deep core of concentrated fruit before a nutty finish of soft acidity. A real return to form for this label.

| | | | |
|---|---|---|---|
| 2002 | 93 | 2004 | 2007+ |
| 2001 | 89 | 2003 | 2006 |
| 2000 | 91 | 2002 | 2005+ |
| 1998 | 80 | 1999 | 2000 |
| 1996 | 88 | 1998 | 2001 |
| 1995 | 91 | 2000 | 2003 |
| 1993 | 88 | 1998 | 2001 |
| 1991 | 94 | 1996 | 1999 |

## RESERVE CHAMBOURCIN

| Hastings River | $20–$29 |
|---|---|
| **Current vintage: 2002** | **81** |

Meaty, earthy, herbal aromas of plums, raspberries and cherries, before a lean, green-edged palate whose light small berry fruit is underpinned by sweet vanilla oak but wrapped in searing, steely acidity.

| | | | |
|---|---|---|---|
| 2002 | 81 | 2004 | 2007 |
| 2001 | 79 | 2003 | 2006 |
| 2000 | 82 | 2002 | 2005 |
| 1998 | 87 | 2003 | 2008 |
| 1997 | 79 | 1999 | 2002 |
| 1996 | 87 | 1998 | 2001 |
| 1995 | 83 | 1997 | 2000 |

## SEMILLON

RANKING **5**

| Hastings River | $12–$19 |
|---|---|
| **Current vintage: 2003** | **87** |

Honest, refreshing and citrusy semillon with a lightly grassy aroma of lime zest, melon and sherbet. Lean, moderately long and shapely palate whose fresh melon/lemon fruit overlies a chalky spine. Finishes with pleasing harmony and fresh acidity.

| | | | |
|---|---|---|---|
| 2003 | 87 | 2005 | 2008 |
| 2002 | 87 | 2004 | 2007 |
| 2001 | 89 | 2003 | 2006+ |
| 2000 | 85 | 2001 | 2002 |
| 1998 | 88 | 2000 | 2003 |
| 1997 | 87 | 2002 | 2005 |
| 1996 | 88 | 2001 | 2004 |
| 1993 | 90 | 2001 | 2005 |
| 1992 | 87 | 1997 | 2000 |

## SHIRAZ

RANKING **5**

| Hastings River | $20–$29 |
|---|---|
| **Current vintage: 2002** | **88** |

Meaty, Rhôney shiraz with a pungent, slightly reductive and black pepper aroma of musky plum and cassis fruit over restrained vanilla oak. Full to medium weight, its supple palate of spicy plum and blackberry fruit culminates in a fine-grained and savoury finish. Loads of evolution and complexity, pleasing depth and brightness, but it remains a fraction short and herbal.

| | | | |
|---|---|---|---|
| 2002 | 88 | 2007 | 2010+ |
| 2001 | 86 | 2003 | 2006 |
| 2000 | 87 | 2002 | 2005+ |
| 1999 | 81 | 2001 | 2004 |
| 1998 | 88 | 2003 | 2006 |
| 1997 | 83 | 1999 | 2002 |
| 1996 | 80 | 1998 | 2001 |

# Castagna

Ressom Lane, Beechworth Vic 3747. Tel: (03) 5728 2888. Fax: (P03) 5728 2898.
Website: www.castagna.com.au  Email: castagna@ enigma.com.au
Region: **Beechworth** Winemaker: **Julian Castagna** Viticulturist: **Julian Castagna**
Chief Executive: **Julian Castagna**

Castagana is one of Beechworth's emergent clan of high-quality and high-elevation small vineyards whose principal wine is a very spicy, Rhône-like shiraz of fineness, elegance and complexity. Its ripe, punchy and spicy Allegro Rosé and meaty La Chiave Sangiovese have also developed a cult following.

## GENESIS SYRAH

RANKING **4**

| Beechworth | $30–$49 |
|---|---|
| **Current vintage: 2001** | **91** |

CASTAGNA

Complex, musky fragrance of red and black berry fruits, briar, plums and dark cherries, lifted by cloves and cinnamon, hints of meat, apricots and forest floor. A fraction spirity, but otherwise restrained and ethereal. Long, supple and fine-grained, it presents almost searingly intense raspberry and dark cherry flavours despite its relative elegance and tightness. Earthy hints of farmyard and cured meats add complexity. Would be marked higher, but a portion of the vineyard appears to have been harvested riper, with some suggestion of dehydration and a loss of freshness. Otherwise an excellent effort.

| | | | |
|---|---|---|---|
| 2001 | 91 | 2003 | 2006+ |
| 2000 | 90 | 2002 | 2005 |
| 1999 | 95 | 2006 | 2007 |

# Castle Rock Estate

Porongorup Road, Porongorup WA 6324. Tel: (08) 9853 1035. Fax: (08) 9853 1010.
Website: www.castlerockestate.com.au  Email: diletti@castlerockestate.com.au

Region: **Great Southern** Winemaker: **Robert Diletti** Viticulturist: **Angelo Diletti** Chief Executive: **Angelo Diletti**

A small cool-climate in the Porongorups whose leading wine is a very floral, slightly Germanic Riesling, but whose performance from year to year is very much subject to the region's ability to fully ripen its fruit.

## CABERNET SAUVIGNON MERLOT

RANKING **5**

**Great Southern** $20–$29
**Current vintage: 2000** 72

Very green, under-ripe and herbaceous, with shaded fruit characters suggestive of capsicum soup.

| 2000 | 72 | 2002 | 2005 |
|------|----|------|------|
| 1999 | 81 | 2001 | 2004 |
| 1998 | 88 | 2003 | 2006+ |
| 1997 | 87 | 2002 | 2005 |
| 1996 | 84 | 2001 | 2004 |

## PINOT NOIR

RANKING **5**

**Great Southern** $20–$29
**Current vintage: 2002** 86

Slightly confectionary, herbal and tomatoey pinot with a smooth, fleshy palate and some penetrative sweet fruit wound around fine-grained tannins. Rather dilute and herbal mid-palate, but some pleasing and vibrant forward fruit.

| 2002 | 86 | 2004 | 2007 |
|------|----|------|------|
| 2001 | 90 | 2003 | 2006 |
| 2000 | 84 | 2001 | 2002 |
| 1999 | 84 | 2000 | 2001 |
| 1998 | 88 | 2000 | 2003 |

## RIESLING

RANKING **4**

**Great Southern** $12–$19
**Current vintage: 2003** 94

Fine, slightly nervy and very stylish and shapely riesling whose musky, floral fragrance of lime juice, lemon, stonefruit and minerals precedes a refreshingly racy, chalky palate. Flavours of lemon, lime, apple and pear are tightly wrapped in fine phenolics and mineral acids.

| 2003 | 94 | 2008 | 2011+ |
|------|----|------|------|
| 2002 | 90 | 2007 | 2010+ |
| 2001 | 86 | 2006 | 2009 |
| 2000 | 89 | 2008 | 2012 |
| 1999 | 80 | 2000 | 2001 |
| 1998 | 93 | 2006 | 2010 |
| 1997 | 88 | 2002 | 2005 |

# Chandon

Green Point Maroondah Highway, Coldstream Vic 3770. Tel: (03) 9739 1110. Fax: (03) 9739 1095.
Website: www.chandon.com.au  Email: info@domainechandon.com.au

Region: **Southern Australia** Winemakers: **Dr Tony Jordan, James Gosper, John Harris**
Viticulturist: **Bernie Wood** Managing Director: **Dr Tony Jordan**

With its opening in the mid 1980s, Domaine Chandon not only re-invented Australia's approach and attitude towards sparkling wine, but it single-handedly created a market for cool climate-grown wines from classic Champagne varieties which were then made with a philosophy and technique almost indistinguishable from Champagne itself. For the first time, Australians believed this country could make wine to rival non-vintage Champagne, setting the scene for a small number of other makers to follow.

## PRESTIGE CUVÉE (formerly Millennium Cuvée)

RANKING **2**

| Southern Australia | $30–$49 |
|---|---|
| **Current vintage: 1995** | **91** |

A developed mushroomy, toasty, buttery and honeyed fragrance of developed floral fruit and hay-like aromas. Rich, chewy and toasty, it's smooth and mature, with an assertive and creamy palate still revealing small berry fruit flavours.

| 1995 | 91 | 2000 | 2003 |
|---|---|---|---|
| 1994 | 95 | 1999 | 2002 |
| 1993 | 95 | 1998 | 2001+ |
| 1992 | 95 | 1997 | 2000 |
| 1989 | 95 | 1997 | 2001+ |

## VINTAGE BLANC DE BLANCS

RANKING **3**

| Southern Australia | $30–$49 |
|---|---|
| **Current vintage: 2000** | **90** |

A fresh bouquet of cumquat and candied citrus rind fruit is scented with nuances of dried flowers, hazelnuts and wheatmeal. Forward and juicy, its generous, creamy palate of tangy citrus flavour culminates in a nutty, savoury finish.

| 2000 | 90 | 2002 | 2005+ |
|---|---|---|---|
| 1999 | 89 | 2004 | 2007 |
| 1998 | 95 | 2003 | 2006 |
| 1997 | 94 | 2002 | 2005 |
| 1996 | 91 | 1998 | 2001 |
| 1995 | 93 | 2000 | 2003 |
| 1993 | 95 | 1998 | 2001+ |
| 1992 | 93 | 1997 | 2000 |
| 1991 | 95 | 1999 | 2003 |
| 1990 | 93 | 1995 | 1998 |

## VINTAGE BLANC DE NOIRS

RANKING **2**

| Southern Australia | $30–$49 |
|---|---|
| **Current vintage: 1997** | **95** |

Delightfully evolved and complex, with a meaty, bready and nutty bouquet plus a chewy, long and elegant palate of restrained power. Long, rich and creamy, it's assertive and punchy, revealing a deep, spicy core of fruit, before finishing long and savoury.

| 1997 | 95 | 2002 | 2005+ |
|---|---|---|---|
| 1996 | 89 | 2001 | 2004 |
| 1994 | 95 | 1999 | 2002 |
| 1993 | 94 | 1998 | 2001 |
| 1992 | 95 | 1997 | 2000 |

## VINTAGE BRUT

RANKING **3**

| Southern Australia | $30–$49 |
|---|---|
| **Current vintage: 2001** | **95** |

Elegant, measured and creamy sparkling wine whose appealingly pungent and floral aromas of pristine cumquat, melon and raspberries are backed by dough-like and meaty cracked yeast influences. Long and smooth, it's vibrant but restrained, with lively fruit and bakery-like yeast qualities culminating in a soft, but crackly finish with lingering fruit flavour. Rather classy.

| 2001 | 95 | 2003 | 2006+ |
|---|---|---|---|
| 1999 | 94 | 2004 | 2007 |
| 1998 | 89 | 2003 | 2006+ |
| 1997 | 89 | 1999 | 2002+ |
| 1996 | 87 | 1998 | 2001+ |
| 1995 | 89 | 1997 | 2000 |
| 1994 | 94 | 1999 | 2002 |
| 1993 | 93 | 1998 | 2001 |
| 1992 | 92 | 1994 | 1997 |

## VINTAGE BRUT ROSÉ

RANKING

**Southern Australia**     $30–$49
**Current vintage: 1999**     88

Developing, and rather phenolic, with a spicy and lightly citrusy fragrance of raspberries, maraschino cherries and hazelnut-like, creamy yeast influences. Its initially lively impression of raspberry and cherry fruit leads into a moderately long, savoury palate whose tangy flavours are drying out, leaving lingering and slightly hard, oaky edges.

| | | | |
|---|---|---|---|
| 1999 | 88 | 2001 | 2004+ |
| 1998 | 94 | 2003 | 2006 |
| 1997 | 94 | 2002 | 2005 |
| 1996 | 93 | 2001 | 2004 |
| 1995 | 91 | 2000 | 2003 |
| 1994 | 94 | 1996 | 1999 |

# Chapel Hill

Chapel Hill Road, McLaren Vale SA 5171. Tel: (08) 8323 8429. Fax: (08) 8323 9245.
Website: www.chapelhillwine.com.au  Email: winery@chapelhillwine.com.au

Region: **McLaren Vale** Winemakers: **Michael Fragos, Angela Meaney** Viticulturist: **Danny Higgins**
Chief Executive: **Pamela Dunsford**

Chapel Hill is a consistent maker of ripe, juicy and slightly old-fashioned and oaky reds from McLaren Vale and Coonawarra fruit. Michael Fragos, until recently with Tatachilla, should make an interesting contribution to the style and quality of these wines, and I look forward to tasting his new wines.

## CABERNET SAUVIGNON

RANKING

**McLaren Vale, Coonawarra**    $30–$49
**Current vintage: 2001**     88

Honest, firm and earthy cabernet with an uncomplicated aroma of sweet red berries and cedary vanilla oak. Moderately full in weight, with a good length of sweet dark berry flavours and assertive oak framed by firm, bony tannins.

| | | | |
|---|---|---|---|
| 2001 | 88 | 2006 | 2009+ |
| 2000 | 87 | 2005 | 2008 |
| 1999 | 88 | 2001 | 2004 |
| 1998 | 83 | 2003 | 2006 |
| 1997 | 93 | 2005 | 2009 |
| 1996 | 93 | 2004 | 2008+ |
| 1995 | 89 | 2000 | 2003 |
| 1994 | 92 | 2002 | 2006 |
| 1993 | 93 | 2001 | 2005 |
| 1992 | 92 | 1997 | 2000 |
| 1991 | 92 | 1999 | 2003 |
| 1990 | 94 | 2002 | 2010 |

## McLAREN VALE SHIRAZ

RANKING

**McLaren Vale**     $30–$49
**Current vintage: 2001**     89

Ripe, rustic shiraz whose meaty aroma of slightly stewed plum and prune-like fruit has already developed earthy and leathery complexity. There's plenty of fruit and oak sweetness on the palate, with menthol-like flavours of blackberries and plums offset by assertive chocolate and pencil-shavings like oak. Good length and structure.

| | | | |
|---|---|---|---|
| 2001 | 89 | 2009 | 2013 |
| 2000 | 86 | 2003 | 2005+ |
| 1999 | 90 | 2004 | 2007 |
| 1998 | 92 | 2006 | 2010+ |
| 1997 | 94 | 2005 | 2009 |
| 1996 | 94 | 2001 | 2004+ |
| 1995 | 92 | 2000 | 2003 |
| 1994 | 93 | 1999 | 2002 |
| 1993 | 94 | 2001 | 2005 |
| 1992 | 93 | 2000 | 2004 |
| 1991 | 94 | 1999 | 2003 |
| 1990 | 91 | 2002 | 2010 |

## RESERVE CHARDONNAY

RANKING

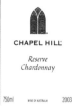

**McLaren Vale**     $20–$29
**Current vintage: 2003**     89

A generously flavoured, round and approachable drink-me-soon chardonnay. Fresh aromas of sweet peachy, buttery fruit with nuances of lemon and tobacco precede a soft, unctuous palate whose voluptuous expression of varietal fruit is cleverly balanced with oak and acidity.

| | | | |
|---|---|---|---|
| 2003 | 89 | 2005 | 2008 |
| 2002 | 90 | 2004 | 2007 |
| 2001 | 89 | 2003 | 2006 |
| 2000 | 86 | 2001 | 2002+ |
| 1999 | 87 | 2000 | 2001 |
| 1998 | 89 | 2000 | 2003+ |
| 1997 | 89 | 1999 | 2002 |
| 1996 | 93 | 2001 | 2004 |
| 1995 | 92 | 2000 | 2003 |
| 1994 | 95 | 2002 | 2006 |

## THE VICAR

| McLaren Vale | $30–$49 |
|---|---|
| **Current vintage: 2001** | **89** |

Firm, old-fashioned, rather jammy and oaky red blend with a fractionally green-edged and salty finish. Its earthy, cedary bouquet of cassis, dark olives and violets reveals a whiff of white pepper and cinnamon. Tarry, rather jammy and licorice-like berry, currant and plum-like fruit is handsomely wrapped in smoky chocolate oak, before a slightly sappy, but savoury finish. It should settle down with time.

| | | | |
|---|---|---|---|
| 2001 | 89 | 2009 | 2013+ |
| 1998 | 90 | 2003 | 2006 |
| 1996 | 94 | 2004 | 2008+ |
| 1994 | 92 | 2002 | 2006 |
| 1993 | 89 | 1998 | 2001 |

## UNWOODED CHARDONNAY

| Padthaway | $12–$19 |
|---|---|
| **Current vintage: 2003** | **89** |

With fresh, nutty aromas of stonefruit, lemon rind and green olives, plus a tangy, juicy palate whose lively melon and peachy flavours offer both length and freshness, this is one of the better unwooded chardonnays around. There's creaminess and a refreshing crispness.

| | | | |
|---|---|---|---|
| 2003 | 89 | 2004 | 2005 |
| 2002 | 90 | 2003 | 2004 |
| 2001 | 82 | 2002 | 2003 |
| 2000 | 86 | 2001 | 2002 |

## VERDELHO

| McLaren Vale | $12–$19 |
|---|---|
| **Current vintage: 2003** | **86** |

Refreshing, tobaccoey verdelho with some attractive, but very restrained melon and citrus fruit. It's clean and lively, with a nutty, savoury finish and a hint of mineral about its acids, but beneath all this lies a thread of slightly cabbagey, cashew-like herbaceousness.

| | | | |
|---|---|---|---|
| 2003 | 86 | 2003 | 2004+ |
| 2002 | 87 | 2003 | 2004 |
| 2001 | 89 | 2002 | 2003+ |
| 2000 | 84 | 2001 | 2002 |
| 1999 | 86 | 2000 | 2001 |
| 1998 | 91 | 2000 | 2003 |

# Charles Melton

Krondorf Road, Tanunda SA 5352. Tel: (08) 8563 3606. Fax: (08) 8563 3422.
Website: www.charlesmeltonwines.com.au  Email: cmw@charlesmeltonwines.com.au
Region: **Barossa Valley** Winemaker: **Graeme Melton** Viticulturist: **Peter Wills** Chief Executive: **Graeme Melton**
Charles Melton is a champion of traditional Barossa styles, although in its mischievously-named Nine Popes it was one of the first to 'rediscover' the virtues of the blend between shiraz, grenache and mourvèdre. Its 2001 vintage reds clearly reflect the unprecedented heat of this once-in-a-lifetime South Australian season.

## CABERNET SAUVIGNON (SHIRAZ)

| Barossa Valley | $30–$49 |
|---|---|
| **Current vintage: 2001** | **87** |

Fast-maturing cabernet with both under and over-ripe qualities. Its dusty, leafy nuances contrast with its tarry, currant and prune-like aspects, while despite some lively blackberry and raspberry fruit flavours, it finishes a little flat and dull. Deftly made, its palate is smooth and elegant, with pleasingly tight-knit fine tannins.

| | | | |
|---|---|---|---|
| 2001 | 87 | 2006 | 2009 |
| 2000 | 87 | 2002 | 2005 |
| 1999 | 82 | 2001 | 2004 |
| 1998 | 93 | 2003 | 2006+ |
| 1996 | 87 | 2001 | 2004 |
| 1993 | 87 | 2001 | 2005 |

## GRENACHE

**Barossa Valley**    $20–$29
**Current vintage: 2000**    **88**

Meaty, herby and savoury wine whose boiled lolly-like aromas of raspberries and red cherries are backed by cedary nuances of vanilla oak. Smooth and elegant, it's earthy but lively, with familiar grenache flavours. An honest, shorter-term wine with some green edges, and a slightly thin finish.

| | | | |
|---|---|---|---|
| 2000 | 88 | 2002 | 2005 |
| 1999 | 88 | 2001 | 2004+ |
| 1998 | 88 | 2000 | 2003 |
| 1996 | 93 | 2004 | 2008 |
| 1994 | 87 | 1996 | 1999 |

## NINE POPES

**Barossa Valley**    $30–$49
**Current vintage: 2001**    **88**

Spicy, musky, dusty cinnamon-like aromas of grenache, with earthy undertones of polished old furniture. Thick, rather cooked and dehydrated flavours of prunes and currants, plums and licorice have some impact and generosity, but dry out to a rather thin and simple, but meaty and savoury finish.

| | | | |
|---|---|---|---|
| 2001 | 88 | 2003 | 2006+ |
| 2000 | 86 | 2002 | 2005 |
| 1999 | 89 | 2004 | 2007 |
| 1998 | 92 | 2006 | 2010 |
| 1997 | 88 | 1999 | 2002 |
| 1996 | 95 | 2004 | 2008 |
| 1995 | 94 | 2003 | 2007+ |
| 1994 | 89 | 1999 | 2002 |
| 1993 | 87 | 2001 | 2005 |
| 1990 | 92 | 1998 | 2002 |

## BAROSSA SHIRAZ

**Barossa Valley**    $30–$49
**Current vintage: 2001**    **85**

Rather overcooked and dehydrated shiraz whose stewed aromas of red berries and plums, currants and prunes are supported by restrained vanilla oak. Lacking customary depth and richness, the palate finishes rather short and flat, with currant-like flavours.

| | | | |
|---|---|---|---|
| 2001 | 85 | 2003 | 2006 |
| 2000 | 88 | 2005 | 2008 |
| 1999 | 90 | 2004 | 2007+ |
| 1998 | 95 | 2003 | 2006 |
| 1997 | 89 | 2005 | 2009 |
| 1995 | 94 | 2003 | 2007 |
| 1990 | 92 | 1998 | 2002+ |

# Chateau Reynella

Reynell Road, Reynella SA 5161. Tel: (08) 8392 2222. Fax: (08) 8392 2202.

Region: **McLaren Vale** Winemakers: **Simon White, Robert Mann** Viticulturist: **Brenton Baker** Chief Executive: **David Woods**

Chateau Reynella has traditionally made the expression of Australian 'Vintage Port' against which others are compared. As the exceptional 1998 vintage illustrates, it has nothing to do with the Portuguese style, but is a typically ripe, jammy and astringent wine, usually fortified with fabulous spirit, that can develop in the bottle for decades. The Basket Press Cabernet Sauvignon is a deep, powerful and long-living regional red.

## BASKET PRESS CABERNET SAUVIGNON

**(Formerly sold under the 'Reynell' brand)**

**McLaren Vale**    $30–$49
**Current vintage: 1998**    **95**

A finely crafted and structured wine whose fragrant, dusty and lightly leathery perfume of cassis, plums, violets and dark olives suggests a hint of cigarbox. Beneath some classical and youthful cabernet flavours of cassis, violets and cedar lies a substantial undercarriage of tightly-knit, firm and fine-grained tannins. Wonderful balance, integration and structure.

| | | | |
|---|---|---|---|
| 1998 | 95 | 2010 | 2018+ |
| 1997 | 89 | 2005 | 2009+ |
| 1996 | 92 | 2008 | 2016 |
| 1995 | 91 | 2007 | 2015 |

# VINTAGE PORT

| **McLaren Vale** | $30–$49 | 1998 | 97 | 2018 | 2028 |
|---|---|---|---|---|---|
| **Current vintage: 1998** | **97** | 1997 | 90 | 2009 | 2017 |

About as good as it gets for traditional Australian vintage port. A heady, spicy, spirity and deeply concentrated aroma of briary cassis, plums and violets overlies a tarry, treacle-like background and chocolate/vanilla oak. Warm, ripe and spirity, its velvet-smooth and sumptuous palate reveals layers of dark plum and berry fruit before finishing long and savoury with a firm spine of powdery tannins. Excellent balance and integration.

| 1996 | 93 | 2008 | 2016 |
|---|---|---|---|
| 1994 | 96 | 2014 | 2024 |
| 1993 | 94 | 2013 | 2023 |
| 1990 | 95 | 2010 | 2020 |
| 1987 | 96 | 2007 | 2017 |
| 1983 | 93 | 2003 | 2013 |
| 1982 | 90 | 2002 | 2012 |
| 1981 | 93 | 2001 | 2009 |
| 1980 | 90 | 2000 | 2005 |

# Chatsfield

O'Neill Road, Mount Barker WA 6324. Tel: (08) 9851 1704. Fax: (08) 9851 1704.
Website: www.chatsfield.com.au  Email: sales@chatsfield.com.au
Region: **Mount Barker** Winemaker: **Diane Miller** Viticulturist: **Mount Barker Viticultural**
Chief Executive: **Ken Lynch**
Chatsfield is a small Mount Barker vineyard whose wines have from time to time shown considerable promise. Some difficult recent vintages have not helped its cause.

## CABERNET FRANC

| **Mount Barker** | $20–$29 | 2001 | 82 | 2003 | 2006 |
|---|---|---|---|---|---|
| **Current vintage: 2001** | **82** | 2000 | 81 | 2001 | 2002 |

Slightly porty, overcooked wine with stewed, varnishy aromas of dark plums, red cherries, cloves and cinnamon, whose cedar/vanilla oak reveals game-like characters. Rather baked, it's forward and hollow, with initial dark cherry flavours becoming dusty and rather meaty. Lacks fruit sweetness and texture.

| 1999 | 88 | 2000 | 2001 |
|---|---|---|---|
| 1998 | 88 | 1999 | 2000 |

## RIESLING

| **Mount Barker** | $12–$19 | 2002 | 77 | 2003 | 2004+ |
|---|---|---|---|---|---|
| **Current vintage: 2002** | **77** | 2001 | 89 | 2006 | 2009 |

Herbal, mouldy aromas of dried apricots precede a lean, tinny palate whose forward pear and stone-fruit flavours tend to lack brightness and length. Finishes rather stressed and slightly sweet.

| 2000 | 89 | 2005 | 2008 |
|---|---|---|---|
| 1999 | 80 | 2000 | 2001 |
| 1998 | 90 | 2003 | 2006+ |
| 1997 | 88 | 1999 | 2002 |
| 1996 | 91 | 1998 | 2001 |
| 1995 | 88 | 2000 | 2003 |
| 1994 | 94 | 2002 | 2006 |
| 1993 | 95 | 1998 | 2001 |

# Chestnut Grove

Chestnut Grove Road, Manjimup WA 6258. Tel: (08) 9772 4345. Fax: (08) 9758 5988.
Website: www.chestnutgrove.com.au   Email: winery@chestnutgrove.com.au
Region: **Manjimup** Winemaker: **Mark Aitken** Viticulturist: **Mark Aitken** Chief Executive: **Mike Calneggia**

Chestnut Grove is a substantial wine producer from the Pemberton/Manjimup region, whose reds are typically sweet and affected by under-ripe influences. While it produces a full range of table wine, it has been most successful on the show circuit with its rather oaky, tomatoey and very herbaceous Merlot.

## MERLOT                                                                     RANKING 5

| Manjimup | $30–$49 |
|---|---|
| Current vintage: 2002 | 87 |

Smoky, herbaceous aromas of red berries, plums and cherries are lifted by sweet cedar/vanilla oak. There's plenty of richness and suppleness, as intense maraschino cherry and cherry tomato fruit is given creaminess and texture by some assertive oak and smooth tannin. Its underlying herbal nature does leave a strong impression at the finish.

| | | | |
|---|---|---|---|
| 2002 | 87 | 2004 | 2007 |
| 2001 | 88 | 2003 | 2006+ |
| 2000 | 87 | 2002 | 2005 |
| 1999 | 89 | 2001 | 2004 |
| 1998 | 75 | 1999 | 2000 |
| 1997 | 81 | 1998 | 1999 |

# Clairault

Caves Road, Willyabrup WA 6280. Tel: (08) 9755 6225. Fax: (08) 9755 6229.
Website: www.clairaultwines.com.au   Email: clairault@clairaultwines.com.au
Region: **Margaret River** Winemaker: **Will Shields** Viticulturist: **Nick Macpherson** Chief Executive: **Bill Martin**

Clairault has a solid tradition of making supple, elegant and rather classy blends of Bordeaux varieties, red and white. Its new ownership and management team is gradually reworking its wines into a new tiered quality system of estate and regional wines.

## RESERVE (Formerly The Clairault)                                           RANKING 4

| Margaret River | $30–$49 |
|---|---|
| Current vintage: 1999 | 81 |

Minty, green and varnishy, with sweet berry fruits and typical earthy regional influences matched by firm, assertive tannins. Very oaky, and a little too volatile.

| | | | |
|---|---|---|---|
| 1999 | 81 | 2001 | 2004+ |
| 1998 | 92 | 2006 | 2010+ |
| 1997 | 81 | 2002 | 2005 |
| 1996 | 87 | 2001 | 2004+ |
| 1995 | 94 | 2003 | 2007 |
| 1994 | 94 | 2006 | 2014 |
| 1993 | 88 | 2001 | 2005 |
| 1991 | 95 | 2003 | 2011 |
| 1990 | 93 | 2002 | 2010 |
| 1989 | 91 | 1997 | 2001 |
| 1988 | 91 | 1996 | 2000 |
| 1987 | 87 | 1995 | 1999 |
| 1986 | 93 | 1998 | 2006 |

## SAUVIGNON BLANC                                                            RANKING 5

| Margaret River | $12–$19 |
|---|---|
| Current vintage: 2003 | 87 |

Lightly herbal aromas of passionfruit and blackberries precede a delicate, fine palate of moderate intensity. There's some pleasing grassiness and tropical/berry fruit, but it's a little too thin for a higher score.

| | | | |
|---|---|---|---|
| 2003 | 87 | 2004 | 2005 |
| 2002 | 85 | 2003 | 2004 |
| 2001 | 87 | 2002 | 2003 |
| 2000 | 87 | 2002 | 2005 |
| 1999 | 84 | 2000 | 2001 |
| 1998 | 89 | 1999 | 2000 |
| 1997 | 92 | 1999 | 2002 |
| 1996 | 95 | 1998 | 2001 |
| 1995 | 94 | 2000 | 2003 |
| 1994 | 94 | 1996 | 1999 |

| Margaret River | $12–$19 |
|---|---|
| **Current vintage: 2003** | **86** |

Lemony, estery confection-like aromas precede a round, juicy and generous palate that tends to lack shape, focus and finish.

| 2003 | 86 | 2004 | 2005 |
|---|---|---|---|
| 2002 | 86 | 2002 | 2003 |
| 2001 | 92 | 2006 | 2009 |
| 2000 | 88 | 2002 | 2005 |
| 1998 | 90 | 2000 | 2003 |
| 1997 | 94 | 1999 | 2002+ |
| 1996 | 93 | 1998 | 2001 |
| 1995 | 89 | 1997 | 2000 |
| 1994 | 94 | 1999 | 2002 |

# Clarendon Hills

Lot 11Brookman Road, Blewitt Springs SA 5171. Tel: (08) 8383 0544. Fax: (08) 8383 0544.
Email: clarendonhills@bigpond.com

Region: **McLaren Vale** Winemaker: **Roman Bratasiuk** Viticulturist: **Various** Chief Executive: **Roman Bratasiuk**

Clarendon Hills has developed a surprisingly large folio of wines made from a complex matrix of varieties and vineyards. As a group, the reds are generally firm and quite rustic, made in a very hands-off fashion that certainly involves some taking of winemaking risk. As a consequence, consistency is not a strong point, but when they are good (as the Astralis and 2002 Hickinbotham Vineyard Syrah illustrate), they can be astonishingly complex and powerful.

## ASTRALIS SYRAH (Formerly Shiraz)
RANKING **2**

| McLaren Vale | $50+ |
|---|---|
| **Current vintage: 2002** | **93** |

A very oaky shiraz whose underlying fruit will take some time to fully emerge, this is a meaty, rustic wine with reductive, charcuterie-like undertones beneath its sweet, spicy and peppery aromas of smoky vanilla oak and small dark berries. Smooth and sumptuous, it's slightly unpolished and unfinished, delivering a deep, concentrated core of blackberry and raspberry flavours slightly hemmed in by its assertive oak and astringent, but slightly blocky tannins. Finishes dusty and oaky.

| 2002 | 93 | 2010 | 2014+ |
|---|---|---|---|
| 1999 | 96 | 2011 | 2019 |
| 1998 | 93 | 2010 | 2018 |
| 1997 | 93 | 2009 | 2017 |
| 1996 | 95 | 2008 | 2016 |
| 1995 | 96 | 2007 | 2015 |
| 1994 | 94 | 2006 | 2014 |

## BLEWITT SPRINGS VINEYARD GRENACHE
RANKING **4**

| McLaren Vale | $30–$49 |
|---|---|
| **Current vintage: 2002** | **88** |

Some herbal and slightly varnishy influences lurk beneath its sweet, earthy aromas of flavours of red berries, plums and polished leather. Smooth and ripe, it's slightly soupy and currant-like, but delivers a pleasing length of fruit and persistent spicy flavours.

| 2002 | 88 | 2004 | 2007+ |
|---|---|---|---|
| 1999 | 87 | 2001 | 2004+ |
| 1998 | 92 | 2003 | 2006 |
| 1997 | 90 | 2002 | 2005 |
| 1995 | 95 | 2003 | 2007+ |
| 1994 | 91 | 2002 | 2006 |

## BROOKMAN VINEYARD MERLOT
RANKING **5**

| McLaren Vale | $30–$49 |
|---|---|
| **Current vintage: 2002** | **88** |

Earthy, reductive merlot with some pleasing violet-like aromas of black cherries, plums and currants supported by cedar/vanilla/chocolate oak influences. Firm, assertive and powerful, its mulberry, cherry and plum-like fruit finishes a little hard and raw-edged.

| 2002 | 87 | 2010 | 2014+ |
|---|---|---|---|
| 2001 | 88 | 2013 | 2021 |
| 1998 | 87 | 2003 | 2006 |

### CLARENDON VINEYARD GRENACHE

RANKING

**McLaren Vale** — $50+
**Current vintage: 2002** — **89**

Rustic, elegant grenache with a spicy, meaty bouquet of red cherries, plums and blueberries over notes of white pepper and vanilla oak. Smooth and supple, full to medium in weight, its up-front confection-like raspberry/plum fruit is framed by fine tannins. Finishes meaty and savoury, but lacks some cut and polish.

| | | | |
|---|---|---|---|
| 2002 | 89 | 2004 | 2007+ |
| 2001 | 89 | 2006 | 2009 |
| 1999 | 89 | 2001 | 2004+ |
| 1998 | 92 | 2003 | 2006 |
| 1997 | 80 | 1999 | 2002 |
| 1996 | 85 | 2004 | 2008 |

### HICKINBOTHAM VINEYARD SYRAH (Formerly Shiraz)

RANKING 4

**McLaren Vale** — $50+
**Current vintage: 2002** — **95**

Top-class shiraz whose penetrative and slightly meaty aromas of dark small berries, plums and restrained cedar/vanilla oak overlie spicy nuances of cloves, cinnamon, white pepper and undergrowth. Smooth, elegant and seamless, the fine, tight-knit palate of intense berry fruits overlies nuances of dark olives and licorice. Framed by firm but fine-grained tannins, its elegant and tightly balanced.

| | | | |
|---|---|---|---|
| 2002 | 95 | 2010 | 2014+ |
| 2001 | 83 | 2006 | 2009 |
| 1999 | 88 | 2004 | 2007 |
| 1998 | 91 | 2003 | 2006 |

### LIANDRA VINEYARD SYRAH (Formerly Shiraz)

RANKING 3

**McLaren Vale** — $50+
**Current vintage: 2002** — **88**

Very reductive and meaty, with earthy, peppery and spicy aromas of dark plums, cherries and onion skin. Long, smooth and spicy, the palate builds in the mouth, delivering intense dark berry and plums flavours before a firm, but slightly bitter finish. Rustic, very evolved and definitely not for the technocrats.

| | | | |
|---|---|---|---|
| 2002 | 88 | 2010 | 2014 |
| 2001 | 89 | 2006 | 2009 |
| 1999 | 95 | 2007 | 2011 |
| 1998 | 91 | 2003 | 2006 |
| 1997 | 93 | 2005 | 2009+ |

### PIGGOT RANGE SYRAH (Formerly Shiraz)

RANKING 4

**McLaren Vale** — $30–$49
**Current vintage: 2002** — **89**

Powerful, earthy, leathery and meaty wine with deep, penetrative small berry, currant and plum flavours backed by complex, evolved and reductive undertones and nuances of sea salt. Very ripe, very powerful and concentrated, given plenty of chocolate-like oak, it does lack some fruit vitality, as well as revealing some suggestions of oxidation.

| | | | |
|---|---|---|---|
| 2002 | 89 | 2010 | 2014+ |
| 1999 | 94 | 2007 | 2011 |
| 1998 | 90 | 2003 | 2006+ |
| 1997 | 88 | 2002 | 2005+ |

# Clayfield

Wilde Lane, Moyston Vic 3377. Tel: (03) 5354 2689, Fax: (03) 5354 2689,
Email:clayfieldwines@netconnect.com.au
Region: **Grampians** Winemaker: **Simon Clayfield** Viticulturist: **Simon Clayfield** Chief Executive: **Simon Clayfield**
Simon Clayfield is an experienced and talented maker of Victorian red wines, and under his own label he crafts classically elegant and exotically spiced Shiraz of considerable finesse and longevity.

### SHIRAZ

RANKING 3

**Grampians** — $30–$49
**Current vintage: 2002** — **95**

Fine-grained, elegant and tightly presented shiraz densely packed with fruit and spice. Its dusty black pepper fragrance of dried herbs, violets and spices reveals ripe aromas of plums and blackberries, suggestions of meat and musk, and restrained cedar/vanilla oak. Its palate is saturated by searingly intense flavours of wild, dark and red berries, above dark chocolate oak. Framed by fine, bony tannins, it finishes taut and lean.

| | | | |
|---|---|---|---|
| 2002 | 95 | 2014 | 2022 |
| 2001 | 95 | 2009 | 2013+ |
| 2000 | 87 | 2005 | 2008 |

**74**

# Clonakilla

Crisps Lane, Murrumbateman NSW 2582. Tel: (02) 6227 5877. Fax: (02) 6227 5871.
Website: www.clonakilla.com.au Email: wine@clonakilla.com.au

Region: **Canberra** Winemaker: **Tim Kirk** Viticulturist: **Michael Lahiff** Chief Executive: **John Kirk**

Clonakilla is a small vineyard at Murrumbateman in the Canberra region that was the first in Australia to produce wines closely modelled on those of Côte-Rôtie in the northern Rhône Valley, using viognier to contribute musky complexity and palate feel to its excellent shiraz. Tim Kirk, who assumed winemaking duties from his father and founder of the company, John Kirk, has also made a string of elegant Cabernet Merlot blends, some very stylish and musky Rieslings and, most recently, some Viogniers of staggering varietal purity and freshness.

## CABERNET MERLOT

RANKING **3**

| Canberra | $30–$49 |
|---|---|
| **Current vintage: 2002** | **90** |

Lean, high acid style with a dusty herbal note to its delicate aromas of dark berries, plums and vanilla oak. Fine and supple, smooth and creamy, its rather polished palate of small berry fruits culminates in a firm, assertive finish of slightly green-edged tannins. Should develop well over medium term.

| | | | |
|---|---|---|---|
| 2002 | 90 | 2007 | 2010 |
| 2001 | 93 | 2009 | 2013+ |
| 2000 | 93 | 2008 | 2012+ |
| 1999 | 91 | 2007 | 2011 |
| 1998 | 93 | 2003 | 2006+ |
| 1997 | 88 | 2005 | 2009+ |
| 1996 | 84 | 1998 | 2001 |
| 1995 | 88 | 2003 | 2007 |
| 1994 | 92 | 2002 | 2006 |

## HILLTOPS SHIRAZ

RANKING **4**

| Canberra | $20–$29 |
|---|---|
| **Current vintage: 2003** | **87** |

A meaty, spicy and rather concentrated shorter-term red with a perfume of dark plums and cherries, violets, mint and black pepper. Oak plays second fiddle behind some rather cooked, spicy and thickly coated confiture-like plum fruit. What would appear to be vine stress shows through as a general lack of brightness and vitality, while the palate finishes earthy, savoury and just a little short.

| | | | |
|---|---|---|---|
| 2003 | 87 | 2005 | 2008 |
| 2002 | 87 | 2004 | 2007 |
| 2001 | 92 | 2003 | 2006+ |
| 2000 | 91 | 2002 | 2005+ |

## RIESLING

RANKING **3**

| Canberra | $20–$29 |
|---|---|
| **Current vintage: 2003** | **88** |

Closed, slightly reductive aromas of dried flowers and lemon rind reveal a marginally cooked and confectionary aspect. Fine, dry and austere, the powdery palate presents some lively lemon and lime-juice flavours and clean, refreshing acidity, but lacks the real depth of fruit expressed in top seasons.

| | | | |
|---|---|---|---|
| 2003 | 88 | 2005 | 2008+ |
| 2002 | 93 | 2004 | 2007+ |
| 2001 | 88 | 2003 | 2006+ |
| 2000 | 92 | 2008 | 2012 |
| 1999 | 95 | 2004 | 2007+ |
| 1998 | 94 | 2003 | 2006+ |
| 1997 | 93 | 2005 | 2009 |
| 1996 | 94 | 2001 | 2004 |
| 1995 | 92 | 2003 | 2007 |

## SHIRAZ VIOGNIER

RANKING **1**

| Canberra | $50+ |
|---|---|
| **Current vintage: 2003** | **96** |

Ripe, generous and assertive, this northern Rhône-like blend has a meaty fragrance whose viognier-derived perfume enhances the muskiness and spiciness of its earthy, red berry shiraz. Despite its sumptuous texture and powerful flavours, it's a silky, fine and elegant wine richly endowed with dark fruits and framed by firm, fine-grained tannins. Savoury, tightly focused and supremely balanced.

| | | | |
|---|---|---|---|
| 2003 | 96 | 2011 | 2015+ |
| 2002 | 96 | 2010 | 2014 |
| 2001 | 97 | 2009 | 2013+ |
| 2000 | 90 | 2005 | 2008+ |
| 1999 | 89 | 2003 | 2007 |
| 1998 | 96 | 2010 | 2018 |
| 1997 | 95 | 2009 | 2017 |
| 1996 | 90 | 2001 | 2004+ |
| 1995 | 89 | 2003 | 2007+ |
| 1994 | 93 | 2002 | 2006+ |
| 1993 | 89 | 1998 | 2001+ |
| 1992 | 89 | 1997 | 2000 |
| 1991 | 88 | 1996 | 1999 |
| 1990 | 82 | 1992 | 1995 |

## VIOGNIER

RANKING **3**

| Canberra | $50+ |
|---|---|
| Current vintage: 2003 | 94 |

First-class viognier with a delicate and alluring perfume of honeysuckle, lemon blossom, cloves, cinnamon and apricot. Very supple, round and elegant, finishing taut and savoury, the palate reveals a restrained sweet core of delicate stonefruit, citrus and spice flavours framed by tangy acids. Precisely measured and delivered, with tightly integrated and restrained oak qualities, it's a lesson in varietal viognier.

| 2003 | 94 | 2004 | 2005+ |
|---|---|---|---|
| 2002 | 95 | 2004 | 2007 |
| 2001 | 92 | 2003 | 2006 |
| 2000 | 93 | 2002 | 2005 |
| 1999 | 92 | 2000 | 2003 |

# Clover Hill

60 Clover Hill Road, Lebrina Tas 7254. Tel: (03) 6395 6114. Fax: (03) 6395 6257.
Website: www.taltarni.com.au  Email: enquiries@taltarni.com.au
Region: **Pipers River**  Winemakers: **Loic Le Calvez, Mark Laurence, Leigh Clarnette**
Viticulturist: **Michael Ciavarella**  Chief Executive: **Peter Steer**
Clover Hill is a Taltarni-owned operation in northern Tasmania that specialises in sparkling wine. Its wines are typically fragrant, creamy and crisply defined, with a fruit profile often slightly herbaceous and tropical.

## VINTAGE

RANKING **4**

| Pipers River | $30–$49 |
|---|---|
| Current vintage: 1999 | 94 |

A delicate bouquet of light melon and tobacco fruit is backed by creamy, bready and mushroomy complexity, with a hint of mature cheese. The palate is long and refined, with pleasing creaminess and suppleness prior to a refreshing finish of racy mineral acids. Very elegant and harmonious.

| 1999 | 94 | 2004 | 2007+ |
|---|---|---|---|
| 1998 | 87 | 2000 | 2003+ |
| 1997 | 82 | 1999 | 2002 |
| 1996 | 92 | 2001 | 2004 |
| 1995 | 91 | 1997 | 2000 |
| 1994 | 94 | 1999 | 2002 |

# Coldstream Hills

31 Maddens Lane, Coldstream Vic 3770. Tel: (03) 5964 9388. Fax: (03) 5964 9389.
Website: www.coldstreamhills.com.au
Region: **Yarra Valley**  Winemaker: **Andrew Fleming**  Viticulturist: **Nicky Harris**  Chief Executive: **John Ballard**
Founded by wine scribe James Halliday, who remains a consultant to this label, Coldstream Hills is a Southcorp-owned brand based in Victoria's cool Yarra Valley region. Over the years it has proven capable of some truly extraordinary wines from a cross-section of varieties including pinot noir, chardonnay, cabernet sauvignon and merlot, but its most reliable labels are indeed made from the Burgundian varieties. Early indications would suggest that 2003 could be the label's best vintage since the uniformly well-performed 2000 season.

## CHARDONNAY

RANKING **4**

| Yarra Valley | $20–$29 |
|---|---|
| Current vintage: 2003 | 90 |

Quite a stylish, smooth and savoury little chardonnay with a slightly closed and withdrawn aroma of sweet buttery, creamy and peachy lemon fruit. There's a pleasing hint of fattiness about its soft and nutty palate whose vibrant stonefruit and melon flavours finish with a hint of tobacco.

| 2003 | 90 | 2004 | 2005+ |
|---|---|---|---|
| 2001 | 92 | 2003 | 2006 |
| 2000 | 88 | 2002 | 2005 |
| 1999 | 87 | 2001 | 2004 |
| 1998 | 90 | 2000 | 2003 |
| 1997 | 92 | 1999 | 2002 |
| 1996 | 91 | 1998 | 2001 |

## MERLOT

RANKING **5**

| Yarra Valley | $20–$29 |
|---|---|
| Current vintage: 2001 | 89 |

A leaner, medium term merlot with an earthy, tobaccoey aroma of plummy fruit, cedary oak and animal hide. Long, fine and supple, the palate presents tightly focused sweet plum and cherry fruit wrapped around fine tannins, but overlying a thread of herbal flavour. There's some attractive firmness and shape.

| 2001 | 89 | 2003 | 2006+ |
|---|---|---|---|
| 2000 | 83 | 2002 | 2005 |
| 1997 | 89 | 1999 | 2002 |

## PINOT NOIR

RANKING **4**

| Yarra Valley | | $20–$29 | |
|---|---|---|---|
| **Current vintage: 2002** | | | **86** |

| | | | |
|---|---|---|---|
| 2002 | 86 | 2003 | 2004 |
| 2001 | 90 | 2003 | 2006 |
| 2000 | 91 | 2002 | 2005+ |
| 1999 | 93 | 2001 | 2004 |
| 1998 | 86 | 1999 | 2000 |
| 1997 | 91 | 2002 | 2005 |
| 1996 | 92 | 1998 | 2001 |

Rather stewed and herbaceous pinot whose raspberry/cherry-like fruit is supported to an extent by some sweet mocha and vanilla oak, but still appears dilute and rather weedy in the middle of the palate. Failed to ripen fully, finishing sappy and green-edged.

## RESERVE CABERNET SAUVIGNON

RANKING **4**

| Yarra Valley | | $30–$49 | |
|---|---|---|---|
| **Current vintage: 2000** | | | **95** |

| | | | |
|---|---|---|---|
| 2000 | 95 | 2008 | 2012+ |
| 1998 | 82 | 2000 | 2003 |
| 1997 | 84 | 2002 | 2005 |
| 1995 | 90 | 2000 | 2003 |
| 1994 | 91 | 2002 | 2006 |
| 1993 | 93 | 1998 | 2002 |
| 1992 | 96 | 2004 | 2012+ |
| 1991 | 93 | 1999 | 2003 |
| 1990 | 93 | 1995 | 1998 |

Silky-smooth Yarra cabernet whose alluring fragrance of cassis, violets and dark chocolate is punctuated with scents of black olives and capsicum. Briary jujube-like cassis and plum fruit bursts its way down the long and tightly integrated palate of fine tannins and smoky, cedary oak. There's a persistent hint of undergrowth and a faint herbal, tobaccoey edge.

## RESERVE CHARDONNAY

RANKING **3**

| Yarra Valley | | $30–$49 | |
|---|---|---|---|
| **Current vintage: 2000** | | | **90** |

| | | | |
|---|---|---|---|
| 2000 | 90 | 2002 | 2005 |
| 1999 | 90 | 2001 | 2004+ |
| 1998 | 94 | 2003 | 2006 |
| 1997 | 90 | 2002 | 2005 |
| 1996 | 93 | 2001 | 2004+ |
| 1995 | 94 | 2000 | 2003 |
| 1994 | 95 | 1999 | 2002 |
| 1993 | 90 | 1995 | 1998 |
| 1992 | 96 | 2000 | 2004 |

A mature, toasty and honeyed chardonnay with a delicate fragrance of restrained stonefruit, citrus and melon aromas over nuances of oatmeal and butter. Soft and creamy, its juicy core of citrus and melon fruit is just starting to become dominated by toasty, buttery characters.

## RESERVE PINOT NOIR

RANKING **2**

| Yarra Valley | | $30–$49 | |
|---|---|---|---|
| **Current vintage: 2002** | | | **88** |

| | | | |
|---|---|---|---|
| 2002 | 88 | 2004 | 2007 |
| 2000 | 93 | 2005 | 2008+ |
| 1998 | 94 | 2003 | 2006+ |
| 1997 | 94 | 2002 | 2005 |
| 1996 | 92 | 1998 | 2001 |
| 1995 | 90 | 1997 | 2000 |
| 1994 | 94 | 1999 | 2002 |
| 1993 | 88 | 1995 | 1998 |
| 1992 | 94 | 1997 | 2000 |
| 1991 | 88 | 1993 | 1996 |

Pretty, peppery and dusty pinot with some lively and forward cherry/plum fruit qualities rather reliant for sweetness on some assertive chocolate/vanilla oak. Lacks real length and finishes rather green-edged.

## RESERVE MERLOT

RANKING **3**

| Yarra Valley | | $30–$49 | |
|---|---|---|---|
| **Current vintage: 2000** | | | **93** |

| | | | |
|---|---|---|---|
| 2000 | 93 | 2005 | 2008 |
| 1998 | 92 | 2003 | 2006 |
| 1997 | 87 | 2002 | 2005+ |

Very smart merlot with strength, ripeness and structure. There's some tobaccoey and herbal complexity behind its varietally correct expression of dark cherries, mulberries and plums, while its assertive vanilla and mocha oak is tightly integrated. It has perfume, length and finish, with pleasing balance and texture.

## SAUVIGNON BLANC

RANKING **5**

| Yarra Valley | | $20–$29 | |
|---|---|---|---|
| **Current vintage: 2003** | | | **86** |

| | | | |
|---|---|---|---|
| 2003 | 86 | 2004 | 2005 |
| 2002 | 91 | 2002 | 2003+ |
| 2001 | 81 | 2001 | 2002 |
| 2000 | 82 | 2001 | 2002 |
| 1999 | 89 | 2000 | 2001 |

Grassy, slightly cooked and confectionary semillon developing toastiness and broadness. Some forward juiciness and punch, but lacks brightness and vitality at the finish.

# Coriole

Chaffeys Road, McLaren Vale SA 5171. Tel: (08) 8323 8305. Fax: (08) 8323 9136.
Website: www.coriole.com Email: info@coriole.com

Region: **McLaren Vale** Winemaker: **Grant Harrison** Viticulturist: **Rachel Steer** Chief Executive: **Mark Lloyd**

Artful and sensitive winemaking is a hallmark of Coriole's consistent and reliable range, which given half a chance in a good season will usually result in distinctive and regional McLaren Vale wines of excellence and balance. Given that it makes Australia's raciest and most refreshing Chenin Blanc, its real signature efforts based around shiraz and other Rhône varieties tend to avoid the overcooked qualities so popular in some circles today. The excellent quality of the 2002 reds released to date suggest big things forthcoming down the pipeline from the more prestigious labels. One of the pioneers of sangiovese in Australia, its reds from this variety retain a delightfully rustic edge. Not unsurprisingly, it appears to have fared better in 2002 than 2001 and 2000.

## CHENIN BLANC
RANKING **5**

McLaren Vale $12–$19
**Current vintage: 2003** **89**

Genuinely tight, finely balanced, austere and refreshing chenin blanc; in itself no small achievement. There's a dusty herbal aspect to its lightly tropical aromas, while its palate is generous and approachable, with some varietal vegetal notes behind its tropical/melon/apricot flavours. Long and dry.

| | | | |
|---|---|---|---|
| 2003 | 89 | 2004 | 2005+ |
| 2002 | 87 | 2003 | 2004+ |
| 2001 | 87 | 2002 | 2003 |
| 2000 | 88 | 2000 | 2001 |
| 1999 | 89 | 2001 | 2004 |

## SEMILLON (formerly Lalla Rookh Semillon)
RANKING **4**

McLaren Vale $20–$29
**Current vintage: 2002** **88**

Smooth, oily semillon with some elegance and refinement. Its concentrated fragrance of floral, tropical and gooseberry/melon fruit overlies a suggestion of bubblegum, while its reserved and creamy palate offers an interesting combination of intensity and delicacy. Finishes long and soft, with a restrained solidsy grip.

| | | | |
|---|---|---|---|
| 2002 | 88 | 2004 | 2007+ |
| 2001 | 90 | 2006 | 2009 |
| 2000 | 89 | 2002 | 2005 |
| 1999 | 88 | 2001 | 2004+ |
| 1998 | 94 | 2003 | 2006 |
| 1997 | 91 | 2002 | 2005 |
| 1996 | 89 | 2001 | 2004 |
| 1995 | 90 | 1997 | 2000 |
| 1994 | 87 | 1996 | 1999 |

## LLOYD RESERVE SHIRAZ
RANKING **2**

McLaren Vale $50+
**Current vintage: 2001** **94**

Slightly closed and meaty aromas of dark plums, cinnamon and cloves, backed by creamy oak. Its chewy, velvet-smooth and multi-layered palate opens to reveal dark, spicy strata of blackberries, plums, chocolates, prunes and currants, culminating in an earthy, savoury finish. Impressively concentrated, rich and unctuous, it's a powerful but approachable package for the moderately long term.

| | | | |
|---|---|---|---|
| 2001 | 94 | 2013 | 2021 |
| 2000 | 87 | 2005 | 2008+ |
| 1999 | 94 | 2007 | 2011+ |
| 1998 | 96 | 2010 | 2018+ |
| 1997 | 90 | 2005 | 2009 |
| 1996 | 95 | 2008 | 2016 |
| 1995 | 95 | 2007 | 2015 |
| 1994 | 94 | 2006 | 2012 |
| 1993 | 89 | 2001 | 2005 |
| 1992 | 95 | 2004 | 2012 |
| 1991 | 94 | 2003 | 2011+ |
| 1990 | 91 | 2002 | 2010 |
| 1989 | 93 | 2001 | 2009 |

## MARY KATHLEEN RESERVE CABERNET MERLOT
RANKING **3**

McLaren Vale $50+
**Current vintage: 2001** **91**

A balanced, structured red blend; firm, fine-grained and elegant. Earthy, cedary aromas of red plums, red berries and cedar/vanilla oak reveal a hint of polished leather. Above its chassis of tightly knit tannins lies a long and supple palate of lingering sweet fruit and integrated, restrained oak, before a lingering and harmonious finish.

| | | | |
|---|---|---|---|
| 2001 | 91 | 2013 | 2021 |
| 2000 | 88 | 2005 | 2008 |
| 1999 | 92 | 2011 | 2019 |
| 1998 | 93 | 2010 | 2018 |
| 1997 | 89 | 2005 | 2009 |
| 1996 | 93 | 2004 | 2008+ |
| 1995 | 90 | 2003 | 2007 |
| 1994 | 89 | 2002 | 2006 |

### REDSTONE SHIRAZ CABERNET (GRENACHE)  RANKING 4

| McLaren Vale | $20–$29 |
|---|---|
| **Current vintage: 2001** | **91** |

Finely balanced, elegant and harmonious blend with a peppery, violet-like fragrance of intense cassis and cedar/vanilla oak. Smooth and supple, long and elegant, its juicy palate of ripe raspberries, cherries, plums and dark berries is framed by fine, tight-knit tannins and supported by creamy vanilla oak. It finishes with a hint of bramble.

| 2001 | 91 | 2006 | 2009 |
|---|---|---|---|
| 2000 | 91 | 2005 | 2008+ |
| 1999 | 87 | 2004 | 2007 |
| 1998 | 89 | 2003 | 2006+ |
| 1997 | 87 | 2002 | 2005 |
| 1996 | 87 | 2004 | 2008 |
| 1995 | 89 | 2001 | 2004 |
| 1994 | 91 | 2002 | 2006 |
| 1993 | 86 | 1998 | 2001 |
| 1992 | 89 | 2000 | 2004 |

### SANGIOVESE  RANKING 5

| McLaren Vale | $12–$19 |
|---|---|
| **Current vintage: 2002** | **89** |

Dusty, slightly earthy, floral and candied aromas of red cherries, cloves and nutmeg precede a generous, reasonably firm but smooth palate whose vibrant sweet cherry-like fruit finishes with fine tannins, soft acids and lingering earthy dustiness. A good wine which perhaps could have used a fraction more acid.

| 2002 | 89 | 2004 | 2007+ |
|---|---|---|---|
| 2001 | 87 | 2003 | 2006+ |
| 1999 | 88 | 2004 | 2007 |
| 1998 | 86 | 2000 | 2003 |
| 1997 | 90 | 2002 | 2005 |
| 1996 | 90 | 2001 | 2004 |
| 1995 | 90 | 2003 | 2007 |
| 1994 | 89 | 1999 | 2002 |
| 1993 | 88 | 2001 | 2005 |
| 1992 | 84 | 1997 | 2000 |

### SHIRAZ  RANKING 4

| McLaren Vale | $20–$29 |
|---|---|
| **Current vintage: 2002** | **93** |

Delightfully flavoursome and uncomplicated shiraz with a sweet perfume of fragrant cassis, raspberries and sweet plums, vanilla/chocolate oak and dusty pepper/clove aromas. Alluring and elegant, its supple but exceptionally expressive palate of vibrant small black and red berries, plums and licorice is framed by firm, but velvet-smooth tannins, before a tangy savoury finish.

| 2002 | 93 | 2007 | 2010+ |
|---|---|---|---|
| 2001 | 92 | 2006 | 2009+ |
| 2000 | 86 | 2002 | 2005+ |
| 1999 | 89 | 2004 | 2007 |
| 1998 | 89 | 2006 | 2010 |
| 1997 | 89 | 2002 | 2005 |
| 1996 | 92 | 2001 | 2004 |
| 1995 | 93 | 2002 | 2007 |
| 1994 | 89 | 2002 | 2006 |
| 1993 | 91 | 2001 | 2005 |
| 1992 | 93 | 1997 | 2000 |
| 1991 | 89 | 1999 | 2003+ |
| 1990 | 93 | 1995 | 1998 |

# Craiglee

Sunbury Road, Sunbury Vic 3429. Tel: (03) 9744 4489. Fax: (03) 9744 4489.
Email: patatcraiglee@hotmail.com

Region: **Sunbury** Winemaker: **Patrick Carmody** Viticulturist: **Patrick Carmody**
Chief Executive: **Patrick Carmody**

While his prayers for rain have been met with disdain from the weather gods in recent years, Pat Carmody is making the best wines of his life. The Shiraz, always known for its savoury spiciness and elegance, has stepped up a notch in structure and breeding, while the 2002 Chardonnay is a taut and mineral wine of fine pedigree.

### CHARDONNAY  RANKING 4

| Sunbury | $20–$29 |
|---|---|
| **Current vintage: 2002** | **93** |

Restrained floral aromas of honeysuckle and cinnamon over an underlying core of citrusy fruit. Reserved and elegant, with an excellent length of tight-knit lemony, melon and citrus flavour finishing taut and mineral, leaving a savoury, nutty finish of steely austerity. Keep it.

| 2002 | 93 | 2007 | 2010 |
|---|---|---|---|
| 2001 | 89 | 2003 | 2006+ |
| 2000 | 88 | 2002 | 2005+ |
| 1999 | 90 | 2001 | 2004 |
| 1998 | 80 | 1999 | 2000 |
| 1997 | 90 | 2002 | 2005 |
| 1996 | 91 | 2001 | 2004 |
| 1995 | 91 | 2000 | 2003 |
| 1994 | 94 | 2002 | 2006 |
| 1993 | 92 | 1998 | 2001 |
| 1992 | 93 | 1997 | 2000 |

## SHIRAZ

RANKING 2

| Sunbury | $30–$49 |
|---|---|
| **Current vintage: 2002** | **94** |

Long, supple and savoury shiraz whose delicate perfume of violets and dark cherries is accentuated with sneezy nuances of black pepper, musky spices and licorice. Presenting a long, creamy palate of vibrant dark fruits, tightly-knit fine tannins and restrained oak, it finishes long and spicy.

| | | | |
|---|---|---|---|
| 2002 | 94 | 2010 | 2014 |
| 2001 | 93 | 2009 | 2013 |
| 2000 | 95 | 2012 | 2020 |
| 1999 | 91 | 2004 | 2007+ |
| 1998 | 89 | 2003 | 2006+ |
| 1997 | 95 | 2005 | 2009 |
| 1996 | 93 | 2004 | 2008 |
| 1995 | 88 | 2000 | 2003+ |
| 1994 | 95 | 2002 | 2006+ |
| 1993 | 95 | 2001 | 2005 |
| 1992 | 89 | 1997 | 2000 |
| 1991 | 91 | 1999 | 2003 |
| 1990 | 93 | 2002 | 2010 |
| 1989 | 91 | 1991 | 1994 |
| 1988 | 94 | 1996 | 2000 |

# Crawford River

Upper Hotspur Road, Crawford via Condah Vic 3303. Tel: (03) 5578 2267. Fax: (03) 5578 2240. Email: crawforddriver@h140.aone.net.au

Region: **Western Victoria** Winemaker: **John Thomson** Viticulturist: **John Thomson**
Chief Executive: **John Thomson**

Crawford River's most popular wine is perhaps its rather accentuated, estery and spicy Riesling, but in my view its elegant, succulent and shapely Cabernet Sauvignon (and occasional Reserve releases of this wine) are its finest. Its tangy 2003 Semillon Sauvignon Blanc offers vibrant fruit and herbaceousness with a clean and lemony cut of acid.

## CABERNET SAUVIGNON

RANKING 3

| Western Victoria | $30–$49 |
|---|---|
| **Current vintage: 2001** | **93** |

A perfume of violets, cassis and cedary/vanilla oak precedes a smooth, elegant palate of pristine berry flavours harmoniously integrated with fine, silky tannins. Its sweet oak and earthy, meaty undertones of forest floor provide complexity and a creamy texture, but the wine is a shade too herbal for an even higher rating.

| | | | |
|---|---|---|---|
| 2001 | 93 | 2009 | 2013+ |
| 2000 | 89 | 2005 | 2008 |
| 1999 | 95 | 2007 | 2011+ |
| 1997 | 90 | 2005 | 2009 |
| 1996 | 95 | 2004 | 2008+ |
| 1995 | 93 | 2003 | 2007+ |
| 1992 | 89 | 2000 | 2004 |
| 1991 | 95 | 1999 | 2003+ |
| 1990 | 89 | 1995 | 1998 |
| 1989 | 88 | 1994 | 1997 |

## RIESLING

RANKING 3

| Western Victoria | $20–$29 |
|---|---|
| **Current vintage: 2003** | **90** |

A delicate, lightly herbal fragrance of apricots, pears and peaches reveals estery undertones of lime juice and lemon rind. Forward and juicy, its tangy, confection-like palate culminates in a long, austere and slightly mineral finish of refreshing acidity.

| | | | |
|---|---|---|---|
| 2003 | 90 | 2005 | 2008+ |
| 2001 | 94 | 2006 | 2009 |
| 2000 | 87 | 2002 | 2005 |
| 1999 | 92 | 2004 | 2007 |
| 1995 | 91 | 2003 | 2007+ |
| 1994 | 94 | 2002 | 2006 |
| 1993 | 95 | 2001 | 2005 |
| 1992 | 94 | 1997 | 2000 |
| 1991 | 90 | 1996 | 1999 |
| 1990 | 93 | 1999 | 2002 |

## SEMILLON SAUVIGNON BLANC

RANKING 4

| Western Victoria | $20–$29 |
|---|---|
| **Current vintage: 2003** | **90** |

Toasty, buttery aromas of candied citrus fruit, talcum powder and vanilla oak, with grassy undertones precede a round, soft and juicy palate of brightness and length. It finishes long and lemony, with lingering tropical and melon-like fruit, plus an attractive grassiness.

| | | | |
|---|---|---|---|
| 2003 | 90 | 2004 | 2005+ |
| 2002 | 82 | 2002 | 2003 |
| 2001 | 93 | 2003 | 2006 |
| 2000 | 89 | 2002 | 2005+ |

# Cullen

Caves Road, Willyabrup via Cowaramup WA 6284. Tel: (08) 9755 5277. Fax: (08) 9755 5550.
Website: www.cullenwines.com.au  Email: enquiries@cullenwines.com.au
Region: **Margaret River** Winemakers: **Vanya Cullen, Trevor Kent** Viticulturist: **Michael Sleegers**
Chief Executive: **Vanya Cullen**

One of Australia's signature wineries blessed with excellent vineyards and the winemaking experience and intellect to get the best from them. One of our elite makers of cabernet blends and chardonnay, the company hallmark is the delivery of complex undertones beneath first-rate primary fruit, fashioned in a wine usually capable of maturing gracefully over a long period of time. The 2002 Chardonnay sets a new benchmark for this maker, while the meaty and affordable Mangan red blend affords a taste of Cullen red to a new audience.

## CHARDONNAY

RANKING 2

| | Margaret River | $50+ |
|---|---|---|
| | **Current vintage: 2002** | **96** |

Supremely elegant, fine and polished chardonnay with a tight-knit and grainy aroma of lemon, melon, white peach and grapefruit backed by nuances of cloves, cashew and sweet vanilla oak. Juicy and forward, its palate begins with intense, punchy flavours of pear, peach and tropical fruit, before becoming more taut and trim, culminating in a zesty lemon sherbet finish framed by very fine, chalky phenolics.

| Year | Score | | |
|---|---|---|---|
| 2002 | 96 | 2007 | 2010+ |
| 2001 | 95 | 2006 | 2009+ |
| 2000 | 94 | 2005 | 2008 |
| 1999 | 95 | 2004 | 2007 |
| 1998 | 94 | 2000 | 2003 |
| 1997 | 96 | 2002 | 2005+ |
| 1996 | 95 | 2001 | 2004+ |
| 1995 | 94 | 2000 | 2003 |
| 1994 | 95 | 2002 | 2006 |
| 1993 | 94 | 1998 | 2001 |
| 1992 | 95 | 1997 | 2000 |
| 1990 | 95 | 1995 | 1998 |
| 1989 | 87 | 1994 | 1997 |
| 1987 | 91 | 1995 | 1999 |
| 1982 | 90 | 1987 | 1990+ |

## DIANA MADELINE CABERNET SAUVIGNON MERLOT

RANKING 1

| | Margaret River | $50+ |
|---|---|---|
| | **Current vintage: 2002** | **95** |

Restrained, supple and elegant cooler season cabernet blend with a spicy, petit verdot-driven aroma of dark plums, mulberries, cassis and violets, supported by lightly smoky and fine-grained cedar/mocha oak. There's a dusty whiff of herbaceousness and mint, also present beneath the fine, but surprisingly firm palate. Dark olives and small berry fruits, green pepper and creamy oak are framed by fine-grained but grippy tannins, finishing long but a fraction closed. Should develop more charm and complexity with time.

| Year | Score | | |
|---|---|---|---|
| 2002 | 95 | 2014 | 2022 |
| 2001 | 97 | 2013 | 2021+ |
| 2000 | 97 | 2012 | 2020+ |
| 1999 | 97 | 2019 | 2029 |
| 1998 | 96 | 2010 | 2018+ |
| 1997 | 93 | 2009 | 2017 |
| 1996 | 95 | 2008 | 2016 |
| 1995 | 96 | 2015 | 2025 |
| 1994 | 95 | 2006 | 2014 |
| 1993 | 94 | 2005 | 2013+ |
| 1992 | 94 | 2004 | 2012+ |
| 1991 | 89 | 2003 | 2011 |
| 1990 | 90 | 2002 | 2010 |
| 1989 | 95 | 2001 | 2009 |
| 1988 | 86 | 1996 | 2000 |
| 1987 | 89 | 1999 | 2007 |
| 1986 | 89 | 2006 | 2016 |
| 1985 | 93 | 2005 | 2015 |
| 1984 | 95 | 2004 | 2014 |
| 1983 | 94 | 1995 | 2003+ |
| 1982 | 91 | 1994 | 2002 |
| 1981 | 90 | 1993 | 2001+ |

## MANGAN (Malbec, Petit Verdot, Merlot)

RANKING 4

| | Margaret River | $30–$49 |
|---|---|---|
| | **Current vintage: 2003** | **88** |

Spicy, meaty, earthy medium weight red whose floral, cedary aromas of dark cherries, blueberries and cranberry overlie suggestions of game meat and dark chocolate. Beginning with some palate-staining dark fruit, the wine then finishes surprisingly thin and hollow, just lacking the real structure to support its pleasing flavours.

| Year | Score | | |
|---|---|---|---|
| 2003 | 88 | 2005 | 2008 |
| 2002 | 93 | 2007 | 2010 |
| 2001 | 89 | 2004 | 2007 |

## SEMILLON SAUVIGNON BLANC BLEND

| Margaret River | $30–$49 |
|---|---|
| **Current vintage: 2003** | **89** |

Slightly raw and confected, indeed comparatively ripe and luscious for this vintage, this wine reveals a delicate, dusty, herbal and lightly oaky bouquet of juicy green melon fruit. Its tangy palate of luscious citrus and green melon flavours is supported by sweet vanilla oak over herbaceous undertones.

| | | | |
|---|---|---|---|
| 2003 | 89 | 2005 | 2008 |
| 2002 | 96 | 2004 | 2007+ |
| 2001 | 96 | 2006 | 2009 |
| 2000 | 95 | 2002 | 2005+ |
| 1999 | 96 | 2007 | 2011 |
| 1998 | 91 | 2000 | 2003 |
| 1997 | 94 | 2005 | 2009 |
| 1995 | 91 | 2000 | 2003 |
| 1994 | 93 | 1996 | 1999 |
| 1993 | 95 | 1998 | 2001 |

# d'Arenberg

Osborn Road, McLaren Vale SA 5171. Tel: (08) 8323 8206. Fax: (08) 8323 8423.
Website: www.darenberg.com.au  Email: winery@darenberg.com.au

Regions: **McLaren Vale, Fleurieu Peninsula** Winemakers: **Chester Osborn, Phillip Dean**
Viticulturists: **David Hunt, Giulio Dimasi** Managing Director: **d'Arry Osborn**

d'Arenberg clearly did well in the 2002 vintage, the coolest ever recorded in South Australia, making wines of more flesh and succulent fruit than for several years. From the easy-drinking (but not to be under-estimated) Laughing Magpie blend to the Dead Arm Shiraz, these are delightfully flavoured and composed reds of generosity and softness, although The Ironstone Pressings is underpinned by its customarily firm and structured chassis.

## d'ARRY'S ORIGINAL SHIRAZ GRENACHE

| McLaren Vale | $12–$19 |
|---|---|
| **Current vintage: 2002** | **90** |

Harmoniously crafted, vibrant and elegant soft dry red whose intense and lightly confectionary flavours of red plums, blueberries and raspberries are lifted by some attractive spiciness and enhanced by a modest treatment in oak. The aromas are fresh and perfumed, while the palate is tightly knit with moderately firm and fine-grained tannins.

| | | | |
|---|---|---|---|
| 2002 | 90 | 2010 | 2014+ |
| 2001 | 87 | 2006 | 2009 |
| 2000 | 90 | 2005 | 2008+ |
| 1999 | 89 | 2004 | 2007+ |
| 1998 | 90 | 2006 | 2010+ |
| 1997 | 89 | 2002 | 2005+ |
| 1996 | 89 | 2004 | 2008 |
| 1995 | 92 | 2003 | 2007 |
| 1994 | 92 | 2002 | 2006 |
| 1993 | 89 | 2001 | 2005 |
| 1992 | 91 | 2000 | 2004 |
| 1991 | 88 | 1999 | 2003 |
| 1990 | 91 | 1998 | 2002 |
| 1989 | 87 | 1997 | 2001 |
| 1988 | 93 | 2000 | 2008 |
| 1987 | 88 | 1997 | 1999 |
| 1986 | 90 | 1996 | 1998 |

## THE BROKEN FISHPLATE SAUVIGNON BLANC

| McLaren Vale | $12–$19 |
|---|---|
| **Current vintage: 2003** | **86** |

Simple, straightforward sauvignon blanc with herby, grassy aromas of lychees, passionfruit and banana-like estery undertones. Broad and generous, with sweet passionfruit and herbal qualities, it finishes rather flat and lacking definition, with suggestions of green cashew and talcum powder.

| | | | |
|---|---|---|---|
| 2003 | 86 | 2003 | 2004+ |
| 2002 | 90 | 2003 | 2004 |
| 2001 | 87 | 2001 | 2002 |
| 2000 | 90 | 2001 | 2002 |
| 1999 | 90 | 2001 | 2004 |
| 1998 | 82 | 1999 | 2000 |

## THE COPPERMINE ROAD CABERNET SAUVIGNON

| McLaren Vale | $50+ |
|---|---|
| **Current vintage: 2002** | **91** |

Very elegant, almost cooler climate cabernet from McLaren Vale reflective of the 2002 vintage. Its ripe perfume of cassis, red plums and cedary oak reveals undertones of tobacco and dried herbs, while its palate is long, tight and powdery, firm but fine-grained, presenting brightly lit small black and red berry fruits. There's a hint of grittiness that should soften with time, with a lingering note of dark olives.

| | | | |
|---|---|---|---|
| 2002 | 91 | 2010 | 2014+ |
| 2001 | 93 | 2009 | 2013+ |
| 2000 | 93 | 2012 | 2020 |
| 1999 | 89 | 2007 | 2011+ |
| 1998 | 94 | 2010 | 2018+ |
| 1997 | 90 | 2005 | 2009+ |
| 1996 | 89 | 2008 | 2016 |

# THE CUSTODIAN GRENACHE

| McLaren Vale | $20–$29 |
|---|---:|
| **Current vintage: 2002** | **92** |

Very drinkable, harmonious and approachable grenache without the excessively confected flavours of so many, and with rare cellaring potential for this variety in Australia. Its sweet fragrance of raspberries, blueberries, dark cherries and plums is distinctively floral, with a whiff of white pepper and restrained oak. Long and smooth, full to medium in weight, it's packed with pristine small berry flavours before a drying, savoury finish.

| 2002 | 92 | 2010 | 2014+ |
|---|---|---|---|
| 2001 | 89 | 2009 | 2013 |
| 2000 | 92 | 2005 | 2008+ |
| 1999 | 91 | 2004 | 2007+ |
| 1998 | 87 | 2003 | 2006 |
| 1997 | 92 | 2002 | 2005 |
| 1996 | 91 | 2004 | 2008 |
| 1995 | 93 | 2003 | 2007 |

# THE DEAD ARM SHIRAZ

| McLaren Vale | $50+ |
|---|---:|
| **Current vintage: 2002** | **94** |

A more elegant, controlled and tightly focused Dead Arm with pleasing fruit and balance, but an unmistakable thread of herbaceousness beneath. Its spicy and lightly smoky fragrance of cassis, blackberries, violets and raspberries is offset by creamy vanilla oak. Silky smooth and velvet-like, its very measured palate of vibrant small black and red berries, licorice and spice culminates in a long, rather minty, eucalypt-like and herbal finish.

| 2002 | 94 | 2010 | 2014 |
|---|---|---|---|
| 2001 | 89 | 2013 | 2021+ |
| 2000 | 93 | 2012 | 2020 |
| 1999 | 89 | 2007 | 2011 |
| 1998 | 93 | 2010 | 2018 |
| 1997 | 92 | 2005 | 2009 |
| 1996 | 95 | 2008 | 2016 |
| 1995 | 94 | 2007 | 2015 |
| 1994 | 93 | 2006 | 2014 |

# THE DRY DAM RIESLING

| McLaren Vale | $12–$19 |
|---|---:|
| **Current vintage: 2003** | **90** |

Fragrant, floral and limey aromas of fresh apples and pear precede a fruity, forward and concentrated palate whose juicy apple/pear fruit culminates in a crisp finish of racy acidity. Punchy, varietal and assertive.

| 2003 | 90 | 2008 | 2011+ |
|---|---|---|---|
| 2002 | 90 | 2007 | 2010 |
| 2001 | 87 | 2003 | 2006 |
| 2000 | 87 | 2005 | 2008 |
| 1999 | 92 | 2004 | 2007 |
| 1997 | 87 | 2002 | 2005 |
| 1996 | 87 | 2001 | 2004 |

# THE FOOTBOLT SHIRAZ

| McLaren Vale | $20–$29 |
|---|---:|
| **Current vintage: 2001** | **87** |

Grippy, generously flavoured shiraz with some intense blackberry, redcurrant and plum flavours in addition to some rather stewed, dehydrated prune and currant influences. Up-front and vibrant, but lacks vitality on the palate, finishing rather stale and cooked.

| 2001 | 87 | 2003 | 2006+ |
|---|---|---|---|
| 2000 | 87 | 2002 | 2005+ |
| 1999 | 89 | 2004 | 2007+ |
| 1998 | 90 | 2006 | 2010 |
| 1997 | 87 | 2002 | 2005+ |
| 1996 | 90 | 2004 | 2008 |
| 1995 | 90 | 2003 | 2007 |
| 1994 | 91 | 2006 | 2014 |
| 1993 | 90 | 2001 | 2005 |
| 1992 | 90 | 2004 | 2012 |
| 1991 | 93 | 2003 | 2011 |
| 1990 | 90 | 1998 | 2002 |

# THE HIGH TRELLIS CABERNET SAUVIGNON

| McLaren Vale | $20–$29 |
|---|---:|
| **Current vintage: 2002** | **89** |

Compact cooler season cabernet whose lightly briary aromas of earthy red berries, redcurrants and raspberries are enhanced with sweet cedary oak. A pleasingly elegant and long palate of small berry flavours is complemented by a very fine cut of tight-knit tannins and measured oak.

| 2002 | 89 | 2007 | 2010+ |
|---|---|---|---|
| 2001 | 85 | 2006 | 2009 |
| 2000 | 87 | 2005 | 2008 |
| 1999 | 87 | 2004 | 2007 |
| 1998 | 93 | 2006 | 2010 |
| 1997 | 88 | 2002 | 2005+ |
| 1995 | 92 | 2003 | 2007 |
| 1994 | 88 | 1999 | 2002 |
| 1993 | 87 | 2001 | 2005 |
| 1992 | 87 | 1997 | 2000 |
| 1991 | 92 | 2003 | 2011 |
| 1990 | 92 | 2002 | 2010 |

## THE IRONSTONE PRESSINGS (Grenache Shiraz)

RANKING 3

**McLaren Vale** $50+
**Current vintage: 2002** 94

A powerful, long-term wine that flaunts its total disregard for modern wine fashion. Its profoundly concentrated and pristine aromas of dark plums and cherry kernels are enhanced by meaty, musky undertones of sweet earth and leather. Long and astringent, its thick, weighty palate of dark plum, blackberry, chocolate and leathery flavours finishes firm and savoury with clove and cinnamon spices. Time is essential.

| | | | |
|---|---|---|---|
| 2002 | 94 | 2014 | 2022+ |
| 2001 | 92 | 2013 | 2021 |
| 2000 | 89 | 2005 | 2008 |
| 1999 | 89 | 2007 | 2011 |
| 1998 | 89 | 2010 | 2018 |
| 1997 | 91 | 2005 | 2009 |
| 1996 | 94 | 2008 | 2016 |
| 1995 | 93 | 2007 | 2015 |
| 1994 | 89 | 2006 | 2014 |
| 1993 | 91 | 2005 | 2013 |
| 1992 | 95 | 2000 | 2004 |
| 1991 | 91 | 2003 | 2011 |
| 1990 | 90 | 2002 | 2010 |
| 1989 | 89 | 2001 | 2009 |

## THE LAST DITCH VIOGNIER

RANKING 5

**McLaren Vale** $12–$19
**Current vintage: 2003** 82

Varnishy, spicy oatmeal-like aromas of citrus and banana, with a rather coarse and oily palate with plenty of spice, but insufficient shape and definition. Finishes a little hot and bitter.

| | | | |
|---|---|---|---|
| 2003 | 82 | 2004 | 2005 |
| 2002 | 87 | 2003 | 2004+ |
| 2001 | 89 | 2003 | 2006 |

## THE NOBLE RIESLING

RANKING 5

**McLaren Vale** $50+
**Current vintage: 2001** 82

Tiring, ageing, varnishy and citrusy sweet white with sweet sherry-like development. Thins out towards a rather simple finish lacking in fruit sweetness and intensity.

| | | | |
|---|---|---|---|
| 2001 | 82 | 2002 | 2003 |
| 2000 | 88 | 2002 | 2005+ |
| 1999 | 88 | 2001 | 2004+ |
| 1998 | 84 | 2000 | 2003 |
| 1997 | 90 | 2002 | 2005 |
| 1996 | 87 | 1998 | 2001 |
| 1995 | 90 | 2000 | 2003 |
| 1994 | 93 | 2002 | 2006 |
| 1993 | 89 | 1995 | 1998 |

## THE OLIVE GROVE CHARDONNAY

RANKING 5

**McLaren Vale** $12–$19
**Current vintage: 2003** 87

Ripe aromas of citrus, apricots and green olives, with sweet vanilla oak. Round, ripe and juicy, it's rather syrupy and oily, with up-front primary fruit and a slightly cloying finish.

| | | | |
|---|---|---|---|
| 2003 | 87 | 2005 | 2008 |
| 2002 | 90 | 2004 | 2007 |
| 2001 | 81 | 2002 | 2003 |
| 2000 | 88 | 2002 | 2005 |
| 1999 | 92 | 2001 | 2004+ |
| 1998 | 92 | 2003 | 2006 |
| 1997 | 88 | 1999 | 2002 |
| 1996 | 87 | 1997 | 1998 |

## THE PEPPERMINT PADDOCK CHAMBOURCIN

**McLaren Vale** $20–$29
**Current vintage: 2000** 82

Lean, rather hard, high acid red with a not unattractive bouquet of sweet dark chocolate, cassis and plums, leather and iron filings. Its forward palate begins with some lively, bright fruits, but then falls short, leaving a searingly acidic finish.

| | | | |
|---|---|---|---|
| 2000 | 82 | 2002 | 2005+ |
| 1999 | 82 | 2001 | 2004 |
| 1998 | 88 | 2003 | 2006 |
| 1997 | 86 | 2002 | 2005 |
| 1996 | 89 | 2001 | 2004 |
| 1995 | 88 | 2000 | 2003 |
| 1994 | 87 | 1999 | 2002 |
| 1993 | 88 | 1998 | 2001 |

## THE STUMP JUMP RED BLEND

**McLaren Vale** $12–$19
**Current vintage: 2002** 89

Developed and gamey aromas of spicy plums, blueberries and mulberries over light cedar/vanilla oak and tarry, leathery nuances. Vibrant and forward, it presents a rich, generous palate of grenache-driven flavour that finishes smooth and silky, with rustic, spicy undertones.

| | | | |
|---|---|---|---|
| 2002 | 89 | 2004 | 2007+ |
| 2001 | 86 | 2003 | 2006 |
| 2000 | 86 | 2002 | 2005 |
| 1999 | 77 | 1999 | 2000 |

## THE TWENTYEIGHT ROAD MOURVÈDRE     RANKING

**McLaren Vale** $30–$49
**Current vintage: 2002** 90

Firm, fine-grained red wine whose jib is cut with a little more elegance than usual. Its spicy, briary aromas of dark plums, berries and freshly turned earth precede a richly flavoured, smooth and choco-latey palate whose fruit flavours are brightly lit and harmoniously married to powdery tannins and restrained oak. Very dry and savoury, destined to open up nicely.

| | | | |
|---|---|---|---|
| 2002 | 90 | 2010 | 2024+ |
| 2001 | 93 | 2009 | 2013+ |
| 2000 | 87 | 2005 | 2008 |
| 1999 | 88 | 2007 | 2011 |
| 1998 | 89 | 2003 | 2006+ |
| 1997 | 87 | 2002 | 2005 |
| 1996 | 92 | 2004 | 2008+ |
| 1995 | 89 | 2003 | 2007 |

## VINTAGE DECLARED PORT SHIRAZ (formerly Vintage Port) RANKING

**McLaren Vale** $30–$49
**Current vintage: 2001** 94

d'Arenberg's re-named Australian vintage port-style is made from old vine McLaren Vale shiraz. Steeped in dark liqueur fruits, its powerful, licorice-like aromas of blackberries and cassis are scented with cloves and cinnamon. Warm and spirity, its sumptuous palate of ripe black and red fruits is framed by firm, powdery tannin. Given its depth and intensity of fruit, it's very smooth and even, finishing typically sweet with lingering notes of currants, prunes and licorice.

| | | | |
|---|---|---|---|
| 2001 | 94 | 2013 | 2021+ |
| 2000 | 95 | 2020 | 2030+ |
| 1999 | 90 | 2011 | 2019+ |
| 1998 | 93 | 2010 | 2018 |
| 1997 | 93 | 2005 | 2009+ |
| 1995 | 94 | 2007 | 2015 |
| 1993 | 93 | 2005 | 2013 |
| 1987 | 94 | 2007 | 2017 |
| 1978 | 90 | 1998 | 2008 |
| 1976 | 93 | 1996 | 2006 |
| 1975 | 93 | 1995 | 2005 |
| 1973 | 95 | 1993 | 2003 |

# Dalfarras

Goulburn Valley Highway, Nagambie Vic 3608. Tel: (03) 5794 2637. Fax: (03) 5794 2360.
Email: admin@tahbilk.com.au

Regions: **Nagambie Lakes, Coonawarra, McLaren Vale** Winemaker: **Alister Purbrick** Viticulturist: **Ian Hendy**
Chief Executive: **Alister Purbrick**

Always competent and sound, Dalfarras' wines are however lacking a shot of vitality and point of difference. Recent years have witnessed something of a movement away from their traditional home of Nagambie Lakes.

## CABERNET SAUVIGNON     RANKING

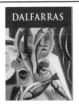

**Coonawarra**
**(Formerly Nagambie Lakes)** $12–$19
**Current vintage: 1998** 84

Green-edged, minty/menthol aromas of black-berries, plums and cedary/vanilla oak, before a dusty, herbal and modestly oaked palate of sweet cassis and raspberry fruit that finishes with firm, astringent and under-ripe tannins.

| | | | |
|---|---|---|---|
| 1998 | 84 | 2006 | 2010 |
| 1997 | 89 | 2005 | 2009+ |
| 1996 | 85 | 2008 | 2016 |
| 1995 | 88 | 2003 | 2007 |
| 1993 | 82 | 2001 | 2005 |
| 1992 | 87 | 2004 | 2012 |
| 1991 | 92 | 2011 | 2021 |
| 1990 | 87 | 2002 | 2010 |

## MERLOT

| Various | $12–$19 |
|---|---|
| **Current vintage: 2002** | **86** |

Firm, slightly lean expression of merlot with meaty, earthy and smoky aromas of maraschino and dark cherries over sweet creamy vanilla oak and vegetal undertones. Smooth and generous, its lively merlot fruit overlies a fine and bony extract, while its rather assertive oak is just a little over-done.

| 2002 | 86 | 2004 | 2007+ |
|---|---|---|---|
| 2001 | 82 | 2003 | 2006 |
| 2000 | 87 | 2002 | 2005+ |

## SAUVIGNON BLANC

| Nagambie Lakes, McLaren Vale | $12–$19 |
|---|---|
| **Current vintage: 2002** | **85** |

Honest, if slightly grassy and flat sauvignon blanc appearing slightly cooked and lifeless. Lean and herbaceous, its palate begins promisingly with some tangy fruit, but finishes a little nondescript, with soft, lemony acids.

| 2002 | 85 | 2002 | 2003 |
|---|---|---|---|
| 2001 | 80 | 2001 | 2001 |
| 2000 | 87 | 2001 | 2002 |
| 1999 | 87 | 2000 | 2001 |

## SHIRAZ

| Nagambie Lakes | $12–$19 |
|---|---|
| **Current vintage: 2000** | **83** |

Meaty, cooked and stewy shiraz whose vegetal expression of berry/plum fruit lacks vitality and generosity. Rather tight, retentive and green-edged, finishing with hard acids and spicy oak.

| 2000 | 83 | 2005 | 2008 |
|---|---|---|---|
| 1999 | 84 | 2004 | 2007+ |
| 1998 | 87 | 2003 | 2006 |
| 1997 | 87 | 2002 | 2005 |
| 1996 | 91 | 2004 | 2008+ |
| 1995 | 92 | 2003 | 2007+ |
| 1994 | 89 | 2006 | 2014 |
| 1993 | 84 | 2001 | 2005 |
| 1992 | 88 | 2000 | 2004 |
| 1991 | 92 | 1999 | 2003 |
| 1990 | 88 | 1998 | 2002 |

# Dalwhinnie

448 Taltarni Road, Moonambel Vic 3478. Tel: (03) 5467 2388. Fax: (03) 5467 2237.
Website: www.dalwhinnie.com.au Email: dalwines@iinet.net.au

Region: **Pyrenees** Winemaker: **David Jones** Viticulturist: **David Jones** Chief Executive: **David Jones**

A benchmark Victorian vineyard, Dalwhinnie is located in one of the regions to have experienced the very worst of the ongoing drought, the Pyrenees. Its signature variety is shiraz, which can express incredible depth of spicy aroma and flavour in good vintages. The lack of water is the single reason for the very slight decline in wine quality over recent seasons, although if all is considered, the wines have held up remarkably well.

## CHARDONNAY

| Pyrenees | $30–$49 |
|---|---|
| **Current vintage: 2002** | **90** |

Long, austere and finely balanced chardonnay with a creamy bouquet of nougat, oatmeal, peach and melon, with undertones of toffee. Already slightly toasty, the palate offers a pleasing core of melon and citrus fruit enhanced with mealy, nutty complexity, but finishes with an edgy, oaky rawness.

| 2002 | 90 | 2004 | 2007+ |
|---|---|---|---|
| 2001 | 93 | 2006 | 2009 |
| 2000 | 92 | 2002 | 2005+ |
| 1999 | 87 | 2001 | 2004 |
| 1998 | 94 | 2003 | 2006 |
| 1997 | 94 | 2002 | 2005 |
| 1996 | 92 | 2001 | 2004 |
| 1995 | 94 | 2000 | 2003 |
| 1994 | 94 | 2002 | 2006 |
| 1993 | 95 | 1998 | 2001 |
| 1992 | 93 | 2000 | 2004 |
| 1991 | 93 | 1999 | 2003 |
| 1990 | 94 | 1998 | 2002 |

## EAGLE SERIES SHIRAZ

RANKING **2**

| Pyrenees | $50+ |
| **Current vintage: 2000** | **95** |

Its complex, herbal aromas of meaty, peppery and rather gamey small black and red berry fruits reveal a dusty, stalky background that continues throughout its firm and drying palate, but which should evolve with time towards more smoky, cedary characters. It's forward and succulent, with intense flavours of mulberries and cassis, before finishing slightly herbal and astringent.

| 2000 | 95 | 2012 | 2020 |
|---|---|---|---|
| 1998 | 93 | 2003 | 2006 |
| 1997 | 97 | 2005 | 2009 |
| 1992 | 94 | 2000 | 2004 |
| 1986 | 93 | 1998 | 2006 |

## MOONAMBEL CABERNET

RANKING **3**

| Pyrenees | $30–$49 |
| **Current vintage: 2002** | **92** |

A very elegant, fine and stylish cabernet from this vineyard, which traditionally has produced a firmer cabernet of considerable astringency. There's a minty whiff of menthol and sweet cedar/vanilla oak beneath its concentrated cassis and violet aromas, while the long and slightly sinewy palate reveals pleasing integration of vibrant plum and blackberry flavours.

| 2002 | 92 | 2014 | 2022 |
|---|---|---|---|
| 2000 | 91 | 2012 | 2020 |
| 1999 | 93 | 2011 | 2019 |
| 1998 | 94 | 2010 | 2018 |
| 1997 | 92 | 2009 | 2017 |
| 1996 | 86 | 2004 | 2008 |
| 1995 | 93 | 2003 | 2007+ |
| 1994 | 90 | 2002 | 2006 |
| 1993 | 85 | 2001 | 2005+ |
| 1992 | 94 | 2004 | 2012+ |
| 1991 | 92 | 2003 | 2011 |
| 1990 | 88 | 2002 | 2010 |
| 1989 | 91 | 1997 | 2001 |
| 1988 | 89 | 1996 | 2000+ |
| 1987 | 82 | 1992 | 1995 |
| 1986 | 93 | 1998 | 2006 |
| 1985 | 86 | 1990 | 1993 |
| 1984 | 80 | 1989 | 1992 |
| 1983 | 87 | 1995 | 2003 |

## MOONAMBEL SHIRAZ

RANKING **2**

| Pyrenees | $30–$49 |
| **Current vintage: 2002** | **90** |

Rather a savoury, herbal Rhôney shiraz with a musky, meaty and peppery aroma of small black and red berries and dried herbs. There's plenty of softness and round, generous earthy dark berry flavour, while it finishes nutty, spicy and savoury, with just a hint of herby sappiness. It's a polished wine, but a closer look does suggest it struggled for ripeness.

| 2002 | 90 | 2007 | 2010+ |
|---|---|---|---|
| 2001 | 94 | 2009 | 2013+ |
| 2000 | 95 | 2008 | 2012+ |
| 1999 | 94 | 2007 | 2011+ |
| 1998 | 95 | 2006 | 2010 |
| 1997 | 94 | 2005 | 2009 |
| 1996 | 95 | 2004 | 2008 |
| 1995 | 92 | 2003 | 2007 |
| 1994 | 93 | 2002 | 2006 |
| 1993 | 87 | 2001 | 2005 |
| 1992 | 97 | 2004 | 2012 |
| 1991 | 95 | 1999 | 2003+ |
| 1990 | 93 | 2002 | 2010 |
| 1989 | 82 | 1994 | 1997 |
| 1988 | 89 | 2000 | 2008 |
| 1987 | 83 | 1995 | 1999 |
| 1986 | 88 | 1994 | 1998+ |

## PINOT NOIR

RANKING **5**

| Pyrenees | $30–$49 |
| **Current vintage: 2002** | **85** |

Minty aromas of stewed, rather stressed fruits with slightly medicinal nuances of dried herbs. Slightly sour-edged and sappy, the palate reveals sour cherry and rhubarb-like fruit bound by greenish, sappy tannins.

| 2002 | 85 | 2004 | 2007+ |
|---|---|---|---|
| 2001 | 89 | 2006 | 2009 |
| 2000 | 84 | 2002 | 2005 |
| 1999 | 88 | 2001 | 2004 |
| 1998 | 90 | 2003 | 2006+ |
| 1996 | 85 | 2001 | 2004 |
| 1995 | 92 | 2000 | 2003 |

# David Traeger

139 High Street, Nagambie Vic 3608. Tel: (03) 5794 2514. Fax: (03) 5794 1776. Email: traeger@eck.net.au
Region: **Nagambie Lakes** Winemaker: **David Traeger** Viticulturist: **David Traeger**
Chief Executive: **Richard Green**

Now owned by Dromana Estate Ltd, the David Traeger label has made a name for some juicy, if slightly sweet central Victorian Verdelho, as well as some finely crafted, leaner expressions of Cabernet Sauvignon and Shiraz. Its reds are typically tight, lean and protected, and slowly acquire roundness and softness with age.

## CABERNET

RANKING **4**

| Nagambie Lakes | $20–$29 |
|---|---|
| **Current vintage: 1999** | **87** |

Typical central Victorian characters of eucalypt, mint and menthol lie beneath the vibrant plum and small red and black berry aromas of this rustic wine. Perhaps lacking a little intensity and focus, it's lean and tight, slowly revealing some sweetness and softness on the palate. Competent enough, it perhaps could have used more aeration and some better oak.

| 1999 | 87 | 2004 | 2007+ |
|---|---|---|---|
| 1998 | 90 | 2010 | 2018 |
| 1997 | 86 | 2005 | 2009 |
| 1996 | 89 | 2004 | 2008 |
| 1995 | 88 | 2003 | 2007 |
| 1993 | 91 | 2001 | 2005 |
| 1992 | 94 | 2004 | 2012 |
| 1990 | 93 | 2002 | 2010 |
| 1989 | 92 | 1997 | 2001 |
| 1988 | 88 | 1996 | 2000 |

## SHIRAZ

RANKING **3**

| Nagambie Lakes | $20–$29 |
|---|---|
| **Current vintage: 2000** | **92** |

Smooth and intensely flavoured, minty Victorian shiraz with a slightly meaty fragrance of small berries, cherries and plums supported by restrained vanilla oak. Medium to full in weight, its bright, lively palate offers a deliciously spicy spread of plum, blackcurrant and raspberry flavours framed by fine, supple tannins. Tight and balanced, but generous and vibrant.

| 2000 | 92 | 2005 | 2008+ |
|---|---|---|---|
| 1999 | 88 | 2004 | 2007+ |
| 1998 | 92 | 2006 | 2010+ |
| 1997 | 93 | 2005 | 2009+ |
| 1996 | 92 | 2004 | 2008 |
| 1995 | 90 | 2003 | 2007 |
| 1993 | 85 | 1998 | 2001 |
| 1992 | 88 | 2000 | 2004 |
| 1990 | 89 | 1998 | 2002 |
| 1988 | 93 | 1996 | 2000 |

## VERDELHO

RANKING **4**

| Various, Victoria | $12–$19 |
|---|---|
| **Current vintage: 2002** | **87** |

Fragrant, lightly herbal and tropical verdelho with a dusty gooseberry-like aroma and a forward, punchy palate finished by lemon and mineral acidity. Clean and dry, but lacks great length.

| 2002 | 87 | 2003 | 2004 |
|---|---|---|---|
| 2001 | 90 | 2003 | 2006+ |
| 2000 | 82 | 2001 | 2002 |
| 1999 | 93 | 2004 | 2007 |
| 1998 | 91 | 2003 | 2006 |
| 1997 | 88 | 1999 | 2002 |

# De Bortoli

De Bortoli Road, Bilbul NSW 2680. Tel: (02) 6966 0100. Fax: (02) 6966 0199.
Website: www.debortoli.com.au  Email: reception_bilbul@debortoli.com.au
Region: **Riverina** Winemakers: **Ralph Graham, Julie Mortlock** Viticulturist: **Kevin De Bortoli**
Chief Executive: **Darren De Bortoli**

De Bortoli's Noble One has achieved a twenty-year track record of fine late harvest semillon. It is the most emulated expression of its kind in Australia, typically delivering a luscious, sumptuous palate of intense, marmalade-like fruit that finishes clean and citrusy. The luscious, but tightly restrained 2002 vintage reaffirms its place at the forefront of Australian dessert wine.

## NOBLE ONE

RANKING **2**

| Riverina | $20–$29 (375 ml) |
|---|---|
| **Current vintage: 2002** | **96** |

Luscious, concentrated dessert wine with pungent, honeyed and buttery aromas of quince and cumquat, melon and apricot. Deeply concentrated, its lavish, opulent palate offers length and viscosity, delivering vibrant, spotlessly clean flavour and sweetness before a refreshingly clear finish. Great richness and balance.

| 2002 | 96 | 2010 | 2014 |
|---|---|---|---|
| 2001 | 90 | 2003 | 2006 |
| 2000 | 93 | 2005 | 2008 |
| 1999 | 93 | 2004 | 2007 |
| 1998 | 95 | 2010 | 2018 |
| 1997 | 89 | 2002 | 2005 |
| 1996 | 95 | 2004 | 2008 |
| 1995 | 95 | 2003 | 2007 |
| 1994 | 96 | 2002 | 2006 |
| 1993 | 93 | 1998 | 2001 |

# De Bortoli Yarra Valley

Pinnacle Lane, Dixon's Creek Vic 3775. Tel: (03) 5965 2271. Fax: (03) 5965 2442.
Website: www.debortoli.com.au  Email: Yarra_Cellar_Door@debortoli.com.au

Region: **Yarra Valley**  Winemakers: **Stephen Webber, David Slingsby-Smith**  Viticulturist: **Philip Lobley**
Chief Executive: **Darren De Bortoli**

De Bortoli is one of the Yarra Valley's largest winemakers, and given the scale of its operations does an excellent job to deliver consistently flavoursome wines of quality and distinction. It is making every effort to produce ripe, juicy shiraz grapes from recent plantings on warmer Yarra sites, and isn't afraid to administer a decent measure of newish oak to its riper and richer reds. Its restaurant has long been a benchmark in the region.

## CABERNET SAUVIGNON

RANKING **4**

**Yarra Valley**  $30–$49
**Current vintage: 2001**  85

Floral aromas of small red berries, blackberries and restrained cedary oak precede a forward, moderately full palate that dries out quickly towards a meaty, herbal finish of sappy tannins. Lacks structure and fruit substance.

| | | | |
|---|---|---|---|
| 2001 | 85 | 2003 | 2006+ |
| 2000 | 92 | 2008 | 2012 |
| 1999 | 89 | 2004 | 2007 |
| 1998 | 90 | 2003 | 2006 |
| 1997 | 92 | 2005 | 2009 |
| 1996 | 91 | 2001 | 2004 |
| 1995 | 95 | 2007 | 2015 |
| 1994 | 89 | 1999 | 2002 |
| 1993 | 90 | 2001 | 2005 |

## CHARDONNAY

RANKING **3**

**Yarra Valley**  $20–$29
**Current vintage: 2003**  90

Tangy and flavoursome, smooth and refreshing Yarra chardonnay. Its buttery and lightly spicy aroma of fresh honeydew melon, tropical and banana-like fruit is evenly matched by finely integrated oak and creamy lees influences. The juicy, long and even palate is clean and vibrant, even if slightly sweet.

| | | | |
|---|---|---|---|
| 2003 | 90 | 2005 | 2008+ |
| 2002 | 94 | 2007 | 2010 |
| 2001 | 89 | 2003 | 2006 |
| 2000 | 93 | 2002 | 2005+ |
| 1999 | 93 | 2004 | 2007 |
| 1998 | 93 | 2003 | 2006 |
| 1997 | 90 | 1999 | 2002+ |
| 1996 | 94 | 2001 | 2004+ |

## GS RESERVE SHIRAZ

RANKING **4**

**Yarra Valley**  $50+
**Current vintage: 1999**  90

Firm, but reserved and elegant cool climate shiraz with a meaty, leathery bouquet of spicy dark plums and vanilla/mocha oak. There's plenty of vibrant, riper small dark berry flavour, but also some cooler, herbal influence and slightly green-edged tannin. Full to medium in weight, it's packed with licorice and spicy fruitcake flavour but also reveals significant sweet chocolate-like oak.

| | | | |
|---|---|---|---|
| 1999 | 90 | 2007 | 2011 |
| 1998 | 89 | 2003 | 2006+ |
| 1997 | 87 | 2002 | 2005 |
| 1997 | 90 | 2001 | 2004+ |

## MELBA RESERVE

RANKING **4**

**Yarra Valley**  $50+
**Current vintage: 1999**  92

A balanced and stylish wine with finesse and elegance. Intense, but earthy aromas of small black and red berries, mulberries and sweet cedar/vanilla oak reveal meaty and undergrowth-like complexity. Brightly lit with plum, mulberry and cassis flavours, the palate is fine, smooth and restrained, culminating in a fine-grained tight-knit finish of dusty, drying fine tannins and sweet cedary oak.

| | | | |
|---|---|---|---|
| 1999 | 92 | 2007 | 2011 |
| 1998 | 89 | 2006 | 2010 |
| 1997 | 91 | 2005 | 2009 |
| 1995 | 88 | 2000 | 2003+ |
| 1994 | 88 | 2002 | 2006 |
| 1993 | 90 | 1998 | 2001+ |
| 1992 | 87 | 1997 | 2000 |

## PINOT NOIR

RANKING **5**

**Yarra Valley**  $30–$49
**Current vintage: 2002**  89

Elegant, supple pinot with a delicate, spicy aroma of small red cherries, plums and berries meshed with modest oak. Smooth and supple, its confectionary-like palate of raspberries, cherries and sweet vanilla/chocolate oak does reveal some green edges and a lack of genuine stuffing, finishing slightly herbal.

| | | | |
|---|---|---|---|
| 2002 | 89 | 2004 | 2007+ |
| 2001 | 85 | 2002 | 2003+ |
| 2000 | 87 | 2002 | 2005 |
| 1999 | 89 | 2001 | 2004 |
| 1998 | 89 | 2000 | 2003 |
| 1997 | 94 | 2002 | 2005 |
| 1996 | 95 | 2001 | 2004 |

## SHIRAZ

| Yarra Valley | $30–$49 |
|---|---|
| **Current vintage: 2002** | **90** |

Fine-grained, spicy and elegant expression of largely French oak-matured Yarra shiraz whose musky, peppery fragrance of cassis, blackberries, raspberries and plums is offset by lightly smoky chocolate oak influences. Smooth and silky, its long palate of sweet dark berries, creamy oak and fine-grained tannins reveals some slightly herbal/under-growth complexity.

| | | | |
|---|---|---|---|
| 2002 | 90 | 2007 | 2010 |
| 2001 | 89 | 2006 | 2009 |
| 2000 | 88 | 2002 | 2005+ |
| 1999 | 90 | 2004 | 2007 |
| 1998 | 89 | 2003 | 2006+ |
| 1997 | 93 | 2005 | 2009 |
| 1996 | 93 | 2001 | 2004 |
| 1995 | 93 | 2003 | 2007 |
| 1994 | 93 | 1999 | 2002 |
| 1993 | 90 | 1998 | 2001 |

# Deakin Estate

Kulkyne Way Iraak via Red Cliffs Vic 3496. Tel: (03) 5029 1666. Fax: (03) 5024 3316.
Website: www.deakinestate.com.au  Email: deakin@wingara.com.au
Region: **Murray Darling** Winemaker: **Linda Jakubans** Viticulturist: **Jeff Milne**
Chief Executive: **David Yunghanns**

Time and again Deakin Estate's cheerful and uncomplicated cheaper wines stand out in my tastings for their freshness, brightness, intensity and balance, while the slightly more expensive 'Select' range offers just that little bit more richness and attention to detail. All typically represent great value for money.

## CABERNET SAUVIGNON

| Murray Darling | $5–$11 |
|---|---|
| **Current vintage: 2002** | **87** |

Lively, intensely flavoured cabernet with persistence and elegance. Its floral aromas of violets and cassis reveal some earthy riverland undertones plus a whiff of herbaceousness, while the palate is well structured, evenly balanced and generous in its expression of dark plum and small berry flavours.

| | | | |
|---|---|---|---|
| 2002 | 87 | 2004 | 2007 |
| 2001 | 84 | 2002 | 2003 |
| 2000 | 86 | 2001 | 2002 |
| 1999 | 81 | 2000 | 2001 |

## MERLOT

| Murray Darling | $5–$11 |
|---|---|
| **Current vintage: 2002** | **87** |

Supple, clean and flavoursome wine with a slightly jammy aroma of raspberries and cherries laced with sweet, fragrant vanilla and coconut oak. Soft, smooth and mouthfilling, it's generously packed with juicy cherry/berry fruit and framed with slightly sappy, but soft tannins.

| | | | |
|---|---|---|---|
| 2002 | 87 | 2003 | 2004 |
| 2001 | 88 | 2002 | 2003+ |
| 2000 | 84 | 2001 | 2002 |
| 1999 | 87 | 2000 | 2001+ |
| 1998 | 82 | 1999 | 2000 |
| 1997 | 85 | 1998 | 1999 |

## SAUVIGNON BLANC

| Murray Darling | $5–$11 |
|---|---|
| **Current vintage: 2004** | **87** |

Refreshing and well-priced sauvignon blanc, with lively herbal and grassy aromas of gooseberries passionfruit and tropical fruits before a vibrant and up-front palate of punchy varietal flavours. Moderately long, slightly sweet, but clean and honest.

| | | | |
|---|---|---|---|
| 2004 | 87 | 2004 | 2005 |
| 2003 | 83 | 2003 | 2004 |
| 2002 | 84 | 2002 | 2003 |
| 2001 | 87 | 2001 | 2002 |

## SELECT CHARDONNAY

| **Murray Darling** | $12–$19 | 2002 | 89 | 2003 | 2004 |
|---|---|---|---|---|---|
| **Current vintage: 2002** | **89** | 2000 | 83 | 2001 | 2002 |
| | | 1998 | 80 | 1998 | 1999 |
| | | 1997 | 87 | 1998 | 1999 |

Excellent riverland chardonnay with a ripe aroma of peach, nectarine and melon intermeshed with sweet buttery and lightly toasty vanilla oak. Ripe and juicy, the palate is packed with vibrant peach, tropical and citrus flavours before a refreshingly clean finish. Its slightly buttery and creamy/vanilla oak is cleverly integrated, completing a wine of generosity and balance.

## SELECT SHIRAZ

RANKING **5**

| **Murray Darling** | $12–$19 | 2001 | 86 | 2003 | 2006 |
|---|---|---|---|---|---|
| **Current vintage: 2001** | **86** | 1999 | 88 | 2001 | 2004 |
| | | 1998 | 89 | 2000 | 2003+ |

Slightly cooked and tarry, this otherwise pleasing and polished shiraz has a maturing, earthy and leathery bouquet of plum and chocolate/vanilla oak with a faint crushed bullant-like character. Assertively oaked, its toasty, creamy palate of red and black fruits is smooth and sumptuous, but lacks great length.

## SHIRAZ

| **Murray Darling** | $5–$11 | 2002 | 86 | 2004 | 2007 |
|---|---|---|---|---|---|
| **Current vintage: 2002** | **86** | 2001 | 86 | 2002 | 2003+ |
| | | 2000 | 87 | 2001 | 2002 |
| | | 1999 | 82 | 2000 | 2001 |
| | | 1998 | 83 | 1999 | 2000 |

Great value shiraz with a fragrance of white pepper, dark cherries and plums, earthy riverland characters and cedar/vanilla oak. Smooth, polished and spicy, it's long and generous, with a pleasing spine of underlying grip and extract.

# Delatite

cnr Stoney's & Pollard's Roads, Mansfield Vic 3722. Tel: (03) 5775 2922. Fax: (03) 5775 2911.
Email: winery@mansfield.net.au

Region: **Mansfield** Winemaker: **Rosalind Ritchie** Viticulturist: **David Ritchie**
Chief Executives: **Robert & Vivienne Ritchie**

For years I have been an admirer of the cool-climate Delatite vineyard's ability to achieve exceptional intensity in its riesling, gewürztraminer and sauvignon blanc, and recent indications are that pinot gris could well become another top-flight variety. I also enjoy the creamy, crackly nature of the Demelza sparkling white, but most of all the steely minerality and perfume of the occasional releases of VS Riesling.

## CHARDONNAY

RANKING  **5**

| **Mansfield** | $20–$29 | 2002 | 88 | 2004 | 2007+ |
|---|---|---|---|---|---|
| **Current vintage: 2002** | **88** | 2000 | 87 | 2002 | 2005 |
| | | 1999 | 87 | 2001 | 2004 |
| | | 1998 | 84 | 2000 | 2003 |
| | | 1997 | 82 | 1998 | 1999 |
| | | 1996 | 90 | 2001 | 2004 |
| | | 1995 | 87 | 1997 | 2000 |
| | | 1994 | 93 | 1999 | 2002 |
| | | 1993 | 94 | 1998 | 2001 |
| | | 1992 | 91 | 2000 | 2004 |

Restrained, delicate chardonnay with a lightly spicy and floral bouquet of white peach and melon over light creamy/vanilla oak and suggestions of grapefruit. Its reserved but lightly viscous palate of pristine citrus and melon flavour culminates in a savoury, nutty finish.

## DEAD MAN'S HILL GEWÜRZTRAMINER

RANKING **4**

DELATITE
VICTORIA

DEAD MAN'S HILL
GEWÜRZTRAMINER
2003

12.5% vol          750ml

**Mansfield** $20–$29

**Current vintage: 2003** **89**

Moderately intense, pretty and powdery traminer with a musky perfume of rose oil, bathpowder and wet slate. Forward and concentrated, but then more delicately flavoured with musky lemon rind and lychee-like nuances, before drying out towards a tight, taut finish.

| | | | |
|---|---|---|---|
| 2003 | 89 | 2005 | 2008+ |
| 2002 | 87 | 2003 | 2004+ |
| 2001 | 94 | 2006 | 2009 |
| 2000 | 91 | 2005 | 2008 |
| 1999 | 87 | 2001 | 2004 |
| 1998 | 88 | 2000 | 2003 |
| 1997 | 89 | 1999 | 2002 |
| 1996 | 91 | 2004 | 2008 |
| 1995 | 87 | 2000 | 2003 |
| 1994 | 93 | 1999 | 2002 |
| 1992 | 91 | 2000 | 2004+ |

## DEMELZA

RANKING **3**

DELATITE

DEMELZA

N.V.
750ml

**Mansfield** $30–$49

**Current vintage: 2001** **92**

Very fine, elegant and creamy sparkling wine whose delicate, nutty and lightly tropical bouquet of citrus-like fruit precedes a smooth, crackly and fine-beaded palate of freshness and raciness. Just give it a little time on cork.

| | | | |
|---|---|---|---|
| 2001 | 92 | 2006 | 2009 |
| 2000 | 87 | 2002 | 2005 |
| 1996 | 93 | 2001 | 2004+ |
| 94–95 | 93 | 1999 | 2002+ |
| 1991 | 84 | 1996 | 1999 |
| 87–88 | 87 | 1995 | 1997 |

RANKING **3**

DELATITE
VICTORIA

RIESLING
2003

12.0% vol          750ml

**Mansfield** $20–$29

**Current vintage: 2003** **89**

A lightly musky perfume of lime and apple, pear and peach precedes a round and generous, almost broad palate of slightly candied fruit. A little advanced, soft and generous, it offers plenty of fruit and flavour before finishing with lemon detergent-like acids.

| | | | |
|---|---|---|---|
| 2003 | 89 | 2005 | 2008+ |
| 2002 | 92 | 2007 | 2010+ |
| 2001 | 90 | 2006 | 2009 |
| 2000 | 91 | 2005 | 2008+ |
| 1999 | 92 | 2007 | 2011 |
| 1998 | 94 | 2006 | 2010 |
| 1997 | 88 | 2005 | 2009 |
| 1996 | 93 | 2004 | 2008 |
| 1995 | 93 | 2000 | 2003 |
| 1994 | 94 | 2002 | 2005 |
| 1993 | 95 | 2001 | 2005 |
| 1992 | 95 | 2000 | 2004 |

## SAUVIGNON BLANC

RANKING **4**

VICTORIA

DELATITE

SAUVIGNON BLANC
2001
750ml
Product of Australia

**Mansfield** $20–$29

**Current vintage: 2003** **91**

Intense floral and mineral fragrance of slightly nutty gooseberries and passionfruit with a distinctive herbaceousness. The palate is long and tangy, with vibrant varietal fruit and a slippery texture culminating in a lingering mineral and lightly phenolic finish punctuated by clean lemony acids.

| | | | |
|---|---|---|---|
| 2003 | 91 | 2003 | 2004+ |
| 2002 | 87 | 2002 | 2003 |
| 2001 | 89 | 2002 | 2003+ |
| 2000 | 90 | 2001 | 2002 |
| 1999 | 89 | 2000 | 2001+ |
| 1998 | 88 | 1999 | 2002+ |
| 1997 | 92 | 1999 | 2002 |

# Devil's Lair

Rocky Road, via Margaret River WA 6285. Tel: (08) 9757 7573. Fax: (08) 9757 7533.
Website: www.devils-lair.com

Region: **Margaret River** Winemaker: **Stuart Pym** Viticulturist: **Simon Robertson** Chief Executive: **John Ballard**

Founded by David Sexton, whose Giant Steps vineyard in the Yarra Valley will shortly debut in this guide, Devil's Lair is Southcorp's foothold in Western Australia. It boasts a large and well-managed vineyard, plus a well-equipped winery, but while often first-rate, its wines can frustrate. The herbaceous and sappy 2001 Devil's Lair red is a case in point, which is well below the expected low water mark for this label.

## CHARDONNAY

RANKING 2

| Margaret River | $30–$49 |
|---|---|
| **Current vintage: 2002** | **90** |

Delicate herbal and spicy aromas of oatmeal, melon and cumquat, cloves and cinnamon with fragrant vanilla oak precede a generous, richly flavoured and concentrated palate of smoothness and length. Ripe and slightly spirity, it's amply laden with tropical and citrus fruit and sweet oak, while its finish remains a little warm and alcoholic. It should flesh out even more.

| 2002 | 90 | 2004 | 2007+ |
|---|---|---|---|
| 2001 | 91 | 2003 | 2005+ |
| 2000 | 95 | 2005 | 2008 |
| 1999 | 95 | 2004 | 2007 |
| 1998 | 89 | 2000 | 2003+ |
| 1997 | 95 | 2002 | 2005 |
| 1996 | 88 | 1998 | 2001 |
| 1995 | 93 | 2000 | 2003 |
| 1994 | 94 | 1996 | 1999 |

## FIFTH LEG RED

RANKING 4

| Margaret River | $12–$19 |
|---|---|
| **Current vintage: 2002** | **89** |

A neatly crafted young wine based on deliciously ripe and pristine fruit. Its spicy fragrance of cassis, raspberries and cherries reveals nuances of white pepper and fine-grained cedar/vanilla oak, while its smooth and silky palate has length, flavour and a surprisingly firm backbone.

| 2002 | 89 | 2004 | 2007 |
|---|---|---|---|
| 2001 | 89 | 2003 | 2006+ |
| 2000 | 92 | 2002 | 2005+ |
| 1999 | 92 | 2001 | 2004 |
| 1997 | 80 | 1998 | 1999 |
| 1996 | 90 | 1998 | 2001 |

## FIFTH LEG WHITE

RANKING 5

| Margaret River | $12–$19 |
|---|---|
| **Current vintage: 2003** | **82** |

A moderately intense, herbal and tropical nose precedes a palate that begins juicy and forward, but then finishes short and a little hot, revealing slightly cooked fruit and some raw edges.

| 2003 | 82 | 2003 | 2004+ |
|---|---|---|---|
| 2002 | 89 | 2003 | 2004 |
| 2000 | 86 | 2001 | 2002 |
| 1998 | 89 | 1999 | 2000 |

## MARGARET RIVER RED

RANKING 2

| Margaret River | $30–$49 |
|---|---|
| **Current vintage: 2001** | **84** |

Rather green-edged and sappy cabernet with clearly shaded dark berry fruit contributing to its herbal, vegetative character. Some assertive new oak and creamy vanilla/cedar influences fail to conceal the soupy capsicum influences on the palate that mask its delicate cassis flavours.

| 2001 | 84 | 2006 | 2009 |
|---|---|---|---|
| 2000 | 89 | 2008 | 2012+ |
| 1999 | 93 | 2007 | 2011 |
| 1998 | 95 | 2010 | 2018 |
| 1997 | 89 | 2002 | 2005+ |
| 1996 | 95 | 2004 | 2008 |
| 1995 | 94 | 2003 | 2007 |
| 1994 | 93 | 2002 | 2006 |
| 1993 | 94 | 2001 | 2005 |
| 1992 | 93 | 2004 | 2012 |
| 1991 | 91 | 1999 | 2003 |
| 1990 | 94 | 2002 | 2010 |

# Diamond Valley

2130 Kinglake Road, St Andrews Vic 3761. Tel: (03) 9710 1484. Fax: (03) 9710 1369.
Website: www.diamondvalley.com.au Email:enq@diamondvalley.com.au
Region: **Yarra Valley** Winemakers: **David Lance, James Lance** Viticulturist: **David Lance**
Chief Executive: **David Lance**

Diamond Valley was one of the second wave of redevelopments in the Yarra Valley, releasing its first wines in the early 1980s. With a mature vineyard at its disposal, plus the exceptional close-planted block of pinot noir on site, it is enjoying a second youth under the enthusiastic winemaking endeavours of James Lance, son of founders David and Cathy Lance. The 2002 vintage at the Estate vineyard has produced a very complete and stylish range of exceptional cool-climate wines.

## CLOSE-PLANTED PINOT NOIR  RANKING **2**

**Yarra Valley** $50+
**Current vintage: 2002** 95

Silky, velvet-like pinot whose deep aromas of dark cherries and berries reveal earthy, charcuterie-like undertones. Its complete and succulent palate reveals layers of dark fruits harmoniously interwoven with restrained oak. With meaty complexity and undertones of forest floor, it finishes long and savoury.

| | | | |
|---|---|---|---|
| 2002 | 95 | 2007 | 2010+ |
| 2001 | 95 | 2006 | 2009 |
| 2000 | 88 | 2002 | 2005+ |
| 1999 | 91 | 2002 | 2005 |
| 1997 | 94 | 1999 | 2002 |
| 1996 | 94 | 2001 | 2004 |
| 1995 | 93 | 1997 | 2000 |

## ESTATE CABERNET MERLOT  RANKING **3**

**Yarra Valley** $30–$49
**Current vintage: 2000** 93

A lightly herbal, but stylish and measured blend of elegance and balance. Its violet-like perfume of raspberries, redcurrants and slightly meaty, cedary oak reveals underlying nuances of dried herbs. Medium to full weight, it's smooth and supple, with a sweet and lively expression of small red berries, cherries and plums framed by fine tannins and restrained oak.

| | | | |
|---|---|---|---|
| 2000 | 93 | 2012 | 2020 |
| 1999 | 92 | 2007 | 2011+ |
| 1998 | 92 | 2003 | 2006+ |
| 1997 | 93 | 2005 | 2009+ |
| 1996 | 88 | 2001 | 2004+ |
| 1994 | 90 | 2002 | 2006+ |
| 1992 | 85 | 2000 | 2004 |
| 1991 | 85 | 1999 | 2003 |
| 1990 | 93 | 1998 | 2002 |

## ESTATE CHARDONNAY  RANKING **4**

**Yarra Valley** $20–$29
**Current vintage: 2002** 94

A pristine young chardonnay with a delicate, buttery aroma of melon, lemon rind and leesy, bacony complexity. Its fine, supple palate has a fluffy, soft palate of delicate stonefruit, citrus and melon flavours enhanced with subtle creamy, bacony and butterscotch influences. Oak plays a restrained, subdued role. It finishes long and soft, with refreshing acidity.

| | | | |
|---|---|---|---|
| 2002 | 94 | 2007 | 2010 |
| 2001 | 87 | 2003 | 2006 |
| 2000 | 92 | 2005 | 2008 |
| 1999 | 88 | 2001 | 2004 |
| 1998 | 89 | 2000 | 2003 |
| 1997 | 88 | 1999 | 2002 |
| 1996 | 87 | 1998 | 2001 |
| 1995 | 92 | 2000 | 2003 |
| 1994 | 93 | 2002 | 2006 |

## ESTATE PINOT NOIR  RANKING **3**

**Yarra Valley** $50+
**Current vintage: 2002** 93

Briary, meaty and savoury pinot with a complex and high-toned floral perfume of red and black cherries, plums and spicy nuances of undergrowth and turned earth. Fine-grained and silky, its smooth and willowy palate reveals a core of sweet, sappy fruit finishing with a dusty, herbal note.

| | | | |
|---|---|---|---|
| 2002 | 93 | 2007 | 2010 |
| 2001 | 90 | 2003 | 2006+ |
| 1999 | 93 | 2007 | 2011 |
| 1998 | 94 | 2003 | 2006 |
| 1997 | 96 | 2002 | 2005+ |
| 1996 | 89 | 2001 | 2004 |
| 1995 | 90 | 2000 | 2003 |
| 1994 | 88 | 1996 | 1999 |
| 1993 | 91 | 1998 | 2001 |

## YARRA VALLEY CABERNET MERLOT

RANKING 5

**Yarra Valley** $20–$29
**Current vintage: 2002** 90

Smooth, fine and very attractive early-drinking blend with a lightly herbal aroma of sweet red berries, forest floor nuances and cedar/vanilla oak. Long and creamy, it's supple and restrained, delivering pristine, if slightly minty berry/plum fruit and lightly smoky oak framed by fine, tight tannins and refreshing acids.

| | | | |
|---|---|---|---|
| 2002 | 90 | 2004 | 2007+ |
| 2001 | 82 | 2003 | 2006 |
| 2000 | 87 | 2002 | 2005 |
| 1999 | 87 | 2001 | 2004+ |

## YARRA VALLEY CHARDONNAY

RANKING 4

**Yarra Valley** $20–$29
**Current vintage: 2003** 90

Delightful early-drinking chardonnay with a citrusy and tropical aroma of peachy fruit and restrained buttery/vanilla oak. Smooth and creamy, the palate offers lively and pristine tropical and stonefruit flavours, light oak and a refreshingly clean and uncluttered finish.

| | | | |
|---|---|---|---|
| 2003 | 90 | 2005 | 2008 |
| 2002 | 90 | 2003 | 2004+ |
| 2000 | 90 | 2002 | 2005 |
| 1999 | 90 | 2001 | 2004 |
| 1998 | 88 | 2000 | 2003 |
| 1997 | 91 | 1999 | 2000 |
| 1996 | 89 | 1998 | 2001 |

## YARRA VALLEY PINOT NOIR

RANKING 4

**Yarra Valley** $20–$29
**Current vintage: 2002** 89

Supple, smooth and generous, this forward and easy-drinking pinot marries fragrant minty cherry-like pinot with lightly smoky oak and refreshing acids. It's uncomplicated and flavoursome, soft and juicy.

| | | | |
|---|---|---|---|
| 2002 | 89 | 2004 | 2007 |
| 2001 | 89 | 2003 | 2006 |
| 2000 | 89 | 2002 | 2005 |
| 1999 | 90 | 2001 | 2004 |
| 1998 | 90 | 2000 | 2003 |
| 1997 | 94 | 1998 | 2001 |
| 1996 | 91 | 1998 | 2001 |
| 1994 | 85 | 1996 | 1999 |

# Domaine A

105 Tea Tree Road, Campania Tas 7026. Tel: (03) 6260 4174. Fax: (03) 6260 4390.
Website: www.domaine-a.com.au Email: althaus@domaine-a.com.au
Region: **Coal River Valley** Winemaker: **Peter Althaus** Viticulturist: **Peter Althaus** Chief Executive: **Peter Althaus**

Domaine A is the label Peter Althaus uses for the small volumes he bottles of occasionally deluxe wines from his Stoney Vineyard in the Coal River Valley. The aristocratic 2000 Cabernet Sauvignon is a classic example of the astonishing depth, flavour, structure and balance of which this site has proven surprisingly and consistently able to deliver. And if you want a taste of the Merlot, you'll probably have to get to know Peter rather well. It's only made for personal consumption, but its sheer quality forces me to list it within these pages.

## CABERNET SAUVIGNON

RANKING 3

**Coal River Valley** $50+
**Current vintage: 2000** 96

Very classy cabernet of opulence and balance. Its meaty, briary aromas of exceptionally concentrated dark plums, cassis and cranberries are backed by cedary oak and earthy undertones. Powerfully structured and richly textured, it's assertive and astringent, but measured and harmoniously crafted, revealing layers of deep, dark and fruits integrated with creamy, cedary and vanilla oak. Iron-fisted elegance and style.

| | | | |
|---|---|---|---|
| 2000 | 96 | 2012 | 2020+ |
| 1999 | 88 | 2007 | 2011 |
| 1998 | 93 | 2010 | 2018 |
| 1997 | 87 | 2005 | 2009 |
| 1995 | 94 | 2007 | 2015 |
| 1994 | 93 | 2006 | 2014 |
| 1993 | 89 | 2005 | 2013 |
| 1992 | 90 | 2004 | 2012 |
| 1991 | 95 | 2003 | 2011 |
| 1990 | 87 | 1995 | 1998 |

A
B
C
**D**
E
F
G
H
I
J
K
L
M
N
O
P
Q
R
S
T
U
V
W
X
Y
Z

## MERLOT

**Coal River Valley**      **Priceless!**
**Current vintage: 1998**     **94**

Tight, focused, elegant and structurally complete merlot that reveals just a fraction too much alcohol for a super-high score. Its small berry fragrance of cassis, mulberry and black cherries is tightly interwoven with fine-grained creamy cedar oak, while the palate bursts with vital, translucent small berry flavours. Wound around silky-fine tannins and creamy oak, it has length, persistence and long-term stability.

| 1998 | 94 | 2010 | 2018 |
|---|---|---|---|
| 1997 | 83 | 2002 | 2005 |
| 1995 | 93 | 2003 | 2007+ |
| 1994 | 89 | 1999 | 2002+ |

## PINOT NOIR

**Coal River Valley**     **$50+**
**Current vintage: 2001**     **92**

Minty, meaty pinot whose spicy, rose petal-like bouquet of maraschino cherries, liqueur chocolate and dried herbs reveals undertones of restrained oak and eucalypt. Minty eucalypt notes underpin its smooth and richly textured palate. Long and persistent, its intense dark, briary fruits are framed by firm, astringent tannins.

| 2001 | 92 | 2009 | 2013 |
|---|---|---|---|
| 2000 | 92 | 2005 | 2008+ |
| 1999 | 89 | 2004 | 2007 |
| 1998 | 95 | 2003 | 2006+ |
| 1997 | 94 | 2005 | 2009 |
| 1995 | 89 | 1997 | 2000 |
| 1994 | 95 | 1999 | 2002+ |
| 1992 | 94 | 1997 | 2000+ |

# Dromana Estate

RMB 555 Old Moorooduc Road, Tuerong Vic 3915. Tel: (03) 9600 3242. Fax: (03) 9600 3245.
Website: www.dromanaestate.com.au Email:info@dromanaestate.com.au

Region: **Mornington Peninsula** Winemaker: **Rollo Crittenden** Viticulturist: **Rollo Crittenden**
Chief Executive: **Richard Green**

Rollo Crittenden has assumed winemaking duties at Dromana Estate with considerable flair and enthusiasm, although the meagre 2002 vintage hardly gave him a great deal to work with. In 2003 he's also made an amarone-like version of the cabernet sauvignon grapes grown at the home block in Dromana that shows unexpected potential and attitude. Dromana Estate was one of the first of the genuinely commercial viticultural and winemaking operations on Victoria's now crowded and over-planted Mornington Peninsula region.

## CABERNET MERLOT

**Mornington Peninsula**     **$20–$29**
**Current vintage: 2002**     **81**

Spicy, greenish and cedary aromas of herby small red and black berries are lifted by sweet cedary vanilla oak. Rather soupy, greenish and meaty, the palate lacks depth and ripeness, finishing rather thin and sappy.

| 2002 | 81 | 2004 | 2007 |
|---|---|---|---|
| 2001 | 93 | 2009 | 2013 |
| 2000 | 93 | 2008 | 2012+ |
| 1999 | 92 | 2007 | 2011 |
| 1998 | 90 | 2006 | 2010 |
| 1997 | 92 | 2005 | 2009 |
| 1996 | 83 | 1998 | 2001+ |
| 1995 | 86 | 2000 | 2003 |
| 1994 | 86 | 1999 | 2002+ |
| 1993 | 86 | 1998 | 2001+ |

## CHARDONNAY

**Mornington Peninsula**     **$20–$29**
**Current vintage: 2002**     **90**

Melon, citrus and pineapple-like aromas of Peninsula chardonnay combine with sweet toasty vanilla oak and suggestions of cashew nut. Smooth and shapely, the palate marries delightfully intense and brightly lit fruit with lightly smoky, creamy, buttery oak and lees-derived influences, culminating in a lingering savoury, nutty finish with a hint of dustiness.

| 2002 | 90 | 2004 | 2007 |
|---|---|---|---|
| 2001 | 89 | 2003 | 2006 |
| 2000 | 82 | 2001 | 2002 |
| 1999 | 93 | 2001 | 2004 |
| 1998 | 90 | 2000 | 2003 |
| 1997 | 87 | 1999 | 2002 |
| 1996 | 88 | 1998 | 2001 |
| 1995 | 90 | 1997 | 2000 |
| 1994 | 95 | 1999 | 2002 |
| 1993 | 93 | 1998 | 2001 |
| 1992 | 93 | 1997 | 2000 |

# PINOT NOIR

| Mornington Peninsula | $20–$29 |
|---|---|
| **Current vintage: 2002** | **89** |

Pretty, youthful and flavoursome early-drinking pinot with a delicate aroma of cherries and lightly vanilla oak, backed by nuances of under-growth, cinnamon and cloves. Fine and supple, its juicy palate of confiture-like raspberry and red cherry flavours is smooth and creamy, framed by soft acids and fine-grained tannins.

| 2002 | 89 | 2004 | 2007 |
|---|---|---|---|
| 2001 | 85 | 2002 | 2003+ |
| 2000 | 90 | 2005 | 2008 |
| 1999 | 87 | 2001 | 2004 |
| 1998 | 88 | 1999 | 2000 |
| 1997 | 91 | 2002 | 2005 |
| 1996 | 93 | 2001 | 2004 |
| 1995 | 93 | 1997 | 2000 |

## RESERVE CHARDONNAY

| Mornington Peninsula | $30–$49 |
|---|---|
| **Current vintage: 2002** | **92** |

A more powerful expression that the 'standard' chardonnay, with a closed, but creamy leesy bouquet of oatmeal, melon and green olives, lifted by sweet vanilla oak. Sumptuous but very restrained and stylish, with concentrated peach/pineapple/green olive flavours elegantly presented before a tangy finish of soft, but vibrant acids. Tightly integrated, with good refinement.

| 2002 | 92 | 2004 | 2007+ |
|---|---|---|---|
| 2001 | 91 | 2003 | 2006+ |
| 2000 | 90 | 2002 | 2005 |
| 1998 | 91 | 2003 | 2006 |
| 1997 | 95 | 2002 | 2005 |
| 1996 | 91 | 2001 | 2004 |
| 1995 | 92 | 1997 | 2000 |
| 1994 | 94 | 1996 | 1999 |

## RESERVE PINOT NOIR

| Mornington Peninsula | $30–$49 |
|---|---|
| **Current vintage: 2002** | **88** |

Dusty, leafy aromas of cherries and slightly stewed plums are tightly integrated with restrained scents of cedary chocolate/vanilla oak. Forward and rather intense, its slightly meaty and pruney palate does present some sweet currant, plum and berry flavours, offering a good length of velvet-like texture.

| 2002 | 88 | 2004 | 2007 |
|---|---|---|---|
| 2001 | 89 | 2003 | 2006 |
| 2000 | 85 | 2002 | 2005 |
| 1998 | 91 | 2000 | 2003+ |
| 1997 | 95 | 2002 | 2005+ |
| 1996 | 94 | 2001 | 2005+ |
| 1995 | 93 | 2000 | 2003+ |

# Elderton

3–5 Tanunda Road, Nuriootpa SA 5355. Tel: (08) 8562 1058. Fax: (08) 8562 2844.
Website: www.eldertonwines.com.au  Email: elderton@eldertonwines.com.au
Region: **Barossa Valley** Winemaker: **Richard Langford** Viticulturist: **David Young**
Chief Executive: **Lorraine Ashmead**

Elderton is an honest and consistent maker of generously flavoured, fully-ripened and lavishly oaked red wines that have proven to be immensely poplar around the world. They're remarkably consistent and will never fail to please a customer who has enjoyed them before. There has however been a recent change in winemaking personnel behind Elderton's wines, and I'm very interested to discover whether or not this will have any discernible effect on the company's winemaking philosophy.

## ASHMEAD CABERNET SAUVIGNON

| Barossa Valley | $50+ |
|---|---|
| **Current vintage: 2000** | **88** |

Juicy, fleshy cabernet whose lifted aromas of blue-berries, cassis and plums are somewhat over-shadowed by sweet mocha and ashtray-like oak influences. Its intense palate of cassis/plum flavour is supported by creamy, mocha oak and framed by fine, lightly sappy tannins.

| 2000 | 88 | 2002 | 2005+ |
|---|---|---|---|
| 1999 | 89 | 2007 | 2011+ |
| 1998 | 89 | 2006 | 2010 |

## CABERNET SAUVIGNON

**Barossa Valley** $20–$29
**Current vintage: 2001** 86

Very forward, ultra-ripe style with a developed bouquet of prune-like fruit to which coconut-like American oak contributes some sweetness. There's a leathery note also present on the palate, whose up-front flavours of plums, prunes and currants become lean and hollow, before a rather gritty finish. Like many 2001s, it just lacks vibrant fruit.

| | | | |
|---|---|---|---|
| 2001 | 86 | 2003 | 2006 |
| 2000 | 89 | 2005 | 2008 |
| 1999 | 87 | 2004 | 2007 |
| 1998 | 91 | 2003 | 2006 |
| 1997 | 87 | 1999 | 2002+ |
| 1996 | 89 | 2001 | 2004 |
| 1995 | 88 | 2000 | 2003 |
| 1994 | 93 | 1999 | 2002 |
| 1993 | 91 | 1998 | 2001 |
| 1992 | 88 | 1997 | 2000 |
| 1991 | 91 | 1996 | 1999 |

## COMMAND SHIRAZ

**Barossa Valley** $50+
**Current vintage: 2000** 93

I was genuinely surprised by this wine, coming as it does from such a difficult season. It's more restrained but also more driven by genuinely ripe fruit than recent vintages, with an attractive spread of smoky, lightly meaty flavours of raspberries and plum jam. Look further and you'll see suggestions of cassis, prunes and currants, with some herbal edges over some charry vanilla oak. It's very smooth, rich and generous, wrapped in silky tannins. Quite a classy expression of its style, and sure to please many people.

| | | | |
|---|---|---|---|
| 2000 | 93 | 2008 | 2012+ |
| 1999 | 90 | 2004 | 2007 |
| 1998 | 89 | 2006 | 2010 |
| 1997 | 83 | 2002 | 2005 |
| 1996 | 89 | 2004 | 2008 |
| 1995 | 91 | 2003 | 2007 |
| 1994 | 94 | 2002 | 2006 |
| 1993 | 89 | 2001 | 2005 |
| 1992 | 95 | 2000 | 2004+ |
| 1990 | 92 | 1995 | 1998 |
| 1988 | 87 | 1996 | 2000 |
| 1987 | 94 | 1999 | 2004 |
| 1986 | 92 | 1998 | 2003 |

## CSM CABERNET SAUVIGNON SHIRAZ MERLOT

**Barossa Valley** $30–$49
**Current vintage: 2000** 86

A fast developing red with a leathery, tobaccoey bouquet with some earthy greenish undertones. Rather herbal small red berry flavours finish thin and sappy, excessively reliant on its sweet vanilla /chocolate oak.

| | | | |
|---|---|---|---|
| 2000 | 86 | 2002 | 2005 |
| 1999 | 90 | 2004 | 2007+ |
| 1998 | 86 | 2003 | 2006 |
| 1997 | 88 | 1999 | 2002 |
| 1996 | 87 | 2001 | 2004 |
| 1995 | 88 | 1998 | 2001 |
| 1994 | 90 | 1999 | 2002 |

## SHIRAZ

**Barossa Valley** $12–$19
**Current vintage: 2002** 89

Smooth, soft and approachable Barossa shiraz with a vibrant, briary aroma of violets, cassis, sweet plums and dark cherries lifted by a spicy whiff of white pepper, mint and menthol. The sweet oak is also evident on the palate, but remains smooth and creamy, leaving the vibrant, juicy flavours of cassis and raspberries, plums and blueberries attractively uncluttered. Ready to enjoy, it's long, willowy and silky.

| | | | |
|---|---|---|---|
| 2002 | 89 | 2004 | 2007+ |
| 2001 | 89 | 2003 | 2006+ |
| 2000 | 90 | 2005 | 2008 |
| 1999 | 83 | 2001 | 2004 |
| 1998 | 90 | 2003 | 2006 |
| 1997 | 87 | 1999 | 2002 |
| 1996 | 87 | 1998 | 2003+ |
| 1995 | 90 | 2000 | 2003 |
| 1994 | 89 | 1999 | 2002 |
| 1993 | 90 | 1995 | 1998 |
| 1992 | 88 | 2000 | 2004 |
| 1991 | 90 | 1999 | 2003 |

# Elsewhere Vineyard

42 Dillons Hill Road, Glaziers Bay Tas 7109. Tel: (03) 6295 1228. Fax: (03) 6295 1591.
Website: www.elsewherevineyard.com  Email: andrew@elsewherevineyard.com
Region: **Southern Tasmania** Winemakers: **Andrew Hood, Steve Lubiana** Viticulturist: **Andrew Cameron**
Chief Executive: **Andrew Cameron**
A tiny Tasmanian vineyard capable of joyously vibrant and elegant pinot noir, Elsewhere has also produced some of the country's finest and most intensely flavoured sparkling wines.

## PINOT NOIR

RANKING **5**

| Southern Tasmania | $30–$49 |
|---|---|
| Current vintage: 2002 | 80 |

Rather herbal and geranium-scented, with light, confection-like flavours or red cherries and raspberries supported by vanilla oak. Finishes sappy, needing more fruit and structure.

| | | | |
|---|---|---|---|
| 2002 | 80 | 2004 | 2007 |
| 2001 | 85 | 2003 | 2006 |
| 2000 | 89 | 2002 | 2005+ |
| 1999 | 82 | 2000 | 2001 |
| 1998 | 88 | 2000 | 2003+ |
| 1995 | 89 | 1997 | 2000+ |
| 1994 | 92 | 1999 | 2002 |

# Epis

812 Black Forest Drive, Woodend Vic 3442. Tel: (03) 5427 1204. Fax: (03) 5427 1204  Email: domaineepis@iprimus.com
Region: **Macedon Ranges** Winemaker: **Stuart Anderson** Viticulturist: **Alec Epis** Chief Executive: **Alec Epis**
Sourcing fruit from the pinot noir and chardonnay vineyard he planted himself near Woodend as well as the original Flynn & Williams cabernet sauvignon plantings at Kyneton (to which he has added some merlot), former Australian football legend Alec Epis is cultivating some of Victoria's finest cool climate fruit. Stuart Anderson, an Australian wine legend and the founder of Balgownie, is the Epis winemaker, and right now he's making some of the best wine of his life.

## CHARDONNAY

RANKING **2**

| Macedon Ranges | $30–$49 |
|---|---|
| Current vintage: 2003 | 95 |

Tangy, long and mineral chardonnay with an intense fragrance of white peaches, nectarines and grapefruit backed by hints of honeysuckle and cashew, cloves and cinnamon, with tightly integrated buttery/vanilla oak. Fine and shapely, in a Macon-like style, its flavour builds in the mouth towards a powerful crescendo of ripe stonefruit and citrus, finishing long and savoury with crackly, refreshing acidity.

| | | | |
|---|---|---|---|
| 2003 | 95 | 2008 | 2011 |
| 2001 | 96 | 2006 | 2009+ |
| 2000 | 95 | 2005 | 2008+ |
| 1998 | 95 | 2003 | 2006+ |

## EPIS & WILLIAMS CABERNET SAUVIGNON

RANKING **3**

| Macedon Ranges | $30–$49 |
|---|---|
| Current vintage: 2003 | 93 |

Lightly herbal and minty central Victorian cabernet with a fragrance of raspberries, cassis and plums tightly knit with sweet cedar/vanilla/chocolate oak. Fine and elegant, smooth and willowy, it's a vibrant and deeply flavoured wine of smoothness and approachability, harmoniously structured around fine tannins and restrained oak.

| | | | |
|---|---|---|---|
| 2003 | 93 | 2011 | 2015+ |
| 2002 | 89 | 2007 | 2010+ |
| 2001 | 94 | 2013 | 2021 |
| 2000 | 95 | 2008 | 2012+ |
| 1999 | 93 | 2007 | 2011+ |

## PINOT NOIR

RANKING **2**

| Macedon Ranges | $30–$49 |
|---|---|
| Current vintage: 2003 | 96 |

Deeply flavoured but fine and elegant, a fragrant pinot noir with a musky rose petal aroma of red cherries and forest floor, with earthy undertones of duck fat. Smooth, supple and silky, its pristine palate of cherry/raspberry flavour is framed by fine-grained and bony tannins, finishing with exceptional length of fruit.

| | | | |
|---|---|---|---|
| 2003 | 96 | 2008 | 2011 |
| 2001 | 96 | 2006 | 2009+ |
| 2000 | 96 | 2005 | 2008+ |
| 1998 | 95 | 2003 | 2006+ |

# Evans Family

Broke Road, Pokolbin NSW 2320. Tel: (02) 4998 7237. Fax: (02) 4998 7798.
Email: evansfamilywines@bigpond.com

Region: **Lower Hunter Valley** Winemaker: **Keith Tulloch** Viticulturist: **Alan Townley** Chief Executive: **Len Evans**

Evans Family Wines is a small Hunter producer whose range includes such interesting diversities as a local Gamay and Pinot Noir, but whose premier wines are its Shiraz and richly textured Chardonnay.

## CHARDONNAY                                    RANKING 5

| Lower Hunter Valley | $30–$49 |
|---|---|
| **Current vintage: 2003** | **85** |

Soft, early-maturing chardonnay whose forward, tobaccoey flavours of cumquat and quince, melon and green olives are underpinned by sweet, buttery and slightly varnishy vanilla oak.

| | | | |
|---|---|---|---|
| 2003 | 85 | 2005 | 2008 |
| 2002 | 88 | 2004 | 2007+ |
| 1999 | 80 | 2000 | 2001 |
| 1998 | 91 | 2003 | 2006 |
| 1997 | 89 | 2002 | 2005 |
| 1996 | 95 | 2001 | 2004 |
| 1995 | 94 | 2003 | 2007 |
| 1994 | 89 | 1999 | 2002 |
| 1993 | 93 | 1998 | 2001 |
| 1990 | 91 | 1992 | 1995 |

# Evans & Tate

cnr Caves & Metricup Rds Willyabrup WA 6280. Tel: (08) 9755 6244. Fax: (08) 9755 6346.
Website: www.evansandtate.com.au  Email: et@evansandtate.com.au

Region: **Margaret River** Winemaker: **Richard Rowe** Viticulturist: **Murray Edmonds**
Chief Executive: **Franklin Tate**

Australia's eighth largest Australian wine company is on a fast growth track. Still caught in the space between medium-sized and substantial, it has taken good initiatives by securing its own distribution channels in key markets such as the US. The current crop of releases, with the notable exception of the 1998 Cabernet Sauvignon, do not quite live up to the expectations generated by the company's own previous success.

## GNANGARA SHIRAZ                                    RANKING 5

| Swan Valley | $12–$19 |
|---|---|
| **Current vintage: 2002** | **82** |

Light, inoffensive red with simple confectionary-like red berry flavours, light vanilla/cedary oak and a whiff of spiciness. Soft, gentle and approachable, with a slightly sappy chassis of green-edged tannins and soft acids.

| | | | |
|---|---|---|---|
| 2002 | 82 | 2003 | 2004 |
| 2000 | 87 | 2002 | 2005 |
| 1999 | 80 | 2000 | 2000 |
| 1998 | 88 | 2000 | 2003+ |
| 1997 | 80 | 1999 | 2002 |
| 1996 | 89 | 1998 | 2001 |

## MARGARET RIVER CABERNET SAUVIGNON            RANKING 4

| Margaret River | $30–$49 |
|---|---|
| **Current vintage: 1998** | **93** |

Firm, quite astringent cabernet that needs plenty of time in the glass. Its pungent, cedary, smoky aromas of blackberry jam, plums and violets precede a sumptuous and well-structured wine whose rich expression of dark berry flavours is framed by firm, if very slightly tough tannins.

| | | | |
|---|---|---|---|
| 1998 | 93 | 2006 | 2010 |
| 1997 | 87 | 2002 | 2005 |
| 1996 | 90 | 2004 | 2008 |
| 1995 | 86 | 2003 | 2007 |
| 1994 | 84 | 1996 | 1999 |
| 1993 | 93 | 2001 | 2005 |
| 1992 | 94 | 2000 | 2004 |
| 1991 | 93 | 1999 | 2003 |

## MARGARET RIVER CLASSIC                            RANKING 5

| Margaret River | $12–$19 |
|---|---|
| **Current vintage: 2003** | **86** |

Leafy aromas of gooseberries, passionfruit and melon precede a forward, juicy palate of moderate intensity that begins with the customary fleshy texture, but then thins out to rather a greenish finish.

| | | | |
|---|---|---|---|
| 2003 | 86 | 2003 | 2003 |
| 2002 | 88 | 2002 | 2003 |
| 2001 | 82 | 2001 | 2002 |
| 2000 | 89 | 2000 | 2000 |

## MARGARET RIVER MERLOT

RANKING **4**

**Margaret River** $30–$49
**Current vintage: 2001** 82

Firm, uncomplicated and drying merlot whose simple cooked and confection-like berry/cherry and plum aromas and jammy, astringent palate are already past their best.

| | | | |
|---|---|---|---|
| 2001 | 82 | 2002 | 2003+ |
| 1999 | 92 | 2004 | 2007 |
| 1998 | 91 | 2006 | 2010 |
| 1996 | 91 | 2004 | 2010 |
| 1995 | 89 | 2000 | 2003 |
| 1994 | 89 | 1999 | 2002 |
| 1993 | 90 | 2001 | 2005 |
| 1992 | 90 | 1997 | 2000 |
| 1991 | 94 | 1999 | 2003 |
| 1990 | 93 | 1998 | 2002 |
| 1989 | 92 | 1994 | 1997 |
| 1988 | 88 | 1993 | 1996 |

## MARGARET RIVER SAUVIGNON BLANC SEMILLON

RANKING **4**

**Margaret River** $30–$49
**Current vintage: 2003** 88

Mainstream Margaret River white blend whose dusty, herbal aromas of melon and gooseberries are lifted by lightly spicy, toasty vanilla oak. Long, smooth and grassy, its generous, succulent palate presents attractive depth of fruit and refreshing acidity, while its oak is perhaps a shade splintery.

| | | | |
|---|---|---|---|
| 2003 | 88 | 2003 | 2006+ |
| 2002 | 89 | 2003 | 2004+ |
| 2000 | 90 | 2000 | 2000 |
| 1999 | 90 | 2000 | 2000 |
| 1998 | 90 | 1999 | 2000 |

## MARGARET RIVER SEMILLON

RANKING **4**

**Margaret River** $20–$29
**Current vintage: 2003** 86

Dusty, leafy and asparagusy, pepper and nettle-like aromas of shaded fruit are lifted by scents of passionfruit and lemon, but rather flattened by some assertively charry vanilla oak. Oily, coarse and vegetal, the palate is lightly tropical and rather oaky, finishing slightly sweet without sufficiently refreshing acidity.

| | | | |
|---|---|---|---|
| 2003 | 86 | 2004 | 2005+ |
| 2002 | 84 | 2004 | 2007 |
| 2001 | 90 | 2003 | 2006 |
| 2000 | 90 | 2005 | 2008 |
| 1997 | 94 | 2002 | 2005+ |
| 1996 | 91 | 1998 | 2001 |
| 1995 | 94 | 2000 | 2003 |
| 1994 | 93 | 1999 | 2002 |
| 1993 | 94 | 2001 | 2005 |

## MARGARET RIVER SHIRAZ

RANKING **4**

**Margaret River** $30–$49
**Current vintage: 2002** 87

Lightly smoky, peppery aromas of red and black plums and berries set against a background of cedary oak. Restrained and elegant, lacking any real punch, it's an honest if rather simple shiraz whose jammy berry flavours are offset by sweet smoky oak and framed by slightly sappy tannins.

| | | | |
|---|---|---|---|
| 2002 | 87 | 2004 | 2007+ |
| 2001 | 90 | 2006 | 2009 |
| 2000 | 90 | 2005 | 2008 |
| 1999 | 90 | 2004 | 2007 |
| 1998 | 91 | 2003 | 2006+ |
| 1997 | 89 | 2005 | 2009 |
| 1996 | 90 | 2004 | 2008 |
| 1995 | 92 | 2007 | 2015 |
| 1994 | 94 | 2002 | 2006 |
| 1993 | 86 | 2001 | 2005 |
| 1992 | 93 | 2000 | 2004 |
| 1991 | 93 | 1999 | 2003 |

A
B
C
D
E
F
G
H
I
J
K
L
M
N
O
P
Q
R
S
T
U
V
W
X
Y
Z

# Ferngrove

Ferngrove Road, Frankland WA 6396. Tel: (08) 9227 8506. Fax: (08) 9227 9742.
Website: www.ferngrove.com.au Email: info@ferngrove.com.au

Region: **Frankland River** Winemaker: **Kim Horton** Viticulturist: **Wayne Barnett** Chief Executive: **Murray Burton**

Ferngrove is an aggressive and relatively young Frankland River-based producer whose management decided to address export markets before establishing a beachhead in Australia itself. The strategy has worked, and today Ferngrove makes and sells good volumes of distinctive and regional wine made by Kim Horton.

## COSSACK RIESLING

RANKING

| Frankland River | $20–$29 |
| --- | --- |
| **Current vintage: 2004** | **88** |

Floral and limey aromas of apple and pear reveal dusty notes of minerals and youthful sulphide pongs that should soon diminish. Long, fine and even, its tightly knit and chalky palate of pear/apple flavours finishes totally dry with lingering citrus notes. Likely to develop well.

| | | | |
| --- | --- | --- | --- |
| 2004 | 88 | 2012 | 2016 |
| 2003 | 90 | 2005 | 2008 |
| 2002 | 94 | 2007 | 2010+ |
| 2001 | 86 | 2003 | 2006 |

# Fire Gully

Caves Road, Willyabrup WA 6280. Tel: (08) 9755 6220. Fax: (08) 9755 6308.

Region: **Margaret River** Winemaker: **Mike Peterkin** Viticulturist: **Mike Peterkin** Chief Executive: **Mike Peterkin**

Fire Gully is a long-established Margaret River brand bought by Pierro's Mike Peterkin in 1998. Its vineyard is kept entirely separate from Pierro's own production, and is responsible for a steadily improving series of reds, along with some punchy dry whites from semillon and sauvignon blanc.

## CABERNET SAUVIGNON MERLOT

RANKING 5

| Margaret River | $20–$29 |
| --- | --- |
| **Current vintage: 2001** | **90** |

A herbal, floral and earthy regional Margaret River blend whose lightly confectionary expression of cassis, raspberries and plums is wound around firm, fine and drying bony tannins. Sweet vanilla oak lifts its aroma, while it finishes with pleasing length of pristine fruit and attractive balance.

| | | | |
| --- | --- | --- | --- |
| 2001 | 90 | 2009 | 2013+ |
| 2000 | 89 | 2002 | 2005+ |
| 1999 | 86 | 2004 | 2007 |
| 1998 | 89 | 2000 | 2003 |
| 1997 | 82 | 1999 | 2002+ |

# Flinders Bay

Wilson Road, Karridale WA 6288. Tel: (08) 9757 6281. Fax: (08) 9757 6353. Email: winecor@tpgi.com.au

Region: **Margaret River** Viticulturist: **Alastair Gillespie** Chief Executive: **Bill Ireland & Alastair Gillespie**

Flinders Bay is a maker of red and white wines from its cool Margaret River vineyard which includes a firm, but deeply fruited Merlot, a musky and licorice-like Shiraz and its herbal and lively Pericles white blend.

## PERICLES SAUVIGNON BLANC SEMILLON

RANKING 5

| Margaret River | $12–$19 |
| --- | --- |
| **Current vintage: 2003** | **87** |

Pungent, slightly sweaty aromas of grassy capsicum, asparagus, squashed melon and gooseberries, before a punchy, ripe and oily palate. Despite some richness and roundness, the fruit is just a little too peppery and herbaceous; while the finish is clean enough, but just a little too cloying.

| | | | |
| --- | --- | --- | --- |
| 2003 | 87 | 2003 | 2004 |
| 2002 | 87 | 2003 | 2004 |
| 2001 | 84 | 2002 | 2003 |
| 1999 | 91 | 2000 | 2001 |

# Fox Creek

Malpas Road, Willunga SA 5171. Tel: (08) 8556 2403. Fax: (08) 8556 2104.
Website: www.foxcreekwines.com  Email: sales@foxcreekwines.com
Region: **McLaren Vale**  Winemakers: **Chris Dix and Tony Walker**  Viticulturist: **Paul Watts**
Chief Executives: **Jim and Helen Watts**

Fox Creek is emerging as a mature wine company with strong convictions on style and quality. As the scores below illustrate, it performs at a consistently high quality level across a number of varieties, and from time to time can produce wines of top class. Its flagship Reserve Shiraz has found a niche that offers something very positive to both enthusiasts of ultra-ripe shiraz as well as those who enjoy more finesse and balance.

## JSM SHIRAZ CABERNET FRANC

RANKING **4**

| McLaren Vale | $20–$29 |
|---|---|
| **Current vintage: 2002** | **88** |

Vibrant, intense early-drinking wine whose lightly spicy and meaty aromas of blackberries, plums and cedar/vanilla oak precede a smooth and supple palate framed by slightly sappy tannins. Lively, translucent redcurrant, blackcurrant and plum-like flavours reveal good fruit sweetness and a hint of confection.

| | | | |
|---|---|---|---|
| 2002 | 88 | 2004 | 2007+ |
| 2001 | 91 | 2003 | 2006+ |
| 2000 | 90 | 2002 | 2005+ |
| 1999 | 89 | 2001 | 2004 |
| 1998 | 89 | 2003 | 2006 |
| 1997 | 87 | 1999 | 2002 |
| 1996 | 84 | 1998 | 2001+ |

## RESERVE CABERNET SAUVIGNON

RANKING **4**

| McLaren Vale | $30–$49 |
|---|---|
| **Current vintage: 2002** | **92** |

Very powerful and structured cabernet that marries its Amarone-like qualities with a deep core of more vibrant and intense fruit. There's a meaty, earthy aspect to its aromas of prunes, currants and dark olives, plums and chocolate oak, while the sweet plum, dark olive and cassis flavours on the palate appear slightly cooked. However there's plenty of power, fruit depth and balance. Given time it should certainly flesh out well.

| | | | |
|---|---|---|---|
| 2002 | 92 | 2010 | 2014+ |
| 2001 | 92 | 2009 | 2013+ |
| 2000 | 89 | 2005 | 2008 |
| 1999 | 90 | 2004 | 2007+ |
| 1998 | 89 | 2006 | 2010 |
| 1997 | 90 | 2005 | 2009+ |
| 1996 | 92 | 2004 | 2008+ |
| 1995 | 88 | 2000 | 2003 |

## RESERVE MERLOT

RANKING **4**

| McLaren Vale | $30–$49 |
|---|---|
| **Current vintage: 2001** | **92** |

Firm, generous and honest merlot with a fresh and lightly perfumed bouquet of black and red cherries and sweet, smoky vanilla and mocha oak. Its vibrant, up-front flavours of dark cherries, plums and cassis then reveal more interesting nuances of licorice, tar and game meats. Framed by fine-grained but drying tannins, it finishes with lingering clove and nutmeg-like flavours with balanced chocolate/vanilla oak.

| | | | |
|---|---|---|---|
| 2001 | 92 | 2006 | 2009 |
| 2000 | 90 | 2005 | 2008+ |
| 1999 | 88 | 2001 | 2004 |
| 1998 | 87 | 2003 | 2006+ |
| 1997 | 87 | 2002 | 2005+ |

## RESERVE SHIRAZ

RANKING **3**

| McLaren Vale | $50+ |
|---|---|
| **Current vintage: 2002** | **93** |

Firm, long and very smooth shiraz that holds its 15% of alcohol with relative ease. Its peppery, spicy fragrance is a complex one, with briary blackberry, cassis and slightly meaty aromas of dark olives offset by sweet milk chocolate and vanilla oak. Very intense and assertive, its long, smooth palate of deep blackberry, redcurrant and dark plum flavours is bound by fine, yet firm tannins. There's some spirity warmth, plus a suggestion of tarry, spicy currant-like flavour. Long and complete, it finishes with just a hint of mint and menthol.

| | | | |
|---|---|---|---|
| 2002 | 93 | 2010 | 2014+ |
| 2001 | 96 | 2013 | 2021 |
| 2000 | 88 | 2005 | 2008 |
| 1999 | 95 | 2007 | 2011+ |
| 1998 | 90 | 2003 | 2006+ |
| 1997 | 88 | 2002 | 2005+ |
| 1996 | 95 | 2008 | 2016 |
| 1995 | 89 | 1997 | 2002 |
| 1994 | 94 | 2006 | 2014 |

## SHORT ROW SHIRAZ

| McLaren Vale | $20–$29 |
|---|---|
| **Current vintage: 2002** | **88** |

Slightly clunky, clumsy and overcooked shiraz with a meaty, menthol-like aroma of cassis and currants before a plush, plump palate of rather subdued intensity, finishing slightly flat and lacking in vitality.

| 2002 | 88 | 2004 | 2007 |
|---|---|---|---|
| 2001 | 91 | 2003 | 2006+ |
| 2000 | 87 | 2002 | 2005 |
| 1999 | 90 | 2001 | 2004 |

## VERDELHO

| McLaren Vale | $12–$19 |
|---|---|
| **Current vintage: 2003** | **90** |

A refreshing, chalky Verdelho with a citrusy aroma of melon, lemon and herbal influences, with a suggestion of soapy detergent. It's rich and concentrated, with a pleasing length of vibrant melon/citrus fruit finishing long and tangy with mineral acidity. Good shape and varietal quality.

| 2003 | 90 | 2004 | 2005+ |
|---|---|---|---|
| 2002 | 86 | 2003 | 2004 |
| 2001 | 86 | 2002 | 2003+ |
| 2000 | 82 | 2001 | 2002 |

# Frankland Estate

Frankland Road, Frankland WA 6396. Tel: (08) 9855 1544. Fax: (08) 9855 1549.
Email: info@franklandestate.com.au

Region: **Frankland River** Winemakers: **Barrie Smith, Judi Cullam** Viticulturist: **Elizabeth Smith**
Chief Executives: **Barrie Smith, Judi Cullam**

Frankland Estate's leadership stance on riesling is paying off handsomely, with some excellent releases under the Cooladerra, Poison Hill, Rivermist and Isolation Ridge vineyard labels. These wines are steadily gaining in aromaticity and fineness, occasionally finishing with austerity reminiscent of leading Austrian examples. The red wines appear to tire quickly, tending to lack intensity of fruit, sweetness, depth and structure.

## ISOLATION RIDGE CABERNET SAUVIGNON

| Frankland River | $20–$29 |
|---|---|
| **Current vintage: 2001** | **83** |

Astringent, drying red with a minty, green-edged and varnishy aspect about its plum-like fruit. Its overly cigarboxy oak could use a little more freshness, while it finishes flat and rather gritty.

| 2001 | 83 | 2006 | 2009 |
|---|---|---|---|
| 1998 | 84 | 2003 | 2006 |
| 1997 | 89 | 2002 | 2005 |
| 1996 | 91 | 2008 | 2016 |
| 1995 | 87 | 2007 | 2015 |
| 1994 | 87 | 1999 | 2002 |
| 1993 | 91 | 2005 | 2013 |
| 1992 | 88 | 1997 | 2000 |
| 1991 | 88 | 1996 | 1999 |

## ISOLATION RIDGE CHARDONNAY

| Frankland River | $20–$29 |
|---|---|
| **Current vintage: 2002** | **84** |

Tiring, butyric aromas of rather beer-like cumquat and melon fruit with pungent cheesy, leesy complexity. Its pleasing quince/cumquat fruit is steadily replaced down the palate by rather stale buttery/vanilla oak, before a flat, cardboard-like finish.

| 2002 | 84 | 2004 | 2007 |
|---|---|---|---|
| 2001 | 90 | 2003 | 2006 |
| 2000 | 77 | 2002 | 2005 |
| 1999 | 85 | 2001 | 2004 |
| 1998 | 80 | 1999 | 2000 |
| 1997 | 87 | 2002 | 2005 |
| 1996 | 87 | 2001 | 2004 |
| 1994 | 94 | 1992 | 2002 |
| 1993 | 85 | 1998 | 2001 |
| 1992 | 88 | 1994 | 1997 |

## ISOLATION RIDGE RIESLING

RANKING **3**

**Frankland River**  $20–$29
**Current vintage: 2003**  93

Refreshing, sculpted and stylish riesling with obvious Austrian connotations. Its delicate floral perfume of limejuice and wet slate precedes an austere and shapely palate whose powdery texture culminates in a dry, lingering slatey finish. It finishes with a bright, persistent core of tangy acidity and citrus/stonefruit flavour.

| | | | |
|---|---|---|---|
| 2003 | 93 | 2008 | 2011+ |
| 2002 | 89 | 2004 | 2007 |
| 2001 | 95 | 2006 | 2009+ |
| 2000 | 93 | 2005 | 2008 |
| 1999 | 85 | 2001 | 2004 |
| 1998 | 93 | 2006 | 2010 |
| 1997 | 88 | 2002 | 2005 |
| 1996 | 91 | 2001 | 2004 |
| 1995 | 91 | 2000 | 2003 |
| 1994 | 88 | 1999 | 2002 |
| 1993 | 87 | 1995 | 1998 |
| 1992 | 89 | 1997 | 2000 |
| 1991 | 90 | 1993 | 1996 |

## ISOLATION RIDGE SHIRAZ

**Frankland River**  $20–$29
**Current vintage: 2001**  81

Tired, stale and meaty, revealing cooked and herbal fruit with vegetal undertones. Restrained plum and cassis flavours are underpinned by a greenish thread of vegetal and dried herb influences, finishing a little short and raw. It appears to have been made from very stressed fruit.

| | | | |
|---|---|---|---|
| 2001 | 81 | 2003 | 2006 |
| 2000 | 77 | 2002 | 2005 |
| 1999 | 82 | 2001 | 2004 |
| 1998 | 86 | 2003 | 2006 |
| 1997 | 84 | 2002 | 2005 |
| 1996 | 89 | 2001 | 2004 |
| 1995 | 90 | 2000 | 2003 |
| 1994 | 91 | 1999 | 2002 |
| 1993 | 87 | 2001 | 2005 |
| 1992 | 88 | 2000 | 2004 |

## OLMO'S REWARD

RANKING **5**

**Frankland River**  $30–$49
**Current vintage: 2001**  82

Ageing, reductive and leathery red with some creamy smoothness, but a thin, green and tiring finish. Very advanced for its age.

| | | | |
|---|---|---|---|
| 2001 | 82 | 2003 | 2006 |
| 2000 | 82 | 2005 | 2008 |
| 1998 | 91 | 2006 | 2010 |
| 1997 | 82 | 2002 | 2005 |
| 1996 | 83 | 2001 | 2004 |
| 1995 | 95 | 2007 | 2015 |
| 1994 | 88 | 2002 | 2006 |
| 1993 | 91 | 1998 | 2001 |
| 1992 | 90 | 1997 | 2000 |

# Freycinet Vineyard

15919 Tasman Highway, Bicheno Tas 7215. Tel: (03) 6257 8574. Fax: (03) 6257 8454.
Email: freycinetwines@tassie.net.au

Region: **East Coast Tasmania** Winemaker: **Claudio Radenti** Viticulturists: **Claudio Radenti & Lindy Bull**
Chief Executive: **Geoff Bull**

One of Tasmania's finest vineyards, Freycinet's wine is made by a very talented guy in Claudio Radenti, whose recent efforts with the Cabernet Merlot, Pinot Noir and Riesling present a consistency still rare in wine from this state. At its best, Freycinet's willowy and fragrant Pinot Noir is one of the country's most complex and convincing.

## CABERNET MERLOT

RANKING **3**

**East Coast Tasmania**  $30–$49
**Current vintage: 2001**  88

Earthy, herbal aromas of confection-like jammy fruit precede a slightly lean, green and hard-edged palate of full to medium weight. There's some pleasing fruit sweetness, structure and richness, but its flavours of plums and cherries are a little too green-edged to cure the wine of its sappy leanness.

| | | | |
|---|---|---|---|
| 2001 | 88 | 2006 | 2009 |
| 2000 | 95 | 2012 | 2020 |
| 1999 | 89 | 2005 | 2007+ |
| 1998 | 93 | 2006 | 2010+ |
| 1997 | 87 | 2002 | 2005 |
| 1995 | 87 | 2000 | 2003 |
| 1994 | 94 | 2002 | 2006 |

## CHARDONNAY

**East Coast Tasmania**    $30–$49
**Current vintage: 2002**    87

Pleasing shorter-term, if surprisingly sugary chardonnay with some apparently botrytis-derived influences. Its lightly smoky bouquet of tropical fruits, cumquat, fig, melon and nutmeal overlies some creamy, leesy complexity and newish oak character. Slightly herby and tinny, its palate reveals pineapple, apricot and melon flavours that are just beginning to break up a little at the finish.

| | | | |
|---|---|---|---|
| 2002 | 87 | 2004 | 2007 |
| 2001 | 88 | 2003 | 2006 |
| 2000 | 87 | 2002 | 2005 |
| 1999 | 93 | 2004 | 2007 |
| 1998 | 90 | 2000 | 2003+ |
| 1997 | 87 | 1999 | 2002 |
| 1996 | 89 | 1998 | 2001 |
| 1995 | 95 | 2003 | 2007 |
| 1994 | 93 | 2002 | 2006 |

## PINOT NOIR

RANKING 2

**East Coast Tasmania**    $50+
**Current vintage: 2002**    90

Delicate, lightly herbal and stalky aromas of raspberries, cherries, blackberries and plums with an underlying meatiness and floral perfume. Ripe, juicy and assertive, with intense, positive primary flavour bound by firm, grippy tannins and tart acidity. A fuller, riper and blockier style for this vineyard, lacking customary focus, but likely to flesh out in time.

| | | | |
|---|---|---|---|
| 2002 | 90 | 2007 | 2010+ |
| 2001 | 95 | 2006 | 2009+ |
| 2000 | 92 | 2005 | 2008 |
| 1999 | 93 | 2004 | 2007+ |
| 1998 | 95 | 2006 | 2010 |
| 1997 | 93 | 2005 | 2009 |
| 1996 | 89 | 2001 | 2004 |
| 1995 | 93 | 2000 | 2003+ |
| 1994 | 95 | 1999 | 2002+ |

## RIESLING

RANKING 3

**East Coast Tasmania**    $20–$29
**Current vintage: 2003**    95

Intense, penetrative slate/mineral aromas with a floral perfume and slightly leesy, funky primary aromas of apples and limes. Bracingly austere, the palate is long and racy, presenting fresh and perfectly defined citrus fruits culminating in a taut and steely finish of mineral acids. Give it time.

| | | | |
|---|---|---|---|
| 2003 | 95 | 2011 | 2015+ |
| 2002 | 93 | 2007 | 2010 |
| 2001 | 88 | 2003 | 2006+ |
| 2000 | 95 | 2005 | 2008 |
| 1999 | 92 | 2004 | 2007 |
| 1998 | 94 | 2006 | 2010 |

# Gapsted

Great Alpine Road, Gapsted Vic 3737. Tel: (03) 5751 1383. Fax: (03) 5751 1368.
website: www.gapstedwines.com.au  Email: admin@gapstedwines.com.au

Region: **Alpine Valleys** Winemaker: **Shayne Cunningham & Michael Cope-Williams**
Viticulturist: **Stephen Lowe** Chief Executive: **Shayne Cunningham**

Gapsted is the brand owned by a contract wine producer in northern Victoria, the Victorian Alps Wine Company, whose wines feature the canopy system chosen to maximise sunlight penetration and fruit exposure in this chilly segment of the viticultural world. The often silky-fine and tightly structured Cabernet Sauvignon is usually the best of these wines. Gapsted also releases one of the few Australian wines made from saperavi.

## BALLERINA CANOPY CABERNET SAUVIGNON

RANKING 4

**East Coast Tasmania**    $20–$29
**Current vintage: 2001**    88

Elegant, smooth and cedary red with a lightly herbal, minty aroma of red berries, cherries and plums supported by restrained vanilla oak. Supple and tight-knit, its palate is more powerful than the nose would suggest, presenting intense small red and black berry fruit entwined with creamy cedary oak and framed by tight-knit tannins.

| | | | |
|---|---|---|---|
| 2001 | 88 | 2006 | 2009+ |
| 2000 | 92 | 2008 | 2012+ |
| 1999 | 87 | 2007 | 2011 |
| 1998 | 90 | 2006 | 2010+ |

# Garry Crittenden 'i'

RMB 555 Old Moorooduc Road, Tuerong, Vic 3915. Tel: (03) 9600 3242. Fax: (03) 9600 3245.
Website: www.dromanaestate.com.au  Email: info@dromanaestate.com.au
Region: **Alpine Valleys** Winemaker: **Rollo Crittenden** Viticulturist: **Rollo Crittenden**
Chief Executive: **Richard Green**
Made by Dromana Estate, this range of Italian varieties is usually the country's best and most convincing collection
of its kind. Like all Australian efforts with these varieties, the concept is still very much a 'work in progress',
but as a group the wines reliably display genuinely varietal flavours and textures.

## 'i' ARNEIS

RANKING **5**

**Alpine Valleys**                    $20–$29
**Current vintage: 2003**                  **90**

A punchy varietal wine whose fresh aromas of pear,
apple and peach reveal a hint of chalk and
mineral. Luscious, round and smooth, just fractionally
hot, with lingering pear/apple fruit culminating
in a tangy mineral finish. Bigger and rounder than
previous releases.

| | | | |
|---|---|---|---|
| 2003 | 90 | 2003 | 2004 |
| 2002 | 77 | 2002 | 2003 |
| 2001 | 89 | 2003 | 2006 |
| 2000 | 89 | 2001 | 2002+ |
| 1999 | 86 | 2000 | 2001 |

## 'i' BARBERA

RANKING **5**

**Alpine Valleys**                    $12–$19
**Current vintage: 2001**                  **89**

Highly enjoyable if not entirely flawless barbera
with a pungent, slightly wild and reductive,
smoky and oily aroma of nicotine and dark
cherries. Honest, rustic and uncomplicated, its
medium-weight palate offers bright cherry and
raspberry flavours before a slightly bitter and
reductive finish. It's long and savoury, with
lingering earthy diesel oil flavours.

| | | | |
|---|---|---|---|
| 2001 | 89 | 2003 | 2006 |
| 2000 | 89 | 2001 | 2002+ |
| 1999 | 86 | 2000 | 2001 |
| 1998 | 84 | 2000 | 2003 |
| 1997 | 89 | 2002 | 2005 |
| 1996 | 89 | 1998 | 2001+ |
| 1995 | 90 | 2000 | 2003 |

## 'i' DOLCETTO

RANKING **5**

**Alpine Valleys**                    $12–$19
**Current vintage: 2002**                  **87**

Minty, spicy dolcetto with a musky aroma of red
cherries, rhubarb and red earth over nuances of
mint and eucalypt. Medium in weight, it's a fine
and elegant early-drinker, with pleasing fruitiness
framed by dusty tannins. Finishes clean and
savoury.

| | | | |
|---|---|---|---|
| 2002 | 87 | 2003 | 2004 |
| 2001 | 77 | 2001 | 2002 |
| 2000 | 88 | 2002 | 2005 |
| 1999 | 83 | 2001 | 2004 |
| 1998 | 87 | 2000 | 2003 |
| 1997 | 82 | 1998 | 1999 |
| 1996 | 87 | 1998 | 2001 |

## 'i' NEBBIOLO

RANKING **4**

**Alpine Valleys**                    $20–$29
**Current vintage: 2000**                  **88**

Wild and spicy suggestions of rose petals, cooked
meats and raisins precede a long, firm and
savoury palate of weight structure and integrity.
While its citrus and currant fruit is a little faded
and dull, its earthy, meaty and leathery development
and firm astringency offer some genuine varietal
quality.

| | | | |
|---|---|---|---|
| 2000 | 88 | 2005 | 2008 |
| 1999 | 89 | 2007 | 2011 |
| 1998 | 93 | 2003 | 2006+ |
| 1997 | 91 | 2002 | 2005+ |
| 1996 | 88 | 2004 | 2008 |
| 1995 | 89 | 2002 | 2007 |
| 1994 | 87 | 2002 | 2006 |
| 1993 | 83 | 19998 | 2001 |

**Alpine Valleys** $12–$19
**Current vintage: 2002** 84

Meaty, herbal and lightly dusty, stalky aromas of red berries and plums over herby, menthol-like and meaty nuances. Firm and astringent, with some lively red berry/plum flavours, it lacks genuine ripeness, finishing slightly green-edged and raw.

| | | | |
|---|---|---|---|
| 2002 | 84 | 2004 | 2007 |
| 2001 | 90 | 2003 | 2006 |
| 2000 | 89 | 2001 | 2002 |
| 1999 | 94 | 2004 | 2007 |
| 1998 | 93 | 2000 | 2003+ |
| 1997 | 89 | 1999 | 2002 |
| 1996 | 90 | 2001 | 2004 |

# Gembrook Hill

Launching Place Road, Gembrook Vic 3783. Tel: (03) 5968 1622. Fax: (03) 5968 1699.
Website: www.gembrookhill.com.au Email: gemhill@nex.net.au

Region: **Yarra Valley** Winemaker: **Timo Mayer** Viticulturist: **Ian Marks** Chief Executive: **Ian Marks**

Gembrook Hill is a genuinely cool-climate Yarra Valley vineyard that is steadily coming of age. Its Sauvignon Blanc can be spectacular, its Chardonnay long and mineral, while its Pinot Noir is gaining flesh and structure. Alongside a typically bitey and savoury Sauvignon Blanc, its best wine from 2002 is the charming and deeply flavoured Pinot Noir sourced from the vineyard of the company's winemaker, Timo Mayer.

## CHARDONNAY  RANKING 3

**Yarra Valley** $30–$49
**Current vintage: 2002** 84

Forward, botrytised chardonnay whose toasty nose of apricots, honey and citrus and simple forward and rather lean palate are showing plenty of advancement. Finishes lean and thin, with greenish acids.

| | | | |
|---|---|---|---|
| 2002 | 84 | 2004 | 2007 |
| 2001 | 95 | 2006 | 2009 |
| 2000 | 92 | 2005 | 2008 |
| 1997 | 86 | 1999 | 2002 |
| 1995 | 91 | 2000 | 2003 |
| 1994 | 89 | 1999 | 2002 |
| 1993 | 92 | 1998 | 2001 |

## PINOT NOIR  RANKING 3

**Yarra Valley** $30–$49
**Current vintage: 2002** 87

With some wild, firm and Volnay-like qualities over its greenish undertones, this earthy, oaky pinot has a significant degree of power and structure. Its oaky aromas of prunes and currants, plus herbal and meaty notes precede a firm, but slightly cooked and under-ripe palate whose core of deep plum-like fruit is surrounded by prune and currant-like nuances.

| | | | |
|---|---|---|---|
| 2002 | 87 | 2007 | 2010 |
| 2001 | 93 | 2003 | 2006+ |
| 2000 | 94 | 2005 | 2008 |
| 1998 | 91 | 2003 | 2006 |
| 1997 | 89 | 1999 | 2002 |

## SAUVIGNON BLANC  RANKING 4

**Yarra Valley** $30–$49
**Current vintage: 2002** 93

Dry, complex and succulent cool climate sauvignon blanc with a lightly smoky, dusty and nutty bouquet of herbal and lightly sweaty citrus and gooseberry aromas. Long, vibrant and juicy, it's penetrative yet also fine, restrained and slightly chalky, but finishes with a steely austerity. There's some pleasing yeasty funkiness, and some clean acids that could have been even more bitey and Loire-like.

| | | | |
|---|---|---|---|
| 2002 | 93 | 2004 | 2007 |
| 2001 | 90 | 2003 | 2006 |
| 2000 | 90 | 2002 | 2005 |
| 1999 | 86 | 2000 | 2001 |
| 1998 | 94 | 2000 | 2003 |

# Geoff Merrill

291 Pimpala Road, Woodcroft SA 5162. Tel: (08) 8381 6877. Fax: (08) 8322 2244.
Email: merrill@geoffmerrillwines.com

Region: **McLaren Vale** Winemakers: **Geoff Merrill, Scott Heidrich** Viticulturist: **Goe DiFabio**
Chief Executive: **Geoff Merrill**

While they are released to the market with impressive age, there is a steady improvement evident in the Reserve level Geoff Merrill wines, of which the velvet-smooth and spicy 1998 Reserve Shiraz is the finest of recent times. The flagship Henley Shiraz produced another powerfully flavoured and tightly constructed wine in 1997.

## RESERVE CABERNET SAUVIGNON

RANKING **5**

**Coonawarra, McLaren Vale, Goulburn Valley** $30–$49
**Current vintage: 1998** 87

Old-fashioned sweet and leathery red with a dusty and herbal fragrance of Ribena and sweet plums backed by cedar/vanilla oak. Firm and linear, its earthy palate of ripe mulberry and slightly over-ripe currant-like fruit is rather disjointed, lacking in brightness and freshness. It finishes with a hint of saltiness.

| | | | |
|---|---|---|---|
| 1998 | 87 | 2006 | 2010+ |
| 1997 | 81 | 1999 | 2002 |
| 1996 | 82 | 1998 | 2001 |
| 1995 | 90 | 2003 | 2007 |
| 1994 | 88 | 1999 | 2002 |
| 1993 | 90 | 2005 | 2013 |
| 1992 | 87 | 2000 | 2004 |
| 1991 | 82 | 1999 | 2003 |
| 1990 | 88 | 1998 | 2002 |
| 1989 | 93 | 1997 | 2001 |
| 1988 | 91 | 1996 | 2000 |
| 1987 | 90 | 1995 | 1999 |
| 1986 | 91 | 1994 | 1998 |

## RESERVE SHIRAZ

RANKING **4**

**McLaren Vale** $30–$49
**Current vintage: 1998** 92

Well constructed, flavoursome shiraz whose aromas of cassis, blackberries and plums are slightly subdued by assertive vanilla oak. Velvet smooth, generous and spicy, its uncomplicated palate of sweet ripe blackberry fruit and smoky vanilla oak is framed by surprisingly firm tannins. Has a good future.

| | | | |
|---|---|---|---|
| 1998 | 92 | 2006 | 2010+ |
| 1997 | 90 | 2005 | 2009 |
| 1996 | 87 | 2001 | 2004+ |
| 1995 | 88 | 2000 | 2003+ |
| 1994 | 85 | 1999 | 2002 |

## SHIRAZ

**McLaren Vale** $20–$29
**Current vintage: 2001** 82

Old-fashioned, cooked, leathery and chocolatey shiraz whose sweaty, pruney bouquet precedes an oaky palate of baked currants and cassis. There's some palate softness and a firm grip of tannin, but the finish is a little stale and even salty.

| | | | |
|---|---|---|---|
| 2001 | 82 | 2006 | 2009 |
| 2000 | 82 | 2002 | 2005 |
| 1999 | 81 | 2001 | 2004 |
| 1998 | 75 | 1999 | 2000 |
| 1997 | 87 | 2002 | 2005 |
| 1996 | 89 | 2001 | 2004 |
| 1995 | 87 | 2000 | 2003 |
| 1994 | 90 | 1999 | 2002 |
| 1992 | 89 | 1998 | 2001 |
| 1991 | 88 | 1997 | 2000 |

# Geoff Weaver

2 Gilpin Lane, Mitcham SA 5062. Tel: (08) 8272 2105. Fax: (08) 8271 0177.
Website: www.geoffweaver.com.au  Email: weaver@adelaide.on.net

Region: **Lenswood** Winemaker: **Geoff Weaver** Viticulturist: **Geoff Weaver** Chief Executive: **Geoff Weaver**

Geoff Weaver makes some of the finest and most elegant white wines in the cool Adelaide Hills wine region.
His Chardonnay typically reveals intense grapefruit and guava-like flavours, while the finely sculpted Riesling
is perfumed and fragrant, with attractive pear and apple qualities. Weaver's red blend of Bordeaux varieties
is typically fine in structure, with delicate fruit influences and fine-grained tannins.

## CABERNET SAUVIGNON MERLOT   RANKING 4

Lenswood                          $30–$49
**Current vintage: 2000**               **87**

Supple, elegant cabernet blend with lightly
dusty, leafy aromas of fresh cassis and small red
berries overlying nuances of violets and forest floor
and partnered by restrained and integrated
creamy cedary oak. Smooth and fine-grained, its
intense core of vibrant small berry fruit is tightly
knit with lightly smoky cedary oak. Deftly made,
but ultimately a little green-edged and sappy.

| 2000 | 87 | 2002 | 2005+ |
|------|----|------|-------|
| 1999 | 90 | 2007 | 2011+ |
| 1998 | 89 | 2003 | 2006+ |
| 1997 | 86 | 2009 | 2017 |
| 1994 | 92 | 2002 | 2006 |
| 1993 | 93 | 2001 | 2005 |
| 1991 | 87 | 1999 | 2003 |
| 1990 | 94 | 1998 | 2002 |

## CHARDONNAY   RANKING 3

Lenswood                          $20–$29
**Current vintage: 2001**               **93**

Restrained, complex aromas of peach and pear,
apple and lime juice are intermeshed with
restrained, creamy and lightly leesy barrel ferment
influences. Tangy, vibrant guava and grapefruit flavour
extends down the rather fine and fluffy palate which
presents a measured balance between winemaking
artefact and natural fruit. Pleasingly long and harmonious.

| 2001 | 93 | 2003 | 2006+ |
|------|----|------|-------|
| 2000 | 86 | 2002 | 2005 |
| 1999 | 84 | 2001 | 2004 |
| 1998 | 88 | 2003 | 2006 |
| 1997 | 94 | 2002 | 2005+ |
| 1996 | 92 | 1998 | 2001 |
| 1995 | 94 | 2000 | 2003+ |
| 1994 | 90 | 1999 | 2002 |

## RIESLING   RANKING 3

Lenswood                          $12–$19
**Current vintage: 2003**               **93**

Racy, lean and refreshing cool climate riesling with
a musky floral note to its lime/apple fragrance.
Finely sculpted, its penetrative apple, pear and lime
flavours finish fresh and citrusy with a lingering
powdery finish. Pristine, tight and balanced.

| 2003 | 93 | 2008 | 2011+ |
|------|----|------|-------|
| 2001 | 91 | 2006 | 2009+ |
| 2000 | 93 | 2008 | 2012+ |
| 1999 | 92 | 2007 | 2011 |
| 1998 | 93 | 2003 | 2006 |
| 1997 | 94 | 2005 | 2009 |
| 1996 | 87 | 1998 | 2001 |
| 1995 | 92 | 2003 | 2007 |
| 1994 | 77 | 1995 | 1996 |
| 1993 | 94 | 2001 | 2005 |

## SAUVIGNON BLANC   RANKING 4

Lenswood                          $20–$29
**Current vintage: 2003**               **89**

Slightly reductive, nutty aromas of melon, gooseberries and baby powder with a light grassiness.
Moderate in weight, with some fleshiness and
roundness, it offers a pleasing length of attractively concentrated varietal flavours along its fine
and reserved palate, building towards a gentle
acid finish.

| 2003 | 89 | 2004 | 2005+ |
|------|----|------|-------|
| 2002 | 94 | 2003 | 2004+ |
| 2001 | 87 | 2001 | 2002 |
| 2000 | 87 | 2001 | 2002 |
| 1999 | 84 | 2000 | 2001 |
| 1998 | 94 | 2000 | 2003 |

# Giaconda

Cnr Wangaratta & McClay Road, s Beechworth Vic 3747. Tel: (03) 5727 0246. Fax: (03) 5727 0246.
Website: www.giaconda.com.au  Email: sales@giaconda.com.au

Region: **Beechworth** Winemaker: **Rick Kinzbrunner** Viticulturist: **Rick Kinzbrunner**
Chief Executive: **Rick Kinzbrunner**

The arrival of its Warner Vineyard Shiraz and Aeolia Roussanne amongst the best of their kind in Australia
has done little to reduce Giaconda's lustrous profile and the global demand for its scarce wines. This domaine-
like operation in the hills of Beechworth is responsible for some of the best and most finely crafted wines of
this country, of which the Chardonnay is the most well-known. Recent vintages of Cabernet Sauvignon, especially
from 1999 onwards, suggest to me that another Giaconda wine might reach similarly stratospheric heights.

## AEOLIA ROUSSANNE

RANKING **2**

**Beechworth**                         $50+
**Current vintage: 2003**              **94**

Deeply perfumed, musky and spicy, exotically
scented with honeysuckle and rose water. Its
luscious, opulent and powerful palate is lavishly
coated with concentrated spicy, citrusy fruit
before a fresh and tightly balance finish of exceptional length.

| 2003 | 94 | 2005 | 2008 |
|------|----|------|------|
| 2002 | 92 | 2004 | 2007 |
| 2001 | 94 | 2003 | 2006 |
| 2000 | 95 | 2002 | 2005+ |

## CABERNET SAUVIGNON

RANKING **2**

**Beechworth**                         $50+
**Current vintage: 2002**              **97**

It has fleshed out rather considerably since the
bottling sample I tasted late in 2003, attaining the
weight and texture one might associate with a
respected Pauillac growth from a fine warm
vintage. There's pristine violet, cassis and dark olive-
like cabernet aroma aplenty, with the tightness,
firmness and integration that we used to seek in
Australian wine long before over-ripe shiraz
became the Holy Grail for so many of our winemakers. It's a positive, assertive claret style whose
harmonious integration between fruit, oak and tannin
suggest to me an exceptionally long cellar life.

| 2002 | 97 | 2014 | 2022+ |
|------|----|------|-------|
| 2001 | 96 | 2013 | 2021 |
| 1999 | 96 | 2011 | 2019 |
| 1998 | 95 | 2006 | 2010 |
| 1997 | 95 | 2005 | 2009+ |
| 1996 | 94 | 2004 | 2008+ |
| 1995 | 94 | 2003 | 2007 |
| 1994 | 93 | 2002 | 2006 |
| 1993 | 93 | 1998 | 2001 |
| 1992 | 95 | 2004 | 2012 |
| 1991 | 96 | 1999 | 2003 |
| 1990 | 92 | 1998 | 2002 |
| 1988 | 94 | 1996 | 2000 |
| 1987 | 82 | 1995 | 1999 |
| 1986 | 89 | 1994 | 1998 |

## CHARDONNAY

RANKING **1**

**Beechworth**                         $50+
**Current vintage: 2002**              **97**

Sumptuous and seamless, perhaps revealing
less artefact and more fruit purity than the
signature 1996 vintage, but it looks capable of
attaining similar complexity with bottle-age.
Beneath fresh melon and stonefruit flavours,
nutty and oatmeal-like influences lie suggestions
of earth and mineral, while the palate's succulent
babyfat texture culminates in a lingering, dry and
savoury. Should develop classically.

| 2002 | 97 | 2007 | 2010+ |
|------|----|------|-------|
| 2001 | 96 | 2006 | 2009+ |
| 2000 | 96 | 2008 | 2012 |
| 1999 | 97 | 2007 | 2011 |
| 1998 | 96 | 2003 | 2006+ |
| 1997 | 95 | 2002 | 2005 |
| 1996 | 97 | 2004 | 2008 |
| 1995 | 92 | 2003 | 2007 |
| 1994 | 94 | 2002 | 2006 |
| 1993 | 94 | 1998 | 2001+ |
| 1992 | 96 | 1997 | 2000 |
| 1991 | 94 | 1995 | 1999 |
| 1990 | 95 | 1998 | 2002 |
| 1989 | 92 | 1991 | 1994 |
| 1988 | 93 | 1993 | 1996 |
| 1987 | 91 | 1992 | 1995 |
| 1986 | 93 | 1991 | 1994 |

# PINOT NOIR

| Beechworth | $50+ |
| --- | --- |
| **Current vintage: 2002** | **95** |

There's a suggestion of Chinese fivespice beneath its rather pungent and assertive aromas of raspberries, redcurrants and dark cherries, offset by a pleasing background of slightly musk, meaty aromas. It's a powerful, sumptuous pinot whose spicy expression of cherries and plums settles down towards a fine, elegant finish.

| | | | |
| --- | --- | --- | --- |
| 2002 | 95 | 2010 | 2014 |
| 2001 | 94 | 2006 | 2009+ |
| 2000 | 95 | 2008 | 2012+ |
| 1999 | 92 | 2007 | 2011 |
| 1998 | 93 | 2006 | 2010 |
| 1997 | 95 | 2002 | 2005+ |
| 1996 | 91 | 2001 | 2004+ |
| 1995 | 81 | 1997 | 2000 |
| 1994 | 93 | 1999 | 2002 |
| 1993 | 92 | 1998 | 2001 |
| 1992 | 96 | 1997 | 2000+ |
| 1991 | 94 | 1996 | 1999 |
| 1990 | 91 | 1995 | 1998 |
| 1989 | 95 | 1994 | 1997 |
| 1988 | 95 | 1993 | 1996 |
| 1987 | 87 | 1989 | 1992 |

# SHIRAZ

| Beechworth | $50+ |
| --- | --- |
| **Current vintage: 2002** | **97** |

A more substantial shiraz, despite the fact that some tobaccooey, slightly herbal notes lurk beneath its bright array of genuinely ripe fruit flavours. An essay in pepper and spice, its wild and briary dark and red berry fruits offer more than a suggestion of the charcuterie. It's a fine Hermitage in style, but a spotlessly clean one in top form. It has depth, richness and structure, but despite its dramatic dimensions, remains perfectly harmonious, balanced and tightly composed. A treat.

| | | | |
| --- | --- | --- | --- |
| 2002 | 97 | 2010 | 2014+ |
| 2001 | 96 | 2009 | 2013 |
| 2000 | 96 | 2008 | 2012 |
| 1999 | 95 | 2007 | 2011 |
| 1998 | 93 | 2003 | 2006 |

# Glaetzer

34 Barossa Valley Way Tanunda SA 5352. Tel: (08) 8563 0288. Fax: (08) 8563 0218.
Website: www.glaetzer.com. Email: glaetzer@glaetzer.com
Region: **Barossa Valley** Winemaker: **Colin & Ben Glaetzer** Chief Executive: **Colin Glaetzer**
Colin and Ben Glaetzer make small volumes of sumptuously flavoured red wines from 80 year-old vines in the Ebenezer district in the Barossa's northwest. The 2000 reds were not considered sufficiently good for release under this label, but the 2001 vintage has produced some delightful wine. Of the two main reds, 'The Bishop' Shiraz tends to express more vitality and brightness than the more powerful, meaty and deeply ripened Shiraz.

# SHIRAZ

| Barossa Valley | $50+ |
| --- | --- |
| **Current vintage: 2001** | **89** |

Sweet, concentrated aromas of red and black berries, currants and plums are given deluxe treatment in lightly smoky cedar/vanilla oak, revealing nuances of white pepper, undergrowth and a hint of funkiness. An up-front fruit bomb with oak playing a significant role, it's smooth and silky, concentrated and voluptuous, but reveals a greenish thread of herbal flavours. Intense cassis, dark plum flavours and assertive cedar/chocolate oak finish just slightly sappy and herbal, with a suggestion of smoked bacon.

| | | | |
| --- | --- | --- | --- |
| 2001 | 89 | 2009 | 2013 |
| 1999 | 86 | 2001 | 2004+ |
| 1997 | 88 | 1999 | 2002 |

**THE AUSTRALIAN WINE ANNUAL**
**www.onwine.com.au**

**2005**

# Goundrey

Langton, Muir Highway, Mount Barker WA 6324. Tel: (08) 9851 1777. Fax: (08) 9851 1997.
Website: www.goundreywines.com.au Email: info@goundreywines.com.au

Region: **Mount Barker** Winemaker: **David Martin** Viticulturist: **Cate Finlay** Chief Executive: **Rich Hanen**

Goundrey is one of the new acquisitions of Vincor, the giant Canadian producer and distributor. It's a long-established name in Western Australia, with a chequered history of ownership and wine quality, although its potential to make excellent wine at the expensive and more affordable extremes of the market has never been seriously doubted. The recent releases of Reserve level white wines are an impressive return to form.

## HOMESTEAD CABERNET MERLOT

RANKING **5**

**Mount Barker**          $12–$19
**Current vintage: 2002**      84

Honest, if slightly herbal and sappy cabernet blend with a sweet fragrance of small black and red berries, cedar/vanilla oak and floral undertones. Smooth and elegant, it's gentle and lively, with green-edged fruit framed by fine tannins.

| | | | |
|---|---|---|---|
| 2002 | 84 | 2004 | 2007 |
| 2001 | 88 | 2003 | 2006+ |
| 2000 | 81 | 2002 | 2005 |
| 1999 | 90 | 2001 | 2004+ |

## RESERVE CABERNET SAUVIGNON

RANKING **5**

**Mount Barker**          $20–$29
**Current vintage: 2002**      87

Elegant, if rather sappy and green-edged cabernet with light aromas of red berries and plums over cedary oak and capsicum-like notes. Vibrant and creamy, with a smooth and supple palate of fresh black and red berry flavours, plus fine-grained cedar/vanilla oak.

| | | | |
|---|---|---|---|
| 2002 | 87 | 2004 | 2007+ |
| 1998 | 78 | 2000 | 2003 |
| 1997 | 80 | 1999 | 2002 |
| 1996 | 90 | 2002 | 2008 |
| 1995 | 90 | 2003 | 2007 |
| 1993 | 87 | 2001 | 2005 |
| 1992 | 85 | 1997 | 2000 |
| 1991 | 93 | 2003 | 2011 |
| 1990 | 85 | 1998 | 2002 |

## RESERVE CHARDONNAY

RANKING **5**

**Mount Barker**          $20–$29
**Current vintage: 2002**      91

A generous, typically Western Australian chardonnay with a pungent, buttery aroma of ripe ruby grapefruit and pineapples, with a whiff of toastiness and leesy nuttiness. The palate remains just the right side of cloying, with pleasing fattiness and texture, finishing with lingering tropical and stonefruit flavours. There's a herbal note throughout the wine, reflective of its cool climate origins.

| | | | |
|---|---|---|---|
| 2002 | 91 | 2004 | 2007 |
| 2001 | 86 | 2003 | 2006 |
| 1999 | 81 | 2000 | 2001 |
| 1998 | 85 | 2000 | 2003 |
| 1997 | 88 | 1999 | 2002 |
| 1995 | 87 | 1997 | 2000 |

## RESERVE RIESLING

RANKING **5**

**Mount Barker**          $12–$19
**Current vintage: 2003**      93

A delicate perfume of lemon blossom, lemon meringue, apple and pear, before an intense, forward palate that becomes long, fine and austere. Very refreshing, but would have been more so were it not for a distinct note of bound sulphide at the finish.

| | | | |
|---|---|---|---|
| 2003 | 93 | 2008 | 2011 |
| 2002 | 84 | 2002 | 2004 |
| 2000 | 84 | 2005 | 2008 |
| 1999 | 82 | 2001 | 2004 |
| 1998 | 88 | 2000 | 2003 |
| 1997 | 90 | 2002 | 2005 |
| 1996 | 93 | 2004 | 2008 |
| 1995 | 87 | 2003 | 2007 |
| 1994 | 94 | 2002 | 2006 |
| 1993 | 95 | 1998 | 2001 |

## RESERVE SHIRAZ

RANKING **5**

**Mount Barker**          $20–$29
**Current vintage: 2001**      82

Earthy, rather flat and woolly, with smoky/mocha oak influences dominating its rather thin, green-edged fruit. Over-oaked and under-fruited.

| | | | |
|---|---|---|---|
| 2001 | 82 | 2003 | 2006 |
| 2000 | 85 | 2002 | 2005+ |
| 1999 | 90 | 2004 | 2007 |
| 1998 | 80 | 2000 | 2003 |
| 1997 | 83 | 1999 | 2002 |
| 1996 | 81 | 1997 | 1998 |
| 1994 | 93 | 2002 | 2006 |
| 1993 | 91 | 2001 | 2005 |
| 1992 | 94 | 2000 | 2004 |

# Gramp's

Barossa Valley Way Rowland Flat SA 5352. Tel: (08) 8521 3111. Fax: (08) 8521 3100.
Region: **Barossa Valley** Winemakers: **Philip Laffer, Sam Kurtz, Bernie Hickin** Viticulturist: **Joy Dick**
Chief Executive: **Laurent Lacassgne**

A really smart Chardonnay from 2002 and a restrained and savoury Botrytis Semillon are the two best wines under the Orlando Wyndham-owned Gramp's label. While being sound and flawless, more work is required for the reds to represent classic Barossa richness and generosity.

## BOTRYTIS SEMILLON

RANKING 4

**Barossa Valley** $12–$19 (375 ml)
**Current vintage: 2003** 90

Luscious, but not overly concentrated expression of late-harvest semillon whose vibrant tropical aromas of melon, mango and pineapple are backed by nuances of honeysuckle and restrained oak. Its sumptuous, savoury palate offers a pleasing length of vibrant fruit punctuated by fresh acids and lifted by smoky, buttery nuances of pastry and marmalade.

| 2003 | 90 | 2005 | 2008+ |
|------|----|------|-------|
| 2002 | 91 | 2004 | 2007+ |
| 2001 | 88 | 2003 | 2006 |
| 1999 | 90 | 2001 | 2004+ |
| 1998 | 83 | 1999 | 2000 |
| 1997 | 89 | 1999 | 2002 |
| 1996 | 89 | 1998 | 2001 |
| 1994 | 82 | 1995 | 1996 |

## CABERNET MERLOT

RANKING 5

**Barossa Valley** $12–$19
**Current vintage: 2001** 82

Light aromas of cassis, raspberries and plums are partnered by vanilla and lightly smoky oak, while its forward palate of plums and small berries becomes rather hollow, lean and green. Lacks weight and substance.

| 2001 | 82 | 2002 | 2005 |
|------|----|------|------|
| 1999 | 86 | 2001 | 2004 |
| 1998 | 88 | 2003 | 2006 |
| 1997 | 89 | 2002 | 2005 |
| 1996 | 86 | 1998 | 2001 |
| 1995 | 85 | 1997 | 2000 |
| 1994 | 82 | 1999 | 2002 |
| 1993 | 75 | 1995 | 1998 |

## CHARDONNAY

RANKING 5

**Barossa Valley** $12–$19
**Current vintage: 2002** 89

Flavoursome and assertive, if indeed rather oaky chardonnay with a forward and spicy aroma of apple, cloves, nutmeg and oatmeal. While the palate reveals plenty of sweet toasty vanilla oak, there's some restrained buttery chardonnay flavour of peaches and nectarines beneath, before a soft, creamy finish. It should develop rather nicely, fleshing out and becoming better balanced.

| 2002 | 89 | 2004 | 2007 |
|------|----|------|------|
| 2001 | 80 | 2002 | 2003 |
| 2000 | 87 | 2001 | 2002 |
| 1999 | 87 | 2001 | 2004 |
| 1998 | 82 | 1999 | 2000 |

## GRENACHE

RANKING 5

**Barossa Valley** $12–$19
**Current vintage: 2002** 83

A leaner, tighter grenache lacking real vitality and freshness. Its sweet, jammy aroma of currants, stewed plums, spicy blueberries and light vanilla oak precedes a raw and fairly thin palate excessively reliant on its vanilla and chocolate oak for sweetness.

| 2002 | 83 | 2003 | 2004 |
|------|----|------|------|
| 1999 | 89 | 2004 | 2007 |
| 1998 | 87 | 2000 | 2003+ |
| 1997 | 88 | 1999 | 2002 |

# Grant Burge

Barossa Valley Way Jacob's Creek Tanunda SA 5352. Tel: (08) 8563 3700. Fax: (08) 8563 2807.
Website: www.grantburgewines.com.au  Email: admin@grantburgewines.com.au

Region: **Barossa Valley**  Winemaker: **Grant Burge**  Viticulturist: **Michael Schrapel**  Chief Executive: **Grant Burge**

Owned and managed by former Krondorf wizzkid Grant Burge, this is an energetic wine company that offers excellent Barossa richness and flavour across a steadily increasing spread of different tiers of quality and price. The Meschach fully deserves its place amongst Australia's classic dry reds, while the Filsell Shiraz offers a more affordable but very serious glimpse of Barossa shiraz. Just as importantly, the 2002 vintage Barossa Vines reds offer exceptional quaffing value.

## BAROSSA VINES SHIRAZ

**Barossa Valley**                     $12–$19
**Current vintage: 2002**                   87

A soft, easy-drinking and crowd-pleasing style of shiraz. Its jammy nose of red and black berries, plums and light vanilla oak reveals some spice and perfume. Warm, generous and mouthfilling, is smooth, approachable palate is packed with vibrant flavour and framed by soft tannins and acidity. Uncomplicated, but fun.

| | | | |
|---|---|---|---|
| 2002 | 87 | 2002 | 2004+ |
| 2001 | 86 | 2003 | 2006 |
| 2000 | 82 | 2001 | 2002 |
| 1999 | 88 | 2001 | 2004 |
| 1998 | 85 | 1999 | 2000 |

## CAMERON VALE CABERNET SAUVIGNON

RANKING **5**

**Barossa Valley**                     $20–$29
**Current vintage: 2001**                   89

Approachable, elegant and flavoursome short to medium-term cabernet. Dusty herbal aromas of ripe blackcurrants, plums and raspberries are evenly matched by sweet vanilla oak. Its smooth, supple palate is framed by soft, fine tannins and packed with lively jujube-like mulberry, plum and blackberry flavours, gently supported by cedar/vanilla oak influences.

| | | | |
|---|---|---|---|
| 2001 | 89 | 2006 | 2009 |
| 2000 | 82 | 2002 | 2005 |
| 1999 | 82 | 2001 | 2004 |
| 1998 | 88 | 2006 | 2010 |
| 1997 | 87 | 2002 | 2005 |
| 1996 | 91 | 2004 | 2008 |
| 1995 | 91 | 2003 | 2007 |
| 1994 | 89 | 2002 | 2006 |
| 1993 | 88 | 2001 | 2005 |

## FILSELL SHIRAZ

RANKING **3**

**Barossa Valley**                     $20–$29
**Current vintage: 2002**                   90

Elegant, tightly focused Barossa shiraz from a cooler season, whose delicate floral aromas of small dark berries are laced with suggestions of mint and menthol. Relatively lean and fine-grained, the vibrant, minty palate presents translucent cassis-like fruit neatly partnered by chocolate/vanilla oak. Framed by a fine-grained cut of powdery tannins, it finishes long and lingering, with a refreshing acid balance.

| | | | |
|---|---|---|---|
| 2002 | 90 | 2010 | 2014+ |
| 2001 | 86 | 2003 | 2006+ |
| 2000 | 93 | 2008 | 2012 |
| 1999 | 88 | 2001 | 2004+ |
| 1998 | 94 | 2006 | 2010 |
| 1997 | 88 | 2002 | 2005 |
| 1996 | 95 | 2004 | 2008+ |
| 1995 | 91 | 2000 | 2003 |
| 1994 | 95 | 2002 | 2006+ |
| 1993 | 82 | 1998 | 2001 |
| 1992 | 90 | 2000 | 2004 |
| 1991 | 93 | 2003 | 2011 |
| 1990 | 92 | 2002 | 2010 |
| 1989 | 87 | 1997 | 2001 |
| 1988 | 89 | 1996 | 2000 |

## HILLCOT MERLOT

RANKING **5**

**Barossa Valley**                     $30–$49
**Current vintage: 2002**                   86

Light, minty merlot with some floral cassis, violet, dark cherry and plum flavours with regional notes of eucalypt and mint. Smooth, fine-grained and elegant, with some assertive added acidity.

| | | | |
|---|---|---|---|
| 2002 | 86 | 2004 | 2007 |
| 2001 | 81 | 2002 | 2003+ |
| 2000 | 81 | 2002 | 2005 |
| 1999 | 88 | 2001 | 2004 |
| 1998 | 89 | 2000 | 2003+ |
| 1997 | 86 | 1999 | 2002 |
| 1996 | 87 | 1998 | 2001 |
| 1995 | 88 | 2000 | 2003 |
| 1994 | 89 | 1999 | 2002 |

# KRAFT SAUVIGNON BLANC

**Eden Valley** $12–$19
**Current vintage: 2003** 81

Reductive, sweaty aromas of asparagus and capsicum smother some underlying nuances of gooseberries and passionfruit. The palate begins with some forward tropical flavours, but becomes syrupy and metallic, finishing lean and hard with a persistent character of tinned pineapple.

| | | | |
|---|---|---|---|
| 2003 | 81 | 2003 | 2004 |
| 2002 | 89 | 2002 | 2003+ |
| 2001 | 83 | 2001 | 2002 |
| 2000 | 87 | 2001 | 2002 |
| 1999 | 84 | 2000 | 2000 |
| 1998 | 90 | 1999 | 2000 |

# MESHACH

**Barossa Valley** $50+
**Current vintage: 2000** 93

A very good wine from this vintage, with a musky, brambly aroma of blackberries and raspberries, sweet mocha/chocolate-like oak and hints of prune, currant and white pepper. Very fine and elegant, with a velvet-like mouthfeel, it offers plenty of briary flavour alongside some tarry, prune-like nuances. Fractionally cooked and lacking the length of the top vintages, but a very solid wine.

| | | | |
|---|---|---|---|
| 2000 | 93 | 2008 | 2012+ |
| 1999 | 96 | 2007 | 2011+ |
| 1998 | 97 | 2010 | 2018+ |
| 1996 | 93 | 2008 | 2016 |
| 1995 | 96 | 2007 | 2015 |
| 1994 | 95 | 2006 | 2014 |
| 1993 | 93 | 2001 | 2005 |
| 1992 | 93 | 2000 | 2004 |
| 1991 | 95 | 2003 | 2011 |
| 1990 | 93 | 1998 | 2002+ |
| 1988 | 94 | 1996 | 2000 |

# MIAMBA SHIRAZ

**Barossa Valley** $12–$19
**Current vintage: 2002** 84

Slightly herbaceous shiraz with a spicy white pepper fragrance of redcurrants, plums and restrained oak. Medium-weight, it's forward and elegant, with some green edges and high-toned acidity.

| | | | |
|---|---|---|---|
| 2002 | 84 | 2004 | 2007 |
| 2001 | 87 | 2003 | 2006 |
| 2000 | 88 | 2002 | 2005+ |
| 1999 | 89 | 2001 | 2004+ |

# MSJ RESERVE CABERNET SHIRAZ BLEND

**Barossa Valley** $50+
**Current vintage: 1998** 91

Slightly old-fashioned Barossa blend, with an earthy, meaty aroma of sweet cassis, plums and mulberries, suggestions of pepper and spice, with a healthy dollop of new chocolate and vanilla oak. Smooth and cedary, with a pleasingly long palate of intense berry fruit and earthy complexity supported by rather a firm and rod-like spine of drying tannins.

| | | | |
|---|---|---|---|
| 1998 | 91 | 2006 | 2010 |
| 1996 | 93 | 2004 | 2008+ |
| 1994 | 95 | 2006 | 2014 |

# SHADRACH CABERNET SAUVIGNON

**Barossa Valley** $50+
**Current vintage: 1999** 87

Developed and leathery, with a weedy undercurrent of herby flavour, this oaky red wine does reveal some lively small berry aromas with some rather greenish shaded fruit characters. Despite a reasonable length of smooth and rather jammy fruit, it finishes without much definition.

| | | | |
|---|---|---|---|
| 1999 | 87 | 2004 | 2007 |
| 1998 | 93 | 2006 | 2010+ |
| 1996 | 92 | 2008 | 2016 |
| 1994 | 93 | 2006 | 2014 |
| 1993 | 90 | 2013 | 2023 |

## SUMMERS CHARDONNAY

RANKING **5**

**Eden Valley, Adelaide Hills**   $12–$19
**Current vintage: 2003**   **87**

Soft, generous and approachable chardonnay whose uncomplicated, honest expression of fresh peaches, apple and cream are lightly oaked and smooth to finish. Great value.

| | | | |
|---|---|---|---|
| 2003 | 87 | 2004 | 2005 |
| 2002 | 88 | 2002 | 2004+ |
| 2001 | 80 | 2002 | 2003 |
| 2000 | 88 | 2002 | 2005 |
| 1999 | 87 | 2001 | 2004 |

## THE HOLY TRINITY (Grenache Shiraz Mourvèdre)

RANKING **4**

**Barossa Valley**   $20–$29
**Current vintage: 2000**   **87**

Ageing, leathery expression of the traditional Australian burgundy style of red with a chocolatey, licorice-like aroma of slightly baked blackberries and plums backed by nuances of sweet cedary oak. Soft and sweet, it offers some lively forward fruit but finishes with a drying and rather metallic finish. Not bad from this vintage.

| | | | |
|---|---|---|---|
| 2000 | 87 | 2002 | 2005 |
| 1999 | 92 | 2004 | 2007 |
| 1998 | 90 | 2000 | 2003+ |
| 1997 | 89 | 1999 | 2002 |
| 1996 | 89 | 1998 | 2001 |
| 1995 | 86 | 1997 | 2000 |

## THORN RIESLING

RANKING **4**

**Eden Valley**   $12–$19
**Current vintage: 2002**   **90**

Despite a fractionally sugary finish to please the crowds, this is a fragrant, musky riesling with a long, mineral palate and a hint of austerity. Its perfumed aromas suggest talcum powder, musky apples and pears, while its chalky palate finishes with lingering lemony flavours.

| | | | |
|---|---|---|---|
| 2002 | 90 | 2007 | 2010 |
| 2001 | 91 | 2006 | 2009+ |
| 2000 | 87 | 2002 | 2005+ |
| 1999 | 88 | 2001 | 2004+ |
| 1998 | 93 | 2003 | 2006 |
| 1997 | 87 | 1999 | 2002 |

## ZERK SEMILLON

RANKING **5**

**Barossa Valley**   $12–$19
**Current vintage: 2002**   **92**

Terrific young Barossa semillon with a lively, herby aroma of melon and lightly dusty vanilla oak. Juicy, round and generous, its long and evenly balanced palate of bright melon flavour is tightly knit with toasty vanilla oak and bound by lively, refreshing mineral and lemony acids.

| | | | |
|---|---|---|---|
| 2002 | 92 | 2003 | 2004+ |
| 2001 | 84 | 2002 | 2003 |
| 2000 | 87 | 2001 | 2002 |
| 1999 | 92 | 2001 | 2004+ |
| 1998 | 88 | 2000 | 2003 |
| 1997 | 87 | 2002 | 2005 |

# Green Point

Green Point Maroondah Highway, Coldstream Vic 3770. Tel: (03) 9739 1110. Fax: (03) 9739 1095.
Website: www.greenpointwines.com.au

Region: **Yarra Valley, Various** Winemakers: **Dr Tony Jordan, James Gosper, John Harris**
Viticulturist: **Bernie Wood Managing Director: Dr Tony Jordan**

Green Point is the label by which Domaine Chandon's Australian sparkling wines are sold in overseas markets, as well as the company's brand of still table wines sold in Australia. The 2003 Chardonnays represent a very positive move from the brand's juicy, confectionary wines of past years towards a style of fineness, refreshing length of tangy fruit and lively lemony acidity.

## McLAREN VALE SHIRAZ

RANKING **5**

| McLaren Vale | | $20–$29 |
|---|---|---|
| **Current vintage: 2002** | | **88** |

A very oaky fragrance of cedar and vanilla gives lift and vitality to currant-like aromas of plums and cassis. Smooth, restrained and elegant, the palate offers vibrant dark fruit flavours along its entire willowy palate, while some roasted vanilla oak tends to conceal some greenish fruit aspects.

| 2002 | 88 | 2004 | 2007 |
|---|---|---|---|
| 2001 | 87 | 2003 | 2006+ |
| 2000 | 84 | 2002 | 2005 |
| 1999 | 87 | 2001 | 2004 |
| 1998 | 91 | 2003 | 2006 |

## RESERVE CHARDONNAY

RANKING **5**

| Yarra Valley | | $20–$29 |
|---|---|---|
| **Current vintage: 2002** | | **89** |

Delicate floral and citrusy aromas and sweet scents of vanilla oak precede a fine, lean and elegant palate. Very restrained, its sappy expression of citrus and melon flavour, nutty vanilla oak and tight, refreshing acids are pleasingly balanced, culminating in a lingering finish of tangy fruit.

| 2002 | 89 | 2007 | 2010 |
|---|---|---|---|
| 2001 | 88 | 2003 | 2006 |
| 2000 | 87 | 2002 | 2005 |

## RESERVE PINOT NOIR

RANKING **5**

| Yarra Valley | | $20–$29 |
|---|---|---|
| **Current vintage: 2002** | | **90** |

An improvement in Domaine Chandon's still pinot noir, with a minty, perfumed aroma of sweet red cherries and rose petals, plus a musky, meaty whiff of the charcuterie. Supple, smooth and willowy, with spotless berry/cherry fruit offset by lightly smoky and sweet vanilla oak. Framed by fine tannins, it's a pristine young wine just about too pretty to be taken too seriously.

| 2002 | 90 | 2004 | 2007 |
|---|---|---|---|
| 2001 | 87 | 2003 | 2006 |
| 2000 | 89 | 2005 | 2008 |

## YARRA VALLEY CHARDONNAY

RANKING **5**

| Yarra Valley | | $20–$29 |
|---|---|---|
| **Current vintage: 2003** | | **90** |

Tightly knit, restrained and refreshing chardonnay whose delicate and floral aromas of peaches and pears are backed by restrained vanilla oak. Supple, fine and elegant, it reveals a core of bright and juicy peach, pear and apple flavours, before finishing crisp and dry, with assertive, but gentle acids.

| 2003 | 90 | 2005 | 2008 |
|---|---|---|---|
| 2002 | 87 | 2004 | 2007 |
| 2001 | 84 | 2003 | 2006 |
| 2000 | 86 | 2000 | 2003 |
| 1999 | 81 | 2000 | 2001 |
| 1998 | 83 | 2000 | 2003 |
| 1996 | 82 | 1996 | 1997 |
| 1995 | 93 | 2000 | 2003 |
| 1994 | 92 | 1999 | 2002 |
| 1993 | 89 | 1998 | 2001 |
| 1992 | 92 | 1997 | 2000 |

## YARRA VALLEY PINOT NOIR   RANKING 5

| Yarra Valley | $20–$29 | 2002 | 83 | 2004 | 2007 |
|---|---|---|---|---|---|
| **Current vintage: 2002** | **83** | 2001 | 90 | 2003 | 2006 |
| | | 2000 | 87 | 2002 | 2005 |
| | | 1998 | 87 | 2000 | 2003 |

Lightly cooked cherry aromas with herbal undertones precede a fruit-driven and rather simple palate. Soft and sappy, with confection-like flavours of raspberries and cherries.

# Grosset

King Street, Auburn SA 5451. Tel: (08) 8849 2175. Fax: (08) 8849 2292.
Website: www.grosset.com.au  Email: info@grosset.com.au
Region: **Clare Valley** Winemaker: **Jeffrey Grosset** Viticulturist: **Jeffrey Grosset** Chief Executive: **Jeffrey Grosset**
The name of Jeffrey Grosset has become synonymous with riesling in Australia, based on an exceptional run of class and consistency from his twin labels of Polish Hill and Watervale Riesling. However the most exciting new wine from this maker is handsomely the finest and most seamless Chardonnay he has yet released from the Piccadilly Valley in the Adelaide Hills. The 2003 Pinot Noir from the same region is also fragrant and juicy.

## GAIA (Cabernet blend)   RANKING 3

| Clare Valley | $30–$49 | 2002 | 90 | 2014 | 2022+ |
|---|---|---|---|---|---|
| **Current vintage: 2002** | **90** | 2001 | 94 | 2013 | 2021 |
| | | 2000 | 91 | 2008 | 2012+ |
| | | 1999 | 90 | 2007 | 2011 |
| | | 1998 | 95 | 2010 | 2018 |
| | | 1996 | 91 | 2004 | 2008 |
| | | 1995 | 93 | 2007 | 2015 |
| | | 1994 | 94 | 2006 | 2014 |
| | | 1993 | 94 | 2005 | 2013 |
| | | 1992 | 95 | 2004 | 2012 |
| | | 1991 | 88 | 1996 | 1999 |
| | | 1990 | 89 | 2002 | 2010 |

A long-term but very retentive red of tightness and some raw, reductive edges. Its violet and cassis-like fragrance of small berries, cedar/chocolate oak reveals a delicate background of menthol and eucalypt, plus some greenish sulphide-like characters. Long, firm and tightly knit, its rather lean palate of pristine small berry and plum fruit is supported by a bony spine of astringent tannins. It just needs plenty of time.

## PICCADILLY (Chardonnay)   RANKING 2

| Piccadilly Valley | $30–$49 | 2003 | 96 | 2008 | 2011 |
|---|---|---|---|---|---|
| **Current vintage: 2003** | **96** | 2002 | 95 | 2007 | 2010 |
| | | 2001 | 94 | 2006 | 2009 |
| | | 2000 | 95 | 2005 | 2008 |
| | | 1999 | 95 | 2004 | 2007+ |
| | | 1998 | 90 | 2003 | 2006 |
| | | 1997 | 94 | 2002 | 2005 |
| | | 1996 | 95 | 2001 | 2004 |
| | | 1995 | 94 | 2000 | 2003 |
| | | 1994 | 94 | 2002 | 2006 |

Seamlessly elegant chardonnay with a complex and restrained bouquet of peach, melon and grilled nuts, fine-grained vanilla oak and a hint of lanolin. Its stylish, silky palate presents a bright core of peach, nectarine and tropical fruit delivered with a delicate, fluffy texture. Tightly knit with creamy oak and fine phenolics, it's the finest chardonnay yet from this maker.

## PINOT NOIR   RANKING 3

| Piccadilly Valley | $30–$49 | 2003 | 93 | 2005 | 2008+ |
|---|---|---|---|---|---|
| **Current vintage: 2003** | **93** | 2002 | 92 | 2007 | 2010+ |
| | | 2001 | 88 | 2003 | 2006 |
| | | 2000 | 82 | 2002 | 2005 |
| | | 1998 | 93 | 2003 | 2006 |
| | | 1997 | 95 | 2002 | 2005+ |
| | | 1996 | 94 | 2004 | 2008 |
| | | 1995 | 91 | 1997 | 2000 |
| | | 1994 | 93 | 1999 | 2002 |
| | | 1993 | 90 | 1998 | 2001 |

Tight, fine and fragrant pinot with a youthfully oaky bouquet of small berries, plums and a hint of currant. Generous, long and complete, it's presently firm and fine-grained, but its balance, depth of vibrant fruit and structure suggest it will flesh out nicely.

**Clare Valley**    $30–$49
**Current vintage: 2003**    **96**

Exemplary Clare riesling, whose intense, musky, rose garden perfume of apples, pears and lime juice reveals an underlying fragrance of wet slate and mineral. Concentrated and exceptionally long, it's searingly intense and citrusy, with forward, open flavours with a soft, juicy palate over a slatey foundation. Superbly fashioned, culminating in an austere, persistent and slightly chalky finish.

There were two bottlings of this wine in 2000, of which the Stelvin-sealed version is marginally superior and likely to live slightly longer.

| | | | |
|---|---|---|---|
| 2003 | 96 | 2015 | 2023 |
| 2002 | 97 | 2014 | 2022 |
| 2001 | 96 | 2009 | 2013+ |
| 2000 | 95 | 2008 | 2012 |
| 1999 | 95 | 2007 | 2011+ |
| 1998 | 92 | 2006 | 2010 |
| 1997 | 97 | 2009 | 2017+ |
| 1996 | 94 | 2004 | 2008 |
| 1995 | 93 | 2003 | 2007+ |
| 1994 | 95 | 2006 | 2014 |
| 1993 | 90 | 2001 | 2005 |
| 1992 | 93 | 2004 | 2012 |
| 1991 | 89 | 1996 | 1999 |
| 1990 | 94 | 2002 | 2010 |
| 1989 | 82 | 1991 | 1994 |
| 1988 | 91 | 1993 | 1996 |
| 1987 | 93 | 1999 | 2004 |
| 1986 | 94 | 1998 | 2006 |
| 1985 | 95 | 1997 | 2005 |

## SEMILLON SAUVIGNON BLANC     RANKING 3

**Clare Valley**    $20–$29
**Current vintage: 2003**    **92**

Delightfully scented, vibrant and delicate aromas of lightly herbal, dusty gooseberry and melon fruit are backed by a reserved dash of vanilla oak. Tangy, ripe and juicy, the palate punches out plenty of bright, pristine melon and citrus flavour, before finishing clean and refreshing with lingering lemony acids and a hint of mineral.

| | | | |
|---|---|---|---|
| 2003 | 92 | 2004 | 2005+ |
| 2002 | 90 | 2004 | 2007 |
| 2001 | 92 | 2006 | 2009 |
| 2000 | 91 | 2002 | 2005 |
| 1999 | 90 | 2004 | 2007 |
| 1998 | 93 | 2003 | 2006 |
| 1997 | 90 | 1998 | 1999 |
| 1996 | 93 | 1998 | 2001 |
| 1995 | 94 | 1997 | 2000 |
| 1994 | 94 | 1999 | 2003 |
| 1993 | 94 | 2001 | 2005 |
| 1992 | 91 | 1997 | 2000 |

## WATERVALE RIESLING     RANKING 2

**Clare Valley**    $30–$49
**Current vintage: 2003**    **96**

Typically perfumed, fragrant aromas of ripe guava, mango and citrus fruits with a whiff of stonefruit and lemon zest. Tangy, long and austere, with a rich, juicy palate bursting with vibrant fruit. Underneath lies a slightly phenolic backbone, while racy acids tie it neatly together.

There were two bottlings of this wine in 2000, of which the Stelvin-sealed version is marginally inferior, but likely to live slightly longer.

| | | | |
|---|---|---|---|
| 2003 | 96 | 2008 | 2011+ |
| 2002 | 96 | 2010 | 2014+ |
| 2001 | 95 | 2009 | 2013 |
| 2000 | 95 | 2008 | 2012+ |
| 1999 | 95 | 2004 | 2007+ |
| 1998 | 90 | 2003 | 2006+ |
| 1997 | 95 | 2002 | 2005+ |
| 1996 | 94 | 2001 | 2004+ |
| 1995 | 92 | 2000 | 2003 |
| 1994 | 94 | 2002 | 2006 |
| 1993 | 90 | 1998 | 2001 |
| 1992 | 90 | 1997 | 2000 |
| 1991 | 96 | 2003 | 2011 |
| 1990 | 94 | 2002 | 2010 |

# Gulf Station

Pinnacle Lane, Dixon's Creek Vic 3775. Tel: (03) 5965 2271. Fax: (03) 5965 2442.
Website: www.debortoli.com.au  Email: dbw@debortoli.com.au

Region: **Yarra Valley** Winemakers: **Stephen Webber, David Slingsby-Smith** Viticulturist: **Philip Lobley**
Chief Executive: **Darren De Bortoli**

Gulf Station is a De Bortoli label that offers affordable and easy drinking from Yarra Valley vineyards. Its best and most consistent wine is its lightly-oaked, lively and refreshing Chardonnay.

## CABERNET SAUVIGNON

**Yarra Valley**                    $12–$19
**Current vintage: 2001**              87

Honest, flavoursome varietal wine with a lightly cooked and confiture-like aroma of cassis and red berries supported by fresh vanilla oak. There's length and smoothness about its vibrant, generous palate whose blackcurrant and raspberry fruit qualities overlie a lightly herbal note. Framed by fine tannins, it's ready to enjoy.

| 2001 | 87 | 2003 | 2006 |
|------|----|------|------|
| 2000 | 86 | 2002 | 2005 |
| 1999 | 86 | 2001 | 2004 |
| 1998 | 85 | 2000 | 2003 |
| 1997 | 86 | 1999 | 2002+ |

## CHARDONNAY

RANKING **5**

**Yarra Valley**                    $12–$19
**Current vintage: 2003**              89

Smart, tangy and vibrant Chablis-like chardonnay whose fresh aromas of lemon, melon and restrained vanilla oak have a pleasing floral aspect. Trim and taut, it has plenty of concentration and generosity of melon and peachy fruit, before finishing long and dry with refreshing lemon sherbet acids.

| 2003 | 89 | 2004 | 2005+ |
|------|----|------|-------|
| 2002 | 89 | 2003 | 2004+ |
| 2001 | 81 | 2002 | 2003 |
| 2000 | 80 | 2001 | 2002 |
| 1999 | 90 | 2000 | 2001 |

## RIESLING

**Yarra Valley**                    $12–$19
**Current vintage: 2003**              81

Vegetal, rubbery wine with simple tinned fruit flavours, finishing rather short, stale and dirty. It's more than possible that the screwtop seal exacerbated the deficiencies of this wine.

| 2003 | 81 | 2003 | 2004 |
|------|----|------|------|
| 2002 | 87 | 2002 | 2003 |
| 2001 | 77 | 2001 | 2002 |
| 2000 | 82 | 2001 | 2002 |
| 1999 | 80 | 2000 | 2001 |
| 1998 | 91 | 2003 | 2006 |
| 1997 | 87 | 2002 | 2005 |

## SHIRAZ

RANKING **5**

**Yarra Valley**                    $12–$19
**Current vintage: 2002**              89

A great value quaffer with some genuine quality. Fragrant, musky and meaty, its sweet and violet-like aromas of small berries and fresh vanilla oak precede a generous, juicy palate whose spicy flavours of dark berries and plums are framed by moderately firm tannins.

| 2002 | 89 | 2004 | 2007 |
|------|----|------|------|
| 2001 | 85 | 2003 | 2006 |
| 2000 | 88 | 2001 | 2002+ |
| 1999 | 83 | 2001 | 2004 |
| 1998 | 83 | 2000 | 2003 |
| 1996 | 92 | 2008 | 2016 |

# Hanging Rock

88 Jim Road, Newham Vic 3442. Tel: (03) 5427 0542. Fax: (03) 5427 0310.
Website: www.hangingrock.com.au  Email: hrw@hangingrock.com.au

Region: **Macedon Ranges** Winemaker: **John Ellis** Viticulturist: **John Ellis** Chief Executive: **John Ellis**

Hanging Rock is best known for its assertive, robust and deeply concentrated Heathcote Shiraz, which was reintroduced to its range from the 1997 vintage after a change in vineyard sourcing. Its sparkling 'Macedon' is a unique wine in that it is fermented in barrel (old oak only), then blended back to a solera-like 'reserve' of older vintages. It is deliberately made to encourage advanced oxidative characters whose intensity does vary from release to release. The white wines from the home Jim Jim vineyard can be exceptionally intense.

## HEATHCOTE SHIRAZ    RANKING **3**

**Heathcote** $30–$49
**Current vintage: 2001** 89

An intensely flavoured but slightly cooked and raw-edged wine from a hot year. Its spicy, briary aromas of blackberries, plums and violets over sweet chocolate and cedary oak precede a moderately full palate whose confiture-like raspberry, cherry and blackberry fruit is framed by very forward and slightly raw tannins. A good effort, with a reasonable length of flavour.

| Year | Score | Year | Score |
|------|------|------|------|
| 2001 | 89 | 2006 | 2009 |
| 2000 | 91 | 2008 | 2012+ |
| 1999 | 93 | 2011 | 2019 |
| 1998 | 93 | 2010 | 2018 |
| 1997 | 90 | 2005 | 2009 |
| 1992 | 95 | 2012 | 2022 |
| 1991 | 95 | 2003 | 2011+ |
| 1990 | 95 | 2002 | 2010+ |
| 1989 | 89 | 1997 | 2001+ |
| 1988 | 91 | 2000 | 2008 |

## MACEDON    RANKING **4**

**Macedon Ranges** $30–$49
**Current vintage: Cuvée X** 89

Its smoky, meaty and slightly aldehydic bouquet is complex and pungent, revealing citrus and melon-like fruit. Chewy and crunchy, the palate is rich and meaty, with candied citrus flavours and meaty, vegetal influences providing a genuinely distinctive and vinous experience. Finishes long and austere, with slightly green edges and varnishy nuances of oak.

| Cuvée | Score | Year | Year |
|-------|------|------|------|
| Cuvée X | 89 | 2004 | 2007+ |
| Cuvée IX | 87 | 2003 | 2005 |
| Cuvée VIII | 91 | 2002 | 2006+ |
| Cuvée VII | 94 | 2000 | 2003 |
| Cuvée VI | 88 | 1999 | 2002 |
| Cuvée V | 87 | 1997 | 2000 |
| Cuvée IV | 94 | 1996 | 1999 |
| Cuvée III | 91 | 1995 | 1999 |

## THE JIM JIM SAUVIGNON BLANC    RANKING **5**

**Macedon Ranges** $20–$29
**Current vintage: 2003** 88

Lightly sweaty and vegetative aromas lurk beneath its dusty, herbaceous aromas of citrus, passionfruit and wet slate, while its slightly cloying, broad and confectionary palate lacks its usual shape and freshness. It finishes with both sweetness and austerity, and would appear to have been made from both under and over-ripe fruit.

| Year | Score | Year | Year |
|------|------|------|------|
| 2003 | 88 | 2004 | 2005 |
| 2002 | 87 | 2003 | 2003 |
| 2001 | 90 | 2003 | 2006 |
| 2000 | 87 | 2001 | 2002 |
| 1999 | 86 | 2000 | 2001 |
| 1998 | 90 | 2000 | 2003 |

# Hardys

Reynell Road, Reynella SA 5161. Tel: (08) 8392 2222. Fax: (08) 8392 2202.
Website: www.hardywines.com.au  Email: corporate@hardywines.com.au

Regions: **South Australia, Tasmania** Winemakers: **Peter Dawson (chief), Paul Lapsley (red),**
**Tom Newton (white), Ed Carr (sparkling).** Viticulturist: **Brenton Baker** Chief Executive: **David Woods**

Part of one of the world's largest wine companies in Constellation Wines, The Hardy Wine Company appears to be getting on with business at the production level, despite significant recent changes in key winemaking personnel. Its leading labels of the Arras sparkling wine, the Eileen Hardy pair of Shiraz and Chardonnay, plus the Thomas Hardy Cabernet Sauvignon are well supported by the reliable and regional Tintara brand.

## ARRAS SPARKLING CHARDONNAY PINOT NOIR

RANKING **2**

Tasmania $50+
**Current vintage: 1999** 95

Developing toasty, meaty and brioche-like bouquet of citrus and honeysuckle, before an elegant and restrained palate whose tightly focused core of intense fruit delivers explosive impact. There's creaminess and richness in the middle, but the wine finishes lean and sculpted, with lingering fresh fruit flavours over a chalky backbone.

| | | | |
|---|---|---|---|
| 2000 | 93 | 2008 | 2012 |
| 1999 | 95 | 2007 | 2011 |
| 1998 | 94 | 2003 | 2006+ |
| 1997 | 90 | 1999 | 2002 |
| 1995 | 95 | 2003 | 2007 |

## EILEEN HARDY CHARDONNAY

RANKING **2**

1999 CHARDONNAY
The best Chardonnay from each vintage is selected by the winemakers for release under the 'Eileen Hardy' label

Pipers River, Padthaway,
McLaren Vale $30–$49
**Current vintage: 2002** 94

Pristine, fragrant aromas of tangy grapefruit, mango and melon over spicy, creamy undertones of matchstick-like oak with nuances of lime, ginger and cinnamon. Smooth and fleshy, the palate has a baby-fat like juiciness and a bright core of vibrant tropical fruit and grapefruit flavour tightly knit with creamy oak. Very good.

| | | | |
|---|---|---|---|
| 2002 | 94 | 2004 | 2007+ |
| 2001 | 95 | 2006 | 2009+ |
| 2000 | 95 | 2005 | 2008 |
| 1999 | 96 | 2004 | 2007+ |
| 1998 | 94 | 2003 | 2006 |
| 1997 | 92 | 1999 | 2002 |
| 1996 | 95 | 2001 | 2004+ |
| 1995 | 93 | 2000 | 2003 |
| 1994 | 91 | 1996 | 1999 |
| 1993 | 90 | 1998 | 2001 |
| 1992 | 85 | 1997 | 2000 |
| 1991 | 93 | 1996 | 1999+ |

## EILEEN HARDY SHIRAZ

RANKING **2**

2000 SHIRAZ
The best Shiraz from each vintage is selected by the winemakers for release under the 'Eileen Hardy' label

McLaren Vale, Padthaway $50+
**Current vintage: 2001** 93

Tightly knit, rather closed but pristine shiraz of intensity and elegance. Its musky, meaty aromas of blackberries, blackcurrants and redcurrants are a little hemmed in at present by sweet cedar/mocha oak, which also overshadows the palate's tightly packed small berry and plum flavours. Moderately firm and very spicy, this sweet-fruited shiraz should emerge into a refined and polished wine.

| | | | |
|---|---|---|---|
| 2001 | 93 | 2009 | 2013+ |
| 2000 | 93 | 2008 | 2012+ |
| 1999 | 96 | 2011 | 2019 |
| 1998 | 97 | 2010 | 2018 |
| 1997 | 93 | 2005 | 2009 |
| 1996 | 96 | 2016 | 2026 |
| 1995 | 95 | 2003 | 2007 |
| 1994 | 95 | 2006 | 2014 |
| 1993 | 89 | 2001 | 2005 |
| 1992 | 90 | 2000 | 2004 |
| 1991 | 92 | 1999 | 2003 |
| 1990 | 93 | 2002 | 2010+ |
| 1989 | 90 | 1997 | 2001 |
| 1988 | 93 | 2000 | 2008+ |
| 1987 | 91 | 1995 | 1999 |

## NOTTAGE HILL CABERNET SHIRAZ

South Australia $12–$19
**Current vintage: 2002** 81

An earthy, rather confectionary riverland red with raspberry and plum flavours. It's lightly spicy, with some forward plummy fruit, but then thins out to rather a hollow finish.

| | | | |
|---|---|---|---|
| 2002 | 81 | 2003 | 2004+ |
| 2001 | 78 | 2002 | 2003 |
| 2000 | 80 | 2001 | 2002 |
| 1999 | 80 | 2000 | 2001 |
| 1998 | 88 | 2000 | 2003+ |
| 1996 | 82 | 2001 | 2004 |
| 1995 | 83 | 1997 | 2000 |
| 1994 | 85 | 1996 | 1999 |

A B C D E F G H I J K L M N O P Q R S T U V W X Y Z

## SIEGERSDORF RIESLING

RANKING 5

**Clare Valley** $12–$19
**Current vintage: 2003** 84

Estery, floral and lemony aromas of tinned pineapples and other tropical fruits, with a confection-like babypowder quality. Toasty and honeyed, with generous and candied fruit flavours, it is fast developing breadth and a little coarseness.

| 2003 | 84 | 2004 | 2005+ |
|------|----|------|-------|
| 2002 | 89 | 2007 | 2010 |
| 2001 | 89 | 2003 | 2006+ |
| 2000 | 89 | 2005 | 2008 |
| 1999 | 80 | 2004 | 2007+ |
| 1998 | 89 | 2003 | 2006+ |
| 1997 | 89 | 2002 | 2005 |
| 1996 | 88 | 2001 | 2004 |
| 1995 | 86 | 1996 | 1997 |

## THOMAS HARDY CABERNET SAUVIGNON

RANKING 3

**Margaret River, McLaren Vale, Coonawarra** $50+
**Current vintage: 1999** 93

Complex earthy aromas of small red and black berries, smoky vanilla/cedar oak, undergrowth and dusty, herbal undertones. Long and astringent, with a deep, dark expression of small berry fruits, it does however present a herbal aspect suggestive of slightly shaded fruit influences.

| 1999 | 93 | 2011 | 2019 |
|------|----|------|------|
| 1996 | 94 | 2008 | 2016 |
| 1995 | 92 | 2003 | 2007+ |
| 1994 | 94 | 2006 | 2012 |
| 1993 | 90 | 2001 | 2005 |
| 1992 | 93 | 2000 | 2004 |
| 1991 | 94 | 2003 | 2011 |
| 1990 | 95 | 2002 | 2010 |
| 1989 | 94 | 2001 | 2009 |

## TINTARA GRENACHE

RANKING 4

**McLaren Vale** $30–$49
**Current vintage: 2002** 90

Pungent reductive and leathery charcuterie-like aromas of cured meats, spicy red plums, raspberries and blueberries, with a background of creamy oak. Presently closed and restrained, it's firm and fine-grained, offering sweet small berry fruits, chocolatey spiciness and a lingering nutty, savoury finish punctuated by pleasing acidity. It should flesh out nicely with time.

| 2002 | 90 | 2007 | 2010+ |
|------|----|------|-------|
| 1999 | 89 | 2004 | 2007 |
| 1998 | 95 | 2003 | 2006+ |
| 1997 | 89 | 2002 | 2005 |
| 1996 | 92 | 2001 | 2004+ |
| 1995 | 93 | 2003 | 2007 |

## TINTARA SHIRAZ

RANKING 3

**McLaren Vale** $30–$49
**Current vintage: 2001** 90

Slightly closed aromas of blackberries, plums, redcurrants and polished cedary oak precede a generous and robust palate. Rich and chocolatey, it's slightly tarry, cooked and forward, with a menthol, currant and prune-like edge to its plum and blackberry fruit. Sweet and creamy vanilla oak lends palate softness and approachability. A well-handled red, but lacking its usual structure and longevity.

| 2001 | 90 | 2006 | 2009+ |
|------|----|------|-------|
| 2000 | 89 | 2005 | 2008 |
| 1999 | 88 | 2004 | 2007 |
| 1998 | 95 | 2006 | 2010+ |
| 1997 | 89 | 2002 | 2005 |
| 1996 | 94 | 2004 | 2008 |
| 1995 | 95 | 2000 | 2003+ |

# Heathcote Winery

183 High Street, Heathcote Vic 3523. Tel: (03) 5433 2595. Fax: (03) 5433 3081.
Website: www.heathcotewinery.com.au Email: winemaker@heathcotewinery.com.au
Region: **Heathcote** Winemaker: **Jonathan Mepham** Viticulturist: **Andrew Mepham**
Chief Executive: **Steve Wilkins**

The Heathcote Winery is without doubt making some of the finest and most long-living of all the shirazes emerging from this highly-rated region. While neither the Mail Coach nor the flagship Curagee Shirazes are in any way shrinking violets, they certainly avoid the overcooked and porty characters sought after by so many other Heathcote-based wineries. A recent tasting of older vintages confirms their class and individuality.

## CHARDONNAY

RANKING **5**

| Heathcote | $20–$29 |
| --- | --- |
| **Current vintage: 2002** | **89** |

Enlivened with a spicy fragrance of honeysuckle, this restrained and savoury chardonnay might just have received a small shot of viognier. Nutty, peachy and lemony, its lightly oaked and creamy aromas precede a round, generous and slightly oily palate. Ripe stonefruit-like flavours of melon and green olives culminate in a chalky, almost dusty finish.

| | | | |
| --- | --- | --- | --- |
| 2002 | 89 | 2004 | 2007 |
| 2001 | 89 | 2003 | 2006 |
| 2000 | 89 | 2002 | 2005 |
| 1998 | 88 | 2000 | 2003+ |
| 1997 | 81 | 1998 | 1999 |
| 1996 | 89 | 1998 | 2001 |

## CURAGEE SHIRAZ

RANKING **2**

| Heathcote | $30–$49 |
| --- | --- |
| **Current vintage: 2002** | **91** |

A big, rich, ripe and chocolatey Heathcote shiraz that unlike so many others from this region in 2002 is focused around fruit qualities that are genuinely ripe and not over-cooked. There's some spicy, meaty complexity behind its floral, earthy aromas, while its powerfully constructed but still eminently approachable palate is thickly coated with deep black fruit flavours. There are smooth, rounded edges to its firm extract.

| | | | |
| --- | --- | --- | --- |
| 2002 | 91 | 2010 | 2014 |
| 2001 | 95 | 2009 | 2013 |
| 1999 | 87 | 2004 | 2007+ |
| 1998 | 95 | 2006 | 2010+ |
| 1997 | 94 | 2005 | 2009 |

## MAIL COACH SHIRAZ

RANKING **3**

| Heathcote | $20–$29 |
| --- | --- |
| **Current vintage: 2002** | **89** |

Firm, meaty and amarone-like shiraz whose dark and musky aromas of dark plums, prunes, currants and treacle precede a velvet-smooth but slightly charry, oaky palate. It's marginally overcooked, but delivers plenty of bright flavours of cherries and dark plums, before an astringent and savoury finish.

| | | | |
| --- | --- | --- | --- |
| 2002 | 89 | 2010 | 2014 |
| 2001 | 91 | 2006 | 2009+ |
| 2000 | 93 | 2008 | 2012 |
| 1999 | 92 | 2007 | 2011 |
| 1998 | 93 | 2006 | 2010+ |
| 1997 | 93 | 2002 | 2005+ |
| 1995 | 85 | 1997 | 2000 |
| 1994 | 91 | 1999 | 2002 |

## MAIL COACH VIOGNIER (Formerly Curagee)

RANKING **5**

| Heathcote | $20–$29 |
| --- | --- |
| **Current vintage: 2003** | **86** |

Little oaky, perhaps rather oxidative and varnishy expression of viognier with some floral perfume, juicy texture and savoury finish, but a slightly overdone level of oxidation. Oaky, and quite fast-maturing.

| | | | |
| --- | --- | --- | --- |
| 2003 | 86 | 2004 | 2005 |
| 2002 | 86 | 2003 | 2004+ |
| 2001 | 88 | 2003 | 2006 |
| 2000 | 91 | 2002 | 2005 |
| 1998 | 89 | 2000 | 2003 |

# Heggies Vineyard

Heggies Range Road, Eden Valley SA 5235. Tel: (08) 8561 3200. Fax: (08) 8561 3393.
Website: www.heggiesvineyard.com  Email: info@heggiesvineyard.com
Region: **Eden Valley** Winemaker: **Peter Gambetta** Viticulturist: **Robin Nettelbeck**
Chief Executive: **Robert Hill Smith**
A mature Eden Valley vineyard producing reliable and flavoursome wine, Heggies is part of the Yalumba family.
The 2003 vintage produced a rather full-blown Viognier, a punchy and savoury Chardonnay, plus a typically
tangy and restrained Riesling.

## CHARDONNAY

RANKING **4**

| Eden Valley | $20–$29 |
| --- | --- |
| **Current vintage: 2003** | **90** |

Punchy, assertive chardonnay with a floral aroma
of peaches and nutmeal over some measured vanilla
oak. There's a musky apricot, viognier-like quality
to the wine's penetrative melon flavours. Round
and generous, it offers a pleasing length of fruit
before finishing rather savoury, with lingering nutty
and stonefruit flavours.

| 2003 | 90 | 2005 | 2008 |
| --- | --- | --- | --- |
| 2002 | 93 | 2004 | 2007 |
| 2001 | 90 | 2003 | 2006 |
| 2000 | 85 | 2002 | 2005 |
| 1998 | 89 | 2000 | 2003+ |
| 1997 | 87 | 1999 | 2002 |
| 1996 | 87 | 1998 | 2001 |
| 1995 | 91 | 2000 | 2003 |

## MERLOT (Formerly Cabernet Blend)

RANKING **4**

| Eden Valley | $30–$49 |
| --- | --- |
| **Current vintage: 2001** | **89** |

A big, almost brassy merlot whose slightly jammy
and confectionary expression of dark cherries and
small berries is tightly matched with fairly
assertive and lightly toasty creamy vanilla oak. The
mocha and dark chocolate influences on the nose
suggest a level of barrel ferment, while the fruit
is just a little too cooked and the tannins marginally too raw and astringent for a higher rating.

| 2001 | 89 | 2006 | 2009 |
| --- | --- | --- | --- |
| 2000 | 87 | 2002 | 2005+ |
| 1999 | 88 | 2001 | 2004+ |
| 1998 | 89 | 2003 | 2006 |
| 1996 | 90 | 2001 | 2004 |
| 1995 | 90 | 2000 | 2003+ |
| 1994 | 93 | 2002 | 2006 |
| 1993 | 94 | 2001 | 2005 |
| 1992 | 87 | 2000 | 2004 |
| 1991 | 88 | 1996 | 1999 |
| 1990 | 91 | 1998 | 2002 |

## RIESLING

RANKING **3**

| Eden Valley | $12–$19 |
| --- | --- |
| **Current vintage: 2003** | **92** |

Tangy, elegant, fine and supple riesling with a fresh
and delicate aroma of lime juice and green
apples over subtle floral and powdery nuances.
Long, clean and restrained, with a reserved core
of intense apple, lemon and pear fruit, it finishes
long and citrusy, with refreshing lemony acids.

| 2003 | 92 | 2008 | 2011+ |
| --- | --- | --- | --- |
| 2002 | 92 | 2010 | 2024+ |
| 2001 | 90 | 2006 | 2009 |
| 2000 | 90 | 2005 | 2008+ |
| 1999 | 95 | 2007 | 2011 |
| 1998 | 96 | 2006 | 2010+ |
| 1997 | 89 | 2002 | 2005 |
| 1996 | 88 | 2003 | 2007 |
| 1995 | 94 | 2003 | 2007 |
| 1994 | 77 | 1996 | 1999 |
| 1993 | 94 | 2005 | 2013 |
| 1992 | 93 | 1997 | 2000 |

## VIOGNIER

RANKING **4**

| Eden Valley | $12–$19 |
| --- | --- |
| **Current vintage: 2003** | **89** |

Feisty and forward viognier whose restrained
perfume of honeysuckle, apricot blossom, cloves
and cinnamon reveal some underlying
nutmeal/almond aromas. Quite full-blown, viscous
and chewy, this is a warm, slightly sweet and nutty
wine with good varietal qualities but a little rawness.

| 2003 | 89 | 2004 | 2005+ |
| --- | --- | --- | --- |
| 2002 | 94 | 2004 | 2007 |
| 2001 | 90 | 2002 | 2003+ |
| 2000 | 89 | 2002 | 2005 |
| 1999 | 82 | 2001 | 2004 |
| 1998 | 93 | 2000 | 2003 |
| 1997 | 92 | 1999 | 2002 |
| 1996 | 86 | 1997 | 1998 |
| 1995 | 80 | 1996 | 1997 |
| 1994 | 90 | 1999 | 2002 |

# Henschke

Henschke Road, Keyneton SA 5353. Tel: (08) 8564 8223. Fax: (08) 8564 8294.
Website: www.henschke.com.au  Email: info@henschke.com.au

Region: **Eden Valley** Winemaker: **Stephen Henschke** Viticulturist: **Prue Henschke**
Chief Executive: **Stephen Henschke**

Henschke is a small and iconic Australian winery in the Eden Valley region with access to several landmark old vine vineyards in the Eden Valley itself, plus some steep but relatively modern plantings at Lenswood in the Adelaide Hills. While a string of variable and challenging vintages has left an imprint in some recent wines, there are positive indications that Henschke's wines are returning to their customary and expected levels of excellence.

## ABBOTTS PRAYER

RANKING **3**

Lenswood                         $50+
**Current vintage: 2000**          **85**

Earthy, greenish aromas of small red berries and sweet, smoky oak precede a thin, sour-edged palate lacking length and ripeness.

| | | | |
|---|---|---|---|
| 2000 | 85 | 2002 | 2005 |
| 1999 | 92 | 2011 | 2019 |
| 1998 | 82 | 2000 | 2003 |
| 1997 | 87 | 2005 | 2009 |
| 1996 | 94 | 2004 | 2008+ |
| 1995 | 94 | 2003 | 2007 |
| 1994 | 95 | 2006 | 2014 |
| 1993 | 94 | 2005 | 2013 |
| 1992 | 92 | 2000 | 2004 |
| 1991 | 93 | 2003 | 2011 |
| 1990 | 96 | 2002 | 2010 |
| 1989 | 89 | 1994 | 1997 |

## CRANES EDEN VALLEY CHARDONNAY

RANKING **4**

Eden Valley                      $20–$29
**Current vintage: 2000**          **82**

Forward, candied and toffee-like aromas of citrus and melon fruit with dusty vanilla oak. Simple, juicy palate whose tobaccoey melon fruit lacks length and finish.

| | | | |
|---|---|---|---|
| 2000 | 82 | 2002 | 2005 |
| 1999 | 82 | 2000 | 2001 |
| 1998 | 92 | 2003 | 2006 |
| 1997 | 90 | 2002 | 2005 |
| 1996 | 93 | 2001 | 2004 |
| 1995 | 90 | 1997 | 2000 |
| 1994 | 93 | 1999 | 2002 |
| 1993 | 91 | 1995 | 1998 |
| 1992 | 92 | 1997 | 2000 |
| 1991 | 94 | 1996 | 1999 |
| 1990 | 95 | 1998 | 2002 |

## CROFT CHARDONNAY

RANKING **4**

Lenswood                         $30–$49
**Current vintage: 2002**          **87**

Nutty aromas of citrus, green cashews, light vanilla oak and creamy lees-derived influences precede a palate that begins with some forward richness and fattiness, but then fades towards a lean finish enlivened by lemon/vanilla oak.

| | | | |
|---|---|---|---|
| 2002 | 87 | 2004 | 2007 |
| 2000 | 87 | 2002 | 2005 |
| 1999 | 84 | 2001 | 2004 |
| 1998 | 94 | 2003 | 2006+ |
| 1997 | 87 | 2002 | 2005 |
| 1996 | 94 | 2001 | 2004 |
| 1995 | 90 | 1997 | 2000 |
| 1994 | 94 | 1999 | 2003 |
| 1993 | 89 | 1995 | 1998 |
| 1990 | 94 | 1995 | 1998 |

## CYRIL HENSCHKE CABERNET SAUVIGNON

RANKING 4

**Eden Valley**     $50+
**Current vintage: 2000**     88

Sweet, forward aromas of herby red berries and plums with cedar/vanilla oak. Medium to full in weight, its sweet forward fruit thins out in the middle palate, before a raw-edged finish of greenish tannins. Lacking ripeness and real integrity, it finishes with slightly sour fruit and stale oak-derived influences suggestive of older cooperage.

| | | | |
|---|---|---|---|
| 2000 | 88 | 2005 | 2008 |
| 1999 | 81 | 2004 | 2007 |
| 1997 | 88 | 2005 | 2009 |
| 1996 | 95 | 2008 | 2016+ |
| 1995 | 91 | 2003 | 2007 |
| 1994 | 89 | 2002 | 2006+ |
| 1993 | 87 | 2001 | 2005 |
| 1992 | 94 | 2004 | 2012 |
| 1991 | 95 | 2003 | 2011 |
| 1990 | 95 | 2002 | 2010 |
| 1989 | 91 | 2001 | 2009 |
| 1988 | 96 | 1996 | 2000 |
| 1987 | 87 | 1992 | 1995 |
| 1986 | 92 | 1998 | 2003 |
| 1985 | 93 | 1997 | 2002 |
| 1984 | 95 | 1992 | 1996 |
| 1983 | 90 | 1995 | 2000 |
| 1982 | 87 | 1987 | 1990 |
| 1981 | 94 | 1993 | 1998 |
| 1980 | 90 | 1992 | 1997 |
| 1979 | 87 | 1987 | 1991 |
| 1978 | 91 | 1990 | 2000 |

## GILES PINOT NOIR

RANKING 5

**Lenswood**     $30–$49
**Current vintage: 2002**     82

Rustic and dusty, with meaty, herbal fruit aromas and sweet vanilla oak before a simple, herbal and up-front palate whose jujube-like flavours are lifted by sweet oak.

| | | | |
|---|---|---|---|
| 2002 | 82 | 2004 | 2007 |
| 2001 | 87 | 2003 | 2006+ |
| 1999 | 89 | 2004 | 2007 |
| 1998 | 84 | 2003 | 2006+ |
| 1997 | 90 | 2002 | 2005 |
| 1996 | 90 | 2001 | 2004 |
| 1994 | 89 | 1999 | 2002 |

## GREEN'S HILL RIESLING

RANKING 4

**Lenswood**     $20–$29
**Current vintage: 2002**     87

Lightly sweaty, but delicate, earthy and confection-like aromas of apple, pear, peaches and lime juice, before a slightly sappy palate. Beginning with juicy, creamy textures and slightly herbal fruit flavours, it finishes a little too cloying and green-edged.

| | | | |
|---|---|---|---|
| 2002 | 87 | 2004 | 2007 |
| 2001 | 82 | 2003 | 2006 |
| 2000 | 87 | 2002 | 2005+ |
| 1999 | 90 | 2001 | 2004 |
| 1998 | 93 | 2003 | 2006+ |
| 1997 | 94 | 2005 | 2009 |
| 1996 | 95 | 2004 | 2008 |
| 1995 | 93 | 2003 | 2007 |
| 1994 | 93 | 2002 | 2006 |
| 1993 | 94 | 1998 | 2001 |

## HILL OF GRACE

RANKING 1

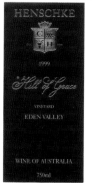

**Eden Valley**     $50+
**Current vintage: 1999**     90

Powerful, rather advanced and meaty shiraz with a complex earthy bouquet of dark plums, blackberries and reductive complexity. Heavily worked, savoury and drying, its chocolatey palate has evolved into the meaty, leathery flavour spectrum, finishing astringent and slightly raw-edged.

| | | | |
|---|---|---|---|
| 1999 | 90 | 2011 | 2019 |
| 1998 | 96 | 2018 | 2028 |
| 1997 | 95 | 2017 | 2027 |
| 1996 | 97 | 2008 | 2016+ |
| 1995 | 93 | 2015 | 2025 |
| 1994 | 93 | 2002 | 2006+ |
| 1993 | 91 | 2013 | 2023 |
| 1992 | 95 | 2012 | 2022 |
| 1991 | 95 | 2011 | 2021 |
| 1990 | 94 | 2002 | 2010+ |
| 1989 | 87 | 1994 | 1997 |
| 1988 | 96 | 2008 | 2018 |
| 1987 | 88 | 1999 | 2007+ |
| 1986 | 97 | 2006 | 2016 |
| 1985 | 91 | 2005 | 2015 |
| 1984 | 88 | 1996 | 2004 |
| 1983 | 84 | 1991 | 1995 |
| 1982 | 94 | 1994 | 2002 |
| 1981 | 84 | 1986 | 1989 |
| 1980 | 89 | 1992 | 2000 |

continued next page...

# HILL OF GRACE

...continued

| | | | |
|---|---|---|---|
| 1979 | 90 | 1991 | 1999 |
| 1978 | 95 | 1998 | 2008 |
| 1977 | 90 | 1989 | 1997+ |
| 1976 | 94 | 1996 | 2006 |
| 1975 | 87 | 1983 | 1987 |
| 1973 | 95 | 1993 | 2003 |
| 1972 | 94 | 1992 | 2002 |
| 1971 | 94 | 1991 | 2001 |
| 1970 | 93 | 1990 | 2000 |
| 1969 | 86 | 1981 | 1989 |

## JULIUS RIESLING

RANKING 3

Eden Valley      $20–$29
**Current vintage: 2003**    **90**

Opulent aromas of pear and apple, with a suggestion of dried hay. Broad, generous palate with pleasing fruit and an underlying phenolic spine. Not hugely complex, but full, broad and generous.

| | | | |
|---|---|---|---|
| 2003 | 90 | 2008 | 2011 |
| 2002 | 94 | 2010 | 2014 |
| 2001 | 88 | 2009 | 2013 |
| 2000 | 84 | 2002 | 2005 |
| 1999 | 93 | 2004 | 2007 |
| 1998 | 91 | 2006 | 2010 |
| 1997 | 94 | 2005 | 2009 |
| 1996 | 94 | 2004 | 2008 |
| 1995 | 91 | 1997 | 2000 |
| 1994 | 95 | 2006 | 2014 |
| 1993 | 95 | 2000 | 2005 |
| 1992 | 94 | 2000 | 2004 |
| 1991 | 95 | 1999 | 2003 |
| 1990 | 95 | 1995 | 1998 |
| 1989 | 87 | 1994 | 1997 |
| 1988 | 88 | 1993 | 1996 |
| 1987 | 94 | 1999 | 2007 |
| 1986 | 90 | 1991 | 1994 |

## KEYNETON ESTATE

RANKING 3

Eden Valley      $30–$49
**Current vintage: 2001**    **86**

Meaty, vegetal aromas of small red and black berries with undertones of sweet, smoky vanilla oak. Supple and smooth, but framed by fine but green-edged tannins, the palate lacks genuine freshness and vitality, and despite having some firmness and structure, finishes rather raw and dull.

| | | | |
|---|---|---|---|
| 2001 | 86 | 2006 | 2009 |
| 1999 | 86 | 2004 | 2007 |
| 1998 | 92 | 2006 | 2010 |
| 1997 | 87 | 2002 | 2005 |
| 1996 | 93 | 2004 | 2008+ |
| 1994 | 93 | 2002 | 2006 |
| 1993 | 94 | 2005 | 2013 |
| 1992 | 93 | 1997 | 2000 |
| 1991 | 95 | 2003 | 2011 |
| 1990 | 88 | 1995 | 1998 |
| 1989 | 87 | 1994 | 1997 |
| 1988 | 93 | 1996 | 2000 |
| 1987 | 85 | 1992 | 1995 |
| 1986 | 94 | 1998 | 2003 |

## LOUIS EDEN VALLEY SEMILLON

RANKING 5

Eden Valley      $20–$29
**Current vintage: 2002**    **90**

Herby, slightly sweaty and greenish semillon aromas of melon and lemon rind with some earthy burned matchstick-like bound sulphide complexity. Lean, dry and citrusy, with a bright core of intense, vibrant fruit finishing long and mineral, with attractive steely austerity. Refreshing and lively.

| | | | |
|---|---|---|---|
| 2002 | 90 | 2007 | 2010 |
| 2000 | 87 | 2002 | 2005 |
| 1999 | 83 | 2001 | 2004 |
| 1998 | 88 | 2003 | 2006 |
| 1997 | 90 | 2002 | 2005 |
| 1996 | 86 | 1998 | 2003 |
| 1995 | 94 | 2000 | 2003 |
| 1994 | 93 | 2002 | 2006 |
| 1993 | 95 | 1998 | 2001 |

## MOUNT EDELSTONE

**Eden Valley**     $50+
**Current vintage: 2001**     92

A developing, old-fashioned red whose choco-latey, meaty and spicy aromas of plums, redcur-rants and sweet, spicy vanilla and lightly toasty oak reveal nuances of mint and menthol. Earthy and leathery, but built on a solid foundation of firm and slightly drying tannins, it offers rich, spicy flavours of redcurrants and mulberries, culminating in a lingering, if slightly gritty finish.

| | | | |
|---|---|---|---|
| 2001 | 92 | 2009 | 2013 |
| 2000 | 82 | 2002 | 2005+ |
| 1999 | 92 | 2007 | 2011 |
| 1998 | 88 | 2000 | 2003+ |
| 1997 | 87 | 2005 | 2009 |
| 1996 | 90 | 2004 | 2008 |
| 1995 | 93 | 2007 | 2015 |
| 1994 | 92 | 2002 | 2006 |
| 1993 | 95 | 2005 | 2013 |
| 1992 | 94 | 2004 | 2012 |
| 1991 | 95 | 2003 | 2011 |
| 1990 | 95 | 2002 | 2010 |
| 1989 | 89 | 1997 | 2003 |
| 1988 | 94 | 2000 | 2005 |
| 1987 | 87 | 1995 | 2001 |
| 1986 | 93 | 1998 | 2003 |
| 1985 | 87 | 2005 | 2015 |
| 1984 | 88 | 1996 | 2001 |
| 1983 | 90 | 1995 | 2000 |
| 1982 | 90 | 1994 | 1999 |
| 1981 | 82 | 1993 | 1998 |
| 1980 | 90 | 2000 | 2005 |

# Hewitson

66 London Road, Mile End SA 5031. Tel: (08) 8443 6466. Fax: (08) 8443 6866.
Website: www.hewitson.com.au Email: dean@hewitson.com.au

Regions: **Barossa Valley, Fleurieu Peninsula** Winemaker: **Dean Hewitson** Chief Executive: **Dean Hewitson**

Dean Hewitson appears to be enjoying himself thoroughly at his self-appointed task of making small parcels of wine from ancient vineyards. His wines reflect not only a technical stability and correctness, but a level of artisan craftsmanship rare in Australian wine. Typically full-flavoured, firm and tightly structured, his savoury and earthy red wines combine rusticity with flair.

## EDEN VALLEY RIESLING

**HEWITSON**
*Riesling*
2003
*Eden Valley*
750ML AUSTRALIAN WINE

**Eden Valley**     $12–$19
**Current vintage: 2003**     91

Estery, fragrant, lightly spicy and chalky lime-juice aromas precede rather a round, juicy and thickly pro-portioned palate for riesling from this region. A fine chalky spine supports the wine's fleshiness and generous length of lively, lingering varietal fruit. Just lacks the definition of fruit and acid for a top score.

| | | | |
|---|---|---|---|
| 2003 | 91 | 2008 | 2011 |
| 2002 | 88 | 2004 | 2007 |
| 1998 | 90 | 2003 | 2006 |

## L'OIZEAU SHIRAZ

**HEWITSON**
*L'Oizeau*
2001
*Shiraz*
*McLaren Vale*
750ML AUSTRALIAN WINE

**Fleurieu Peninsula**     $30–$49
**Current vintage: 2001**     88

A generous but elegant shiraz whose slightly closed and earthy aromas of plums and prunes, chocolate and leather overlie pleasing walnut-like aromas. Moderately rich, it reveals an old-fashioned, spicy and slightly overcooked palate with pleasing softness and fruit sweetness. It finishes soft and savoury.

| | | | |
|---|---|---|---|
| 2001 | 88 | 2003 | 2006+ |
| 2000 | 93 | 2008 | 2012+ |
| 1999 | 86 | 2004 | 2007 |
| 1997 | 87 | 1999 | 2002 |
| 1996 | 86 | 2001 | 2004 |

## MISS HARRY (Grenache Shiraz Mourvèdre)

**HEWITSON**
*Miss Harry*
2003
DRY GROWN & ANCIENT
*Barossa Valley*
750ML AUSTRALIAN WINE · 43% VOL

**Fleurieu Peninsula**     $20–$29
**Current vintage: 2003**     90

Tight, focused and dry, this meaty and savoury early-drinker has a restrained, spicy aroma of small red berries over earthy nuances of cloves, cinnamon and nutmeg. Smooth and silky, its up-front flavours of plums and redcurrants herald a long and juicy palate that culminates in a lingering and fine-grained finish.

| | | | |
|---|---|---|---|
| 2003 | 90 | 2004 | 2005+ |
| 2002 | 91 | 2003 | 2004+ |
| 2001 | 90 | 2003 | 2006 |

## OLD GARDEN MOURVÈDRE

| Barossa Valley | $30–$49 | 2002 | 92 | 2010 | 2014+ |
|---|---|---|---|---|---|
| **Current vintage: 2002** | **92** | 2001 | 91 | 2009 | 2013 |
| | | 2000 | 95 | 2012 | 2020 |

Complex rustic, meaty and earthy aromas of briary dark berries and plums, laced with sweet scents of flowers and chocolate. Its long, smooth and creamy palate of pristine dark plum and berry flavours reveals suggestions of currant and menthol. Lingering, dark and spicy, it's surprisingly soft given its substantial extract.

# Highbank Vineyards

Riddoch Highway, Coonawarra SA 5263. Tel: (08) 8736 3311. Fax: (08) 8736 3122.
Website: www.highbank.com.au  Email: winemaker@highbank.com.au
Region: **Coonawarra** Winemakers: **Dennis Vice, Trevor Mast** Viticulturist: **Dennis Vice**
Chief Executive: **Dennis Vice**

Highbank is a small individual vineyard in Coonawarra cultivated without the use of chemical herbicides or insecticides whose major wine is its blend of red Bordeaux varieties. As a glance at the scores indicates, recent vintages have been remarkably inconsistent. When they are good, however, they are excellent.

## COONAWARRA BASKET PRESS

| Coonawarra | $30–$49 | 2002 | 82 | 2004 | 2007 |
|---|---|---|---|---|---|
| **Current vintage: 2002** | **82** | 2001 | 93 | 2009 | 2013 |
| | | 2000 | 81 | 2002 | 2005 |
| Light, rather simple and soupy red whose herby, | | 1999 | 79 | 2000 | 2001 |
| greenish aromas of mint and menthol, small berries | | 1998 | 96 | 2010 | 2018 |
| and plums precedes a forward, but ultimately short | | 1997 | 95 | 2005 | 2009 |
| palate whose forward flavours of raspberries and | | 1996 | 95 | 2008 | 2016 |
| mulberries finish slightly sappy. | | 1994 | 95 | 2002 | 2006 |
| | | 1993 | 93 | 1998 | 2001 |
| | | 1992 | 94 | 2000 | 2004 |
| | | 1991 | 89 | 1996 | 1999+ |

# Hill Smith Estate

Flaxman's Valley Road, Eden Valley SA 5235. Tel: (08) 8561 3200. Fax: (08) 8561 3393.
Website: www.hillsmithestate.com  Email: info@hillsmithestate.com
Region: **Eden Valley** Winemaker: **Louisa Rose** Viticulturist: **Robin Nettlebeck**
Chief Executive: **Robert Hill Smith**

Hill Smith Estate is another mature Eden Valley vineyard linked through ownership to the Yalumba winery, where its sole remaining wine — a lively, intense and occasionally excellent sauvignon blanc — is made.

## SAUVIGNON BLANC

| Eden Valley | $12–$19 | 2003 | 90 | 2004 | 2005+ |
|---|---|---|---|---|---|
| **Current vintage: 2003** | **90** | 2002 | 88 | 2003 | 2004 |
| | | 2001 | 81 | 2001 | 2002 |
| Offering more style and complexity than most | | 2000 | 81 | 2001 | 2002 |
| Australian sauvignon blanc, this racy, almost | | 1999 | 92 | 2000 | 2001 |

steely wine has a smoky, herbal Loire-like aroma of gooseberries and lychees. Racy and austere, its initially smooth palate of gooseberry and passionfruit flavours has a herbal quality, finishing with lively acids and a note of capsicum.

# Hollick

cnr Ravenswood Lane & Riddoch Highway, Coonawarra SA 5263. Tel: (08) 8737 2318. Fax: (08) 8737 2952.
Website: www.hollick.com Email: admin@hollick.com

Region: **Coonawarra** Winemakers: **Ian Hollick, David Norman** Viticulturist: **Ian Hollick**
Chief Executive: **Ian Hollick**

Ian Hollick is a highly experienced Coonawarra viticulturist whose wines, with the exceptional of the occasionally first-class Ravenswood (a varietal cabernet sauvignon), tend to be fine, herbal, cedary and rather ethereal.

## CABERNET SAUVIGNON MERLOT

**Coonawarra** $20–$29
**Current vintage: 2002** 77

Leafy, dusty and greenish red blend whose light fruit is masked by intense green capsicum influences.

| | | | |
|---|---|---|---|
| 2002 | 77 | 2003 | 2004+ |
| 2001 | 86 | 2003 | 2006 |
| 2000 | 82 | 2002 | 2005 |
| 1999 | 84 | 2001 | 2004 |
| 1998 | 88 | 2000 | 2003+ |
| 1997 | 82 | 1999 | 2002 |
| 1996 | 80 | 1997 | 1998 |
| 1995 | 87 | 1997 | 2000 |
| 1994 | 91 | 1999 | 2002 |
| 1993 | 90 | 1998 | 2001 |
| 1992 | 89 | 1997 | 2000 |

## RAVENSWOOD (CABERNET SAUVIGNON)    RANKING 4

**Coonawarra** $50+
**Current vintage: 2000** 89

A well-made wine from a difficult vintage. Its herbal, tobaccoey aromas of cassis, mulberries and cedary oak reveal hints of undergrowth, raisins and varnish. Smooth, supple and very restrained, the palate presents slightly herbal small red and black berry flavours, cedar and tobacco over a slightly sappy, but fine-grained backbone. Finishes with some elegance and style, but a hint of sweet-sour fruit.

| | | | |
|---|---|---|---|
| 2000 | 89 | 2005 | 2008 |
| 1999 | 84 | 2004 | 2007 |
| 1998 | 94 | 2006 | 2010+ |
| 1996 | 87 | 2001 | 2004 |
| 1994 | 89 | 2002 | 2006+ |
| 1993 | 92 | 2001 | 2005 |
| 1992 | 93 | 2000 | 2004 |
| 1991 | 95 | 2003 | 2011 |
| 1990 | 94 | 2002 | 2010 |
| 1989 | 92 | 2001 | 2009 |
| 1988 | 93 | 2000 | 2005 |

## RESERVE CHARDONNAY

**Coonawarra** $20–$29
**Current vintage: 2003** 81

Rather simple chardonnay whose cumquat, melon and quince flavours have a herby, soapy edge. Forward, lacks great length, and finishes rather thin and steely.

| | | | |
|---|---|---|---|
| 2003 | 81 | 2004 | 2005 |
| 2002 | 89 | 2003 | 2004+ |
| 2001 | 84 | 2002 | 2003 |
| 2000 | 82 | 2001 | 2002 |
| 1999 | 89 | 2001 | 2004 |
| 1998 | 83 | 2000 | 2003 |
| 1997 | 82 | 1998 | 1999 |
| 1996 | 87 | 1998 | 2001 |
| 1995 | 83 | 2000 | 2003 |
| 1994 | 92 | 1999 | 2002 |

## RIESLING

**Coonawarra** $12–$19
**Current vintage: 2003** 87

Well-made riesling with a lightly herbal and floral talcum powder-like scent of lime juice. Tight, quite forward and austere, its tangy lemon/lime fruit lacks great length but finishes clean and refreshing.

| | | | |
|---|---|---|---|
| 2003 | 87 | 2005 | 2008 |
| 2002 | 85 | 2003 | 2004 |
| 2001 | 86 | 2003 | 2006 |
| 2000 | 87 | 2002 | 2005 |
| 1999 | 86 | 2001 | 2004 |
| 1998 | 85 | 2000 | 2003 |
| 1997 | 83 | 1999 | 2002 |
| 1995 | 88 | 2000 | 2003 |
| 1994 | 88 | 1999 | 2002 |
| 1992 | 94 | 1997 | 2000 |
| 1991 | 91 | 1993 | 1996 |

## SHIRAZ CABERNET SAUVIGNON

**Coonawarra** $20–$29
**Current vintage: 2002** 84

Meaty, spicy earthy aromas of restrained berry fruit and white pepper, with a fine, supple palate whose light flavours, berry/plum fruit and restrained cedary oak just finish a little thin and sappy.

| | | | |
|---|---|---|---|
| 2002 | 84 | 2004 | 2007 |
| 2001 | 83 | 2003 | 2006 |
| 2000 | 90 | 2001 | 2002 |
| 1998 | 90 | 2000 | 2003+ |
| 1997 | 82 | 1999 | 2002 |

## WILGHA SHIRAZ

**Coonawarra** $30–$49
**Current vintage: 2000** 87

Slightly varnishy early-drinking shiraz with a dusty, spicy bouquet of small red berries and plums backed by earthy nuances of cedar/vanilla oak. Forward, slightly cooked and jammy, it's restrained and approachable, with spicy red berry fruit partnered by smoky chocolate oak, framed by light tannins. Just drying out a shade.

| | | | |
|---|---|---|---|
| 2000 | 87 | 2002 | 2005 |
| 1999 | 88 | 2001 | 2004+ |
| 1998 | 81 | 2000 | 2003 |
| 1997 | 86 | 1999 | 2002 |
| 1996 | 82 | 1998 | 2001 |
| 1994 | 91 | 1996 | 1999 |
| 1993 | 90 | 1998 | 2001 |
| 1992 | 89 | 1997 | 2000 |
| 1991 | 92 | 1996 | 1999 |
| 1990 | 91 | 1995 | 1998 |

# Houghton

Dale Road, Middle Swan WA 6056. Tel: (08) 9274 5100. Fax: (08) 9250 3872.
Website: www.houghton-wines.com.au

Region: **Various WA** Winemaker: **Rob Bowen** Viticulturist: **Ron Page** Chief Executive: **David Woods**

With its Crofters label plus its very consistent range of different combinations of region and variety, Houghton has been reinvented as one of the best and most reliable of Western Australian wines. Its Chardonnay and Sauvignon Blanc from Pemberton are two of the finest wines to come from this region, while the upmarket pairing of the Jack Mann red and the Gladstones Shiraz add sharp-edge excitement. And, against all odds (not to mention logic), the White Burgundy still lives!

## CROFTERS CABERNET MERLOT

**Various WA** $12–$19
**Current vintage: 2001** 87

Slightly earthy, meaty aromas of briary dark fruit are offset by resiny, sweet vanilla and cedary oak. Long, firm and stylish, its reserved expression of small black and red berry fruits is framed by slightly metallic tannins and underpinned by a herbal, greenish aspect. The wine has its qualities, but it is too vegetal and its assertive oak is excessively resiny.

| | | | |
|---|---|---|---|
| 2001 | 87 | 2006 | 2009 |
| 2000 | 90 | 2008 | 2012+ |
| 1999 | 87 | 2007 | 2011 |
| 1998 | 88 | 2003 | 2006 |

## CROFTERS SEMILLON SAUVIGNON BLANC

**Various WA** $12–$19
**Current vintage: 2003** 84

Rather sweaty and botrytised aromas of apricots and candy, with weedy, silage-like undertones. Simple and confectionary, the palate's mango and paw paw flavours culminate in a green-edged lemon drop finish.

| | | | |
|---|---|---|---|
| 2003 | 84 | 2004 | 2005 |
| 2002 | 88 | 2004 | 2007 |
| 2001 | 85 | 2002 | 2003 |

## FRANKLAND RIVER SHIRAZ

RANKING 5

**Frankland River** $20–$29
**Current vintage: 2001** 87

| | | | |
|---|---|---|---|
| 2001 | 87 | 2006 | 2009+ |
| 2000 | 89 | 2008 | 2012 |
| 1999 | 90 | 2004 | 2007 |

A spicy red berry and dark plum shiraz of moderately full weight and pleasing focus. Long, fine-grained and savoury, with some pleasing leathery development but reveals some excessively resiny and gluey oak influences.

## GLADSTONES SHIRAZ

RANKING 2

**Frankland River** $50+
**Current vintage: 2001** 88

| | | | |
|---|---|---|---|
| 2001 | 88 | 2009 | 2013+ |
| 2000 | 95 | 2012 | 2020 |
| 1999 | 96 | 2007 | 2011+ |

A rather closed, slightly retentive and reductive shiraz. Its musky, meaty and tomato-like aromas of red and black berries and plums are offset by creamy vanilla oak, while its assertive, grippy palate presents a silky centre of raspberry, cassis and plum-like fruit framed by some hard edges. Likely to age slowly.

## JACK MANN RED

RANKING 2

**Various WA,**
**mainly Great Southern** $50+
**Current vintage: 2000** 86

| | | | |
|---|---|---|---|
| 2000 | 86 | 2008 | 2012+ |
| 1999 | 94 | 2011 | 2019 |
| 1998 | 95 | 2010 | 2018+ |
| 1996 | 95 | 2004 | 2008+ |
| 1995 | 93 | 2003 | 2007+ |
| 1994 | 92 | 2002 | 2005 |

Matched to cedar/chocolate oak, its sweet earthy, leathery and vegetal malbec-influenced aromas of dark plums, prunes and currants push the limits of genuine fruit ripeness. Robust and sinewy, this firm and leathery wine reveals some advancing red berry qualities and some excessive vegetable-like malbec flavour. Rather disappointing and clumsy, with too much tired meaty fruit, and too much malbec.

## MARGARET RIVER CABERNET SAUVIGNON

RANKING 5

**Margaret River** $20–$29
**Current vintage: 2001** 87

| | | | |
|---|---|---|---|
| 2001 | 87 | 2006 | 2009+ |
| 2000 | 90 | 2005 | 2008+ |
| 1999 | 85 | 2001 | 2004+ |

A sound and quite impressive wine with just enough of a green thread lurking beneath to detract from its earthy aromas of cassis, plums and cedary oak, and its supple, loose-knit palate of pleasing intensity. Good firmness and suppleness.

## PEMBERTON CHARDONNAY

RANKING 3

**Pemberton** $20–$29
**Current vintage: 2003** 93

| | | | |
|---|---|---|---|
| 2003 | 93 | 2005 | 2008+ |
| 2002 | 91 | 2004 | 2007+ |
| 2001 | 92 | 2003 | 2006 |

Complete and balanced chardonnay whose lightly tropical aromas of melon and peach are tightly integrated with restrained sweet vanilla oak. Long and seamless, the palate reveals a luxuriantly creamy texture bursting with intense flavours of pineapple, peaches and ruby grapefruit before finishing with refreshingly clean citrusy acids. Very smooth and harmonious, with lightly toasty oak playing second fiddle.

## PEMBERTON SAUVIGNON BLANC

RANKING 4

Pemberton $20–$29
**Current vintage: 2003** 91

| | | | |
|---|---|---|---|
| 2003 | 91 | 2003 | 2004+ |
| 2002 | 93 | 2003 | 2004+ |
| 2001 | 85 | 2002 | 2003 |

Refreshingly honest and uncompromisingly varietal sauvignon blanc with a vibrant, juicy and grassy aroma of passionfruit and cassis whose pungency borders on the sweaty. Intense and forward, round and almost oily, its generous passionfruit and herbaceous flavours finish clean and dry with lemony acids.

## WHITE BURGUNDY

RANKING 5

HOUGHTON

Swan Valley $12–$19
**Current vintage: 2003** 87

| | | | |
|---|---|---|---|
| 2003 | 87 | 2003 | 2004+ |
| 2002 | 82 | 2002 | 2003 |
| 2001 | 87 | 2002 | 2003+ |
| 2000 | 77 | 2001 | 2002 |
| 1999 | 87 | 2001 | 2004 |
| 1998 | 87 | 2000 | 2003 |
| 1997 | 87 | 1999 | 2002 |
| 1996 | 86 | 1998 | 2001 |

Good honest white wine with plenty of value. Its delicate, dusty aromas of citrus, peach and tropical fruit have a lightly herbal edge, while the palate is fruity and clean, generously flavoured and slightly sweet to finish.

# Howard Park

1 Scotsdale Road, Denmark WA 6333. Tel: (08) 9848 2345. Fax: (08) 9848 2064.
Miamup Road, Cowaramup, WA, 6284 Tel: (08) 9755 9988. Fax: (08) 9755 9048.
Email:hpw@hpw.com.au Website: www.howardparkwines.com.au.

Regions: **Great Southern, Margaret River** Winemaker:s **Michael Kerrigan, Andy Browning**
Chief Executive: **Jeff Burch**

Howard Park began its existence as an iconic, but tiny producer of a Cabernet Sauvignon and Riesling from the Great Southern region. Merlot from Margaret River was introduced to the red during the early 1990s, before the gradual incorporation of new company-owned Margaret River vineyards into the equation. Today, the Cabernet Sauvignon Merlot is principally sourced from Great Southern, unless quality is prohibitive. A second tier of labels and a Margaret River winery were then developed, as this well-resourced wine business significantly expanded its production. While I have been less taken by recent vintages than some of my peers, I am very impressed with the focused and tightly sculpted 2003 Riesling.

## CABERNET SAUVIGNON MERLOT

RANKING 3

HOWARD PARK

Great Southern $50+
**Current vintage: 2001** 89

| | | | |
|---|---|---|---|
| 2001 | 89 | 2009 | 2013+ |
| 2000 | 90 | 2005 | 2008+ |
| 1999 | 92 | 2004 | 2007+ |
| 1998 | 83 | 2003 | 2006 |
| 1997 | 86 | 2002 | 2005+ |
| 1996 | 96 | 2008 | 2016 |
| 1995 | 83 | 2000 | 2003 |
| 1994 | 96 | 2014 | 2024 |
| 1993 | 92 | 2001 | 2005+ |
| 1992 | 97 | 2004 | 2012+ |
| 1991 | 93 | 2003 | 2011 |
| 1990 | 90 | 1998 | 2002 |
| 1989 | 95 | 2001 | 2009 |
| 1988 | 96 | 2008 | 2018 |
| 1987 | 90 | 1995 | 1999+ |
| 1986 | 95 | 2006 | 2016 |

Elegant, polished but assertively oaked cabernet whose earthy, cedary aromas of slightly herbal small berries reveal some spirity aromas as well as a light varnishy volatility. Supple and sappy, the palate is long and smooth, delivering some attractive small red and black berry flavours tightly knit with creamy vanilla oak and fine-grained tannins.

# CHARDONNAY

| Great Southern, Marg. River $30–$49 | | | |
|---|---|---|---|
| **Current vintage: 2002** | | | **87** |

Two different regions have produced a split personality wine that marries celery, sweetcorn and cashew-like cool-climate Great Southern chardonnay with juicier, pineapple and cumquat-like Margaret River fruit. It's nutty and savoury, with some mineral and oatmeal-like complexity, but finishes rather syrupy and metallic, with green-edged and slightly sour acids.

| 2002 | 87 | 2004 | 2007 |
|---|---|---|---|
| 2001 | 86 | 2006 | 2009 |
| 2000 | 89 | 2002 | 2005 |
| 1999 | 90 | 2001 | 2004 |
| 1998 | 90 | 2000 | 2003 |
| 1997 | 87 | 1999 | 2002 |
| 1996 | 91 | 1998 | 2001 |
| 1995 | 94 | 2000 | 2003 |
| 1994 | 94 | 1999 | 2002 |
| 1993 | 93 | 1998 | 2001 |

# LESTON SHIRAZ

| Margaret River | $30–$49 |
|---|---|
| **Current vintage: 2002** | **88** |

Vibrant aromas of juicy raspberries, red cherries and assertive chocolate/vanilla/cedary oak reveal light tomato-like and herbal undertones. Sweet vanilla/chocolate oak helps to smooth out the slightly sappy and green-edged palate that offers some lively and juicy red berry fruits.

| 2002 | 88 | 2004 | 2007+ |
|---|---|---|---|
| 2001 | 88 | 2003 | 2006+ |
| 2000 | 89 | 2005 | 2008+ |
| 1999 | 87 | 2001 | 2004 |

# RIESLING

| Great Southern | $20–$29 |
|---|---|
| **Current vintage: 2003** | **95** |

Delightfully elegant, restrained and long-term riesling whose delicate floral perfume of lemon, lime and talcum powder precedes a very slightly confected palate of fineness and tightness. There's a chalky texture beneath its vibrant expression of racy pear/apple riesling flavour, before a lingering lemon rind finish. Tightly sculpted and focused; the best under this label for some years.

| 2003 | 95 | 2011 | 2015 |
|---|---|---|---|
| 2002 | 84 | 2004 | 2007+ |
| 2001 | 88 | 2006 | 2009 |
| 2000 | 87 | 2008 | 2012 |
| 1999 | 86 | 2001 | 2004+ |
| 1998 | 92 | 2003 | 2006 |
| 1997 | 94 | 2005 | 2009+ |
| 1996 | 93 | 2004 | 2008 |
| 1995 | 94 | 2000 | 2003+ |
| 1994 | 92 | 2002 | 2006 |
| 1993 | 95 | 2001 | 2005 |
| 1992 | 95 | 2004 | 2012 |
| 1991 | 94 | 2003 | 2011 |

# SCOTSDALE CABERNET SAUVIGNON

| Great Southern | $30–$49 |
|---|---|
| **Current vintage: 2001** | **93** |

Earthy, cedary fragrance of red berries, violets, chocolates and cassis, with hints of vanilla. Supple, elegant palate whose bright small berry fruits are framed by firm, fine-grained tannins with a velvet feel. There's a cool herbal note just beneath the surface.

| 2001 | 93 | 2006 | 2009+ |
|---|---|---|---|
| 2000 | 82 | 2002 | 2005 |
| 1999 | 87 | 2001 | 2004 |

# SCOTSDALE SHIRAZ

| Great Southern | $30–$49 |
|---|---|
| **Current vintage: 2002** | **93** |

A lively floral and black pepper fragrance of sweet raspberries, cherries and plums with undertones of cloves, cinnamon and cedary oak precedes a palate of style and searing intensity. Smooth and shapely, it's medium to full in weight but laced with vibrant flavours of raspberries, strawberries, cassis and plums. Framed with smooth and fine-grained tannins, it finishing with brightness and intensity.

| 2002 | 93 | 2007 | 2010 |
|---|---|---|---|
| 2001 | 88 | 2003 | 2006+ |
| 2000 | 91 | 2002 | 2005+ |

# Hugo

RSD 230Elliott Road, McLaren Flat SA 5171. Tel: (08) 8383 0098. Fax: (08) 8383 0446.

Region: **McLaren Vale** Winemaker: **John Hugo** Viticulturist: **John Hugo** Chief Executive: **John Hugo**

Made to be enjoyed without extended cellaring, Hugo's red wines are ripe and juicy, honest, flavoursome and oaky, although some might find their use of American cooperage bordering on the excessive. The 2002 Chardonnay is another bright, punchy and generous wine offering surprising complexity and finesse.

## CABERNET SAUVIGNON

RANKING **5**

| | McLaren Vale | $12–$19 |
|---|---|---|
| | **Current vintage: 2001** | **86** |

A punchy, flavoursome cabernet with juicy ripeness and approachability. Its slightly stewed aromas of blackberries and redcurrants, menthol and eucalypt overlie some lightly smoky creamy oak. Smooth, generous and uncomplicated, the palate is soft and round, with sweet cassis/plum flavours and chocolate-like oak influences.

| | | | |
|---|---|---|---|
| 2001 | 86 | 2003 | 2006+ |
| 2000 | 87 | 2005 | 2008 |
| 1999 | 89 | 2004 | 2007 |
| 1998 | 91 | 2006 | 2010 |
| 1997 | 82 | 2002 | 2005+ |
| 1996 | 90 | 2001 | 2004 |
| 1995 | 89 | 2000 | 2003 |
| 1994 | 88 | 1992 | 2002 |
| 1993 | 91 | 2001 | 2005 |

## CHARDONNAY

RANKING **5**

| | McLaren Vale | $12–$19 |
|---|---|---|
| | **Current vintage: 2002** | **89** |

Sweet aromas of peaches and cream, tropical fruit and assertive coconut/vanilla American oak. Forward and approachable, the vibrant, juicy and generously flavoured palate marries ripe stone-fruits with grilled nuts, sweet oak and soft acids. It's very honest and open, with some hints of barrel fermentation and bound sulphide complexity. Great value.

| | | | |
|---|---|---|---|
| 2002 | 89 | 2003 | 2004+ |
| 1999 | 89 | 2001 | 2004 |
| 1998 | 86 | 1999 | 2000 |
| 1997 | 90 | 2002 | 2005 |
| 1996 | 87 | 1999 | 2001 |
| 1994 | 90 | 1999 | 2002 |
| 1993 | 93 | 2001 | 2005 |

## SHIRAZ

RANKING **5**

| | McLaren Vale | $12–$19 |
|---|---|---|
| | **Current vintage: 2001** | **77** |

Rather neutral, earthy and meaty, cooked and thin, lacking in richness and weight of primary fruit. Finishes stale and flat.

| | | | |
|---|---|---|---|
| 2001 | 77 | 2003 | 2006 |
| 2000 | 86 | 2002 | 2005 |
| 1999 | 87 | 2001 | 2004 |
| 1998 | 90 | 2003 | 2006 |
| 1997 | 87 | 1999 | 2002+ |
| 1996 | 91 | 2001 | 2004 |
| 1995 | 90 | 2000 | 2003 |
| 1994 | 90 | 1999 | 2002 |
| 1993 | 90 | 2001 | 2005 |
| 1992 | 92 | 1997 | 2000 |

# Huntington Estate

Cassilis Road, Mudgee NSW 2850. Tel: (02) 6373 3825. Fax: (02) 6373 3730. Email: huntwine@hwy.com.au

Region: **Mudgee** Winemaker: **Susan Roberts** Viticulturist: **Colin Millott** Chief Executive: **Bob Roberts**

Huntington Estate makes ripe, firm and rustic red wines that offer both value and longevity. Its Special Reserve releases offer an extra degree of intensity and structure, and receive additional time in newer oak. The dark, black-fruited and meaty 2001 Special Reserve Cabernet is a typical example, while the 1999 vintage is more restrained, fruit-driven and creamy.

## CABERNET SAUVIGNON

RANKING **5**

| | Mudgee | $12–$19 |
|---|---|---|
| | **Current vintage: 2001** | **87** |

Very firm, astringent cabernet whose meaty, leathery fruit reveals some greenish undertones. Its herbal aromas of red berries and plums suggest a hint of under and over-ripeness, while the palate is robust and rustic, with a slightly hollow sappiness. Quite thick and chocolatey, with older oak characters.

| | | | |
|---|---|---|---|
| 2001 | 87 | 2009 | 2013 |
| 1999 | 89 | 2007 | 2011+ |
| 1998 | 88 | 2006 | 2010 |
| 1997 | 85 | 2002 | 2005+ |
| 1995 | 88 | 2003 | 2007 |
| 1994 | 88 | 2002 | 2006 |
| 1993 | 89 | 2001 | 2005 |
| 1992 | 93 | 2004 | 2012 |
| 1991 | 90 | 1996 | 1999 |

## SEMILLON

| Mudgee | $12–$19 |
|---|---|
| **Current vintage: 2003** | **83** |

Savoury, slightly bitter semillon whose candied, marmalade-like citrus and tobaccoey fruit is offset by rather cardboard-like oak. It's quite herbal and vegetal, with refreshing acidity, but also with what appears to be hop-like, leesy influences.

| 2003 | 83 | 2005 | 2008 |
|---|---|---|---|
| 2002 | 87 | 2004 | 2007 |
| 2000 | 90 | 2002 | 2005 |
| 1999 | 84 | 2001 | 2004 |
| 1998 | 86 | 2000 | 2003 |
| 1997 | 90 | 2002 | 2005 |
| 1996 | 93 | 2001 | 2004 |
| 1995 | 92 | 2000 | 2003 |

RANKING 5

| Mudgee | $12–$19 |
|---|---|
| **Current vintage: 2001** | **84** |

Leathery, meaty and developing aromas of violets and camphor, plums and red berries, with earthy undertones. Forward, stewed and meaty flavours of blackberries and redcurrants, then become thin and astringent, lacking real depth and focus of fruit.

| 2001 | 84 | 2003 | 2006+ |
|---|---|---|---|
| 1999 | 87 | 2004 | 2007+ |
| 1998 | 81 | 2003 | 2006 |
| 1997 | 90 | 2005 | 2009 |
| 1995 | 89 | 2003 | 2007+ |
| 1994 | 86 | 1999 | 2002 |
| 1993 | 95 | 2005 | 2013 |
| 1992 | 89 | 1997 | 2000 |
| 1991 | 91 | 1999 | 2003 |

## SPECIAL RESERVE CABERNET SAUVIGNON

RANKING 4

| Mudgee | $20–$29 |
|---|---|
| **Current vintage: 2001** | **93** |

Developing sweet, earthy, leathery aromas with scents of violets, cassis and raspberry confiture. Smooth, generous and surprisingly elegant, it's a long, deeply concentrated and sumptuous red whose sweet small black and red berry flavours are matched to assertive cedar/vanilla oak and offset by meaty, earthy and savoury complexity. Good balance and future.

| 2001 | 93 | 2013 | 2021 |
|---|---|---|---|
| 1999 | 92 | 2011 | 2019 |
| 1997 | 87 | 2005 | 2009 |
| 1994 | 80 | 2002 | 2006 |

# Ingoldby

Ingoldby Road, McLaren Flat SA 5171. Tel: (08) 8383 0005. Fax: (08) 8383 0790.
Region: **McLaren Vale** Winemaker: **Charles Hargrave** Viticulturist: **Guy Rayner** Chief Executive: **Jamie Odell**
Ingoldby is a slightly lost soul, being one of Beringer Blass' acquisitions in the McLaren Vale region, but lacking the renewed focus presently being given to the neighbouring Maglieri label. The reds tend to be sturdy, firm and awkward.

## CABERNET SAUVIGNON

RANKING 5

| McLaren Vale | $12–$19 |
|---|---|
| **Current vintage: 2002** | **87** |

Firm, slightly blocky and hard-edged cabernet with a light, floral and herbal aroma of meaty small berries, mint and menthol, plus some light vanilla oak influence. It opens up slowly to reveal some attractive raspberry, cassis, mulberry and plum flavours but over a thread of herbal nuances. Robust, but perhaps a little too extracted for its fruit.

| 2002 | 87 | 2007 | 2010 |
|---|---|---|---|
| 1999 | 87 | 2004 | 2007 |
| 1998 | 85 | 2003 | 2006 |
| 1997 | 82 | 1999 | 2002+ |
| 1996 | 82 | 1998 | 2001 |
| 1995 | 89 | 2000 | 2003 |
| 1994 | 90 | 1999 | 2002 |
| 1993 | 89 | 2000 | 2005 |
| 1992 | 93 | 2000 | 2004 |
| 1991 | 95 | 2003 | 2011 |
| 1990 | 90 | 2002 | 2010 |

## RESERVE SHIRAZ

| McLaren Vale | $30–$49 | 2001 | 88 | 2006 | 2009 |
| **Current vintage: 2001** | **88** | 1999 | 86 | 2001 | 2004 |
| | | 1998 | 86 | 2000 | 2003 |

Ripe, slightly cooked and jammy aromas of dark plums and prunes together with overt new cedar/chocolate oak influences. Rich and soft, it reveals some pleasing fruit sweetness, but an excess of tarry, overcooked characters typical of so many 2001 shirazes. Flavoursome and generous, certain to please many, but too awkward, over-cooked and simplistic for its price.

# Jacob's Creek

Barossa Valley Way Rowland Flat SA 5352. Tel: (08) 8521 3140. Fax: (08) 8521 3425.
Region: **Southern Australia** Winemaker: **Philip Laffer** Viticulturist: **Joy Dick** Chief Executive: **Laurent Lacassgne**
While it's hard to disagree with those who perceive a slightly oxymoronic notion to the concept of a Jacob's Creek Limited Release label, its detractors tend to quieten and take notice once they taste the wines. Similarly, the value and quality offered by the Reserve wines takes some beating. And what about the 'standard' label? They still represent great drinkability and enjoyment, just as they have always done.

## CHARDONNAY

| Southern Australia | $5–$11 | 2003 | 86 | 2004 | 2005 |
| **Current vintage: 2003** | **86** | 2002 | 82 | 2002 | 2003 |
| | | 2001 | 82 | 2001 | 2002 |

Tangy, peachy and buttery chardonnay with lightly floral, creamy and citrusy aromas before a fine, shapely palate of citrus, cashew and peaches. Bound by refreshing acidity, it offers some fleshiness and roundness, and despite a slightly thin and greenish/metallic finish, remains a very good commercial wine.

## LIMITED RELEASE CHARDONNAY

| Southern Australia | $20–$29 | 2001 | 90 | 2003 | 2006+ |
| **Current vintage: 2001** | **90** | 2000 | 88 | 2002 | 2005 |
| | | 1999 | 82 | 2000 | 2001 |
| | | 1998 | 86 | 1999 | 2000 |
| | | 1996 | 88 | 1997 | 1998 |

Elegant, well-made chardonnay whose delicate tobaccoey and smoky bouquet of honeydew melon, peach and floral complexity precedes a smooth and supple palate with bright citrus, melon and cashew-like flavours, lightly toasty vanilla oak, a generous, almost fatty texture and a lingering savoury finish. Attractively balanced and refined.

## LIMITED RELEASE SHIRAZ CABERNET

| Southern Australia | $50+ | 1998 | 95 | 2010 | 2018+ |
| **Current vintage: 1998** | **95** | 1997 | 86 | 1999 | 2002 |
| | | 1996 | 93 | 2004 | 2008 |
| | | 1994 | 88 | 1999 | 2002 |

Classic Australian blend with a restrained fragrance of small black and red berries, dark chocolates, creamy, smoky oak, violets and white pepper, cedar, cloves and cinnamon. Smooth and satiny, with concentrated small berry flavours matched by tightly integrated mocha/coconut oak and tight-knit tannins. Superbly balanced, long and elegant.

## RESERVE CABERNET SAUVIGNON

**Southern Australia**    $12–$19
**Current vintage: 2001**    86

Slightly herbal and weedy white pepper and capsicum aromas of berry fruits lifted by perfumed vanilla oak, with some underlying and slightly under-ripe spicy tea tin-like influences. Simultaneously cooked, minty and herbal, the palate combines meaty berry flavours with green-edged herbaceous undertones, framed by sappy, raw-ish tannins. Flavoursome, but lacks charm and fruit sweetness.

| | | | |
|---|---|---|---|
| 2001 | 86 | 2003 | 2006 |
| 2000 | 89 | 2005 | 2008 |
| 1999 | 87 | 2001 | 2004+ |
| 1998 | 87 | 2000 | 2003 |

## RESERVE CHARDONNAY

**Southern Australia**    $12–$19
**Current vintage: 2002**    90

Stylish, integrated and compact chardonnay of elegance and fineness. Delicate, slightly dusty green cashew and citrusy aromas precede an elegant and fluffy, babyfat palate of melon and peaches, creamy oak and fine, refreshing acids. It culminates in a nutty finish with lingering fruit sweetness. Excellent value.

| | | | |
|---|---|---|---|
| 2002 | 90 | 2004 | 2007 |
| 2001 | 88 | 2003 | 2006 |
| 2000 | 87 | 2002 | 2005 |
| 1999 | 88 | 2001 | 2004 |

## RESERVE RIESLING

**Southern Australia**    $12–$19
**Current vintage: 2003**    93

A stylist's riesling, whose flowery rose oil and musky perfume of citrus aromas and long, silky palate are tightly woven around a fine chalkiness and racy acidity. It's long, delicate and pristine; a finely sculpted wine of freshness and shape, with lingering stonefruit and pear-like flavours.

| | | | |
|---|---|---|---|
| 2003 | 93 | 2008 | 2011+ |
| 2002 | 92 | 2007 | 2010 |
| 2001 | 88 | 2003 | 2006 |

## RESERVE SHIRAZ

**Southern Australia**    $12–$19
**Current vintage: 2001**    89

Slightly overcooked, meaty and flavoursome soft shiraz with a lightly smoky, spicy and plummy, aroma of confectionary-like blackberry jam and sweet creamy oak. Smooth, soft and generous, it's firm and balanced, with generous, if slightly simple ripe to ultra-ripe flavours.

| | | | |
|---|---|---|---|
| 2001 | 89 | 2006 | 2009 |
| 2000 | 87 | 2002 | 2005+ |
| 1999 | 89 | 2001 | 2004+ |
| 1998 | 87 | 2000 | 2003 |

## RIESLING

**Southern Australia**    $5–$11
**Current vintage: 2003**    89

Generous, quite broad and tangy riesling with a delicate floral and estery aroma of pear and lime, and underlying nuances of apple and pear. It's fine and chalky, with a pleasing length of varietal flavours, finishing with lemony acids.

| | | | |
|---|---|---|---|
| 2003 | 89 | 2005 | 2008+ |
| 2002 | 86 | 2003 | 2004+ |
| 2001 | 89 | 2003 | 2006 |
| 2000 | 88 | 2005 | 2008 |
| 1999 | 89 | 2001 | 2004 |
| 1998 | 86 | 1999 | 2000 |
| 1997 | 88 | 1999 | 2002 |
| 1996 | 89 | 2001 | 2004 |

## SHIRAZ CABERNET

**Southern Australia**    $5–$11
**Current vintage: 2002**    87

Fresh aromas of small black and red berries, toasty vanilla oak and a decent whiff of spiciness precede a smooth, fine-grained palate bursting with vibrant berry/plum flavours. Lifted by lightly smoky vanilla oak, it finishes with good length and freshness.

| | | | |
|---|---|---|---|
| 2002 | 87 | 2004 | 2007 |
| 2001 | 84 | 2003 | 2006 |
| 2000 | 83 | 2002 | 2005 |
| 1999 | 84 | 2001 | 2004 |
| 1998 | 85 | 2000 | 2003+ |
| 1997 | 85 | 2002 | 2005 |
| 1996 | 82 | 1998 | 2001 |

# James Irvine

Roeslers Road, Eden Valley SA 5235. Tel: (08) 8564 1046. Fax: (08) 8546 1314.
Email: merlotbiz@ irvinewines.com.au

Region: **Eden Valley** Winemaker: **James Irvine** Viticulturist: **James Irvine** Chief Executive: **Marjorie Irvine**

James Irvine has achieved an international reputation for his robust and extensively oak-matured Grand Merlot. Made in a traditional Australian fashion, it has made something of a habit of collecting major international awards. Irvine's second-tier label, Eden Crest, produced a smooth, if rather vegetal and confectionary merlot in 2001.

## GRAND MERLOT

RANKING **4**

| Eden Valley | $50+ |
|---|---|
| Current vintage: 1999 | 90 |

A developing earthy, leathery bouquet of slightly cooked plums, maraschino cherries and red berries overlies lightly varnishy and smoky vanilla/cedar oak. Velvet-smooth and creamy, its super-ripe and forward flavours of prunes, currants and raisins glides towards a savoury, walnut-like finish. It does dry out, leaving a slightly raw extract.

| | | | |
|---|---|---|---|
| 1999 | 90 | 2007 | 2011 |
| 1998 | 91 | 2003 | 2006+ |
| 1997 | 87 | 2005 | 2009 |
| 1996 | 89 | 2004 | 2008 |
| 1995 | 92 | 2003 | 2007 |
| 1994 | 95 | 2006 | 2014 |
| 1993 | 95 | 2005 | 2013 |
| 1992 | 89 | 2000 | 2004 |
| 1991 | 94 | 1999 | 2003 |
| 1990 | 93 | 2002 | 2010 |

# Jamiesons Run

Riddoch Highway, Coonawarra SA 5263. Tel: (08) 8736 3380. Fax: (08) 8736 3071.
Website www.jamiesonsrun.com.au  Email: cellardoor@jamiesonsrun.com.au

Region: **Coonawarra** Winemaker: **Andrew Hales** Viticulturist: **Vic Patrick** Chief Executive: **Jamie Odell**

Beringer Blass is investing a lot of capital in the Jamiesons Run concept, which it has gradually adapted from a one-horse wine (a blend of shiraz, cabernet sauvignon and merlot) to a multi-tiered structure incorporating a base varietal range, a slightly snazzier Red Terra range, an individual vineyard range (Alexander's Block, McShane's Block and O'Dea's Block), culminating in a Limited Release Cabernet Sauvignon and a Reserve red blend. That's wine marketing in the 21st century! And without being too facetious, by and large, I'm rather impressed!

## CABERNET SAUVIGNON (Formerly blended with Shiraz & Merlot)

| Coonawarra | $12–$19 |
|---|---|
| Current vintage: 2001 | 83 |

Tough, rather unyielding, lacking sweetness and brightness of fruit. Its simple confectionary aromas of red berries, plums and cedar/vanilla oak reveal vegetal, under-ripe nuances, while the palate is raw, extracted and herbal, finishing thin and sappy.

| | | | |
|---|---|---|---|
| 2001 | 83 | 2003 | 2006 |
| 2000 | 82 | 2002 | 2005 |
| 1999 | 81 | 2001 | 2004 |
| 1998 | 84 | 2000 | 2003 |
| 1997 | 88 | 2002 | 2005 |
| 1996 | 88 | 2001 | 2004 |
| 1995 | 90 | 2000 | 2003 |
| 1994 | 93 | 2002 | 2006 |

## CHARDONNAY

RANKING **5**

| Coonawarra | $12–$19 |
|---|---|
| Current vintage: 2003 | 89 |

Very complete, honest and enjoyable commercially priced chardonnay with bright tropical and lemon/lime fruit carefully married with restrained nutty and vanilla oak. Smooth and citrusy, with a soft buttery oak influence on the palate before a soft acid finish.

| | | | |
|---|---|---|---|
| 2003 | 89 | 2003 | 2004+ |
| 2002 | 89 | 2003 | 2004 |
| 2001 | 87 | 2002 | 2003 |

## MERLOT

RANKING **5**

| Coonawarra | $12–$19 |
|---|---|
| Current vintage: 2001 | 88 |

Very quaffable velvet-like merlot, right on the popular button. Toasty bubblegum-like oak complements its sweet aromas of violets, black cherries and cassis, while its juicy, toasty palate has plenty of depth, flavour and roundness.

| | | | |
|---|---|---|---|
| 2001 | 88 | 2003 | 2006 |
| 2000 | 77 | 2001 | 2002 |
| 1999 | 82 | 2001 | 2004 |
| 1998 | 88 | 2000 | 2003 |

**2005** **THE AUSTRALIAN WINE ANNUAL** **141**
www.onwine.com.au

## RESERVE COONAWARRA CABERNET BLEND

| Coonawarra | $30–$49 |
| --- | --- |
| **Current vintage: 2001** | **95** |

Deeply perfumed with scents of violets, cassis, sweet plums and mulberries, with attractively integrated cedar/vanilla oak and a pronounced suggestion of peppermint. Its smooth, plush palate sumptuously marries deeply flavoured small berry fruits with harmoniously integrated oak. Pleasingly long and complete, with just the merest hint of salty/stressed 2001 characters.

| 2001 | 95 | 2009 | 2013 |
| --- | --- | --- | --- |
| 2000 | 89 | 2005 | 2008 |
| 1999 | 88 | 2004 | 2007 |
| 1998 | 93 | 2006 | 2010+ |
| 1996 | 84 | 1998 | 2001 |
| 1995 | 82 | 1997 | 2000 |

# Jansz

Pipers Brook Road, Pipers Brook Tas 7254. Tel: (03) 6382 7066. Fax: (03) 6382 7088.
Website: www.jansz.com Email: info@jansz.com

Region: **Pipers River** Winemaker: **Natalie Fryar** Viticulturist: **Robin Nettelbeck**
Chief Executive: **Robert Hill Smith**

Owned by S. Smith & Son of Yalumba fame, Jansz is a cutting-edge Australian sparkling label able to source exceptional cool-climate fruit from northern Tasmania. With its new interactive wine visitor centre in Pipers Brook and a developing track record of fine, tightly sculpted and beautifully presented sparkling wines, Jansz is going to take some beating. A recent vertical tasting of all its releases showed that despite an evolution in style towards a rounder and creamier structure, its characteristic longevity and complexity should remain unhindered. Time will ultimately reveal whether or not the Late Disgorged Cuvée from the excellent 1997 vintage outperforms the classy and stylish 'standard' edition from the same year.

## VINTAGE CUVÉE (Formerly Brut Cuvée)

| Pipers River | $30–$49 |
| --- | --- |
| **Current vintage: 1999** | **93** |

There's a hint of herbal influence beneath the nutty, biscuity and pastry-like cracked yeast aromas of this lively, creamy sparkling wine. Its palate is fresh and citrusy, with a round, chewy texture and a pleasingly length of flavour, finished with soft, lemony acids. Already revealing some toasty development, it's ready to drink.

| 1999 | 93 | 2007 | 2011+ |
| --- | --- | --- | --- |
| 1997 | 95 | 2005 | 2009+ |
| 1996 | 89 | 2001 | 2004+ |
| 1995 | 87 | 2000 | 2003 |
| 1994 | 95 | 2002 | 2006 |
| 1993 | 86 | 1998 | 2001 |
| 1992 | 94 | 1997 | 2000+ |
| 1991 | 89 | 1996 | 1999+ |
| 1990 | 95 | 1998 | 2002 |
| 1989 | 94 | 1997 | 2001+ |

## LATE DISGORGED CUVÉE

| Pipers River | $30–$49 |
| --- | --- |
| **Current vintage: 1996** | **87** |

Intense aromas of pineapple, passionfruit and quince, with undertones of apricot and melon. Forward and juicy, tropical and toasty, it lacks length and freshness, becoming quite broad and short. Shows clear signs of botrytis infection.

| 1996 | 87 | 2001 | 2004 |
| --- | --- | --- | --- |
| 1995 | 90 | 2003 | 2007 |
| 1992 | 95 | 2000 | 2004 |

# Jasper Hill

Drummonds Lane, Heathcote Vic 3523. Tel: (03) 5433 2528. Fax: (03) 5433 3143.

Region: **Heathcote** Winemaker: **Ron Laughton** Viticulturist: **Ron Laughton** Chief Executive: **Ron Laughton**

The lofty status achieved by the Jasper Hill vineyard by the mid 1990s, as well as the exceptional balance and longevity of its wines to that time, have much to do with the modern viticultural equivalent of the Gold Rush — the frenzy to buy and plant land in the Heathcote region to shiraz vines. While I believe there is now a strong will at Jasper Hill to return to more balanced levels of alcohol in its signature wines, recent dry vintages have not given the operators of this dryland vineyard the flexibility they might once have anticipated.

## EMILY'S PADDOCK SHIRAZ CABERNET FRANC  RANKING 3

**Heathcote** $50+
**Current vintage: 2002** 88

Jasper Hill has experienced some of the worst of the Victorian drought, and there's little doubt that this wine does reveal some of the stress endured by this now-famous dryland vineyard. There's a meaty animal hide quality to its aroma of dried herbs and vanilla oak, while its palate is massively tannic and extracted. Bordering into nuances of prunes and currants, its briary flavours of blackberries and plums intermingle with chocolate oak and exotic spices. Neither for the faint-hearted, nor the impatient.

| | | | |
|---|---|---|---|
| 2002 | 88 | 2010 | 2014 |
| 2001 | 95 | 2013 | 2021+ |
| 2000 | 93 | 2008 | 2012+ |
| 1999 | 86 | 2004 | 2007 |
| 1998 | 90 | 2006 | 2010+ |
| 1997 | 94 | 2009 | 2017 |
| 1996 | 89 | 2000 | 2008 |
| 1995 | 87 | 2000 | 2003 |
| 1994 | 88 | 2002 | 2006 |
| 1993 | 93 | 2001 | 2005+ |
| 1992 | 87 | 2012 | 2022 |
| 1991 | 96 | 2003 | 2011 |
| 1990 | 94 | 2002 | 2010 |
| 1989 | 81 | 1994 | 1997 |
| 1988 | 95 | 2000 | 2008+ |

## GEORGIA'S PADDOCK RIESLING  RANKING 4

**Heathcote** $20–$29
**Current vintage: 2003** 90

Distinctively taut, lemony and minerally riesling poles apart from the mainstream Australian style. Its accentuated aromas of honeysuckle and lemon rind precede a steely, austere palate revealing a pleasing depth of apple, candied lemon rind and mineral flavours.

| | | | |
|---|---|---|---|
| 2003 | 90 | 2008 | 2011+ |
| 2002 | 90 | 2007 | 2010+ |
| 2001 | 87 | 2006 | 2009+ |
| 2000 | 91 | 2005 | 2008 |
| 1998 | 90 | 2003 | 2006 |
| 1997 | 93 | 2005 | 2009 |
| 1996 | 87 | 1998 | 2001 |
| 1994 | 90 | 1999 | 2002 |

## GEORGIA'S PADDOCK NEBBIOLO  RANKING 3

**Heathcote** $50+
**Current vintage: 2002** 83

Significantly greener than previous releases of this wine, with a dusty, spicy and peppery aroma of wild, brandied preserved fruits, meaty and floral nuances. Powerful and assertive, its minty expression of licorice-like fruit has a spirity grappa-like quality, before an exceptionally astringent finish.

| | | | |
|---|---|---|---|
| 2002 | 83 | 2010 | 2014 |
| 2001 | 92 | 2006 | 2009+ |
| 2000 | 92 | 2005 | 2008+ |

## GEORGIA'S PADDOCK SHIRAZ  RANKING 3

**Heathcote** $50+
**Current vintage: 2002** 90

Revealing more primary fruit qualities than its more celebrated stablemate, this is a wine of considerable power but surprising elegance. Its slightly closed aromas of redcurrants, cassis and plums are laced with white pepper, cinnamon and cloves, plus tarry, currant-like nuances. Despite its opulent dimensions and its concentrated expression of musky red berry fruit, there's some silkiness, fineness and integration with sweet vanilla/cedar/dark chocolate oak and fine-grained powdery tannins.

| | | | |
|---|---|---|---|
| 2002 | 90 | 2014 | 2022 |
| 2001 | 95 | 2009 | 2013+ |
| 2000 | 90 | 2008 | 2012+ |
| 1999 | 87 | 2004 | 2007 |
| 1998 | 88 | 2006 | 2010+ |
| 1997 | 93 | 2009 | 2017 |
| 1996 | 94 | 2008 | 2016 |
| 1995 | 96 | 2007 | 2015 |
| 1994 | 95 | 2002 | 2006+ |
| 1993 | 96 | 2005 | 2013 |
| 1992 | 95 | 2004 | 2012 |
| 1991 | 89 | 1999 | 2003 |
| 1990 | 94 | 2002 | 2010 |
| 1989 | 86 | 1997 | 2001 |
| 1988 | 95 | 2008 | 2018 |

# Jim Barry

Craigs Hill Road, (Off Main North Road, ) Clare SA 5453. Tel: (08) 8842 2261. Fax: (08) 8842 3752.
Email: jbwines@jimbarry.com

Region: **Clare Valley** Winemaker: **Mark Barry** Viticulturist: **Peter Barry** Chief Executive: **Peter Barry**

There's little doubt that given a return to a more moderate weather pattern that Jim Barry's leading red wines will again rate at their customarily high levels, but the exceptionally hot and dry 2000 and 2001 seasons have taken their toll, producing both meaty over-ripe and vegetal characteristics.

## CABERNET SAUVIGNON

**Clare Valley** $12–$19
**Current vintage: 2000** 82

Varnishy, rather meaty aromas of cassis, raspberries, smallgoods and polished oak, before a lean, apparently stressed palate lacking fruit depth and framed by cedary oak.

| | | | |
|---|---|---|---|
| 2000 | 82 | 2002 | 2005 |
| 1999 | 82 | 2004 | 2007+ |
| 1998 | 88 | 2006 | 2010 |
| 1997 | 84 | 2002 | 2005 |
| 1996 | 84 | 2001 | 2004 |
| 1995 | 92 | 2003 | 2007 |
| 1994 | 88 | 1999 | 2002 |
| 1993 | 88 | 1998 | 2001 |
| 1992 | 91 | 2000 | 2004 |
| 1990 | 88 | 1995 | 1998 |

## McRAE WOOD SHIRAZ RANKING 5

**Clare Valley** $30–$49
**Current vintage: 2001** 82

Shorter-term and rather forward, soupy red with a slightly varnishy, cooked aroma of currants and prunes, plums and creamy vanilla oak. Medium to full in weight, it's sumptuous and meaty, but over-ripened and dehydrated, lacking the stuffing to back up its initial delivery of prune/currant flavours. Finishes drying and minty, with moderately firm tannins.

| | | | |
|---|---|---|---|
| 2001 | 82 | 2003 | 2006+ |
| 2000 | 87 | 2002 | 2005+ |
| 1999 | 88 | 2004 | 2007 |
| 1998 | 89 | 2003 | 2006 |
| 1997 | 84 | 2002 | 2005 |
| 1996 | 93 | 2004 | 2008 |
| 1995 | 91 | 2000 | 2003 |
| 1994 | 94 | 2002 | 2006 |
| 1993 | 87 | 1995 | 1998 |
| 1992 | 93 | 2000 | 2004+ |

## THE ARMAGH SHIRAZ RANKING 2

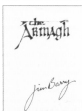

**Clare Valley** $50+
**Current vintage: 2001** 89

Rather thick, meaty and pruney shiraz with a tarry, menthol-like aroma of sweet vanilla oak, currants and licorice. It's velvet-smooth and finely crafted, but the thick layers of ultra-ripe and dehydrated fruit tend to lack freshness and vitality. It relies excessively on its tightly integrated creamy vanilla oak for palate sweetness, while some slightly greenish notes lurk beneath the lingering finish.

| | | | |
|---|---|---|---|
| 2001 | 89 | 2009 | 2013 |
| 2000 | 91 | 2005 | 2008+ |
| 1999 | 95 | 2011 | 2019 |
| 1998 | 92 | 2006 | 2010 |
| 1997 | 95 | 2005 | 2009+ |
| 1996 | 93 | 2004 | 2008 |
| 1995 | 95 | 2003 | 2007+ |
| 1994 | 93 | 2006 | 2014 |
| 1993 | 88 | 1998 | 2001+ |
| 1992 | 94 | 2004 | 2012 |
| 1991 | 93 | 2003 | 2011 |
| 1990 | 95 | 2010 | 2020 |
| 1989 | 94 | 2009 | 2019 |
| 1988 | 93 | 2000 | 2005 |
| 1987 | 93 | 2007 | 2017 |

## WATERVALE RIESLING RANKING 3

**Clare Valley** $12–$19
**Current vintage: 2003** 89

Approachable and fragrant riesling whose floral bouquet of lime, lemon and wet slate reveal a hint of estery, candied citrus aroma. Tangy, juicy and spicy, it's forward and soft, with lemon candy and baby powder flavours bound by soft acids.

| | | | |
|---|---|---|---|
| 2003 | 89 | 2005 | 2008 |
| 2002 | 94 | 2007 | 2010+ |
| 2001 | 92 | 2009 | 2013 |
| 2000 | 89 | 2005 | 2008 |
| 1999 | 95 | 2004 | 2007 |
| 1998 | 93 | 2003 | 2006+ |
| 1997 | 93 | 2005 | 2009 |
| 1996 | 89 | 2004 | 2008 |
| 1995 | 91 | 2003 | 2007+ |
| 1994 | 88 | 1999 | 2002 |
| 1993 | 91 | 2001 | 2005 |
| 1992 | 85 | 1994 | 1997 |
| 1991 | 90 | 1993 | 1996 |

# Katnook Estate

Riddoch Highway, Coonawarra SA 5263. Tel: (08) 8737 2394. Fax: (08) 8737 2397.
Website: www.katnookestate.com.au  Email: katnook@wingara.com.au
Region: **Coonawarra** Winemakers: **Wayne Stehbens, Tony Milanowski** Viticulturist: **Chris Brodie**
Chief Executive: **David Yunghanns**
A powerful Cabernet Sauvignon from 2001, a zesty and stylish Sauvignon Blanc from 2003 and a juicy, fully-ripened Chardonnay from 2002 are the three highlights in Katnook Estate's current folio. A series of challenging recent vintages has not aided wine quality for this stand-out Coonawarra producer. Wayne Stehbens is celebrating 25 years of winemaking achievement, that have taken Katnook from obscurity to international recognition.

## CABERNET SAUVIGNON

RANKING **2**

**Coonawarra** $30–$49
**Current vintage: 2001** 92

A powerful, assertive Coonawarra cabernet whose deep, earthy fragrance of meaty, olive-like cassis and plums is underpinned by vanilla oak. Deep, ripe and creamy, with a plumcake-like richness, the palate is just slightly overcooked, with dark berry fruits, currants and cedary oak framed by firm, astringent tannins.

| 2001 | 92 | 2009 | 2013+ |
|---|---|---|---|
| 2000 | 86 | 2002 | 2005 |
| 1999 | 95 | 2007 | 2011 |
| 1998 | 95 | 2010 | 2018 |
| 1997 | 95 | 2009 | 2017 |
| 1996 | 95 | 2008 | 2016 |
| 1995 | 88 | 2000 | 2003 |
| 1994 | 94 | 2002 | 2006 |
| 1993 | 94 | 2005 | 2013 |
| 1992 | 87 | 2004 | 2012 |
| 1991 | 94 | 2003 | 2011 |
| 1990 | 92 | 2002 | 2010 |
| 1988 | 87 | 1996 | 2000+ |
| 1987 | 88 | 1991 | 1995 |
| 1986 | 94 | 1998 | 2003 |

## CHARDONNAY

RANKING **4**

**Coonawarra** $30–$49
**Current vintage: 2002** 92

Ripe, punchy aromas of melon, peaches and cream, backed by creamy, smoky vanilla oak and a very assertive butterscotch-like malolactic influence. Round, smooth and silky, the palate is long and evenly balanced between juicy ripe fruit, creamy oak and soft acids, while I find its buttery malolactic characters just a little overdone.

| 2002 | 92 | 2004 | 2007+ |
|---|---|---|---|
| 2001 | 88 | 2003 | 2006+ |
| 2000 | 86 | 2002 | 2005 |
| 1999 | 87 | 2001 | 2004 |
| 1998 | 90 | 2000 | 2003 |
| 1997 | 89 | 1999 | 2002 |
| 1996 | 93 | 2001 | 2004 |
| 1995 | 94 | 2000 | 2003 |
| 1994 | 94 | 1999 | 2002 |
| 1993 | 94 | 1998 | 2001 |

## CHARDONNAY BRUT

RANKING **4**

**Coonawarra** $20–$29
**Current vintage: 2002** 87

Simply, fruity and varietal sparkling chardonnay whose light, spicy aromas of lime and lemon and vibrant, fluffy and lemony palate offer freshness, flavour and a hint of toastiness. Uncomplicated, lively and clean.

| 2002 | 87 | 2004 | 2007 |
|---|---|---|---|
| 2001 | 85 | 2003 | 2006 |
| 1996 | 93 | 2001 | 2004 |
| 1995 | 90 | 2000 | 2003 |
| 1994 | 82 | 1996 | 1999 |
| 1993 | 90 | 1995 | 1998 |
| 1990 | 94 | 1995 | 1998 |

## MERLOT

RANKING **4**

**Coonawarra** $30–$49
**Current vintage: 2001** 82

Meaty, earthy and sweaty merlot whose very developed, herbal fruit is bound by green-edged tannins. Needs more fruit and freshness.

| 2001 | 82 | 2003 | 2006 |
|---|---|---|---|
| 2000 | 87 | 2002 | 2005 |
| 1999 | 82 | 2001 | 2004 |
| 1998 | 96 | 2006 | 2010+ |
| 1997 | 93 | 2002 | 2005+ |
| 1996 | 94 | 2004 | 2008 |
| 1995 | 87 | 1997 | 2001 |
| 1994 | 94 | 1999 | 2002 |
| 1993 | 94 | 1998 | 2001 |
| 1992 | 93 | 1997 | 2000 |

# ODYSSEY

| Coonawarra | $50+ |
| --- | --- |
| **Current vintage: 2000** | **87** |

Very oaky, slightly varnishy cabernet with lifted meaty, herbal and smoky aromas of jammy raspberries, plums and blackberries. The palate begins with the promise of richness and structure, but its briary flavours of cassis and red berries then become leafy, as the varnishy oak takes over. It finishes with slightly metallic tannins and cooked fruit.

| 2000 | 87 | 2008 | 2012 |
| --- | --- | --- | --- |
| 1999 | 95 | 2011 | 2019 |
| 1998 | 90 | 2006 | 2010 |
| 1997 | 90 | 2005 | 2009+ |
| 1996 | 97 | 2008 | 2016+ |
| 1994 | 95 | 2006 | 2014 |
| 1992 | 94 | 2004 | 2012 |
| 1991 | 96 | 2003 | 2011+ |

# PRODIGY SHIRAZ

RANKING

| Coonawarra | $50+ |
| --- | --- |
| **Current vintage: 2000** | **88** |

Rustic, shorter-term Coonawarra shiraz with a developing, gamey, earthy bouquet of leathery, peppery and dusty cassis/mulberry/blueberry fruit with greenish, herbal tinges. Moderately full in weight, its herby, green-edged and dusty palate does present some pleasingly intense forward fruit and smoky new oak, but lacks genuine length, structure and ripeness.

| 2000 | 88 | 2002 | 2005+ |
| --- | --- | --- | --- |
| 1999 | 89 | 2004 | 2007 |
| 1998 | 97 | 2006 | 2010 |
| 1997 | 91 | 2005 | 2009 |

# RIESLING

RANKING

| Coonawarra | $12–$19 |
| --- | --- |
| **Current vintage: 2003** | **89** |

Rather closed aromas of apple, pear and lime juice with some honey and tropical aromatics precede a generous, broad but concentrated palate that culminates in a clean, refreshing and limey finish of racy lemony acidity.

| 2003 | 89 | 2005 | 2008+ |
| --- | --- | --- | --- |
| 2002 | 90 | 2004 | 2007+ |
| 2001 | 87 | 2003 | 2006+ |
| 2000 | 89 | 2005 | 2008 |
| 1999 | 82 | 2001 | 2004 |
| 1998 | 91 | 2003 | 2006+ |
| 1997 | 86 | 1999 | 2002 |
| 1996 | 87 | 2001 | 2004 |
| 1995 | 82 | 2000 | 2003 |

# SAUVIGNON BLANC

RANKING

| Coonawarra | $20–$29 |
| --- | --- |
| **Current vintage: 2003** | **90** |

Delicate, focused aromas of fresh tropical and citrus fruits with a suggestion of grassiness. Pristine and refreshing, its piercing, yet restrained core of pure sauvignon blanc flavour culminates in a soft acid finish.

| 2003 | 90 | 2004 | 2005+ |
| --- | --- | --- | --- |
| 2002 | 90 | 2003 | 2004 |
| 2001 | 88 | 2001 | 2002 |
| 2000 | 82 | 2001 | 2002 |
| 1999 | 82 | 1999 | 2000 |
| 1998 | 88 | 1998 | 1999 |

# SHIRAZ

RANKING

| Coonawarra | $20–$29 |
| --- | --- |
| **Current vintage: 2002** | **87** |

Spicy, meaty early-drinking shiraz whose closed, slightly confection-like aromas of spicy raspberries, animal felt and licorice reveal underlying vegetal influences. Similarly, the palate is pleasing and forward, with earthy, meaty spicy fruit and sweet gamey oak that culminates in a green-edged and lightly sappy, metallic finish.

| 2002 | 87 | 2004 | 2007+ |
| --- | --- | --- | --- |
| 2001 | 89 | 2003 | 2006+ |
| 2000 | 88 | 2002 | 2005+ |
| 1999 | 88 | 2001 | 2004+ |
| 1998 | 86 | 2006 | 2010 |

# Kay's Amery

Kays Road, McLaren Vale SA 5171. Tel: (08) 8323 8201. Fax: (08) 8323 9199.
Website: www.kaybrothersamerywines.com.au Email: amery@senet.com.au

Region: **McLaren Vale** Winemaker: **Colin Kay** Viticulturist: **Colin Kay** Chief Executive: **Colin Kay**

Kay's Amery is a traditional maker of McLaren Vale wine able to achieve remarkable concentration and depth of juicy dark fruit in its low-cropped reds from old vines. Oddly enough, the reds I have tasted from the cooler 2002 season are more alcoholic than from the extremely hot 2001 vintage, which is responsible for a significant number of high-alcohol red wines in McLaren Vale. And furthermore, the 2002 Shiraz easily carries its 15.5%!

## BLOCK 6 SHIRAZ

RANKING **4**

| McLaren Vale | $50+ |
|---|---|
| Current vintage: 2001 | 90 |

Plush, concentrated shiraz with a complex bouquet of spicy leather, chocolate and briary influences beneath aromas of raspberries, plums and sweet vanilla/mocha oak. Sumptuous but velvet-smooth, it's richly flavoured with intense dark fruits but avoids excessive over-ripeness, finishing savoury with some elegance and tightness.

| | | | |
|---|---|---|---|
| 2001 | 90 | 2009 | 2013 |
| 2000 | 87 | 2005 | 2008+ |
| 1999 | 90 | 2004 | 2007 |
| 1998 | 90 | 2006 | 2010 |
| 1997 | 82 | 2002 | 2005 |
| 1996 | 95 | 2004 | 2008+ |
| 1995 | 93 | 2003 | 2007+ |
| 1994 | 94 | 2006 | 2014 |
| 1993 | 93 | 2005 | 2013 |
| 1992 | 94 | 2004 | 2012 |
| 1991 | 93 | 1999 | 2003 |
| 1990 | 93 | 2002 | 2010 |
| 1989 | 90 | 1994 | 1997 |

## CABERNET SAUVIGNON

RANKING **5**

| McLaren Vale | $20–$29 |
|---|---|
| Current vintage: 2002 | 86 |

An honest, earthy and rather reserved cabernet made in a lighter style than usual for this region. Its musky, spicy aromas of light plummy fruit and mocha/chocolate oak precede a flavoursome, but restrained palate whose uncomplicated and up-front fruit is supported by fine tannins.

| | | | |
|---|---|---|---|
| 2002 | 86 | 2007 | 2010 |
| 2001 | 89 | 2009 | 2013 |
| 2000 | 87 | 2005 | 2008 |
| 1999 | 89 | 2004 | 2007 |
| 1998 | 89 | 2006 | 2010+ |
| 1997 | 90 | 2005 | 2009 |
| 1996 | 92 | 2004 | 2008 |
| 1995 | 89 | 2003 | 2007 |
| 1994 | 90 | 2006 | 2014 |
| 1993 | 87 | 2001 | 2005 |

## HILLSIDE SHIRAZ

RANKING **4**

| McLaren Vale | $20–$29 |
|---|---|
| Current vintage: 2001 | 89 |

Concentrated blackberry confiture aromas with plums and licorice, cinnamon and cloves over sweet coconut and vanilla oak. Ripe, round and smooth, if slightly soupy expression of sweet plums and dark berries well integrated with chocolate/vanilla oak with a good fine tannin structure inserted beneath.

| | | | |
|---|---|---|---|
| 2001 | 89 | 2006 | 2009 |
| 2000 | 92 | 2005 | 2008 |
| 1999 | 87 | 2004 | 2007 |
| 1998 | 89 | 2003 | 2006 |
| 1997 | 91 | 2002 | 2005+ |

## MERLOT

| McLaren Vale | $20–$29 |
|---|---|
| Current vintage: 2002 | 87 |

Plummy, meaty merlot with sweet earthy aromas of slightly overcooked prune-like and leathery fruit supported by assertive sweet chocolate/vanilla oak. Generous, round and plummy, the minty fruitcake-like palate is smooth and richly flavoured, if slightly cooked and forward. Drink soon.

| | | | |
|---|---|---|---|
| 2002 | 87 | 2004 | 2007 |
| 2000 | 84 | 2005 | 2008+ |
| 1999 | 82 | 2001 | 2004 |
| 1998 | 89 | 2006 | 2010 |

## SHIRAZ

| | | | |
|---|---|---|---|
| **McLaren Vale** | **$20–$29** | | |
| **Current vintage: 2002** | **88** | | |

A lively fragrance of raspberries, red cherries and plums brings a hint of sweet vanilla oak, floral perfume and confection. Smooth, supple and creamy, the palate is vibrant, fleshy and juicy, with boiled lolly-like small berry flavours and creamy vanilla oak easily carrying its stated 15.5% alcohol. Sumptuous and soft, it's an attractive, if uncomplicated riper style.

| | | | |
|---|---|---|---|
| 2002 | 88 | 2007 | 2010+ |
| 2001 | 88 | 2006 | 2009 |
| 1999 | 89 | 2001 | 2004 |
| 1998 | 94 | 2006 | 2010 |
| 1997 | 88 | 2002 | 2005+ |
| 1996 | 94 | 2004 | 2008 |
| 1995 | 91 | 2007 | 2015 |
| 1994 | 90 | 2006 | 2014 |
| 1993 | 87 | 2001 | 2005 |

# Killerby

Caves Road, Willyabrup WA 6285. Tel: 1-800 655 722. Fax: 1-800 679 578.
Website: www.killerby.com.au  Email: grapevine@killerby.com.au
Region: **Geographe, Margaret River** Winemaker: **Mark Matthews** Viticulturist: **Travis Schultz**
Chief Executive: **Ben Killerby**

You have to hand it to Killerby, for having made the transition from Geographe into Margaret River. Its taut and savoury white wines are consistently first-rate, often presenting surprising complexity and definition, while both the Shiraz and Cabernet Sauvignon have performed well in recent years.

## CABERNET SAUVIGNON

| | | | |
|---|---|---|---|
| **Geographe, Margaret River** | **$20–$29** | | |
| **Current vintage: 2002** | **89** | | |

Honest, early-drinking cabernet with a lightly musky and herbal aroma of sweet, slightly jammy raspberries and red plums over spicy, cedary oak. It's smooth and creamy, with vibrant, if uncomplicated red fruit flavours over an assertive spine and cedar/vanilla oak.

| | | | |
|---|---|---|---|
| 2002 | 89 | 2007 | 2010 |
| 2001 | 89 | 2009 | 2013 |
| 2000 | 93 | 2008 | 2012+ |
| 1999 | 87 | 2004 | 2007 |
| 1998 | 86 | 2003 | 2006+ |
| 1997 | 86 | 2002 | 2005 |
| 1996 | 83 | 2004 | 2008 |
| 1995 | 87 | 2003 | 2007 |
| 1994 | 82 | 1999 | 2002 |
| 1993 | 93 | 2005 | 2013 |
| 1992 | 94 | 2000 | 2004 |
| 1991 | 87 | 2003 | 2011 |

## CHARDONNAY

| | | | |
|---|---|---|---|
| **Geographe, Margaret River** | **$20–$29** | | |
| **Current vintage: 2002** | **92** | | |

An austere, stylish and crafted chardonnay whose pungent, creamy aromas of melon and citrus fruit overlie nuances of oatmeal, tobacco and grilled nuts, with lightly smoky vanilla oak. Reined in by its tight-knit acidity, its palate of peach, melon and grapefruit flavour remains elegant and dry, finely balanced and savoury.

| | | | |
|---|---|---|---|
| 2002 | 92 | 2007 | 2010 |
| 2001 | 89 | 2003 | 2006 |
| 2000 | 92 | 2005 | 2008 |
| 1999 | 80 | 2000 | 2000 |
| 1998 | 86 | 2000 | 2003+ |
| 1997 | 84 | 1999 | 2002 |
| 1996 | 93 | 2001 | 2004 |
| 1995 | 93 | 2000 | 2003 |

## SAUVIGNON BLANC

| | | | |
|---|---|---|---|
| **Geographe, Margaret River** | **$20–$29** | | |
| **Current vintage: 2003** | **92** | | |

There's a nutty whiff of lightly smoky vanilla oak beneath some fresh, grassy aromas of gooseberries and passionfruit. Relatively lean and acidic, it's a stylish, taut and trim wine, with some slightly aggressive oak peeking through its nutty, herbal sauvignon flavours of gooseberries and lychees. Long and zesty, with pleasing shape and balance, it should flesh out in the bottle.

| | | | |
|---|---|---|---|
| 2003 | 92 | 2004 | 2005+ |
| 2002 | 93 | 2004 | 2007 |
| 2001 | 88 | 2003 | 2006 |

## SEMILLON

RANKING 4

**Geographe, Margaret River** $20–$29
**Current vintage: 2003**     **90**

Distinctive, unusual and slightly oxidative semillon with a lightly cheesy, leesy and even sweaty perfume of ripe honeydew melon over hints of mineral and greenish Loire-like smokiness. Unashamedly reductive, it's long, mineral, even meaty, creating an assertive presence in the mouth punctuated by taut, clean acidity. It should settle into a complex and savoury food style.

| | | | |
|---|---|---|---|
| 2003 | 90 | 2005 | 2008+ |
| 2002 | 91 | 2004 | 2007+ |
| 2001 | 90 | 2003 | 2006 |
| 1999 | 93 | 2004 | 2007 |
| 1998 | 84 | 2000 | 2003 |
| 1997 | 90 | 2002 | 2005 |
| 1996 | 93 | 2001 | 2004 |
| 1995 | 94 | 2000 | 2003 |
| 1994 | 91 | 2002 | 2006 |
| 1993 | 90 | 1998 | 2001 |
| 1992 | 91 | 1997 | 2000 |
| 1991 | 91 | 1999 | 2003 |
| 1990 | 87 | 1995 | 1998 |

## SHIRAZ

RANKING 3

**Geographe, Margaret River** $20–$29
**Current vintage: 2001**     **89**

Ripe aromas of plums, blackcurrants and blueberries with sweet, slightly varnishy vanilla/mocha oak precede a juicy palate of intensity and polish. Ripe, juicy fruit sweetness easily handles its assertive vanilla oak. Generous, up-front and flavoursome, it finishes savoury with length and persistence.

| | | | |
|---|---|---|---|
| 2001 | 89 | 2009 | 2013 |
| 2000 | 89 | 2005 | 2008+ |
| 1999 | 95 | 2007 | 2011 |
| 1998 | 93 | 2006 | 2010 |
| 1997 | 86 | 2002 | 2005 |
| 1996 | 89 | 2001 | 2004 |
| 1995 | 94 | 2003 | 2007 |
| 1994 | 94 | 2002 | 2006 |
| 1993 | 93 | 2001 | 2005 |
| 1992 | 82 | 1997 | 2000 |
| 1991 | 94 | 1999 | 2003 |
| 1989 | 89 | 1997 | 2001 |

# Knappstein

2 Pioneer Avenue Clare SA 5453. Tel: (08) 8842 2600. Fax: (08) 8842 3831.
Website: www.knappsteinwines.com.au  Email: knappsteinwines@knappstein.com.au
Region: **Clare Valley** Winemaker: **Andrew Hardy** Viticulturist: **Ray Klavins** Chief Executive: **Peter Cowan**
Knappstein is a long-established Clare Valley label with a solid all-round reputation for its broad range of varietal table wines. That said, with the possible exception of its very consistent Riesling, not enough Knappstein wine fits into the 'must have' category. None of this is news to those individuals close to the brand, who have some very interesting developments to reveal over the next few years...

## CABERNET MERLOT

RANKING 5

**Clare Valley**      $20–$29
**Current vintage: 2001**     **86**

Light, minty aromas of boiled lolly-like red berries, vanilla oak and menthol, plus a lighter palate of some fleshiness and texture whose forward berry fruits dry out a little towards the finish.

| | | | |
|---|---|---|---|
| 2001 | 86 | 2003 | 2006+ |
| 2000 | 82 | 2002 | 2005 |
| 1999 | 88 | 2004 | 2007 |
| 1998 | 90 | 2003 | 2006 |
| 1997 | 89 | 2002 | 2005 |
| 1996 | 91 | 2001 | 2004 |
| 1995 | 89 | 2000 | 2003 |
| 1994 | 89 | 2002 | 2006 |
| 1993 | 87 | 1998 | 2001 |
| 1992 | 88 | 1997 | 2000 |
| 1991 | 91 | 1999 | 2003 |
| 1990 | 90 | 1992 | 1995 |

## CHARDONNAY

RANKING 5

**Clare Valley, Lenswood**      $20–$29
**Current vintage: 2003**     **82**

Pungent almost over-ripe aromas of squashed melons and bananas, quince and tobacco precede a fast-developing, juicy, round and forward palate that lacks length and brightness.

| | | | |
|---|---|---|---|
| 2003 | 82 | 2004 | 2005 |
| 2002 | 90 | 2004 | 2007 |
| 2001 | 84 | 2002 | 2003 |
| 2000 | 86 | 2002 | 2005 |
| 1998 | 83 | 1999 | 2000 |
| 1996 | 88 | 1998 | 2001 |
| 1995 | 90 | 2000 | 2003 |
| 1994 | 82 | 1996 | 1999 |

## ENTERPRISE CABERNET SAUVIGNON

RANKING 3

**Clare Valley** $50+
**Current vintage: 2000** 86

Slightly porty, meaty red whose jammy aromas of minty berry fruit and sweet oak reveal some dead fruit influences. Cooked, leathery and fast-developing, the palate is reliant on its impressive, but sweet oak, since its desiccated, pruney and dehydrated fruit lacks freshness and bounce.

| | | | |
|---|---|---|---|
| 2000 | 86 | 2002 | 2005+ |
| 1999 | 89 | 2004 | 2007+ |
| 1998 | 95 | 2010 | 2018+ |
| 1997 | 93 | 2005 | 2009+ |
| 1996 | 95 | 2008 | 2016+ |
| 1995 | 90 | 2003 | 2007+ |
| 1994 | 89 | 2006 | 2014 |

## ENTERPRISE SHIRAZ

RANKING 2

**Clare Valley** $50+
**Current vintage: 2000** 88

Meaty, concentrated shiraz whose minty, menthol-like expression of pruney, plummy and currant-like fruit is reliant for sweetness and depth on its rather assertive chocolate/mocha oak. It's rich, soft and generous, fine for early drinking, but lacks the length, freshness and structure for longer cellaring.

| | | | |
|---|---|---|---|
| 2000 | 88 | 2005 | 2008 |
| 1999 | 95 | 2007 | 2011+ |
| 1998 | 91 | 2003 | 2006+ |
| 1997 | 94 | 2005 | 2009+ |
| 1996 | 95 | 2004 | 2008+ |
| 1995 | 93 | 2003 | 2007 |
| 1994 | 95 | 2006 | 2014 |

## GEWÜRZTRAMINER

RANKING 4

**Clare Valley** $12–$19
**Current vintage: 2003** 82

Spicy, varnishy aromas of lychees and gooseberries are rather cooked and lacking freshness. Broad, but finishing lean and hard-edged, its palate is framed by some stark acidity.

| | | | |
|---|---|---|---|
| 2003 | 82 | 2003 | 2004+ |
| 2002 | 93 | 2007 | 2010+ |
| 2001 | 83 | 2002 | 2003 |
| 2000 | 91 | 2005 | 2008 |
| 1999 | 89 | 2004 | 2007 |
| 1998 | 93 | 2003 | 2006 |
| 1997 | 94 | 2002 | 2005 |
| 1996 | 93 | 2001 | 2004 |
| 1995 | 89 | 2000 | 2003 |
| 1994 | 91 | 2002 | 2006 |
| 1993 | 94 | 1998 | 2001 |
| 1992 | 90 | 1994 | 1997 |

## RIESLING

RANKING 2

**Clare Valley** $12–$19
**Current vintage: 2003** 94

Spicy, tightly focused aromas of apple, pear and flowers are fresh and vibrant. Bursting with clear, concentrated riesling flavour, it's long and chalky with a refreshing lemon/lime finish.

| | | | |
|---|---|---|---|
| 2003 | 94 | 2008 | 2011 |
| 2002 | 93 | 2007 | 2010+ |
| 2001 | 94 | 2009 | 2013+ |
| 2000 | 95 | 2008 | 2012 |
| 1999 | 93 | 2004 | 2007 |
| 1998 | 95 | 2006 | 2010 |
| 1997 | 94 | 2005 | 2009 |
| 1996 | 93 | 2004 | 2008+ |
| 1995 | 90 | 2003 | 2007 |
| 1994 | 94 | 2006 | 2014 |
| 1993 | 95 | 2001 | 2005 |
| 1992 | 91 | 1997 | 2000 |
| 1991 | 90 | 1996 | 1999 |
| 1990 | 93 | 1998 | 2002 |

## SEMILLON SAUVIGNON BLANC

RANKING 5

**Clare Valley** $20–$29
**Current vintage: 2003** 81

Herbal, rather cooked and citrusy aromas lack freshness, while the palate is confection-like and advanced, becoming hard-edged and austere. Lacks fruit and freshness.

| | | | |
|---|---|---|---|
| 2003 | 81 | 2003 | 2004 |
| 2001 | 90 | 2003 | 2006 |
| 2000 | 83 | 2000 | 2001 |
| 1998 | 86 | 2000 | 2003 |
| 1997 | 87 | 1999 | 2002 |
| 1996 | 92 | 2001 | 2004 |
| 1995 | 93 | 1997 | 2000 |
| 1994 | 89 | 1999 | 2002 |
| 1993 | 94 | 1995 | 1998 |
| 1992 | 93 | 1997 | 2000 |

## SHIRAZ

RANKING **4**

| Clare Valley | $20–$29 |
|---|---|
| **Current vintage: 2002** | **90** |

Youthful licorice-like aromas of red and black berries, dark plums, white pepper, cinnamon and cloves precede a smooth, willowy and restrained palate of medium to full weight over fine, powdery tannins. Brightly flavoured, it's developing some leathery complexity, is just a little warm and spirity, but remains very approachable.

| 2002 | 90 | 2007 | 2010+ |
|---|---|---|---|
| 2001 | 89 | 2006 | 2009+ |
| 2000 | 86 | 2002 | 2005 |
| 1999 | 90 | 2004 | 2007 |
| 1998 | 92 | 2003 | 2006+ |
| 1997 | 88 | 2002 | 2005 |
| 1996 | 83 | **1998** | **2001** |

# Knight Granite Hills

1481 Burke & Wills Track Baynton Kyneton Vic 3444. Tel: (03) 5423 7288. Fax: (03) 5423 7288.
Email: knights@ granitehills.com.au
Region: **Macedon Ranges** Winemakers: **Llew Knight, Ian Gunter**
Chief Executives: **Gordon, Heather & Llew Knight**
Located at one of the coolest and latest vineyard sites on mainland Australia, Knight has a history of deeply perfumed, intensely flavoured and minerally Riesling, a elegant, fine-grained Cabernet Sauvignon plus a sneezy black pepper Shiraz. Its musky and chalky 2003 Riesling is perhaps its finest wine ever made, and sits well with the very best from the Eden Valley, which also enjoyed a stellar riesling vintage in 2003.

## CABERNET SAUVIGNON

RANKING **4**

| Macedon Ranges | $20–$29 |
|---|---|
| **Current vintage: 2001** | **82** |

Earthy, herbal and meaty, cedary aromas precede and up-front palate of green-edged small red berries, finishing lean and sappy.

| 2001 | 82 | 2003 | 2006 |
|---|---|---|---|
| 2000 | 77 | 2002 | 2005 |
| 1999 | 94 | 2007 | 2011+ |
| 1998 | 90 | 2006 | 2010 |
| 1997 | 86 | 2002 | 2005 |
| 1996 | 84 | 2001 | 2004 |
| 1995 | 89 | 2003 | 2007 |
| 1992 | 86 | 1997 | 2000 |
| 1991 | 87 | 2003 | 2011 |
| 1989 | 86 | 1991 | 1994 |
| 1988 | 82 | 1996 | 2000 |

## CHARDONNAY

RANKING **5**

| Macedon Ranges | $20–$29 |
|---|---|
| **Current vintage: 2003** | **88** |

An unusual, very distinctive and heavily worked chardonnay with pungent oxidative influences. Its floral aromas of quince and melon reveal nuances of aldehyde and oatmeal, while its sweet, buttery palate is chewy and savoury. With a generous core of apple, melon and pear-like fruit, it gradually freshens in the glass, shedding some reductive complexity.

| 2003 | 88 | 2005 | 2008 |
|---|---|---|---|
| 2002 | 88 | 2003 | 2006 |
| 2001 | 82 | 2002 | 2003 |
| 2000 | 87 | 2002 | 2005 |
| 1999 | 85 | 2000 | 2001 |
| 1998 | 86 | 2000 | 2003 |
| 1997 | 83 | 1999 | 2002 |
| 1996 | 90 | 2001 | 2004 |
| 1995 | 93 | 2003 | 2007 |
| 1994 | 83 | 1996 | 1999 |
| 1993 | 92 | 1998 | 2001 |

## RIESLING

RANKING **3**

| Macedon Ranges | $20–$29 |
|---|---|
| **Current vintage: 2003** | **96** |

Classic cool climate riesling with a musky perfume of lemon, lime and apple beneath alluring scents of rose petals. Long and crunchy, with a juicy, fleshy core of vibrant stonefruit, pear and apple flavours bound by crackly acidity. Wonderfully generous, tight and austere, before a long and powdery slate-like finish.

| 2003 | 96 | 2011 | 2015 |
|---|---|---|---|
| 2002 | 92 | 2007 | 2010 |
| 2001 | 89 | 2003 | 2006 |
| 2000 | 87 | 2002 | 2005 |
| 1999 | 92 | 2007 | 2011 |
| 1998 | 91 | 2003 | 2006+ |
| 1997 | 94 | 2009 | 2017 |
| 1995 | 93 | 2003 | 2007 |
| 1994 | 89 | 2002 | 2006 |
| 1993 | 85 | 1998 | 2001 |
| 1992 | 94 | 2000 | 2004 |

## SHIRAZ

**Macedon Ranges**      $20–$29
**Current vintage: 2001**      89

Spicy, almost sneezy bouquet of black pepper, cassis, dark plums and cedary oak over nuances of violets and underlying meaty, herbal influences. Pristine and penetrative, smooth and polished, it's bursting with dark plums, berries and cherries framed by tight-knit fine tannins, but does reveal an underlying thread of herbaceousness.

| 2001 | 89 | 2009 | 2013+ |
|------|----|------|-------|
| 2000 | 88 | 2005 | 2008  |
| 1999 | 86 | 2001 | 2004+ |
| 1998 | 87 | 2003 | 2006  |
| 1997 | 82 | 1999 | 2002  |
| 1996 | 80 | 1998 | 2003  |

# Kooyong

110 Hunts Road, Tuerong Vic 3933. Tel: (03) 5989 7355. Fax: (02) 5989 7677.
Website: www.kooyong.com  Email: wines@kooyong.com

Region: **Mornington Peninsula** Winemaker: **Sandro Mosele** Viticulturist: **Sandro Mosele**
Chief Executive: **Giorgio Gjergja**

Kooyong is the most exciting winemaking development to occur in Victoria's Mornington Peninsula region for more than a decade. A comparatively large-scale project, with high expectations of quality and genuine restrictions on quantity, its vineyard offers Sandro Mosele an exceptionally broad range of options with respect to sites and clones. The business is now owned by the owner of Port Phillip Estate, whose wines have been contract-made at Kooyong for a short period. Kooyong recently released three 2001 individual vineyard wines of exceptional poise and complexity.

## CHARDONNAY

**Mornington Peninsula**      $30–$49
**Current vintage: 2001**      95

Beautifully presented chardonnay with a grainy aroma of oatmeal, lemon blossom and underlying dusty, mineral notes. Long, supple and elegant, the palate is evenly measured and balanced, delivering spotlessly pure stonefruit flavours backed by suggestions of grilled nuts, cream and earthy wild yeast nuances. It finishes refreshing and savoury, with a lingering minerality.

| 2001 | 95 | 2006 | 2009  |
|------|----|------|-------|
| 2000 | 94 | 2002 | 2005+ |
| 1999 | 92 | 2001 | 2004  |

## PINOT NOIR

**Mornington Peninsula**      $30–$49
**Current vintage: 2001**      95

Very stylish pinot of Pommard-like weight and style. Its perfume of rose petals and red cherries, cinnamon and cloves, musk and undergrowth is supported by restrained cedar/vanilla oak, while its supple, bony palate is both chewy and elegant. Its meaty core of cherry/plum fruit is framed by firm, fine-grained tannins before a nutty, savoury finish. Excellent texture and weight, with lingering animal hide-like complexity.

| 2001 | 95 | 2006 | 2009+ |
|------|----|------|-------|
| 2000 | 90 | 2005 | 2008  |
| 1999 | 92 | 2001 | 2004+ |

# Lake's Folly

Broke Road, Pokolbin NSW 2320. Tel: (02) 4998 7507. Fax: (02) 4998 7322.
Website: www.lakesfolly.com.au  Email: folly@ozemail.com.au
Region: **Lower Hunter Valley**  Winemaker: **Rodney Kempe**  Viticulturist: **Jason Locke**
Chief Executive: **Peter Fogarty**
The renaissance of Lake's Folly, Australia's first 'boutique' or 'weekend' winery, goes from strength to strength.
Another first-class Cabernet blend from 2002 and a silky, seamless Chardonnay from 2003 should be enough
to convince any doubters that Rodney Kempe is guiding this top-class vineyard to the next quality level. He
attributes much of the development in the red to the increasingly important role played by petit verdot.

## LAKE'S FOLLY (Cabernet blend)  RANKING 2

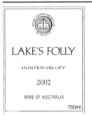

| Lower Hunter Valley | $30–$49 |
|---|---|
| **Current vintage: 2002** | **95** |

A very polished successor to the stellar 2001 release. This blend of four red varieties presents a restrained and delicate petit verdot-dominant perfume of spicy violet aromas, cedar, cassis and rosemary, with underlying nuances of blackberries and dark plums. Very fine, supple, long and stylish, the palate bursts with pure small berry flavours tightly integrated with restrained cedar/vanilla oak and a fine-grained undercarriage of silky tannins before a finish of turned earth and dried herbs.

| | | | |
|---|---|---|---|
| 2002 | 95 | 2014 | 2022 |
| 2001 | 96 | 2013 | 2021+ |
| 2000 | 96 | 2012 | 2020+ |
| 1999 | 93 | 2011 | 2019 |
| 1998 | 95 | 2010 | 2018 |
| 1997 | 89 | 2005 | 2009+ |
| 1996 | 82 | 2001 | 2004 |
| 1995 | 88 | 2003 | 2007 |
| 1994 | 95 | 2002 | 2006+ |
| 1993 | 94 | 2001 | 2005 |
| 1992 | 87 | 1997 | 2000 |
| 1991 | 90 | 2003 | 2011 |
| 1990 | 87 | 1998 | 2002+ |
| 1989 | 92 | 2001 | 2009 |

## CHARDONNAY  RANKING 2

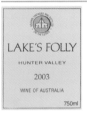

| Lower Hunter Valley | $30–$49 |
|---|---|
| **Current vintage: 2003** | **96** |

Classic modern chardonnay of exceptional finesse and elegance. Its peachy perfume of cumquat, quince and nectarine reveals tightly integrated and fine-grained vanilla and clove-like new French oak. Exceptionally long, fine and seamless, its palate reveals an almost fluffy silkiness. Its delightful purity of restrained, but precisely focused peach/citrus fruit is framed by clean, perfectly punctuated acidity.

| | | | |
|---|---|---|---|
| 2003 | 96 | 2008 | 2011+ |
| 2002 | 95 | 2007 | 2010+ |
| 2001 | 96 | 2009 | 2013 |
| 2000 | 95 | 2005 | 2008 |
| 1999 | 89 | 2001 | 2004 |
| 1998 | 94 | 2003 | 2006+ |
| 1997 | 89 | 1999 | 2002 |
| 1996 | 95 | 2001 | 2004+ |
| 1995 | 89 | 2000 | 2003 |
| 1994 | 90 | 1999 | 2002 |
| 1993 | 89 | 1998 | 2001+ |
| 1992 | 92 | 2000 | 2004 |
| 1991 | 95 | 1999 | 2003+ |
| 1990 | 88 | 1995 | 1998 |
| 1989 | 89 | 1994 | 1997+ |
| 1988 | 88 | 1993 | 1996 |

# Langmeil

cnr Langmeil & Para Rds, Tanunda SA 5352. Tel: (08) 8563 2595. Fax: (08) 8563 3622.
Website: www.langmeilwinery.com.au  Email: langmeilwinery@ozemail.com.au
Region: **Barossa Valley**  Winemaker: **Paul Lindner**  Viticulturist: **Carl Lindner**  Chief Executive: **Richard Lindner**
It hasn't taken Langmeil long to cement its place amongst the better small makers in the Barossa Valley. A
red wine specialist, its wines marry their ripeness and juicy flavours with meaty, earthy complexity. The company's
flagship red, The Freedom Shiraz, is made from vines planted in the 1840s. And some say Australian wine was
born yesterday! The 2002 reds look very exciting indeed.

## CABERNET SAUVIGNON  RANKING 4

| Barossa Valley | $20–$29 |
|---|---|
| **Current vintage: 2001** | **86** |

Fragrant, but herbal, even unusually tropical and gooseberry-like aromas with a greenish, sappy and cedary palate of vibrant cassis, plum and cherry flavours framed by soft tannins with a surprisingly firm grip.

| | | | |
|---|---|---|---|
| 2001 | 86 | 2003 | 2006+ |
| 2000 | 88 | 2005 | 2008 |
| 1999 | 91 | 2007 | 2011+ |
| 1998 | 90 | 2006 | 2010 |

## THE FREEDOM SHIRAZ

| Barossa Valley | $50+ |
| --- | --- |
| Current vintage: 2001 | 91 |

Pungent, tarry, meaty aromas of cassis and dark plums, prunes and currants are very spicy and slightly spirity, and lifted by sweet coconut/vanilla oak. Its deeply concentrated, warm and spirity palate with assertive, if slightly dehydrated fruit flavours, finishes slightly sweet. Sumptuous, velvety and firm, wrapped in fine, drying tannins and finishing slightly salty. Impressive depth of fruit, but lacks the brightness and freshness for a really high score.

| | | | |
| --- | --- | --- | --- |
| 2001 | 91 | 2006 | 2009+ |
| 2000 | 91 | 2005 | 2008+ |
| 1999 | 96 | 2011 | 2019 |
| 1998 | 93 | 2006 | 2010+ |
| 1997 | 90 | 2002 | 2005+ |

## THREE GARDENS (Shiraz Grenache Mourvèdre)

| Barossa Valley | $20–$29 |
| --- | --- |
| Current vintage: 2002 | 90 |

Joyous little southern Rhône blend with a delicate, floral and spicy aroma of fresh, confectionary small red berries backed by musky nuances of animal hide. Smooth, long and pristine, with a crystal-clear expression of cassis, raspberries, blueberries and plums gently framed by fine tannins and finished with refreshing acidity.

| | | | |
| --- | --- | --- | --- |
| 2002 | 90 | 2004 | 2007 |
| 2001 | 91 | 2006 | 2009 |
| 2000 | 90 | 2005 | 2008 |

## VALLEY FLOOR SHIRAZ

| Barossa Valley | $20–$29 |
| --- | --- |
| Current vintage: 2002 | 88 |

Uncomplicated, early-drinking shiraz with a lively aroma of raspberry confiture, plums and cedar/vanilla oak over spicy notes of cinnamon. Moderately long, its juicy palate of raspberry/cherry flavours finishes marginally sappy, with attractive fruit sweetness.

| | | | |
| --- | --- | --- | --- |
| 2002 | 88 | 2004 | 2007 |
| 2001 | 89 | 2003 | 2006+ |
| 2000 | 88 | 2002 | 2005 |
| 1999 | 93 | 2011 | 2019 |
| 1998 | 89 | 2003 | 2006+ |

# Leasingham

7 Dominic Street, Clare SA 5453. Tel: (08) 8842 2555. Fax: (08) 8842 3293.
Website: www.leasingham-wines.com.au  Email: cellardoor@leasingham-wines.com.au
Region: **Clare Valley** Winemakers: **Kerri Thompson, Cynthea Semmens** Viticulturist: **Ian Smith**
Chief Executive: **David Woods**
Wisely choosing not to produce its Classic Clare reds from the 2000 vintage, Leasingham has moved a step closer to ultra-ripeness with the 2001 releases. Naturally, the shiraz handled the extreme heat better than cabernet sauvignon, but the pick of Leasingham's 2001 reds is for me the more vibrant and delightfully open Bin 61 Shiraz. The perfectly sculpted Classic Clare Riesling from 2002 is one of the very best from this classic riesling vintage, while the 2003 Bin 7 is perfumed, racy and austere.

## BASTION SHIRAZ CABERNET

| Clare Valley | $12–$19 |
| --- | --- |
| Current vintage: 2002 | 88 |

Smooth, polished and very affordable red with an intense minty/menthol fragrance of blackberry jam, cinnamon cake and sweet vanilla/coconut oak. Its long and creamy palate presents lively, briary blackberry and redcurrant fruit with cedary oak and earthy complexity framed by moderately firm tannins.

| | | | |
| --- | --- | --- | --- |
| 2001 | 88 | 2007 | 2010 |
| 2001 | 86 | 2002 | 2003 |
| 2000 | 87 | 2005 | 2008 |

## BIN 7 RIESLING

RANKING 4

RIESLING

| Clare Valley | $12–$19 |
| Current vintage: 2003 | 95 |

This vibrant and refreshing riesling has a musky fragrance of rose petals, white peaches and pear, lime juice and lemon, plus an appealing spiciness. Bursting with concentrated citrus and tropical riesling flavour, it's long, racy and austere, with a chalky texture culminating in a refreshing slate-like finish.

| | | | |
|------|----|------|-------|
| 2003 | 95 | 2008 | 2011 |
| 2002 | 88 | 2004 | 2007 |
| 2001 | 91 | 2003 | 2006 |
| 2000 | 94 | 2008 | 2012 |
| 1999 | 89 | 2004 | 2007 |
| 1998 | 92 | 2006 | 2010 |
| 1997 | 85 | 2002 | 2005 |
| 1996 | 90 | 2001 | 2004+ |

## BIN 56 CABERNET MALBEC

RANKING 4

CABERNET
MALBEC

| Clare Valley | $20–$29 |
| Current vintage: 2001 | 87 |

Lacking its customary richness and fruit sweetness, this meaty, chocolatey red offers a plummy, pruney aroma with some developing leathery complexity. Forward and meaty, it's spicy, earthy and slightly overcooked. Sweet mocha and chocolate oak helps to smooth over its slightly raw and astringent finish.

| | | | |
|------|----|------|-------|
| 2001 | 87 | 2006 | 2009+ |
| 2000 | 86 | 2005 | 2008 |
| 1999 | 90 | 2004 | 2007+ |
| 1998 | 92 | 2006 | 2010 |
| 1997 | 86 | 2002 | 2005+ |
| 1996 | 90 | 2004 | 2008 |
| 1995 | 90 | 2000 | 2003 |
| 1994 | 90 | 1999 | 2002 |
| 1993 | 89 | 2001 | 2005 |
| 1992 | 93 | 2000 | 2004 |
| 1991 | 90 | 1999 | 2003+ |
| 1990 | 90 | 1998 | 2002 |
| 1989 | 86 | 1994 | 1997 |
| 1988 | 90 | 1993 | 1996 |

## BIN 61 SHIRAZ

RANKING 3

SHIRAZ

| Clare Valley | $20–$29 |
| Current vintage: 2001 | 90 |

Maturing, spicy shiraz with a developing and sneezy bouquet of black pepper and blackberries, cassis and plums, cloves and cinnamon above some assertive chocolate and vanilla oak. Rich, dark and meaty, the palate is firm, long and drying, with lingering meaty flavours of slightly cooked dark fruits. A great effort from this vintage.

| | | | |
|------|----|------|-------|
| 2001 | 90 | 2006 | 2009 |
| 2000 | 88 | 2005 | 2008 |
| 1999 | 93 | 2004 | 2007+ |
| 1998 | 94 | 2003 | 2006+ |
| 1997 | 91 | 2005 | 2009 |
| 1996 | 90 | 2001 | 2004 |
| 1995 | 93 | 2003 | 2007 |
| 1994 | 93 | 1999 | 2002 |
| 1993 | 89 | 2001 | 2005 |
| 1992 | 87 | 1997 | 2000 |

## CLASSIC CLARE CABERNET SAUVIGNON

RANKING 4

CLASSIC CLARE

| Clare Valley | $30–$49 |
| Current vintage: 2001 | 89 |

Powerful and assertively oaked cabernet with minty, menthol aromas of slightly cooked plums and pruney fruit over sweet cedar/vanilla oak. Its robust and tarry palate of prunes, cassis, plums and raspberries pushes the limits of ripeness and oak influence, leaving an impression of richness and concentration, but not necessarily of balance and harmony.

| | | | |
|------|----|------|-------|
| 2001 | 89 | 2009 | 2013 |
| 1999 | 94 | 2011 | 2019 |
| 1998 | 92 | 2006 | 2010+ |
| 1997 | 86 | 2002 | 2005 |
| 1996 | 91 | 2004 | 2008 |
| 1995 | 87 | 2000 | 2003 |
| 1994 | 91 | 2002 | 2006 |
| 1993 | 93 | 2001 | 2005 |

## CLASSIC CLARE RIESLING

RANKING 3

CLASSIC CLARE

| Clare Valley | $20–$29 |
| Current vintage: 2002 | 96 |

Stunning, perfectly shaped and stylish riesling with length and minerality. Its musky rose petal fragrance of lime juice, stonefruit and wet slate precedes a tangy, sculpted palate with many layers of flavour. Limey nuances of lemon rind, talcum powder and even a complex lees-derived earthiness contribute character to its profound core of vibrant fruit. A classic Clare indeed.

| | | | |
|------|----|------|-------|
| 2002 | 96 | 2010 | 2014+ |
| 2000 | 93 | 2008 | 2012 |
| 1998 | 88 | 2000 | 2003 |
| 1996 | 93 | 2004 | 2008 |
| 1995 | 94 | 2003 | 2007 |
| 1994 | 95 | 2002 | 2006+ |

## CLASSIC CLARE SHIRAZ

RANKING **3**

| Clare Valley | $30–$49 |
|---|---|
| **Current vintage: 2001** | **91** |

Monumentally powerful shiraz with just enough fruit brightness and vitality not to be clobbered into submission by its overt American oak and sumptuous extract. Smoky mocha and tarry aromas of jammy plums and blackberries, treacle and dark chocolate reveal an underlying meatiness, spiciness and even a floral perfume. Meaty, ripe and juicy, its raisined fruit and velvet-smooth tannins ease back into their luxuriant cushion of sweet, caramel-like oak.

| | | | |
|---|---|---|---|
| 2001 | 91 | 2006 | 2009+ |
| 1999 | 90 | 2004 | 2007 |
| 1998 | 95 | 2006 | 2010+ |
| 1997 | 93 | 2005 | 2009 |
| 1996 | 95 | 2001 | 2004+ |
| 1995 | 92 | 2003 | 2007 |
| 1994 | 95 | 2006 | 2014 |
| 1993 | 94 | 2001 | 2005 |
| 1992 | 88 | 1997 | 2000 |
| 1991 | 94 | 2003 | 2011 |

# Leconfield

Riddoch Highway, Coonawarra SA 5263. Tel: (08) 8737 2326. Fax: (08) 8737 2285.
Website: www.leconfieldcoonawarra.com.au  Email: leconfield@coonawarra.limestonecoast.net.au

Region: **Coonawarra** Winemaker: **Paul Gordon** Viticulturist: **Dean Whiteman**
Chief Executive: **Dr Richard Hamilton**

Paul Gordon is slowly developing Leconfield's red wine quality to the level expected of its first-rate location in downtown Coonawarra, although the cool 2002 vintage made life difficult with shiraz and merlot. Leconfield has followed its fine 2002 Riesling with another appealingly tight and mineral edition from 2003.

## CABERNET SAUVIGNON

| Coonawarra | $30–$49 |
|---|---|
| **Current vintage: 2001** | **91** |

The best wine under this label for several years has a bright, lightly herbal and violet-like aroma of cassis, dark plums and dusty cedar/vanilla oak. Plump and juicy, its generous and creamy palate of concentrated and succulent varietal flavours is supported by a firm, fine-grained tannic backbone and well-integrated cedar/vanilla oak. It finishes with good length of flavour, but lightly herbal edges.

| | | | |
|---|---|---|---|
| 2001 | 91 | 2009 | 2013+ |
| 2000 | 84 | 2002 | 2005 |
| 1999 | 84 | 2001 | 2004+ |
| 1998 | 83 | 2003 | 2006 |
| 1997 | 86 | 2009 | 2011 |
| 1996 | 87 | 2001 | 2004 |
| 1995 | 82 | 2000 | 2003 |
| 1994 | 89 | 1999 | 2002 |

## CHARDONNAY

RANKING **5**

| Coonawarra | $20–$29 |
|---|---|
| **Current vintage: 2003** | **82** |

Light buttery, tropical aromas of melon and banana are juicy and confected, while the palate is lean, tropical, relatively simple and green-edged.

| | | | |
|---|---|---|---|
| 2003 | 82 | 2003 | 2004 |
| 2002 | 88 | 2003 | 2004+ |
| 2000 | 86 | 2002 | 2005 |
| 1999 | 84 | 2000 | 2001 |
| 1998 | 90 | 2000 | 2003 |

## MERLOT

RANKING **5**

| Coonawarra | $30–$49 |
|---|---|
| **Current vintage: 2002** | **81** |

Vegetal aromas of violets, geraniums and sweet cedar/vanilla oak precede a herbaceous, soupy and under-ripe palate that finishes short, raw and green.

| | | | |
|---|---|---|---|
| 2002 | 81 | 2004 | 2007 |
| 2001 | 87 | 2006 | 2009 |
| 2000 | 88 | 2002 | 2005 |
| 1998 | 90 | 2003 | 2006 |
| 1997 | 92 | 2005 | 2009 |
| 1996 | 95 | 2004 | 2008 |

## OLD VINES RIESLING

RANKING 4

| Coonawarra | $20–$29 |
|---|---|
| **Current vintage: 2003** | **90** |

A lean, bony cellar style of riesling with a delicate and floral apple/pear fragrance. A fine, austere and slightly chalky palate of delicate fruit is tightly wound around lemon and mineral acids.

| | | | |
|---|---|---|---|
| 2003 | 90 | 2008 | 2011 |
| 2002 | 93 | 2004 | 2007+ |
| 2001 | 88 | 2003 | 2006 |
| 1999 | 77 | 2000 | 2001 |
| 1998 | 89 | 2003 | 2006+ |
| 1997 | 90 | 2002 | 2005 |
| 1996 | 87 | 2001 | 2004 |
| 1995 | 91 | 2000 | 2003 |

## SHIRAZ

| Coonawarra | $20–$29 |
|---|---|
| **Current vintage: 2002** | **83** |

Earthy, minty and herbal shiraz with nuances of green beans and capsicum beneath its light raspberry and cassis flavours. Medium to full in weight, but rather too vegetal and rustic.

| | | | |
|---|---|---|---|
| 2002 | 83 | 2003 | 2006 |
| 2001 | 82 | 2003 | 2006 |
| 2000 | 87 | 2002 | 2005 |
| 1999 | 81 | 2001 | 2004 |
| 1998 | 85 | 2003 | 2006 |
| 1997 | 92 | 2002 | 2005 |
| 1996 | 92 | 1998 | 2001 |
| 1995 | 93 | 2003 | 2007 |
| 1994 | 92 | 1999 | 2002 |
| 1993 | 93 | 2001 | 2005 |
| 1992 | 93 | 1997 | 2000 |
| 1990 | 95 | 1998 | 2002 |

# Leeuwin Estate

Stevens Road, Witchcliffe WA 6285. Tel: (08) 9759 0000. Fax: (08) 9750 0001.
Website: www.leeuwinestate.com.au  Email: info@leeuwinestate.com.au
Region: **Margaret River** Winemaker: **Bob Cartwright** Viticulturist: **David Winstanley**
Chief Executive: **Tricia Horgan**

Leeuwin Estate makes more top-drawer chardonnay in Australia than any other maker. Its flagship wine is, naturally enough, its sought-after Art Series Chardonnay, a wine that has only infrequently dipped below gold medal standard since its very first vintage in 1980. Typically sumptuous, assertive and deeply flavoured, it is perhaps the longest-living of all Australian chardonnays, and typically gives of its best between 8–12 years of age. New Leeuwin additions to this edition include the rustic and spicy Art Series Shiraz and the vibrant, herbaceous and citrusy Siblings blend of semillon and sauvignon blanc.

## ART SERIES CABERNET SAUVIGNON

RANKING 5

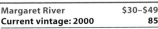

| Margaret River | $30–$49 |
|---|---|
| **Current vintage: 2000** | **85** |

Light violet, raspberry and cassis aromas with greenish undertones of menthol and mint are matched with sweet vanilla and cedary oak. Fine and elegant, the palate presents some rather confection-like raspberry, mulberry and cassis flavours that lack their customary freshness. There is a suggestion of stress about the fruit, while the tannins are fine, firm and drying.

| | | | |
|---|---|---|---|
| 2000 | 85 | 2005 | 2008+ |
| 1999 | 87 | 2004 | 2007+ |
| 1998 | 89 | 2006 | 2010+ |
| 1997 | 82 | 2005 | 2009 |
| 1996 | 83 | 2001 | 2004 |
| 1995 | 80 | 2003 | 2007 |
| 1994 | 89 | 2006 | 2014 |
| 1993 | 88 | 2001 | 2005 |
| 1992 | 95 | 2000 | 2004 |
| 1991 | 95 | 2003 | 2011+ |
| 1990 | 95 | 2002 | 2010 |
| 1989 | 95 | 2001 | 2009 |
| 1988 | 86 | 2000 | 2008 |
| 1987 | 87 | 1999 | 2004 |

A B C D E F G H I J K L M N O P Q R S T U V W X Y Z

# ART SERIES CHARDONNAY

RANKING **1**

**Margaret River** $50+
**Current vintage: 2001** 96

A classically sumptuous, luxuriant chardonnay from this celebrated maker, with a lightly smoky, floral perfume of minerals, grapefruit and lemon zest. Very reserved despite being so richly succulent, unfolding layers of deep fruit flavours, creamy oak and cashew nuts, before a wonderfully long and crystalline finish of exceptional freshness and balance. Absolutely seamless and harmonious.

| | | | |
|---|---|---|---|
| 2001 | 96 | 2009 | 2013+ |
| 2000 | 95 | 2008 | 2012 |
| 1999 | 95 | 2007 | 2011 |
| 1998 | 95 | 2006 | 2010 |
| 1997 | 97 | 2005 | 2009 |
| 1996 | 95 | 2004 | 2008 |
| 1995 | 97 | 2003 | 2007 |
| 1994 | 94 | 2002 | 2006 |
| 1993 | 93 | 1998 | 2001 |
| 1992 | 93 | 1997 | 2000 |
| 1991 | 93 | 1999 | 2003 |
| 1990 | 95 | 2002 | 2010 |
| 1989 | 94 | 1997 | 2001 |
| 1988 | 93 | 1996 | 2000 |
| 1987 | 97 | 1999 | 2007 |
| 1986 | 97 | 1998 | 2006 |
| 1985 | 94 | 1993 | 1997+ |
| 1984 | 91 | 1992 | 1996+ |
| 1983 | 95 | 1995 | 2003 |
| 1982 | 95 | 1990 | 1994+ |
| 1981 | 94 | 1989 | 1993+ |
| 1980 | 92 | 1988 | 1992 |

# ART SERIES RIESLING

RANKING **5**

**Margaret River** $12–$19
**Current vintage: 2003** 89

Broad, rich and tangy riesling with a dusty nose of slightly over-ripe tropical and stonefruit aromas. Spicy, long and savoury, it's packed with punchy lime/lemon and tropical flavour.

| | | | |
|---|---|---|---|
| 2003 | 89 | 2008 | 2011 |
| 2002 | 88 | 2004 | 2007+ |
| 2001 | 89 | 2006 | 2009 |
| 2000 | 87 | 2002 | 2005 |
| 1999 | 91 | 2001 | 2004 |
| 1998 | 83 | 1999 | 2000 |
| 1997 | 87 | 2002 | 2005 |
| 1996 | 90 | 2001 | 2004 |
| 1995 | 89 | 2000 | 2003 |
| 1994 | 87 | 1999 | 2002 |
| 1993 | 88 | 1998 | 2001 |
| 1992 | 89 | 1997 | 2000 |

# ART SERIES SAUVIGNON BLANC

RANKING **4**

**Margaret River** $30–$49
**Current vintage: 2003** 88

Rather exaggerated leafy aromas of capsicum and asparagus tend to mask much of its gooseberry and passionfruit-like fruit aroma, while the juicy, viscous palate is rich, ripe and punchy, offering a broad spread of herbaceous and tropical varietal characters.

| | | | |
|---|---|---|---|
| 2003 | 88 | 2004 | 2005 |
| 2002 | 91 | 2003 | 2004 |
| 2001 | 93 | 2002 | 2003+ |
| 2000 | 87 | 2001 | 2002 |
| 1999 | 91 | 2000 | 2001+ |
| 1998 | 93 | 1999 | 2000 |
| 1997 | 94 | 1999 | 2002 |
| 1996 | 95 | 1998 | 2001 |
| 1995 | 94 | 1997 | 2000 |
| 1994 | 94 | 1996 | 1999 |

# ART SERIES SHIRAZ

RANKING **4**

**Margaret River** $30–$49
**Current vintage: 2001** 90

Meaty, spicy aromas of cracked pepper and cloves, red plums and cherries, with sweet cedar/vanilla oak over a hint of greenness. The lean, bony palate presents a mouthful of ripe tomatoey cherry fruit bound by firm tannins. Quite refined, but on the other hand, also rather rustic and green-edged.

| | | | |
|---|---|---|---|
| 2001 | 90 | 2006 | 2009 |
| 2000 | 83 | 2002 | 2005 |
| 1999 | 90 | 2007 | 2011 |

## PRELUDE CABERNET MERLOT

| Margaret River | $20–$29 |
|---|---|
| **Current vintage: 2001** | **89** |

Elegant and measured cabernet blend whose earthy and lightly musky aromas of cassis and mulberries reveal suggestions of undergrowth, cedary oak and some floral qualities. Smooth and supple, the palate is richer, riper and more structured than the nose would indicate, with several layers of fruit well integrated with oak and tannins, plus a relatively light herbal influence.

| | | | |
|---|---|---|---|
| 2001 | 89 | 2006 | 2009+ |
| 2000 | 81 | 2002 | 2005 |
| 1999 | 78 | 2004 | 2007 |
| 1998 | 83 | 2000 | 2003 |
| 1997 | 82 | 1999 | 2002+ |
| 1996 | 88 | 2001 | 2004 |
| 1994 | 86 | 2002 | 2006 |
| 1993 | 85 | 1998 | 2001 |
| 1991 | 89 | 1999 | 2003 |
| 1990 | 90 | 2002 | 2010 |
| 1989 | 93 | 2001 | 2009 |
| 1988 | 90 | 2000 | 2008 |

## PRELUDE CHARDONNAY

RANKING **4**

| Margaret River | $20–$29 |
|---|---|
| **Current vintage: 2002** | **87** |

A floral, toasty, marmalade-like aroma of lemon rind and tinned pineapple precedes a soft, generous palate whose developing quince/grapefruit flavours and brassy vanilla oak just lack a little freshness and finesse.

| | | | |
|---|---|---|---|
| 2002 | 87 | 2004 | 2007 |
| 2001 | 93 | 2003 | 2006+ |
| 2000 | 90 | 2002 | 2005 |
| 1999 | 90 | 2001 | 2004+ |
| 1998 | 92 | 2000 | 2003+ |
| 1997 | 87 | 1999 | 2002 |
| 1996 | 82 | 1997 | 1998 |
| 1994 | 92 | 1999 | 2002 |
| 1993 | 93 | 1998 | 2001 |
| 1992 | 89 | 1997 | 2000 |

## SIBLINGS SAUVIGNON BLANC SEMILLON

RANKING **5**

| Margaret River | $20–$29 |
|---|---|
| **Current vintage: 2003** | **88** |

A well-made wine with dusty, herbal and lightly smoky aromas of pungent honeydew melon and passionfruit precede a rather polished, succulent palate that lacks its usual length and raciness. It finishes soft, smooth and slightly oily.

| | | | |
|---|---|---|---|
| 2003 | 88 | 2003 | 2004+ |
| 2002 | 92 | 2002 | 2003+ |
| 2001 | 89 | 2001 | 2002 |

# Lenswood Vineyards

Croft Road, Lenswood SA 5240. Tel: (08) 8333 3113. Fax: (08) 8333 3136.
Website: www.lenswoodvineyards.com.au  Email: admin@lenswoodvineyards.com.au

Region: **Lenswood** Winemaker: **Tim Knappstein** Viticulturists: **Tim Knappstein, Paul Smith**
Chief Executive: **Annie Knappstein**

Tim and Annie Knappstein developed their Lenswood property, which is closely adjacent to both Geoff Weaver's and the Henschke vineyards in the same sub-region, in the early 1980s. The vineyard has achieved a strong following for its deeply textured Chardonnay, juicy Sauvignon Blanc and ripe, punchy Pinot Noir, which can develop excellent complexity with time in the bottle. Comparatively recent arrivals include the Gewürztraminer and the very stylish and tightly-knit The Palatine blend of red Bordeaux varieties.

## CHARDONNAY

RANKING **3**

| Lenswood | $30–$49 |
|---|---|
| **Current vintage: 2001** | **87** |

Fast-developing toasty chardonnay with a slightly brassy bouquet of toffee, melon and citrus, with honeyed, buttery, mealy and vanilla undertones. Becoming quite broad and even hard-edged, it does lack elegance but delivers ripe citrus/melon fruit and punchy oak before finishing with a nutmeal-like savoury finish.

| | | | |
|---|---|---|---|
| 2001 | 87 | 2002 | 2003+ |
| 2000 | 94 | 2005 | 2008 |
| 1999 | 93 | 2001 | 2004+ |
| 1998 | 93 | 2003 | 2006 |
| 1997 | 90 | 1999 | 2002 |
| 1996 | 92 | 2001 | 2004 |
| 1995 | 95 | 2000 | 2003+ |
| 1994 | 91 | 1999 | 2002 |
| 1993 | 92 | 1998 | 2001 |
| 1992 | 94 | 1997 | 2000 |
| 1991 | 93 | 1996 | 1999+ |

A
B
C
D
E
F
G
H
I
J
K
**L**
M
N
O
P
Q
R
S
T
U
V
W
X
Y
Z

## GEWÜRZTRAMINER

RANKING 4

| Lenswood | $20–$29 |
|---|---|
| **Current vintage: 2003** | **93** |

| | | | |
|---|---|---|---|
| 2003 | 93 | 2005 | 2008+ |
| 2001 | 91 | 2003 | 2006 |
| 1999 | 86 | 2001 | 2004+ |

Spotlessly clean, pristine traminer aromas of musky rose petals and spices, lychees, passionfruit and tropical fruits. Very fine and elegant despite its enormous concentration of fruit, finishing pleasingly dry with zesty acids. While it's not particularly oily now, I'd expect it to gain more texture with time.

## PINOT NOIR

RANKING 3

| Lenswood | $30–$49 |
|---|---|
| **Current vintage: 2002** | **91** |

| | | | |
|---|---|---|---|
| 2002 | 91 | 2007 | 2010+ |
| 2000 | 95 | 2005 | 2008+ |
| 1999 | 93 | 2007 | 2011 |
| 1998 | 95 | 2003 | 2006+ |
| 1997 | 87 | 2002 | 2005 |
| 1996 | 92 | 2004 | 2008 |
| 1995 | 87 | 1997 | 2000 |
| 1994 | 91 | 1999 | 2002+ |
| 1993 | 90 | 1998 | 2001+ |
| 1992 | 88 | 1997 | 2000 |
| 1991 | 94 | 1996 | 1999+ |

Deeply ripened, concentrated and slightly cooked aromas of cherries, plums and prunes, with a musky, smoky and lightly dusty herbal background. A powerful, assertive palate deeply flavoured with small red berries and cherries, blackberries and plums is framed by firm, fine tannins and assertive oak. Fractionally blocky and over-ripe for classic pinot.

## SAUVIGNON BLANC

RANKING 3

| Lenswood | $20–$29 |
|---|---|
| **Current vintage: 2003** | **93** |

| | | | |
|---|---|---|---|
| 2003 | 93 | 2003 | 2004+ |
| 2002 | 95 | 2003 | 2004+ |
| 2001 | 93 | 2001 | 2002+ |
| 2000 | 89 | 2000 | 2001 |
| 1999 | 94 | 2001 | 2004 |
| 1998 | 94 | 1999 | 2000 |
| 1997 | 91 | 1998 | 1999 |

Pungent, complex dusty and lightly sweaty, herbaceous aromas of tropical fruits, gooseberries, passionfruit and cassis. Round and juicy, with pronounced forward grassy varietal flavours, becoming long and mineral.

## THE PALATINE (Merlot, Malbec, Cabernet blend)

RANKING 3

| Lenswood | $30–$49 |
|---|---|
| **Current vintage: 2001** | **90** |

| | | | |
|---|---|---|---|
| 2001 | 90 | 2009 | 2013+ |
| 1999 | 95 | 2007 | 2011+ |
| 1998 | 94 | 2006 | 2010 |
| 1997 | 89 | 2005 | 2009 |

Powerful, almost Amarone-like cabernet blend whose cedary fragrance of small berries and plums, game and tobacco is supported by vanilla oak and reveals slightly cooked prune/currant-like nuances. Its substantial palate presents good weight of very ripe fruit, with a firm underlying extract. Give it time.

# Lenton Brae

Caves Road, Willyabrup Valley Margaret River WA 6295. Tel: (08) 9755 6255. Fax: (08) 9755 6268.
Website: www.lentonbrae.com  Email: info@lentonbrae.com

Region: **Margaret River** Winemaker: **Edward Tomlinson** Viticulturist: **Mark Groat**
Chief Executive: **Jeanette Tomlinson**

One of the emergent breed of fine new Margaret River wineries, Lenton Brae is presently doing best with its smoky and savoury Chardonnay, plus its steely, herbal Semillon Sauvignon Blanc blend.

## CABERNET MERLOT

RANKING 5

| Margaret River | $20–$29 |
|---|---|
| **Current vintage: 2002** | **87** |

| | | | |
|---|---|---|---|
| 2002 | 87 | 2004 | 2007 |
| 2001 | 87 | 2003 | 2006 |
| 2000 | 90 | 2002 | 2005+ |
| 1999 | 89 | 2004 | 2007 |
| 1998 | 87 | 2000 | 2003 |
| 1997 | 82 | 1998 | 1999 |
| 1996 | 87 | 2001 | 2004 |
| 1995 | 89 | 2000 | 2003 |
| 1993 | 82 | 1995 | 1998 |

A lighter, short-term blend whose earthy aromas of lightly herbal berry fruits and vanilla/mocha oak precede a palate of moderate weight and some elegance. While it lacks genuine depth of fruit, it reveals some pretty, bright small berry fruits and restrained oak framed by slightly lean, green-edged tannins.

## CHARDONNAY

RANKING **4**

LENTON BRAE

2000 MARGARET RIVER
CHARDONNAY

**Margaret River** $20–$29
**Current vintage: 2003** **91**

Toasty, lightly smoky aromas of honeydew melon, green olives and wheatmeal precede an elegant but round and succulent palate. Its assertive vanilla oak should ease back, leaving a savoury and refreshing wine of length and dryness.

| 2003 | 91 | 2005 | 2008+ |
|------|----|------|-------|
| 2002 | 88 | 2004 | 2007+ |
| 2001 | 94 | 2003 | 2006+ |
| 2000 | 91 | 2002 | 2005+ |
| 1999 | 93 | 2001 | 2004+ |
| 1998 | 92 | 2000 | 2003 |
| 1997 | 89 | 1999 | 2002+ |
| 1996 | 89 | 2001 | 2004 |

## MARGARET RIVER (Formerly Cabernet Sauvignon)

RANKING **4**

LENTON BRAE

1998
MARGARET RIVER

**Margaret River** $30–$49
**Current vintage: 2001** **85**

A taut, lean cabernet blend whose dusty, leafy aromas of light berry fruit and vanilla oak precede a palate that lacks its usual richness and fruit, finishing greenish and grainy.

| 2001 | 85 | 2003 | 2006+ |
|------|----|------|-------|
| 2000 | 89 | 2008 | 2012 |
| 1999 | 94 | 2007 | 2011+ |
| 1998 | 88 | 2006 | 2010 |
| 1997 | 87 | 2002 | 2005 |
| 1996 | 95 | 2004 | 2008+ |
| 1995 | 93 | 2003 | 2007 |
| 1994 | 92 | 2006 | 2014 |

## SEMILLON SAUVIGNON BLANC

RANKING **4**

1999

MARGARET RIVER
SEMILLON
SAUVIGNON BLANC

LENTON

**Margaret River** $20–$29
**Current vintage: 2003** **89**

Nutty, herbal and dusty, grassy aromas of gooseberries and passionfruit precede a juicy, grapey palate of typically regional herbaceous berry flavours. Its racy lemony acids and austerity do however reflect a partial lack of fruit concentration and brightness.

| 2003 | 89 | 2004 | 2005+ |
|------|----|------|-------|
| 2002 | 90 | 2003 | 2004+ |
| 2001 | 90 | 2001 | 2002+ |
| 2000 | 91 | 2001 | 2002 |
| 1999 | 89 | 1999 | 2000 |
| 1998 | 86 | 2000 | 2003 |
| 1997 | 88 | 1999 | 2002 |
| 1996 | 93 | 2001 | 2004 |

# Leo Buring

Tanunda Road, Nuriootpa SA 5355. Tel: (08) 8560 9389. Fax: (08) 8562 1669.
Website: www.leoburing.com.au
Region: **Eden Valley, Clare Valley** Winemaker: **Oliver Crawford** Viticulturist: **John Matz**
Chief Executive: **John Ballard**

After a few short years in the wilderness, Leo Buring is back where history suggests it belongs — at the forefront of riesling production in Australia. Its trio of 2003 releases, which includes the Eden Valley Riesling which is not yet listed in this book, are each astonishingly pure, tightly sculpted and pristine expressions of this resurgent variety. So, Leo Buring is again a specialist riesling maker of some repute, and its Leonay Eden Valley riesling rightly earns its place as a '1' Ranking in this guide, one of just sixteen Australian wines accorded this status.

## CLARE VALLEY RIESLING

RANKING **3**

LeoBuring

CLARE VALLEY
RIESLING

**Clare Valley** $12–$19
**Current vintage: 2003** **94**

Punchy, forward aromas of lemon and lime precede a juicy, concentrated and fleshy palate assertive in its weight and texture. Dry and mineral, steeped in penetrative fruit, finishing with lingering citrus flavour.

| 2003 | 94 | 2011 | 2015+ |
|------|----|------|-------|
| 2002 | 93 | 2010 | 2014 |
| 2000 | 87 | 2005 | 2008 |
| 1999 | 93 | 2007 | 2011 |
| 1998 | 89 | 2000 | 2003 |
| 1997 | 91 | 2005 | 2009 |
| 1996 | 91 | 2004 | 2008 |
| 1995 | 86 | 2000 | 2003 |
| 1994 | 93 | 2002 | 2006 |
| 1993 | 94 | 2001 | 2005 |

## LEONAY EDEN VALLEY RIESLING

**Eden Valley** $20–$29
**Current vintage: 2003** **97**

Complex aromas of Fuji apple, slate and lifted floral and mineral nuances over slightly funky, leesy bound sulphide influences. Silky smooth, fine and complete, the palate is supremely long, austere and elegant. Its taut, fine-grained texture and its tightly-sharpened finish of pristine mineral and lime juice qualities set it up for the very long term.

| | | | |
|---|---|---|---|
| 2003 | 97 | 2015 | 2023 |
| 1999 | 96 | 2011 | 2019+ |
| 1998 | 92 | 2006 | 2010 |
| 1997 | 93 | 2005 | 2009 |
| 1995 | 96 | 2003 | 2007 |
| 1994 | 96 | 2006 | 2014+ |
| 1993 | 93 | 2001 | 2005 |
| 1991 | 94 | 2003 | 2012 |
| 1990 | 94 | 2002 | 2010 |
| 1984 | 93 | 1996 | 2004+ |

## LEONAY WATERVALE RIESLING

**Clare Valley** $20–$29
**Current vintage: 2002** **95**

Stylish, assertive and focused riesling with substance and longevity. Its rose garden perfume of apple, guava, baby powder and wet slate precedes a fine and powdery palate whose concentration of fruit is tightly harnessed by appropriately bracing acidity. Wonderful length and balance, especially for a dry riesling of 13% alcohol.

| | | | |
|---|---|---|---|
| 2002 | 95 | 2010 | 2014+ |
| 1994 | 92 | 2002 | 2006 |
| 1992 | 94 | 2000 | 2004 |
| 1991 | 95 | 2003 | 2011 |
| 1990 | 93 | 1998 | 2002 |
| 1988 | 93 | 1996 | 2000 |
| 1981 | 80 | 1989 | 1993 |
| 1980 | 87 | 1988 | 1992 |
| 1973 | 94 | 1981 | 1985 |
| 1972 | 96 | 1992 | 1997 |

# Lillydale Estate

Lot 10 Davross Court, Seville Vic 3139. Tel: (03) 5964 2016. Fax: (03) 5964 3009.
Website: www.mcwilliams.com.au  Email: liloffice@mcwilliams.com.au

Region: **Yarra Valley** Winemakers: **Max McWilliam, Jim Brayne** Viticulturist: **Alex Van Driel**
Chief Executive: **Kevin McLintock**

One of the larger operations in the Yarra Valley, Lillydale is owned by the McWilliam family. While its wines are typically elegant, flavoursome and ready to drink at or shortly after release, it would be interesting to see what this highly capable wine producer could achieve if it decided to take the brand up-market. The spicy, floral and racy Gewürztraminer is often my pick of the releases.

## CABERNET MERLOT

Lillydale Estate
Cabernet Merlot 2002

**Yarra Valley** $20–$29
**Current vintage: 2002** **83**

Light earthy and floral aromas of dark cherries and berries with restrained cedary oak are over-powered by vegetal sulphide influences. Firm and structured, with assertive sweet chocolate-like oak and drying tannins, it presents some attractive small berry and plum flavours.

| | | | |
|---|---|---|---|
| 2002 | 83 | 2004 | 2007 |
| 2001 | 84 | 2003 | 2006 |
| 2000 | 88 | 2002 | 2005+ |
| 1999 | 89 | 2001 | 2004+ |
| 1998 | 89 | 2003 | 2006 |
| 1997 | 89 | 2002 | 2005 |
| 1996 | 86 | 1998 | 2001 |
| 1995 | 84 | 1997 | 2000 |
| 1994 | 89 | 1999 | 2002 |
| 1992 | 91 | 1997 | 2000 |
| 1991 | 91 | 1999 | 2003 |
| 1990 | 88 | 1995 | 1998 |

## CHARDONNAY

Lillydale Estate
Chardonnay 2002

**Yarra Valley** $12–$19
**Current vintage: 2003** **87**

A good wine that would have appreciated a little less charry oak. It presents a toasty bouquet of peaches and honeydew melon and rather a woody palate whose punchy, juicy melon and stonefruit flavours finish a little sappy.

| | | | |
|---|---|---|---|
| 2003 | 87 | 2004 | 2005+ |
| 2002 | 89 | 2004 | 2007 |
| 2001 | 84 | 2002 | 2003+ |
| 2000 | 87 | 2002 | 2005 |
| 1999 | 87 | 2001 | 2004 |
| 1998 | 88 | 1999 | 2000 |
| 1997 | 90 | 1999 | 2002 |
| 1996 | 87 | 1998 | 2001 |
| 1995 | 86 | 1997 | 2000 |
| 1994 | 82 | 1996 | 1999 |

## GEWÜRZTRAMINER

RANKING 4

| Yarra Valley | $12–$19 |
|---|---|
| **Current vintage: 2003** | **90** |

| | | | |
|---|---|---|---|
| 2003 | 90 | 2005 | 2008+ |
| 2002 | 83 | 2002 | 2003 |
| 2000 | 92 | 2002 | 2005 |
| 1998 | 89 | 2000 | 2003 |
| 1996 | 90 | 2001 | 2004 |
| 1995 | 94 | 2000 | 2003 |
| 1993 | 85 | 1995 | 1996 |

Pleasingly punchy, spicy and varietal, with some Alsatian pretensions. A musky perfume of rose oil, lychees, pineapple and mango precedes a round and juicy palate of length, brightness and clarity. It finishes slightly meaty and savoury, with just a hint of sugar.

## PINOT NOIR

RANKING 5

| Yarra Valley | $20–$29 |
|---|---|
| **Current vintage: 2003** | **87** |

| | | | |
|---|---|---|---|
| 2003 | 87 | 2008 | 2011 |
| 2002 | 89 | 2004 | 2007 |
| 2001 | 86 | 2003 | 2006 |
| 2000 | 83 | 2002 | 2005 |
| 1999 | 89 | 2001 | 2004 |
| 1998 | 85 | 1999 | 2000 |
| 1997 | 89 | 1999 | 2002 |
| 1996 | 90 | 1998 | 2001 |
| 1995 | 87 | 1997 | 2000 |
| 1994 | 88 | 1996 | 1999 |

A flavoursome, smoky and surprisingly firm young pinot likely to build in the bottle. Its aromas of dark cherries and raspberries are backed by meaty nuances of duck fat, but the palate shows good depth of fruit. Just a little soupy for a higher score.

# Lindemans

Karadoc Winery, Edey Road, Karadoc via Red Cliffs Vic 3496. Tel: (03) 5051 3285. Fax: (03) 5051 3390.
Wynns Coonawarra Estate, Memorial Drive, Coonawarra SA 5263. Tel: (08) 8736 3266. Fax: (08) 8736 3202.
Website: www.lindemans.com.au

Regions: **Coonawarra and Padthaway** Winemakers: **Greg Clayfield, Emma Wood, Chris Dix**
Viticulturist: **Alan Jenkins** Chief Executive: **John Ballard**

Some recent difficult vintages have taken their toll on the quality of the three Lindemans Coonawarra flagships, which have lacked their customary cut and polish since 1999. Southcorp is presently undergoing a major renovation of its Coonawarra vineyards, and from 2003 the first positive results have begun to emerge. I perceive a strong commitment to the quality of this label within Southcorp, but it might take a little time for the reworked vineyards and better vintages to show through.

## BIN 65 CHARDONNAY

| Southern Australia | $5–$11 |
|---|---|
| **Current vintage: 2004** | **83** |

| | | | |
|---|---|---|---|
| 2004 | 83 | 2004 | 2005 |
| 2003 | 83 | 2003 | 2004+ |
| 2002 | 86 | 2002 | 2003 |
| 2001 | 81 | 2001 | 2002 |

Sweet, lightly toasty aromas of peach, cumquat and mandarin over vanilla oak. Forward, soft and approachable, its juicy palate of slightly candied citrus/melon fruit finishes with some raw-edged oak, but also lacking a little freshness.

## LIMESTONE RIDGE SHIRAZ CAB. SAUVIGNON

RANKING 2

| Coonawarra | $50+ |
|---|---|
| **Current vintage: 2000** | **86** |

| | | | |
|---|---|---|---|
| 2000 | 86 | 2005 | 2008 |
| 1999 | 95 | 2011 | 2011+ |
| 1998 | 96 | 2006 | 2010+ |
| 1997 | 90 | 2005 | 2009+ |
| 1996 | 94 | 2004 | 2008+ |
| 1994 | 95 | 2014 | 2024 |
| 1993 | 91 | 2001 | 2005 |
| 1992 | 88 | 1997 | 2000 |
| 1991 | 94 | 2003 | 2011 |
| 1990 | 88 | 1995 | 1998 |
| 1989 | 89 | 1991 | 1994 |
| 1987 | 87 | 1989 | 1992 |
| 1986 | 88 | 1994 | 1998 |
| 1985 | 87 | 1990 | 1993 |
| 1984 | 87 | 1989 | 1992 |
| 1982 | 90 | 1987 | 1990 |
| 1981 | 90 | 1989 | 1993 |
| 1980 | 94 | 1998 | 1992 |

Disappointingly meaty, herbal and sappy wine suggestive of uneven fruit ripeness. Its bouquet offers scents of small red and black berries, but they're shrouded around herbal influence, while the palate is simultaneously green-edged and cooked. There's some decent cedary oak, but the wine is too skinny and vegetal to do justice to this famous vineyard.

## PYRUS

RANKING **3**

| Coonawarra | $50+ | | |
|---|---|---|---|
| **Current vintage: 2000** | **90** | | |

Fine-grained, tight and supple cabernet blend with a herbal note beneath its aromas of slightly stewed plums, small berries and sweet vanilla oak. Forward and lively, its palate of attractive red cherry, cassis and plum flavours and dusty cedar/vanilla oak presents both length and elegance.

| 2000 | 90 | 2005 | 2008 |
|---|---|---|---|
| 1999 | 93 | 2007 | 2011+ |
| 1998 | 95 | 2006 | 2010+ |
| 1997 | 89 | 2002 | 2005+ |
| 1996 | 89 | 2004 | 2008 |
| 1995 | 88 | 2000 | 2003+ |
| 1994 | 90 | 2002 | 2006+ |
| 1993 | 89 | 1998 | 2001 |
| 1992 | 88 | 1997 | 2000 |
| 1991 | 95 | 1999 | 2003+ |
| 1990 | 90 | 1998 | 2002+ |

## RESERVE CHARDONNAY

RANKING **4**

| South Australia | $12–$19 | | |
|---|---|---|---|
| **Current vintage: 2003** | **86** | | |

Savoury, slightly drying young chardonnay revealing cooked citrus/melon fruit, toasty, toffee-like development and buttery vanilla oak. It opens up after some time in the glass, finishing nutty and savoury.

| 2003 | 86 | 2004 | 2005+ |
|---|---|---|---|
| 2000 | 88 | 2002 | 2005 |
| 1999 | 91 | 2004 | 2007 |
| 1998 | 93 | 2003 | 2006 |
| 1997 | 93 | 2002 | 2005 |
| 1996 | 87 | 2001 | 2004 |

## ST. GEORGE CABERNET SAUVIGNON

RANKING **2**

| Coonawarra | $50+ | | |
|---|---|---|---|
| **Current vintage: 2001** | **88** | | |

Showing signs of over-ripeness, this slightly disjointed cabernet of medium to full weight and firmish tannin lacks sufficient fruit weight to last its customary distance. Its plummy aromas reveal leathery development, while the cassis, plum and mulberry fruits present on the palate are forward and beginning to dry out. Fine-grained cedar/chocolate oak does lend sweetness and mouthfeel.

| 2001 | 88 | 2006 | 2009 |
|---|---|---|---|
| 2000 | 88 | 2005 | 2008 |
| 1999 | 94 | 2007 | 2019 |
| 1998 | 95 | 2010 | 2018 |
| 1997 | 90 | 2002 | 2005+ |
| 1996 | 94 | 2008 | 2016 |
| 1995 | 94 | 2003 | 2007+ |
| 1994 | 94 | 2006 | 2014 |
| 1993 | 87 | 1998 | 2001 |
| 1992 | 89 | 2000 | 2004 |
| 1991 | 95 | 2003 | 2011 |
| 1990 | 92 | 2002 | 2010 |
| 1989 | 87 | 1994 | 1997 |
| 1988 | 93 | 1993 | 1996 |
| 1987 | 82 | 1989 | 1992 |
| 1986 | 94 | 1998 | 2006 |

# Madew

Lake George via Collector NSW 2581. Tel: (02) 4848 0026. Fax: (02) 4848 0164.
Website: www.madewwines.com.au  Email: cellardoor@madewwines.com.au

Region: **Canberra** Winemaker: **David Madew** Chief Executive: **David Madew**

Just as I'm beginning to enjoy the exciting new quality levels that Madew wines have achieved in the past few years comes news that the business is for sale. I can't be the only one hoping that this vineyard falls into safe hands, since I have come to relish the prospect of tasting its new releases of complex, slightly sweet and Germanic rieslings, and its citrusy, savoury expressions of pinot gris.

## RIESLING

RANKING **4**

| Canberra | $20–$29 | | |
|---|---|---|---|
| **Current vintage: 2003** | **88** | | |

Toasty, developing riesling with a delightfully fragrant bouquet of lemon detergent and lime juice, plus a fractionally sweet and beautifully presented palate of juicy pear, peach and apple flavours. It's long and tangy, but does reveal some sweet volatility.

| 2003 | 88 | 2005 | 2008 |
|---|---|---|---|
| 2002 | 94 | 2010 | 2014 |
| 2001 | 86 | 2002 | 2003 |
| 2000 | 90 | 2002 | 2005 |

# Maglieri

Douglas Gully Road, McLaren Flat SA 5171. Tel: (08) 8383 2211. Fax: (08) 8383 0735.
Website: www.maglieri.com.au

Region: **McLaren Vale** Winemaker: **Trevor Tucker** Viticulturist: **Chris Dundon** Chief Executive: **Jamie Odell**

Beringer Blass might be in the process of selling the Maglieri winery and its surrounding vineyard, but it still has strong plans for the future of this brand. Despite the fact that it is best-known in Queensland for its best-selling Lambrusco (?!), Maglieri is destined to become the stable for some interesting McLaren Vale-grown red wines from Italian varieties, plus of course, shiraz. The initial 2002 release of Italian material produced some vibrant Barbera and some varietally correct (and delightfully drinkable) Nebbiolo and Sangiovese.

## CABERNET SAUVIGNON

RANKING **5**

| McLaren Vale | $20–$29 |
| --- | --- |
| **Current vintage: 2002** | **88** |

Soft and ready to drink, with a sweet, smoky aroma of mocha/vanilla barrel ferment oak and slightly floral, menthol-like cassis and plums. Smooth and sappy, it's long and smooth, made in a modern crowd-pleasing style with sweet fruit, smoky oak and fine, soft tannins.

| | | | |
| --- | --- | --- | --- |
| 2002 | 88 | 2004 | 2007+ |
| 2001 | 81 | 2003 | 2006 |
| 2000 | 82 | 2002 | 2005 |
| 1999 | 83 | 2001 | 2004 |
| 1997 | 90 | 2002 | 2005 |
| 1995 | 91 | 2003 | 2007 |
| 1999 | 84 | 2001 | 2004 |

## SHIRAZ

RANKING **5**

| McLaren Vale | $20–$29 |
| --- | --- |
| **Current vintage: 2001** | **88** |

Approachable medium-weight shorter-term shiraz with a slightly varnishy and confectionary aroma of sweet raspberries, cassis and light vanilla oak. There's flavour, smoothness and elegance, but the fine, creamy palate is relatively simple and oaky.

| | | | |
| --- | --- | --- | --- |
| 2001 | 88 | 2003 | 2006 |
| 2000 | 82 | 2002 | 2005 |
| 1999 | 83 | 2001 | 2004 |
| 1998 | 87 | 2000 | 2003 |
| 1997 | 90 | 2002 | 2005 |
| 1996 | 89 | 2004 | 2008 |
| 1995 | 91 | 2003 | 2007 |

## STEVE MAGLIERI SHIRAZ

RANKING **3**

| McLaren Vale | $50+ |
| --- | --- |
| **Current vintage: 1999** | **88** |

Evolving, rustic and meaty shiraz with an advanced, earthy bouquet of currants, treacle, plums and prunes, with undertones of fennel and gluey oak. Smooth and restrained, the palate borders on over-ripeness, with dollops of dark plums, prunes and chocolates offset by spicy vanilla and creamy coconut-like American oak. It finishes rustic and earthy.

| | | | |
| --- | --- | --- | --- |
| 1999 | 88 | 2004 | 2007+ |
| 1998 | 90 | 2003 | 2006 |
| 1997 | 93 | 2005 | 2009 |
| 1995 | 95 | 2003 | 2007 |
| 1994 | 94 | 2002 | 2006 |
| 1993 | 82 | 1995 | 1998 |

# Main Ridge Estate

80 William Road, Red Hill Vic 3937. Tel: (03) 5989 2686. Fax: (03) 5931 0000.
Website: www.mre.com.au  Email: mrestate@mre.com.au

Region: **Mornington Peninsula**  Winemaker: **Nat White**  Viticulturist: **Nat White**
Chief Executives: **Rosalie & Nat White**

Main Ridge Estate was one of the first vineyards on Victoria's much-hyped Mornington Peninsula region, but through thick and thin, this tiny estate has justified all the accolades it has modestly collected. Its Chardonnay begins life rather introverted, with slightly angular pineapple and citrus flavours, before settling down into a classic cellaring style, while its feted Half Acre Pinot Noir marries delicate varietal perfume with tightness, integrity and longevity.

## CHARDONNAY                                         RANKING **3**

| Mornington Peninsula | $30–$49 |
|---|---|
| **Current vintage: 2003** | **93** |

Plump, juicy Peninsula chardonnay with a youthful aroma of tangy citrus fruit, tobacco, green cashew and slightly varnishy oak that should come together after more time in the bottle. Round and generous, it's long and stylish, with lingering citrus, melon and tropical fruit flavours tightly knit with butterscotch and oatmeal-like complexity, before a lingering finish punctuated by soft, refreshing acids.

| 2003 | 93 | 2008 | 2011 |
|---|---|---|---|
| 2002 | 86 | 2004 | 2007 |
| 2001 | 89 | 2003 | 2006+ |
| 2000 | 93 | 2005 | 2008 |
| 1999 | 93 | 2004 | 2007 |
| 1998 | 95 | 2006 | 2010 |
| 1997 | 88 | 1999 | 2002+ |
| 1996 | 88 | 1998 | 2001 |
| 1995 | 82 | 1997 | 2000 |
| 1994 | 94 | 1999 | 2002 |
| 1993 | 89 | 1998 | 2001 |

## HALF ACRE PINOT NOIR                               RANKING **2**

| Mornington Peninsula | $30–$49 |
|---|---|
| **Current vintage: 2002** | **90** |

A minty perfume of rose petals, red cherries and briar precedes a supple, smooth and elegant palate delivering pristine small berry/cherry fruit over a tight-knit backbone of fine tannins. Some underlying herbal and sappy influences suggest this tightly-crafted wine will drink best in its youth.

| 2002 | 90 | 2004 | 2007+ |
|---|---|---|---|
| 2001 | 95 | 2006 | 2009+ |
| 2000 | 95 | 2008 | 2012 |
| 1999 | 94 | 2007 | 2011 |
| 1998 | 93 | 2003 | 2006 |
| 1997 | 95 | 2002 | 2005+ |
| 1996 | 87 | 2001 | 2004 |
| 1995 | 88 | 1997 | 2000 |
| 1994 | 93 | 2002 | 2006 |
| 1993 | 90 | 2001 | 2005 |

# Majella

Lynn Road, Coonawarra SA 5263. Tel: (08) 8736 3055. Fax: (08) 8736 3057.
Website: www.majellawines.com.au  Email: prof@majellawines.com.au

Region: **Coonawarra**  Winemaker: **Bruce Gregory**  Viticulturist: **Anthony Lynn**  Chief Executive: **Brian Lynn**

Majella is one of the recent successes of Australian wine. The long-established grape-growing Lynn family have taken to the business of making and marketing wine like ducks to water, electing to create sumptuous, oaky and deeply concentrated reds of approachability and sweetness. Their key resource is a terrific mature vineyard, and their wines simply reflect some great fruit.

## CABERNET                                           RANKING **3**

| Coonawarra | $20–$29 |
|---|---|
| **Current vintage: 2002** | **88** |

Restrained, perfumed cabernet whose aromas of cassis and violets, mulberries and plums overlie dusty nuances of crushed vine leaves. Long, smooth and restrained, it's stylish and tightly integrated, but its savoury finish does reveal herbal undertones and sappy, metallic edges to its tight-knit spine of firm tannins.

| 2002 | 88 | 2010 | 2014 |
|---|---|---|---|
| 2001 | 95 | 2009 | 2013+ |
| 2000 | 93 | 2005 | 2008 |
| 1999 | 90 | 2004 | 2007 |
| 1998 | 95 | 2006 | 2010+ |
| 1997 | 93 | 2005 | 2009 |
| 1996 | 93 | 2001 | 2004 |
| 1995 | 86 | 1997 | 2000 |
| 1994 | 82 | 1996 | 1999 |

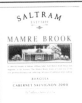

## SHIRAZ

**Coonawarra** $20–$29
**Current vintage: 2002** 87

RANKING 2

Pristine violet-like aromas of sweet red and black berries with nuances of plums, cedar/vanilla oak, plus earthy hints of dried herbs and menthol. Its initial burst of intense cassis/mulberry flavour becomes a little dilute, herbal and sappy down the palate. Framed by slightly under-ripe tannins smoothed over to an extent by sweet vanilla oak, it's a pretty but early-drinking wine.

| Year | Score | Drink | Drink |
|---|---|---|---|
| 2002 | 87 | 2004 | 2007 |
| 2001 | 95 | 2009 | 2013 |
| 2000 | 89 | 2005 | 2008 |
| 1999 | 90 | 2004 | 2007 |
| 1998 | 95 | 2003 | 2006+ |
| 1997 | 94 | 2002 | 2005+ |
| 1996 | 94 | 2001 | 2004 |
| 1995 | 87 | 1997 | 2000 |
| 1994 | 93 | 2002 | 2006 |
| 1993 | 86 | 1995 | 1998 |
| 1992 | 84 | 1994 | 1997 |
| 1991 | 86 | 1993 | 1996 |

## THE MALLEEA

RANKING 3

**Coonawarra** $50+
**Current vintage: 2001** 91

Rich and generous, this assertively oaked Coonawarra red has a spicy and slightly treacle-like aroma of cassis and dark plums over nuances of undergrowth and up-front sweet mocha/chocolate oak. Firmly structured, its long, smooth palate reveals deep plum, cassis and mulberry flavours and plenty of sweet new oak, framed by tight, grippy tannins.

| Year | Score | Drink | Drink |
|---|---|---|---|
| 2001 | 91 | 2009 | 2013+ |
| 2000 | 87 | 2005 | 2008 |
| 1999 | 92 | 2004 | 2007 |
| 1998 | 95 | 2006 | 2010+ |
| 1997 | 92 | 2002 | 2005+ |
| 1996 | 94 | 2001 | 2004 |

# Mamre Brook

Angaston Road, Angaston SA 5353. Tel: (08) 8564 3355. Fax: (08) 8564 2209.
Website: www.saltramwines.com.au  Email: cellardoor@saltramestate.com.au
Region: **Barossa Valley** Winemaker: **Nigel Dolan** Viticulturist: **Murray Heidenreich** Chief Executive: **Jamie Odell**

Mamre Brook represents some of the best buying in South Australian wine. Overseen by the talents of Nigel Dolan, its reds present the richness and generosity for which the Barossa is famous, and they're tailored into a balanced, cellaring style that ensures plenty of longevity. Buy them before Beringer Blass wakes up!

## CABERNET SAUVIGNON (formerly Cabernet Shiraz)

RANKING 4

**Barossa Valley** $20–$29
**Current vintage: 2001** 88

Ripe plummy aromas of baked blackberries and currants, with a restrained background of sweet vanilla oak with lightly herbal nuances. Initially bright and jammy, with richness of dark plum and berry fruits, it does become a little thin and sappy down the palate.

| Year | Score | Drink | Drink |
|---|---|---|---|
| 2001 | 88 | 2006 | 2009 |
| 2000 | 88 | 2005 | 2008 |
| 1999 | 90 | 2004 | 2007 |
| 1998 | 94 | 2010 | 2018 |
| 1997 | 93 | 2005 | 2009 |
| 1996 | 95 | 2008 | 2016+ |
| 1995 | 88 | 1997 | 2000 |
| 1994 | 90 | 2002 | 2006 |
| 1993 | 91 | 1998 | 2001 |
| 1988 | 85 | 1993 | 1998 |
| 1986 | 93 | 2006 | 2016 |

## CHARDONNAY

RANKING 4

**South Australia** $20–$29
**Current vintage: 2002** 90

A lively, elegant and willowy wine with plenty of elegance as well as depth of flavour. Its vibrant, slightly smoky bouquet of peaches, cumquats, grapefruit and pineapple reveals undertones of creamy leesy quality and fresh vanilla oak. Smooth and supple, the palate delivers restrained but juicy citrus/melon fruit before a lingering and soft finish of lemon sherbet.

| Year | Score | Drink | Drink |
|---|---|---|---|
| 2002 | 90 | 2004 | 2007 |
| 2001 | 89 | 2003 | 2006 |
| 2000 | 90 | 2002 | 2005+ |
| 1999 | 87 | 2000 | 2001 |
| 1998 | 87 | 2000 | 2003 |
| 1997 | 83 | 1998 | 1999 |
| 1996 | 89 | 1998 | 2001 |

## SHIRAZ

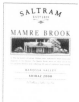

**Barossa Valley**   $20–$29
**Current vintage: 2001**   **88**

Concentrated, almost exaggerated aromas of cassis, blackberries and plums with assertive smoky vanilla/coconut new oak deliver a spicy floral perfume. Super-ripe, sweet and forward, the palate begins with brightly lit flavours of cassis and raspberries and sweet smoky chocolate oak before fading towards a currant and prune-like finish.

| | | | |
|---|---|---|---|
| 2001 | 88 | 2003 | 2006+ |
| 2000 | 89 | 2005 | 2008 |
| 1999 | 90 | 2004 | 2007 |
| 1998 | 95 | 2006 | 2010 |
| 1997 | 95 | 2005 | 2009+ |
| 1996 | 94 | 2004 | 2008 |

# Margan

1238 Milbrodale Road, Ceres Hill Broke NSW 2330. Tel: (02) 6579 1317. Fax: (02) 6579 1317.
Website: www.margan.com.au Email: di@margan.com.au
Region: **Lower Hunter Valley** Winemakers: **Andrew Margan, Chris Mennie** Viticulturist: **Andrew Margan**
Chief Executive: **Andrew Margan**

Margan is a family-owned wine business in the Hunter Valley that deliberately makes its wines to mature early. The results are pleasing, approachable and generous. As the vibrant and lightly spicy 2002 Shiraz illustrates, the reds are typically vibrant and juicy; the whites lively and refreshing, exemplified by the 2003 Semillon.

## BOTRYTIS SEMILLON

**Lower Hunter Valley**   $20–$29
**Current vintage: 2003**   **93**

A fine, elegant, harmonious and moderately sweet dessert wine that you can really drink. Its lightly tropical, floral and honeydew melon aromas are lifted by delicate vanilla oak, while its vibrant and refreshing palate has a controlled measure of lusciousness that prevents it from cloying.

| | | | |
|---|---|---|---|
| 2003 | 93 | 2005 | 2008 |
| 2002 | 89 | 2004 | 2007 |
| 2001 | 86 | 2003 | 2006+ |

## CABERNET SAUVIGNON

**Lower Hunter Valley**   $20–$29
**Current vintage: 2002**   **87**

Slightly cooked and confectionary, with dusty, earthy aromas of sweet black and red berries and vanilla oak, plus a supple, medium-weight palate whose smooth delivery of cherry/plum fruit is bound by fine, powdery tannins. Finishes savoury, with nutty influences.

| | | | |
|---|---|---|---|
| 2002 | 87 | 2004 | 2007+ |
| 2001 | 87 | 2003 | 2006 |
| 2000 | 90 | 2005 | 2008 |
| 1999 | 87 | 2001 | 2004+ |
| 1997 | 84 | 2002 | 2005 |

## CHARDONNAY

**Lower Hunter Valley**   $12–$19
**Current vintage: 2003**   **88**

Lightly dusty aromas of lemon sherbet, peach and melon with nutty undertones precede a smooth, gentle palate of medium intensity and richness. Its restrained peach and melon flavours culminate in a refreshing green apple finish with nuances of tobacco.

| | | | |
|---|---|---|---|
| 2003 | 88 | 2004 | 2005+ |
| 2002 | 86 | 2003 | 2004+ |
| 2001 | 82 | 2002 | 2003+ |
| 2000 | 86 | 2001 | 2002 |
| 1998 | 91 | 1999 | 2000 |

## SEMILLON

**Lower Hunter Valley**   $12–$19
**Current vintage: 2003**   **90**

Clean, juicy and slightly oily semillon with an earthy, slightly cheesy and grassy aroma of lemon juice and honeydew melon. Soft, round and generous, with vibrant melon/lemon flavours, it finishes slightly chalky with refreshing citrusy acids.

| | | | |
|---|---|---|---|
| 2003 | 90 | 2008 | 2011+ |
| 2002 | 90 | 2004 | 2007 |
| 2001 | 85 | 2001 | 2002+ |
| 2000 | 89 | 2002 | 2005 |
| 1998 | 87 | 2003 | 2006 |

| Lower Hunter Valley | $20–$29 |
|---|---|
| Current vintage: 2002 | 90 |

A dash of creamy vanilla oak is all that this spicy and slightly jammy aroma of cassis and mulberries, plums and raspberries requires. The palate is ripe and juicy, brightly lit with peppery, lightly spicy small berry fruits, finishing with length and softness, bound by fine, powdery tannins. Again, the oak is restrained but ample.

RANKING 4

| 2002 | 90 | 2004 | 2007 |
|---|---|---|---|
| 2001 | 89 | 2003 | 2006 |
| 2000 | 92 | 2005 | 2008+ |
| 1999 | 90 | 2004 | 2007 |
| 1998 | 85 | 2000 | 2003 |
| 1997 | 89 | 2002 | 2005 |

# McAlister Vineyards

RMB 6810 Golden Beach Road, Longford South-East Gippsland Vic 3851. Tel: (03) 5149 7229.
Fax: (03) 5149 7229

Region: **Gippsland** Winemaker: **Peter Edwards** Viticulturist: **Peter Edwards** Chief Executive: **Peter Edwards**

The McAlister is a single vineyard red blend of Bordeaux varieties that in normal seasons exhibits vibrant, complex flavours delivered in a refined and elegant package. Its wines are not the sort that stands out in a tasting; indeed they require a level of interest over a period of time for their flavours and structure to emerge fully. There's absolutely nothing wrong with that: these are wines for drinking, not showing.

## THE McALISTER

RANKING 4

| Gippsland | $30–$49 |
|---|---|
| Current vintage: 2001 | 90 |

An elegant, restrained cabernet blend made with great sensitivity. Its meaty, undergrowth-like aromas of small red and black berries precede a soft, slightly herbal and smooth palate whose intensity and richness build in the mouth. Underpinned by a fine, but evident firmness, it needs time to develop its intended complexity.

| 2001 | 90 | 2009 | 2013 |
|---|---|---|---|
| 2000 | 91 | 2005 | 2008 |
| 1999 | 87 | 2004 | 2007 |
| 1998 | 85 | 2003 | 2006+ |
| 1997 | 87 | 2005 | 2009 |
| 1996 | 84 | 1998 | 2001 |
| 1995 | 87 | 2000 | 2003 |
| 1994 | 95 | 2002 | 2006 |
| 1993 | 90 | 1998 | 2001 |
| 1992 | 93 | 2000 | 2004 |
| 1991 | 93 | 1999 | 2003 |
| 1990 | 94 | 2002 | 2010 |
| 1989 | 87 | 1997 | 2001 |
| 1988 | 93 | 2000 | 2005 |
| 1987 | 92 | 1999 | 2004 |
| 1986 | 90 | 1994 | 1998 |

# McWilliam's

Doug McWilliam Road, Yenda NSW 2681. Tel: (02) 6968 1001. Fax: (02) 6968 1312.
Website: www.mcwilliams.com.au Email: mcwines@mcwilliams.com.au

Region: **Riverina** Winemakers: **Jim Brayne, Scott Zrna, Russell Cody** Viticulturist: **Jeff Dance**
Chief Executive: **Kevin McLintock**

Under Kevin McLintock, McWilliams is moving headlong through a period of brand expansion, based on the 'McWilliams Territory' theme which has seen the Riverina-based company move into Coonawarra, the Eden Valley and even the Margaret River. Some clear wins have emerged along the way, like the 2003 Eden Valley Riesling and the consistent success of the new Australian hybrid variety Tyrian at its home near Griffith. I remain an unabashed fan of the company's Riverina Botrytis Semillon, which is made in a more complex and savoury fashion than most of its competitors.

## 1877 CABERNET SAUVIGNON SHIRAZ

RANKING 4

| Coonawarra, Hilltops | $50+ |
|---|---|
| Current vintage: 2001 | 93 |

Cedary, leathery and slightly old-fashioned red, with scents of white pepper and spice beneath aromas of sweet vanilla oak, red berries and redcurrants. It's firm and well structured, with depth, length and grip. The fruit is ripe, vibrant and generous without a hint of over-ripeness, while the tannins are approachable and integrated.

| 2001 | 93 | 2009 | 2013 |
|---|---|---|---|
| 2000 | 87 | 2005 | 2008 |
| 1999 | 87 | 2004 | 2007 |
| 1998 | 95 | 2006 | 2010+ |

## EDEN VALLEY RIESLING

RANKING 5

**Eden Valley**     $12–$19
**Current vintage: 2003**    91

Delightfully fresh, perfumed and refreshing young riesling whose delicate floral and baby-powder-like perfume of lime juice, apple and pear precede a vibrant, racy palate. Its lingering lime juice flavours are supported by fine, powdery phenolics, before a clean and austere finish.

| 2003 | 91 | 2008 | 2011+ |
| 2002 | 86 | 2004 | 2007 |
| 2001 | 89 | 2006 | 2009 |
| 1996 | 89 | 2001 | 2004 |

## MARGARET RIVER SEMILLON SAUVIGNON BLANC

RANKING 5

**Eden Valley**     $12–$19
**Current vintage: 2003**    89

Early-drinking generous and grassy regional blend with a lifted, juicy and herbal fragrance of gooseberries and passionfruit. Round, generous and vibrant, it's succulent and flavoursome, finishing fresh with just a hint of sweetness.

| 2003 | 89 | 2004 | 2005 |
| 2002 | 88 | 2003 | 2004 |
| 2001 | 86 | 2002 | 2003 |

## RIVERINA BOTRYTIS SEMILLON

RANKING 2

**Riverina**     $20–$29
**Current vintage: 2001**    95

Rather more punchy and feisty than its predecessors, this is however a very worthwhile dessert wine that takes some time to reveal its smoothness and integration. Citrusy, honeysuckle and pastry aromas with nuances of melon and butter precede a punchy, concentrated palate of lusciousness and measured sweetness. It finishes nutty and savoury, with length and freshness.

| 2001 | 95 | 2003 | 2006 |
| 2000 | 94 | 2005 | 2008 |
| 1999 | 96 | 2004 | 2007 |
| 1998 | 95 | 2003 | 2006 |
| 1997 | 92 | 2002 | 2005 |
| 1996 | 88 | 1998 | 2001 |

## TYRIAN

RANKING 4

**Riverina**     $12–$19
**Current vintage: 2002**    89

A little closed, but a firm, generous and rather robust red with some very promising dark berry and plum fruit. Slightly confectionary aromas of raspberries, cherries and redcurrants with meaty, gamey undertones precede a long, linear palate whose intense fruit and cedar/chocolate oak conceal just a hint of herbal greenness. Finishes tight and astringent, with lingering walnut-like flavours.

| 2002 | 89 | 2007 | 2010 |
| 2001 | 92 | 2005 | 2009 |
| 2000 | 90 | 2005 | 2008 |
| 1999 | 88 | 2001 | 2004+ |

# Meadowbank

699 Richmond Road, Cambridge Tas 7170. Tel: (03) 6248 4484. Fax: (03) 6248 4485.
Website: www.meadowbankwines.com.au  Email: bookings@meadowbankwines.com.au
Region: **Derwent Valley**  Winemaker: **Andrew Hood**  Viticulturist: **Adrian Hallam**  Chief Executive: **Gerald Ellis**
Meadowbank's cool climate wines are refreshing, herbal and uncomplicated, but better years present bright, vibrant fruit flavours tightly wrapped in zesty acids. In good years the pinot noirs are bright and cherry-like.

## CHARDONNAY

**Derwent Valley**     $20–$29
**Current vintage: 2003**    86

Delicate, lightly herbal aromas of pineapple, peaches and grapefruit, with a slightly rancid note. Reasonably long, its palate of stonefruit, melon and butter finishes lightly grassy and with a suggestion of sweetness.

| 2003 | 86 | 2004 | 2005 |
| 2002 | 77 | 2002 | 2003 |
| 2001 | 88 | 2002 | 2003 |
| 1999 | 87 | 2001 | 2004 |
| 1998 | 86 | 2000 | 2003 |
| 1997 | 82 | 1998 | 1999 |
| 1995 | 87 | 1997 | 2000 |
| 1994 | 88 | 1999 | 2002 |
| 1993 | 90 | 1998 | 2001 |

## GRACE ELIZABETH CHARDONNAY

RANKING **5**

| Derwent Valley | | $30–$49 | | | | |
|---|---|---|---|---|---|---|
| **Current vintage: 2003** | | **87** | 2003 | 87 | 2005 | 2008 |
| | | | 2002 | 89 | 2004 | 2007 |
| | | | 2000 | 87 | 2002 | 2005 |
| | | | 1998 | 82 | 2000 | 2003 |
| | | | 1997 | 83 | 1998 | 1999 |
| | | | 1995 | 95 | 2003 | 2007 |

Its nutty, quite oxidative and spicy aromas of dried flowers and delicate melon fruit are enhanced by hints of tobacco and creamy, leesy influences. Soft, smooth and elegant, it's clean, nutty and savoury, with a slightly reserved expression of fruit intensity and brightness.

## HENRY JAMES PINOT NOIR

RANKING **5**

| Derwent Valley | | $30–$49 | | | | |
|---|---|---|---|---|---|---|
| **Current vintage: 2001** | | **88** | 2001 | 88 | 2003 | 2006 |
| | | | 2000 | 91 | 2002 | 2005 |
| | | | 1999 | 89 | 2001 | 2004+ |
| | | | 1998 | 82 | 2000 | 2003+ |
| | | | 1997 | 84 | 1999 | 2002 |

Up-front, early-drinking pinot with a musky cinnamon-like perfume of rose petals and maraschino cherries over stalky nuances of game meat. Smooth and supple, it's long and fine-grained, with a lively length of cherry-like flavours before a slightly thin and herbal finish bound by fine, but sappy tannins.

# Metala

Nuriootpa Road, Angaston SA 5353. Tel: (08) 8564 3355. Fax: (08) 8564 2209.
Website: www.beringerblass.com.au

Region: **Langhorne Creek** Winemaker: **Nigel Dolan** Viticulturists: **Tom and Guy Adams**
Chief Executive: **Jamie Odell**

Metala is an historic Australian brand made by Nigel Dolan and sourced from a very old vineyard in Langhorne Creek. In better vintages its oldest vines contribute to the Black Label Shiraz, while the 'standard' white label blend of shiraz with cabernet sauvignon is consistently one of the best sub-$20 wines around.

## BLACK LABEL SHIRAZ

RANKING **3**

| Langhorne Creek | | $30–$49 | | | | |
|---|---|---|---|---|---|---|
| **Current vintage: 2000** | | **94** | 2000 | 94 | 2008 | 2012 |
| | | | 1998 | 90 | 2003 | 2006 |
| | | | 1996 | 95 | 2004 | 2008 |
| | | | 1995 | 90 | 2003 | 2007 |
| | | | 1994 | 95 | 2002 | 2006 |

Rich, velvety crowd-pleasing red of generosity and ripeness, plus a little elegance on the side. It already reveals a developing leathery, meaty bouquet of slightly cooked and plummy berry/blackcurrant fruit set against a background of chocolate/vanilla and lightly smoky bubblegum-like oak. Polished and voluptuous, but tightly balanced and harmonious.

## SHIRAZ CABERNET

RANKING **4**

| Langhorne Creek | | $12–$19 | | | | |
|---|---|---|---|---|---|---|
| **Current vintage: 2001** | | **89** | 2001 | 89 | 2006 | 2009 |
| | | | 2000 | 90 | 2005 | 2008 |
| | | | 1999 | 86 | 2001 | 2004 |
| | | | 1998 | 93 | 2006 | 2010 |
| | | | 1997 | 89 | 2002 | 2005 |
| | | | 1996 | 91 | 2001 | 2004 |
| | | | 1995 | 90 | 2000 | 2003 |
| | | | 1994 | 91 | 2002 | 2006 |
| | | | 1993 | 92 | 2001 | 2005 |
| | | | 1992 | 91 | 2000 | 2004 |
| | | | 1991 | 87 | 1999 | 2003 |
| | | | 1988 | 80 | 1993 | 1996 |

Delicate aromas of cassis, plums and lightly smoky chocolate/vanilla oak with cedary undertones of cloves and cinnamon. Medium to full in weight, fine and elegant, its spicy red and black berry flavours are underpinned by a slightly raw extract and finish with a faint suggestion of saltiness.

# Mildara Coonawarra

Riddoch Highway, Coonawarra SA 5263. Tel: (08) 8736 3380. Fax: (08) 8736 3307.
Website: www.beringerblass.com.au

Region: **Coonawarra** Winemaker: **Andrew Hales** Viticulturist: **Brendan Provis** Chief Executive: **Jamie Odell**

Mildara's white label Cabernet Sauvignon has been overtaken by more fashionable wines in the Beringer Blass stable, but smart drinkers will always consider this Coonawarra red above many others priced more expensively. It's a typically elegant, fine-grained regional style usually suited to medium-term cellaring.

## CABERNET SAUVIGNON

RANKING **5**

| Coonawarra | $20–$29 |
|---|---|
| **Current vintage: 2002** | **92** |

Very elegant, fine and tightly structured cabernet with a violet-like fragrance of sweet cassis, redcurrant and plums, over dusty herbal notes and cedary oak. Smooth, tine and fine-grained, its palate has length, firmness and integration. Its sweet cassis, mulberry and plum fruit works neatly with chocolate/vanilla oak and its fine, firm extract. Marginally herbal; a fine cool season wine.

| | | | |
|---|---|---|---|
| 2002 | 92 | 2010 | 2014 |
| 2000 | 87 | 2005 | 2008 |
| 1999 | 88 | 2004 | 2007+ |
| 1998 | 93 | 2006 | 2010+ |
| 1997 | 83 | 1999 | 2002 |
| 1996 | 88 | 2004 | 2008 |
| 1995 | 87 | 2000 | 2003 |
| 1994 | 93 | 2002 | 2006 |
| 1993 | 95 | 2001 | 2005 |
| 1992 | 94 | 2000 | 2004 |
| 1991 | 90 | 1996 | 1999 |
| 1990 | 94 | 1995 | 1998 |
| 1989 | 87 | 1994 | 1997 |
| 1988 | 94 | 1996 | 2000 |

# Miranda

57 Jondaryan Avenue Griffith NSW 2680. Tel: (02) 8345 6300. Fax: (02) 8345 6366.
Website: www.mirandawines.com.au  Email: info@mirandawines.com.au

Regions: **Riverina, King Valley, Barossa** Winemakers: **Garry Wall, Sam Miranda**
Viticulturist: **Ross Turkington** Chief Executive: **David Hammond**

Unable to keep up with the hectic expansion of Australian wine in recent years, the Miranda family sold its business to the aggressively expanding McGuigan Simeon company, one of the big five producers in this country. Before the sale, the quality of recent vintages did reflect the scarcity of adequate funding required to finish the wines properly.

## GOLDEN BOTRYTIS SEMILLON

RANKING **4**

| Riverina | $12–$19 (375 ml) |
|---|---|
| **Current vintage: 2002** | **87** |

Slightly cooked and candied aromas of tinned pineapple, melon and citrus, without a significant level of quality botrytis. Quite luscious, concentrated and syrupy, with some intense tropical fruit flavours and reasonable length, but finishes a little flat and varnishy.

| | | | |
|---|---|---|---|
| 2002 | 87 | 2004 | 2007 |
| 2001 | 91 | 2003 | 2006 |
| 2000 | 91 | 2002 | 2005 |
| 1999 | 89 | 2001 | 2004 |
| 1998 | 90 | 2003 | 2006 |
| 1997 | 94 | 2002 | 2005 |
| 1996 | 92 | 1998 | 2001 |
| 1995 | 87 | 1997 | 2000 |
| 1994 | 87 | 1996 | 1999 |

## HIGH COUNTRY MERLOT

| King Valley | $12–$19 |
|---|---|
| **Current vintage: 2001** | **82** |

Rather stressed, cooked and leathery aromas of stewed plums, raspberries and cherries with a background of mint and overt cedary oak. Hard and linear, the palate lacks fruit sweetness and softness, finishing astringent and lean.

| | | | |
|---|---|---|---|
| 2001 | 82 | 2003 | 2006 |
| 2000 | 84 | 2002 | 2005 |
| 1999 | 83 | 2001 | 2004 |
| 1998 | 89 | 2000 | 2003+ |

# Mitchell

Hughes Park Road, Sevenhill via Clare SA 5453. Tel: (08) 8843 4258. Fax: (08) 8843 4340
Website: www.mitchellwines.com.au Email: amitchell@mitchellwines.com.au
Region: **Clare Valley** Winemaker: **Simon Pringle** Viticulturist: **Leon Schramm**
Chief Executives: **Andrew Mitchell & Jane Mitchell**

Mitchell is a highly-rated small Clare Valley producer that has moved headlong into the screwcap revolution by adopting these seals for each of its wines. It has long held a strong reputation for its Riesling and Peppertree Shiraz, but the pick of its current releases is its supple and creamy oak-matured Semillon.

## PEPPERTREE VINEYARD SHIRAZ

RANKING **5**

**Clare Valley** $20–$29
**Current vintage: 2002** 87

Musky aromas of red plums and red berries reveal slightly resinous oak and obvious sulphide undertones. Smooth, soft and generous, its rustic expression of dark berry/plum fruit is offset by clove/cinnamon-like spiciness and framed by fine, almost silky tannins. It finishes with an unusual green-edged meatiness, but offers good structure and potential.

| | | | |
|---|---|---|---|
| 2002 | 87 | 2007 | 2010+ |
| 2001 | 85 | 2003 | 2006 |
| 2000 | 81 | 2005 | 2008 |
| 1999 | 88 | 2004 | 2007 |
| 1998 | 92 | 2006 | 2010 |
| 1997 | 87 | 1999 | 2002 |
| 1996 | 93 | 2001 | 2004 |
| 1995 | 82 | 2000 | 2003 |
| 1994 | 90 | 1999 | 2003 |
| 1993 | 93 | 2001 | 2005 |
| 1992 | 92 | 2000 | 2004 |
| 1991 | 91 | 1996 | 1999 |
| 1990 | 94 | 1998 | 2002 |
| 1989 | 93 | 1994 | 1997 |

## SEVENHILL VINEYARD CABERNET SAUVIGNON

RANKING **5**

**Clare Valley** $20–$29
**Current vintage: 2001** 87

A well-made wine from under-ripe and cooked fruit. Its herby, meaty and slightly stewy plum-like aromas reveal some greenish notes, while its palate is long and assertive, with intense plum/small berry flavours and cedar/vanilla oak framed by robust, if marginally sappy tannins.

| | | | |
|---|---|---|---|
| 2001 | 87 | 2006 | 2009+ |
| 2000 | 88 | 2005 | 2008 |
| 1998 | 91 | 2006 | 2010 |
| 1997 | 85 | 2002 | 2005 |
| 1996 | 89 | 2004 | 2008 |
| 1995 | 82 | 2000 | 2003 |
| 1994 | 91 | 2002 | 2006 |
| 1992 | 91 | 2004 | 2012 |
| 1991 | 93 | 2003 | 2011 |
| 1990 | 94 | 2002 | 2010 |
| 1988 | 88 | 1996 | 2000 |

## THE GROWERS GRENACHE

RANKING **5**

**Clare Valley** $20–$29
**Current vintage: 2001** 86

Earthy reductive influences show through some spicy confectionary blueberry-like grenache aromas backed by sweet vanilla oak and undertones of raspberries, cherries and plums. Meaty, forward and jammy, with a pleasing core of juicy fruit flavours, the wine then becomes rather hard, even bitter and slightly spirity.

| | | | |
|---|---|---|---|
| 2001 | 86 | 2003 | 2009 |
| 2000 | 87 | 2002 | 2005 |
| 1999 | 86 | 2001 | 2004 |
| 1998 | 88 | 2000 | 2003 |
| 1997 | 90 | 1999 | 2002 |
| 1996 | 86 | 1998 | 2001 |

## THE GROWERS SEMILLON

RANKING **5**

**Clare Valley** $12–$19
**Current vintage: 2002** 92

Smooth, stylish oak-matured semillon with a delicate perfume of lightly herbal melon and honeycomb over nuances of toasty vanilla oak. Its creamy, elegant palate marries juicy ripe fruit with well-integrated oak and malolactic buttery characters, finishing with soft, supple acids. Just perhaps a fraction sweet.

| | | | |
|---|---|---|---|
| 2002 | 92 | 2007 | 2010 |
| 2001 | 89 | 2003 | 2006 |
| 2000 | 88 | 2002 | 2005 |
| 1999 | 89 | 2001 | 2004+ |
| 1998 | 88 | 2000 | 2003 |
| 1997 | 89 | 2002 | 2005 |
| 1996 | 90 | 2001 | 2004 |
| 1995 | 88 | 2000 | 2003 |
| 1994 | 93 | 2002 | 2006 |
| 1993 | 95 | 2001 | 2005 |

## WATERVALE RIESLING

RANKING 3

**Clare Valley** $12–$19
**Current vintage: 2003** 88

Toasty, rich and developing riesling with a slightly cooked and apple-like aroma with buttery undertones. Quite broad and generous, even rather firm and phenolic, it just lacks the freshness and tightness of the best vintages.

| | | | |
|---|---|---|---|
| 2003 | 88 | 2005 | 2008 |
| 2002 | 91 | 2007 | 2010 |
| 2001 | 95 | 2009 | 2013+ |
| 2000 | 95 | 2008 | 2012 |
| 1999 | 80 | 2001 | 2004 |
| 1998 | 94 | 2006 | 2010+ |
| 1997 | 92 | 2005 | 2009 |
| 1996 | 87 | 2001 | 2004 |
| 1995 | 94 | 2003 | 2007 |
| 1994 | 88 | 1999 | 2003 |
| 1993 | 93 | 2001 | 2005 |
| 1992 | 91 | 1997 | 2000 |

# Mitchelton

Mitchellstown Road, Nagambie Vic 3608. Tel: (03) 5736 2222. Fax: (03) 5736 2266.
Website: www.mitchelton.com.au  Email: mitchelton@mitchelton.com.au
Region: **Nagambie Lakes** Winemakers: **Don Lewis, Toby Barlow** Viticulturist: **John Beresford**
Chief Executive: **Michael Kluczko**

Predictably, for me at least, Mitchelton changed several label designs yet again just prior to the printing of this edition! This time however I can't fault their logic, since a contemporary and Rhône-ish look has been fashioned for its affordable but distinctly up-town trio of the Airstrip, Crescent and Parish (a classy new blend of shiraz and viognier). Personally, I'd add the spicy and very varietal Viognier to this range, even at the risk of having to insert yet another new label for the 2006 edition. Under some tight brand control and some very proficient winemaking, Mitchelton is finally becoming easier to understand and to enjoy.

## AIRSTRIP (Marsanne Viognier Roussanne blend)

RANKING 3

**Nagambie Lakes** $20–$29
**Current vintage: 2002** 93

A stylish, measured and harmonious blend with a spicy, lightly tropical fragrance of citrus, apple and pear, with nuances of lemon, tea leaves and minerals. It's sumptuous and juicy, but long, supple and evenly paced, culminating in a lingering and savoury finish of lemony and mineral acids. Oak is reserved and secondary.

| | | | |
|---|---|---|---|
| 2002 | 93 | 2004 | 2007 |
| 2001 | 93 | 2003 | 2006 |
| 2000 | 89 | 2002 | 2005+ |
| 1999 | 90 | 2001 | 2005+ |
| 1998 | 85 | 2000 | 2003 |
| 1994 | 92 | 1999 | 2002+ |

## BLACKWOOD PARK BOTRYTIS RIESLING

RANKING 5

**Nagambie Lakes** $30–$49
**Current vintage: 2003** 83

Rather forward, marmalade-like dessert wine whose palate of tinned tropical fruit lacks its customary lusciousness, length and brightness. Moderately sweet, but slightly flat and stale to finish.

| | | | |
|---|---|---|---|
| 2003 | 83 | 2004 | 2005 |
| 2001 | 87 | 2003 | 2006 |
| 2000 | 86 | 2001 | 2002 |
| 1998 | 92 | 2003 | 2006 |
| 1997 | 89 | 1999 | 2002 |
| 1996 | 93 | 2001 | 2004 |

## BLACKWOOD PARK CABERNET SAUVIGNON

RANKING 4

**Nagambie Lakes** $12–$19
**Current vintage: 2002** 89

Tight-knit, leaner cabernet with meaty, earthy aromas of dark plums and blackberries over smoky, cedary oak and gamey nuances. The palate is taut and bony, with a firm, powdery chassis beneath some slightly underpowered fruit. With its fresh acidity and balance, it should develop well.

| | | | |
|---|---|---|---|
| 2002 | 89 | 2007 | 2010+ |
| 2001 | 92 | 2006 | 2009+ |
| 2000 | 91 | 2005 | 2008 |
| 1999 | 87 | 2004 | 2007 |
| 1997 | 81 | 1998 | 1999 |
| 1996 | 93 | 2004 | 2008+ |

# BLACKWOOD PARK CHARDONNAY

RANKING 4

**Nagambie Lakes** $12–$19
**Current vintage: 2002** 88

Generous, round and soft, if rather woody chardonnay, with aromas of toasted cashews, buttery vanilla oak, bran and oatmeal, banana and melon. There's more tropical fruit on the palate, which finishes with citrusy acids.

| | | | |
|---|---|---|---|
| 2002 | 88 | 2003 | 2004+ |
| 2000 | 88 | 2002 | 2005 |
| 1999 | 90 | 2001 | 2004 |
| 1998 | 93 | 2003 | 2006 |
| 1997 | 94 | 2002 | 2005 |

# BLACKWOOD PARK RIESLING

RANKING 3

**Nagambie Lakes** $12–$19
**Current vintage: 2004** 93

Shapely, sculpted and aromatic riesling with zesty crispness and raciness. Its fresh lime juice, pear and apple perfume reveal lightly spicy and musky lemongrass undertones. Long and elegant, tight and lean, with powdery phenolics and a pleasing juiciness about its lime/lemon fruit.

| | | | |
|---|---|---|---|
| 2004 | 93 | 2009 | 2012+ |
| 2003 | 90 | 2008 | 2011 |
| 2002 | 90 | 2007 | 2010+ |
| 2001 | 88 | 2003 | 2006+ |
| 2000 | 93 | 2008 | 2012 |
| 1999 | 87 | 2001 | 2004 |
| 1998 | 93 | 2006 | 2010 |
| 1997 | 90 | 2002 | 2005+ |
| 1996 | 93 | 2004 | 2008 |
| 1995 | 93 | 2000 | 2003 |
| 1994 | 93 | 1999 | 2002 |
| 1993 | 91 | 1998 | 2001 |
| 1992 | 92 | 1994 | 1997 |
| 1991 | 94 | 1999 | 2003 |

# CENTRAL VICTORIA SHIRAZ

RANKING 4

**Nagambie Lakes** $20–29
**Current vintage: 2002** 93

Very drinkable, savoury and meaty shiraz with a brooding, peppery, spicy and slightly gamey perfume of plums and blackcurrants. Smooth, generous and sumptuous, its vibrant and brightly lit palate of intense minty dark fruits and creamy oak is framed by fine-grained, moderately firm tannins and lively acidity. Remarkable intensity, style and balance for its price.

| | | | |
|---|---|---|---|
| 2002 | 93 | 2007 | 2010+ |
| 2001 | 90 | 2006 | 2009+ |
| 2000 | 92 | 2005 | 2008 |
| 1999 | 89 | 2004 | 2007 |
| 1997 | 85 | 1999 | 2002 |
| 1996 | 83 | 1998 | 2001 |
| 1995 | 87 | 2000 | 2003 |
| 1994 | 85 | 1996 | 2001 |

# CENTRAL VICTORIAN VIOGNIER

RANKING 4

**Nagambie Lakes** $20–$29
**Current vintage: 2003** 90

Attractive early-drinking viognier whose delicate perfume of spicy, musky and slightly candied apricot aromas precedes an intense, forward and slippery palate of up-front fruit, juicy viscosity and refreshing but soft acidity.

| | | | |
|---|---|---|---|
| 2003 | 90 | 2004 | 2005+ |
| 2002 | 89 | 2003 | 2004+ |
| 2001 | 88 | 2002 | 2003+ |
| 2000 | 79 | 2000 | 2001 |
| 1998 | 84 | 1999 | 2000 |

# CLASSIC RELEASE MARSANNE

RANKING 4

**Nagambie Lakes** $20–$29
**Current vintage: 1998** 89

A mature dry white for drinking now with a developed, toasty and buttery bouquet whose sweet vanilla oak slightly dominates its waxy, nutty and spicy fruit qualities. Round and generous, its lightly sappy and oily palate of butter, toast and grilled nut flavours finishes a little sweet and alcoholic, with clean soft acids. Not hugely varietal.

| | | | |
|---|---|---|---|
| 1998 | 89 | 2003 | 2006 |
| 1997 | 89 | 1999 | 2002+ |
| 1996 | 90 | 2000 | 2003 |
| 1995 | 88 | 1997 | 2000+ |
| 1994 | 82 | 1995 | 1998 |
| 1993 | 95 | 1998 | 2001 |
| 1992 | 94 | 2000 | 2004 |

## CRESCENT (Shiraz Mourvèdre Grenache blend)

| | | | |
|---|---|---|---|
| **Nagambie Lakes** | $20–$29 | | |
| **Current vintage: 2001** | **89** | | |

A sweet, slightly confected and spicy perfume of plums, blueberries, raspberries and cassis is scented with white pepper, cinnamon and cloves over dusty vanilla oak. A moderately firm chassis of grippy tannins finishes long and minty. Earthy, savoury undertones, frame its smooth and generous palate of lively berry and currant flavours. of pleasing depth and integration.

| 2001 | 91 | 2006 | 2009 |
|---|---|---|---|
| 2000 | 93 | 2005 | 2008 |
| 1999 | 89 | 2004 | 2007+ |
| 1998 | 89 | 2003 | 2006+ |
| 1997 | 84 | 1999 | 2002 |

## PRINT SHIRAZ

| | |
|---|---|
| **Nagambie Lakes** | $50+ |
| **Current vintage: 2001** | **93** |

Rich, ripe and minty central Victorian shiraz with grip and grunt. Its spicy, white pepper fragrance of cassis, plums and mulberries is backed by creamy, meaty oak, while its robust and generous palate offers a rich, sweet core of dark fruit. Tightly integrated with linear, rod-like tannins and lightly smoky cedary oak, it's balanced and stable, with a plush, smooth middle.

| 2001 | 93 | 2009 | 2013+ |
|---|---|---|---|
| 2000 | 90 | 2005 | 2008+ |
| 1999 | 92 | 2007 | 2011 |
| 1998 | 93 | 2010 | 2018 |
| 1997 | 91 | 2005 | 2009 |
| 1996 | 89 | 2001 | 2004 |
| 1995 | 92 | 2003 | 2007 |
| 1994 | 88 | 2002 | 2006 |
| 1993 | 94 | 2005 | 2013 |
| 1992 | 88 | 2000 | 2004+ |
| 1991 | 94 | 2003 | 2011 |
| 1990 | 90 | 1998 | 2002 |

# Montalto

33 Shoreham Road, Red Hill South Vic 3937. Tel: (03) 5989 8412. Fax: (03) 5989 8417.
Web: montalto.com.au  Email: info@montalto.com.au
Region: **Mornington Peninsula** Winemaker: **Robin Brockett** Viticulturist: **Geoff Clarke**
Chief Executive: **John Mitchell**

Montalto is an emergent brand in the Mornington Peninsula that combines a first-rate vineyard site with an olive grove and wetlands development. There are two tiers to its wines, Montalto and the second 'Pennon' label, each of which offer excellent value for their price-points. Montalto's fine restaurant has quickly become one of the most popular in the region. Although the wines are made at Scotchman's Hill, this is a serious wine business indeed, as illustrated by the very classy 2003 releases.

## CHARDONNAY

| | |
|---|---|
| **Mornington Peninsula** | $20–$29 |
| **Current vintage: 2003** | **94** |

Restrained, delicate perfume of peaches and melon, nectarines and pineapple over slightly nutty, dusty vanilla oak. Long, fine and delicate, with a babyfat middle palate revealing some alluringly pristine and penetrative fruit. It finishes soft, nutty and savoury, with a lingering note of mineral.

| 2003 | 94 | 2008 | 2011 |
|---|---|---|---|
| 2001 | 93 | 2003 | 2006+ |
| 2000 | 92 | 2002 | 2005 |
| 1999 | 91 | 2001 | 2004 |

## PINOT NOIR

| | |
|---|---|
| **Mornington Peninsula** | $30–$49 |
| **Current vintage: 2003** | **93** |

Ripe, deeply flavoured and quite firm, bony Peninsula pinot with genuine cellaring potential. There's an earthy, animal hide note beneath its fragrant and musky aromas of dark cherries, plums and vanilla oak. Firm, tight and fine-grained, its palate is richly flavoured with dark, spicy berry/cherry flavours. Excellent balance and structure.

| 2003 | 93 | 2005 | 2008+ |
|---|---|---|---|
| 2001 | 93 | 2003 | 2006+ |
| 2000 | 90 | 2002 | 2005 |
| 1999 | 80 | 2001 | 2004 |

# Montrose

Poet's Corner Wines, Craigmoor Road, Mudgee NSW 2850. Tel: (02) 6372 2208. Fax: (02) 6372 4464
Email: info@poetscornerwines.com

Region: **Mudgee** Winemaker: **James Manners** Viticulturist: **Frank Hellwig** Chief Executive: **Laurent Lacassgne**

Montrose has delivered handsomely in the 2002 vintage, the first solid season it has experienced for some years. The Italian varietals of Sangiovese and Barbera plus the Chardonnay have each made generous and flavoursome wines of varietal integrity and correctness.

## BARBERA

RANKING **4**

| Mudgee | $20–$29 |
|---|---|
| Current vintage: 2002 | 92 |

Vibrant, elegant and varietally correct barbera, with some regional notes of eucalypt and mint. Sweet and spicy, its briary aromas of tomato bush small red berries, nicotine and diesel oil are backed by sweet vanilla oak. Smooth, sumptuous and pristine, it offers a long and lingering palate of piercing small red berries, plums and cherries, evenly matched to restrained vanilla oak and framed by powder-fine tannins.

| 2002 | 92 | 2004 | 2007+ |
|---|---|---|---|
| 2000 | 83 | 2002 | 2005 |
| 1999 | 91 | 2001 | 2004+ |
| 1997 | 92 | 2002 | 2005+ |
| 1996 | 89 | 2001 | 2004+ |

## BLACK SHIRAZ

RANKING **5**

| Mudgee | $12–$19 |
|---|---|
| Current vintage: 2001 | 81 |

Under-ripe, greenish and confection-like dark fruit with stale, smoky vanilla and ashtray-like oak.

| 2001 | 81 | 2002 | 2003 |
|---|---|---|---|
| 1999 | 90 | 2004 | 2007+ |
| 1998 | 84 | 2000 | 2003 |
| 1997 | 89 | 2005 | 2009 |
| 1996 | 89 | 1998 | 2001 |
| 1995 | 88 | 1997 | 2000 |
| 1994 | 87 | 1996 | 1999 |

## SANGIOVESE

RANKING **4**

| Mudgee | $20–$29 |
|---|---|
| Current vintage: 2002 | 90 |

Spicy aromas of dried herbs, maraschino cherries and raspberries with a modest oak influence and a background of marzipan. Smooth and supple, but finely crafted over a spine of chalky dry tannins, it presents a tight and varietally correct palate of sour-edged red berry fruits.

| 2002 | 90 | 2003 | 2004+ |
|---|---|---|---|
| 1998 | 89 | 2000 | 2003+ |
| 1997 | 90 | 1999 | 2002 |
| 1996 | 89 | 2001 | 2004 |

## STONY CREEK CHARDONNAY

RANKING **4**

| Mudgee | $12–$19 |
|---|---|
| Current vintage: 2002 | 90 |

Restrained aromas of honeysuckle and peaches integrate tightly with slightly charry, fine-grained vanilla oak, plus a hint of spice. Smooth, elegant and creamy, offering rather juicy, concentrated peachy chardonnay fruit, it's long and finely balanced, culminating in a lingering finish of nutty flavours and soft acidity.

| 2002 | 90 | 2007 | 2010 |
|---|---|---|---|
| 2001 | 88 | 2003 | 2006 |
| 1999 | 90 | 2001 | 2004+ |
| 1997 | 91 | 2002 | 2005 |
| 1996 | 90 | 1998 | 2001+ |
| 1994 | 90 | 1999 | 2002 |

# Moondah Brook

Dale Road, Middle Swan WA 6056. Tel: (08) 9274 5372. Fax: (08) 9274 5372.
Region: **Western Australia** Winemaker: **Rob Bowen** Viticulturist: **Ron Page** Chief Executive: **David Woods**
Moondah Brook has been slowly downgraded to a generic Western Australian brand of cheap, cheerful and well-made wines of lively varietal flavours and short-term appeal. Its ripe, tropical and punchy 2003 Verdelho is clearly its best current release.

## CABERNET SAUVIGNON                          RANKING 5

| Western Australia | $12–$19 |
|---|---|
| Current vintage: 2001 | 77 |

Lightly cooked, slightly dirty and meaty, greenish and stemmy aromas precede a simultaneously weedy, green and cooked palate simply lacking in fruit.

| Year | Score | | |
|---|---|---|---|
| 2001 | 77 | 2003 | 2006 |
| 2000 | 86 | 2002 | 2005+ |
| 1999 | 88 | 2004 | 2007 |
| 1998 | 88 | 2003 | 2006+ |
| 1997 | 82 | 1999 | 2002 |
| 1996 | 90 | 2004 | 2008 |
| 1995 | 87 | 2000 | 2003 |
| 1993 | 84 | 1995 | 1998 |

## CHARDONNAY

| Western Australia | $12–$19 |
|---|---|
| Current vintage: 2003 | 80 |

Light, floral and slightly rancid aromas of peach and grapefruit precede a simple, oily palate of slightly cooked fruit that lacks freshness and length.

| Year | Score | | |
|---|---|---|---|
| 2003 | 80 | 2003 | 2004+ |
| 2002 | 88 | 2003 | 2004+ |
| 2001 | 83 | 2001 | 2002 |
| 2000 | 86 | 2002 | 2005 |
| 1999 | 83 | 2000 | 2001 |
| 1998 | 90 | 2000 | 2003 |

## CHENIN BLANC

| Western Australia | $12–$19 |
|---|---|
| Current vintage: 2003 | 86 |

Dusty, grassy aromas of lightly tangy citrusy fruit precede a forward, herbal and lightly tropical palate whose slightly confectionary and juicy, peachy fruit finishes crisp and clean, with attractive acidity and a hint of sweetness.

| Year | Score | | |
|---|---|---|---|
| 2003 | 86 | 2004 | 2005+ |
| 2002 | 81 | 2002 | 2003 |
| 2001 | 82 | 2002 | 2003 |
| 2000 | 82 | 2001 | 2002 |
| 1998 | 86 | 2000 | 2003+ |
| 1997 | 86 | 2002 | 2005 |

## SHIRAZ                          RANKING 5

| Western Australia | $12–$19 |
|---|---|
| Current vintage: 2001 | 83 |

Herby, tomatoey expression of Western Australian shiraz whose relatively simple expression of berry fruits present a smooth, soft palate lacking real varietal intensity and length.

| Year | Score | | |
|---|---|---|---|
| 2001 | 83 | 2003 | 2006 |
| 2000 | 86 | 2002 | 2005+ |
| 1999 | 88 | 2004 | 2007 |
| 1998 | 87 | 2003 | 2006 |
| 1997 | 86 | 1999 | 2002 |
| 1996 | 88 | 2001 | 2004 |

## VERDELHO                          RANKING 5

| Western Australia | $12–$19 |
|---|---|
| Current vintage: 2003 | 87 |

Slightly pungent and grassy aromas of fresh tropical fruit precede a round, fruit palate whose pleasing length and punch of mango and melon-like fruit finishes clean, dry and refreshing, with a hint of mineral.

| Year | Score | | |
|---|---|---|---|
| 2003 | 87 | 2004 | 2005+ |
| 2002 | 88 | 2003 | 2004 |
| 2001 | 89 | 2002 | 2006 |
| 2000 | 89 | 2002 | 2005 |
| 1999 | 87 | 2001 | 2004+ |
| 1998 | 89 | 2000 | 2003+ |
| 1997 | 83 | 1999 | 2002 |

# Moondarra

Browns Road, Moondarra via Erica Vic 3825. Fax: (03) 9598 0766.

Region: **Gippsland** Winemakers: **Sandro Mosele, Neil Prentice** Viticulturist: **Neil Prentice**
Chief Executive: **Neil Prentice**

Moondarra is a tiny Gippsland vineyard whose wines are amongst the many others made at Kooyong on the Mornington Peninsula. Its premier wines, the Conception and Samba Side pinot noirs, have quickly acquired cult status. Neil Prentice made the hard but admirable decision that the pitifully small 2002 vintage was not of sufficiently high standard for any wine to be bottled under these labels.

## CONCEPTION PINOT NOIR

RANKING **4**

**Gippsland** $50+
**Current vintage: 2001** 90

This wine has a hint of mint and menthol about its aroma of briary and slightly jammy dark cherries and plums, while there's also a whiff of clove, cinnamon and a sniff of funk. A touch of what appears to be oak-derived volatility pokes through, coming across slightly prickly on the palate. Firm and fine-grained, it's deeply fruited and stalky. My only concerns relate to the regional influences and how they will evolve, plus the faint volatility.

| | | | |
|---|---|---|---|
| 2001 | 90 | 2003 | 2006+ |
| 2000 | 90 | 2005 | 2008 |
| 1999 | 88 | 2004 | 2007 |

# Moorilla Estate

655 Main Road, Berriedale Tas 7011. Tel: (03) 6277 9900. Fax: (03) 6249 4093.
Website: www.moorilla.com  Email: wine@moorilla.com.au

Region: **Southern Tasmania** Winemaker: **Michael Glover** Viticulturist: **Michael Glover**
Chief Executive: **Tim Goddard**

Moorilla Estate has taken huge strides in recent years, especially with its premier wine, the Reserve Pinot Noir. The exceptionally cool 2002 vintage provided something of an unwanted challenge for this and other southern Tasmanian wine producers. However, I have faith in what Moorilla is working towards, and believe that given reasonable conditions, that this company will again excel.

## CABERNET SAUVIGNON

RANKING **5**

**Southern Tasmania** $20–$29
**Current vintage: 2002** 77

Very green, under-ripe cabernet whose capsicum-like expression of cassis and plum fruit is partnered by sweet vanilla oak, but finishes lean and metallic, with high-toned sappy acids.

| | | | |
|---|---|---|---|
| 2002 | 77 | 2004 | 2007+ |
| 2001 | 86 | 2003 | 2006 |
| 2000 | 91 | 2008 | 2012 |
| 1999 | 88 | 2004 | 2007 |
| 1998 | 88 | 2003 | 2006 |
| 1997 | 86 | 2002 | 2005+ |
| 1995 | 81 | 2000 | 2003 |
| 1994 | 93 | 2002 | 2006 |
| 1993 | 82 | 2001 | 2005 |

## CHARDONNAY

**Southern Tasmania** $20–$29
**Current vintage: 2002** 84

Light, creamy aromas of nectarines, cloves and dusty, cardboard-like oak precede a syrupy palate whose green-edged tropical fruits are framed by sappy and rather tinny acids.

| | | | |
|---|---|---|---|
| 2002 | 84 | 2004 | 2007 |
| 2001 | 85 | 2003 | 2006 |
| 2000 | 87 | 2002 | 2005 |
| 1999 | 83 | 2001 | 2004 |
| 1998 | 81 | 2000 | 2003+ |
| 1996 | 83 | 1998 | 2001 |
| 1995 | 94 | 2003 | 2007 |

# GEWÜRZTRAMINER

**Southern Tasmania** $20–$29
**Current vintage: 2003** 86

A high-acid traminer with a slightly sweaty, musky perfume of rose oil, lychees and hair oil. Its generous and oily palate has reasonable length, revealing confectionary and bathpowder notes that finish with some steely edges. Lacks a little freshness and varietal intensity.

| | | | |
|---|---|---|---|
| 2003 | 86 | 2004 | 2005+ |
| 2001 | 83 | 2002 | 2003 |
| 2000 | 94 | 2005 | 2008 |
| 1999 | 90 | 2004 | 2007 |
| 1998 | 89 | 2003 | 2006 |
| 1997 | 90 | 2002 | 2005 |
| 1996 | 82 | 1997 | 1998 |

# PINOT NOIR

**Southern Tasmania** $20–$29
**Current vintage: 2003** 81

Unlike its recent predecessors, this under-ripened pinot is varnishy, confectionary, herby and stewed, with green edges and excessive volatility.

| | | | |
|---|---|---|---|
| 2003 | 81 | 2004 | 2005+ |
| 2002 | 86 | 2004 | 2007 |
| 2001 | 89 | 2003 | 2006+ |
| 2000 | 90 | 2005 | 2008 |
| 1999 | 87 | 2001 | 2004 |
| 1998 | 87 | 2000 | 2004 |
| 1997 | 92 | 2002 | 2005 |
| 1996 | 90 | 2001 | 2004 |
| 1995 | 88 | 2000 | 2003 |
| 1994 | 91 | 1999 | 2002 |

# RESERVE PINOT NOIR

**Southern Tasmania** $30–$49
**Current vintage: 2001** 93

Floral, perfumed pinot with delicate, lightly stalky herbal aromas of sweet red berries and cherries. Restrained, supple palate whose hints of musk and cloves overlay a core of earthy pinot fruit, bound in fine-grained tannins and neatly interwoven with restrained vanilla/cedar oak. A little too herbal for top marks.

| | | | |
|---|---|---|---|
| 2001 | 93 | 2006 | 2009 |
| 2000 | 91 | 2002 | 2005+ |
| 1999 | 91 | 2004 | 2007 |
| 1998 | 83 | 2000 | 2003 |
| 1997 | 88 | 2002 | 2005 |
| 1996 | 87 | 1998 | 2001 |

# RIESLING

**Southern Tasmania** $20–$29
**Current vintage: 2003** 84

Slightly tinny, greenish riesling with sweaty, herbal aromas of lightly spicy lime and lemon. Long, lean and austere, its restrained apple, pear and lime fruits finish with a rather metallic acidity.

| | | | |
|---|---|---|---|
| 2003 | 84 | 2005 | 2008+ |
| 2002 | 80 | 2003 | 2004+ |
| 2001 | 93 | 2006 | 2009+ |
| 2000 | 87 | 2008 | 2012 |
| 1999 | 87 | 2004 | 2007 |
| 1998 | 90 | 2003 | 2006 |
| 1997 | 87 | 1999 | 2002 |
| 1996 | 91 | 2001 | 2004 |
| 1995 | 88 | 1997 | 2000 |
| 1994 | 95 | 2006 | 2014 |

# Mourooduc Estate

501 Derril Road, Mourooduc Vic 3933. Tel: (03) 5971 8506. Fax: (03) 5971 8550.
Website: www.mourooduc-estate.com.au  Email: us@mourooduc-estate.com.au
Region: **Mornington Peninsula**  Winemaker: **Dr Richard McIntyre**  Chief Executive: **Dr Richard McIntyre**
Mourooduc Estate was one of the first makers from the Mornington Peninsula to fashion table wines of genuine class. After a few years during which the makers have perhaps sought to achieve too much complexity too quickly in the life of their wines, the 2002 Pinot Noir makes a very welcome return to the vineyard's former elevated status.

## CHARDONNAY
RANKING 5

| Mornington Peninsula | $30–$49 |
|---|---|
| **Current vintage: 2002** | **83** |

Fast-ageing chardonnay whose spicy, varnishy and gluey oak-derived aromas detract from its stone-fruit and pineapple flavours. Juicy but green-edged, it's forward and syrupy, finishing with varnishy notes and sappy acids.

| | | | |
|---|---|---|---|
| 2002 | 83 | 2003 | 2004 |
| 2001 | 77 | 2002 | 2003 |
| 2000 | 77 | 2002 | 2005 |
| 1999 | 87 | 2001 | 2004 |
| 1998 | 92 | 2000 | 2003 |
| 1997 | 88 | 2002 | 2005 |
| 1996 | 93 | 2001 | 2004 |
| 1995 | 93 | 2000 | 2003 |
| 1994 | 95 | 1999 | 2002 |
| 1993 | 92 | 1998 | 2001 |

## PINOT NOIR
RANKING 4

| Mornington Peninsula | $30–$49 |
|---|---|
| **Current vintage: 2002** | **91** |

Fragrant scents of rose petals, sweet red berries and cherries with a herbal, dusty, undergrowth-like background. Its velvet-smooth, juicy palate of sweet red fruit has warmth and generosity, with a lingering finish punctuated by fresh acids. The wine has an earthy spiciness, attractive balance and composition and is likely to build in the bottle.

| | | | |
|---|---|---|---|
| 2002 | 91 | 2004 | 2007+ |
| 2001 | 84 | 2003 | 2006 |
| 2000 | 84 | 2002 | 2005 |
| 1998 | 88 | 2003 | 2006 |
| 1997 | 93 | 2002 | 2005 |
| 1996 | 87 | 2001 | 2004 |
| 1995 | 93 | 2000 | 2003 |
| 1994 | 92 | 1999 | 2002 |
| 1993 | 93 | 1998 | 2001 |
| 1992 | 95 | 2000 | 2004 |
| 1991 | 84 | 1996 | 1999 |

## THE MOOROODUC CHARDONNAY
RANKING 5

| Mornington Peninsula | $50+ |
|---|---|
| **Current vintage: 2002** | **84** |

Heavily worked, spiky and varnishy chardonnay whose peachy melon flavours lack great length and richness. Smooth and creamy, but also hot, a little awkward and angular.

| | | | |
|---|---|---|---|
| 2003 | 84 | 2004 | 2007+ |
| 2001 | 86 | 2003 | 2006 |
| 2000 | 76 | 2002 | 2005 |
| 1999 | 84 | 2001 | 2004 |
| 1998 | 91 | 2003 | 2006 |

## THE MOOROODUC PINOT NOIR
RANKING 5

| Mornington Peninsula | $50+ |
|---|---|
| **Current vintage: 2001** | **87** |

Meaty, rustic pinot with an aroma of raspberries and maraschino cherries over sweet vanilla oak. Rather forward, juicy and green-edged, its palate reveals some vibrant red berry and cherry fruit. It has also evolved meaty, farmyard characters and has begun to dry out at the finish.

| | | | |
|---|---|---|---|
| 2001 | 87 | 2003 | 2006 |
| 2000 | 81 | 2002 | 2005 |
| 1998 | 77 | 2000 | 2003 |
| 1997 | 94 | 2005 | 2009 |

# Morris

Mia Mia Road, Rutherglen Vic 3685. Tel: (02) 6026 7303. Fax: (02) 6026 7445
Email: morriswines@orlando-wyndham.com

Region: **Rutherglen Winemaker: David Morris** Chief Executive: **Laurent Lacassgne**

Morris is one of the traditional makers of red wines in Victoria's northeasterly and warm to hot-climate Rutherglen region. Despite the fact that it is owned by one of the world's largest beverage companies in Pernod-Ricard, Morris makes its reds quite autonomously. The results are everything you'd hope for — traditionally-crafted 'country' wines of integrity, character and authenticity. The 2001s are right on the button. It also goes without saying that Morris is one of the elite makers of Rutherglen's unique tokay and muscat.

## BLUE IMPERIAL
RANKING **5**

**Rutherglen** $20–$29
**Current vintage: 2002** 87

Honest, but lighter wine whose meaty, spicy aromas of plums and blueberries, prunes and currants, have sweet vanilla oak and floral undertones. Ripe and forward, then slightly hollow, its sweet, rather cooked and meaty prune/currant fruit qualities overlie nuances of blueberries and blackberries, before finishing soft and smooth.

| | | | |
|---|---|---|---|
| 2002 | 87 | 2007 | 2010 |
| 2001 | 89 | 2006 | 2009 |
| 1999 | 88 | 2007 | 2011 |
| 1998 | 86 | 2003 | 2006 |

## CABERNET SAUVIGNON
RANKING **5**

**Rutherglen** $12–$19
**Current vintage: 2001** 89

Rich, ripe and uncomplicated Rutherglen cabernet with a slightly confectionary aroma of plums, black-currants and raspberries with earthy and vanilla/cedary undertones. Rustic and earthy, its tarry and chocolatey palate offers plenty of thickness and ripeness. Should cellar well.

| | | | |
|---|---|---|---|
| 2001 | 89 | 2009 | 2013 |
| 2000 | 86 | 2008 | 2012 |
| 1999 | 89 | 2007 | 2011+ |
| 1998 | 89 | 2006 | 2010 |
| 1997 | 82 | 1999 | 2002+ |
| 1996 | 88 | 2004 | 2008+ |
| 1995 | 87 | 2003 | 2007 |
| 1994 | 89 | 2006 | 2014 |
| 1993 | 87 | 2005 | 2013 |
| 1992 | 88 | 2000 | 2004 |
| 1990 | 91 | 2002 | 2010 |
| 1989 | 91 | 2001 | 2009 |
| 1988 | 91 | 2000 | 2005 |
| 1987 | 88 | 1995 | 1999 |

## CHARDONNAY
RANKING **5**

**Rutherglen** $12–$19
**Current vintage: 2003** 88

Generous, soft and easy-drinking chardonnay with a restrained and nutty aroma of peach and melon, backed by nuances of dried herbs and green olives. Sweet, ripe and juicy, it's a smooth and steady peaches and cream style whose pleasing weight and flavour finishes soft and refreshing.

| | | | |
|---|---|---|---|
| 2003 | 88 | 2005 | 2008 |
| 2002 | 89 | 2004 | 2007 |
| 2001 | 87 | 2003 | 2006 |
| 2000 | 88 | 2002 | 2005 |
| 1999 | 87 | 2000 | 2001 |
| 1998 | 86 | 2000 | 2003 |
| 1997 | 83 | 1999 | 2002 |

## DURIF
RANKING **4**

**Rutherglen** $20–$29
**Current vintage: 2001** 90

About as concentrated and as robust as Rutherglen reds should ever be, this powerful, tarry red has rather a wild and meaty aroma of briary cooked prune-like fruit, chocolate and creamy oak and a whiff of antiseptic. Youthful, firm and linear, its thickly proportioned depth of plum/prune flavour stays just this side of over-ripe, delivering deeply spicy and lingering game-like qualities.

| | | | |
|---|---|---|---|
| 2001 | 90 | 2013 | 2021 |
| 2000 | 90 | 2012 | 2020 |
| 1999 | 87 | 2007 | 2011 |
| 1998 | 93 | 2010 | 2018+ |
| 1997 | 91 | 2009 | 2017 |
| 1996 | 88 | 2004 | 2008+ |
| 1995 | 93 | 2007 | 2015 |
| 1994 | 93 | 2002 | 2006 |
| 1993 | 87 | 2001 | 2005 |
| 1992 | 90 | 2004 | 2012 |
| 1991 | 93 | 2003 | 2011 |
| 1990 | 93 | 2002 | 2010 |
| 1989 | 88 | 2001 | 2009 |
| 1988 | 88 | 2000 | 2005 |

## SHIRAZ

RANKING **5**

| Rutherglen | $12–$19 |
|---|---|
| Current vintage: 2001 | 90 |

Earthy, typically regional Rutherglen shiraz of richness, smoothness and structure. Sweet, lightly gamey aromas of red berries and plums are concentrated and spicy, with spicy oaky undertones. A natural, uncomplicated countryside wine of pleasing weight, texture and harmony.

| | | | |
|---|---|---|---|
| 2001 | 90 | 2009 | 2013 |
| 2000 | 85 | 2005 | 2008 |
| 1999 | 88 | 2004 | 2007+ |
| 1998 | 89 | 2003 | 2006+ |
| 1997 | 85 | 2005 | 2009 |
| 1996 | 89 | 2004 | 2008+ |
| 1995 | 87 | 2000 | 2003 |
| 1994 | 87 | 2002 | 2006 |
| 1993 | 82 | 1998 | 2001 |
| 1992 | 91 | 2004 | 2012 |
| 1991 | 90 | 2003 | 2011 |
| 1990 | 88 | 1998 | 2002 |
| 1989 | 86 | 1994 | 1997 |

# Moss Wood

Metricup Road, Willyabrup WA 6280. Tel: (08) 9755 6266. Fax: (08) 9755 6303.
Website: www.mosswood.com.au  Email: mosswood@mosswood.com.au
Region: **Margaret River** Winemaker: **Keith Mugford** Viticulturist: **Matthew Bowden**
Chief Executives: **Keith & Clare Mugford**

Honest as ever, Keith Mugford has spoken recently about his desire to shave a percentage or so of alcohol strength from his red wines, something he believes he will achieve by returning to inoculating with cultured yeasts ahead of the 'wild' or 'indigenous' yeasts he deployed for the three years up to and including 2000. If the 2001 vintage is anything to go by, he's succeeded handsomely, in the process making a wine that we both believe is the best red ever released (to this time, at least) by Moss Wood. It's nothing short of awe-inspiring.

## CABERNET SAUVIGNON

RANKING **2**

| Margaret River | $50+ |
|---|---|
| Current vintage: 2001 | 97 |

Alluringly deep, complex perfume of pristine small dark berries, mulberries and redcurrants, scented with violets, perfectly integrated cedar/mocha oak and a dusty suggestion of dark olives. Sumptuous, silky palate whose deep core of intense small dark berry flavour is lavishly coated with chocolate/vanilla/cedar oak and bound by supremely fine, satiny tannins. Suggestions of tar and prune reveal some slightly riper fruit, while its structure, power and integration stamp it as a significant wine, perhaps the finest Moss Wood ever.

| | | | |
|---|---|---|---|
| 2001 | 97 | 2013 | 2021+ |
| 2000 | 93 | 2008 | 2012+ |
| 1999 | 93 | 2011 | 2021 |
| 1998 | 90 | 2006 | 2010+ |
| 1997 | 89 | 2005 | 2009 |
| 1996 | 96 | 2008 | 2016 |
| 1995 | 96 | 2015 | 2025 |
| 1994 | 95 | 2014 | 2024 |
| 1993 | 87 | 2001 | 2005 |
| 1992 | 89 | 2000 | 2004 |
| 1991 | 96 | 2003 | 2011+ |
| 1990 | 95 | 2002 | 2010+ |
| 1989 | 91 | 2001 | 2009 |
| 1988 | 89 | 2000 | 2008 |
| 1987 | 89 | 1999 | 2007 |
| 1986 | 95 | 2006 | 2016 |
| 1985 | 97 | 2005 | 2015 |

## CHARDONNAY

RANKING **2**

| Margaret River | $30–$49 |
|---|---|
| Current vintage: 2003 | 95 |

Very stylish chardonnay whose pungent aromas of sweet spicy tropical fruit, quince and lemon essence, cloves and cinnamon, are supported by fine-grained oak. It presents a long, concentrated and assertive palate whose fleshy, sappy texture is likely to build handsomely in weight and structure.

| | | | |
|---|---|---|---|
| 2003 | 95 | 2008 | 2011 |
| 2002 | 95 | 2007 | 2010+ |
| 2001 | 95 | 2006 | 2009 |
| 2000 | 91 | 2005 | 2008 |
| 1999 | 96 | 2007 | 2011 |
| 1998 | 90 | 2003 | 2006+ |
| 1997 | 95 | 2002 | 2005 |
| 1996 | 93 | 1998 | 2001 |
| 1995 | 93 | 2003 | 2007 |
| 1994 | 95 | 2002 | 2006 |
| 1993 | 92 | 1998 | 2001 |
| 1992 | 94 | 2000 | 2004 |
| 1991 | 91 | 2003 | 2011 |
| 1990 | 94 | 2002 | 2010 |

A
B
C
D
E
F
G
H
I
J
K
L
**M**
N
O
P
Q
R
S
T
U
V
W
X
Y
Z

## GLENMORE VINEYARD CABERNET SAUVIGNON

| Margaret River | $30–$49 |
| --- | --- |
| Current vintage: 2001 | 89 |

Delicate aromas of raspberries, cherries and cassis with cedar/vanilla oak and a lightly herbal and tobaccoey background. Its pretty, vibrant, forward red berry fruit is slightly jammy, while its tannins are fine and gentle.

| 2001 | 89 | 2003 | 2006+ |
| --- | --- | --- | --- |
| 2000 | 93 | 2008 | 2012 |
| 1999 | 93 | 2004 | 2007+ |

## LEFROY BROOK VINEYARD CHARDONNAY

| Pemberton | $30–$49 |
| --- | --- |
| Current vintage: 2003 | 93 |

Lightly floral, estery aromas of tropical fruits, nectarines, bananas and oatmeal, with undertones of fine-grained vanilla/clove oak. Long, elegant and tightly focused, with a creamy, peachy palate of vibrant melon/cumquat flavours aided by slightly dusty vanilla oak. Finishing with fresh, but smooth acidity, its flavours persist with brightness and length.

| 2003 | 93 | 2005 | 2008+ |
| --- | --- | --- | --- |
| 2002 | 89 | 2004 | 2007+ |
| 2001 | 91 | 2003 | 2006 |
| 1997 | 92 | 1999 | 2002 |

## PINOT NOIR

| Margaret River | $30–$49 |
| --- | --- |
| Current vintage: 2001 | 87 |

Lightly floral rose petal aromas of berries, cherries and boiled lollies precede a palate of medium to full weight. Its sweet vanilla oak lends creaminess and smokiness to its light, uncomplicated expression of raspberries and strawberries, but does finish a little too brassy. Framed by soft acids and tannins.

| 2001 | 87 | 2006 | 2009 |
| --- | --- | --- | --- |
| 2000 | 81 | 2002 | 2005 |
| 1999 | 81 | 2004 | 2007 |
| 1998 | 88 | 2003 | 2006 |
| 1997 | 86 | 2002 | 2005 |
| 1996 | 89 | 2001 | 2004 |
| 1995 | 93 | 2003 | 2007 |
| 1994 | 87 | 1999 | 2002 |
| 1993 | 83 | 1998 | 2001 |

## RIBBON VALE VINEYARD CABERNET BLEND

| Margaret River | $30–$49 |
| --- | --- |
| Current vintage: 2002 | 91 |

Very smooth, plush and intensely flavoured cabernet whose pristine floral fragrance of maraschino cherries, raspberries and redcurrants conceals a whiff of spirit and presents a generous measure of cedar/vanilla oak. Its deep flavours of bright red and dark berries are offered along a luscious but measured palate framed by velvet-like tannins and vanilla oak. Just lacks the complexity required for a higher score.

| 2002 | 91 | 2010 | 2014+ |
| --- | --- | --- | --- |
| 2001 | 92 | 2009 | 2013 |
| 2000 | 93 | 2008 | 2012 |
| 1999 | 90 | 2011 | 2019 |
| 1998 | 77 | 2000 | 2003 |
| 1997 | 93 | 2005 | 2009 |
| 1996 | 90 | 2004 | 2008+ |
| 1995 | 87 | 2003 | 2007+ |
| 1994 | 87 | 2002 | 2006 |
| 1993 | 84 | 1995 | 1998 |
| 1992 | 89 | 1997 | 2000 |
| 1991 | 88 | 2003 | 2011 |
| 1990 | 93 | 1995 | 1998 |
| 1989 | 90 | 1994 | 1997 |

## RIBBON VALE VINEYARD MERLOT

| Margaret River | $30–$49 |
| --- | --- |
| Current vintage: 2002 | 88 |

Sweet, dusty aromas of spicy plums and dark cherries over creamy vanilla oak, with vegetal, leathery undertones. Elegant and polished, its palate of intense dark fruit and classy sweet oak overlies a slightly modest extract of fine-grained tannins, finishing with tobaccoey, herbal complexity.

| 2002 | 88 | 2007 | 2010+ |
| --- | --- | --- | --- |
| 2001 | 90 | 2006 | 2009+ |
| 2000 | 91 | 2005 | 2008 |
| 1999 | 92 | 2007 | 2011 |
| 1998 | 77 | 2000 | 2003 |
| 1997 | 91 | 2002 | 2005 |
| 1996 | 90 | 2004 | 2008 |
| 1995 | 90 | 2000 | 2003 |
| 1994 | 80 | 1999 | 2002 |
| 1993 | 89 | 2001 | 2005 |
| 1992 | 92 | 2000 | 2004 |
| 1991 | 93 | 1999 | 2003 |
| 1990 | 88 | 1995 | 1998 |

... 

## SEMILLON

RANKING 3

| Margaret River | $20–$29 |
|---|---|
| **Current vintage: 2003** | **93** |

Tangy, juicy, punchy Margaret River semillon whose lightly herbal and citrusy aromas reveal some lightly reductive and cheesy characters that dissipate in the glass. Pristine and lightly grassy, with vibrant and mouthfilling honeydew melon and rockmelon fruit qualities culminating in a refreshingly clean finish.

| | | | |
|---|---|---|---|
| 2003 | 93 | 2005 | 2008+ |
| 2001 | 95 | 2006 | 2009 |
| 2000 | 92 | 2002 | 2005+ |
| 1999 | 91 | 2001 | 2004 |
| 1998 | 87 | 2000 | 2003 |
| 1997 | 84 | 1998 | 1999 |
| 1994 | 86 | 1996 | 1999 |
| 1993 | 87 | 1998 | 2001 |
| 1992 | 90 | 2000 | 2004 |
| 1991 | 90 | 1996 | 1999 |
| 1990 | 86 | 1995 | 1998 |
| 1989 | 85 | 1994 | 1997 |
| 1988 | 91 | 1993 | 1996 |

# Mount Gisborne

83 Waterson Road, Gisborne Vic 3437. Tel: 03 5428 2834. Fax: 03 5428 2834. Email: mgw@hotkey.net.au

Region: **Macedon Ranges** Winemaker: **Stuart Anderson** Viticulturist: **David Ell**
Chief Executives: **David & Mary Ell**

Mount Gisborne is a cool-climate Victorian vineyard from an exposed and windy site whose best vintages of Chardonnay and Pinot Noir are classically proportioned wines of genuine intensity and longevity.

## CHARDONNAY

RANKING 4

| Macedon Ranges | $30–$49 |
|---|---|
| **Current vintage: 2001** | **89** |

Already maturing and losing some youthful freshness, this forward and brassy chardonnay has a toasty bouquet of cumquats and figs, nuts and spices. Its up-front and juicy palate is initially rather oily before falling away to leave slightly tired and candied fruit.

| | | | |
|---|---|---|---|
| 2001 | 89 | 2003 | 2006 |
| 2000 | 87 | 2002 | 2005 |
| 1999 | 87 | 2000 | 2001+ |
| 1998 | 95 | 2003 | 2006+ |
| 1997 | 94 | 2002 | 2005 |
| 1995 | 93 | 2000 | 2003 |

## PINOT NOIR

RANKING 3

| Macedon Ranges | $30–$49 |
|---|---|
| **Current vintage: 2001** | **89** |

An old-fashioned Pommard-like pinot whose spicy bouquet of minty red cherries and stewed plums reveals slightly vegetal, greenish undertones and nuances of menthol. Firm and grippy, it's evolving some meaty, animal hide-like complexity, but also possesses a little hotness and spiciness. With a little time it should become quite charming and rustic.

| | | | |
|---|---|---|---|
| 2001 | 89 | 2006 | 2009 |
| 2000 | 90 | 2005 | 2008 |
| 1999 | 93 | 2004 | 2007 |
| 1998 | 90 | 2003 | 2006 |
| 1997 | 94 | 2002 | 2005+ |
| 1996 | 91 | 2004 | 2008 |
| 1995 | 93 | 2000 | 2003+ |

# Mount Horrocks

The Old Railway Station Curling Street, Auburn SA 5451. Tel: (08) 8849 2202. Fax: (08) 8849 2243.
Website: www.mounthorrocks.com  Email: sales@mounthorrocks.com
Region: **Clare Valley** Winemaker: **Stephanie Toole** Chief Executive: **Stephanie Toole**

Mount Horrocks is an energetic Clare Valley wine producer whose proprietor and maker, Stephanie Toole, is restlessly working to refine her range of wines towards classic status. Her 2003 vintage white wines take her considerably closer, for this season has produced an exceptionally classy and flavoursome Semillon, steeped in complexity and attitude. The austere and minerally Riesling hits a similarly high note.

## CABERNET MERLOT

RANKING  4

**Clare Valley**  $30–$49
**Current vintage: 2001**  90

A lean and polished red with a sweet, slightly confection-like aroma of raspberries and blackberries, sweet cedar/vanilla oak and a floral background of mint, eucalypt and menthol. Firm and assertive, its long and persistent palate of brightly lit and lightly stewy small red and black berry flavours culminates in a finish of refreshing acids and slightly raw tannins. Just give it a few years.

| 2001 | 90 | 2009 | 2013 |
|---|---|---|---|
| 2000 | 89 | 2005 | 2008 |
| 1999 | 91 | 2007 | 2011 |
| 1998 | 90 | 2003 | 2006+ |
| 1996 | 94 | 2004 | 2008+ |
| 1995 | 90 | 2000 | 2003 |
| 1994 | 91 | 1999 | 2002 |
| 1993 | 87 | 1998 | 2001 |
| 1992 | 89 | 1997 | 2000 |

## CHARDONNAY

RANKING 4

**Clare Valley**  $20–$29
**Current vintage: 2003**  85

Developed buttery aromas of peaches, cashews and vanilla oak, before a fast-maturing palate of greenish cashew flavours.

| 2003 | 85 | 2003 | 2004+ |
|---|---|---|---|
| 2002 | 90 | 2004 | 2007 |
| 2000 | 90 | 2002 | 2005+ |
| 1999 | 90 | 2001 | 2004 |
| 1998 | 80 | 1999 | 2000 |

## CORDON CUT

RANKING 2

**Clare Valley**  $30–$49
**Current vintage: 2003**  90

Early-drinking and concentrated dessert wine with penetrative, if slightly cooked and varnishy aromas of lemon and pineapple. Forward and toasty, it's smooth and luscious, but its initial viscosity and juiciness falls away to a slightly leaner, tighter finish than usual.

| 2003 | 90 | 2004 | 2005+ |
|---|---|---|---|
| 2002 | 96 | 2002 | 2007 |
| 2001 | 94 | 2003 | 2006 |
| 2000 | 95 | 2002 | 2005 |
| 1999 | 91 | 2001 | 2004 |
| 1998 | 90 | 1999 | 2000 |
| 1997 | 87 | 1999 | 2002 |
| 1996 | 93 | 2001 | 2004 |
| 1995 | 90 | 2000 | 2003 |
| 1994 | 95 | 1999 | 2002 |
| 1993 | 95 | 1998 | 2001 |
| 1992 | 90 | 1994 | 1997 |

## RIESLING

RANKING 3

**Clare Valley**  $20–$29
**Current vintage: 2003**  95

Delicately scented with a floral perfume of tropical fruits, lemon rind and zest of lime, this very elegant, finely structured and refined riesling will surely cellar well. Lean and austere, its piercingly pure citrus flavours build slowly in the mouth, delivered over a chalky backbone. It culminates in a lingering, dry and savoury finish of fresh mineral acids.

| 2003 | 95 | 2011 | 2015 |
|---|---|---|---|
| 2002 | 95 | 2010 | 2014+ |
| 2001 | 92 | 2006 | 2009+ |
| 2000 | 87 | 2002 | 2005 |
| 1999 | 93 | 2004 | 2007 |
| 1998 | 93 | 2003 | 2006 |
| 1997 | 90 | 2002 | 2005 |
| 1996 | 90 | 1998 | 2001 |
| 1995 | 90 | 1997 | 2000 |
| 1994 | 93 | 1999 | 2002 |
| 1993 | 94 | 2001 | 2005 |
| 1992 | 91 | 2000 | 2004 |

## SEMILLON (Formerly blended with Sauvignon Blanc) RANKING 3

| Clare Valley | $20–$29 |
|---|---|
| **Current vintage: 2003** | **94** |

Full-on semillon whose rich, luscious flavours and textures effortlessly absorb some pretty high-class oak. Lightly grassy melon and stonefruit aromas knit tightly with creamy wheatmeal oak qualities, while the generous, tangy palate presents a deep, vibrant core of lemon/melon fruit framed by sweet oak and racy mineral acids. Plenty of cut and polish, loads of attitude.

| Year | Score | | |
|---|---|---|---|
| 2003 | 94 | 2005 | 2008+ |
| 2002 | 91 | 2004 | 2007 |
| 2001 | 95 | 2006 | 2009 |
| 2000 | 90 | 2002 | 2005 |
| 1999 | 92 | 2004 | 2007+ |
| 1998 | 90 | 2000 | 2003 |
| 1997 | 91 | 1999 | 2002 |
| 1996 | 88 | 1998 | 2001 |

## SHIRAZ RANKING 4

| Clare Valley | $30–$49 |
|---|---|
| **Current vintage: 2001** | **88** |

Good, firm and honest red wine from a very hot vintage. Meaty, earthy aromas of stewed plums, menthol and dark chocolate oak precede a smooth and tightly worked palate whose very ripe flavours of plums and blackcurrants, slightly shrivelled currants and raisins are given sweetness through assertive vanilla oak.

| Year | Score | | |
|---|---|---|---|
| 2001 | 88 | 2006 | 2009 |
| 2000 | 92 | 2005 | 2008+ |
| 1999 | 91 | 2004 | 2007 |
| 1998 | 93 | 2003 | 2006+ |
| 1997 | 82 | 1999 | 2002 |
| 1996 | 86 | 1998 | 2001 |

# Mount Ida

Northern Highway, Heathcote Vic 3523. Tel: (03) 9730 1022.
Website: www.beringerblass.com.au
Region: **Victoria** Winemaker: **Matt Steel** Chief Executive: **Jamie Odell**

Mount Ida is a tiny Heathcote vineyard that through a series of historical accidents has ended up in the hands of Beringer Blass, one of the world's largest wine producers. Given that the substantially below-par performance of the 2001 vintage wine was very likely a reflection of the filthy hot vintage and accumulated drought experienced at Mount Ida, this excellent vineyard has indeed prospered, instead of falling through the cracks at Beringer Blass. Expect big things from Mount Ida in future, whose wines have traditionally been more elegant than the contemporary Heathcote norm of blockbuster weight.

## SHIRAZ RANKING 3

| Victoria | $20–$29 |
|---|---|
| **Current vintage: 2001** | **84** |

Rather soupy and overcooked wine from this excellent vineyard, whose closed, spicy aromas of dark cherries and plums are partnered by slightly charry vanilla oak and nuances of cloves and cinnamon. Powerful, overripe and porty, the palate lacks brightness and focus, finishing slightly medicinal with metallic tannins.

| Year | Score | | |
|---|---|---|---|
| 2001 | 84 | 2003 | 2006 |
| 1999 | 92 | 2004 | 2007 |
| 1998 | 96 | 2003 | 2006+ |
| 1997 | 91 | 2002 | 2005 |
| 1996 | 93 | 2001 | 2004 |
| 1995 | 96 | 2003 | 2007 |
| 1994 | 94 | 1999 | 2002 |
| 1992 | 95 | 1997 | 2000 |
| 1991 | 94 | 1999 | 2003 |
| 1990 | 93 | 1995 | 1998 |

# Mount Langi Ghiran

Warrak–Buangor Road, Buangor Vic 3375. Tel: (03) 5354 3207. Fax: (03) 5354 3277.
Website: www.langi.com.au Email: sales@langi.com.au

Region: **Grampians** Winemaker: **Trevor Mast** Viticulturist: **Damien Sheehan** Chief Executive: **Gordon Gebbie**

Mount Langi Ghiran has not only been at the forefront of the modern, stylish and peppery expression of western Victorian shiraz, but its Langi Shiraz was right there when the American market discovered top-notch Australian wine. It's now in the hands of the Rathbone family, owners of Yering Station and, more recently, Parker Coonawarra. The potential represented by Mount Langi Ghiran is phenomenal; the challenge faced by its owners and makers is to realise it.

## BILLI BILLI (Shiraz & Grenache)

RANKING **5**

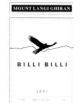

Grampians $20–$29
Current vintage: 2001    83

A tight, lean red with an earthy, bony aroma of light plum and red cherry fruit over spicy, fruitcake-like notes of grenache. Sappy, under-ripe notes lurk beneath some meaty, spicy plummy fruit, while the finish is a little mean and ungenerous.

| 2001 | 83 | 2003 | 2006+ |
|------|----|------|-------|
| 2000 | 92 | 2005 | 2008 |
| 1999 | 86 | 2001 | 2004 |
| 1998 | 82 | 2000 | 2003 |

## CLIFF EDGE SHIRAZ

RANKING **5**

Grampians $20–$29
Current vintage: 2001    88

Elegant, spicy short term shiraz with a vibrant, earthy bouquet of blackcurrant and black pepper, plums and cinnamon, backed by floral undertones. Smooth, reserved and slightly overcooked, it's also minty and herbal, supported by sweet vanilla and lightly toasty oak.

| 2001 | 88 | 2003 | 2006 |
|------|----|------|------|
| 2000 | 92 | 2002 | 2005 |
| 1999 | 86 | 2001 | 2004 |

## LANGI CABERNET SAUVIGNON MERLOT

RANKING **4**

Grampians $30–$49
Current vintage: 2000    85

Earthy, meaty aromas of lightly spicy and herbal berry fruit, leather and camphor, before a smooth, up-front palate of small berry and plum flavours. Rather a hollow middle palate precedes a lean, hard-edged finish of greenish undertones.

| 2000 | 85 | 2005 | 2008 |
|------|----|------|-------|
| 1999 | 93 | 2007 | 2011+ |
| 1998 | 88 | 2006 | 2010 |
| 1997 | 91 | 2005 | 2009+ |
| 1996 | 90 | 2004 | 2008+ |
| 1994 | 95 | 2006 | 2014 |
| 1993 | 94 | 2001 | 2005 |
| 1992 | 95 | 2000 | 2004 |
| 1991 | 93 | 1999 | 2003 |
| 1990 | 92 | 1995 | 1998 |
| 1989 | 91 | 1997 | 2001 |
| 1988 | 90 | 1993 | 1996 |

## LANGI SHIRAZ

RANKING **3**

Grampians $50+
Current vintage: 200?    94

Stylish, long term shiraz with a hint of mint and pepper beneath some complex, spicy, earthy aromas of dark berries, cherries and plums. Long, fine and focused, with an intense core of peppery dark fruits, becoming more meaty and savoury towards its lingering, spicy finish. It's tightly balanced, with well-integrated cedary oak, fine tannins and regional menthol/mint influences.

| 2000 | 94 | 2008 | 2020 |
|------|----|------|-------|
| 1999 | 88 | 2001 | 2004+ |
| 1998 | 90 | 2003 | 2006 |
| 1997 | 86 | 2002 | 2005 |
| 1996 | 94 | 2004 | 2008 |
| 1995 | 94 | 2003 | 2007 |
| 1994 | 97 | 2006 | 2014 |
| 1993 | 80 | 2001 | 2005 |
| 1992 | 93 | 2004 | 2012 |
| 1991 | 90 | 1999 | 2003 |
| 1990 | 93 | 2002 | 2010 |
| 1989 | 95 | 2001 | 2009 |
| 1988 | 91 | 1996 | 2000 |

## PINOT GRIS

RANKING **5**

| Grampians | $20–$29 |
|---|---|
| **Current vintage: 2003** | **90** |

Dusty, dry and genuinely varietal pinot gris with a delicate floral perfume of spices, citrus blossom, apple and pear. Forward and juicy, it's then long and smooth, finishing savoury, nutty and chalky.

| | | | |
|---|---|---|---|
| 2003 | 90 | 2004 | 2005+ |
| 2002 | 86 | 2003 | 2004+ |
| 2001 | 89 | 2001 | 2002+ |

## RIESLING

RANKING **3**

| Grampians | $20–$29 |
|---|---|
| **Current vintage: 2003** | **93** |

Germanic, cooler climate expression of perfumed, fragrant riesling with fresh aromas of lime juice, pear and apple over suggestions of stonefruit and spice. Long and smooth, silky and seamless, its sculpted palate of crisply defined pear, apple and peach flavours culminates in a refreshing citrusy finish.

| | | | |
|---|---|---|---|
| 2003 | 93 | 2008 | 2011 |
| 2002 | 93 | 2007 | 2010 |
| 2000 | 92 | 2005 | 2008 |
| 1999 | 80 | 2000 | 2001 |
| 1998 | 83 | 2000 | 2003 |
| 1997 | 82 | 1999 | 2002 |
| 1996 | 94 | 2004 | 2008 |
| 1995 | 94 | 2003 | 2007 |
| 1994 | 91 | 1999 | 2002 |
| 1993 | 94 | 1998 | 2001 |

# Mount Mary

Coldstream West Road, Lilydale Vic 3140. Tel: (03) 9739 1761. Fax: (03) 9739 0137.

Region: **Yarra Valley** Winemakers: **John Middleton & Rob Hall** Viticulturists: **John Middleton & Rob Hall** Chief Executive: **John Middleton**

Mount Mary is one of Australia's iconic vineyards. Its dryland vineyard is planted to a broad array of clones of its constituent varieties, from which a local selection has been made. Its yields are modest to very low, and its wines nurtured according to the very disciplined approach of John Middleton, who now has a significantly expanded winery to work within. I am an unashamed admirer of Middleton and his wines, whose string of excellent recent vintages have introduced a remarkable measure of consistency.

## CABERNET 'QUINTET'

RANKING **1**

| Yarra Valley | $50+ |
|---|---|
| **Current vintage: 2002** | **94** |

Very fine, elegant, cool-climate cabernet blend whose pristine fruit and finely handled oak integrate tightly with a satiny spine of fine-grained tannins. Its perfume of cassis and violets reveals a hint of dusty herbal influence, undergrowth and tightly measured cedar/dark chocolate oak. Smooth and stylish, it's pristine and silky, presenting exceptional length and brightness of fruit over lightly herbal and tobaccoey nuances of undergrowth and sweet oak.

| | | | |
|---|---|---|---|
| 2002 | 94 | 2014 | 2022 |
| 2001 | 97 | 2013 | 2021 |
| 2000 | 97 | 2012 | 2020+ |
| 1999 | 97 | 2011 | 2019 |
| 1998 | 97 | 2010 | 2018 |
| 1997 | 91 | 2002 | 2005+ |
| 1996 | 95 | 2004 | 2008+ |
| 1995 | 91 | 2007 | 2015 |
| 1994 | 96 | 2006 | 2014 |
| 1993 | 90 | 2001 | 2005 |
| 1992 | 95 | 2000 | 2004 |
| 1991 | 95 | 2009 | 2003 |
| 1990 | 97 | 2002 | 2010 |
| 1989 | 85 | 1994 | 1997 |
| 1988 | 97 | 2000 | 2008 |
| 1987 | 90 | 1995 | 1999 |
| 1986 | 95 | 1998 | 2006 |
| 1985 | 91 | 1997 | 2002 |
| 1984 | 95 | 2004 | 2014 |
| 1983 | 87 | 1991 | 1995 |

## CHARDONNAY

RANKING **2**

| Yarra Valley | $50+ |
|---|---|
| **Current vintage: 2003** | **96** |

Wonderfully balanced, smooth and composed chardonnay of seamless length and exceptional concentration. Its youthful aromas of tropical fruits, melon and white peach reveal underlying notes of chalk and minerals, with reserved oak influences and suggestions of cashew. Its long, sumptuous babyfat-like palate of sweet melon and tangy tangerine flavours culminates in a tight and harmonious finish with lingering mealy and nutmeg-like subtleties.

| | | | |
|---|---|---|---|
| 2003 | 96 | 2008 | 2011+ |
| 2002 | 95 | 2007 | 2010+ |
| 2001 | 96 | 2006 | 2009+ |
| 2000 | 95 | 2008 | 2012 |
| 1999 | 94 | 2004 | 2007 |
| 1998 | 92 | 2003 | 2006+ |
| 1997 | 90 | 2002 | 2005 |
| 1996 | 93 | 2004 | 2008 |
| 1995 | 92 | 2003 | 2007 |
| 1994 | 90 | 1997 | 2002 |
| 1993 | 90 | 1998 | 2001 |
| 1992 | 94 | 2000 | 2004 |
| 1991 | 95 | 1999 | 2003 |

## PINOT NOIR

**Yarra Valley** $50+
**Current vintage: 2002** 92

A pretty, floral and charming pinot with a fragrance of rose petals, strawberries and red cherries over nuances of cinnamon, cloves, herbal undertones and restrained vanilla oak. Sweet, smooth and juicy, its palate has some flesh and pleasing fine-grained support, presenting lively up-front and slightly confectionary flavours of cherry and berries. Fine and supple, with a herbal thread beneath, it's a delightful wine for shorter term cellaring.

| | | | |
|---|---|---|---|
| 2002 | 92 | 2004 | 2007+ |
| 2001 | 93 | 2006 | 2009 |
| 2000 | 97 | 2008 | 2012 |
| 1999 | 95 | 2007 | 2011 |
| 1998 | 89 | 2003 | 2006 |
| 1997 | 89 | 2002 | 2005+ |
| 1996 | 89 | 1998 | 2001 |
| 1995 | 88 | 2000 | 2003 |
| 1994 | 94 | 2002 | 2006 |
| 1993 | 88 | 1998 | 2001 |
| 1992 | 94 | 2000 | 2004 |
| 1991 | 93 | 1999 | 2003 |
| 1990 | 92 | 1995 | 1998 |
| 1989 | 95 | 1997 | 2001 |
| 1988 | 91 | 1996 | 2000 |

## TRIOLET

**Yarra Valley** $50+
**Current vintage: 2003** 95

A riper expression of this wine with a lightly herbal aroma of honeydew melon and lemon over grassy nuances of gooseberries and restrained vanilla oak. Smooth and juicy, it's exceptionally rich and concentrated, delivering an unctuous, long and textured palate underpinned by powdery phenolics. Delicious, but limited, with a faint suggestion of sweetness balanced by citrusy acids.

| | | | |
|---|---|---|---|
| 2003 | 95 | 2005 | 2008+ |
| 2002 | 95 | 2007 | 2010 |
| 2001 | 95 | 2006 | 2009 |
| 2000 | 95 | 2005 | 2008 |
| 1999 | 94 | 2004 | 2007 |
| 1998 | 95 | 2003 | 2006+ |
| 1997 | 92 | 2002 | 2005 |
| 1996 | 95 | 2001 | 2004 |
| 1995 | 95 | 2000 | 2003 |
| 1994 | 93 | 1999 | 2002 |
| 1993 | 95 | 1995 | 1998 |
| 1992 | 95 | 1997 | 2000+ |
| 1991 | 94 | 1996 | 1999 |
| 1990 | 94 | 1998 | 2002 |

# Mount Pleasant

Marrowbone Road, Pokolbin NSW 2321. Tel: (02) 4998 7505. Fax: (02) 4998 7761.
Website: www.mcwilliams.com.au Email: mcwines@mcwillliams.com.au
Region: **Lower Hunter Valley** Winemaker: **Phillip Ryan** Viticulturist: **Graham Doran**
Chief Executive: **Kevin McLintock**

Mount Pleasant is the McWilliams family's beachhead in the Hunter Valley, and home to a stable of classic, traditional wines made from ancient and historic vineyards. Its efforts with semillon under the Elizabeth and Lovedale labels are the stuff of legend, while the rustic, earthy and typically regional reds from the OP & OH and Rosehill Vineyards can be spectacular. The label's best current red is the rich and chocolatey Maurice O'Shea Shiraz, named after Mount Pleasant's first and most famous winemaker.

## ELIZABETH (Semillon)

**Lower Hunter Valley** $12–$19
**Current vintage: 2002** 95

Classic Hunter semillon with a delicate, but pristine aroma of honeydew melon, lemon and tobacco leaf. Long, smooth and polished, it's perhaps more concentrated that usual, delivering a refined, if slightly soapy palate of lingering fruit and dusty, herbal nuances. Very restrained, fine and elegant, likely to develop great complexity.

| | | | |
|---|---|---|---|
| 2002 | 95 | 2010 | 2014+ |
| 2001 | 89 | 2006 | 2009 |
| 2000 | 90 | 2005 | 2008+ |
| 1999 | 88 | 2001 | 2004+ |
| 1998 | 90 | 2003 | 2006+ |
| 1997 | 93 | 2005 | 2009 |
| 1996 | 95 | 2008 | 2016 |
| 1995 | 93 | 2003 | 2007+ |
| 1994 | 95 | 2006 | 2014 |
| 1993 | 93 | 2001 | 2005 |
| 1992 | 87 | 2000 | 2004 |
| 1991 | 88 | 1993 | 1996 |
| 1990 | 87 | 1995 | 1998 |
| 1989 | 93 | 2001 | 2009 |
| 1988 | 88 | 1990 | 1993 |
| 1987 | 91 | 1995 | 1999+ |
| 1986 | 95 | 1998 | 2006+ |

# HUNTER VALLEY CHARDONNAY

RANKING **5**

**Lower Hunter Valley** $12–$19
**Current vintage: 2003** 88

Elegant, uncluttered, tight and shapely chardonnay with lightly smoky aromas of fresh melon and buttery vanilla oak. Generous, juicy flavours of peach and melon with tobaccoey undertones deliver freshness and fruit along a slightly grippy palate.

| | | | |
|---|---|---|---|
| 2003 | 88 | 2005 | 2008 |
| 2002 | 87 | 2002 | 2003 |
| 2001 | 89 | 2003 | 2006 |
| 2000 | 87 | 2002 | 2005 |
| 1999 | 89 | 2001 | 2004 |
| 1997 | 88 | 1999 | 2002 |
| 1996 | 90 | 2001 | 2004 |
| 1995 | 87 | 2000 | 2003 |
| 1994 | 85 | 1996 | 1999 |

# HUNTER VALLEY MERLOT

RANKING **5**

**Lower Hunter Valley** $12–$19
**Current vintage: 2002** 86

Very rustic, horsey and farmyard-like merlot whose sweaty, leathery aromas of plums, cherries and cedary oak precede a very evolved mid-weight palate framed by firm metallic tannins. There's plenty of sour-edged plum/cherry flavour, but it's very old-fashioned, astringent and hard-edged.

| | | | |
|---|---|---|---|
| 2002 | 86 | 2004 | 2007+ |
| 2001 | 89 | 2006 | 2009 |
| 2000 | 89 | 2002 | 2005+ |
| 1999 | 89 | 2001 | 2004+ |
| 1998 | 86 | 2000 | 2003 |
| 1997 | 82 | 1999 | 2002 |
| 1996 | 89 | 1998 | 2001 |

# LOVEDALE SEMILLON

RANKING **2**

**Lower Hunter Valley** $50+
**Current vintage: 1998** 95

Classic Hunter semillon with a developing bouquet of lightly smoky, creamy toasty baby powder-like aromas of fresh honeydew melon and lemon. Delightfully vibrant and pure in its concentrated and silky-smooth expression of citrus fruit, beneath which runs a fine-grained thread of powdery, talcum-like phenolics. Finishes long, with an almost Chablis-like tartness, but building in concentration and intensity.

| | | | |
|---|---|---|---|
| 2003 | 95 | 2015 | 2023 |
| 2000 | 89 | 2005 | 2008+ |
| 1998 | 95 | 2010 | 2018 |
| 1997 | 91 | 2005 | 2009+ |
| 1996 | 96 | 2008 | 2016 |
| 1995 | 90 | 2007 | 2015 |
| 1986 | 95 | 1998 | 2006+ |
| 1984 | 96 | 1996 | 2004 |
| 1979 | 94 | 1991 | 1999+ |

# MAURICE O'SHEA SHIRAZ

RANKING **3**

**Lower Hunter Valley** $30–$49
**Current vintage: 2000** 94

Impressive, if slightly stressed Hunter shiraz whose opulent, smoky aromas of violets, cassis, prunes, currants and sweet mocha/chocolate barrel fermentation influences reveal undertones of spices and licorice. Moderately full in weight, delivering an impressively concentrated palate dripping with small dark berry/currant flavours and some more dehydrated characters, it's smooth, polished and persistent. Likely to cellar well.

| | | | |
|---|---|---|---|
| 2000 | 94 | 2012 | 2020 |
| 1999 | 92 | 2007 | 2011 |
| 1998 | 93 | 2006 | 2010+ |
| 1997 | 91 | 2005 | 2009 |
| 1996 | 88 | 2001 | 2004+ |
| 1994 | 88 | 2002 | 2006 |
| 1993 | 91 | 1998 | 2001 |

# OLD PADDOCK & OLD HILL SHIRAZ

RANKING **4**

**Lower Hunter Valley** $30–$49
**Current vintage: 2002** 90

Rustic, evolved and old-fashioned Australian burgundy style with musky aromas of Chesterfield leather, suede and meaty reduction. Charmingly complex and earthy, its farmyard-like cherry/plum fruit is framed by hard-edged and surprisingly assertive tannins. There's more than a hint of reduction and horsey complexity about this wine, which is less likely to please the technocrats than the aesthetes.

| | | | |
|---|---|---|---|
| 2002 | 90 | 2010 | 2014 |
| 2001 | 89 | 2009 | 2013+ |
| 1999 | 89 | 2004 | 2007 |
| 1998 | 94 | 2006 | 2010+ |
| 1997 | 88 | 2002 | 2005 |
| 1996 | 92 | 2004 | 2008+ |
| 1995 | 90 | 2003 | 2007 |

### PHILIP (Shiraz)

| Lower Hunter Valley | $12–$19 |
|---|---|
| Current vintage: 2000 | 85 |

Dry, leathery and old-fashioned shiraz made from slightly cooked and confectionary red berry fruit. Relatively simple, with a reasonable length of fruit sweetness, it dries out to finish rather thin in fruit but moderately firm and leathery.

| 2000 | 85 | 2005 | 2008 |
|---|---|---|---|
| 1999 | 88 | 2004 | 2007 |
| 1998 | 83 | 2003 | 2006 |
| 1997 | 82 | 1999 | 2002 |
| 1996 | 84 | 1998 | 2001 |
| 1995 | 88 | 2000 | 2003 |
| 1994 | 83 | 1999 | 2002 |
| 1993 | 77 | 1995 | 1998 |

### ROSEHILL SHIRAZ

RANKING 3

| Lower Hunter Valley | $20–$29 |
|---|---|
| Current vintage: 2000 | 84 |

Earthy, simple, slightly under-ripe and confected aromas of raspberries and cassis are supported by sweet mocha/vanilla oak. Some lively forward raspberry/cassis/plum fruit then thins out as the palate becomes fragile and ethereal, leaving a green-edged finish supported by sweet oak.

| 2000 | 84 | 2005 | 2008 |
|---|---|---|---|
| 1999 | 91 | 2004 | 2007+ |
| 1998 | 93 | 2006 | 2010+ |
| 1997 | 93 | 2002 | 2005 |
| 1996 | 93 | 2004 | 2008 |
| 1995 | 84 | 1997 | 2000 |
| 1991 | 91 | 1996 | 1999 |
| 1990 | 80 | 1992 | 1995 |

# Mountadam

High Eden Road, Eden Valley SA 5235. Tel: (08) 8564 1900 Fax: (08) 8564 1999
Website: www.mountadam.com  Email: office@mountadam.com

Region: **Eden Valley**  Winemakers: **Andrew Ewart, Tim Heath**  Viticulturist: **Mary Retallack**
General Manager: **Tony Jordan**

Owned by Cape Mentelle, Mountadam is potentially one of the finest wine producers in South Australia. Blessed with a mature vineyard and a winery that still looks innovative more than two decades after its completion, Mountadam's challenge is to get its vineyard delivering fruit of genuine physiological ripeness. Until it does, its wines will always be on the back foot. Now that Cape Mentelle has bought the place and Tony Jordan is faced with the challenge, I reckon it has its best chance to fulfil its potential for seval years.

### CABERNET SAUVIGNON

RANKING 5

| Eden Valley | $30–$49 |
|---|---|
| Current vintage: 1998 | 84 |

Confectionary flavours of raspberries and cherries with some creamy, musky complexity precede a green-edged and hollow palate of mulberry/raspberry fruit that finishes with a sappy cut of tannin.

| 1998 | 84 | 2003 | 2006 |
|---|---|---|---|
| 1997 | 83 | 1999 | 2002+ |
| 1996 | 86 | 1998 | 2001 |
| 1995 | 92 | 2000 | 2003 |
| 1994 | 91 | 2002 | 2006 |

### CHARDONNAY

RANKING 5

| Eden Valley | $30–$49 |
|---|---|
| Current vintage: 2002 | 87 |

Toasty, buttery aromas of peaches and nectarines reveal tobaccoey and nutty undertones. Very toasty and unusually viscous, its nutty, savoury palate lacks fruit freshness. Rather coarse and hot, it's entwined with hessian-like oak, before finishing hot and spirity.

| 2002 | 87 | 2004 | 2007 |
|---|---|---|---|
| 2001 | 77 | 2002 | 2003 |
| 2000 | 86 | 2002 | 2005 |
| 1999 | 87 | 2001 | 2004 |
| 1998 | 87 | 2000 | 2003+ |
| 1997 | 80 | 1999 | 2002 |
| 1996 | 86 | 1998 | 2001 |
| 1995 | 87 | 1997 | 2000 |
| 1994 | 94 | 1999 | 2002 |
| 1993 | 88 | 1998 | 2001 |
| 1992 | 91 | 1995 | 2000 |
| 1991 | 93 | 1996 | 1999 |
| 1990 | 92 | 1998 | 2002 |
| 1989 | 91 | 1994 | 1997 |

# PINOT NOIR

| Eden Valley | $30–$49 |
|---|---|
| **Current vintage: 2002** | **89** |

Meaty, youthful pinot with a spicy, rose petal perfume of maraschino cherries and red plums before a soft, stalky palate of medium weight and some grip. Likely to build in the bottle, acquiring a good depth of varietal flavour.

| 2002 | 89 | 2004 | 2007+ |
|---|---|---|---|
| 2001 | 86 | 2006 | 2009 |
| 1999 | 89 | 2004 | 2007 |
| 1998 | 92 | 2003 | 2006 |
| 1997 | 87 | 2002 | 2005 |
| 1996 | 87 | 2004 | 2008 |
| 1995 | 87 | 2000 | 2003 |
| 1994 | 89 | 1999 | 2002 |
| 1993 | 90 | 2001 | 2005 |
| 1992 | 89 | 1997 | 2000 |
| 1991 | 93 | 1999 | 2002 |

# PINOT NOIR CHARDONNAY

| Eden Valley | $30–$49 |
|---|---|
| **Current vintage: 1998** | **82** |

A little too far on the wild side for mine, this interesting, but almost feral expression of savoury, meaty sparkling wine combines bright, lolly-like and creamy berry fruits with profoundly complex lees-derived influences. Very dry, with fine, soft acids.

| 1998 | 82 | 2000 | 2003 |
|---|---|---|---|
| 1994 | 77 | 1996 | 1999 |
| 1992 | 94 | 1997 | 2000 |
| 1991 | 93 | 1996 | 1999 |
| 1990 | 94 | 1995 | 1998 |

# DW SHIRAZ (Formerly Patriarch)

| Eden Valley | $30–$49 |
|---|---|
| **Current vintage: 2001** | **91** |

A closed, withdrawn, but quite robust shiraz that should flesh out well given time in the bottle. Slightly dull aromas of dark cherries, plums and licorice precede a moderately full palate whose super-ripe flavours of currants and raisins are lifted by more vibrant red and black berry qualities, plus some sweet chocolate and vanilla oak.

| 2001 | 91 | 2009 | 2013+ |
|---|---|---|---|
| 1999 | 85 | 2001 | 2004 |
| 1998 | 92 | 2006 | 2010 |
| 1997 | 88 | 2002 | 2005 |
| 1996 | 88 | 2004 | 2008 |
| 1995 | 94 | 2003 | 2007 |
| 1994 | 92 | 1999 | 2002 |
| 1993 | 92 | 2001 | 2005 |
| 1992 | 91 | 2002 | 2004 |
| 1991 | 94 | 1999 | 2003 |
| 1990 | 92 | 1998 | 2002 |

# THE RED

| Eden Valley | $30–$49 |
|---|---|
| **Current vintage: 1999** | **83** |

Both cooked and under-ripe, this earthy, leathery and advancing red presents green-edged plums and dark berry flavours and very cedary, pencil-shavings-like oak aromas. Moderately long, its meaty palate of herbal fruit is framed by raw, sappy, tannins.

| 1999 | 83 | 2004 | 2007 |
|---|---|---|---|
| 1998 | 87 | 2003 | 2006 |
| 1997 | 82 | 1999 | 2002+ |
| 1996 | 86 | 2001 | 2004 |
| 1995 | 90 | 2000 | 2003 |
| 1994 | 94 | 2006 | 2014 |
| 1992 | 89 | 2000 | 2004 |
| 1990 | 93 | 1995 | 1998 |
| 1989 | 87 | 1994 | 1997 |
| 1988 | 90 | 1996 | 2000 |

# Murrindindi

Cummins Lane, Murrindindi Vic 3717. Tel: (03) 5797 8217. Fax: (03) 5797 8422.
Region: **Yea Valley** Winemaker: **Hugh Cuthbertson** Viticulturist: **Alan Cuthbertson**
Chief Executive: **Janet Cuthbertson**

Located in the Yea Valley of central Victoria, Murrindindi is a small vineyard devoted to the making of Bordeaux-influenced reds and a traditionally-made Chardonnay. Its red wines have reflected a lack of genuine ripeness in recent seasons, while the Chardonnay delivers pleasing complexity and texture.

## CABERNET MERLOT
RANKING **5**

**Yea Valley**      $20–$29
**Current vintage: 2002**      83

Leafy capsicum and snow-pea aromas of light cassis and cherry fruit supported by restrained vanilla oak, with a forward, but hollow and sappy palate whose under-ripe fruit finishes long, but lean and greenish.

| | | | |
|---|---|---|---|
| 2002 | 83 | 2004 | 2007 |
| 1998 | 85 | 2003 | 2006 |
| 1997 | 80 | 1999 | 2002 |
| 1995 | 93 | 2003 | 2007 |
| 1994 | 90 | 2002 | 2006 |
| 1992 | 83 | 1994 | 1997 |
| 1985 | 84 | 1993 | 1997 |

## CHARDONNAY
RANKING **4**

**Yea Valley**      $20–$29
**Current vintage: 2001**      89

Drink-now style of chardonnay with pleasing toasty, buttery and honeyed complexity. Its nutty, fig-like aromas of dried flowers are lifted by lightly smoky oak, while its soft, creamy palate overlies fine, chalky phenolics.

| | | | |
|---|---|---|---|
| 2001 | 89 | 2003 | 2006 |
| 2000 | 91 | 2002 | 2005+ |
| 1999 | 87 | 2001 | 2004 |
| 1998 | 89 | 2003 | 2006 |
| 1997 | 94 | 2002 | 2005+ |
| 1996 | 90 | 2001 | 2004 |
| 1994 | 90 | 1999 | 2002 |

# Nepenthe

Jones Road, Balhannah SA 5242. Tel: (08) 8388 4439. Fax: (08) 8398 0488.
Website: www.nepenthe.com.au  Email: paul@nepenthe.com.au
Region: **Adelaide Hills** Winemakers: **Peter Leske, Matt Wenk** Viticulturist: **Murray Leake**
Chief Executive: **James Tweddell**

Nepenthe is a significant Adelaide Hills producer whose amusingly esoteric range of wines are steadily improving in direct reflection of the increasing age of the vineyards that supply them. The heat experienced in 2000 and 2001 clearly affected the quality of several wines, while 2002 appears to have been the company's best season to date.

## CHARDONNAY
RANKING **5**

**Adelaide Hills**      $20–$29
**Current vintage: 2002**      87

Early-drinking, lively and uncomplicated chardonnay with a fragrant, if slightly green-edged perfume of tropical fruits and creamy, leesy and oak-derived complexity. Juicy and slightly syrupy, its forward palate of tropical fruits, lime and green cashew flavours finishes a little short and punctuated by slightly sappy acids.

| | | | |
|---|---|---|---|
| 2002 | 87 | 2003 | 2004 |
| 2000 | 86 | 2002 | 2005 |
| 1999 | 88 | 2001 | 2004+ |
| 1998 | 90 | 2000 | 2003 |
| 1997 | 87 | 1998 | 1999 |

## LENSWOOD ZINFANDEL
RANKING **5**

**Adelaide Hills**      $30–$49
**Current vintage: 2001**      89

Jammy, briary rose garden and earthy aromas of raspberries and red plums, before a rich, long and smooth palate of meaty ripeness. Its earthy, leathery and plummy fruit is framed by firm, very fine astringency, leaving a finish of refreshing acids and lingering tarry licorice flavours. Advanced, but genuinely varietal.

| | | | |
|---|---|---|---|
| 2001 | 89 | 2003 | 2006+ |
| 2000 | 76 | 2002 | 2005 |
| 1999 | 91 | 2004 | 2007 |
| 1998 | 81 | 2000 | 2003 |
| 1997 | 87 | 1999 | 2002+ |

**THE AUSTRALIAN WINE ANNUAL**
www.onwine.com.au
**2005**

# PINOT GRIS

RANKING 5

| Adelaide Hills | $20–$29 |
|---|---|
| **Current vintage: 2003** | **88** |

Attractive pinot gris whose dusty lemon rind and floral aromas of honeydew melon, stonefruits and cashews precede a long and elegant palate of brightness and focused nutty, dusty and citrusy fruit finishing lingering, herb-edged and savoury.

| | | | |
|---|---|---|---|
| 2003 | 88 | 2004 | 2005+ |
| 2002 | 92 | 2003 | 2004+ |
| 2001 | 77 | 2001 | 2002 |
| 2000 | 82 | 2000 | 2001 |

# PINOT NOIR

RANKING 5

| Adelaide Hills | $20–$29 |
|---|---|
| **Current vintage: 2002** | **89** |

Slightly confection-like pinot of village Burgundy-like quality with a floral, slightly cooked aroma of sweet, spicy plums, maraschino cherries and vanilla oak. The palate is lively, minty and brightly flavoured with jam-like sweet berries and cherries, drying out to a fine-grained, firm finish.

| | | | |
|---|---|---|---|
| 2002 | 89 | 2004 | 2007 |
| 2001 | 86 | 2003 | 2006 |
| 2000 | 86 | 2002 | 2005 |
| 1999 | 87 | 2001 | 2004+ |
| 1998 | 88 | 2000 | 2003+ |
| 1997 | 81 | 1998 | 1999 |

# SAUVIGNON BLANC

RANKING 4

| Adelaide Hills | $20–$29 |
|---|---|
| **Current vintage: 2003** | **91** |

Its penetrative, complex and slightly sweaty varietal aromas of cut grass, capsicum, passionfruit, gooseberries and cassis precede a juicy and forward palate that becomes attractively tight and sculpted, finishing with good length, mineral acids and lingering fruit flavour.

| | | | |
|---|---|---|---|
| 2003 | 91 | 2004 | 2005 |
| 2002 | 91 | 2002 | 2003+ |
| 2001 | 91 | 2002 | 2003 |
| 2000 | 87 | 2001 | 2002 |
| 1999 | 94 | 2000 | 2001 |
| 1998 | 92 | 1999 | 2000+ |
| 1997 | 92 | 1997 | 1998 |

# SEMILLON

RANKING 5

| Adelaide Hills | $20–$29 |
|---|---|
| **Current vintage: 2001** | **87** |

Rather oaky, with assertive toasty and vanilla wood-derived aromas over attractive scents of mineral and lemon sherbet. Clean and fresh, its classy citrus/melon fruit is somewhat subdued by its sweet vanilla oak, which tends to shorten the palate.

| | | | |
|---|---|---|---|
| 2001 | 87 | 2003 | 2006 |
| 2000 | 82 | 2002 | 2005 |
| 1999 | 87 | 2000 | 2001 |
| 1998 | 87 | 2000 | 2003 |
| 1997 | 83 | 1998 | 1999 |

# THE FUGUE (Cabernet Sauvignon, Merlot, Cabernet Franc)

RANKING 4

| Adelaide Hills | $20–$29 |
|---|---|
| **Current vintage: 2000** | **85** |

Reveals both under and over-ripe characters, with meaty, pruney and chocolatey aromas and herbal undertones. Its jammy forward fruits lack real impact and intensity, while the finish is meaty, sappy and green-edged.

| | | | |
|---|---|---|---|
| 2000 | 85 | 2005 | 2008 |
| 1999 | 90 | 2007 | 2011 |
| 1998 | 89 | 2003 | 2006 |
| 1997 | 93 | 2005 | 2009 |

# THE ROGUE (Cabernet Merlot Shiraz)

RANKING 5

| Adelaide Hills | $20–$29 |
|---|---|
| **Current vintage: 2002** | **82** |

Spicy, dusty and capsicum-like aromas of white pepper and vegetable soup over a light expression of red berry fruit precede a forward, but rather minty and oak-dominated palate. Light, bright flavours of sweet red and black berries offer some vitality, but finish a little thin and green-edged.

| | | | |
|---|---|---|---|
| 2002 | 82 | 2004 | 2007 |
| 2001 | 90 | 2006 | 2009+ |
| 2000 | 88 | 2002 | 2005+ |

# Ninth Island

1216 Pipers Brook Road, Pipers Brook Tas 7252. Tel: (03) 6382 7527. Fax: (03) 6382 7226.
Website: www.pipersbrook.com  Email: enquiries@pipersbrook.com
Regions: **Pipers River, Tamar River**  Winemaker: **Rene Bezemer**
Viticulturist: **Bruce McCormack**  Managing Director: **Paul de Moor**

Sourced from several Tasmanian regions, Ninth Island is Pipers Brook's second label, typically offering a range of delightfully up-front early-drinking table wines of brightness and vitality.

## CHARDONNAY

| Pipers River, Tamar River | $12–$19 |
|---|---|
| **Current vintage: 2003** | **83** |

Light, but honest cool climate chardonnay, this fruit-driven wine has a lightly sweaty, candied aroma of green-edged tropical fruit, plus a forward palate of juicy stonefruit, apple and pear flavours. It's a little short, with some greenish acidity.

| | | | |
|---|---|---|---|
| 2003 | 83 | 2004 | 2005+ |
| 2002 | 82 | 2002 | 2003 |
| 2001 | 83 | 2002 | 2003 |
| 2000 | 89 | 2001 | 2002 |
| 1999 | 85 | 2000 | 2001 |

## PINOT NOIR

RANKING **5**

| Pipers River, Tamar River | $20–$29 |
|---|---|
| **Current vintage: 2003** | **87** |

Pleasing, fruity pinot with a slightly cooked and prune-like aroma of ripe cherries and plums, with a surprisingly rich and generous palate whose core of ripe fruit is underpinned by some firm, integrated tannin.

| | | | |
|---|---|---|---|
| 2003 | 87 | 2004 | 2005+ |
| 2001 | 89 | 2002 | 2003 |
| 2000 | 89 | 2001 | 2002 |
| 1999 | 87 | 2000 | 2001+ |
| 1998 | 88 | 2000 | 2003 |

## SAUVIGNON BLANC

| Pipers River, Tamar River | $12–$19 |
|---|---|
| **Current vintage: 2003** | **83** |

Pungent, lightly sweaty and vegetal aromas of gooseberries, green cashews and cassis precede a juicy, nutty, green-edged and generous palate whose oily texture just lacks great length, finishing a little thin and short.

| | | | |
|---|---|---|---|
| 2003 | 83 | 2003 | 2004 |
| 2002 | 84 | 2002 | 2003 |
| 2001 | 83 | 2001 | 2002 |
| 2000 | 92 | 2001 | 2002 |
| 1999 | 80 | 2000 | 2001 |
| 1998 | 84 | 1999 | 2000 |

# Normans

Xanadu Adelaide Hills, Grants Gully Road, Clarendon SA 5157. Tel: (08) 8383 5555. Fax: (08) 8383 5551.
Website: www.xanadunormans.com.  Email: info@xanadunormans.com.
Region: **Various**  Winemakers: **Natasha Mooney, Joel Tilbrook**  Viticulturists: **Graeme Dun, Bruce Phillips**
Chief Executive: **Sam Atkins**

Normans has been bought by the aggressively expanding but lately troubled Xanadu Wines. Its new owners will maintain the labels listed in this guide, plus the competitively-priced Encounter Bay brand. Gotta be honest — quality ain't what it used to be. But then again, neither are the prices...

## CHAIS CLARENDON CABERNET SAUVIGNON

RANKING **4**

| McLaren Vale | $30–$49 |
|---|---|
| **Current vintage: 2002** | **89** |

An honest, flavoursome cabernet with an elegant, fine-grained structure, but without the complexity of higher rating wines. Its slightly greenish, stressed aromas of sweet cassis, raspberries and plums are entwined with sweet mocha oak, nuances of mint and eucalypt. There's length and clarity on the palate, with vibrant berry fruits neatly meshed with creamy mocha oak.

| | | | |
|---|---|---|---|
| 2002 | 89 | 2007 | 2010+ |
| 1999 | 83 | 2001 | 2004 |
| 1998 | 91 | 2006 | 2010 |
| 1996 | 88 | 2004 | 2008 |
| 1995 | 86 | 1997 | 2000 |
| 1994 | 93 | 2000 | 2006 |
| 1992 | 90 | 2000 | 2004 |
| 1991 | 94 | 2003 | 2011 |
| 1990 | 93 | 2002 | 2010 |
| 1989 | 93 | 1997 | 2001 |

## CHAIS CLARENDON SHIRAZ

RANKING 3

| | McLaren Vale | $30–$49 |
|---|---|---|
| | **Current vintage: 2002** | **88** |

Uncomplicated, smooth, willowy and pretty early-drinking lighter expression of shiraz with a floral perfume of lively blackcurrant, plum and raspberry fruit plus minty undertones of cloves and vanilla oak. Supple and elegant, revealing pristine, but delicate berry fruits, it's framed by silky fine tannins, finishing savoury and very slightly salty.

| | | | |
|---|---|---|---|
| 2002 | 88 | 2004 | 2007 |
| 2001 | 90 | 2009 | 2013 |
| 1999 | 93 | 2007 | 2011 |
| 1998 | 94 | 2006 | 2010 |
| 1997 | 89 | 1999 | 2002 |
| 1996 | 90 | 2001 | 2004 |
| 1995 | 93 | 2003 | 2007 |
| 1994 | 89 | 1999 | 2002 |
| 1992 | 90 | 1997 | 2000 |
| 1991 | 93 | 1999 | 2003 |
| 1990 | 93 | 2002 | 2010 |
| 1989 | 93 | 1997 | 2001 |
| 1988 | 94 | 2000 | 2008 |

## LANGHORNE CREEK CABERNET BLEND

RANKING 5

| | Langhorne Creek | $20–$29 |
|---|---|---|
| | **Current vintage: 1999** | **86** |

Forward, rather basic and ageing cabernet with minty, medicinal aromas of blackberry fruit with nutty, cedary oak. Its generous, but tiring palate of confectionary berry fruit is losing brightness, leaving a minty/menthol finish of slightly raw tannins.

| | | | |
|---|---|---|---|
| 1999 | 86 | 2004 | 2007 |
| 1998 | 94 | 2006 | 2010 |
| 1997 | 87 | 1999 | 2002 |
| 1996 | 84 | 2001 | 2004 |

# Oakridge

864 Maroondah Highway, Coldstream Vic 3770. Tel: (03) 9739 1920. Fax: (03) 9739 1923.
Website: www.oakridgeestate.com.au Email: info@oakridgeestate.com.au
Region: **Yarra Valley** Winemaker: **David Bicknell** Viticulturist: **Steve Sadlier** Chief Executive: **Franklin Tate**
Oakridge began as a small vineyard high above Seville in the higher reaches of the Yarra Valley, where it made some truly spectacular cabernets and blends. The Zitzlaff family then floated the company, sold the farm and moved to another, larger and more visible site on the Maroondah Highway. The concept failed to catch on, and the business was bought by Evans & Tate. So, with only the name remaining from the initial idea, Oakridge is today a thoroughly competent, if perhaps unspectacular maker of Yarra Valley table wine.

## CABERNET MERLOT

RANKING 5

| | Yarra Valley | $20–$29 |
|---|---|---|
| | **Current vintage: 2001** | **86** |

Smooth, early-drinking blend with lightly, earthy and cedary aromas of plums and dark berries. Framed by soft tannins, its confection-like expression of raspberry and plum flavours offers some fruit sweetness and suppleness, finishing earthy and herbal.

| | | | |
|---|---|---|---|
| 2001 | 86 | 2003 | 2006 |
| 2000 | 89 | 2005 | 2008 |
| 1999 | 87 | 2001 | 2004 |
| 1998 | 87 | 2000 | 2003 |
| 1997 | 84 | 2002 | 2005 |
| 1995 | 87 | 1997 | 2000 |
| 1994 | 82 | 1996 | 1999 |
| 1993 | 87 | 1998 | 2001 |
| 1992 | 93 | 2000 | 2004 |

## CABERNET SAUVIGNON (formerly Reserve)

RANKING 4

| | Yarra Valley | $30–$49 |
|---|---|---|
| | **Current vintage: 2001** | **86** |

Light, simple and confectionary aromas of red berries and light cedary oak with herbal undertones. Simple, forward and cedary, with some juiciness and sweetness before a greenish, slightly raw finish.

| | | | |
|---|---|---|---|
| 2001 | 86 | 2003 | 2006 |
| 2000 | 90 | 2008 | 2012+ |
| 1999 | 93 | 2007 | 2011+ |
| 1997 | 88 | 2005 | 2009+ |
| 1995 | 89 | 2000 | 2003+ |
| 1994 | 93 | 2002 | 2006 |
| 1991 | 96 | 2003 | 2011 |
| 1990 | 94 | 2002 | 2010 |
| 1987 | 82 | 1992 | 1995 |
| 1986 | 94 | 1994 | 1998 |

## CHARDONNAY

**Yarra Valley**      $20–$29
**Current vintage: 2003**     89

Elegant, creamy chardonnay with a restrained and lightly smoky aroma of melon, peach and tropical fruits. With a bright core of vibrant flavour, its smooth, lively palate of tightly integrated grapefruit, melon and creamy oak finishes fresh and lemony.

| 2003 | 89 | 2005 | 2008 |
|------|----|------|------|
| 2002 | 92 | 2007 | 2010 |
| 1999 | 82 | 2001 | 2004 |
| 1998 | 89 | 2003 | 2006 |
| 1997 | 93 | 2002 | 2005 |
| 1996 | 94 | 2001 | 2004 |
| 1995 | 85 | 1997 | 2000 |
| 1994 | 87 | 1996 | 1999 |

## PINOT NOIR

RANKING 5

**Yarra Valley**      $20–$29
**Current vintage: 2003**     89

Candied, floral aromas of red cherries, raspberries and light vanilla oak precede a juicy, fleshy palate with a pleasing core of intense cherry flavour. Fine and supple, framed by smooth, creamy tannins, and likely to flesh out over time.

| 2003 | 89 | 2005 | 2008 |
|------|----|------|------|
| 2002 | 80 | 2004 | 2007 |
| 2000 | 87 | 2002 | 2005 |
| 1999 | 81 | 2000 | 2001 |
| 1998 | 82 | 1999 | 2000 |
| 1997 | 89 | 1999 | 2002+ |

## SHIRAZ

**Yarra Valley**      $20–$29
**Current vintage: 2002**     86

Up-front, spicy and oaky, with a peppery aroma of raspberries, plums, cherries and aromatic vanilla oak. Medium to full-bodied, its palate begins with sweet berry fruit, but becomes lean and sappy, finishing with green edged-tannins and sweet oak.

| 2002 | 86 | 2004 | 2007 |
|------|----|------|------|
| 2000 | 81 | 2002 | 2005 |
| 1999 | 83 | 2001 | 2004 |
| 1998 | 89 | 2003 | 2006 |

# Omrah

Albany Highway, Mount Barker WA 6324. Tel: (08) 9851 2150. Fax: (08) 9851 1839.
Website: www.plantagenetwines.com  Email: sales@plantagenetwines.com
Region: **Great Southern**  Winemakers: **Richard Robson**  Viticulturists: **Roger Pattenden, Peter Glen**
Omrah is the highly-rated second label of Plantagenet, one of the Great Southern's leading wineries. Its Shiraz offers plenty of peppery, spicy dark fruit and richness, while the Sauvignon Blanc is vibrant, herby and tropical.

## SAUVIGNON BLANC

RANKING 5

**Great Southern**      $12–$19
**Current vintage: 2003**     91

Punchy, ripe sauvignon blanc with a lightly soapy, grassy fragrance of asparagus, gooseberries and passionfruit. Its concentrated and slippery palate of intense tropical and berry fruits culminates in an austere, steely finish. Just a little phenolic and grippy for a higher score.

| 2003 | 91 | 2003 | 2004+ |
|------|----|------|-------|
| 2002 | 88 | 2003 | 2004 |
| 2000 | 86 | 2001 | 2002 |
| 1999 | 77 | 1999 | 2000 |

## SHIRAZ

RANKING 5

**Great Southern**      $12–$19
**Current vintage: 2002**     89

Honest, varietal shiraz of genuine flavour and value. Its lightly earthy, meaty bouquet of spicy plums and its sappy palate of blackberry/plum fruit do suggest a lightly herbal thread, but offer plenty of flavour and Rhône-like character. There's plenty of spiciness, richness and generosity.

| 2002 | 89 | 2004 | 2007+ |
|------|----|------|-------|
| 2001 | 87 | 2003 | 2006 |
| 2000 | 89 | 2001 | 2002+ |
| 1999 | 90 | 2001 | 2004 |
| 1998 | 82 | 2000 | 2003 |

## UNOAKED CHARDONNAY

| Great Southern | $12–$19 | 2003 | 88 | 2004 | 2005 |
|---|---|---|---|---|---|
| **Current vintage: 2003** | **88** | 2002 | 88 | 2003 | 2004 |
| | | 2001 | 84 | 2001 | 2002 |
| | | 2000 | 87 | 2001 | 2002 |

Floral, tropical and lightly sweaty aromas of ripe, punchy melon, citrus and mango aromas with some grassy undertones, before a round, sweet and juicy palate that culminates in a soft refreshing finish of citrus and melon fruit.

# Orlando

Barossa Valley Way Rowland Flat SA 5352. Tel: (08) 8521 3111. Fax: (08) 8521 3100.
Website: www.orlandowyndhamgroup.com Email: contact_us@orlando.com.au
Region: **South Australia** Winemakers: **Philip Laffer, Sam Kurtz, Bernie Hickin** Viticulturist: **Joy Dick**
Chief Executive: **Laurent Lacassgne**

You don't see too many wines bearing an Orlando label, yet when you do, they're usually worth buying. The Saints range is as thorough and professional as you'll see in the mid to upper end of the market, consistently producing Riesling, Chardonnay and Cabernet Sauvignon significantly better than their prices would suggest. At the top end lie several labels including the Lawson's Shiraz, Centenary Hill Shiraz, Jacaranda Ridge Cabernet Sauvignon and Steingarten Riesling, each of which compete with consummate ease against more assumptively priced wines from makers large and small.

## CENTENARY HILL SHIRAZ

| Barossa Valley | $50+ | 1997 | 87 | 2002 | 2005+ |
|---|---|---|---|---|---|
| **Current vintage: 1997** | **87** | 1996 | 94 | 2008 | 2016 |
| | | 1995 | 94 | 2003 | 2007 |
| | | 1994 | 96 | 2006 | 2014+ |

Earthy, minty and slightly medicinal aromas of cooked plums and cassis with vanilla/chocolate oak and a whiff of varnish. Rich and forward, with plenty of concentrated plummy, prune and currant-like fruit, it then dries out at little towards a leathery, slightly old-fashioned finish of sweet gamey fruit and firm tannin.

## JACARANDA RIDGE CABERNET SAUVIGNON

| Coonawarra | $50+ | 1998 | 97 | 2010 | 2018+ |
|---|---|---|---|---|---|
| **Current vintage: 1998** | **97** | 1997 | 92 | 2009 | 2017 |
| | | 1996 | 97 | 2008 | 2016 |
| | | 1994 | 95 | 2006 | 2014 |
| | | 1992 | 89 | 2000 | 2004 |
| | | 1991 | 94 | 2003 | 2011 |
| | | 1990 | 94 | 2002 | 2010 |
| | | 1989 | 93 | 1997 | 2001 |
| | | 1988 | 91 | 1993 | 1996 |
| | | 1987 | 91 | 1995 | 1999 |
| | | 1986 | 87 | 1991 | 1994 |
| | | 1982 | 92 | 1987 | 1990 |

Deep, dark and brooding aromas of dark plums, black olives and cassis scented with dusty dried herbs, capsicum and sweet vanilla oak. Powerful, full-flavoured and spotlessly clean palate bursting with perfectly ripened small black and red berries tightly knit with vanilla/chocolate/cedar oak over a firm, integrated spine of gravelly tannins. Builds to a long, assertive finish of exceptional length and balance, with underlying dusty and herbal influences.

## LAWSON'S SHIRAZ

| Padthaway | $50+ | 1999 | 93 | 2007 | 2011+ |
|---|---|---|---|---|---|
| **Current vintage: 1999** | **93** | 1998 | 94 | 2010 | 2018 |
| | | 1997 | 93 | 2005 | 2009+ |
| | | 1996 | 95 | 2004 | 2008+ |
| | | 1995 | 90 | 2003 | 2007 |
| | | 1994 | 96 | 2006 | 2014+ |
| | | 1993 | 90 | 2001 | 2005 |
| | | 1992 | 86 | 2004 | 2012 |
| | | 1991 | 95 | 2003 | 2011 |
| | | 1990 | 93 | 2002 | 2010 |

From a warm, then later cool and damp season comes a lighter, but fragrant, floral and minty wine with fresh, spicy aromas of sweet small berry fruit beginning to integrate with bubblegum and mocha American oak.

# ST HELGA RIESLING

RANKING 2

**Eden Valley** $12–$19
**Current vintage: 2003** 90

Elegant, long-term riesling of balance and finesse, with a slightly chalky, nutty perfume of pear and apple. Long and tangy, its pristine palate reveals lime, lemon and apple flavours with a suggestion of baby powder, finishing clean, dry and persistent.

| | | | |
|---|---|---|---|
| 2003 | 90 | 2011 | 2015 |
| 2002 | 95 | 2010 | 2014+ |
| 2001 | 94 | 2006 | 2009+ |
| 2000 | 88 | 2002 | 2005+ |
| 1999 | 95 | 2007 | 2011 |
| 1998 | 94 | 2006 | 2010 |
| 1997 | 89 | 2002 | 2005 |
| 1996 | 95 | 2004 | 2010 |
| 1995 | 89 | 2003 | 2007 |
| 1994 | 95 | 2002 | 2006+ |
| 1993 | 87 | 1995 | 1998 |
| 1992 | 95 | 2000 | 2004+ |
| 1991 | 92 | 1999 | 2003+ |
| 1990 | 93 | 1995 | 1998 |
| 1989 | 90 | 1991 | 1994 |
| 1988 | 80 | 1990 | 1993 |
| 1987 | 90 | 1992 | 1995 |

# ST HILARY CHARDONNAY

RANKING 4

**Padthaway** $12–$19
**Current vintage: 2003** 88

Pleasing, if rather oaky chardonnay with a lemon bathpowder fragrance suggestive of grapefruit, melon and creamy vanilla oak. Smooth, restrained and even, with a herbal note beneath its lively peach, apple, grapefruit and melon flavours. Finishes quite tightly, with refreshing lemony acids.

| | | | |
|---|---|---|---|
| 2003 | 88 | 2005 | 2008 |
| 2002 | 89 | 2004 | 2007 |
| 2001 | 86 | 2002 | 2003+ |
| 2000 | 90 | 2002 | 2005+ |
| 1999 | 88 | 2001 | 2004 |
| 1998 | 90 | 2003 | 2006 |
| 1997 | 90 | 1999 | 2002 |
| 1996 | 90 | 2001 | 2004 |
| 1995 | 85 | 1996 | 1997 |

# ST HUGO CABERNET SAUVIGNON

RANKING 3

**Coonawarra** $30–$49
**Current vintage: 2001** 90

Elegant Coonawarra red from a challenging vintage. Its lightly smoky fragrance of raspberries, cassis, plums and violets is tightly knit with chocolate/mocha/vanilla oak, while its smooth and refined palate is framed by a fine-grained structure of powdery tannins. Typical regional cabernet flavours of cassis, plums, blackberries and mulberries are long and persistent.

| | | | |
|---|---|---|---|
| 2001 | 90 | 2006 | 2009 |
| 2000 | 87 | 2005 | 2008 |
| 1999 | 90 | 2007 | 2011 |
| 1998 | 94 | 2006 | 2010 |
| 1997 | 89 | 2005 | 2009 |
| 1996 | 93 | 2004 | 2008+ |
| 1994 | 95 | 2006 | 2014+ |
| 1993 | 91 | 2001 | 2005 |
| 1992 | 88 | 1997 | 2000 |
| 1991 | 95 | 2003 | 2011+ |
| 1990 | 94 | 2002 | 2010 |
| 1989 | 94 | 1997 | 2001 |
| 1988 | 91 | 1996 | 2000 |
| 1987 | 89 | 1995 | 1999 |
| 1986 | 90 | 1994 | 1998 |
| 1985 | 92 | 1990 | 1993 |
| 1984 | 93 | 1989 | 1992 |
| 1983 | 85 | 1985 | 1988 |
| 1992 | 94 | 1990 | 1994 |

# STEINGARTEN RIESLING

RANKING 2

**Eden Valley** $20–$29
**Current vintage: 2001** 96

Classic Australian riesling at a ridiculous price for a wine of this stature. A penetrative and pristine floral perfume of lime, lemon and talcum powder heralds a long, fine palate whose perfect delivery of fresh lemon, lime, green apple and peach-like fruit is interwoven with fine chalky phenolics. Punctuated by refreshing acidity, it's a timely reminder that Eden Valley riesling is as fine as anyone else's.

| | | | |
|---|---|---|---|
| 2001 | 96 | 2009 | 2013+ |
| 2000 | 95 | 2008 | 2012+ |
| 1999 | 94 | 2007 | 2011 |
| 1998 | 95 | 2010 | 2018 |
| 1997 | 95 | 2005 | 2009 |
| 1996 | 97 | 2004 | 2008+ |
| 1995 | 91 | 2000 | 2003 |
| 1994 | 96 | 1999 | 2002+ |
| 1992 | 93 | 2004 | 2012 |
| 1991 | 96 | 2003 | 2011 |
| 1990 | 95 | 1998 | 2002+ |
| 1989 | 88 | 1991 | 1994 |
| 1988 | 90 | 1993 | 1996 |
| 1987 | 90 | 1999 | 2004 |
| 1979 | 94 | 1987 | 1991+ |

# Oxford Landing

PMB 31 Waikerie SA 5330. Tel: (08) 8561 3200. Fax: (08) 8561 3393.
Website: www.yalumba.com  Email: jhindleycooke@yalumba.com
Region: **Riverlands** Winemaker: **Teresa Heuzenroeder** Viticulturist: **Bill Wilksch**
Chief Executive: **Robert Hill Smith**

Its excellent 2002 Cabernet Sauvignon Shiraz confirms the place of Oxford Landing amongst the best and often most surprising of the Riverlands' wine labels. Its deep dark, berry flavours, carefully balanced oak and tight-knit tannins are underpinned by minty/menthol influences.

## CABERNET SAUVIGNON SHIRAZ
RANKING **5**

| Riverlands | $12–$19 | 2002 | 89 | 2004 | 2007 |
|---|---|---|---|---|---|
| **Current vintage: 2002** | **89** | 2001 | 86 | 2003 | 2006 |
| | | 2000 | 84 | 2002 | 2005 |
| | | 1999 | 84 | 2000 | 2001 |
| | | 1998 | 81 | 1999 | 2000 |
| | | 1997 | 89 | 1998 | 1999 |
| | | 1996 | 87 | 1998 | 2001 |
| | | 1995 | 80 | 1996 | 1997 |

Very surprising, this lively, fresh and very complete wine offers truly remarkable value for money. Its vibrant, spicy aromas of slightly earthy and muddy small black and red berries over vanilla and coconut oak reveals nuances of mint and menthol. A long, intense and moderately firm palate of pristine primary small berry fruit and sweet vanilla oak is tightly wound around fine, tight tannins.

## CHARDONNAY

| Riverlands | $12–$19 | 2003 | 80 | 2003 | 2004 |
|---|---|---|---|---|---|
| **Current vintage: 2003** | **80** | 2002 | 81 | 2002 | 2003 |
| | | 2001 | 80 | 2001 | 2002 |
| | | 2000 | 88 | 2001 | 2002 |
| | | 1999 | 86 | 2000 | 2001 |
| | | 1998 | 87 | 1999 | 2000+ |
| | | 1997 | 87 | 1998 | 1999 |

Simple, forward and candied wine whose peachy, creamy flavours are supported by light, splintery oak but lack length, fruit and freshness.

## MERLOT

| Riverlands | $12–$19 | 2002 | 87 | 2004 | 2007 |
|---|---|---|---|---|---|
| **Current vintage: 2002** | **87** | 2000 | 83 | 2002 | 2005 |
| | | 1999 | 80 | 2000 | 2001 |

Meaty, leathery merlot with some, lightly sweaty complexity, but revealing a sweet, intense core of dark plums and sweet cherries tightly supported by vanilla oak. Supple and smooth, its polished, meaty palate finishes with some appealing reductive and savoury influences. Great value.

# Paringa Estate

44 Paringa Road, Red Hill South Vic 3937. Tel: (03) 5989 2669. Fax: (03) 5931 0135.
Email: paringa@cdi.com.au
Region: **Mornington Peninsula** Winemaker: **Lindsay McCall** Viticulturists: **Lindsay McCall, Nick Power**
Chief Executives: **Lindsay & Margaret McCall**

Paringa Estate has made a name for its deeply coloured, dark-fruited and spicy Pinot Noir, and its fragrant and peppery Shiraz, each of which are typically given generous treatment in new oak. At their best, these are exceptional wines, grown at one of the Mornington Peninsula's premier vineyards.

## CHARDONNAY
RANKING **4**

| Mornington Peninsula | $30–$49 | 2002 | 85 | 2004 | 2007 |
|---|---|---|---|---|---|
| **Current vintage: 2002** | **85** | 2001 | 90 | 2003 | 2006 |
| | | 2000 | 89 | 2002 | 2005 |
| | | 1999 | 89 | 2001 | 2004 |
| | | 1998 | 91 | 2000 | 2003 |
| | | 1997 | 93 | 2002 | 2005 |
| | | 1996 | 84 | 1997 | 1998 |
| | | 1995 | 92 | 2000 | 2003 |
| | | 1994 | 93 | 1996 | 1999 |
| | | 1993 | 92 | 1998 | 2001 |
| | | 1992 | 89 | 1997 | 2000 |

Spicy, nutty and mealy aromas of closed, citrusy fruit precede a juicy, forward palate that lacks genuine length and brightness, becoming nutty and savoury before a soft, oak-dominated finish.

## PINOT NOIR

**RANKING 3**

**Mornington Peninsula** $50+
**Current vintage: 2002** 88

Meaty, savoury and early-drinking pinot with a sweet, spicy aroma of slightly stewed plums, dark cherries and meaty, currant-like qualities. Smooth, polished and marginally stressed, its concentrated and forward palate of dark plum, berry and currant flavours finishes soft and savoury.

| | | | |
|---|---|---|---|
| 2002 | 88 | 2004 | 2007 |
| 2001 | 89 | 2003 | 2006 |
| 2000 | 93 | 2002 | 2005+ |
| 1999 | 89 | 2004 | 2007 |
| 1998 | 95 | 2003 | 2006+ |
| 1997 | 95 | 2002 | 2005 |
| 1996 | 87 | 1998 | 2001 |
| 1995 | 93 | 2000 | 2003 |
| 1994 | 87 | 1996 | 1999 |
| 1993 | 93 | 1998 | 2001 |
| 1992 | 92 | 1997 | 2000 |
| 1991 | 81 | 1996 | 1999 |

## SHIRAZ

**RANKING 4**

**Mornington Peninsula** $50+
**Current vintage: 2001** 88

Oaky, with some under and over-ripe characters. Its delicate, lightly confectionary and cinnamon-like perfume of raspberries, red cherries and plums reveals rosemary and mint/eucalypt undertones over sweet vanilla oak. Forward and pristine, its cherry/berry fruit and sweet oak overlie smooth, creamy tannins.

| | | | |
|---|---|---|---|
| 2001 | 88 | 2003 | 2006+ |
| 2000 | 90 | 2005 | 2008 |
| 1999 | 88 | 2001 | 2004+ |
| 1998 | 88 | 2003 | 2006 |
| 1997 | 95 | 2005 | 2009 |
| 1996 | 88 | 2001 | 2004 |
| 1995 | 88 | 2000 | 2003 |
| 1994 | 94 | 1999 | 2002 |
| 1993 | 93 | 2001 | 2005 |
| 1992 | 86 | 2000 | 2004 |
| 1991 | 91 | 1999 | 2003 |

# Parker Coonawarra Estate

Riddoch Highway, Coonawarra SA 5263. Tel: (08) 8737 3525. Fax: (08) 8737 3527.
Website: www.parkercoonawarraestate.com.au  Email: cellardoor@parkercoonawarraestate.com.au
Region: **Coonawarra** Winemaker: **Peter Bissell** Viticulturist: **Doug Balnaves** Chief Executive: **Gordon Gebbie**
Parker Coonawarra Estate is the brainchild of the late John Parker. It was Parker's aim to create a definitive marque of Coonawarra red wines, offering the depth of fruit and longevity for which the region is famous. The business was recently acquired by the Rathbone family, owners of both Yering Station and Mount Langi Ghiran. Parker is a good logical fit into this business, and the Rathbones have demonstrated that they are serious about producing wine of exceptional quality. Parker should go from strength to strength.

## TERRA ROSSA CABERNET SAUVIGNON

**RANKING 5**

**Coonawarra** $20–$29
**Current vintage: 2002** 83

Meaty, greenish and soupy vegetative aromas of capsicum, sweet plums, berries and vanilla oak precede a herbal, cedary and rather thin palate that lacks genuine ripeness.

| | | | |
|---|---|---|---|
| 2002 | 83 | 2004 | 2007+ |
| 2001 | 89 | 2006 | 2009 |
| 1999 | 90 | 2001 | 2004+ |
| 1998 | 87 | 2003 | 2006 |
| 1997 | 86 | 1999 | 2002+ |
| 1996 | 84 | 1998 | 2001 |
| 1995 | 87 | 2000 | 2003 |
| 1994 | 84 | 1999 | 2002 |
| 1992 | 82 | 1997 | 2000 |
| 1991 | 88 | 1999 | 2003 |
| 1989 | 87 | 1991 | 1994 |

## TERRA ROSSA FIRST GROWTH

**RANKING 2**

**Coonawarra** $50+
**Current vintage: 2001** 93

Firm, long-living and complete cabernet. Its dark, deep and concentrated, leathery aroma of meaty merlot and plummy/cassis cabernet opens into a powerful, plush palate of length, concentration and firmness. Deep, dark berry fruits are tightly knit with new oak and fine, astringent tannins.

| | | | |
|---|---|---|---|
| 2001 | 93 | 2013 | 2021 |
| 2000 | 95 | 2008 | 2012+ |
| 1999 | 88 | 2004 | 2007 |
| 1998 | 95 | 2018 | 2028 |
| 1996 | 97 | 2008 | 2016+ |
| 1994 | 84 | 1999 | 2002 |
| 1993 | 90 | 2001 | 2005 |
| 1991 | 95 | 2003 | 2011+ |
| 1990 | 97 | 2002 | 2010 |
| 1989 | 92 | 1997 | 1991 |
| 1988 | 95 | 2000 | 2008 |

## TERRA ROSSA MERLOT

RANKING **4**

| Coonawarra | $30–$49 |
|---|---|
| **Current vintage: 2001** | **83** |

Splintery, oaky merlot with some pretty impressive plum and dark cherry fruit totally overwhelmed by its polished, varnishy and chocolate/vanilla oak that tends to wring it dry from the mid-palate backwards.

| | | | |
|---|---|---|---|
| 2001 | 83 | 2006 | 2009 |
| 2000 | 91 | 2002 | 2005+ |
| 1999 | 89 | 2004 | 2007 |
| 1998 | 93 | 2006 | 2010 |

# Passing Clouds

Kurting Road, Kingower Vic 3517. Tel: (03) 5438 8257. Fax: (03) 5438 8246.
Region: **Bendigo** Winemaker: **Graeme Leith** Viticulturist: **Graeme Leith**
Chief Executives: **Graeme Leith, Sue Mackinnon**
The minty, meaty Shiraz from 2002 suggests that this cooler season might have been a little kinder to this central Victorian property. Based near Bendigo, its mature vineyard typically produces firm, robust and long-living red wines of searingly concentrated fruit firmly wrapped in powdery tannins.

## ANGEL BLEND (Cabernet Sauvignon & Merlot)

RANKING **4**

| Bendigo | $30–$49 |
|---|---|
| **Current vintage: 2001** | **86** |

Minty aromas of violets, cassis and raspberries over nuances of green capsicum, mint and sweet vanilla oak. Full to medium weight, its minty expression of small berry fruits and sweet oak offers length and some firmness, although its tannins are a little sappy and under-ripe.

| | | | |
|---|---|---|---|
| 2001 | 86 | 2006 | 2009+ |
| 2000 | 87 | 2005 | 2008 |
| 1999 | 91 | 2007 | 2011 |
| 1998 | 90 | 2010 | 2018 |
| 1997 | 93 | 2005 | 2009+ |
| 1996 | 90 | 2008 | 2016 |
| 1995 | 94 | 2007 | 2015 |
| 1994 | 91 | 2006 | 2014 |
| 1992 | 93 | 2000 | 2004 |
| 1991 | 90 | 1999 | 2003 |
| 1990 | 89 | 2002 | 2010 |
| 1987 | 87 | 1995 | 1999 |
| 1985 | 93 | 1993 | 1997 |
| 1984 | 87 | 1989 | 1992 |
| 1982 | 94 | 1990 | 1994 |

## GRAEME'S BLEND (Cabernet Sauvignon & Shiraz)

RANKING **4**

| Bendigo | $20–$29 |
|---|---|
| **Current vintage: 2001** | **87** |

Spicy, meaty aromas of cooked currants and raisins, with undertones of cloves and cinnamon, redcurrants, plums and older cedary/vanilla cooperage. Supple and restrained, with evolved, meaty and savoury flavours over a fragile spine of fine-grained tannins, finishing a little short and sappy. Suggestive of rather cooked fruit.

| | | | |
|---|---|---|---|
| 2001 | 87 | 2006 | 2009 |
| 2000 | 83 | 2002 | 2005+ |
| 1999 | 89 | 2011 | 2019 |
| 1998 | 91 | 2006 | 2010+ |
| 1997 | 90 | 2005 | 2009 |
| 1996 | 89 | 2004 | 2008+ |
| 1995 | 94 | 2003 | 2007 |
| 1994 | 88 | 2006 | 2014 |
| 1992 | 94 | 2004 | 2012 |
| 1991 | 91 | 1996 | 1999 |
| 1990 | 88 | 2002 | 2010 |
| 1989 | 85 | 1994 | 1997 |

## SHIRAZ

RANKING **4**

| Bendigo | $30–$49 |
|---|---|
| **Current vintage: 2002** | **90** |

A more supple, smooth and elegant wine from this central Victorian maker that combines pleasing regional mint and pepper with a decent measure of cut and polish. Its pungent, meaty aroma of blackberries, violets and plums is scented with cracked pepper, spices and a whiff of menthol. Long, fine and evenly ripened, its vibrant palate of blackcurrant and blackberry flavours finishes with powdery tannins and lingering savoury, meaty complexity.

| | | | |
|---|---|---|---|
| 2002 | 90 | 2010 | 2014+ |
| 2001 | 93 | 2009 | 2013+ |
| 1998 | 87 | 2010 | 2018 |
| 1997 | 87 | 2005 | 2009 |
| 1996 | 89 | 2004 | 2008 |
| 1994 | 93 | 2002 | 2006+ |

# Pauletts

Polish Hill Road, Polish Hill River SA 5453. Tel: (08) 8843 4328. Fax: (08) 8843 4202.
Email: paulwine@rbe.net.au

Region: **Clare Valley** Winemaker: **Neil Paulett** Viticulturist: **Matthew Paulett** Chief Executive: **Neil Paulett**

Led by its spicy, peppery Shiraz, of which the 2001 is more forward and generously oaked than usual, Pauletts is a small maker of a typically regional selection of Clare Valley wine, including an austere and citrusy riesling.

## CABERNET MERLOT   RANKING 5

**Clare Valley** $20–$29
**Current vintage: 2001** 88

Honest medium-term cabernet blend whose violet-like aromas of slightly stewed small red and black berries also reveal some meatiness and herbal undertones. Medium in weight, the palate presents some intense berry fruit flavour augmented by slightly varnishy, cedar/vanilla oak, finishing with herbal edges and firm, fine tannins.

| | | | |
|---|---|---|---|
| 2001 | 88 | 2006 | 2009+ |
| 2000 | 89 | 2008 | 2012 |
| 1999 | 88 | 2004 | 2007 |
| 1998 | 81 | 2000 | 2003 |
| 1997 | 88 | 2002 | 2005 |
| 1996 | 93 | 2004 | 2008 |
| 1995 | 89 | 2000 | 2003 |
| 1994 | 90 | 1996 | 1999 |
| 1993 | 84 | 1995 | 1998 |
| 1992 | 93 | 2000 | 2004 |
| 1991 | 93 | 1999 | 2003 |
| 1990 | 94 | 1995 | 1998 |
| 1989 | 93 | 1994 | 1997 |
| 1987 | 87 | 1992 | 1995 |

## RIESLING   RANKING 5

**Clare Valley** $12–$19
**Current vintage: 2003** 88

Dry, austere riesling with toasty, slightly cooked aromas of apple and pear before a round and generous palate whose lemon-lime flavours culminate in a minerally finish.

| | | | |
|---|---|---|---|
| 2003 | 88 | 2008 | 2011+ |
| 2001 | 85 | 2003 | 2006 |
| 2000 | 87 | 2005 | 2008 |
| 1999 | 89 | 2004 | 2007 |
| 1998 | 89 | 2000 | 2003+ |
| 1997 | 82 | 2002 | 2005 |
| 1996 | 88 | 2001 | 2004 |
| 1995 | 93 | 2003 | 2007 |
| 1994 | 93 | 2002 | 2006 |
| 1993 | 90 | 1995 | 1998 |
| 1992 | 93 | 2000 | 2004 |
| 1991 | 90 | 1999 | 2003 |
| 1990 | 93 | 1998 | 2002 |

## SHIRAZ   RANKING 4

**Clare Valley** $20–$29
**Current vintage: 2001** 89

Oakier than usual from this maker, here is a rustic but flavoursome shiraz full of charm and character. Its meaty, spicy aromas of raspberries, cassis and dark plums overlie polished new oak and minty, farmyard-like influences. Generous, ripe and succulent, its velvet-like palate of deep dark and red berry flavours is framed by fine, firm tannins. It finishes with licorice-like and meaty, savoury complexity.

| | | | |
|---|---|---|---|
| 2001 | 89 | 2009 | 2013+ |
| 2000 | 90 | 2005 | 2008 |
| 1999 | 90 | 2004 | 2007 |
| 1998 | 86 | 2000 | 2003+ |
| 1997 | 86 | 2002 | 2005 |
| 1996 | 88 | 2001 | 2004 |
| 1995 | 89 | 2000 | 2003 |
| 1994 | 91 | 1999 | 2002 |
| 1993 | 94 | 2001 | 2005 |
| 1992 | 91 | 2000 | 2004 |
| 1991 | 91 | 1996 | 1999 |
| 1990 | 91 | 1995 | 1998 |
| 1989 | 90 | 1994 | 1997 |
| 1988 | 85 | 1993 | 1996 |

# Paxton

Sand Road, McLaren Vale SA 5171. Tel: (08) 8323 8645. Fax: (08) 8323 8903.
Website: www.paxtonvineyards.com  Email: paxton@tnenet.net.au

Region: **McLaren Vale**  Winemaker: **Contract**  Viticulturist: **Toby Bekkers**  Chief Executive: **David Paxton**

Paxton is a McLaren Vale label developed by one of Australia's leading viticulturists, whose 2002 Shiraz is a flavoursome, but finer and more elegant version than its more sumptuous and ultra-ripe predecessors.

## SHIRAZ

RANKING **5**

| McLaren Vale | $30–$49 |
|---|---|
| Current vintage: 2002 | 92 |

Relatively rich, but youthful McLaren Vale shiraz, with a sweet, meaty and cedary aroma of currants, white pepper and red plums supported by lightly smoky vanilla oak. Smooth and polished, with lively, generous flavours of raspberries, cassis and plums neatly matched to lightly charry, creamy vanilla oak. Framed by firm tannins and fresh acids, it's pleasingly varietal and attractively balanced.

| 2002 | 92 | 2010 | 2014 |
|---|---|---|---|
| 2001 | 86 | 2003 | 2006 |
| 2000 | 87 | 2002 | 2005+ |
| 1999 | 88 | 2001 | 2004+ |
| 1998 | 90 | 2000 | 2003+ |

# Penfolds

Magill Estate Winery 78 Penfold Road, Magill SA 5072. Tel: (08) 8568 9389 Fax: (08) 8364 3961.
Website: www.penfolds.com.au  Email: penfolds.bv@cellar-door.com.au

Region: **South Australia**  Winemaker: **Peter Gago**  Viticulturist: **Nick Gill**  Chief Executive: **John Ballard**

Penfolds is a Australia's most significant maker of red wine, and is a lynchpin brand within the Southcorp empire. Today it is recognised around the world for its famous hierarchy of red wines that begin with the budget Rawson's Retreat label and extend all the way upwards to the country's most feted wine, Grange. Recent corporate difficulties within Southcorp have attracted widespread attention, although there are many positive signs that John Ballard is steering the big ship to safety. While many observers are pointing a finger at Penfolds for making a decision to change its wine style to a finer and fruitier model, the overriding cause for this movement in style has been vintage variation. Of all the major Australian brands, Penfolds has been hardest hit by the recent string of unprecedented seasonal change and diversity.

## ADELAIDE HILLS CHARDONNAY

RANKING **4**

| Adelaide Hills | $20–$29 |
|---|---|
| Current vintage: 2000 | 89 |

Perhaps a little clinical and contrived, this remains a pleasing wine whose ripe peach, green melon and lemony fruit is augmented by an array of winemaking artefact. The nose is delicate but quite complex, with nutty, bacon and buttery qualities. Forward and toasty, with a ripe, fleshy texture and sweet oak, there's a lightly oxidative aspect to the palate that's expressed as sweet toffee and caramel flavour.

| 2000 | 89 | 2002 | 2005 |
|---|---|---|---|
| 1999 | 89 | 2001 | 2004 |
| 1998 | 93 | 2003 | 2006 |
| 1997 | 88 | 2002 | 2005 |
| 1996 | 93 | 2001 | 2004 |
| 1995 | 89 | 1997 | 2000 |

## ADELAIDE HILLS SEMILLON

RANKING **4**

| Adelaide Hills | $20–$29 |
|---|---|
| Current vintage: 2000 | 85 |

Oaky, lightly charry aromas of restrained honeydew melon and lychees. Ripe and juicy but excessively woody, its phenolic palate of melon/tropical fruit finishes with some coarseness.

| 2000 | 85 | 2002 | 2005 |
|---|---|---|---|
| 1998 | 95 | 2006 | 2010 |
| 1997 | 88 | 1999 | 2002 |
| 1996 | 91 | 1998 | 2001 |
| 1995 | 89 | 1997 | 2000 |
| 1994 | 93 | 1999 | 2002+ |
| 1993 | 94 | 2001 | 2005 |

# BIN 128 COONAWARRA SHIRAZ

**Coonawarra** $20–$29
**Current vintage: 2001** 93

The best of the recent Penfolds releases, for the first time in my memory. Its earthy, leathery, rather old-fashioned aroma of animal hide and small berries is spicy and charming. While there's some plumpness and generosity, the palate is very smooth, spicy and restrained, framed by fine tannins and pierced throughout by flavours of white pepper, red cherries, cassis and plums.

| | | | |
|---|---|---|---|
| 2001 | 93 | 2009 | 2013+ |
| 2000 | 83 | 2002 | 2005 |
| 1999 | 90 | 2004 | 2007 |
| 1998 | 93 | 2010 | 2018 |
| 1997 | 87 | 2002 | 2005 |
| 1996 | 94 | 2008 | 2016 |
| 1995 | 86 | 2000 | 2003 |
| 1994 | 93 | 2002 | 2006 |
| 1993 | 88 | 2001 | 2005 |
| 1992 | 93 | 2000 | 2004 |
| 1991 | 89 | 1999 | 2003 |
| 1990 | 92 | 1998 | 2002 |
| 1989 | 86 | 1994 | 1997 |
| 1988 | 90 | 2000 | 2005 |
| 1987 | 82 | 1992 | 1995 |
| 1986 | 93 | 1994 | 1998 |
| 1985 | 88 | 1993 | 1997 |

# BIN 138 OLD VINE RHÔNE BLEND

**Barossa Valley** $20–$29
**Current vintage: 2002** 91

Vibrant, racy, juicy southern Rhône blend with some pleasing meaty complexity beneath its spicy floral fragrance and its plump, concentrated palate of dark berries and plums. Smooth and very silky, its long, lingering and fruit-driven.

| | | | |
|---|---|---|---|
| 2002 | 91 | 2004 | 2007+ |
| 2001 | 88 | 2003 | 2006+ |
| 1999 | 89 | 2004 | 2007 |
| 1998 | 92 | 2006 | 2010 |
| 1997 | 90 | 2005 | 2009 |
| 1996 | 92 | 2004 | 2008 |
| 1995 | 86 | 1997 | 2000 |
| 1994 | 92 | 2002 | 2006 |
| 1993 | 89 | 2001 | 2005 |

# BIN 389 CABERNET SHIRAZ

**South Australia** $30–$49
**Current vintage: 2001** 91

Elegant, polished and restrained wine dominated by the mint/menthol characters of the Padthaway proportion of its fruit. Leafy small berry cabernet influences combine with leathery, spicy shiraz, while creamy oak and velvet-smooth tannins provide gentle support. A very different Bin 389.

| | | | |
|---|---|---|---|
| 2001 | 91 | 2009 | 2013 |
| 2000 | 89 | 2005 | 2008+ |
| 1999 | 92 | 2007 | 2011 |
| 1998 | 96 | 2010 | 2018+ |
| 1997 | 93 | 2005 | 2009+ |
| 1996 | 97 | 2008 | 2016 |
| 1995 | 92 | 2004 | 2008 |
| 1994 | 95 | 2006 | 2014+ |
| 1993 | 93 | 2005 | 2013 |
| 1992 | 92 | 2004 | 2012 |
| 1991 | 94 | 2003 | 2011 |
| 1990 | 95 | 2002 | 2010 |
| 1989 | 87 | 1994 | 1997 |
| 1988 | 93 | 1996 | 2000 |
| 1987 | 91 | 1995 | 1999 |
| 1986 | 95 | 1998 | 2006 |

# BIN 407 CABERNET SAUVIGNON

**South Australia** $30–$49
**Current vintage: 2001** 87

Dusty herbal and greenish characters combine with slightly overcooked and earthy qualities in this fine and more elegant Bin 407. There are some pleasing small berry fruits, but overall the wine is too vegetal, displaying almost silage-like influences.

| | | | |
|---|---|---|---|
| 2001 | 87 | 2006 | 2009 |
| 2000 | 87 | 2005 | 2008 |
| 1999 | 90 | 2004 | 2007+ |
| 1998 | 91 | 2006 | 2010 |
| 1997 | 89 | 2005 | 2009 |
| 1996 | 95 | 2004 | 2008 |
| 1995 | 90 | 2003 | 2007+ |
| 1994 | 94 | 2002 | 2006 |
| 1993 | 93 | 2001 | 2005 |
| 1992 | 88 | 1997 | 2000 |
| 1991 | 94 | 2003 | 2011 |
| 1990 | 93 | 2002 | 2010 |

## BIN 707 CABERNET SAUVIGNON

**Barossa Valley, Coonawarra**    **$50+**
**Current vintage: 2001**    **93**

Firmly constructed cabernet with a floral perfume of violets and briary small berry fruit and sweet new vanilla oak before a deeply concentrated and astringent palate saturated with flavours of black-berry, plum and cassis. There are some slightly cooked and currant-like undertones to its fruitcake-like fruit, while the assertive chocolate oak and drying tannins contribute to its impressive structure.

| | | | |
|---|---|---|---|
| 2001 | 93 | 2013 | 2021+ |
| 1999 | 95 | 2007 | 2011+ |
| 1998 | 97 | 2010 | 2018+ |
| 1997 | 93 | 2005 | 2009+ |
| 1996 | 96 | 2008 | 2016+ |
| 1994 | 94 | 2006 | 2014 |
| 1993 | 95 | 2005 | 2013 |
| 1992 | 94 | 2004 | 2012 |
| 1991 | 97 | 2003 | 2011+ |
| 1990 | 95 | 2010 | 2018 |
| 1989 | 91 | 1997 | 2001 |
| 1988 | 95 | 2000 | 2008 |
| 1987 | 93 | 1999 | 2007 |
| 1986 | 95 | 2006 | 2016 |
| 1985 | 91 | 1997 | 2005 |
| 1984 | 93 | 1996 | 2004 |
| 1983 | 91 | 1995 | 2003 |
| 1982 | 89 | 1994 | 2002 |
| 1980 | 93 | 1992 | 2000 |
| 1978 | 91 | 1990 | 1998 |

## GRANGE

**Barossa Valley (predominantly) $50+**
**Current vintage: 1999**    **96**

Superbly elegant and harmonious wine, with a deep red ruby hue. Perfumed with violets and rasp-berries, cassis and redcurrants, it is lifted by hints of briar and blueberries, plus some assertive, but integrated vanilla/coconut oak. Smooth and silky, a beautifully complete and controlled wine of fineness and tightness; whose pristine small black and red berry fruit and integration present this refined vintage at its absolute best.

| | | | |
|---|---|---|---|
| 2001 | 95 | 2021 | 2031 |
| 2000 | 88 | 2008 | 2012 |
| 1999 | 96 | 2019 | 2029+ |
| 1998 | 97 | 2018 | 2028+ |
| 1997 | 95 | 2017 | 2027+ |
| 1996 | 98 | 2026 | 2036+ |
| 1995 | 95 | 2025 | 2035+ |
| 1994 | 95 | 2014 | 2024+ |
| 1993 | 89 | 2005 | 2013 |
| 1992 | 94 | 2012 | 2022 |
| 1991 | 97 | 2021 | 2031 |
| 1990 | 97 | 2020 | 2030 |
| 1989 | 95 | 2001 | 2009+ |
| 1988 | 91 | 2000 | 2008+ |
| 1987 | 91 | 1999 | 2007 |
| 1986 | 95 | 2016 | 2026 |
| 1985 | 92 | 2005 | 2015 |
| 1984 | 90 | 2004 | 2014 |
| 1983 | 96 | 2023 | 2033 |
| 1982 | 93 | 2002 | 2012 |
| 1981 | 88 | 2001 | 2011 |
| 1980 | 90 | 2000 | 2010 |
| 1979 | 87 | 1991 | 1999 |
| 1978 | 94 | 1998 | 2008+ |
| 1977 | 92 | 1997 | 2007 |
| 1976 | 94 | 1986 | 1996+ |
| 1975 | 89 | 1987 | 1995 |
| 1974 | 89 | 1986 | 1994+ |
| 1973 | 83 | 1981 | 1985 |
| 1972 | 90 | 1984 | 1992 |
| 1971 | 97 | 2001 | 2011 |
| 1970 | 93 | 1980 | 1990 |
| 1969 | 91 | 1989 | 1994 |
| 1968 | 94 | 1988 | 1998 |
| 1967 | 92 | 1987 | 1997 |
| 1966 | 97 | 1996 | 2006 |
| 1965 | 95 | 1995 | 2005+ |
| 1964 | 96 | 1984 | 1994+ |
| 1963 | 95 | 1983 | 1993+ |
| 1962 | 97 | 1992 | 2002+ |
| 1961 | 95 | 1991 | 2001 |
| 1960 | 90 | 1972 | 1980+ |
| 1959 | 90 | 1979 | 1989 |
| 1958 | 87 | 1966 | 1970 |
| 1957 | 89 | 1969 | 1977+ |
| 1956 | 88 | 1976 | 1981 |

continued next page...

# GRANGE
...continued

| | | | |
|---|---|---|---|
| 1955 | 96 | 1985 | 1990 |
| 1954 | 90 | 1966 | 1974 |
| 1953 | 97 | 1983 | 1993+ |
| 1952 | 95 | 1972 | 1982+ |
| 1951 | 87 | 1963 | 1971 |

## KALIMNA BIN 28 SHIRAZ
RANKING 4

**Barossa Valley**    $20–$29
**Current vintage: 2001**    87

Early-maturing, meaty and rather cooked wine whose tarry, prune-like fruit does reflect its vintage. There's some pleasing perfume, but the palate lacks length and freshness despite some soft, smooth tannins and creamy oak.

| | | | |
|---|---|---|---|
| 2001 | 87 | 2006 | 2009 |
| 2000 | 88 | 2005 | 2008 |
| 1999 | 86 | 2004 | 2007+ |
| 1998 | 95 | 2010 | 2018+ |
| 1997 | 91 | 2005 | 2009 |
| 1996 | 94 | 2008 | 2016 |
| 1995 | 90 | 2003 | 2007 |
| 1994 | 92 | 2002 | 2006 |
| 1993 | 84 | 1998 | 2001 |
| 1992 | 92 | 2000 | 2004 |
| 1991 | 93 | 1999 | 2003 |
| 1990 | 93 | 1998 | 2002 |
| 1989 | 87 | 1994 | 1997 |
| 1988 | 89 | 1996 | 2000 |
| 1987 | 88 | 1995 | 1999 |
| 1986 | 93 | 1998 | 2003 |
| 1985 | 87 | 1993 | 1997 |
| 1984 | 85 | 1989 | 1992 |
| 1983 | 82 | 1995 | 2000 |
| 1982 | 88 | 1990 | 1994 |

## KOONUNGA HILL CHARDONNAY
RANKING 5

**South Australia**    $12–$19
**Current vintage: 2003**    86

Honest, simple peaches and cream chardonnay with light aromas of uncomplicated fruit, nutty vanilla oak and herbal undertones. Forward and tropical, with a slightly hollow centre, it finishes soft, with notes of green cashew.

| | | | |
|---|---|---|---|
| 2003 | 86 | 2004 | 2005 |
| 2002 | 86 | 2002 | 2003 |
| 2001 | 89 | 2002 | 2003+ |
| 2000 | 87 | 2001 | 2002+ |

## KOONUNGA HILL SHIRAZ CABERNET SAUVIGNON
RANKING 5

**South Australia**    $12–$19
**Current vintage: 2001**    81

Disappointing wine with earthy, meaty aromas of prunes and herbal undertones. Under and over-ripe, with a forward, developed and thin palate that finishes sappy and green-edged. A reflection of the extremely hot vintage.

| | | | |
|---|---|---|---|
| 2001 | 81 | 2003 | 2006 |
| 2000 | 86 | 2002 | 2005+ |
| 1999 | 87 | 2004 | 2007 |
| 1998 | 87 | 2003 | 2006+ |
| 1997 | 86 | 2002 | 2005 |
| 1996 | 90 | 2004 | 2008 |
| 1995 | 87 | 2000 | 2003 |
| 1994 | 87 | 1999 | 2002 |
| 1993 | 88 | 2001 | 2005 |
| 1992 | 88 | 2000 | 2004 |
| 1991 | 92 | 1999 | 2003 |
| 1990 | 90 | 1998 | 2002 |
| 1989 | 88 | 1997 | 2001 |
| 1988 | 90 | 1996 | 2000 |
| 1987 | 82 | 1995 | 1999 |
| 1986 | 93 | 1998 | 2006 |
| 1985 | 84 | 1993 | 1997 |
| 1984 | 90 | 1996 | 2004 |
| 1983 | 89 | 1995 | 2003 |
| 1982 | 90 | 1994 | 2002 |
| 1981 | 88 | 1993 | 2001 |
| 1980 | 89 | 1992 | 2000+ |
| 1979 | 87 | 1987 | 1991 |
| 1978 | 93 | 1990 | 1998 |
| 1977 | 91 | 1989 | 1997 |
| 1976 | 88 | 1988 | 1996 |

## MAGILL ESTATE SHIRAZ

RANKING **3**

**Adelaide Metropolitan**    **$50+**
**Current vintage: 2001**    **93**

Fragrant aromas of intense, slightly confiture-like raspberries, red cherries and plums, with undertones of turned earth and creamy, bubblegum-like oak. Sweet, soft and vibrant, it's primary and youthful, with juicy cassis, raspberry and dark cherry flavours and sweet vanilla oak generating a sumptuous, plush mouthfeel. A delightful and vivacious young wine, but a massive departure in style for this vineyard.

| | | | |
|---|---|---|---|
| 2001 | 93 | 2013 | 2021 |
| 2000 | 90 | 2005 | 2008+ |
| 1999 | 95 | 2011 | 2019 |
| 1998 | 93 | 2010 | 2018 |
| 1997 | 92 | 2005 | 2009+ |
| 1996 | 95 | 2008 | 2016 |
| 1995 | 93 | 2003 | 2007 |
| 1994 | 91 | 2002 | 2012 |
| 1993 | 93 | 2005 | 2013 |
| 1992 | 90 | 2000 | 2004 |
| 1991 | 95 | 2011 | 2021 |
| 1990 | 94 | 2002 | 2010 |
| 1989 | 93 | 1997 | 2001 |
| 1988 | 91 | 2000 | 2005 |
| 1987 | 93 | 1995 | 1999 |
| 1986 | 94 | 1998 | 2003 |
| 1985 | 93 | 1993 | 1997 |
| 1984 | 90 | 1989 | 1992 |
| 1983 | 92 | 1995 | 2000 |

## RAWSON'S RETREAT CABERNET SAUVIGNON

**South Australia**    **$12–$19**
**Current vintage: 2002**    **83**

Advanced and pruney cabernet with light, but vibrant aromas of blackcurrant and plums supported by lightly chocolate/vanilla oak. The palate is cooked and jammy, and very developed for its age.

| | | | |
|---|---|---|---|
| 2002 | 83 | 2003 | 2004 |
| 2001 | 86 | 2002 | 2003+ |
| 2000 | 86 | 2002 | 2005 |
| 1999 | 85 | 2001 | 2004 |
| 1998 | 86 | 2000 | 2003 |
| 1997 | 82 | 1998 | 1999 |
| 1996 | 85 | 1998 | 2001 |

## RESERVE AGED RIESLING

RANKING **4**

**Clare Valley**    **$20–$29**
**Current vintage: 1999**    **92**

Fresh, lively and youthful aromas of lime juice and lemon rind, backed by lightly spiced nuances of toast and honey. Long and lively, punctuated by refreshing mineral acidity, it's vital and vibrant, delivering delightfully intense citrus and pear/apple flavour along a smooth palate over fine-grained chalky phenolics.

| | | | |
|---|---|---|---|
| 1999 | 92 | 2007 | 2011 |
| 1998 | 92 | 2006 | 2010 |
| 1997 | 90 | 2005 | 2009 |
| 1993 | 90 | 2001 | 2005 |

## RESERVE BIN CHARDONNAY

RANKING **3**

**Various, Southern Australia**    **$50+**
**Current vintage: 2000**    **94**

A persistent, delightfully balanced and supple wine with generous flavours, poise and elegance. Its smoky, mealy aromas of dusty citrus and peaches, melon and bananas are backed by buttery/vanilla oak and some funky, nutty sulphide influences. Restrained and creamy, it offers a fine length of juicy and brightly lit fruit culminating in a lingering chalky finish.

| | | | |
|---|---|---|---|
| 2000 00A | 94 | 2005 | 2008 |
| 1998 98A | 92 | 2003 | 2006 |
| 1995 95A | 93 | 2000 | 2003 |
| 1994 94A | 93 | 1999 | 2002 |

## RESERVE BIN EDEN VALLEY RIESLING

RANKING **3**

**Eden Valley**    **$20–$29**
**Current vintage: 2003**    **93**

Light, slightly confectionary aromas of lemon sherbet, spicy apple and pear. Long and juicy, but reasonably phenolic and chalky palate whose pleasing varietal flavours culminate in a persistent and tangy finish. Pleasing balance.

| | | | |
|---|---|---|---|
| 2003 | 93 | 2008 | 2011 |
| 2002 | 92 | 2007 | 2010 |
| 2001 | 92 | 2003 | 2006+ |
| 2000 | 93 | 2002 | 2005+ |
| 1999 | 94 | 2004 | 2007+ |

## RWT SHIRAZ

**Barossa Valley** $50+
**Current vintage: 2001** 88

Some excellent winemaking and very smart oak can't hide the pruney, stressed nature of the fruit used for this wine. Its spicy cinnamon spicecake aromas and sweet, forward palate of currants, plums and red berries are deeply flavoured and tightly supported by new cedary oak, but the finish lacks length and brightness.

| | | | |
|------|----|------|-------|
| 2001 | 88 | 2009 | 2013+ |
| 2000 | 91 | 2005 | 2008+ |
| 1999 | 96 | 2011 | 2019 |
| 1998 | 97 | 2010 | 2018+ |
| 1997 | 95 | 2005 | 2009 |

## ST HENRI SHIRAZ

**Barossa Valley, Clare Valley,**
**Coonawarra** $50+
**Current vintage: 1999** 95

Supple, elegant shiraz with a spicy floral perfume of cassis, blackberries and raspberries with peppery undertones of treacle and caramel, star anise and restrained cedary oak. Its long and satiny palate presents pristine, vibrant fruit over a fine-grained chassis, finishing smooth and gentle with delightful intensity.

| | | | |
|------|----|------|-------|
| 1999 | 95 | 2011 | 2019 |
| 1998 | 94 | 2018 | 2028 |
| 1997 | 93 | 2005 | 2009 |
| 1996 | 95 | 2008 | 2016 |
| 1995 | 91 | 2003 | 2007+ |
| 1994 | 94 | 2006 | 2014 |
| 1993 | 92 | 2003 | 2007 |
| 1992 | 90 | 2000 | 2004 |
| 1991 | 94 | 2003 | 2011 |
| 1990 | 96 | 2002 | 2010 |
| 1989 | 94 | 2001 | 2009 |
| 1988 | 93 | 2000 | 2005 |
| 1987 | 93 | 1999 | 2004 |
| 1986 | 96 | 1998 | 2008+ |
| 1985 | 91 | 1997 | 2002 |
| 1984 | 80 | 1992 | 1996 |
| 1983 | 90 | 1995 | 2003 |
| 1982 | 90 | 1990 | 1994 |
| 1981 | 82 | 1993 | 1998 |
| 1980 | 90 | 1992 | 1997 |
| 1979 | 77 | 1987 | 1991 |
| 1978 | 80 | 1990 | 1995 |
| 1977 | 82 | 1989 | 1994 |
| 1976 | 93 | 1996 | 2006+ |

## THE VALLEYS CHARDONNAY

**Clare and Eden Valleys** $12–$19
**Current vintage: 2000** 88

Honest, well-made and uncomplicated candied chardonnay whose banana-like aromas of citrus, tropical fruit and vanilla oak precede a creamy but forward palate whose juicy flavours are integrated with creamy leesy influences and finished with clean, lemony acids. Sound, but predictable.

| | | | |
|------|----|------|-------|
| 2000 | 88 | 2002 | 2005 |
| 1998 | 89 | 2000 | 2003+ |
| 1997 | 92 | 1999 | 2002 |
| 1996 | 88 | 1998 | 2001 |
| 1995 | 88 | 1997 | 2000 |
| 1994 | 92 | 1999 | 2002 |
| 1993 | 91 | 1998 | 2001 |
| 1992 | 90 | 1997 | 2000 |

## YATTARNA CHARDONNAY

**Adelaide Hills, Drumborg,**
**McLaren Vale** $50+
**Current vintage: 2000** 95

Clinically perfect chardonnay, perhaps lacking a little soul. Its minerally fragrance suggests dried flowers, lemon blossom and dusty, spicy cloves, with nutmeg and melon fruit. Elegant, supple and seamless, its juicy, vibrant palate of pineapple, grapefruit and mango perfectly integrates with nutty vanilla oak and finishes with refreshing citrusy acids.

| | | | |
|------|----|------|-------|
| 2000 | 95 | 2005 | 2008 |
| 1999 | 95 | 2004 | 2007+ |
| 1998 | 97 | 2006 | 2010 |
| 1997 | 95 | 2002 | 2005+ |
| 1996 | 95 | 2001 | 2004+ |
| 1995 | 94 | 2000 | 2003 |

# Penley Estate

McLeans Road, Coonawarra SA 5263. Tel: (08) 8736 3211. Fax: (08) 8736 3124.
Website: www.penley.com.au  Email: penley@penley.com.au

Region: **Coonawarra** Winemaker: **Kym Tolley** Viticulturist: **Michael Wetherall** Chief Executive: **Kym Tolley**

Penley Estate is a small and serious maker of Coonawarra wines, principally reds from cabernet sauvignon, merlot and shiraz. Its owner/winemaker Kym Tolley brings his winemaking experience from Penfolds into the equation, but while his wines reveal substantial benefit from oak maturation, they are typically made with riper, juicier fruit flavours than Penfolds wines themselves.

## CHARDONNAY

RANKING 5

**Coonawarra** $12–$19
**Current vintage: 2002** 88

Sweet, creamy aromas of buttery oak, tropical fruits and sweetcorn, with undertones of peaches and oatmeal. Ripe and juicy, smooth and generous, it's round, soft and forward, a smooth easy-drinking peaches and cream chardonnay.

| | | | |
|---|---|---|---|
| 2002 | 88 | 2004 | 2007 |
| 2001 | 90 | 2003 | 2006 |
| 2000 | 81 | 2001 | 2002 |
| 1999 | 82 | 2001 | 2004 |
| 1998 | 87 | 1999 | 2000 |
| 1997 | 90 | 1999 | 2002+ |
| 1996 | 87 | 1998 | 2001 |
| 1995 | 90 | 1997 | 2002 |

## HYLAND SHIRAZ

RANKING 4

**Coonawarra** $12–$19
**Current vintage: 2002** 87

A fruit-driven shiraz with a slightly jammy and herbal aroma of raspberries, plums and sweet cedar/vanilla oak. Up-front, generous and juicy, its lively palate of redcurrants and raspberries, plums and currants begins with intensity and spiciness, but finishes slightly short and flat, lightly sappy and herbal.

| | | | |
|---|---|---|---|
| 2002 | 87 | 2004 | 2007 |
| 2001 | 91 | 2006 | 2009 |
| 2000 | 88 | 2002 | 2005+ |
| 1999 | 91 | 2004 | 2007 |
| 1998 | 87 | 2003 | 2006 |
| 1997 | 89 | 1999 | 2002+ |
| 1996 | 89 | 2001 | 2004 |
| 1994 | 82 | 1996 | 1999 |
| 1993 | 82 | 1995 | 1998 |

## MERLOT

RANKING 5

**Coonawarra** $20–$29
**Current vintage: 2002** 87

Herbal, dusty and cedary aromas of red cherries and plums over nuances of tobacco leaf. Smooth and supple, its elegant and tightly knit palate of sweet cherry/plum fruit and cedary oak is framed by a slightly sappy extract of fine and moderately firm tannins, but finishes with herbal and vegetal nuances.

| | | | |
|---|---|---|---|
| 2002 | 87 | 2004 | 2007+ |
| 1999 | 87 | 2001 | 2004 |
| 1998 | 83 | 2000 | 2003 |
| 1997 | 86 | 1999 | 2002 |
| 1996 | 80 | 1997 | 1998 |

## PHOENIX CABERNET SAUVIGNON

RANKING 5

**Coonawarra** $20–$29
**Current vintage: 2002** 86

Restrained, leafy and meaty cabernet with an earthy, dusty bouquet whose small berry aromas are supported by cedary oak and whose very forward and slightly hollow palate is given sweetness and texture from cedar/vanilla oak.

| | | | |
|---|---|---|---|
| 2002 | 86 | 2004 | 2007 |
| 2001 | 93 | 2006 | 2009+ |
| 2000 | 82 | 2002 | 2005 |
| 1999 | 82 | 2001 | 2004 |
| 1998 | 89 | 2003 | 2006 |
| 1997 | 89 | 1999 | 2002+ |
| 1996 | 90 | 1998 | 2001+ |
| 1995 | 85 | 1997 | 2000 |

## RESERVE (Formerly Cabernet Sauvignon)

RANKING 4

**Coonawarra** $50+
**Current vintage: 2000** 87

A developing cedary, leathery bouquet of sweet berry fruit and chocolate/vanilla oak reveals herbal undertones. Sumptuous and meaty, it begins with intense red berry, blackberry and plum flavours before a slightly sappy middle, then a firm, rather hard-edged grip of greenish tannins and acids. There's plenty of richness and flavour, but the wine lacks genuine length and a truly ripe backbone of tannin.

| | | | |
|---|---|---|---|
| 2000 | 87 | 2005 | 2008 |
| 1999 | 93 | 2007 | 2011 |
| 1998 | 91 | 2006 | 2010 |
| 1997 | 90 | 2002 | 2005+ |
| 1996 | 91 | 2004 | 2008 |
| 1995 | 87 | 2000 | 2003 |
| 1994 | 90 | 1998 | 2002 |
| 1993 | 93 | 2005 | 2013 |
| 1992 | 93 | 2000 | 2004 |
| 1991 | 95 | 2003 | 2011 |
| 1990 | 94 | 1998 | 2002 |
| 1989 | 91 | 1994 | 1997 |

## SHIRAZ CABERNET

| Coonawarra | $20–$29 |
|---|---|
| **Current vintage: 2000** | **88** |

Meaty, earthy and leathery aromas of dark, spicy plums and blackcurrant-like shiraz are matched by sweet cedar/vanilla oak. Packed with sweet cassis/plum fruit, its generous, vibrant palate borders on the sumptuous, but finishing with soft tannins and herbal undertones. Drink soon.

| | | | |
|---|---|---|---|
| 2000 | 88 | 2005 | 2008 |
| 1999 | 88 | 2001 | 2004+ |
| 1998 | 88 | 2003 | 2006 |
| 1997 | 82 | 1999 | 2002 |
| 1996 | 87 | 1998 | 2001 |
| 1995 | 89 | 1997 | 2000 |
| 1994 | 92 | 2002 | 2006 |
| 1993 | 89 | 1995 | 1998 |
| 1992 | 90 | 1997 | 2000 |
| 1991 | 93 | 1999 | 2003 |
| 1990 | 91 | 1995 | 1998 |

# Pepper Tree

Halls Road, Pokolbin NSW 2320. Tel: (02) 4998 7539. Fax: (02) 4998 7746.
Website: www.peppertreewines.com.au  Email: ptwinery@peppertreewines.com.au

Region: **Lower Hunter Valley, Coonawarra, Various** Winemaker: **Chris Cameron** Viticulturist: **Derek Smith**
Chief Executive: **John Martini**

Pepper Tree is an ambitious project whose wines are largely sourced from both the Hunter Valley and Coonawarra. Its winemaker, Chris Cameron, has been an enthusiastic pioneer of modern Australian merlot, made from very ripe Coonawarra fruit. The challenge facing Pepper Tree's Grand Reserve Merlot is to achieve an ageable style in which herbaceous characteristics are fully controlled. The appointment of the experienced executive John Martini will hopefully see this energetic business convert more of its undoubted potential into results.

## GRAND RESERVE CABERNET SAUVIGNON

| Coonawarra | $50+ |
|---|---|
| **Current vintage: 2000** | **92** |

Lightly herbal aromas of meaty, briary small dark plums and blackcurrant, with lightly minty undertones of dark cherries, coffee grounds and sweet cedar/chocolate oak. Long, smooth and elegant, its marginally leafy expression of bright berry/plum fruit knits tightly with a powder-fine astringency and new oak.

| | | | |
|---|---|---|---|
| 2000 | 92 | 2008 | 2012 |
| 1999 | 84 | 2001 | 2004 |
| 1998 | 87 | 2006 | 2010+ |
| 1996 | 83 | 2001 | 2004 |

## GRAND RESERVE MERLOT

| Coonawarra | $50+ |
|---|---|
| **Current vintage: 2000** | **89** |

Early-maturing merlot whose slightly closed bouquet of sweet red an black cherries, dark plums and new cedar/vanilla oak reveals hints of undergrowth. Rich and generous, it's forward and oaky, with some reserved but sweet and slightly candied raspberry, cherry and plum flavours. While there's a reasonable length of fruit and some very assertive oak, the palate is showing signs of drying out.

| | | | |
|---|---|---|---|
| 2000 | 89 | 2005 | 2008 |
| 1998 | 95 | 2006 | 2010 |
| 1996 | 92 | 2001 | 2004 |
| 1995 | 88 | 1997 | 2000 |

## GRAND RESERVE SEMILLON

| Lower Hunter Valley | $20–$29 |
|---|---|
| **Current vintage: 2003** | **87** |

Slightly closed aromas of dusty lime and melon, with a racy, sculpted palate whose initially intense fruit culminates in an austere and steely acidity, but a slightly dulled delivery of flavour.

| | | | |
|---|---|---|---|
| 2003 | 87 | 2008 | 2011+ |
| 2002 | 85 | 2007 | 2010+ |
| 2000 | 82 | 2002 | 2005 |
| 1999 | 82 | 2001 | 2004 |
| 1998 | 88 | 2006 | 2010 |
| 1997 | 93 | 2005 | 2009 |
| 1996 | 90 | 2004 | 2008 |
| 1995 | 95 | 2003 | 2007 |
| 1994 | 90 | 1999 | 2002 |
| 1993 | 88 | 1998 | 2001 |

# Pepperjack

Saltram Estates, Nuriootpa–Angaston Road, Angaston SA 5353. Tel: (08) 8564 3355. Fax: (08) 8564 2209.

Region: **Barossa Valley** Winemaker: **Nigel Dolan** Chief Executive: **Jamie Odell**

Pepperjack is a Beringer Blass-owned brand spawned out of the Saltram business. Its very approachable, soft and flavoursome reds are generously oaked and usually ready to drink by release.

## CABERNET SAUVIGNON

| Barossa Valley | $20–$29 | 2000 | 81 | 2001 | 2002 |
|---|---|---|---|---|---|
| **Current vintage: 2000** | **81** | 1999 | 87 | 2001 | 2004+ |
| | | 1998 | 81 | 2000 | 2003 |

Simple, cooked and jammy cabernet whose minty, plummy aromas precede a sappy, greenish palate of medium weight, given some sweetness through its vanilla oak. Simultaneously under and over-ripe.

## SHIRAZ

RANKING **5**

| Barossa Valley | $20–$29 | 2001 | 86 | 2003 | 2006 |
|---|---|---|---|---|---|
| **Current vintage: 2001** | **86** | 2000 | 86 | 2002 | 2005 |
| | | 1999 | 86 | 2001 | 2004 |
| | | 1998 | 89 | 2003 | 2006 |
| | | 1997 | 82 | 1999 | 2002 |
| | | 1996 | 89 | 2001 | 2004+ |

Sound, honest shiraz with a pungent, earthy and chocolate-like aroma of spicy plums and berries. Ripe and forward, lacking great length and structure; a shorter-term and slightly green-edged wine.

# Pertaringa

cnr Hunt & Rifle Range Roads, McLaren Vale SA 5171. Tel: (08) 8323 8125. Fax: (08) 8323 7766.
Website: www.pertaringa.com.au  Email: wines@pertaringa.com.au

Region: **McLaren Vale** Winemakers: **Geoff Hardy, Ben Riggs** Viticulturist: **Ian Leask**
Chief Executives: **Ian Leask & Geoff Hardy**

Geoff Hardy and Ian Leask are major contract growers for some of Australia's largest wine producers. Their Pertaringa label comprises a range of wines from the McLaren Vale vineyard of the same name. Made with the assistance of the well-known Ben Riggs, the approachable and generously flavoured 2001 reds are a healthy improvement from the difficult 2000 season.

## OVER THE TOP SHIRAZ

RANKING **5**

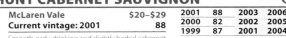

| McLaren Vale | $20–$29 | 2001 | 89 | 2006 | 2009 |
|---|---|---|---|---|---|
| **Current vintage: 2001** | **89** | 2000 | 83 | 2002 | 2005 |
| | | 1999 | 90 | 2004 | 2007 |
| | | 1998 | 88 | 2003 | 2006+ |

Approachable and generous shiraz with an oaky, slightly cooked and soupy aroma of toasty dark plums, currants and cassis. Its smooth palate of licorice-like cassis and plum fruit is wrapped in fine tannins, before finishing with moderate length and refreshing acidity.

## RIFLE AND HUNT CABERNET SAUVIGNON

RANKING **5**

| McLaren Vale | $20–$29 | 2001 | 88 | 2003 | 2006 |
|---|---|---|---|---|---|
| **Current vintage: 2001** | **88** | 2000 | 82 | 2002 | 2005 |
| | | 1999 | 87 | 2001 | 2004 |

Smooth, early-drinking and slightly herbal cabernet with an earthy, slightly dull and minty aroma of cassis and plums. Soft, smooth and delicate, the palate reveals attractive cassis/plum flavour with sweet mocha/vanilla oak over an underlying herbal thread.

# Petaluma

Spring Gully Road, Piccadilly SA 5151. Tel: (08) 8339 4122. Fax: (08) 8339 5253.
Website: www.petaluma.com.au  Email: petaluma@petaluma.com.au
Regions: **Adelaide Hills, Coonawarra** Winemakers: **Brian Croser, Con Moshos** Viticulturist: **Mike Harms**
Chief Executive: **Peter Cowan**

While the attentions of its founder, Brian Croser, are now divided between his duties at Lion Nathan (owners of the Petaluma brand) and his own pet projects that include the Tappanappa venture at Wrattonbully, the team he has assembled over the years deserves great credit for the continued excellence of his long-established labels, as well as the introduction of new wines like the Shiraz and the Viognier. It says something for the integrity of the business that these two wines, each of which are greatly improved, have yet to earn the yellow Petaluma label, the sign they will achieve once they have really been attached to this important wine family.

## CHARDONNAY   RANKING 2

**Piccadilly Valley**                 $30–$49
**Current vintage: 2001**                **94**

A typically fine and focused chardonnay from the Croser stable whose fresh, but delicate aroma of lemon sherbet, apple and pear is backed by suggestions of creamy, clove-like oak and banana. Supple, long and elegant, unfolding a bright core of melon and citrus fruit, it finishes slightly dusty, with refreshing acids.

| Vintage | Score | Drink from | Drink to |
|---|---|---|---|
| 2001 | 94 | 2006 | 2009 |
| 2000 | 92 | 2005 | 2008 |
| 1999 | 95 | 2004 | 2007 |
| 1998 | 94 | 2006 | 2010 |
| 1997 | 95 | 2005 | 2009 |
| 1996 | 95 | 2004 | 2008 |
| 1995 | 95 | 2003 | 2007 |
| 1994 | 94 | 2002 | 2006 |
| 1993 | 93 | 1995 | 1998 |
| 1992 | 95 | 2000 | 2004 |
| 1991 | 91 | 1996 | 1999 |
| 1990 | 93 | 1998 | 2002 |
| 1989 | 90 | 1991 | 1994 |
| 1988 | 88 | 1993 | 1996 |
| 1987 | 92 | 1995 | 1999 |
| 1986 | 88 | 1991 | 1994 |

## COONAWARRA (Cabernet Sauvignon & Merlot)   RANKING 1

**Coonawarra**                       $50+
**Current vintage: 2001**                **95**

Very classy, structured red of typical strength and longevity. Its bright, slightly confectionary aromas of mulberries, raspberries, plums and cassis integrate tightly with sweetly scented chocolate oak. Firm and almost sinewy, the palate of rich plum-like fruit reveals a faint suggestion of pruney, stewed fruit, but is essentially long, firm and complete, supported by sweet vanilla oak and assertive tannins.

| Vintage | Score | Drink from | Drink to |
|---|---|---|---|
| 2001 | 95 | 2013 | 2021 |
| 2000 | 94 | 2008 | 2012 |
| 1999 | 91 | 2007 | 2011 |
| 1998 | 98 | 2018 | 2028 |
| 1997 | 97 | 2009 | 2017+ |
| 1996 | 95 | 2016 | 2026 |
| 1995 | 93 | 2007 | 2015 |
| 1994 | 95 | 2006 | 2014+ |
| 1993 | 92 | 2005 | 2013 |
| 1992 | 95 | 2012 | 2022 |
| 1991 | 95 | 2003 | 2011+ |
| 1990 | 95 | 2002 | 2010 |
| 1988 | 92 | 2000 | 2008+ |
| 1987 | 87 | 1995 | 1999 |
| 1986 | 91 | 1998 | 2006 |
| 1985 | 82 | 1990 | 1993 |
| 1984 | 81 | 1986 | 1989 |
| 1982 | 87 | 1987 | 1990 |
| 1981 | 87 | 1986 | 1989 |
| 1980 | 84 | 1985 | 1988 |
| 1979 | 95 | 1991 | 1999+ |

## CROSER   RANKING 3

**Piccadilly Valley**                 $30–$49
**Current vintage: 2001**                **93**

Pristine and shapely wine with an aromatic bouquet of white peach, apple and pear over a creamy, lightly nutty background. Its smooth and elegant palate presents vibrant strawberry and cherry pinot flavour along its entirety, finishing crisp and creamy.

| Vintage | Score | Drink from | Drink to |
|---|---|---|---|
| 2001 | 93 | 2003 | 2006+ |
| 2000 | 89 | 2005 | 2008 |
| 1999 | 93 | 2001 | 2004+ |
| 1998 | 91 | 2000 | 2003+ |
| 1997 | 92 | 1999 | 2002+ |
| 1996 | 93 | 1998 | 2001 |
| 1995 | 93 | 1997 | 2000 |
| 1994 | 94 | 1996 | 1999 |
| 1993 | 93 | 1995 | 1998 |
| 1992 | 94 | 1997 | 2000 |
| 1991 | 90 | 1999 | 2003 |

# MERLOT

**Coonawarra** $50+
**Current vintage: 1999** 94

Evolving, earthy and gamey aromas and floral perfumes of bright red plums, raspberries and red cherries are tightly matched with cedar/vanilla oak. Supple, restrained and creamy, the palate presents bright red fruits with finely integrated drying tannins and chocolate/cedar oak. Long and elegant, finishing with meaty nuances of small-goods and earth.

| | | | |
|---|---|---|---|
| 2001 | 96 | 2009 | 2013+ |
| 2000 | 93 | 2008 | 2012+ |
| 1999 | 94 | 2007 | 2011+ |
| 1998 | 93 | 2006 | 2010 |
| 1997 | 96 | 2009 | 2017 |
| 1996 | 94 | 2004 | 2008 |
| 1995 | 90 | 2003 | 2007 |
| 1994 | 93 | 2006 | 2014+ |
| 1993 | 89 | 2001 | 2005+ |
| 1992 | 95 | 2004 | 2012+ |
| 1991 | 90 | 2003 | 2011 |
| 1990 | 92 | 2002 | 2010 |

# RIESLING

RANKING 2

PETALUMA
1996 RIESLING
750ml

**Clare Valley** $20–$29
**Current vintage: 2003** 93

Perfumed, delicate but vibrant aromas of candied citrus fruit are lightly musky and spicy. Juicy and forward, with fresh, punchy flavours of lemon and lime, apple and pear culminating in a tangy wet slate finish of moderate length.

| | | | |
|---|---|---|---|
| 2003 | 93 | 2008 | 2011+ |
| 2002 | 96 | 2010 | 2014 |
| 2001 | 95 | 2009 | 2013 |
| 2000 | 91 | 2005 | 2008 |
| 1999 | 95 | 2011 | 2019 |
| 1998 | 91 | 2006 | 2010 |
| 1997 | 94 | 2009 | 2017 |
| 1996 | 95 | 2008 | 2016 |
| 1995 | 96 | 2007 | 2015 |
| 1994 | 94 | 2006 | 2014 |
| 1993 | 87 | 2001 | 2005 |
| 1992 | 90 | 2000 | 2004 |
| 1991 | 93 | 2003 | 2011 |
| 1990 | 95 | 2002 | 2010+ |
| 1989 | 90 | 1997 | 2001+ |
| 1988 | 92 | 2000 | 2008 |

# SHIRAZ

RANKING 3

PETALUMA
ADELAIDE HILLS
2000
*Shiraz*
750ml

**Adelaide Hills** $30–$49
**Current vintage: 2002** 93

A briary, spicy perfume of blackberries and violets, cedar and walnuts, dried herbs and spearmint precedes a firm, oaky palate of full to medium weight. Well-ripened flavours of red cherries, redcurrants, plums and cassis reveal a slightly cooked aspect, while some plush, assertive oak sits above fine-grained and bony tannins. Good modern Rhône-like style with a future.

| | | | |
|---|---|---|---|
| 2002 | 93 | 2010 | 2014 |
| 2001 | 95 | 2009 | 2013 |
| 2000 | 91 | 2005 | 2008 |
| 1999 | 89 | 2004 | 2007 |
| 1998 | 91 | 2003 | 2006 |

# TIERS CHARDONNAY

RANKING 1

PETALUMA
TIERS
PICCADILLY VALLEY
1996 CHARDONNAY

**Piccadilly Valley** $50+
**Current vintage: 2000** 96

A complex, perfumed chardonnay poles apart from the Australian mainstream, scented with honeysuckle, stonefruit, melon and lemon. Initially creamy and fleshy, the palate then become taut and chalky, its peachy fruit finishing savoury with nutty, wheatmeal flavours and a gravely texture. Singularly tight and restrained, yet surprisingly powerful.

| | | | |
|---|---|---|---|
| 2000 | 96 | 2005 | 2008+ |
| 1999 | 93 | 2004 | 2007 |
| 1998 | 97 | 2005 | 2008 |
| 1997 | 97 | 2002 | 2005+ |
| 1996 | 96 | 2004 | 2008 |

# VIOGNIER

RANKING 4

PETALUMA
ADELAIDE HILLS
2001
*Viognier*
750ml

**Adelaide Hills** $30–$49
**Current vintage: 2003** 94

A delicate perfume of apricot blossom, honeysuckle, cloves and cinnamon precedes a generous, yet tightly controlled palate. Beginning forward and quite viscous, it becomes fine and supple, revealing bright and penetrative varietal flavour, some alcoholic warmth and babyfat texture before a clean, savoury and refreshing finish.

| | | | |
|---|---|---|---|
| 2003 | 93 | 2005 | 2008 |
| 2002 | 91 | 2004 | 2007 |
| 2001 | 89 | 2003 | 2006 |
| 2000 | 90 | 2001 | 2002+ |
| 1999 | 90 | 2001 | 2004 |
| 1998 | 90 | 2000 | 2003+ |

# Peter Lehmann

Off Para Road, Tanunda SA 5352. Tel: (08) 8563 2100. Fax: (08) 8563 3402.
Website: www.peterlehmannwines.com.au  Email: plw@lehmannwines.com.au

Region: **Barossa Valley** Winemakers: **Andrew Wigan, Leonie Lange & Ian Hongell,**
Viticulturist: **Peter Nash** Chief Executive: **Douglas Lehmann**

It's business as usual at Peter Lehmann, whose efforts to resist the takeover bid by Allied Domecq in favour of the ultimately successful claim by the significantly smaller Hess Group represent a plot deep enough for at least one TV mini-series. The best news amongst the current releases are the exceptionally vibrant and spotlessly presented Barossa reds from 2002, plus the astonishingly pure, perfumed and pristine Eden Valley Riesling from 2003.

## CLANCY'S (Blend of Shiraz and red Bordeaux varieties)   RANKING 5

| Barossa Valley | $12–$19 |
|---|---|
| Current vintage: 2002 | 89 |

Very generous, flavoursome budget red whose pleasingly intense small black jujube-like fruit flavours are perfectly married with the right amount of smoked oyster American oak influences. Great value.

| | | | |
|---|---|---|---|
| 2002 | 89 | 2004 | 2007 |
| 2000 | 80 | 2002 | 2005 |
| 1999 | 81 | 2000 | 2001 |
| 1998 | 85 | 2000 | 2003 |
| 1997 | 92 | 2002 | 2005 |
| 1996 | 89 | 1998 | 2001 |
| 1995 | 89 | 1997 | 2000 |
| 1994 | 90 | 1996 | 1999 |
| 1993 | 84 | 1995 | 1998 |

## EDEN VALLEY RIESLING (Formerly Blue Eden Riesling)   RANKING 2

| Eden Valley | $12–$19 |
|---|---|
| Current vintage: 2004 | 90 |

A racy young riesling whose punchy limejuice and lemon rind aromas reveal spicy, floral undertones of fresh apple and baby powder. Long, fine and chalky, its brightly lit but slightly candied citrus and apple flavours are punctuated by a refreshingly crisp finish of lemony acids.

| | | | |
|---|---|---|---|
| 2004 | 90 | 2006 | 2009+ |
| 2003 | 95 | 2008 | 2011+ |
| 2002 | 95 | 2007 | 2010 |
| 2001 | 95 | 2009 | 2013 |
| 2000 | 89 | 2005 | 2008 |

## EIGHT SONGS SHIRAZ   RANKING 3

| Barossa Valley | $30–$49 |
|---|---|
| Current vintage: 2000 | 89 |

Smoky vanilla-like aromas of raspberries, cherries, plums and cassis with herbal undertones precedes a silky-smooth and restrained palate whose vibrant berry flavours partner toasty nuances of sweet chocolate/vanilla oak. Finishes a little thin and sappy, just lacking genuine fruit ripeness.

| | | | |
|---|---|---|---|
| 2000 | 89 | 2005 | 2008 |
| 1999 | 92 | 2004 | 2007+ |
| 1998 | 94 | 2006 | 2010+ |
| 1997 | 88 | 2002 | 2005+ |
| 1996 | 96 | 2004 | 2008+ |

## MENTOR   RANKING 3

| Barossa Valley | $30–$49 |
|---|---|
| Current vintage: 2000 | 88 |

Creamy new oak lends sweetness and support to some lightly leafy and stewy berry/prune-like fruit. There's some hollowness, plus a slightly sappy finish.

| | | | |
|---|---|---|---|
| 2000 | 88 | 2005 | 2008+ |
| 1999 | 91 | 2004 | 2007 |
| 1998 | 93 | 2010 | 2018 |
| 1997 | 91 | 2005 | 2009 |
| 1996 | 95 | 2008 | 2016 |
| 1995 | 87 | 2007 | 2015 |
| 1994 | 93 | 2006 | 2014 |
| 1993 | 87 | 2001 | 2005+ |
| 1992 | 93 | 2000 | 2004+ |
| 1991 | 93 | 1999 | 2003 |
| 1990 | 94 | 2002 | 2010 |
| 1989 | 94 | 2001 | 2006 |
| 1986 | 95 | 1998 | 2003 |

## NOBLE SEMILLON

RANKING 5

**Barossa Valley**  $12–$19 (375 ml)
**Current vintage: 2001**  87

Generous, candied dessert wine with a fragrance of lemon rind, honeydew melon, vanilla and brioche. Its concentrated, tangy palate of candied citrus, melon and tinned pineapple is slightly cloying. Lacks a little elegance and tightness.

| | | | |
|---|---|---|---|
| 2001 | 87 | 2003 | 2006+ |
| 2000 | 90 | 2002 | 2005+ |
| 1999 | 82 | 2001 | 2004 |
| 1998 | 84 | 2003 | 2006 |
| 1997 | 86 | 1999 | 2002 |
| 1996 | 81 | 1997 | 1998 |
| 1995 | 87 | 2000 | 2003 |
| 1994 | 91 | 1999 | 2002 |
| 1992 | 84 | 1997 | 2000 |
| 1990 | 87 | 1995 | 1998 |
| 1989 | 87 | 1994 | 1997 |

## RESERVE RIESLING

RANKING 3

**Eden Valley**  $20–$29
**Current vintage: 2000**  90

Faster-maturing and very approachable riesling whose toasty floral perfume of slightly oily lemon juice, green apple and pear precede a slightly confectionary and forward palate of roundness and juiciness. It becomes tighter, more elegant and chalky towards its tangy finish of citrusy acids.

| | | | |
|---|---|---|---|
| 2000 | 90 | 2005 | 2008+ |
| 1998 | 95 | 2006 | 2010+ |
| 1997 | 90 | 2005 | 2009 |
| 1996 | 90 | 2001 | 2004 |
| 1995 | 92 | 2000 | 2003 |
| 1994 | 93 | 2002 | 2006 |
| 1993 | 95 | 2005 | 2013 |
| 1992 | 93 | 2000 | 2004 |
| 1991 | 93 | 1996 | 1999 |
| 1990 | 92 | 1992 | 1997 |
| 1989 | 91 | 1991 | 1996 |
| 1987 | 91 | 1992 | 1995 |

## STONEWELL

RANKING 2

**Barossa Valley**  $50+
**Current vintage: 1999**  95

Deep, dark brooding aromas of blackberry, plum and blackcurrant concentrate, with meaty, rather gamey new oak qualities. Long, smooth and silky, with penetrative minty small berry flavours, suggestions of licorice and spice tightly interwoven with creamy oak. Typical of the better Barossa wines of this vintage.

| | | | |
|---|---|---|---|
| 1999 | 95 | 2007 | 2011+ |
| 1998 | 89 | 2006 | 2010 |
| 1997 | 93 | 2005 | 2008+ |
| 1996 | 96 | 2008 | 2016+ |
| 1995 | 91 | 2003 | 2007+ |
| 1994 | 96 | 2002 | 2006+ |
| 1993 | 95 | 2005 | 2013 |
| 1992 | 93 | 2000 | 2004 |
| 1991 | 95 | 2011 | 2021 |
| 1990 | 89 | 1998 | 2002+ |
| 1989 | 95 | 2001 | 2006+ |
| 1988 | 95 | 2000 | 2008 |
| 1987 | 94 | 1999 | 2004 |

## THE BAROSSA CABERNET SAUVIGNON

RANKING 4

**Barossa Valley**  $20–$29
**Current vintage: 2002**  91

Barossa cabernet of excellent value, drinkability and cellaring potential. Its dusty, herbal fragrance of violets, cassis, plums and sweet cedar/vanilla oak precedes a smooth, forward palate of genuine depth and structure. It's smooth and elegant, but offers pristine small berry flavours tightly married to creamy vanilla oak and firm, crafted tannins. Remarkable for the price.

| | | | |
|---|---|---|---|
| 2002 | 91 | 2007 | 2010 |
| 2001 | 83 | 2003 | 2006 |
| 2000 | 88 | 2002 | 2005+ |
| 1999 | 87 | 2001 | 2004+ |
| 1998 | 93 | 2006 | 2010 |
| 1997 | 93 | 2002 | 2005+ |
| 1996 | 90 | 2001 | 2004 |
| 1995 | 88 | 2000 | 2003 |
| 1994 | 93 | 1999 | 2002 |
| 1993 | 93 | 2001 | 2005 |
| 1992 | 94 | 2000 | 2004 |
| 1991 | 89 | 1999 | 2003 |
| 1990 | 93 | 2002 | 2010 |
| 1989 | 91 | 1997 | 2001 |
| 1988 | 93 | 2000 | 2008 |

## THE BAROSSA CHARDONNAY

RANKING 5

**Barossa Valley** $12–$19
**Current vintage: 2002** 87

Honest, creamy, generous chardonnay with a smoky aroma of peach, melon and green olives, before a fleshy, juicy palate framed by lemony acids that should flesh out even further.

| | | | |
|---|---|---|---|
| 2001 | 87 | 2004 | 2007 |
| 2001 | 84 | 2002 | 2003 |
| 2000 | 81 | 2001 | 2002 |
| 1998 | 88 | 2000 | 2003 |
| 1997 | 88 | 1998 | 1999 |
| 1996 | 83 | 1997 | 1998 |

## THE BAROSSA GRENACHE

RANKING 5

**Barossa Valley** $12–$19
**Current vintage: 2001** 87

Soft, generous boiled confection-like grenache whose lively flavours of raspberries and blueberries are backed by cinnamon and cloves, with underlying earthy complexity. Round and juicy, very supple and approachable.

| | | | |
|---|---|---|---|
| 2001 | 87 | 2002 | 2003+ |
| 2000 | 88 | 2001 | 2002 |
| 1999 | 84 | 2001 | 2004 |
| 1998 | 88 | 2000 | 2003 |
| 1997 | 86 | 1999 | 2002 |

## THE BAROSSA RIESLING (Formerly Eden Valley Riesling)

RANKING 4

**Barossa Valley, Eden Valley** $12–$19
**Current vintage: 2003** 90

Generous, juicy riesling whose fragrant perfume of musk and floral aromas, tropical, lime and apple-like fruits precede a rather broad, luscious palate of softness and length. Very approachable; for shorter-term cellaring.

| | | | |
|---|---|---|---|
| 2003 | 90 | 2005 | 2008+ |
| 2002 | 90 | 2004 | 2007+ |
| 2001 | 88 | 2003 | 2006 |
| 2000 | 86 | 2001 | 2005 |
| 1999 | 85 | 2000 | 2001 |
| 1998 | 90 | 2003 | 2006 |
| 1997 | 87 | 1999 | 2002 |
| 1996 | 90 | 2001 | 2004 |
| 1995 | 82 | 1997 | 2000 |
| 1994 | 88 | 1999 | 2002 |
| 1993 | 93 | 1998 | 2001 |
| 1992 | 92 | 1997 | 2000 |

## THE BAROSSA SEMILLON

RANKING 4

**Barossa Valley** $5–$11
**Current vintage: 2003** 92

Astonishing value for under ten dollars, this very stylish, racy and tightly balanced semillon is one of the best yet under this label. Its lightly dusty and mineral aromas of melon and gooseberries precede a lean but focused palate whose slightly grassy varietal flavours are supported by restrained and integrated oak influences, before a marvellously fresh and vibrant acid finish.

| | | | |
|---|---|---|---|
| 2003 | 92 | 2008 | 2011 |
| 2002 | 91 | 2004 | 2007+ |
| 2001 | 89 | 2001 | 2002+ |
| 2000 | 92 | 2002 | 2005 |
| 1999 | 89 | 2001 | 2004 |
| 1998 | 89 | 2000 | 2003 |
| 1997 | 90 | 1999 | 2002 |
| 1996 | 89 | 1998 | 2001 |

## THE BAROSSA SHIRAZ

RANKING 4

**Barossa Valley** $12–$19
**Current vintage: 2002** 90

This racy, spicy and silky-smooth young shiraz is bursting with intense, slightly jammy and brightly lit varietal flavour. With a heady floral perfume of cassis, plums and sweet smoky chocolate oak, and a long, concentrated palate simply saturated with fruit, it's finely balanced with fresh acids and integrated fine tannins. Great value.

| | | | |
|---|---|---|---|
| 2002 | 90 | 2007 | 2010 |
| 2001 | 90 | 2003 | 2006 |
| 2000 | 89 | 2002 | 2005+ |
| 1999 | 88 | 2001 | 2004+ |
| 1998 | 92 | 2003 | 2006 |
| 1997 | 93 | 2002 | 2005+ |
| 1996 | 91 | 1998 | 2001 |
| 1995 | 87 | 1997 | 2000 |
| 1994 | 91 | 1999 | 2002 |
| 1993 | 90 | 2001 | 2005 |
| 1992 | 93 | 2000 | 2004 |
| 1991 | 91 | 1996 | 1999 |
| 1990 | 90 | 1995 | 1998 |

# THE SEVEN SURVEYS

RANKING **5**

| Barossa Valley | $20–$29 |
|---|---|
| **Current vintage: 1999** | **90** |

Leathery, savoury Rhône blend with a pungent, sweaty and evolving bouquet of jammy raspberry/plum fruit over floral and spicy aromas. Its meaty, farm floor palate is firm, fine and savoury, given sweetness and softness through chocolate and vanilla oak. Very rustic, earlier-drinking style of some charm.

| 1999 | 90 | 2004 | 2007 |
|---|---|---|---|
| 1998 | 89 | 2003 | 2006 |
| 1997 | 88 | 1999 | 2002+ |
| 1996 | 86 | 1998 | 2001 |

# Pewsey Vale

Browns Rd Pewsey Vale SA 5235. Tel: (08) 8561 3200. Fax: (08) 8561 3393.
Website: www.pewseyvale.com  Email: info@pewseyvale.com
Region: **Eden Valley** Winemaker: **Louisa Rose** Viticulturist: **Robin Nettelbeck**
Chief Executive: **Robert Hill Smith**

Pewsey Vale is a riesling vineyard in the Eden Valley whose consistently reliable wines are made by the very talented Louisa Rose into perfumed, delicate expressions of the dry Australian style. The 1998 vintage of The Contours Riesling, the property's reserve wine, is a classical expression of Eden Valley riesling at its finest.

## RIESLING

RANKING **4**

| Eden Valley | $12–$19 |
|---|---|
| **Current vintage: 2003** | **93** |

Stylish and quite classy, with a baby powder and mineral aroma of lime juice and lemon rind. Long, racy palate whose citrusy fruit finishes with a refreshing mineral persistence.

| 2003 | 93 | 2008 | 2011+ |
|---|---|---|---|
| 2002 | 91 | 2007 | 2010+ |
| 2001 | 90 | 2006 | 2009 |
| 2000 | 91 | 2005 | 2008+ |
| 1999 | 95 | 2007 | 2011+ |
| 1998 | 88 | 2003 | 2006 |
| 1997 | 94 | 2005 | 2009 |
| 1996 | 94 | 2008 | 2016 |
| 1995 | 92 | 2003 | 2007 |
| 1994 | 93 | 2006 | 2014 |
| 1993 | 94 | 1998 | 2001 |
| 1992 | 93 | 1997 | 2000 |
| 1991 | 93 | 1999 | 2003 |
| 1990 | 94 | 1998 | 2002 |
| 1989 | 89 | 1997 | 2001 |
| 1988 | 90 | 1993 | 1996 |

## THE CONTOURS RIESLING

RANKING **2**

| Eden Valley | $20–$29 |
|---|---|
| **Current vintage: 1998** | **95** |

Classic Eden Valley riesling, whose lightly toasty, buttery aromas of honey and fresh flowers reveal a dusty suggestion of waxy lemon rind and lime juice. There's also smoky whiff of bound sulphide. Round and generous, with a juicy, fleshy palate of excellent length, it remains an elegant, stylish and chalky wine that has almost outgrown its adolescence to reveal the true benefits of bottle-age.

| 1998 | 95 | 2006 | 2010+ |
|---|---|---|---|
| 1997 | 89 | 2002 | 2005 |
| 1996 | 95 | 2008 | 2016 |
| 1995 | 92 | 2003 | 2007+ |

# Phillip Island

414 Berry's Beach Road, Phillip Island Vic 3922. Tel: (03) 5956 8465. Fax: (03) 5956 8465.
Website: www.phillipislandwines.com.au  Email: enq@phillipislandwines.com.au
Region: **Gippsland** Winemakers: **David Lance, James Lance** Viticulturist: **Michael Bentley**
Chief Executives: **Joanne & Michael Bentley**

Phillip Island Wines is operated by the Lance family from Diamond Valley in the Yarra Valley hills. Its table wines are typically fresh, vibrant and fruit-driven, with pleasing varietal qualities. It's the only winery at Phillip Island, which is perhaps better known for its motor racing circuit and its local penguin population.

## CABERNET SAUVIGNON  RANKING 5

**Gippsland**  $20–$29
**Current vintage: 2001**  89

Earthy, slightly cooked aromas of confectionary-like sweet berries and vanilla oak precede a juicy, soft and generous palate of intense cherry, plum and raspberry flavours and meaty undertones. Its palate builds nicely towards a powerful, firm and drying finish of lingering jammy dark berry/plum flavours.

| 2001 | 89 | 2006 | 2009+ |
|------|----|------|-------|
| 2000 | 87 | 2002 | 2005+ |
| 1999 | 88 | 2004 | 2007 |
| 1997 | 81 | 1999 | 2002 |

## CHARDONNAY  RANKING 5

**Gippsland**  $20–$29
**Current vintage: 2002**  88

Round, juicy chardonnay with aromas of melon, tobacco and buttery/vanilla oak. Forward and slightly cloying, it's generous, broad and slightly oily, for drinking earlier than later.

| 2002 | 88 | 2004 | 2007 |
|------|----|------|------|
| 2001 | 86 | 2003 | 2006 |
| 2000 | 86 | 2001 | 2002 |
| 1998 | 89 | 2000 | 2003 |
| 1997 | 89 | 1999 | 2002 |

## MERLOT  RANKING 5

**Gippsland**  $20–$29
**Current vintage: 2001**  87

Soft, pretty and easy-drinking merlot with a minty, slightly confectionary expression of berry/cherry fruit and cedar/vanilla oak. Smooth and supple, it's creamy and juicy, with a slightly sappy backbone of fine tannins.

| 2001 | 87 | 2003 | 2006 |
|------|----|------|------|
| 2000 | 88 | 2002 | 2005 |
| 1999 | 81 | 2000 | 2001 |
| 1998 | 86 | 1999 | 2000 |

## THE NOBBIES PINOT NOIR  RANKING 5

**Gippsland**  $20–$29
**Current vintage: 2003**  90

Fragrant aromas of red cherries and dark plums over smoky, charry, charcuterie-like forest floor nuances. Pleasingly vibrant but slightly closed berry/cherry fruit overlies fine-grained tannins and smoky new oak. There's length and intensity, and the wine is likely to build rather handsomely in richness.

| 2003 | 90 | 2005 | 2008 |
|------|----|------|-------|
| 2002 | 87 | 2004 | 2007 |
| 2001 | 86 | 2002 | 2003+ |
| 2000 | 82 | 2001 | 2002 |
| 1999 | 85 | 2000 | 2001 |
| 1998 | 90 | 2000 | 2003 |
| 1997 | 93 | 1999 | 2002 |
| 1996 | 90 | 1998 | 2001+ |

# Pierro

Caves Road, Willyabrup via Cowaramup WA 6284. Tel: (08) 9755 6220. Fax: (08) 9755 6308.
Email: pierro@iinet.net.au

Region: **Margaret River** Winemaker: **Mike Peterkin** Viticulturist: **Mike Peterkin** Chief Executive: **Mike Peterkin**

Pierro is one of the few Australian wineries that could claim to have established a trend that many others have followed. Since the mid 1980s Mike Peterkin has crafted a Chardonnay of monumental power, but of simultaneously smooth and silky delivery. Recent years have seen more refinement and gentility about these wines, as typified by the exceptionally stylish 2002 and 2003 editions. While I believe Peterkin to be more of an instinctive maker of white wine than red, he is also fine-tuning Pierro's red blend into a style of more tightness and balance.

## CABERNET SAUVIGNON MERLOT

RANKING **3**

| Margaret River | $50+ |
|---|---|
| Current vintage: 2001 | 92 |

Sumptuous, modern and well-ripened cabernet blend with some slightly reductive and meaty complexity. Its delicate perfume of small red berries and sweet vanilla/cedar oak precedes a plush, very smooth and rounded palate whose intense small berry flavours are married to an assertive combination of oak and firm, fine tannins. Some ultra-ripe currant-like nuances lead me to question its ultimate longevity.

| | | | |
|---|---|---|---|
| 2001 | 92 | 2009 | 2013+ |
| 2000 | 87 | 2002 | 2005+ |
| 1999 | 93 | 2007 | 2011+ |
| 1998 | 90 | 2006 | 2010+ |
| 1997 | 86 | 2002 | 2005 |
| 1996 | 93 | 2004 | 2008+ |
| 1995 | 87 | 2000 | 2003 |

## CHARDONNAY

RANKING **1**

| Margaret River | $50+ |
|---|---|
| Current vintage: 2003 | 97 |

Wonderfully bright, luscious and vibrant chardonnay with rare intensity and concentration of fruit. Its lightly smoky aromas of ruby grapefruit, honeydew melon and fresh pineapple overlie tightly integrated nuances of sweet, fine-grained vanilla oak. Smooth and juicy, its mouthfilling palate simply explodes with pristine and perfectly ripened flavours of tropical fruits and citrus, tightly underpinned by sweet oak and creamy, lees-derived complexity. It finishes long and persistent, with racy, citrusy acids and lingering tropical fruit flavours.

| | | | |
|---|---|---|---|
| 2003 | 97 | 2008 | 2011+ |
| 2002 | 96 | 2010 | 2014 |
| 2001 | 89 | 2003 | 2006 |
| 2000 | 95 | 2005 | 2008+ |
| 1999 | 96 | 2007 | 2011 |
| 1998 | 93 | 2000 | 2003+ |
| 1997 | 95 | 2002 | 2005+ |
| 1996 | 97 | 2001 | 2004 |
| 1995 | 93 | 2000 | 2003 |
| 1994 | 95 | 2002 | 2006 |
| 1993 | 95 | 2001 | 2005 |
| 1992 | 96 | 2000 | 2004 |
| 1991 | 94 | 1996 | 1999 |
| 1990 | 94 | 1998 | 2002 |
| 1989 | 91 | 1994 | 1997 |
| 1988 | 88 | 1990 | 1995 |
| 1987 | 94 | 1995 | 1999 |
| 1986 | 95 | 1994 | 1998 |

## PINOT NOIR

RANKING **5**

| Margaret River | $30–$49 |
|---|---|
| Current vintage: 2001 | 86 |

Dusty, meaty wet wool aromas precede a firm palate of medium weight and some sweet berry fruit framed by drying tannins. Lacks freshness and vitality.

| | | | |
|---|---|---|---|
| 2001 | 86 | 2003 | 2006 |
| 2000 | 81 | 2002 | 2005+ |
| 1999 | 90 | 2004 | 2007 |
| 1998 | 87 | 2000 | 2003+ |
| 1997 | 89 | 2002 | 2005 |
| 1996 | 88 | 2001 | 2004 |
| 1995 | 84 | 2000 | 2003 |
| 1994 | 87 | 1999 | 2002 |
| 1993 | 90 | 2001 | 2005 |
| 1992 | 90 | 2000 | 2004 |
| 1990 | 94 | 1995 | 1998 |
| 1988 | 82 | 1989 | 1990 |
| 1987 | 93 | 1992 | 1995 |

## SEMILLON SAUVIGNON BLANC (LTC)

RANKING 3

**Margaret River** $20–$29
**Current vintage: 2004** **94**

Stylish, flavoursome and vibrant white Bordeaux blend of translucent brightness and vitality. Its fresh, grassy aromas of gooseberries and passionfruit, plus its juicy, vibrant palate of tangy fruit are enhanced by suggestions of butter and citrus from a subliminal addition of chardonnay. Long and refreshing, it sits neatly above a fine, powdery backbone of chalky phenolics. Excellent shape and balance.

| | | | |
|---|---|---|---|
| 2004 | 94 | 2006 | 2009+ |
| 2003 | 91 | 2005 | 2008+ |
| 2002 | 91 | 2004 | 2007 |
| 2001 | 92 | 2003 | 2006+ |
| 2000 | 94 | 2002 | 2005 |
| 1999 | 89 | 2001 | 2004 |
| 1998 | 91 | 2000 | 2003 |
| 1997 | 93 | 2002 | 2005 |
| 1996 | 94 | 2001 | 2004 |
| 1995 | 93 | 1997 | 2000 |
| 1994 | 93 | 1999 | 2002 |
| 1993 | 93 | 1998 | 2001 |
| 1992 | 91 | 1997 | 2000 |
| 1991 | 91 | 1996 | 1999 |
| 1990 | 90 | 1998 | 2002 |

# Pikes

Polish Hill River Road, Sevenhill SA 5453. Tel: (08) 8843 4370. Fax: (08) 8843 4353.
Website: www.pikeswines.com.au  Email: info@pikeswines.com.au
Region: **Clare Valley** Winemakers: **Neil Pike, John Trotter** Viticulturist: **Andrew Pike**
Chief Executives: **Neil Pike & Andrew Pike**

Pikes is an energetic family-owned and operated winery in Clare. It has made an encouraging move into blends with Italian varieties under its Luccio and Premio labels, but its best wines are its meaty Reserve Shiraz and the steely, austere Reserve Riesling. Pikes enjoyed exceptional riesling vintages in both 2002 and 2003.

## CABERNET

RANKING 5

**Clare Valley** $20–$29
**Current vintage: 2001** **87**

A meaty, very ripe, but simultaneously herbal cabernet with a light aroma of cooked plums, red-currants and vanilla oak. Rather reserved, it's marginally hollow and modestly fruited, but offers some pleasing, if slightly vegetal fruit qualities.

| | | | |
|---|---|---|---|
| 2001 | 87 | 2006 | 2009 |
| 2000 | 86 | 2002 | 2005+ |
| 1999 | 89 | 2004 | 2007 |
| 1998 | 91 | 2006 | 2010+ |
| 1997 | 89 | 2005 | 2009 |
| 1996 | 91 | 2004 | 2008+ |
| 1995 | 87 | 1997 | 2000 |
| 1994 | 94 | 2002 | 2006 |
| 1993 | 93 | 1998 | 2001 |
| 1992 | 94 | 2000 | 2004 |
| 1991 | 93 | 1999 | 2003 |
| 1990 | 93 | 1998 | 2002 |

## RESERVE RIESLING

RANKING 2

**Clare Valley** $20–$29
**Current vintage: 2002** **96**

Sherbet-like aromas of lime and wet minerals, fresh flowers and lemon essence. Long and racy, superbly punctuated and presented palate of exceptional fineness and tightness. Pure lime juice, lemon and apple flavours of rare concentration culminate in a long and refreshing finish of razor-like mineral acids. Very stylish and complete.

| | | | |
|---|---|---|---|
| 2002 | 96 | 2010 | 2014+ |
| 2001 | 94 | 2009 | 2013+ |
| 1997 | 95 | 2005 | 2009 |

## RIESLING

RANKING 2

**Clare Valley** $12–$19
**Current vintage: 2003** **94**

A pristine, long and stylish riesling, whose musky, floral perfume of fresh pear and apple aromas precede a long, shapely palate bursting with pure riesling flavours. It finishes long and refreshing, with clean citrusy acids.

| | | | |
|---|---|---|---|
| 2003 | 94 | 2008 | 2011+ |
| 2002 | 94 | 2007 | 2010 |
| 2001 | 92 | 2006 | 2009 |
| 2000 | 94 | 2008 | 2012 |
| 1999 | 95 | 2007 | 2011 |
| 1998 | 93 | 2003 | 2006+ |
| 1997 | 89 | 2002 | 2005 |
| 1996 | 90 | 2001 | 2004 |
| 1995 | 81 | 1997 | 2000 |
| 1992 | 87 | 1997 | 2000 |
| 1990 | 93 | 1998 | 2002 |
| 1988 | 93 | 1993 | 1996 |

## SHIRAZ

RANKING **5**

| Clare Valley | $20–$29 | | |
|---|---|---|---|
| **Current vintage: 2001** | **89** | | |

Fine, spicy and rustic shiraz with a meaty, musky aroma of dark cherries, plums and red berries with slightly herbal undertones of cloves and cinnamon, mint and menthol. Its long, peppery palate is both elegant and complex, with lingering sweet berry flavours finishing tight, spicy and savoury.

| | | | |
|---|---|---|---|
| 2001 | 89 | 2006 | 2009 |
| 2000 | 87 | 2005 | 2008 |
| 1999 | 89 | 2004 | 2007 |
| 1998 | 88 | 2006 | 2010+ |
| 1997 | 90 | 2005 | 2009 |
| 1996 | 87 | 2001 | 2004 |
| 1995 | 93 | 2000 | 2003 |
| 1994 | 91 | 1999 | 2002 |
| 1993 | 90 | 2001 | 2005 |
| 1992 | 94 | 2000 | 2004 |
| 1991 | 94 | 2003 | 2011 |
| 1990 | 94 | 2002 | 2010 |

# Pipers Brook

1216 Pipers Brook Road, Pipers Brook Tas 7254. Tel: (03) 6382 7527. Fax: (03) 6382 7226.
Website: www.pipersbrook.com  Email: enquiries@pipersbrook.com

Region: **Pipers River** Winemaker: **Rene Bezemer** Viticulturist: **Bruce McCormack** Chief Executive: **Paul de Moor**

Pipers Brook is the largest and most significant maker of Tasmanian wine, and has introduced thousands of people to the distinctively different qualities and styles of the wines from the coolest and southernmost Australian state. For a relatively small producer (by mainland standards), it operates a somewhat confusing hierarchy of labels, but the company's intentions to isolate its best sites and to keep separate these wines is entirely laudable. While the company has perhaps achieved most renown with its Burgundian varieties (and the Reserve Chardonnay from 2001 is delightful), I tend to rate its Riesling, Gewürztraminer and Pinot Gris more highly.

## CUVÉE CLARK RIESLING (Late Harvest)

RANKING **3**

| Pipers River | $30–$49 (375 ml) | | |
|---|---|---|---|
| **Current vintage: 2003** | **93** | | |

Nutty, pastry-like scents of fresh flowers, melon and mango, pear and apple, backed by confection-like baby powdery undertones. Pure, bright and lively, it offers a sweet and luscious palate whose concentrated flavours of apricots, lime and pear finish savoury and clean, with racy and refreshing acidity.

| | | | |
|---|---|---|---|
| 2003 | 93 | 2005 | 2008+ |
| 2001 | 95 | 2006 | 2009+ |
| 2000 | 96 | 2005 | 2008+ |

## ESTATE CHARDONNAY

RANKING **3**

| Pipers River | $30–$49 | | |
|---|---|---|---|
| **Current vintage: 2002** | **86** | | |

A slightly green-edged chardonnay with complex nutty aromas of honeysuckle, green cashew and nectarine, apple and melon, with buttery and slightly charry undertones. Rather syrupy, its sappy and slightly spiky palate of green olives, butterscotch and nutty vanilla oak is very forward, lacking genuine depth of fruit.

| | | | |
|---|---|---|---|
| 2002 | 86 | 2004 | 2007 |
| 2001 | 94 | 2006 | 2009 |
| 2000 | 93 | 2005 | 2008 |
| 1999 | 88 | 2001 | 2004 |
| 1998 | 90 | 2003 | 2006 |
| 1997 | 92 | 1999 | 2002 |
| 1996 | 86 | 1998 | 2001 |
| 1995 | 94 | 2003 | 2007 |
| 1994 | 82 | 1996 | 1999 |
| 1993 | 93 | 1998 | 2001 |
| 1992 | 93 | 1997 | 2000 |
| 1991 | 94 | 1999 | 2003 |

## ESTATE GEWÜRZTRAMINER

RANKING **3**

| Pipers River | $20–$29 | | |
|---|---|---|---|
| **Current vintage: 2003** | **93** | | |

Very classical, very Alsatian expression of gewürztraminer, whose musky perfume of rose water and lychees precedes a smooth, round and sumptuous palate that remains just the right side of oiliness. There's excellent length and breadth of flavour, while the finish is both lingering and austere. A shade more acid might have tightened it even further, but it still has improvement ahead.

| | | | |
|---|---|---|---|
| 2003 | 93 | 2008 | 2011+ |
| 2001 | 93 | 2006 | 2009 |
| 2000 | 94 | 2005 | 2008 |
| 1999 | 89 | 2004 | 2007 |
| 1998 | 94 | 2003 | 2006+ |
| 1997 | 90 | 1999 | 2002 |
| 1996 | 86 | 2001 | 2004 |
| 1995 | 94 | 2000 | 2003 |
| 1993 | 90 | 1995 | 1998 |
| 1992 | 93 | 2000 | 2004 |
| 1991 | 90 | 1999 | 2003 |
| 1990 | 89 | 1995 | 1998 |

## ESTATE PINOT GRIS

RANKING 4

PIPERS BROOK VINEYARD
2001 PINOT GRIS
T A S M A N I A

**Pipers River**     $20–$29
**Current vintage: 2003**     82

A leafy, greenish rose garden perfume precedes a lightly fruited and somewhat dilute palate of under-ripe fruit that finishes savoury, sappy and nutty.

| | | | |
|---|---|---|---|
| 2003 | 82 | 2003 | 2004 |
| 2001 | 77 | 2002 | 2003 |
| 2000 | 90 | 2002 | 2005 |
| 1999 | 94 | 2001 | 2004 |
| 1998 | 87 | 1999 | 2000 |

## ESTATE PINOT NOIR (Formerly Pellion)

RANKING 4

PIPERS BROOK VINEYARD
2000 PINOT NOIR
T A S M A N I A

E S T A T E

**Pipers River**     $30–$49
**Current vintage: 2002**     87

Forward, up-front pinot with attractive and slightly jammy maraschino cherry, raspberry and plum-like aromas and grassy, dill pickle-like undertones. Fine bony tannins underpin its juicy cherry/plum flavours, but it lacks the length and intensity for a higher rating.

| | | | |
|---|---|---|---|
| 2002 | 87 | 2004 | 2007 |
| 2001 | 81 | 2002 | 2003 |
| 2000 | 90 | 2002 | 2005 |
| 1999 | 90 | 2004 | 2007 |
| 1998 | 86 | 2000 | 2003+ |
| 1997 | 89 | 2002 | 2005 |
| 1996 | 82 | 2001 | 2004 |
| 1995 | 89 | 1997 | 2000 |
| 1994 | 90 | 1999 | 2002 |
| 1993 | 89 | 1995 | 1998 |
| 1992 | 91 | 1997 | 2000 |
| 1991 | 93 | 1999 | 2003 |

## ESTATE RIESLING

RANKING 3

PIPERS BROOK VINEYARD
2001 RIESLING
T A S M A N I A

**Pipers River**     $20–$29
**Current vintage: 2003**     89

Broad, rather alcoholic and confectionary riesling with a spicy, musky perfume of honeysuckle and lime, with underlying nuances of apricots. It offers some delightful riesling flavour, but its hotness and excessive breadth detract from its harmony and longevity.

| | | | |
|---|---|---|---|
| 2003 | 89 | 2005 | 2008 |
| 2002 | 90 | 2004 | 2007 |
| 2001 | 93 | 2003 | 2006+ |
| 2000 | 95 | 2012 | 2020 |
| 1999 | 93 | 2007 | 2011 |
| 1998 | 95 | 2006 | 2010 |
| 1997 | 90 | 2002 | 2005 |
| 1996 | 93 | 2004 | 2008 |
| 1995 | 93 | 2003 | 2007 |
| 1994 | 91 | 2002 | 2006 |
| 1993 | 94 | 1998 | 2001 |
| 1992 | 86 | 1994 | 1997 |

## OPIMIAN CABERNET BLEND

RANKING 5

PIPERS BROOK VINEYARD
2000 OPIMIAN
Cabernet Sauvignon/Merlot/Cabernet Franc
T A S M A N I A

E S T A T E

**Northern Tasmania**     $30–$49
**Current vintage: 2000**     86

Pungent earthy and seaweed-like aromas of light berry fruit, brown olives and sweet cedar/gamey vanilla oak. Thin and lean, with under-ripe fruit underpinned by very smart new oak, it finishes steely and hard-edged, lacking weight and structure.

| | | | |
|---|---|---|---|
| 2000 | 86 | 2005 | 2008 |
| 1999 | 87 | 2004 | 2007 |
| 1998 | 81 | 2003 | 2006 |
| 1997 | 84 | 2002 | 2005 |
| 1995 | 94 | 2003 | 2007 |
| 1992 | 87 | 1994 | 1997 |
| 1991 | 90 | 1999 | 2003 |
| 1989 | 87 | 1994 | 1997 |
| 1988 | 90 | 1996 | 2000 |

## PIRIE

RANKING 5

**Pipers River**     $50+
**Current vintage: 1998**     87

Varnishy and highly oxidative aromas of dried flowers, brown apple and wheatmeal, before a nutty, savoury palate that does reveal more sweetness of fruit, a good length of flavour and a fine, tight bead. Needs more texture and freshness.

| | | | |
|---|---|---|---|
| 1998 | 87 | 2003 | 2006 |
| 1997 | 86 | 1999 | 2002 |
| 1996 | 83 | 1998 | 2001 |
| 1995 | 95 | 2000 | 2003+ |

**THE AUSTRALIAN WINE ANNUAL**
www.onwine.com.au
**2005**

## SUMMIT CHARDONNAY

| Pipers River | $50+ |
|---|---|
| **Current vintage: 2000** | **89** |

Very pungent wild and meaty smallgoods aromas over nuances of melon, stonefruit and smoky vanilla oak. Rather varnishy, its chewy, buttery palate marries juicy melon and citrus flavours with overtly bacony, nutty and savoury influences. It's oily almost to the point of hardness, finishing with a slightly varnishy sweetness. Very interesting, technically imperfect, but full of character.

| 2000 | 89 | 2002 | 2005 |
|---|---|---|---|
| 1999 | 88 | 2001 | 2004 |
| 1998 | 91 | 2000 | 2003 |
| 1997 | 82 | 1999 | 2002 |

# Plantagenet

Albany Highway, Mount Barker WA 6324. Tel: (08) 9851 2150. Fax: (08) 9851 1839.
Email: planwine@rainbow.agn.net.au

Region: **Mount Barker** Winemaker: **Richard Robson** Viticulturists: **Roger Pattenden, Peter Glen**
Chief Executive: **Tony Smith**

Plantagenet might be located in one of the most challenging and least climatically consistent of Australian wine regions, but does an exceptional job in crafting a range of varietal wines of generous flavours, integrity and cellaring ability. With a sound regime of winemaking in place for each of its key varieties, picking Plantagenet's best wine is really a matter of seeing what season best promotes which varieties in the vineyards.

## CABERNET SAUVIGNON

RANKING 4

| Mount Barker | $30–$49 |
|---|---|
| **Current vintage: 2001** | **90** |

A firm, structured cabernet with some over-cooked and under-ripe influences. Pleasing scents of small berries and suggestions of under-growth lie beneath earthy, leathery and slightly grassy aromas and cedary oak. Smooth and creamy, the velvet-like palate presents pleasing fruit, forest floor and herbaceous elements, framed by fine, but drying tannins.

| 2001 | 90 | 2009 | 2013 |
|---|---|---|---|
| 1999 | 89 | 2004 | 2007+ |
| 1998 | 93 | 2006 | 2010 |
| 1997 | 88 | 2005 | 2009 |
| 1996 | 87 | 2001 | 2004 |
| 1995 | 88 | 2003 | 2007 |
| 1994 | 95 | 2006 | 2014+ |
| 1993 | 90 | 2001 | 2005 |
| 1992 | 94 | 2004 | 2012 |
| 1991 | 92 | 2003 | 2011 |
| 1990 | 94 | 2002 | 2010 |
| 1989 | 93 | 2001 | 2009 |

## CHARDONNAY

RANKING 3

| Mount Barker | $20–$29 |
|---|---|
| **Current vintage: 2003** | **94** |

Elegant, savoury cellar style of chardonnay with a honeysuckle-like fragrance of ruby grapefruit, tinned tropical fruits and grilled nuts supported by light vanilla oak. Its fine, fluffy palate finishes long and tightly integrated, revealing a pristine core of intense fruit, plus creamy wheatmeal complexity.

| 2003 | 94 | 2008 | 2011 |
|---|---|---|---|
| 2001 | 85 | 2003 | 2006 |
| 2000 | 93 | 2005 | 2008 |
| 1999 | 94 | 2004 | 2007+ |
| 1998 | 89 | 2003 | 2006 |
| 1997 | 91 | 2002 | 2005 |
| 1996 | 87 | 2001 | 2004 |
| 1995 | 93 | 2000 | 2003 |

## PINOT NOIR

| Mount Barker | $30–$49 |
|---|---|
| **Current vintage: 2002** | **86** |

Lacking real varietal definition, this sappy and slightly raw-edged pinot is a little rubbery, meaty and sweaty. Its round, tomatoey expression of plum-like fruit is green-edged and stewy, finishing sappy with green bean-like flavours.

| 2002 | 86 | 2004 | 2007 |
|---|---|---|---|
| 2001 | 80 | 2003 | 2006 |
| 2000 | 83 | 2002 | 2005 |
| 1999 | 86 | 2001 | 2004 |
| 1998 | 87 | 2000 | 2003+ |
| 1997 | 90 | 1999 | 2002+ |
| 1996 | 91 | 2001 | 2004 |
| 1995 | 91 | 2000 | 2003 |
| 1994 | 89 | 1996 | 1999 |

A
B
C
D
E
F
G
H
I
J
K
L
M
N
O
**P**
Q
R
S
T
U
V
W
X
Y
Z

## RIESLING

| Mount Barker | $12–$19 |
|---|---|
| **Current vintage: 2003** | **89** |

Dusty aromas of apricot and citrus rind suggest some botrytis influences, but there's plenty of fresh floral and limey fruit as well. Forward and juicy, it's a musky, spicy riesling with attractive fruit sweetness. It finishes clean and dry, with a slight tin-like note and a suggestion of freshly cut apple.

| | | | |
|---|---|---|---|
| 2003 | 89 | 2005 | 2008 |
| 2002 | 88 | 2004 | 2007 |
| 2001 | 94 | 2009 | 2013 |
| 2000 | 95 | 2005 | 2008 |
| 1999 | 93 | 2007 | 2011 |
| 1998 | 95 | 2006 | 2010 |
| 1997 | 94 | 2005 | 2009 |
| 1996 | 94 | 2004 | 2008 |
| 1995 | 94 | 2003 | 2007 |
| 1994 | 94 | 2006 | 2014 |
| 1993 | 94 | 1998 | 2001 |

## SHIRAZ

| Mount Barker | $30–$49 |
|---|---|
| **Current vintage: 2001** | **90** |

Musky, wild and fragrant shiraz whose peppery, briary dark red berry and cherry fruit is backed by undergrowth-like complexity and sweet cedary/vanilla oak. Smooth and silky, medium to full in weight, with developed, earthy complexity, it's a Rhône expression with soft, but rigid tannins that finishes long, meaty and savoury. The flavours might just be evolving ahead of its structure.

| | | | |
|---|---|---|---|
| 2001 | 90 | 2006 | 2009 |
| 2000 | 90 | 2005 | 2008 |
| 1999 | 93 | 2007 | 2011+ |
| 1998 | 95 | 2006 | 2010 |
| 1997 | 86 | 1999 | 2002 |
| 1996 | 87 | 2002 | 2008 |
| 1995 | 93 | 2003 | 2007 |
| 1994 | 96 | 2002 | 2006 |
| 1993 | 94 | 2005 | 2013 |
| 1991 | 91 | 1999 | 2003 |
| 1990 | 93 | 1998 | 2002 |
| 1989 | 90 | 2001 | 2009 |
| 1988 | 90 | 2000 | 2008 |
| 1987 | 90 | 1999 | 2007 |
| 1986 | 88 | 1998 | 2007 |

# Poet's Corner

Craigmoor Road, Mudgee NSW 2850. Tel: (02) 6372 2208. Fax: (02) 6372 4464.
Website: www.poetscornerwines.com Email: info@poetscornerwines.com

Region: **Mudgee** Winemaker: **James Manners** Viticulturist: **Frank Hellwig** Chief Executive: **Laurent Lacassgne**

Poet's Corner is an Orlando Wyndham-owned Mudgee brand that has evolved out of a pair of very good and affordable red and white table wines. It has recently gone up-market with some reasonably good 'Henry Lawson' wines, of which the Chardonnay has been quite classy. I can't help thinking the Henry Lawson theme has rather been done to death.

## HENRY LAWSON CABERNET SAUVIGNON

| Mudgee | $20–$29 |
|---|---|
| **Current vintage: 2001** | **86** |

Meaty, stewy and slightly soupy aromas of cooked plums, prunes and currants, with plenty of assertive sweet vanilla and mocha/chocolate oak plus gamey undertones. Firm and concentrated, but lacking genuine depth of fruit sweetness, it's an over-ripened style with rather assertive, drying tannin.

| | | | |
|---|---|---|---|
| 2001 | 86 | 2006 | 2009 |
| 1998 | 88 | 2003 | 2006 |
| 1997 | 87 | 2002 | 2005+ |

## HENRY LAWSON SHIRAZ

| Mudgee | $20–$29 |
|---|---|
| **Current vintage: 2002** | **89** |

A rustic, spicy medium-term red with an earthy honesty. Its restrained bouquet of redcurrants, briary cassis, plums and blackberries reveal undertones of nutty, cedary/vanilla oak with hints of game meat. Slightly cooked, with confectionary red berry fruit, it's smooth and generous, with up-front earthy, spicy fruit and sweet cedary oak framed by soft tannins.

| | | | |
|---|---|---|---|
| 2002 | 89 | 2007 | 2010+ |
| 2001 | 88 | 2006 | 2009 |
| 1998 | 89 | 2006 | 2010+ |
| 1997 | 83 | 2002 | 2005 |

## SHIRAZ CABERNET BLEND

**Various** $12–$19
**Current vintage: 2002** 87

Very good cheaper red blend with a vibrant, slightly jammy aroma of minty cassis, raspberries and plums, with floral and cedary undertones. Spicy, smooth and creamy, its fresh berry flavours overlie some earthy riverland characters, but are given structure and shape through fine-grained tannins. Good length and value.

| | | | |
|---|---|---|---|
| 2002 | 87 | 2004 | 2007+ |
| 2001 | 85 | 2002 | 2003 |
| 1999 | 82 | 2000 | 2001 |
| 1998 | 83 | 2000 | 2003 |
| 1997 | 86 | 1999 | 2002 |
| 1996 | 88 | 2001 | 2004 |
| 1995 | 87 | 1997 | 2000 |

## UNWOODED CHARDONNAY

RANKING **5**

**Various** $5–$11
**Current vintage: 2003** 86

Lively aromas of peaches, nectarines and melons with slightly rancid green cashew-like nuances. Round, oily and confectionary, rather green-edged and sappy, it finishes without great length or depth.

| | | | |
|---|---|---|---|
| 2003 | 86 | 2004 | 2005 |
| 2001 | 83 | 2002 | 2003 |
| 2000 | 80 | 2000 | 2001 |
| 1999 | 87 | 2000 | 2001 |
| 1998 | 88 | 1999 | 2000 |

## WHITE BLEND

RANKING **5**

**Mudgee** $5–$11
**Current vintage: 2003** 87

Fragrant aromas of mango, paw paw, peach and lemon are slightly grassy, with undertones of lightly dusty vanilla oak. Round, juicy and generous, it's slightly cooked, but lively and fruity, finishing clean and refreshing with lemony acids.

| | | | |
|---|---|---|---|
| 2003 | 87 | 2004 | 2005 |
| 2002 | 88 | 2003 | 2004+ |
| 2000 | 87 | 2001 | 2002 |
| 1999 | 82 | 2001 | 2004 |
| 1998 | 82 | 1999 | 2000 |
| 1997 | 87 | 1998 | 1999 |
| 1996 | 87 | 1997 | 1998 |

# Poole's Rock

DeBeyers Road, Pokolbin NSW 2320. Tel: (02) 4998 7389 Fax: (02) 4998 7682
Website: www.poolesrock.com.au Email: info@poolesrock.com.au
Region: **Lower Hunter Valley** Winemaker: **Partick Auld** Viticulturist: **Evan Powell** Chief Executive: **Peter Russell**

With the purchase of the Tulloch winery from Southcorp in 2002, Poole's Rock acquired a base in the heart of the Hunter Valley. With the more recent appointment of former Tulloch winemaker Patrick Auld, Poole's Rock has bought itself an inestimable resource of Hunter Valley experience and talent. I look forward to seeing how these developments affect the company's premier label, its soft, smooth and approachable Chardonnay.

## CHARDONNAY

RANKING **4**

**Lower Hunter Valley** $20–$29
**Current vintage: 2001** 89

A crafted, winemaker-driven chardonnay whose peachy fruit qualities of melon and tobacco are rather over-awed by its lightly varnishy and dusty oak. Ripe, juicy and tropical, it finishes nutty and savoury with fresh lemony acids, but would have been better and longer living with less overt wood influence.

| | | | |
|---|---|---|---|
| 2001 | 89 | 2003 | 2006 |
| 1999 | 89 | 2001 | 2004 |
| 1998 | 90 | 2003 | 2006 |
| 1997 | 90 | 2002 | 2005 |
| 1996 | 92 | 1998 | 2001 |
| 1995 | 87 | 1997 | 2000 |

# Port Phillip Estate

261 Red Hill Road, Red Hill South Vic 3937. Tel: (03) 5989 2708. Fax: (03) 5989 3017.
Website: www.portphillip.net  Email: sales@portphillip.net

Region: **Mornington Peninsula** Winemaker: **Sandro Mosele** Viticulturist: **Doug Wood**
Chief Executive: **Georgio Gjergja**

Port Phillip Estate is a tiny Mornington Peninsula producer of occasionally stylish and finely balanced Shiraz and heady, spicy Pinot Noir from its tiny vineyard high on Red Hill. it recently moved its contracted winemaking to Kooyong, where Sandro Mosele was beginning to exert an influence. Next thing, the owners of Port Phillip Estate made an offer the owners of Kooyong found impossible to refuse. At very least, Port Phillip Estate's wine will now for the first time ever be made in its own premises.

## PINOT NOIR

RANKING **5**

| Mornington Peninsula | $20–$29 |
|---|---|
| **Current vintage: 2002** | **87** |

Pretty, early-drinking pinot with a herbal aroma of spicy sweet cherries and raspberries over some impressive sweet vanilla oak. Smooth and forward, its jammy berry/cherry flavours are spicy and herbal, lacking real presence in the mouth and finishing slightly sappy.

| | | | |
|---|---|---|---|
| 2002 | 87 | 2003 | 2004+ |
| 2001 | 89 | 2003 | 2006 |
| 2000 | 82 | 2002 | 2005 |
| 1999 | 91 | 2001 | 2004+ |
| 1998 | 88 | 1999 | 2000 |

## SHIRAZ

RANKING **5**

| Mornington Peninsula | $30–$49 |
|---|---|
| **Current vintage: 2001** | **80** |

Gluey, smoky and charry oak detracts from its attractive, if slightly cooked plummy and berry flavours. Its palate is smothered by excessively smoky and splintery oak influences, while a lightly greenish thread still remains evident.

| | | | |
|---|---|---|---|
| 2001 | 79 | 2003 | 2006 |
| 2000 | 89 | 2002 | 2005+ |
| 1999 | 86 | 2000 | 2003 |
| 1998 | 89 | 2002 | 2005+ |

# Preece

Mitchelton, Nagambie Vic 3608. Tel: (03) 5736 2222. Fax: (03) 5736 2266.
Website: www.mitchelton.com.au  Email: mitchelton@mitchelton.com.au

Region: **Goulburn Valley** Winemakers: **Don Lewis, Toby Barlow** Viticulturist: **John Beresford**
Chief Executive: **Peter Cowan**

Preece is a Mitchelton brand comprising a number of varietal table wines grown in the Nagambie Lakes region. Several of the current releases are simply exceptional, especially at their modest price-points.

## CABERNET SAUVIGNON

RANKING **5**

| Nagambie Lakes | $12–$19 |
|---|---|
| **Current vintage: 2002** | **90** |

Very competent cabernet with intense minty aromas of dark plums, berries, restrained vanilla oak and a whiff of menthol. Long, elegant and fully ripe, the palate presents vibrant cassis flavours, measured cedary oak and suggestions of dark olives. Over-delivers for the asking price.

| | | | |
|---|---|---|---|
| 2002 | 90 | 2007 | 2010 |
| 2001 | 88 | 2006 | 2009 |
| 2000 | 89 | 2005 | 2008 |
| 1999 | 89 | 2001 | 2004+ |
| 1998 | 87 | 2000 | 2003+ |
| 1997 | 83 | 2002 | 2005 |
| 1996 | 86 | 1998 | 2001 |
| 1995 | 87 | 2000 | 2003 |
| 1994 | 89 | 1999 | 2002 |
| 1993 | 87 | 1998 | 2001 |

## CHARDONNAY

PREECE

CHARDONNAY
2003

| Nagambie Lakes | $12–$19 |
|---|---|
| **Current vintage: 2003** | **86** |

Lively aromas of lemon, pineapple and fresh apple over light, nutty oak influences. Juicy tropical and cashew-like fruit finishes with good length and soft acids, but some slightly cardboard-like oak.

| | | | |
|---|---|---|---|
| 2003 | 86 | 2004 | 2005 |
| 2002 | 84 | 2002 | 2003 |
| 2001 | 84 | 2001 | 2002 |
| 2000 | 88 | 2001 | 2002 |
| 1999 | 82 | 1999 | 2000 |
| 1998 | 86 | 1999 | 2000 |

## MERLOT

RANKING **5**

PREECE

MERLOT
2002 VICTORIA

| Nagambie Lakes | $12–$19 |
|---|---|
| **Current vintage: 2002** | **90** |

A sumptuous, juicy little merlot with all the right bells and whistles. There's a hint of mint and menthol and a light eucalypt note about its aromas of dark cherries, plums and blackberries, while its pristine palate is textbook easy-drinking merlot. Medium to full in weight, it is also a wine of some substance, supported by fine-grained and drying tannins. Exceptional value.

| | | | |
|---|---|---|---|
| 2002 | 90 | 2004 | 2007+ |
| 2000 | 88 | 2002 | 2005+ |
| 1999 | 89 | 2001 | 2004+ |
| 1998 | 87 | 2003 | 2006 |
| 1997 | 89 | 2002 | 2005 |
| 1996 | 83 | 1998 | 2001 |
| 1995 | 90 | 2000 | 2003 |
| 1994 | 88 | 1999 | 2002 |
| 1993 | 87 | 1998 | 2001 |

## SAUVIGNON BLANC

RANKING **5**

PREECE

SAUVIGNON
BLANC
2003 VICTORIA

| Nagambie Lakes | $12–$19 |
|---|---|
| **Current vintage: 2004** | **87** |

Punchy ripe gooseberry, passionfruit and melon aromas with up-front grassy qualities precede a long, slippery palate of freshness and vitality. Clean as a whistle, its pleasing fruit finishes long and dry.

| | | | |
|---|---|---|---|
| 2004 | 87 | 2004 | 2005+ |
| 2003 | 90 | 2003 | 2004+ |
| 2002 | 86 | 2002 | 2003 |
| 2001 | 87 | 2002 | 2003 |
| 2000 | 87 | 2001 | 2002 |
| 1999 | 89 | 2000 | 2001 |
| 1998 | 90 | 1998 | 1999 |
| 1997 | 82 | 1998 | 1999 |

## SHIRAZ

RANKING **5**

PREECE

1998 SHIRAZ

| Nagambie Lakes | $12–$19 |
|---|---|
| **Current vintage: 2002** | **89** |

Very neat, very flavoursome and affordable shiraz more than capable of causing some embarrassment. Its sweet and slightly meaty fragrance of dark berries, plus and cedar/chocolate oak precedes a smooth and supple palate with a hint of muddy earthiness beneath its vibrant small berry flavours. Its tannins are firm but smooth, and oak plays a contented second fiddle.

| | | | |
|---|---|---|---|
| 2002 | 89 | 2004 | 2007 |
| 2001 | 81 | 2003 | 2006 |
| 2000 | 87 | 2002 | 2005 |
| 1999 | 87 | 2001 | 2004 |
| 1998 | 86 | 2000 | 2003 |

A
B
C
D
E
F
G
H
I
J
K
L
M
N
O
**P**
Q
R
S
T
U
V
W
X
Y
Z

# Primo Estate

Old Port Wakefield Road, Virginia SA 5120. Tel: (08) 8380 9442. Fax: (08) 8380 9696.
Website: www.primoestate.com.au  Email: info@primoestate.com.au

Region: **Adelaide**  Winemakers: **Joe Grilli, David Tait**  Viticulturist: **Peter Grilli**  Chief Executive: **Joe Grilli**

Joe Grilli is one of the most creative and instinctive winemakers in Australia. His list of innovations includes the savoury, fine-grained and long-living Moda Amarone cabernet blend plus the riesling-based La Magia dessert wine under the same label, which incorporates a small portion of musky gewürztraminer. The Sparkling Red Joseph blend includes old vintages of bottle-aged Australian dry reds, while La Biondina Colombard takes this humble variety into hitherto unchartered territory.

## IL BRICCONE SHIRAZ SANGIOVESE     RANKING 5

**Various, South Australia**    $12–$19
**Current vintage: 2002**              86

Earthy, rustic and old-fashioned red with spicy farmyard aromas of sweet leather, cloves and pepper, with horsehair nuances. Initially smooth and elegant, it dries out to a savoury, spicy finish that lacks its customary weight and richness.

| | | | |
|---|---|---|---|
| 2002 | 86 | 2004 | 2007 |
| 2001 | 92 | 2003 | 2006+ |
| 2000 | 89 | 2002 | 2005 |
| 1999 | 89 | 2001 | 2004 |
| 1998 | 82 | 1999 | 2000 |

## JOSEPH MODA AMARONE CABERNET BLEND     RANKING 2

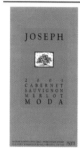

**Fleurieu Peninsula,**
**Limestone Coast**           $50+
**Current vintage: 2001**        93

Lightly cooked, meaty and developing aromas of meaty, nutty fruit and sweet mocha/chocolate oak. Firm, bony tannins and assertive oak handsomely partner smooth, almost sumptuous and concentrated flavours of raisins, currants, plums and cherry jam. It's a powerful and overtly oaky and astringent wine whose deep, slightly cooked fruit and structure remind me of Barolo.

| | | | |
|---|---|---|---|
| 2001 | 93 | 2009 | 2013+ |
| 2000 | 92 | 2008 | 2012 |
| 1999 | 95 | 2011 | 2019 |
| 1998 | 89 | 2003 | 2006 |
| 1997 | 88 | 2002 | 2005 |
| 1996 | 93 | 2008 | 2016 |
| 1995 | 94 | 2007 | 2015 |
| 1994 | 97 | 2006 | 2014 |
| 1993 | 95 | 2005 | 2013 |
| 1992 | 92 | 2004 | 2012 |
| 1991 | 97 | 2003 | 2011 |
| 1990 | 94 | 2002 | 2010 |
| 1989 | 94 | 2001 | 2009 |
| 1988 | 90 | 1996 | 2000 |
| 1987 | 88 | 1995 | 1999 |

## JOSEPH 'LA MAGIA' BOTRYTIS WHITE BLEND     RANKING 2

**Adelaide Plains**          $30–$49
**Current vintage: 2002**          95

An exotic perfume of spicy lemon blossom, honeysuckle and lemon meringue overlies fragrant nuances of pear, apple and lychees, with underlying musky rose oil traminer influences. Syrupy and honeyed, the concentrated, luscious palate of great intensity and sweetness reveals pristine, pure fruit before a lingering, clean finish. Excellent poise and balance.

| | | | |
|---|---|---|---|
| 2002 | 95 | 2004 | 2007+ |
| 2001 | 94 | 2003 | 2006+ |
| 1998 | 86 | 2000 | 2003+ |
| 1996 | 90 | 2001 | 2004 |
| 1995 | 95 | 2000 | 2003 |
| 1994 | 94 | 1999 | 2002 |
| 1993 | 95 | 2001 | 2005 |
| 1991 | 94 | 1999 | 2003 |
| 1989 | 88 | 1994 | 1998 |

## 'LA BIONDINA' COLOMBARD     RANKING 5

**Adelaide Plains**          $12–$19
**Current vintage: 2003**          89

A remarkably complex expression of colombard, with a lightly grassy fragrance of spicy and slightly confectionary citrus and tropical fruit. Its punchy, almost funky palate of pineapple and passionfruit and creamy leesy undertones finishes mineral and austere, with a dusty talcum powder texture.

| | | | |
|---|---|---|---|
| 2003 | 89 | 2004 | 2005 |
| 2002 | 87 | 2002 | 2003 |
| 2001 | 88 | 2002 | 2003 |
| 1999 | 83 | 2000 | 2001 |
| 1997 | 86 | 1997 | 1997 |

# Prince Albert

100 Lemins Road, Waurn Ponds Vic 3216. Tel: (03) 5241 8091. Fax: (03) 5241 8091.

Region: **Geelong** Winemaker: **Bruce Hyett** Viticulturist: **Bruce Hyett** Chief Executive: **Bruce Hyett**

Prince Albert was the first Victorian vineyard to be entirely devoted to pinot noir. While some stress is evident in the 2003 vintage, the property's increasing vine age have both contributed flesh and weight to its wine, which is becoming one of Victoria's most consistent pinot noirs.

## PINOT NOIR

RANKING 3

PRINCE ALBERT
GEELONG

PINOT NOIR
2001

PRODUCE OF AUSTRALIA

| Geelong | $30–$49 |
|---|---|
| Current vintage: 2003 | 87 |

Marzipan-like aromas of slightly stewed cherries, plums and currants, with meaty nuances of undergrowth. Rich, round and smoothly delivered, its forward and assertive palate packs plenty of flavour.

| | | | |
|---|---|---|---|
| 2003 | 87 | 2005 | 2008 |
| 2002 | 84 | 2004 | 2007 |
| 2001 | 92 | 2006 | 2009 |
| 2000 | 95 | 2005 | 2008 |
| 1999 | 89 | 2007 | 2011 |
| 1998 | 91 | 2003 | 2006 |
| 1997 | 93 | 2002 | 2005 |
| 1996 | 82 | 1998 | 2001 |
| 1995 | 93 | 2000 | 2003 |
| 1994 | 90 | 1999 | 2002 |
| 1993 | 86 | 1995 | 1998 |
| 1992 | 94 | 1997 | 2000 |

# Radenti

Freycinet, 15919 Tasman Highway, Bicheno Tas 7215. Tel: (03) 6257 8384. Fax: (03) 6257 8454.

Region: **East Coast Tasmania** Winemaker: **Claudio Radenti & Lindy Bull** Viticulturist: **Geoff Bull**
Chief Executive: **Geoff Bull**

The sparkling wine from the highly-rated Freycinet vineyard, Radenti is usually made in rather a wild, earthy and complex style with ultra-long maturation on lees, whose rich, creamy palate is underpinned by a fine, chalky spine and refreshing acidity.

## CHARDONNAY PINOT NOIR

RANKING 3

RADENTI
CHARDONNAY PINOT NOIR

| East Coast Tasmania | $30–$49 |
|---|---|
| Current vintage: 1997 | 92 |

There's a distinctive and evolved meaty, bakery quality about the fresh melon, peach and lime juice aromas of this small-run Tasmanian sparkler, which offers a fine, restrained and stylish palate of complexity and racy acidity. It's long, dry and savoury, with raspberry and cherry fruit, a creamy leesy texture and lingering nutty flavours.

| | | | |
|---|---|---|---|
| 1997 | 92 | 2002 | 2005+ |
| 1996 | 89 | 2001 | 2004 |
| 1995 | 93 | 2000 | 2003 |
| 1994 | 95 | 1999 | 2002 |
| 1993 | 88 | 1998 | 2001 |

# Redbank

1 Sally's Lane, Redbank Vic 3478. Tel: (03) 5467 7255. Fax: (03) 5467 7248.
Website: www.sallyspaddock.com.au  Email: info@sallyspaddock.com.au
Region: **Pyrenees** Winemaker: **Neill Robb** Viticulturist: **Scott Hutton** Chief Executive: **Neill Robb**

Redbank is simultaneously a maker of several small production, small individual vineyard wines of which Sally's Paddock is rightly famous, while it lends its name to a series of other larger production wines under labels like Long Paddock and Fighting Flat. At its best, Sally's Paddock is an impressively concentrated, firm and balanced red for long-term cellaring. Recent drought seasons have undoubtedly affected the wine.

## SALLY'S PADDOCK

RANKING **3**

| Pyrenees | $50+ |
|---|---|
| **Current vintage: 2001** | **88** |

Minty, slightly meaty aromas of pristine small black and red berries, plums and sweet cedar/vanilla oak with earthy undertones of dried herbs and menthol. Long and firm, with a rod-like chassis of astringent tannins, it presents ripe, searingly intense black and red berry flavour married to creamy, chocolatey oak but reveals some greenish, herbal undertones.

| | | | |
|---|---|---|---|
| 2001 | 88 | 2009 | 2013+ |
| 2000 | 93 | 2012 | 2020+ |
| 1999 | 88 | 2007 | 2011+ |
| 1998 | 96 | 2010 | 2018+ |
| 1997 | 88 | 2005 | 2009 |
| 1996 | 90 | 2004 | 2008+ |
| 1995 | 95 | 2007 | 2015 |
| 1994 | 94 | 2006 | 2014 |
| 1993 | 94 | 2005 | 2013 |
| 1992 | 92 | 2000 | 2004 |
| 1991 | 91 | 2003 | 2011 |
| 1990 | 93 | 2020 | 2030 |
| 1989 | 87 | 2001 | 2009 |
| 1988 | 95 | 2000 | 2008 |
| 1987 | 82 | 1999 | 2004 |
| 1986 | 93 | 2006 | 2016 |
| 1985 | 88 | 1997 | 2005 |
| 1984 | 85 | 1989 | 1992 |
| 1983 | 87 | 2003 | 2013 |
| 1982 | 93 | 2002 | 2012 |
| 1981 | 94 | 2001 | 2011 |
| 1980 | 93 | 1992 | 1997 |
| 1989 | 93 | 1991 | 1999+ |

# Redgate

Boodjidup Road, Margaret River WA 6285. Tel: (08) 9757 6488. Fax: (08) 9757 6308.
Website: www.redgatewines.com.au  Email: info@redgatewines.com.au
Region: **Margaret River** Winemaker: **Andrew Forsell** Viticulturist: **Jeff Cottle** Chief Executive: **Bill Ullinger**

While Redgate's white wines are steadily offering more intensity and brightness, its reds still tend towards excessive greenish, leaner styles. There's little doubt, however, of the potential of this vineyard.

## CABERNET BLEND

RANKING **5**

| Margaret River | $20–$29 |
|---|---|
| **Current vintage: 2001** | **83** |

Meaty, herbal red with slightly cough medicine-like aromas of shaded fruits before a slightly hollow and extracted palate that lacks the intensity of fruit to handle its firm spine of green-edged tannins.

| | | | |
|---|---|---|---|
| 2001 | 83 | 2006 | 2009 |
| 1999 | 89 | 2007 | 2011 |
| 1998 | 80 | 2000 | 2003 |
| 1996 | 86 | 2001 | 2004 |
| 1995 | 94 | 2003 | 2007 |
| 1994 | 92 | 2002 | 2006 |
| 1993 | 84 | 1995 | 1998 |

## CHARDONNAY

RANKING **5**

| Margaret River | $20–$29 |
|---|---|
| **Current vintage: 2003** | **87** |

Lightly hessian-like oaky aromas with tropical, grape-fruit and peachy fruit, before a pleasingly smooth and creamy palate of pineapple and grapefruit flavours and fresh, lightly herbal acids. Better oak would have helped hugely.

| | | | |
|---|---|---|---|
| 2003 | 87 | 2005 | 2008 |
| 2002 | 89 | 2004 | 2007 |
| 2001 | 87 | 2003 | 2006 |
| 1999 | 82 | 1999 | 2000 |

## OFS SEMILLON

RANKING 5

| Margaret River | $12–$19 |
|---|---|
| **Current vintage: 2003** | **89** |

Dusty herbal aromas of green beans and asparagus with nuances of honeydew melon and lightly toasty vanilla oak. Rather exaggerated, the viscous, slightly oily palate presents genuine depth of passionfruit-like varietal flavours and profoundly herbaceous influences, finishing with a touch of sweetness.

| 2003 | 89 | 2003 | 2004+ |
|---|---|---|---|
| 2002 | 88 | 2003 | 2004+ |
| 2001 | 86 | 2002 | 2003 |
| 2000 | 77 | 2001 | 2002 |
| 1999 | 85 | 2000 | 2001 |

## RESERVE SAUVIGNON BLANC

RANKING 5

| Margaret River | $12–$19 |
|---|---|
| **Current vintage: 2003** | **89** |

A toasty sauvignon blanc with an oaky vanilla aroma of green bean and capsicum, gooseberries and lychees before a fleshy, slick and oily palate. Broad and herbal, its restrained palate of cassis, lychees and toasty vanilla oak finishes clean and dry.

| 2003 | 89 | 2004 | 2005 |
|---|---|---|---|
| 2002 | 86 | 2002 | 2003 |
| 2001 | 86 | 2002 | 2003+ |
| 2000 | 87 | 2002 | 2005 |
| 1999 | 82 | 1999 | 2000 |
| 1998 | 90 | 1999 | 2000 |
| 1997 | 87 | 1998 | 1999 |

## SAUVIGNON BLANC SEMILLON

RANKING 5

| Margaret River | $12–$19 |
|---|---|
| **Current vintage: 2003** | **88** |

Typical regional sauvignon blanc with a lively grassy, herbal aroma of passionfruit, melon and other tropical fruits. Elegant and restrained, but tangy and flavoursome, it's fine and steely, with a pleasing length of fruit and a refreshing finish.

| 2003 | 88 | 2004 | 2005+ |
|---|---|---|---|
| 2002 | 88 | 2004 | 2007 |
| 2001 | 83 | 2002 | 2003 |
| 2000 | 87 | 2002 | 2005 |
| 1999 | 88 | 1999 | 2000 |

# Redman

Riddoch Highway, Coonawarra SA 5263. Tel: (08) 8736 3331. Fax: (08) 8736 3013.
Website: www.redman.com.au

Region: **Coonawarra** Winemakers: **Bruce & Malcolm Redman** Viticulturists: **Bruce & Malcolm Redman**
Chief Executives: **Bruce & Malcolm Redman**

Redman's vineyards are amongst the oldest and best in Coonawarra, and on occasions produce exceptional intensity and length of flavour. The style favoured by the Redman brothers is however a finer, leaner and more cedary old-fashioned red which, despite not possessing substantial palate weight and brightness, typically requires several years in the cellar to drink at its best.

## CABERNET SAUVIGNON

RANKING 5

| Coonawarra | $20–$29 |
|---|---|
| **Current vintage: 2002** | **88** |

Complex, meaty, older style of cabernet with leathery aromas of dark olives, cinnamon and prunes. Firm and meaty, it is a firmly structured, chewy and astringent red that might lack primary fruit, but should slowly develop softness and complexity.

| 2002 | 88 | 2014 | 2022 |
|---|---|---|---|
| 2001 | 89 | 2006 | 2009 |
| 2000 | 88 | 2008 | 2012 |
| 1999 | 90 | 2007 | 2011 |
| 1998 | 89 | 2006 | 2010 |
| 1997 | 88 | 2002 | 2005 |
| 1996 | 89 | 2004 | 2008 |
| 1994 | 93 | 2002 | 2006 |
| 1993 | 93 | 2001 | 2005 |
| 1992 | 92 | 2004 | 2012 |
| 1991 | 84 | 2003 | 2011 |
| 1990 | 93 | 2002 | 2010 |
| 1989 | 82 | 1997 | 2001 |
| 1988 | 88 | 2000 | 2008 |
| 1987 | 88 | 1999 | 2004 |

## CABERNET SAUVIGNON MERLOT

RANKING 4

| Coonawarra | $20–$29 |
|---|---|
| **Current vintage: 2000** | **89** |

Firm, structured red with intense minty aromas of cassis and raspberries, plums and slightly herbal, tobaccoey undertones over cedar/vanilla oak. Fullish in weight, with a meaty, herbal expression of plum and cassis flavours framed by slightly drying tannins.

| 2000 | 89 | 2008 | 2012 |
|---|---|---|---|
| 1999 | 86 | 2004 | 2007+ |
| 1998 | 94 | 2010 | 2018 |
| 1997 | 83 | 1999 | 2002 |
| 1996 | 90 | 2004 | 2008+ |
| 1995 | 86 | 2000 | 2003 |
| 1994 | 93 | 2006 | 2014 |
| 1993 | 93 | 2001 | 2005 |
| 1992 | 94 | 2000 | 2004 |
| 1991 | 91 | 1999 | 2003 |
| 1990 | 87 | 1995 | 1998 |

## SHIRAZ

RANKING 5

| Coonawarra | $12–$19 |
|---|---|
| **Current vintage: 2002** | **89** |

Spicy, slightly cooked aromas of red berries and plums with restrained cedar/vanilla oak and earthy undertones. Lightly peppery, its smooth and elegant palate of medium weight offers lively redcurrant, mulberry and plum flavours with smooth, fine tannins and fresh acidity.

| 2002 | 89 | 2010 | 2014 |
|---|---|---|---|
| 2001 | 89 | 2003 | 2006+ |
| 2000 | 89 | 2003 | 2006+ |
| 1999 | 82 | 2001 | 2004 |
| 1998 | 86 | 2003 | 2006 |
| 1997 | 81 | 1998 | 1999 |
| 1996 | 84 | 1998 | 2004+ |
| 1995 | 86 | 1997 | 2000 |
| 1994 | 84 | 1996 | 1999 |
| 1993 | 90 | 2001 | 2005 |
| 1992 | 91 | 2000 | 2004 |
| 1991 | 88 | 1993 | 1996 |
| 1990 | 91 | 1995 | 1998 |

# Reilly's

Cnr Burra & Hill Streets, Mintara SA 5415. Tel: (08) 8843 9013. Fax: (08) 8843 9013.
Website: www.reillyswines.com  Email: admin@reillyswines.com

Region: **Clare Valley** Winemaker: **Justin Ardill** Viticulturist: **Robert Smyth** Chief Executive: **Justin Ardill**

Based at Mintaro in the Clare Valley, Reilly's is a small maker of traditional regional table wines led by its firm, minty and assertively oaked 'Dry Land' Shiraz and Cabernet Sauvignon varietals.

## DRY LAND CABERNET SAUVIGNON

RANKING 5

| Clare Valley | $30–$49 |
|---|---|
| **Current vintage: 2001** | **86** |

Minty, leathery aromas of cassis, plums and chocolate, with a ripe, robust and slightly over-cooked palate whose minty fruit is given sweet, but rather clunky oak.

| 2001 | 86 | 2006 | 2009+ |
|---|---|---|---|
| 2000 | 89 | 2005 | 2008 |
| 1999 | 82 | 2001 | 2004 |
| 1998 | 88 | 2003 | 2006+ |

## DRY LAND SHIRAZ

RANKING 5

| Clare Valley | $30–$49 |
|---|---|
| **Current vintage: 2001** | **89** |

Firm and structured shiraz, if perhaps a fraction raw. Its spicy aromas of violets, cassis and blackberries are matched to assertively creamy/coconut American oak, with undertones of chocolate and licorice. There's strength and richness, if not finesse, but the wine offers plenty of punchy fruit and oak.

| 2001 | 89 | 2009 | 2013 |
|---|---|---|---|
| 2000 | 88 | 2005 | 2008 |
| 1999 | 92 | 2004 | 2007 |
| 1998 | 89 | 2003 | 2006+ |

## WATERVALE RIESLING

RANKING **5**

| Clare Valley | $12–$19 | 2003 | 89 | 2008 | 2011 |
|---|---|---|---|---|---|
| **Current vintage: 2001** | **89** | 2002 | 88 | 2004 | 2007+ |
| | | 2001 | 83 | 2002 | 2003 |

Restrained aromas of pear and apple, with dusty, citrusy undertones. Long, dry and austere, its pleasing length of lemony fruit culminates in a refreshing, steely finish. Should develop well.

# Reynell

Reynell Road, Reynella SA 5161. Tel: (08) 8392 2222. Fax: (08) 8392 2202.

Region: **McLaren Vale** Winemakers: **Simon White, Robert Mann** Viticulturist: **Brenton Baker**
Chief Executive: **David Woods**

Reynell is a low-key but upmarket Hardy Wine Company label which presently just includes a single traditionally made, robust, exceptionally long-term Basket Pressed Shiraz of enormous character. A classic regional style, its fruit has not been supercharged in contemporary fashion with a whammy of new oak.

## BASKET PRESSED SHIRAZ

RANKING **2**

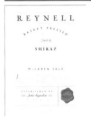

| McLaren Vale | $50+ | 2000 | 90 | 2002 | 2005 |
|---|---|---|---|---|---|
| **Current vintage: 2000** | **90** | 1998 | 94 | 2018 | 2028 |
| | | 1997 | 93 | 2009 | 2017 |
| | | 1996 | 95 | 2008 | 2016 |
| | | 1995 | 94 | 2007 | 2015 |

Tarry, ripe and confected aromas of bright cassis and plums are perfumed and intense, while its background of restrained cedar/vanilla oak partially conceals some rather greenish/vegetal notes beneath. Forward, cooked and alcoholic, with a good presence of fruit at the front of the palate that dries out leaving rather a raw, blocky and alcoholic finish. Obviously made from very stressed fruit, very fast-maturing and already past its best. Somehow collected the trophy as the most outstanding wine of last year's Adelaide show, with another six in the bag as well!

# Richard Hamilton

Main Road, Willunga SA 5172. Tel: (08) 8556 2288. Fax: (08) 8556 2868.
Website: www.hamiltonwines.com  Email: hwg@hamiltonwines.com

Region: **McLaren Vale** Winemaker: **Paul Gordon** Viticulturist: **Lee Harding**
Chief Executive: **Dr Richard Hamilton**

Led by its Centurion Shiraz, the Hamilton wine brand releases a number of complex and savoury individual vineyard reds that typically just lack a little flesh and fruit intensity to break into the next level of prestige and price. The brand also appears to be changing its name yet again, this time back to 'Richard Hamilton'. With other competing wine brands owned by other members of the same family (ie Hamilton's Ewell and Hugh Hamilton), it's no surprise that a significant level of confusion exists within the market and the trade.

## BURTON'S VINEYARD (Grenache Shiraz Blend)

RANKING **4**

| McLaren Vale | $20–$29 | 2001 | 86 | 2006 | 2009 |
|---|---|---|---|---|---|
| **Current vintage: 2001** | **86** | 1999 | 88 | 2004 | 2007 |
| | | 1998 | 93 | 2003 | 2006+ |
| | | 1997 | 86 | 2005 | 2008 |
| | | 1996 | 89 | 2001 | 2004 |
| | | 1995 | 93 | 2003 | 2007 |
| | | 1994 | 88 | 1999 | 2002 |
| | | 1992 | 86 | 1998 | 2001 |

A slightly under and over-ripened wine with minty, meaty aromas of prunes, currants and chocolate/mocha oak over lightly peppery and spicy herbal undertones. Its meaty palate of raisined fruit is supported by a drying cut of astringency that finishes with greenish and metallic undertones. Its sweet oak doesn't quite substitute for sweet fruit.

## CENTURION SHIRAZ

RANKING **3**

| McLaren Vale | $30–$49 |
|---|---|
| **Current vintage: 2001** | **91** |

Deep, rather closed shiraz whose sweaty, lightly herbal, meaty and musky aromas of red berries, sweet leather, plums and dark chocolate precede a smooth, but rather introverted palate. There's pleasing depth of red plum and red berry flavours, with plenty of spice and cedary oak, while its firm, powdery frame of tannins will aid its longevity. It finishes with lingering notes of currants and licorice.

| 2001 | 91 | 2009 | 2013 |
|---|---|---|---|
| 2000 | 87 | 2002 | 2005+ |
| 1999 | 93 | 2007 | 2011+ |
| 1998 | 93 | 2006 | 2010+ |
| 1996 | 88 | 2001 | 2004+ |
| 1995 | 94 | 2003 | 2007 |
| 1994 | 91 | 2002 | 2006 |
| 1992 | 87 | 2000 | 2004 |

## GUMPRS BLOCK SHIRAZ

RANKING **4**

| McLaren Vale | $20–$29 |
|---|---|
| **Current vintage: 2002** | **89** |

Leaner, bony shiraz with some pleasing fruit sweetness, but also some evidently stressed and over-ripe fruit qualities. Its earthy, chocolatey aromas of prunes and currants precede a slightly cooked palate of attractive dark berry and plum-like fruit married to some chocolate/cedary oak and framed by firm but lightly metallic tannins.

| 2002 | 89 | 2007 | 2010 |
|---|---|---|---|
| 2001 | 89 | 2006 | 2009 |
| 2000 | 90 | 2008 | 2012 |
| 1999 | 89 | 2001 | 2004+ |
| 1998 | 91 | 2006 | 2010 |
| 1997 | 89 | 1999 | 2002 |
| 1996 | 83 | 1998 | 2001+ |

## HUT BLOCK CABERNET SAUVIGNON

RANKING **4**

| McLaren Vale | $20–$29 |
|---|---|
| **Current vintage: 2001** | **93** |

Herbal, earthy and meaty aromas of small black berries, plums and olives, with suggestions of fennel, cloves and polished oak. Moderately full but surprisingly elegant palate of lively, bright berry/plum fruit entwined with tight, bony tannins. Harmonious warmer climate cabernet style building to a lingering finish of intense small fruit flavours.

| 2001 | 93 | 2009 | 2013+ |
|---|---|---|---|
| 2000 | 90 | 2005 | 2008+ |
| 1999 | 91 | 2004 | 2007+ |
| 1998 | 94 | 2006 | 2010 |
| 1997 | 88 | 2002 | 2005 |
| 1996 | 84 | 2004 | 2008 |
| 1995 | 91 | 2003 | 2007 |
| 1994 | 89 | 1999 | 2002 |
| 1993 | 87 | 1998 | 2001 |
| 1992 | 90 | 2000 | 2004 |
| 1991 | 94 | 1999 | 2003 |

## LOT 148 MERLOT

RANKING **4**

| McLaren Vale | $20–$29 |
|---|---|
| **Current vintage: 2002** | **86** |

Developing, earthy and leathery wine whose green-edged mulberry, dark cherry and plum fruit qualities are beginning to tire and lose sweetness. Finishes a little flat, with rather sinewy tannins.

| 2002 | 86 | 2004 | 2007+ |
|---|---|---|---|
| 2001 | 89 | 2006 | 2009 |
| 2000 | 90 | 2005 | 2008+ |
| 1999 | 90 | 2001 | 2004+ |
| 1998 | 87 | 2003 | 2006 |
| 1997 | 89 | 2002 | 2005 |

## SIGNATURE CHARDONNAY

RANKING **5**

| McLaren Vale | $12–$19 |
|---|---|
| **Current vintage: 2003** | **87** |

Restrained, lightly oaked aromas of melon and lemon rind, peach and banana precede a soft and surprisingly elegant palate. There's plenty of texture, but refreshingly crisp acids neatly punctuate the wine's generous and vibrant peach/apple flavours.

| 2003 | 87 | 2004 | 2005 |
|---|---|---|---|
| 2002 | 89 | 2004 | 2007 |
| 2000 | 89 | 2001 | 2002 |
| 1999 | 84 | 2001 | 2004 |
| 1998 | 87 | 2000 | 2003 |
| 1997 | 87 | 1999 | 2000 |

## THE SLATE QUARRY RIESLING

RANKING **5**

**McLaren Vale**     $12–$19
**Current vintage: 2003**     **89**

Floral, perfumed and rather estery riesling with a juicy, round and spotless mouthful of concentrated varietal flavour. Rich and juicy, even slightly sweet, it finishes with punchy fruit but a slight lack of shape.

| | | | |
|---|---|---|---|
| 2003 | 89 | 2005 | 2008 |
| 2002 | 87 | 2004 | 2007 |
| 2001 | 80 | 2002 | 2003 |
| 2000 | 89 | 2002 | 2005 |
| 1999 | 87 | 2001 | 2004 |
| 1998 | 86 | 2000 | 2003 |

# Richmond Grove

Para Road, Tanunda SA 5352. Tel: (08) 8563 7303. Fax: (08) 8563 7330.
Website: www.richmondgrovewines.com  Email: info@richmondgrove.com.au
Region: **Various** Winemakers: **John Vickery, Steve Clarkson** Viticulturist: **Joy Dick**
Chief Executive: **Laurent Lacassgne**

Richmond Grove is a popular Orlando Wyndham brand that comprises wines blended from and sourced from a number of prominent Australian regions. Its finest and most consistent wine is its tangy, citrusy and perfumed Watervale Riesling, which hails from South Australia's Clare Valley.

## FRENCH CASK CHARDONNAY

RANKING **5**

**Various**     $12–$19
**Current vintage: 2002**     **87**

Charming, early-drinking chardonnay with a delicate fragrance of peach and nectarine with creamy, buttery and vanilla oak. Lively flavours of stonefruit, pineapple and grapefruit, creamy oak and leesy complexity with undertones of green cashews finish refreshing, with soft acids.

| | | | |
|---|---|---|---|
| 2002 | 87 | 2003 | 2004+ |
| 2001 | 87 | 2002 | 2003 |
| 2000 | 87 | 2002 | 2005 |
| 1997 | 80 | 1998 | 1999 |

## LIMITED RELEASE BAROSSA SHIRAZ

RANKING **5**

**Barossa Valley**     $12–$19
**Current vintage: 2001**     **86**

Rather simple, advanced and confectionary shiraz whose jammy raspberry, plum and cherry aromas reveal stewy, meaty prune-like influences. Drink soon.

| | | | |
|---|---|---|---|
| 2001 | 86 | 2003 | 2006 |
| 2000 | 81 | 2002 | 2005 |
| 1999 | 88 | 2001 | 2004+ |
| 1998 | 88 | 2000 | 2003+ |
| 1997 | 87 | 1999 | 2002 |
| 1996 | 90 | 2001 | 2004 |
| 1995 | 87 | 1997 | 2000 |
| 1994 | 91 | 1999 | 2002 |

## LIMITED RELEASE CABERNET SAUVIGNON

RANKING **5**

**Coonawarra**     $12–$19
**Current vintage: 2001**     **88**

Restrained, lightly floral cassis, mulberry and violet-like aromas, with light cedar/vanilla oak over tobaccoey hints of greenish fruit. Full to medium weight, with good length and slightly gritty firmness, it reveals some attractive primary fruit and oak over an underlying greenish thread.

| | | | |
|---|---|---|---|
| 2001 | 88 | 2006 | 2009 |
| 2000 | 83 | 2002 | 2005 |
| 1999 | 88 | 2004 | 2007 |
| 1998 | 86 | 2003 | 2006 |
| 1997 | 82 | 1999 | 2002 |
| 1996 | 88 | 1998 | 2001 |
| 1995 | 87 | 2000 | 2003 |
| 1994 | 94 | 2002 | 2006 |
| 1993 | 88 | 1998 | 2001 |
| 1992 | 89 | 1997 | 2000 |

## WATERVALE RIESLING

Clare Valley $12–$19
**Current vintage: 2003** 93

Delicate, lively fragrance of rose petals, apple and pear over suggestions of stonefruit and spice. Long, pristine palate whose translucent flavours of pear, apple and lime juice fit neatly over a very fine phenolic backbone. Fine and refreshing, it finishes with an austere note of cold steel, with lingering fruit and acid.

| | | | |
|---|---|---|---|
| 2003 | 93 | 2008 | 2011 |
| 2002 | 95 | 2010 | 2014 |
| 2001 | 93 | 2006 | 2009 |
| 2000 | 93 | 2008 | 2012 |
| 1999 | 94 | 2004 | 2007+ |
| 1998 | 93 | 2006 | 2010 |
| 1997 | 89 | 2006 | 2010 |
| 1996 | 92 | 2001 | 2004 |
| 1995 | 94 | 2003 | 2007 |
| 1994 | 91 | 1999 | 2002 |

# Riddoch

Riddoch Highway, Coonawarra SA 5263. Tel: (08) 8737 2394. Fax: (08) 8737 2397.
Website: www.riddoch.com.au  Email: riddoch@wingara.com.au

Region: **Coonawarra** Winemakers: **Wayne Stehbens, Tony Milanowski** Viticulturist: **Chris Brodie**
Chief Executive: **David Yunghanns**

Riddoch is the second label for Coonawarra high-flier Katnook Estate. Its best wines are its reds, sound wines that typically offer moderate weight, pleasing fruit and oak qualities. The 2002 releases are lighter than usual.

## CABERNET SHIRAZ

Coonawarra $12–$19
**Current vintage: 2002** 82

Dusty herbal and white pepper-like aromas of light berry/plum fruit with cedar/vanilla oak precede a forward, but dilute palate lacking fruit and richness, finishing slightly thin with sappy, metallic tannins.

| | | | |
|---|---|---|---|
| 2002 | 82 | 2004 | 2007 |
| 2001 | 87 | 2003 | 2006+ |
| 2000 | 81 | 2002 | 2005 |
| 1999 | 79 | 2000 | 2001 |
| 1998 | 88 | 2000 | 2003+ |
| 1997 | 81 | 1998 | 1999 |
| 1996 | 88 | 1998 | 2001 |
| 1995 | 84 | 1997 | 2000 |
| 1994 | 90 | 1996 | 1999 |

## CHARDONNAY

Coonawarra $12–$19
**Current vintage: 2002** 87

Attractive early-drinking chardonnay whose lightly creamy aromas of lemon, peach and vanilla oak herald a slightly confectionary, peachy and forward palate of syrupy cumquat-like flavour and soft acids.

| | | | |
|---|---|---|---|
| 2002 | 87 | 2003 | 2004+ |
| 2001 | 87 | 2002 | 2003+ |
| 1999 | 87 | 2000 | 2001 |
| 1998 | 82 | 1999 | 2000 |

## SHIRAZ

Coonawarra $12–$19
**Current vintage: 2002** 82

Earthy, leathery and lightly cooked aromas of plums and cherries, with a simple, earthy palate finishing rather short and thin.

| | | | |
|---|---|---|---|
| 2002 | 82 | 2004 | 2007 |
| 2001 | 83 | 2003 | 2006 |
| 2000 | 88 | 2002 | 2005 |
| 1999 | 81 | 2001 | 2004 |
| 1998 | 90 | 2003 | 2006 |
| 1997 | 83 | 1999 | 2002 |
| 1996 | 90 | 1998 | 2001 |
| 1995 | 85 | 1996 | 1997 |
| 1994 | 90 | 1999 | 2002 |
| 1993 | 82 | 1995 | 1998 |

# Robertson's Well

Riddoch Highway, Coonawarra SA 5263. Tel: (08) 8736 3380. Fax: (08) 8736 3071.
Region: **Coonawarra** Winemaker: **Andrew Hales** Viticulturist: **Vic Patrick** Chief Executive: **Jamie Odell**
The age of its current releases and the increasing prominence of the Jamiesons Run brand as the premier Beringer Blass Coonawarra brand leads one to query the fate of Robertson's Well, which has not lived up to expectations for several years.

## CABERNET SAUVIGNON

RANKING **5**

| Coonawarra | $20–$29 |
|---|---|
| **Current vintage: 2000** | **86** |

Meaty, dusty and herbaceous aromas of raspberries and restrained cedary/vanilla oak precede a lively palate offering some vibrant small black and red berry flavours and cedary oak framed by fine, drying tannins. Too green and vegetal; held together by assertive acidity.

| | | | |
|---|---|---|---|
| 2000 | 86 | 2002 | 2005+ |
| 1999 | 89 | 2004 | 2007+ |
| 1998 | 91 | 2006 | 2010 |
| 1996 | 87 | 2001 | 2004 |
| 1995 | 88 | 2000 | 2003 |
| 1994 | 94 | 2002 | 2006 |
| 1993 | 91 | 2001 | 2005 |
| 1992 | 92 | 2000 | 2004 |

## SHIRAZ

RANKING **5**

| Coonawarra | $20–$29 |
|---|---|
| **Current vintage: 2000** | **81** |

Herbaceous, leathery aromas of dark olives lack fruit freshness and intensity. Some initially vibrant dark plum fruit flavours then fade towards a short, metallic and green-edged finish.

| | | | |
|---|---|---|---|
| 2000 | 81 | 2002 | 2005 |
| 1999 | 81 | 2001 | 2004 |
| 1998 | 91 | 2003 | 2006 |
| 1997 | 87 | 1999 | 2002 |
| 1996 | 89 | 1998 | 2001 |

# Rochford

Cnr Maroondah Highway & Hill Road, Coldstream Vic 3770. Tel: (03) 5962 2119 Fax: (03) 5962 5319.
Website: www.rochfordwines.com  Email: info@rochfordwines.com
Region: **Macedon Ranges** Winemaker: **David Creed**
Chief Executives: **Helmut Konecsny & Yvonne Lodico-Konecsny**
Rochford is an energetic small wine business that acquired Eyton On Yarra in 2001 to complement its existing vineyards in the cool Macedon Ranges region. While there is a strong focus on the development of pinot noir and chardonnay from both regions, I have been taken lately with a nutty 2003 Arneis from the Yarra Valley and a concentrated and complex 2003 Riesling from the Macedon Ranges.

## PINOT NOIR

RANKING **4**

| Macedon Ranges | $30–$49 |
|---|---|
| **Current vintage: 2002** | **86** |

A firm, slightly extracted pinot whose sweet plum flavours and sweet cedar/vanilla oak are underpinned by vegetal, shaded, green bean like influences. Finishes hard, with unyielding tannins.

| | | | |
|---|---|---|---|
| 2002 | 86 | 2004 | 2007 |
| 2001 | 90 | 2006 | 2009 |
| 2000 | 90 | 2005 | 2008 |
| 1999 | 83 | 2001 | 2004 |
| 1996 | 86 | 1998 | 2001 |
| 1995 | 91 | 2000 | 2003 |
| 1994 | 87 | 2002 | 2006 |
| 1993 | 94 | 2001 | 2005 |
| 1992 | 94 | 2000 | 2004 |
| 1991 | 92 | 1999 | 2003 |
| 1990 | 91 | 1995 | 1998 |

# Rockford

Krondorf Road, Tanunda SA 5352. Tel: (08) 8563 2720. Fax: (08) 8563 3787.
Email: info@rockfordwines.com.au

Region: **Barossa Valley** Winemakers: **Robert O'Callaghan, Chris Ringland**
Chief Executive: **David Kalleske**

Rockford simply revels in what it does best, the making of high-class table wines in traditional style from some of the Barossa's best-managed small mature vineyards. Its Cabernet Sauvignon and Basket Press Shiraz provide all the richness and voluptuous fruit the region is known for, without resorting to over-ripeness or over-extraction. The whites are amongst the region's richest and finest. As a group, the 2001 red releases are more forward, rustic and meaty than usual.

## BASKET PRESS SHIRAZ

RANKING **2**

**Barossa Valley** $50+
**Current vintage: 2001** 89

Very ripe, meaty Barossa shiraz matured in some very assertive vanilla and smoked oyster-like oak. It's smoky, creamy aromas of sweet, jammy plums and berries reveal riper notes of raisins and currants. Its palate is smooth and silky, with plenty of forward, if slightly cooked fruit qualities before a slightly herbal finish that does lose some intensity. Not as long-term a wine as usual for this label, but it does offer plenty of rustic charm and flavour from a very hot vintage.

| | | | |
|---|---|---|---|
| 2001 | 89 | 2009 | 2013 |
| 2000 | 93 | 2005 | 2008+ |
| 1999 | 96 | 2007 | 2011+ |
| 1998 | 96 | 2008 | 2018 |
| 1997 | 93 | 2005 | 2009 |
| 1996 | 96 | 2016 | 2026 |
| 1995 | 90 | 2003 | 2007 |
| 1994 | 93 | 2002 | 2006+ |
| 1993 | 88 | 2005 | 2013 |
| 1992 | 89 | 2000 | 2004 |
| 1991 | 96 | 2011 | 2021 |
| 1990 | 91 | 1998 | 2002+ |
| 1989 | 87 | 1997 | 2001 |
| 1988 | 93 | 2000 | 2004+ |

## BLACK SHIRAZ

RANKING **2**

**Barossa Valley** $50+
**Current disgorging: 2003** 90

Sweet earthy farm floor bouquet of liqueur chocolates, polished leathery, wild plums and briary small berry fruits, with undertones of bitumen, cedar and herbal nuances. Full-flavoured and forward, it's a ripe, briary and tarry wine whose up-front palate of blackberries and plums, chocolates and tar finishes slightly herbal and lacking its customary length.

The vintages specified on the right relate to the year of disgorging.

| | | | |
|---|---|---|---|
| 2003 | 90 | 2005 | 2008 |
| 2002 | 96 | 2006 | 2010 |
| 2001 | 95 | 2004 | 2008 |
| 2000 | 97 | 2006 | 2010 |
| 1998 | 91 | 1999 | 2003 |

## HAND PICKED RIESLING

RANKING **3**

**Barossa Valley** $12–$19
**Current vintage: 2001** 93

A round and generous riesling whose delicate lime juice and green apple perfume, reveals undertones of fresh flowers, minerals, dried herbs and lanolin. Soft and approachable, its luscious, juicy palate is underpinned by chalky phenolics, before a refreshing and slightly austere finish of apple and lemon-like acidity.

| | | | |
|---|---|---|---|
| 2001 | 93 | 2009 | 2013 |
| 2000 | 95 | 2005 | 2008+ |
| 1999 | 93 | 2004 | 2007 |
| 1998 | 94 | 2003 | 2006+ |
| 1997 | 88 | 1999 | 2002 |
| 1996 | 92 | 2004 | 2008 |
| 1995 | 93 | 2000 | 2003+ |

## LOCAL GROWERS SEMILLON

RANKING **3**

**Barossa Valley** $20–$29
**Current vintage: 2001** 87

Early-drinking semillon with a spicy and honeyed bouquet of toasty melon fruit, cinnamon and cloves over nuances of green olives and butter. Forward and a fraction short, its candied expression of peaches, melon and sweet buttery oak finishes without its usual vitality.

| | | | |
|---|---|---|---|
| 2001 | 87 | 2003 | 2006 |
| 2000 | 92 | 2002 | 2005+ |
| 1999 | 92 | 2004 | 2007 |
| 1998 | 93 | 2003 | 2006+ |
| 1997 | 91 | 2005 | 2009 |
| 1996 | 90 | 2001 | 2004 |
| 1995 | 94 | 2000 | 2003+ |
| 1994 | 92 | 1999 | 2002 |

## MOPPA SPRINGS (Grenache Shiraz Mataro)

| Barossa Valley | $20–$29 |
|---|---|
| **Current vintage: 2000** | **88** |

| | | | |
|---|---|---|---|
| 2000 | 88 | 2002 | 2005 |
| 1999 | 90 | 2004 | 2007 |
| 1998 | 89 | 2003 | 2006+ |

Developing, leathery and raisiny red with a lightly varnishy aroma of prunes, red plums and currants over sweet vanilla oak. Smooth and chocolatey, it's soft and generous, with rather advanced flavours of dried fruits now showing signs of age. Beginning to dry up, it finishes with soft tannins and lightly vegetal notes

## RIFLE RANGE CABERNET SAUVIGNON

| Barossa Valley | $20–$29 |
|---|---|
| **Current vintage: 2001** | **90** |

| | | | |
|---|---|---|---|
| 2001 | 90 | 2009 | 2013+ |
| 2000 | 89 | 2005 | 2008 |
| 1999 | 94 | 2007 | 2011+ |
| 1998 | 94 | 2010 | 2018 |
| 1997 | 89 | 2005 | 2009 |
| 1996 | 94 | 2004 | 2008+ |
| 1995 | 91 | 2000 | 2003+ |
| 1994 | 89 | 1999 | 2002 |

Long, well-made cabernet from a challenging hot season, delivering plenty of intense small berry and plum-like flavours, balance and harmony. Its slightly jammy aromas of plums and cassis deliver some minty/eucalypt complexity, with nuances of cedary/vanilla oak, bitumen and currants. It's firm and tightly focused, but remains fresh and lively with a finish of vibrant acidity and fine-grained, firm tannins.

## ROD & SPUR (Shiraz Cabernet)

| Barossa Valley | $30–$49 |
|---|---|
| **Current vintage: 2001** | **87** |

| | | | |
|---|---|---|---|
| 2001 | 87 | 2003 | 2006 |
| 2000 | 91 | 2005 | 2008 |
| 1999 | 87 | 2004 | 2007 |

Very reductive, earthy red with dusty, leafy aromas of red and black berries over sweet cedary oak. Forward and slightly jammy, it presents a soft, almost plump middle of sweet berry fruit before a drying, finely astringent finish with herbal undertones. Lacks its customary palate weight.

# Rosemount Estate

Rosemount Road, Denman NSW 2328. Tel: (02) 6549 6400. Fax: (02) 6549 6499.
Website: www.rosemountestate.com.au Email: rosemountestates.hv@cellardoor.com.au
Region: **Various** Winemakers: **Charles Whish, Briony Hoare, Matt Koch** Viticulturist: **Richard Hilder**
Chief Executive: **John Ballard**

Rosemount Estate is the remarkably successful brand developed by the Oatley family that was bought by Southcorp in early 2001. While a number of financial commentators now claim that Southcorp paid too much for the business, they were very silent back then. However, like Southcorp, Rosemount's quality at the top end has suffered through an unprecedented run of difficult vintages. It does however, offer tremendous value throughout its range, and in wines like the Orange Vineyard Chardonnay, remarkably affordable quality.

## BALMORAL SYRAH

| McLaren Vale | $50+ |
|---|---|
| **Current vintage: 1999** | **90** |

| | | | |
|---|---|---|---|
| 2000 | 89 | 2005 | 2008 |
| 1999 | 90 | 2004 | 2007 |
| 1998 | 97 | 2010 | 2018 |
| 1997 | 90 | 2002 | 2005 |
| 1996 | 94 | 2004 | 2008 |
| 1995 | 97 | 2007 | 2015 |
| 1994 | 95 | 2002 | 2006+ |
| 1993 | 88 | 1998 | 2001 |
| 1992 | 96 | 2000 | 2004+ |
| 1991 | 95 | 2003 | 2011 |
| 1990 | 94 | 2002 | 2010 |
| 1989 | 94 | 1997 | 2003+ |

Wild, floral and spicy, aromas of cooked plums and cassis, chocolate/cedar/vanilla oak with earthy, tarry undertones. Forward and creamy, long and linear, it dries out towards a sappy finish of and slightly metallic tannins and green-edged acids. Very ripe, delivering punchy flavours of prunes and currants, it's an atypical Balmoral with some, but significantly less than its usual polish.

## CABERNET SAUVIGNON

**Various** $12–$19
**Current vintage: 2001** 80

Rather caramelised and jammy red whose forward, minty flavours of cassis and plums precede a light, hollow and earthy palate.

| | | | |
|---|---|---|---|
| 2001 | 80 | 2002 | 2003 |
| 2000 | 81 | 2002 | 2005 |
| 1999 | 87 | 2000 | 2001 |
| 1998 | 87 | 2000 | 2003 |
| 1996 | 84 | 1998 | 2001 |

## CHARDONNAY                                                   RANKING **5**

**Various** $12–$19
**Current vintage: 2003** 82

Gluey aromas of peaches and cream with underlying tropical fruit nuances and nutty vanilla oak precede a creamy palate of fleshiness and depth. Similarly gluey oak detracts from some generous fruit with complex butterscotch and nutty influences.

| | | | |
|---|---|---|---|
| 2002 | 87 | 2003 | 2004+ |
| 2001 | 83 | 2002 | 2003 |
| 2000 | 87 | 2001 | 2002 |
| 1999 | 87 | 2000 | 2001 |
| 1998 | 90 | 2000 | 2003 |

## GIANTS CREEK CHARDONNAY (Viognier)        RANKING **3**

**Upper Hunter Valley** $30–$49
**Current vintage: 2002** 93

Very restrained, elegant white blend with slightly oxidative aromas of dried flowers, melon and dusty lemon blossom over nuances of apple, pear and spicy oak. Initially round and generous, it becomes more restrained and elegant down the palate, culminating in a nutty, savoury finish of lemony acids.

| | | | |
|---|---|---|---|
| 2002 | 93 | 2007 | 2010 |
| 2001 | 90 | 2003 | 2006+ |
| 1999 | 93 | 2004 | 2007 |
| 1998 | 90 | 2003 | 2006 |
| 1997 | 87 | 2002 | 2005 |
| 1996 | 90 | 2001 | 2004 |
| 1995 | 89 | 1997 | 2000 |
| 1994 | 90 | 1999 | 2002 |
| 1993 | 94 | 1998 | 2001 |
| 1992 | 84 | 1994 | 1997 |

## GSM                                                             RANKING **4**

**McLaren Vale** $20–$29
**Current vintage: 2001** 91

An up-front show pony style with spicy white pepper and confectionary grenache-driven aromas of red cherries, plums and blueberries offset by polished chocolate/vanilla oak. Jammy and juicy, its chocolatey palate is long and vibrant, underpinned by lively vanilla oak and framed by fine-grained but firm tannins.

| | | | |
|---|---|---|---|
| 2001 | 91 | 2006 | 2009 |
| 1999 | 93 | 2007 | 2011 |
| 1998 | 90 | 2003 | 2006 |
| 1997 | 88 | 1999 | 2002+ |
| 1996 | 90 | 2001 | 2004 |
| 1995 | 86 | 2003 | 2007 |
| 1994 | 88 | 1999 | 2002 |

## MOUNTAIN BLUE                                          RANKING **3**

**Mudgee** $30–$49
**Current vintage: 2000** 87

A medium-weight blend of ripe, almost jammy fruit with plenty of sweet new oak. Its ripe, minty aromas of cassis, black plums, peppermint and cedary/chocolate oak are backed by nuances of spearmint and eucalypt. Oak-driven, its soft, minty palate lacks genuine spine and structure.

| | | | |
|---|---|---|---|
| 2000 | 87 | 2005 | 2008+ |
| 1999 | 82 | 2001 | 2004+ |
| 1998 | 96 | 2010 | 2018 |
| 1997 | 95 | 2005 | 2009 |
| 1996 | 95 | 2008 | 2016 |
| 1995 | 95 | 2007 | 2015 |
| 1994 | 93 | 2006 | 2014 |

## ORANGE VINEYARD CABERNET SAUVIGNON      RANKING **5**

**Orange** $20–$29
**Current vintage: 2000** 90

Polished minty cabernet with a briary fragrance of violets and cassis with a background of cedar/vanilla oak. Long, smooth and creamy, it's a stylish wine with tightly focused cassis and plum flavours neatly meshed with cedary oak and fine, powdery tannins.

| | | | |
|---|---|---|---|
| 2000 | 90 | 2008 | 2012+ |
| 1999 | 86 | 2001 | 2004+ |
| 1998 | 87 | 2003 | 2006 |
| 1997 | 87 | 2002 | 2005 |
| 1996 | 91 | 2004 | 2008 |
| 1995 | 87 | 2003 | 2007 |

# ORANGE VINEYARD CHARDONNAY

RANKING 2

| Orange | $20–$29 |
|---|---|
| **Current vintage: 2002** | **89** |

Lightly herbal aromas of banana, pineapple and cashew with light vanilla oak precede a medium-weight palate of creamy softness. Juicy, but herbal flavours of melon, peach and cashew become leaner and finer down the palate, finishing with some alcoholic hotness.

| | | | |
|---|---|---|---|
| 2002 | 89 | 2004 | 2007+ |
| 2001 | 95 | 2006 | 2009 |
| 2000 | 94 | 2002 | 2005+ |
| 1999 | 95 | 2004 | 2007 |
| 1998 | 93 | 2003 | 2006 |
| 1997 | 94 | 2005 | 2009 |
| 1996 | 93 | 2001 | 2004 |
| 1995 | 93 | 2003 | 2007 |
| 1994 | 94 | 1999 | 2002 |

# ORANGE VINEYARD MERLOT

RANKING 5

| Orange | $20–$29 |
|---|---|
| **Current vintage: 2001** | **89** |

Savoury, but herbal merlot with a meaty, earthy bouquet of plums and tobacco, with underlying fine-grained cedary oak. Elegant, supple and tightly knit, its gentle palate delivers plum and dark cherry flavours and undergrowth-like complexity over sappy, tobaccoey influences.

| | | | |
|---|---|---|---|
| 2001 | 89 | 2006 | 2009+ |
| 2000 | 89 | 2005 | 2008 |
| 1999 | 83 | 2001 | 2004 |
| 1998 | 93 | 2003 | 2006+ |

# ROXBURGH CHARDONNAY

RANKING 2

ROXBURGH
Chardonnay

| Upper Hunter Valley | $50+ |
|---|---|
| **Current vintage: 2002** | **94** |

An oily, but relatively elegant Roxburgh whose delicate nutty aromas of honeysuckle and citrus fruit are lifted by smoky, creamy vanilla oak. Round and generous, it presents a long, textured palate with a core of juicy melon, mango and citrus flavours bordered by greenish suggestions of cashew nuts and fine phenolics. It's full and seamless, finishing with savoury nuances of oatmeal and citrusy acids.

| | | | |
|---|---|---|---|
| 2002 | 94 | 2004 | 2007 |
| 2001 | 91 | 2003 | 2006+ |
| 1999 | 91 | 2004 | 2007 |
| 1998 | 95 | 2003 | 2006+ |
| 1997 | 91 | 2002 | 2005 |
| 1996 | 94 | 2002 | 2006 |
| 1995 | 94 | 2000 | 2003 |
| 1994 | 91 | 1999 | 2001 |
| 1993 | 88 | 1998 | 2001 |
| 1992 | 88 | 1997 | 2000 |
| 1991 | 94 | 2003 | 2011 |
| 1990 | 92 | 1998 | 2002 |
| 1989 | 94 | 1997 | 2001 |
| 1988 | 86 | 1993 | 1996 |
| 1987 | 93 | 1995 | 1999 |

# SHIRAZ

RANKING 5

| Various | $12–$19 |
|---|---|
| **Current vintage: 2002** | **86** |

Vibrant jujube-like aromas of cassis and plums, with a slightly muddy background of chocolate/vanilla oak. Smooth and silky, with lively small berry flavours of some concentration, it finishes with an excess of distinctly muddy riverland undertones.

| | | | |
|---|---|---|---|
| 2002 | 86 | 2003 | 2004+ |
| 2001 | 86 | 2002 | 2003+ |
| 2000 | 86 | 2001 | 2002 |
| 1999 | 87 | 2000 | 2001 |
| 1998 | 89 | 2000 | 2003+ |
| 1997 | 87 | 1999 | 2002 |

# SHOW RESERVE CABERNET SAUVIGNON

RANKING 3

| Coonawarra | $20–$29 |
|---|---|
| **Current vintage: 2001** | **87** |

Dried herbs and sweet cedar/vanilla oak add complexity to its intense fragrance of red and black berries, plums and mulberries, while its palate is juicy and up-front, but lacks genuine length. Supported by sweet oak, it reveals a rather hollow middle, but a moderately firm, if herbal finish of smooth, slightly sappy tannins.

| | | | |
|---|---|---|---|
| 2001 | 87 | 2006 | 2009 |
| 2000 | 93 | 2008 | 2012 |
| 1999 | 91 | 2007 | 2011+ |
| 1998 | 94 | 2010 | 2018 |
| 1997 | 90 | 2002 | 2005+ |
| 1996 | 95 | 2004 | 2008+ |
| 1995 | 88 | 2000 | 2003 |
| 1994 | 95 | 2006 | 2014 |
| 1993 | 93 | 2001 | 2005 |
| 1992 | 94 | 2004 | 2012 |
| 1991 | 87 | 2003 | 2011 |
| 1990 | 93 | 2002 | 2010 |
| 1989 | 87 | 1994 | 1997 |
| 1988 | 91 | 1996 | 2000+ |

# SHOW RESERVE CHARDONNAY

**Upper Hunter Valley**  $20–$29
**Current vintage: 2002**  91

Juicy, oily Hunter chardonnay with a pungent, bubblegum-like aroma of citrus and melon fruit, creamy vanilla oak and earthy, leesy complexity. Sweet and punchy, it's generous and early maturing, offering vibrant bathpowder-like melon and lemon fruit over nuances of tobacco. Finishes soft and round.

| | | | |
|---|---|---|---|
| 2002 | 91 | 2004 | 2007 |
| 2001 | 87 | 2002 | 2003 |
| 2000 | 95 | 2005 | 2008+ |
| 1999 | 94 | 2004 | 2007 |
| 1998 | 93 | 2006 | 2010 |
| 1997 | 93 | 2002 | 2005+ |
| 1996 | 95 | 2004 | 2008+ |
| 1995 | 93 | 2003 | 2007 |
| 1994 | 90 | 2002 | 2006 |
| 1993 | 91 | 1998 | 2001 |

# SHOW RESERVE SEMILLON

**Upper Hunter Valley**  $20–$29
**Current vintage: 2002**  90

Pungent aromas of green olives and tobacco with nutty undertones precedes a long and creamy palate whose juicy melon-like fruit culminates in a lingering nougat-like finish. Nicely balanced and restrained.

| | | | |
|---|---|---|---|
| 2002 | 90 | 2007 | 2010 |
| 2000 | 92 | 2005 | 2008 |
| 1998 | 92 | 2006 | 2010 |
| 1997 | 91 | 2005 | 2009 |
| 1996 | 93 | 2004 | 2008 |
| 1995 | 93 | 2003 | 2007 |
| 1991 | 89 | 1996 | 1999 |
| 1990 | 93 | 1998 | 2002 |
| 1989 | 94 | 1997 | 2001+ |

# SHOW RESERVE SHIRAZ

**McLaren Vale**  $20–$29
**Current vintage: 2000**  87

Sweet leathery and earthy berry/plum fruit with reductive sweet corn-like undertones and slightly varnishy vanilla oak. Slightly jammy and porty, revealing under and over-ripe fruit qualities, it does offer a reasonable length of sweet, juicy fruit and mocha/chocolate oak, but lacks genuine ripeness, harmony and balance.

| | | | |
|---|---|---|---|
| 2000 | 87 | 2002 | 2005+ |
| 1999 | 86 | 2004 | 2007 |
| 1998 | 88 | 2003 | 2006 |
| 1997 | 88 | 2002 | 2005 |
| 1996 | 95 | 2004 | 2008 |
| 1995 | 91 | 2003 | 2007 |

# TRADITIONAL (Cabernet blend)

**McLaren Vale**  $20–$29
**Current vintage: 2001**  89

A plump, succulent and generous young red for short-term enjoyment, this Jimmy Watson winner has a vibrant and slightly jammy aroma of small black and red berries, with earthy, herbal nuances. Its full to medium palate begins with sweet, forward fruit, is then carried along by smooth creamy vanilla oak, before a slightly green-edged finish.

| | | | |
|---|---|---|---|
| 2001 | 89 | 2003 | 2006+ |
| 2000 | 87 | 2002 | 2005+ |
| 1999 | 88 | 2001 | 2004 |
| 1998 | 93 | 2006 | 2010 |
| 1997 | 90 | 2002 | 2005 |
| 1996 | 91 | 2004 | 2008 |

# Ross Estate

Barossa Valley Highway, Lyndoch SA 5351. Tel: (08) 8524 4033. Fax: (08) 8524 4533.
Website: www.rossestate.com.au  Email: rossestate@rossestate.com.au
Region: **Barossa Valley**  Winemaker: **Rod Chapman**  Chief Executive: **Darius Ross**
In 1993 the Ross family bought a 110 ha vineyard near Lyndoch in the Barossa Valley. The property produces some ripe, assertive wines from its mature vineyards, of which the grenache vines are ninety-five years old.

## OLD VINE GRENACHE

RANKING **5**

| Barossa Valley | $20–$29 |
|---|---|
| **Current vintage: 2002** | **83** |

Very ripe, slightly porty and jammy blackberry, plum and sweet vanilla aromas with some varnishy volatility. Forward, sweet and juicy, its pleasing length of juicy dark cherry, plum and dark chocolate flavours is soft and smooth, but spoiled by a spiky, varnishy finish.

| | | | |
|---|---|---|---|
| 2002 | 83 | 2004 | 2007 |
| 2001 | 89 | 2003 | 2006+ |
| 2000 | 88 | 2002 | 2005 |
| 1999 | 81 | 2001 | 2004 |

# Rothbury Estate, The

Broke Road, Pokolbin NSW 2320. Tel: (02) 4998 7555. Fax: (02) 4998 7553.
Website: www.beringerblass.com.au
Region: **Lower Hunter Valley**  Winemaker: **Neil McGuigan**  Viticulturist: **Roger Dixon**
Chief Executive: **Jamie Odell**
Some honest, if unspectacular releases under the Neil McGuigan label have been overshadowed by some fine and very regional Brokenback wines — especially the Semillon and Chardonnay, of which the 2002 editions are a big step forward. There is still much to do before Rothbury regains its place amongst the Hunter's elite.

## BROKENBACK CHARDONNAY

RANKING **5**

| Lower Hunter Valley | $20–$29 |
|---|---|
| **Current vintage: 2002** | **92** |

Smooth, charmingly elegant and flavoursome young chardonnay with a floral and lightly nutty aroma of peachy fruit and restrained vanilla oak, backed by creamy suggestions of extended lees contact. A gentle, supple and fluffy palate of stonefruits and creamy oak finishes with soft acidity.

| | | | |
|---|---|---|---|
| 2002 | 92 | 2004 | 2007 |
| 2001 | 86 | 2002 | 2003 |
| 2000 | 87 | 2002 | 2005 |
| 1996 | 88 | 1998 | 2001 |

## BROKENBACK SEMILLON

RANKING  **4**

| Lower Hunter Valley | $20–$29 |
|---|---|
| **Current vintage: 2002** | **90** |

Likely to mature into a richer Hunter style, its floral aromas of lemon, apple and melon are well ripened, without a hint of grassiness. Initially round and juicy, it becomes tighter and more restrained down the palate, finishing with a fine chalky grip and lemony acids. Tight and focused.

| | | | |
|---|---|---|---|
| 2002 | 90 | 2007 | 2010+ |
| 2001 | 82 | 2003 | 2006 |
| 2000 | 91 | 2008 | 2012 |
| 1998 | 92 | 2003 | 2006 |
| 1997 | 94 | 2005 | 2009 |

# Rufus Stone

Tyrrell's, Broke Road, Pokolbin NSW 2320. Tel: (02) 4993 7000. Fax: (02) 4998 7723.
Website: www.tyrrells.com.au Email: tyrrells@tyrrells.com.au
Region: **Various** Winemakers: **Andrew Spinaze, Mark Richardson** Chief Executive: **Bruce Tyrrell**
A brand owned and operated by Tyrrell's that features red wines sourced from outside the company's native Hunter Valley, Rufus Stone is a well-priced source of medium to full-bodied reds made without excessive ripeness or extract. The McLaren Vale wines are consistent; the Heathcote Shiraz very promising.

## HEATHCOTE SHIRAZ
RANKING **4**

| Heathcote | $20–$29 |
|---|---|
| Current vintage: 2002 | 88 |

Lively and fresh despite some stewed/cooked fruit qualities, this fragrant red offers some attractive suppleness and sappiness. Earthy qualities of small red and black berries, sweet cedar/vanilla oak with nuances of white pepper, cloves and cinnamon deliver a finely integrated, medium to full-bodied palate.

| | | | |
|---|---|---|---|
| 2002 | 88 | 2004 | 2007 |
| 2001 | 87 | 2003 | 2006 |
| 2000 | 92 | 2005 | 2008+ |
| 1999 | 91 | 2004 | 2007 |
| 1998 | 88 | 2006 | 2010 |
| 1997 | 92 | 2002 | 2005+ |

## McLAREN VALE MERLOT
RANKING **4**

| McLaren Vale | $20–$29 |
|---|---|
| Current vintage: 2001 | 91 |

Fresh and aromatic, with a slightly meaty, minty and jammy bouquet of red and black cherries and berries over creamy, vanilla oak influences. Its long, firm palate is saturated with ripe fruits tightly knit with sweet cedar/chocolate oak and framed by firm, fine-grained tannins. Should flesh out well over time.

| | | | |
|---|---|---|---|
| 2001 | 91 | 2006 | 2009 |
| 2000 | 91 | 2002 | 2005+ |
| 1999 | 90 | 2004 | 2007 |

## McLAREN VALE SHIRAZ
RANKING **4**

| McLaren Vale | $20–$29 |
|---|---|
| Current vintage: 2002 | 91 |

Spicy aromas of black pepper, cloves and cinnamon, sweet blackberries, dark plums and sweet chocolate oak precede a taut, long and refined palate of moderate weight. Its pristine expression of dark berries and plums is married to restrained oak and framed by a fine-grained extract. Finishes long, balanced and savoury, with a lively acidity and lingering fruit sweetness.

| | | | |
|---|---|---|---|
| 2002 | 91 | 2010 | 2014+ |
| 2000 | 87 | 2002 | 2005+ |
| 1999 | 90 | 2004 | 2007 |
| 1998 | 93 | 2003 | 2006+ |
| 1997 | 93 | 2002 | 2005 |
| 1996 | 84 | 2001 | 2004 |

# Russet Ridge

cnr Caves Road, & Riddoch Hwy (vyd only) Naracoorte SA 5271. Tel: (08) 8521 3140. Fax: (08) 8521 3425
Email: contact_us@orlando.com
Region: **Limestone Coast** Winemakers: **Philip Laffer, Sam Kurtz, Bernie Hickin** Viticulturist: **Martin Wirper**
Chief Executive: **Laurent Lacassgne**
Russet Ridge is a Limestone Coast-sourced brand of Orlando Wyndham red wine. The tightly focused 2002 vintage represents a strong return to its mid-1990s form.

## CABERNET SHIRAZ MERLOT
RANKING **5**

| Limestone Coast | $12–$19 |
|---|---|
| Current vintage: 2002 | 92 |

Fine, elegant, flavoursome and smoothly structured wine whose lively berry/plum fruits are cleverly integrated into a modestly generous and harmonious palate of freshness and focus. Its sweet oak and fine tannins appropriately offset its vibrant fruit.

| | | | |
|---|---|---|---|
| 2002 | 92 | 2007 | 2010+ |
| 1999 | 82 | 2001 | 2004+ |
| 1998 | 88 | 2003 | 2006 |
| 1997 | 86 | 2002 | 2005 |
| 1996 | 92 | 2001 | 2004+ |
| 1995 | 85 | 2000 | 2003 |
| 1994 | 92 | 1999 | 2002 |
| 1993 | 90 | 2001 | 2005 |
| 1992 | 89 | 2000 | 2004 |
| 1991 | 91 | 1996 | 1999 |

# Rymill

The Riddoch Run Vineyard, Riddoch Highway, Coonawarra SA 5263.
Tel: (08) 8736 5001. Fax: (08) 8736 5040.
Website: www.rymill.com.au   Email: winery@rymill.com.au
Region: **Coonawarra** Winemakers: **John Innes, Clemence Dournois** Viticulturist: **Grant Oschar**
Chief Executive: **John Innes**

Rymill is a small to medium-sized Coonawarra operation that is very serious about making premium wine. Not exactly assisted by the region's recent run of difficult vintages, Rymill's red wines have lately been influenced by significant herbaceous and rustic horse hair-like influences.

## CABERNET SAUVIGNON

RANKING **5**

| | |
|---|---|
| Coonawarra | $20–$29 |
| **Current vintage: 2000** | **84** |

Pruney, currant-like aromas of cassis and plums with assertive cedar/chocolate oak. Lacks vitality, length and structure, with overcooked, meaty and greenish fruit supported by rather thin, unsubstantial tannin.

| 2000 | 84 | 2005 | 2008 |
|---|---|---|---|
| 1999 | 86 | 2004 | 2007 |
| 1998 | 91 | 2006 | 2010 |
| 1997 | 86 | 2002 | 2005 |
| 1996 | 90 | 2004 | 2008 |
| 1995 | 88 | 2000 | 2003+ |
| 1994 | 89 | 2002 | 2006+ |
| 1993 | 83 | 1995 | 1998 |
| 1992 | 88 | 2000 | 2004+ |

## MC² MERLOT CABERNETS

RANKING **5**

| | |
|---|---|
| Coonawarra | $12–$19 |
| **Current vintage: 2001** | **89** |

A fine, elegant, restrained and flavoursome Coonawarra blend with a lively bouquet of sweet red berries, cherries and plums over light nuances of cedar/vanilla oak, violets and undergrowth. Smooth and supple, its attractive fruit flavours are underpinned by neatly integrated creamy oak and supple tannins, finishing clean and savoury with a light dusting of tobaccoey and meaty flavour.

| 2001 | 89 | 2006 | 2009+ |
|---|---|---|---|
| 2000 | 89 | 2005 | 2008 |
| 1999 | 88 | 2001 | 2004 |
| 1998 | 81 | 2000 | 2003 |
| 1997 | 91 | 1999 | 2002 |
| 1996 | 89 | 1998 | 2001 |
| 1995 | 88 | 1997 | 2000 |
| 1994 | 87 | 1996 | 1999 |

## SHIRAZ

RANKING **4**

| | |
|---|---|
| Coonawarra | $20–$29 |
| **Current vintage: 2000** | **77** |

Rustic and evolved, this horsey, meaty shiraz reveals light red berry flavours and cedary, leathery nuances that culminate in a flat, stale and metallic finish.

| 2000 | 77 | 2002 | 2005 |
|---|---|---|---|
| 1999 | 92 | 2004 | 2007+ |
| 1998 | 91 | 2003 | 2006 |
| 1997 | 91 | 2002 | 2006+ |
| 1996 | 89 | 2004 | 2005 |
| 1995 | 88 | 2000 | 2003 |
| 1994 | 82 | 1999 | 2002+ |

# Saltram

Nuriootpa–Angaston Road, Angaston SA 5353. Tel: (08) 8564 3355. Fax: (08) 8564 2209.
Website: www.saltramwines.com.au

Region: **Barossa Valley** Winemaker: **Nigel Dolan** Viticulturist: **Syd Kyloh** Chief Executive: **Jamie Odell**

The launch of the initial 2000 vintage of The Eighth Maker Shiraz, a scarce and very expensive wine hand-crafted by the company's 8th winemaker in Nigel Dolan, has given additional gloss to this now-successful Beringer Blass-owned Barossa brand. Its more established classic, the No1. Shiraz, has also produced a fine wine from the very hot and challenging 2000 vintage.

## NO. 1 SHIRAZ — RANKING 2

**Barossa Valley** $50+
**Current vintage: 2000** 90

There's a slightly cooked, spicy, meaty quality about this wine's sweet, ripe and smoky aroma of violets, cassis, mulberries and raspberries. There's also a hint of licorice and a generous serve of vanilla oak. Forward and intensely flavoured, the richly endowed palate is steeped in slightly meaty cassis and plum-like fruit and cloaked in assertive smoky cedar/vanilla oak. Lightly cooked, uncomplicated but finely crafted, it's a worthy red from a difficult vintage.

| | | | |
|---|---|---|---|
| 2000 | 90 | 2005 | 2008+ |
| 1999 | 94 | 2007 | 2011+ |
| 1998 | 96 | 2010 | 2018 |
| 1997 | 88 | 2005 | 2009 |
| 1996 | 94 | 2008 | 2016 |
| 1995 | 93 | 2003 | 2007+ |
| 1994 | 93 | 2002 | 2006 |

# Sandalford

3210 West Swan Road, Caversham WA 6055. Tel: (08) 9274 5922. Fax: (08) 9274 2154.
Website: www.sandalford.com  Email: sandalford@sandalford.com

Regions: **Various, WA** Winemaker: **Paul Boulden** Viticulturist: **Peter Traeger** Chief Executive: **Grant Brinklow**

Sandalford deserves credit for steadily improving all its premier wines, sourced from a number of Western Australian regions. Released to the market perhaps earlier than ideal, the reds are acquiring richness, fruit weight and structure, while the whites are refreshingly aromatic, with intense varietal flavours.

## CABERNET SAUVIGNON — RANKING 4

**Margaret River** $30–$49
**Current vintage: 2002** 90

A pleasingly stylish and harmonious cabernet with distinctive Margaret River qualities. There's a minty note of dried herbs beneath its oaky fragrance of violets, cassis and plums, while its slender palate presents a pleasing length of lively small red and black berry flavours intermeshed with fine tannins and assertive vanilla, cedar and mocha oak.

| | | | |
|---|---|---|---|
| 2002 | 90 | 2007 | 2010+ |
| 2001 | 90 | 2009 | 2013 |
| 2000 | 88 | 2005 | 2008 |
| 1999 | 87 | 2004 | 2007 |
| 1998 | 84 | 2000 | 2003 |
| 1997 | 84 | 1999 | 2002+ |
| 1996 | 81 | 1998 | 2001 |
| 1995 | 92 | 2000 | 2003 |
| 1994 | 92 | 2002 | 2006 |
| 1993 | 81 | 1998 | 2001 |
| 1992 | 87 | 1994 | 1997 |
| 1991 | 87 | 1999 | 2003 |
| 1990 | 90 | 2002 | 2010 |
| 1989 | 85 | 2001 | 2009 |

## CHARDONNAY — RANKING 4

**Margaret River** $12–$19
**Current vintage: 2003** 89

Good honest chardonnay with a slightly spicy, nutty and oaky aroma of sweet melon and grapefruit, plus undertones of lime juice and oatmeal. Its sumptuous, generous palate of grapefruit, melon and mango flavours brings plenty of fruit sweetness and flavour, before a lingering finish of crisp acids. Just a little too oaky for a higher score.

| | | | |
|---|---|---|---|
| 2003 | 89 | 2005 | 2008 |
| 2002 | 90 | 2004 | 2007 |
| 2001 | 87 | 2003 | 2006 |
| 1999 | 94 | 2004 | 2007 |
| 1998 | 84 | 2000 | 2003 |
| 1997 | 84 | 1998 | 1999 |
| 1996 | 89 | 1998 | 2001 |
| 1995 | 94 | 2000 | 2003 |
| 1994 | 90 | 1999 | 2002 |
| 1993 | 94 | 1998 | 2001 |
| 1992 | 84 | 1993 | 1994 |

## MERLOT

RANKING **5**

| Various, WA | $20–$29 |
|---|---|
| **Current vintage: 2002** | **87** |

Pretty, early-drinking merlot whose rather sweet, lolly-like aromas of plums, cherries and vanilla oak before a forward and slightly hollow palate of primary fruit and soft tannins.

| 2002 | 87 | 2003 | 2004 |
|---|---|---|---|
| 2001 | 87 | 2003 | 2006 |
| 2000 | 90 | 2005 | 2008 |
| 1999 | 75 | 2001 | 2004+ |

## RIESLING

RANKING **4**

| Various, WA | $12–$19 |
|---|---|
| **Current vintage: 2003** | **89** |

Fresh, racy young riesling with a penetrative, punchy aroma of lime juice and lemon rind, green apples and bathpowder. Its palate is lightly spicy, juicy and crunchy, with up-front green apple flavours and texture before a refreshing finish of lemony acids and minerals.

| 2003 | 89 | 2005 | 2008 |
|---|---|---|---|
| 2002 | 90 | 2007 | 2010 |
| 2001 | 83 | 2002 | 2003 |
| 2000 | 93 | 2005 | 2008+ |
| 1998 | 90 | 2006 | 2010 |

## SEMILLON SAUVIGNON BLANC

RANKING **5**

| Margaret River | $12–$19 |
|---|---|
| **Current vintage: 2004** | **88** |

Herbal, lightly sweaty aromas of passionfruit, lychees and capsicum precede a smooth and restrained palate whose pure, delicate fruit flavours are punctuated by racy, lemony acids. Very honest and flavoursome; likely to build more richness in the bottle.

| 2004 | 88 | 2005 | 2006 |
|---|---|---|---|
| 2003 | 89 | 2003 | 2004 |
| 2002 | 85 | 2002 | 2003 |
| 2001 | 82 | 2001 | 2002 |
| 2000 | 90 | 2002 | 2005+ |
| 1999 | 89 | 2001 | 2004 |

## SHIRAZ

| Margaret River, Mt Barker | $20–$29 |
|---|---|
| **Current vintage: 2003** | **84** |

Spicy, peppery aromas of candied cherries and plums with a sweet background of slightly gluey vanilla oak. Up-front, with sweet bubblegum-like small red and black berry flavours, the palate then dries out with nuances of currants and plums, before finishing drying, fine-grained and oaky.

| 2002 | 84 | 2003 | 2004+ |
|---|---|---|---|
| 2001 | 89 | 2006 | 2009 |
| 1999 | 81 | 2001 | 2004 |
| 1998 | 83 | 2000 | 2003 |
| 1997 | 82 | 1999 | 2002+ |
| 1996 | 87 | 2001 | 2004 |
| 1995 | 89 | 2003 | 2007 |
| 1994 | 90 | 2002 | 2006 |
| 1993 | 89 | 1998 | 2001 |

## VERDELHO

RANKING **4**

| Margaret River | $12–$19 |
|---|---|
| **Current vintage: 2004** | **90** |

Refreshing, racy verdelho whose lightly spicy fragrance of kiwifruit, guava and gooseberries reveals a light herbaceousness. Immediately intense, the palate bursts with pristine tropical fruit and gooseberry flavours, culminating in a tangy and lingering citrusy finish.

| 2004 | 90 | 2006 | 2009 |
|---|---|---|---|
| 2003 | 90 | 2005 | 2008 |
| 2002 | 90 | 2004 | 2007 |
| 2001 | 84 | 2006 | 2009 |
| 2000 | 77 | 2001 | 2002 |
| 1999 | 89 | 2001 | 2004 |
| 1998 | 88 | 2003 | 2006 |
| 1997 | 83 | 1998 | 1999 |

# Sandstone

PO Box 558 Busselton WA 6280. Tel: (08) 9755 6271. Fax: (08) 9755 6292.
Email: sandstone@portavin.com.au

Region: **Margaret River** Winemaker: **Jan Davies**

Sandstone is a small and idiosyncratic Margaret River label with a terrific track record of fine oak-matured Semillons and some robust, long-living Cabernet Sauvignons.

## CABERNET SAUVIGNON

RANKING

| Margaret River | $30–$49 |
| --- | --- |
| **Current vintage: 2000** | **86** |

Early-drinking cabernet whose earthy aromas of ripe plums and redcurrants are developing leathery and cedary undertones. Ripe, forward and juicy, it finishes thin and slightly green-edged, lacking its customary length and structure.

| | | | |
| --- | --- | --- | --- |
| 2000 | 86 | 2002 | 2005+ |
| 1999 | 95 | 2011 | 2019 |
| 1998 | 92 | 2006 | 2010 |
| 1996 | 89 | 2004 | 2008 |
| 1995 | 87 | 2003 | 2007 |
| 1993 | 88 | 2001 | 2005 |
| 1992 | 92 | 2004 | 2012 |
| 1991 | 90 | 2003 | 2011 |
| 1990 | 89 | 1998 | 2002 |
| 1989 | 91 | 1997 | 2001 |
| 1988 | 87 | 1993 | 1996 |

## SEMILLON

RANKING

| Margaret River | $20–$29 |
| --- | --- |
| **Current vintage: 2002** | **87** |

Substantial barrel ferment influences pervade the nose and palate of this soft and concentrated wine, whose toasty fragrance of honeysuckle, melon and lemon rind reveals a significant sweet vanilla background. Round and charry, the chewy, buttery palate finishes with softness and an oaky rawness.

| | | | |
| --- | --- | --- | --- |
| 2002 | 87 | 2007 | 2010 |
| 2001 | 91 | 2006 | 2009 |
| 2000 | 84 | 2002 | 2005+ |
| 1999 | 90 | 2004 | 2007 |
| 1998 | 94 | 2003 | 2006 |
| 1997 | 94 | 2002 | 2005 |
| 1995 | 94 | 2003 | 2007 |
| 1994 | 93 | 1999 | 2002 |
| 1993 | 93 | 2001 | 2005 |

# Scotchmans Hill

190 Scotchmans Road, Drysdale Vic 3222. Tel: (03) 5251 3176. Fax: (03) 5253 1743.
Website: www.scotchmanshill.com.au  Email: info@scotchmans.com.au

Region: **Geelong** Winemaker: **Robin Brockett** Viticulturist: **Robin Brockett**
Chief Executives: **David and Vivienne Browne**

Scotchmans Hill is a very successful small winery business located near Geelong, on the dry side of Melbourne's Port Phillip Bay, where the drought hasn't made viticulture easy for the last few years. Its wines are affordably priced, and typically deliver that little bit more than many of their competitors. Despite the dry seasons, in 2003 Scotchmans Hill has still produced Pinot Noir and Sauvignon Blanc of its customary standard, as well as its finest Chardonnay for some years.

## CABERNET SAUVIGNON MERLOT

| Geelong | $20–$29 |
| --- | --- |
| **Current vintage: 2000** | **76** |

Shaded and greenish, with jammy fruit and geranium-like flavours through both nose and palate.

| | | | |
| --- | --- | --- | --- |
| 2000 | 76 | 2002 | 2005 |
| 1999 | 81 | 2001 | 2004 |
| 1998 | 88 | 2003 | 2006 |
| 1996 | 81 | 1998 | 2001 |
| 1995 | 86 | 2000 | 2003 |
| 1994 | 79 | 1996 | 1999 |

## CHARDONNAY

RANKING **5**

| Geelong | $20–$29 |
|---|---|
| **Current vintage: 2003** | **90** |

Ripe, buttery chardonnay with a juicy aroma of nectarines, pineapple and figs, with creamy lees-derived and restrained, slightly toffee-like malolactic influences. Its smooth, fleshy palate does present some refinement in its expression of reserved lemon and stonefruit flavours, finishing with length and freshness. It should flesh out well, overcoming a little alcoholic warmth.

| | | | |
|---|---|---|---|
| 2003 | 90 | 2005 | 2008 |
| 2002 | 86 | 2004 | 2007 |
| 2001 | 83 | 2002 | 2003 |
| 2000 | 86 | 2002 | 2005 |
| 1999 | 82 | 2000 | 2001 |
| 1998 | 87 | 1999 | 2000 |
| 1997 | 91 | 1998 | 2002 |

## PINOT NOIR

RANKING **5**

| Geelong | $20–$29 |
|---|---|
| **Current vintage: 2003** | **90** |

Well-composed and tightly structured young pinot whose floral perfume of raspberries and cherries is supported by sweet vanilla/cedar oak. Fresh and forward, its soft, generous palate has an approachable lusciousness and length, presenting sweet flavours of plums and cherries with an underlying spiciness. It finishes dusty and savoury, with hints of charcuterie.

| | | | |
|---|---|---|---|
| 2003 | 90 | 2005 | 2008+ |
| 2002 | 88 | 2004 | 2007 |
| 2001 | 89 | 2002 | 2006 |
| 2000 | 84 | 2001 | 2002 |
| 1999 | 87 | 2000 | 2001+ |
| 1998 | 86 | 1999 | 2000 |
| 1997 | 93 | 2002 | 2005 |

## SAUVIGNON BLANC

RANKING **5**

| Geelong | $12–$20 |
|---|---|
| **Current vintage: 2003** | **89** |

Honest, clean and generous sauvignon blanc with a pungent, lightly sweaty aroma of tropical fruits and passionfruit backed by capsicum and asparagus. Juicy, smooth and viscous, it's bright and tangy, but just lacks a little acid definition at the finish.

| | | | |
|---|---|---|---|
| 2003 | 89 | 2003 | 2004+ |
| 2002 | 89 | 2003 | 2004 |
| 2001 | 90 | 2002 | 2003+ |
| 2000 | 88 | 2001 | 2002 |

# Seppelt

Moyston Road, Great Western Vic 3377. Tel: (03) 5361 2222. Fax: (03) 5361 2200.
Website: www.seppelt.com.au Email: gwcd@cellar-door.com.au
Seppeltsfield Road, Seppeltsfield via Nuriootpa SA 5355. Tel: (08) 8568 6200. Fax: (08) 8562 8333.
Website: www.seppelt.com.au Email: seppelt.bv@cellar-door.com.au
Regions: **Great Western, Drumborg, Barooga, Barossa**
Winemakers: **Arthur O'Connor, James Godfrey, Steve Goodwin**
Viticulturist: **Paul Dakis** Chief Executive: **John Ballard**

Loaded with more history, tradition and quality vineyard resources than most wine companies could ever dream of, Seppelt remains a problem child within the Southcorp marketing mix. Its cheap Great Western sparkling wines are a national benchmark, while its ancient fortifieds from the Barossa Valley and Rutherglen fall under the same brand. Add to these the exceptional still and sparkling shirazes from Great Western and the occasionally stunning wines from the western Victorian Drumborg vineyard, and it's little wonder that Seppelt is indeed a product manager's perfect nightmare. The consolation, of course, is that you'd get to drink the wines.

## CHALAMBAR SHIRAZ

RANKING **4**

| Victoria | $12–$19 |
|---|---|
| **Current vintage: 2000** | **93** |

Harmoniously crafted cellar-style shiraz, with a peppery bouquet of spicy cassis and plums, with underlying earthy nuances of farm floor and dried herbs. Long and lean, its vibrant, elegant palate of intense berry fruit and vanilla/chocolate oak is framed by powder-fine tannins. Very good persistence.

| | | | |
|---|---|---|---|
| 2000 | 93 | 2008 | 2012+ |
| 1999 | 86 | 2001 | 2004+ |
| 1998 | 93 | 2006 | 2010+ |
| 1997 | 89 | 2002 | 2005+ |
| 1996 | 83 | 1998 | 2001 |
| 1995 | 91 | 2003 | 2007 |
| 1994 | 88 | 1999 | 2002 |
| 1993 | 84 | 1995 | 1998 |
| 1992 | 90 | 1997 | 2000 |
| 1991 | 90 | 1999 | 2003 |
| 1990 | 92 | 1998 | 2002 |
| 1989 | 90 | 1998 | 2001 |

## DORRIEN CABERNET SAUVIGNON

**Barossa Valley**      **$50+**
**Current vintage: 1998**      **93**

Wild, briary aromas of cassis, prunes and currants, with meaty, earthy undertones of licorice and sweet cedar/chocolate oak. Smooth and polished, its elegant, creamy palate offers a fine length of vibrant cassis and plum flavours supported by sweet oak and framed by smooth tannins. Finishes long and tight, with some herbal complexity.

| | | | |
|---|---|---|---|
| 1998 | 93 | 2006 | 2010+ |
| 1997 | 89 | 2005 | 2009+ |
| 1996 | 95 | 2008 | 2016 |
| 1994 | 93 | 2006 | 2014 |
| 1993 | 88 | 2001 | 2005 |
| 1992 | 90 | 2000 | 2004 |
| 1991 | 94 | 2003 | 2011 |
| 1990 | 91 | 2002 | 2010 |
| 1989 | 92 | 1997 | 2001 |
| 1988 | 84 | 1993 | 1996 |

## DRUMBORG RIESLING

**Western Districts**      **$20–$29**
**Current vintage: 2003**      **93**

Its delicate, Germanic perfume of citrus and deciduous fruit aromas and herbal undertones precedes an almost bracing, tightly focused and penetrative palate of lemon meringue and stone-fruits. Long, stylish and drier than most previous vintages, it finishes with refreshing acidity.

| | | | |
|---|---|---|---|
| 2003 | 93 | 2008 | 2011+ |
| 2000 | 94 | 2008 | 2012 |
| 1999 | 94 | 2011 | 2019 |
| 1998 | 89 | 2003 | 2006+ |
| 1997 | 87 | 2002 | 2005 |
| 1996 | 90 | 2001 | 2004 |
| 1993 | 94 | 2001 | 2005 |
| 1991 | 89 | 1999 | 2003 |
| 1988 | 88 | 1996 | 2000 |
| 1981 | 82 | 1989 | 1993 |
| 1978 | 89 | 1990 | 1998 |

## ORIGINAL SPARKLING SHIRAZ

**Victoria**      **$12–$19**
**Current vintage: 2002**      **89**

Lacking the customary lees-derived maturity of many Seppelt sparkling reds, this is more like a carbonated shiraz, albeit a flavoursome and elegant one. Its lightly earthy, spicy aromas of white pepper and cloves, dark red and black berries, cassis and plums reveal light cedary oak, undergrowth and violet-like fragrances. There's plenty of generous primary fruit on the palate, which remains long and fine before a lingering savoury finish.

| | | | |
|---|---|---|---|
| 2002 | 89 | 2004 | 2007+ |
| 1998 | 90 | 2006 | 2010 |
| 1996 | 93 | 2004 | 2008 |
| 1995 | 94 | 2003 | 2007 |
| 1994 | 93 | 2002 | 2006+ |
| 1993 | 92 | 2001 | 2005 |
| 1992 | 87 | 1997 | 2000 |
| 1991 | 93 | 2003 | 2011 |
| 1990 | 91 | 1998 | 2002 |
| 1989 | 85 | 1997 | 2001 |
| 1988 | 88 | 1996 | 2000 |

## SALINGER

**Victoria, Southern Australia**    **$30–$49**
**Current vintage: 2001**      **90**

Fine, elegant and creamy sparking wine with a delicate and lightly spicy aroma of peach and banana, with slightly candied citrus, vanilla oak and floral undertones. Soft and buttery, with toffee-like nuances, it's generous and smooth, with pastry-like notes beneath primary flavours of peach and melon. Very attractive balance, length and lingering fruit sweetness.

| | | | |
|---|---|---|---|
| 2001 | 90 | 2006 | 2009 |
| 2000 | 91 | 2005 | 2008 |
| 1999 | 94 | 2004 | 2007 |
| 1998 | 94 | 2003 | 2006 |
| 1997 | 93 | 2002 | 2005+ |
| 1996 | 91 | 2001 | 2004 |
| 1995 | 91 | 2003 | 2007 |
| 1994 | 92 | 1999 | 2002+ |
| 1993 | 95 | 1998 | 2001 |
| 1992 | 95 | 1997 | 2000 |
| 1991 | 94 | 1996 | 1999 |

## SHOW SPARKLING SHIRAZ

**Great Western**      **$50+**
**Current vintage: 1994**      **92**

Earthy, rather rustic sparkling shiraz with attractive fruit sweetness, undergrowth-like complexity and firmness, but a suggestion of slightly under-ripened fruit. There's a greenish, sweetcorn-like note beneath its peppery, spicy perfume of earthy cassis, plums and cigarboxy influences. Smooth and elegant, its sweet, chewy palate reveals meaty, forest floor and savoury complexity beneath its lingering jujube-like expression of black and red berries.

| | | | |
|---|---|---|---|
| 1994 | 92 | 2006 | 2014 |
| 1993 | 93 | 2005 | 2013 |
| 1990 | 95 | 2002 | 2010+ |
| 1987 | 90 | 1995 | 1999+ |
| 1986 | 95 | 1998 | 2006 |
| 1985 | 91 | 1993 | 1997 |
| 1984 | 94 | 1999 | 2001 |

## ST PETERS SHIRAZ (Formerly Great Western Shiraz)

RANKING **2**

| Great Western | $30–$49 |
| Current vintage: 2000 | **95** |

Long and harmonious, this complex and seamless shiraz has a spicy cracked pepper fragrance of intense cassis, plums and mulberries over nuances of polished leather, undergrowth and sweet truffles. Firm and supple, its silky palate presents perfectly ripened dark berry/plum fruit tightly knit with restrained oak and fine tannins, finishing with lingering savoury notes and fruit sweetness. There's some pleasing rusticity, and a greenish edge to the tannins that should diminish with age.

| | | | |
|---|---|---|---|
| 2000 | 95 | 2012 | 2020+ |
| 1999 | 90 | 2004 | 2007+ |
| 1998 | 96 | 2010 | 2018+ |
| 1997 | 92 | 2009 | 2017 |
| 1996 | 95 | 2008 | 2016 |
| 1995 | 95 | 2007 | 2015 |
| 1993 | 95 | 2005 | 2013 |
| 1992 | 90 | 2000 | 2004 |
| 1991 | 95 | 2003 | 2011 |
| 1988 | 88 | 1996 | 2000 |
| 1987 | 80 | 1992 | 1995 |
| 1986 | 90 | 1998 | 2003 |
| 1985 | 88 | 1997 | 2002 |

## VICTORIAN PREMIUM RESERVE CABERNET MERLOT

RANKING **4**

(Formerly Harpers Range)

| Victoria | $20–$29 |
| Current vintage: 2003 | **82** |

A disappointing earthy, muddy red whose simple berry, plum and currant-like fruit and menthol-like undertones are flattered by its cedary oak. Inexpensive, but uninteresting.

| | | | |
|---|---|---|---|
| 2003 | 82 | 2004 | 2005 |
| 2000 | 91 | 2008 | 2012 |
| 1998 | 90 | 2006 | 2010 |
| 1997 | 91 | 2002 | 2005+ |
| 1996 | 84 | 2001 | 2004 |
| 1995 | 89 | 2003 | 2007 |
| 1994 | 88 | 1999 | 2002 |
| 1993 | 82 | 1995 | 1998 |
| 1992 | 90 | 1997 | 2000 |

# Sevenhill

College Road, Sevenhill via Clare SA 5453. Tel: (08) 8843 4222. Fax: (08) 8843 4382.
Website: www.sevenhillcellars.com.au  Email: sales@sevenhillcellars.com.au
Region: **Clare Valley** Winemakers: **Brother John May & Tim Gneil** Viticulturist: **Craig Richards**
Chief Executive: **Paul McClure**

The oldest Clare winery, Sevenhill is still operated by the same order of Jesuit priests who bought the land it occupies in 1851. Its wines are honest, flavoursome and rather rustic, with the exception of the long, chalky and occasionally steely Riesling.

## CABERNET SAUVIGNON

RANKING **5**

| Clare Valley | $20–$29 |
| Current vintage: 2001 | **87** |

Honest, uncomplicated cabernet with a minty and confectionary fragrance of small black and red berries, slightly cooked plums and vanilla oak. Forward and fruity, it's generous, soft and fruity.

| | | | |
|---|---|---|---|
| 2001 | 87 | 2006 | 2009 |
| 2000 | 83 | 2002 | 2005 |
| 1999 | 88 | 2007 | 2011 |
| 1998 | 86 | 2003 | 2006 |
| 1997 | 86 | 2002 | 2005+ |
| 1996 | 88 | 2004 | 2008 |
| 1995 | 84 | 1997 | 2000 |
| 1994 | 90 | 2006 | 2014 |
| 1993 | 90 | 2005 | 2013 |
| 1992 | 90 | 2000 | 2004 |
| 1991 | 87 | 1999 | 2003 |
| 1990 | 87 | 1998 | 2002 |

## RIESLING

RANKING **4**

| Clare Valley | $12–$19 |
| Current vintage: 2003 | **89** |

Assertive, flavoursome riesling with a lime juice and lemon rind aroma of slate and mineral before a smooth palate that steadily builds in the mouth, becoming broader, more tangy, concentrated and candied. It finishes with lemony acids, but without great definition and shape.

| | | | |
|---|---|---|---|
| 2003 | 89 | 2008 | 2011 |
| 2002 | 87 | 2004 | 2007 |
| 2001 | 90 | 2006 | 2009 |
| 2000 | 91 | 2005 | 2008+ |
| 1999 | 88 | 2004 | 2007 |
| 1998 | 91 | 2003 | 2006 |
| 1997 | 93 | 2002 | 2005 |
| 1996 | 93 | 2004 | 2008 |
| 1995 | 94 | 2000 | 2003 |
| 1994 | 93 | 2002 | 2006 |

## SEMILLON

RANKING **5**

| Clare Valley | $12–$19 | | | | |
|---|---|---|---|---|---|
| **Current vintage: 2003** | **87** | 2003 | 87 | 2005 | 2008 |
| | | 1999 | 90 | 2005 | 2007+ |
| | | 1998 | 89 | 2003 | 2006 |
| | | 1996 | 87 | 1998 | 2001 |
| | | 1995 | 82 | 1997 | 2000 |
| | | 1994 | 87 | 1999 | 2002 |

Ripe, rather pungent and lightly grassy aromas of lemon and melon-like fruit, before a generous and juicy palate of vibrant melon and citrus fruit. There's plenty of length, before an austere and slightly phenolic finish with lemony acids. Likely to develop quickly.

## SHIRAZ

RANKING **4**

| Clare Valley | $20–$29 | | | | |
|---|---|---|---|---|---|
| **Current vintage: 2001** | **89** | 2001 | 89 | 2009 | 2013 |
| | | 1999 | 87 | 2004 | 2007 |
| | | 1998 | 90 | 2003 | 2006 |
| | | 1997 | 89 | 2002 | 2005+ |
| | | 1996 | 91 | 2001 | 2004 |
| | | 1995 | 91 | 2003 | 2007 |
| | | 1994 | 91 | 2002 | 2006 |
| | | 1993 | 93 | 2005 | 2013 |
| | | 1992 | 90 | 2000 | 2004 |

Minty, menthol Clare shiraz with a violet-like fragrance of cassis, cloves and white pepper over sweet vanilla oak. Its reasonably long and flavoursome palate of sweet fruit and oak is framed by fine, moderately firm tannins. Honest and uncomplicated.

## STM (Shiraz Touriga Malbec)

RANKING **5**

| Clare Valley | $12–$19 | | | | |
|---|---|---|---|---|---|
| **Current vintage: 2000** | **82** | 2000 | 82 | 2002 | 2005 |
| | | 1999 | 87 | 2001 | 2004+ |
| | | 1998 | 80 | 2000 | 2003 |
| | | 1997 | 86 | 2002 | 2005 |
| | | 1996 | 88 | 2001 | 2004 |
| | | 1995 | 88 | 2003 | 2007 |
| | | 1994 | 89 | 2002 | 2006 |
| | | 1993 | 90 | 2005 | 2013 |

Under and over-ripe red whose herbal, forest floor and jammy red berry aromas are given gentle oak. Forward, rather sappy and vegetal, supported by cedar/vanilla oak and soft tannins, it lacks sufficient weight of ripe fruit.

# Seville Estate

Linwood Road, Seville Vic 3139. Tel: 1300 880 561. Fax: (03) 5964 2633.
Website: www.sevilleestate.com.au  Email: wine@sevilleestate.com.au
Region: **Yarra Valley** Winemakers: **Iain Riggs, Dylan McMahon** Viticulturist: **Alastair Butt**
Chief Executive: **Rob Hawkings**

Seville Estate is a mature vineyard with one of the cooler sites in the Yarra Valley. Its original plantings of nearly 30 year-old vines are now deployed for its intensely perfumed and complex Reserve Pinot Noir, Reserve Shiraz and Reserve Cabernet Sauvignon labels, that are made into assertively oaked styles. The estate's younger vines provide the fruit for its fine, elegant and seamless 'standard' wines. At time of writing, the precise ownership of the Yarra Valley vineyards is unclear, and the owners of the brand, Brokenwood, are planning to introduce a Victorian range under this label.

## CABERNET SAUVIGNON

RANKING **5**

| Yarra Valley | $20–$29 | | | | |
|---|---|---|---|---|---|
| **Current vintage: 1998** | **84** | 1998 | 84 | 2000 | 2003+ |
| | | 1997 | 89 | 2005 | 2009 |
| | | 1995 | 86 | 2002 | 2006 |
| | | 1994 | 89 | 2002 | 2006 |
| | | 1992 | 94 | 2004 | 2012 |
| | | 1991 | 93 | 1999 | 2003 |

Shaded, dusty and herbaceous aromas of soupy capsicum with nuances of cedary oak precede a lightly fruited palate tending to lack freshness and impact.

# CHARDONNAY

**Yarra Valley**  $20–$29
**Current vintage: 2003**  90

Tight, elegant and savoury chardonnay with a delicate peachy and tropical bouquet supported by creamy vanilla oak. Soft and generous, its juicy melon and peachy fruit is enhanced by nutty lees-derived complexity and texture, finishing long and fresh with soft acidity.

| | | | |
|---|---|---|---|
| 2003 | 90 | 2005 | 2008 |
| 2002 | 87 | 2004 | 2007 |
| 2001 | 88 | 2003 | 2006 |
| 2000 | 87 | 2002 | 2005 |
| 1999 | 89 | 2001 | 2004 |
| 1998 | 89 | 2003 | 2006 |
| 1997 | 94 | 2002 | 2005+ |
| 1996 | 91 | 2001 | 2004 |
| 1995 | 92 | 2000 | 2003 |
| 1994 | 94 | 2002 | 2006 |

# PINOT NOIR

**Yarra Valley**  $20–$29
**Current vintage: 2003**  88

Honest, flavoursome if rather simple pinot whose aroma of raspberries, cherries and red plums reveals sweet vanilla/cedary oak and nuances of dried herbs. Smooth and pretty, its supple and juicy palate delivers a vibrant mouthful of tangy, candied cherry and plum flavours backed by smoky vanilla oak, finishing with soft tannins and fresh acids.

| | | | |
|---|---|---|---|
| 2003 | 88 | 2005 | 2008 |
| 2002 | 86 | 2004 | 2007 |
| 2001 | 88 | 2003 | 2006+ |
| 2000 | 89 | 2002 | 2005 |
| 1999 | 87 | 2001 | 2004 |
| 1998 | 87 | 2000 | 2003+ |
| 1995 | 87 | 2000 | 2003 |
| 1993 | 93 | 1998 | 2001 |
| 1992 | 88 | 2000 | 2004 |

# RESERVE CABERNET SAUVIGNON

**Yarra Valley**  $30–$49
**Current vintage: 2001**  92

Firm, ripe but rather closed cabernet with a sweet, earthy and slightly meaty bouquet of violets, prunes and plums over restrained cedar/vanilla oak and herbal undertones. Long, fine and silky, its palate reveals lively berry fruits plus smooth, creamy and fine-grained oak over a firm, powdery chassis of fine, drying tannins. Well integrated, with a modest substratum of herbal influence.

| | | | |
|---|---|---|---|
| 2001 | 92 | 2009 | 2013+ |
| 2000 | 93 | 2012 | 2020 |
| 1999 | 92 | 2001 | 2004 |

# SHIRAZ

**Yarra Valley**  $20–$29
**Current vintage: 2002**  93

Classy, refined and very elegant cool climate shiraz laced with black pepper and cassis/plum flavours. Its spicy, dusty perfume of penetrative dark fruit is supported by fresh cedar/vanilla oak, while its vibrant, lingering palate is fine, supple and almost sappy. So balanced and even it will surely cellar well, but most will succumb to its immediate appeal.

| | | | |
|---|---|---|---|
| 2002 | 93 | 2010 | 2014+ |
| 2001 | 93 | 2006 | 2009 |
| 2000 | 86 | 2002 | 2005 |
| 1999 | 92 | 2004 | 2007 |
| 1997 | 93 | 2005 | 2009 |
| 1996 | 93 | 2004 | 2008 |
| 1995 | 93 | 2003 | 2007 |
| 1994 | 90 | 2002 | 2006 |
| 1993 | 95 | 2001 | 2005 |
| 1992 | 94 | 2004 | 2012+ |
| 1991 | 91 | 2003 | 2011+ |
| 1990 | 86 | 1995 | 1998+ |
| 1989 | 82 | 1991 | 1994 |
| 1988 | 88 | 1996 | 2000+ |

# Shadowfax

K Road, Werribee Vic 3030. Tel: (03) 9731 4420. Fax: (03) 9731 4421.
Website: www.shadowfax.com.au  Email: shadowfax@mansiongroup.com.au

Region: **Various** Winemaker: **Matt Harrop** Viticulturist: **Andrew Tedder**

Shadowfax is a no-expense-spared winery operation established within the bounds of Werribee Park near Melbourne, where it grows a surprisingly flavoursome Shiraz. Its fruit is generally sourced from all over southeastern Australia, as winemaker Matt Harrop is given a relatively free hand to buy parcels that he believes will produce consistently good wine each year. So far, the results are very positive, especially when the first wines from the company's newly-acquired mature Zuber Estate vineyard at Heathcote are considered as well.

## CHARDONNAY

RANKING 4

| Various, SA, Vic | $20–$29 |
| --- | --- |
| **Current vintage: 2002** | **90** |

Complex, creamy and smoky aromas of ruby grapefruit, melon and peaches with underlying reductive matchstick-like complexity and tightly integrated new oak. Its fluffy, refreshing palate of intense lemon meringue, melon and grapefruit flavour is tightly knit with restrained oak and leesy influences, finishing with freshness and balance.

| 2002 | 90 | 2004 | 2007 |
| --- | --- | --- | --- |
| 2001 | 87 | 2003 | 2006 |
| 2000 | 89 | 2002 | 2005 |
| 1999 | 93 | 2001 | 2004 |

## PINOT GRIS

RANKING 4

| Various, SA, Vic | $20–$29 |
| --- | --- |
| **Current vintage: 2003** | **91** |

Varietally correct, clean, refreshing and well made pinot gris whose slightly oxidative, nutty aromas of apple, pear and peach reveal a hint of dustiness. There's a little hotness on the palate, but it's rich, broad and juicy, punchy and flavoursome, before a dusty, drying and slightly phenolic chalky finish. If you're wondering what the fuss is all about with pinot gris, you could do worse than to try this.

| 2003 | 91 | 2003 | 2004+ |
| --- | --- | --- | --- |
| 2002 | 83 | 2003 | 2004 |
| 2001 | 84 | 2002 | 2003 |
| 2000 | 91 | 2002 | 2005 |

## PINOT NOIR

RANKING 4

| Various, Vic | $20–$29 |
| --- | --- |
| **Current vintage: 2002** | **86** |

Slightly cooked and jammy jujube-like cherry, plum and blackberry aromas over sweet vanilla oak and musky clove and cinnamon-like spices precede a forward, juicy palate that becomes less intense and even dilute towards its oaky finish. Lacks genuine structure.

| 2002 | 86 | 2004 | 2007 |
| --- | --- | --- | --- |
| 2001 | 89 | 2003 | 2006 |
| 2000 | 93 | 2002 | 2005 |

## SAUVIGNON BLANC

RANKING 4

| Adelaide Hills | $12–$19 |
| --- | --- |
| **Current vintage: 2003** | **92** |

Restrained minerally, nettle-like and slightly estery aromas of gooseberries, cassis and passionfruit, with a reserved cut of herbaceousness. Long and racy, with intense, rather funky and earthy sauvignon flavours and angular, slatey mineral notes behind its lively, juicy fruit. Has the acidity and finish of a good Marlborough example.

| 2003 | 92 | 2003 | 2004+ |
| --- | --- | --- | --- |
| 2002 | 84 | 2003 | 2004 |
| 2001 | 90 | 2002 | 2003+ |

# Shantell

1974 Melba Highway, Dixons Creek Vic 3775. Tel: (03) 5965 2264. Fax: (03) 5965 2331.
Website: www.shantellvineyard.com.au  Email: shantell@shantellvineyard.com.au

Region: **Yarra Valley** Winemakers: **Shan & Turid Shanmugam** Viticulturists: **Shan & Turid Shanmugam**
Chief Executive: **Turid Shanmugam**

Shantell's red wines are perfumed and minty, with intense fruit flavours and elegant, fine-grained palates.
With its firm spine of fine, tight-knit tannins, the Cabernet Sauvignon ages very well.

## CABERNET SAUVIGNON

RANKING **4**

**Yarra Valley**      $30–$49
**Current vintage: 2000**      89

Restrained aromas of mulberries, plums and
cassis show through some cedary, pencil-shavings
oak and hints of bell pepper. Fine, long and smooth,
its polished palate offers a pleasing length of fruit
tightly knit with fine, firm tannins, finishing a little
drying with herbal influences.

| | | | |
|---|---|---|---|
| 2000 | 89 | 2008 | 2012 |
| 1999 | 92 | 2007 | 2011+ |
| 1998 | 91 | 2006 | 2010+ |
| 1997 | 87 | 2002 | 2005 |
| 1996 | 84 | 2001 | 2004 |
| 1995 | 84 | 2000 | 2003 |
| 1994 | 91 | 2002 | 2006 |
| 1993 | 88 | 1998 | 2001 |
| 1992 | 95 | 2004 | 2012 |
| 1991 | 93 | 1999 | 2003 |
| 1990 | 93 | 1998 | 2002 |
| 1989 | 88 | 1991 | 1994 |
| 1988 | 93 | 1993 | 1996 |

## CHARDONNAY

**Yarra Valley**      $20–$29
**Current vintage: 2002**      81

Oaky, rather varnishy and slightly butyric aromas
of nutty, melon and peachy fruit precede a
forward and angular palate that dries out to an
oaky, spicy and spiky finish with a hint of
sweetness.

| | | | |
|---|---|---|---|
| 2002 | 81 | 2003 | 2004+ |
| 2001 | 80 | 2002 | 2003+ |
| 2000 | 81 | 2002 | 2005+ |
| 1999 | 86 | 2000 | 2001 |
| 1997 | 87 | 2002 | 2005 |
| 1996 | 89 | 1998 | 2001 |
| 1995 | 93 | 2000 | 2003 |
| 1994 | 94 | 1999 | 2002 |
| 1993 | 94 | 1998 | 2001 |
| 1992 | 93 | 1997 | 2000 |

## PINOT NOIR

RANKING **5**

**Yarra Valley**      $30–$49
**Current vintage: 2001**      80

Minty/menthol aromas of meaty raspberries
and red cherries, with a forward, rather hollow palate
that dries out quickly towards a lean, rather
eucalypt/medicinal finish.

| | | | |
|---|---|---|---|
| 2001 | 80 | 2003 | 2006 |
| 2000 | 88 | 2002 | 2005+ |
| 1999 | 86 | 2004 | 2007 |
| 1998 | 89 | 2000 | 2003+ |
| 1997 | 87 | 2002 | 2005 |
| 1996 | 88 | 2001 | 2004 |
| 1995 | 87 | 2000 | 2003 |
| 1994 | 82 | 1996 | 1999 |
| 1993 | 91 | 1998 | 2001 |
| 1992 | 87 | 1994 | 1997 |
| 1991 | 90 | 1996 | 1999 |
| 1990 | 91 | 1995 | 1998 |

# Shaw and Smith

Lot 4 Jones Road, Balhannah SA 5242. Tel: (08) 8398 0500. Fax: (08) 8398 0600.
Website: www.shawandsmith.com Email: info@shawandsmith.com

Region: **Adelaide Hills** Winemaker: **Martin Shaw** Viticulturist: **Wayne Pittaway**
Chief Executives: **Martin Shaw, Michael Hill Smith**

Shaw and Smith has moved from being a successful 'virtual' wine business to the proud owner of young, developing Adelaide Hills vineyards and a stunningly versatile winery. With a new focus on its exciting Merlot label, plus its first release of 2002 Adelaide Hills Shiraz in the can, Shaw and Smith is proving to be as capable with red winemaking as it is with whites.

## M3 VINEYARD CHARDONNAY    RANKING 2

| Adelaide Hills | $30–$49 |
|---|---|
| **Current vintage: 2003** | **94** |

Tightly focused, refreshing and shapely New World chardonnay with some cellaring potential. Lightly spicy notes of pear, apple and grapefruit colour its delicate aroma, while some tightly integrated oak plays second fiddle. A smooth, creamy and elegant baby fat-like palate offers bright peach, melon and mango flavours neatly woven with fine oak and clean acids.

| 2003 | 94 | 2008 | 2011 |
|---|---|---|---|
| 2002 | 95 | 2007 | 2010 |
| 2001 | 93 | 2003 | 2006+ |
| 2000 | 94 | 2002 | 2005+ |

## MERLOT    RANKING 3

| Adelaide Hills | $30–$49 |
|---|---|
| **Current vintage: 2002** | **94** |

Concentrated, with layers of structure and richness, great balance. Very elegant and fine, with powdery tannins.

| 2002 | 94 | 2010 | 2014 |
|---|---|---|---|
| 2001 | 93 | 2006 | 2009 |
| 2000 | 90 | 2002 | 2005 |
| 1999 | 87 | 2004 | 2007 |

## SAUVIGNON BLANC    RANKING 4

| Adelaide Hills | $20–$29 |
|---|---|
| **Current vintage: 2003** | **88** |

Dusty, leafy aromas of capsicum, gooseberries and lychees with smoky undertones, before a juicy, slippery palate whose forward varietal fruit becomes a little broad, sweaty and fatty, lacking its customary tightness.

| 2003 | 88 | 2003 | 2004 |
|---|---|---|---|
| 2002 | 95 | 2003 | 2004+ |
| 2001 | 91 | 2002 | 2003+ |
| 2000 | 87 | 2000 | 2001 |
| 1999 | 88 | 2000 | 2001 |
| 1998 | 91 | 1998 | 1999 |

## UNOAKED CHARDONNAY    RANKING 4

| Adelaide Hills | $20–$29 |
|---|---|
| **Current vintage: 2003** | **88** |

Lightly buttery melon, cashew and stonefruit flavours are married with creamy leesy influences to complete a fragrant, smooth and refreshing unoaked style that finishes with a soft, clean acidity.

| 2003 | 88 | 2003 | 2004 |
|---|---|---|---|
| 2002 | 87 | 2003 | 2004 |
| 2001 | 90 | 2002 | 2003 |
| 2000 | 90 | 2001 | 2002 |
| 1999 | 82 | 1999 | 2000 |
| 1998 | 90 | 1999 | 2000 |

# Shottesbrooke

Bagshaws Road, McLaren Flat SA 5171. Tel: (08) 8383 0002. Fax: (08) 8383 0222.
Website: www.shottesbrooke.com.au  Email: admin@shottesbrooke.com.au

Region: **McLaren Vale** Winemaker: **Nick Holmes** Viticulturist: **Hamish Maguire** Chief Executive: **Nick Holmes**

Shottesbrooke is a well-established McLaren Vale winery whose well-structured reds have traditionally been finer and more elegant than most in its region. Its Sauvignon Blanc is punchy, pungent and arrestingly varietal.

## CABERNET SAUVIGNON MERLOT MALBEC    RANKING 4

**McLaren Vale** $20–$29
**Current vintage: 2001** 88

Minty, meaty and herbal aromas of shaded small dark berry fruits and plums, with nuances of menthol and cedary oak. Its intense but grippy palate presents sweet flavours of red and black berries with a slightly sappy, green edge, plus some assertive cedar/vanilla oak. Firm and flavoursome; needs time to settle and integrate.

| | | | |
|---|---|---|---|
| 2001 | 88 | 2009 | 2013 |
| 1999 | 83 | 2001 | 2004+ |
| 1998 | 94 | 2006 | 2010 |
| 1997 | 89 | 2005 | 2009 |
| 1996 | 86 | 2001 | 2004 |
| 1995 | 84 | 2000 | 2003 |
| 1994 | 92 | 2002 | 2006 |
| 1993 | 87 | 1998 | 2001 |
| 1992 | 93 | 2000 | 2004 |
| 1991 | 94 | 1999 | 2003 |
| 1990 | 91 | 1998 | 2002 |
| 1989 | 90 | 1997 | 2001 |
| 1988 | 93 | 1993 | 1996 |

## CHARDONNAY    RANKING 5

**McLaren Vale** $12–$19
**Current vintage: 2003** 88

Rich, soft and succulent chardonnay with a creamy and lightly earthy and reductive aroma of marmalade-like citrus/melon fruit, vanilla oak and a smoky meatiness. Ripe and tangy, with some earthy, savoury reductive characters, it opens up with brightness and intensity.

| | | | |
|---|---|---|---|
| 2003 | 88 | 2005 | 2008 |
| 2001 | 88 | 2003 | 2006 |
| 2000 | 87 | 2001 | 2002+ |
| 1999 | 88 | 2001 | 2004 |
| 1998 | 89 | 2000 | 2003+ |
| 1997 | 87 | 1999 | 2002 |
| 1996 | 90 | 2001 | 2004 |

## MERLOT    RANKING 5

**McLaren Vale** $20–$29
**Current vintage: 2002** 83

Minty, leathery, reductive aromas of cooked plums and dark cherries precede an aggressive and rather chunky palate of green-edged fruit framed by slightly raw and metallic tannins.

| | | | |
|---|---|---|---|
| 2002 | 83 | 2004 | 2007+ |
| 2001 | 86 | 2006 | 2009 |
| 2000 | 89 | 2008 | 2012 |
| 1999 | 89 | 2004 | 2007 |
| 1998 | 90 | 2003 | 2006 |
| 1997 | 92 | 2002 | 2005 |
| 1996 | 90 | 2001 | 2004 |
| 1995 | 90 | 2000 | 2003 |
| 1994 | 90 | 1999 | 2002 |

## SAUVIGNON BLANC    RANKING 5

**Fleurieu** $12–$19
**Current vintage: 2003** 87

Early-drinking sauvignon with a pungent, sweaty aroma of gooseberries, kiwifruit and passionfruit, before a broad, rich and almost oily palate of ripe passionfruit and lychee flavours. Finishes soft, without great length.

| | | | |
|---|---|---|---|
| 2003 | 87 | 2004 | 2005 |
| 2002 | 89 | 2003 | 2004 |
| 2001 | 91 | 2002 | 2003+ |
| 2000 | 88 | 2002 | 2005 |
| 1999 | 86 | 2000 | 2001 |

# Skillogalee

Trevarrick Road, Sevenhill via Clare SA 5453. Tel: (08) 8843 4311. Fax: (08) 8843 4343.
Email: skilly@chariot.net.au

Region: **Clare Valley** Winemaker: **Dave Palmer** Viticulturist: **Dave Palmer** Chief Executive: **Dave Palmer**

Skillogalee is one of the Clare Valley's small family-run vineyards. Its rustic, earthy reds are less ripe and assertive than others of the region, and whose Riesling is forward, juicy and toasty.

## RIESLING
RANKING

| Clare Valley | | $12–$19 |
|---|---|---|
| **Current vintage: 2003** | | **87** |

Earlier-drinking riesling whose punchy talc-like aromas of estery tropical and lime juice precede a generous, round and toasty palate with a lemon sherbet finish of soft acids.

| | | | |
|---|---|---|---|
| 2003 | 87 | 2005 | 2008 |
| 2002 | 89 | 2007 | 2010 |
| 2001 | 93 | 2006 | 2008+ |
| 2000 | 89 | 2002 | 2005+ |
| 1999 | 90 | 2004 | 2007 |
| 1998 | 90 | 2003 | 2006 |
| 1997 | 92 | 2005 | 2009 |
| 1996 | 91 | 2001 | 2004 |
| 1995 | 93 | 2003 | 2007 |
| 1994 | 94 | 2006 | 2014 |
| 1993 | 90 | 2001 | 2005 |
| 1992 | 93 | 1997 | 2000 |
| 1991 | 90 | 1996 | 1999 |
| 1990 | 94 | 1998 | 2002 |

## SHIRAZ
RANKING 5

| Clare Valley | | $20–$29 |
|---|---|---|
| **Current vintage: 2001** | | **87** |

Moderately full shiraz whose up-front and minty aromas of concentrated blackberries, raspberries, cherries and plums reveal a light oaky smokiness. Beginning with vibrant, minty berry fruit, it loses some intensity and richness towards the finish.

| | | | |
|---|---|---|---|
| 2001 | 87 | 2003 | 2006+ |
| 2000 | 81 | 2002 | 2005+ |
| 1999 | 85 | 2007 | 2011 |
| 1998 | 84 | 2000 | 2003+ |
| 1997 | 92 | 2002 | 2005+ |
| 1996 | 88 | 1998 | 2001 |
| 1995 | 90 | 2000 | 2003 |
| 1994 | 91 | 1999 | 2002 |
| 1993 | 91 | 2001 | 2005 |
| 1992 | 91 | 2000 | 2004 |
| 1991 | 90 | 1996 | 1999 |
| 1990 | 93 | 1995 | 1998 |

## THE CABERNETS
RANKING 5

| Clare Valley | | $20–$29 |
|---|---|---|
| **Current vintage: 2001** | | **85** |

Earthy, lightly minty and reductive aromas of cassis, redcurrants and plums are offset by restrained vanilla oak. A little more stewy, the palate's berry/plum fruit appears more cooked and stressed, finishing rather lean and skinny.

| | | | |
|---|---|---|---|
| 2001 | 85 | 2006 | 2009 |
| 2000 | 86 | 2005 | 2008 |
| 1999 | 85 | 2007 | 2011 |
| 1998 | 88 | 2003 | 2006 |
| 1997 | 91 | 2002 | 2005+ |
| 1996 | 92 | 2004 | 2008 |
| 1995 | 87 | 2000 | 2003 |
| 1994 | 91 | 2002 | 2006 |
| 1993 | 88 | 2001 | 2005 |
| 1992 | 89 | 2000 | 2004 |
| 1991 | 90 | 1996 | 1999 |
| 1990 | 90 | 1998 | 2002 |

# Smithbrook

Smithbrook Road, Pemberton WA 6260. Tel: (08) 9772 3557. Fax: (08) 9772 3579.
Website: www.smithbrook.com.au  Email: smithbrk@karriweb.com.au
Region: **Pemberton** Winemaker: **Michael Symon** Viticulturist: **Jonathan Farrington**
Chief Executive: **Peter Cowan**

Lion Nathan's Western Australian outpost is a large vineyard in Pemberton that delivers a very consistent Sauvignon Blanc, as well as producing an earthy, leathery merlot of some charm.

## MERLOT RANKING 5

| Pemberton | $20–$29 |
|---|---|
| Current vintage: 2001 | 87 |

A herbal, spicy merlot with an earthy and vegetal aroma of sweet dark plums and cherries supported by restrained cedar/vanilla oak. Lively forward flavours of red and black cherries backed by meaty, gamey nuances and leathery complexity dry out a little, leaving a slightly lean and bony finish.

| 2001 | 87 | 2003 | 2006+ |
|---|---|---|---|
| 2000 | 89 | 2005 | 2008 |
| 1999 | 89 | 2001 | 2004 |
| 1995 | 80 | 1997 | 2000 |

## SAUVIGNON BLANC RANKING 4

| Pemberton | $12–$19 |
|---|---|
| Current vintage: 2003 | 93 |

Finely sculpted, intensely flavoured, racy and vibrant sauvignon blanc with punchy, lightly grassy varietal aromas of gooseberries, passionfruit and tropical fruits. Long, dry and well defined, its juicy, tangy fleshy core of fruit culminates in a tight, austere and mineral finish.

| 2003 | 93 | 2004 | 2005+ |
|---|---|---|---|
| 2002 | 90 | 2003 | 2004 |
| 2001 | 87 | 2002 | 2003 |
| 2000 | 91 | 2000 | 2001 |

# Sorrenberg

Alma Road, Beechworth Vic 3747. Tel: (03) 5728 2278. Fax: (03) 5728 2278.
Website: www.sorrenberg.com
Region: **Beechworth** Winemaker: **Barry Morey** Viticulturist: **Barry Morey** Chief Executive: **Barry Morey**

Sorrenberg is a small and highly rated maker of distinctive and complex wines in the Beechworth hills of north-east Victoria. Its Chardonnay is typically fine, citrusy and mineral, while it can achieve rare Bordeaux-like qualities in its Sauvignon Blanc Semillon blend. Heavily worked and spicy, its Gamay is often delicious drinking despite having very little in common with Beaujolais.

## CABERNET BLEND RANKING 5

| Beechworth | $20–$29 |
|---|---|
| Current vintage: 2001 | 87 |

Smooth, reserved cabernet blend with a leafy and slightly meaty bouquet of small red and black berries, sweet vanilla/cedar oak with nuances of violets and undergrowth-like complexity. Moderately long, elegant and fine-grained, its palate offers sweet berry fruit integrated with fine-grained tannins and cedary oak, but a distinct undercurrent of herbaceousness.

| 2001 | 87 | 2006 | 2009 |
|---|---|---|---|
| 2000 | 90 | 2005 | 2008+ |
| 1999 | 88 | 2004 | 2007 |
| 1998 | 87 | 2003 | 2006 |
| 1997 | 83 | 1999 | 2002 |
| 1994 | 88 | 1998 | 2003 |

## CHARDONNAY RANKING 3

| Beechworth | $30–$49 |
|---|---|
| Current vintage: 2002 | 90 |

It takes a little time for this wine to really open up in the glass, for the rather closed aromas that begin with sweet butter and toast, oatmeal and sweet corn, cumquat and quince do then become more vibrant and less spicy. Fine and elegant, its slightly marmalade-like palate does also reveal more depth of fruit to counter its handsome vanilla and buttery oak. There's softness, fineness and delicacy, but I'd prefer a shade more acidity to better accentuate the acids and fruit.

| 2002 | 90 | 2004 | 2007 |
|---|---|---|---|
| 2001 | 95 | 2003 | 2006+ |
| 2000 | 94 | 2005 | 2008 |
| 1999 | 90 | 2004 | 2007 |
| 1998 | 86 | 2000 | 2003 |
| 1997 | 93 | 2002 | 2005 |

A B C D E F G H I J K L M N O P Q R S T U V W X Y Z

**2005** **THE AUSTRALIAN WINE ANNUAL** **261**
www.onwine.com.au

## GAMAY

| Beechworth | $20–$29 | 2002 | 87 | 2004 | 2007 |
|---|---|---|---|---|---|
| Current vintage: 2002 | 87 | 2001 | 88 | 2003 | 2006 |
| | | 2000 | 91 | 2002 | 2005 |
| | | 1999 | 84 | 2000 | 2001 |
| | | 1998 | 87 | 1999 | 2000 |

Slightly dull and developed aromas of earthy red plums and cherries backed by nuances of cloves and vanilla oak. Penetrative flavours of small red berry/cherry fruit with spicy, undergrowth-like complexity tend to lack length, finishing a little flat and herbal.

## SAUVIGNON BLANC SEMILLON

| Beechworth | $20–$29 | 2003 | 91 | 2005 | 2008 |
|---|---|---|---|---|---|
| Current vintage: 2002 | 91 | 2002 | 95 | 2007 | 2010 |
| | | 2001 | 93 | 2006 | 2009 |
| | | 2000 | 90 | 2002 | 2005 |
| | | 1999 | 87 | 2001 | 2004 |
| | | 1998 | 88 | 2000 | 2003 |

A delicate, dusty perfume of gooseberries, passionfruit and dried herbs with lightly smoky nuances of vanilla oak precedes a smooth, silky palate of length and refinement. The wine builds nicely in the mouth, revealing a pleasing marriage between dusty herbal fruit and sweet vanilla oak. However the wine just lacks the raciness and vitality that might have been evident with a shade more acidity.

# St Hallett

St Hallett's Road, Hallet Valley Tanunda SA 5352. Tel: (08) 8563 7000. Fax: (08) 8563 7001.
Website: www.sthallett.com.au  Email: sthallett@sthallett.com.au

Region: **Barossa Valley** Winemakers: **Stuart Blackwell, Di Ferguson, Matt Gant** Viticulturist: **Chris Rogers**
Chief Executive: **Peter Cowan**

Another hot Barossa vintage in 2001 prevented St Hallett, alongside many of its neighbours, from enjoying a classic vintage. Like many others, its reds tend towards the cooked and meaty, while some fine winemaking has given some polish to the leading labels of Old Block and Blackwell Shiraz. St Hallett is owned and operated by Lion Nathan's wine division.

## BLACKWELL SEMILLON (Formerly Semillon Select)

| Barossa Valley | $12–$19 | 2002 | 86 | 2004 | 2007+ |
|---|---|---|---|---|---|
| Current vintage: 2002 | 86 | 2001 | 87 | 2003 | 2006 |
| | | 1999 | 84 | 2001 | 2004 |
| | | 1998 | 88 | 2000 | 2003 |
| | | 1997 | 90 | 1999 | 2002 |
| | | 1996 | 88 | 1998 | 2001 |
| | | 1995 | 83 | 1996 | 1997 |

Smoky, toasty aromas of honeydew melon are slightly subdued by assertive oak influences, while its generous, broad and oaky palate matches slightly cloying and honeyed fruit with sticky, almost flabby oak. An older style, lacking real shape and balance.

## BLACKWELL SHIRAZ

| Barossa Valley | $20–$29 | 2001 | 92 | 2006 | 2009+ |
|---|---|---|---|---|---|
| Current vintage: 2001 | 92 | 1999 | 92 | 2004 | 2007+ |
| | | 1998 | 95 | 2006 | 2010+ |
| | | 1997 | 88 | 2002 | 2005 |
| | | 1996 | 91 | 2004 | 2008 |
| | | 1995 | 87 | 2000 | 2003 |
| | | 1994 | 92 | 1999 | 2002+ |

Meaty, dark and pruney aromas of currants, blackberries and plums with sweet chocolate and vanilla oak. Smooth, black and briary, its sumptuous palate reveals a fine depth of plush, velvet-like texture and concentrated licorice and cassis-like fruit. There's a faint suggestion of meaty over-ripeness, but the wine has plenty of richness and substance.

## CABERNET SHIRAZ (Formerly Cabernet Sauvignon)

| Barossa Valley | $20–$29 | 2001 | 83 | 2003 | 2006+ |
|---|---|---|---|---|---|
| Current vintage: 2001 | 83 | 2000 | 83 | 2002 | 2005 |
| | | 1999 | 89 | 2004 | 2007+ |
| | | 1998 | 89 | 2006 | 2010 |
| | | 1996 | 87 | 2001 | 2004 |
| | | 1995 | 87 | 1997 | 2000 |
| | | 1994 | 89 | 1996 | 1999 |
| | | 1993 | 90 | 1998 | 2001 |
| | | 1992 | 91 | 2000 | 2004 |
| | | 1991 | 88 | 1999 | 2003 |

Greenish, also cooked young blend whose leathery, earthy fragrance of plums, dark berries and currants overlies nuances of chocolate and spice. Up-front and fruity, initially smooth and generous, it then falls a little short, revealing stressed, greenish fruit influences that lack intensity and brightness.

## EDEN VALLEY RIESLING

RANKING **3**

| | Eden Valley | $12–$19 |
| --- | --- | --- |
| | **Current vintage: 2003** | **92** |

Finely sculpted, fractionally sweet but stylish riesling with a floral, mineral fragrance of dried flowers, lime juice and lemon with slatey under-tones of lees-derived complexity. Long and vibrant, with a clean and refreshing palate of apple, pear and citrus flavours over chalky phenolics, finishing clean and tangy.

| | | | |
| --- | --- | --- | --- |
| 2003 | 92 | 2008 | 2011+ |
| 2002 | 93 | 2007 | 2010 |
| 2001 | 89 | 2006 | 2009 |
| 2000 | 90 | 2005 | 2008 |
| 1999 | 90 | 2004 | 2007 |
| 1998 | 90 | 2003 | 2006+ |
| 1997 | 93 | 2002 | 2005+ |
| 1996 | 88 | 2001 | 2004 |

## FAITH SHIRAZ

RANKING **4**

| | Barossa Valley | $20–$29 |
| --- | --- | --- |
| | **Current vintage: 2002** | **89** |

Smooth, early-drinking Australian burgundy style with a violet and bubblegum-like aroma of minty raspberry, cherry and cassis fruit. Soft and supple, it's vibrant and minty, delivering pristine and chocolatey small berry flavours framed by soft tannins and refreshing acids.

| | | | |
| --- | --- | --- | --- |
| 2002 | 89 | 2004 | 2007 |
| 2001 | 86 | 2003 | 2006 |
| 2000 | 82 | 2002 | 2005 |
| 1999 | 92 | 2004 | 2009 |
| 1998 | 90 | 2003 | 2006 |
| 1997 | 88 | 1998 | 1999 |
| 1996 | 86 | 1998 | 2001 |
| 1995 | 88 | 2000 | 2003 |
| 1994 | 89 | 1996 | 1999+ |

## OLD BLOCK SHIRAZ

RANKING **3**

| | Barossa Valley | $50+ |
| --- | --- | --- |
| | **Current vintage: 2001** | **89** |

Moderately powerful but slightly overcooked shiraz lacking genuine life and vitality. Its stewy redcurrant, plum, blackberry and currant-like aromas are backed by sweet vanilla/cedar oak, while its quite con-centrated, cooked and fullish palate doesn't quite deliver on its promises. There's plenty of smoothness, but it finishes slightly gritty.

| | | | |
| --- | --- | --- | --- |
| 2001 | 89 | 2009 | 2013 |
| 2000 | 84 | 2002 | 2005+ |
| 1999 | 94 | 2007 | 2011 |
| 1998 | 95 | 2010 | 2018 |
| 1997 | 82 | 1999 | 2002 |
| 1996 | 89 | 2001 | 2004 |
| 1995 | 89 | 2000 | 2003+ |
| 1994 | 94 | 2002 | 2006 |
| 1993 | 91 | 1998 | 2001 |
| 1992 | 92 | 1997 | 2000 |
| 1991 | 95 | 2003 | 2011 |
| 1990 | 95 | 2002 | 2010 |
| 1989 | 91 | 1997 | 2001 |
| 1988 | 95 | 2000 | 2008 |
| 1987 | 90 | 1995 | 1999 |
| 1986 | 94 | 1998 | 2003 |
| 1985 | 91 | 1993 | 1997 |

# St Huberts

St Huberts Road, Coldstream Vic 3770. Tel: (03) 9739 1118. Fax: (03) 9739 1096.
Website; www.beringerblass.com.au

Region: **Yarra Valley** Winemaker: **Matt Steel** Viticulturist: **Damien de Castella** Chief Executive: **Jamie Odell**

St Huberts is one of those small large company labels whose integrity and consistency can sneak beneath the radar of wine enthusiasts. Rarely showy, its fine, elegant and brightly flavoured wines typically reveal structure and longevity, and usually stand up favourably when compared to the efforts of its boutique neighbours.

## CABERNET SAUVIGNON

RANKING **3**

| | Yarra Valley | $20–$29 |
| --- | --- | --- |
| | **Current vintage: 2001** | **90** |

Long, restrained cabernet with a little cut and polish. Its delicate, lightly minty and herbal fragrance of slightly prune and currant-like berry/plum fruits is tightly matched with creamy vanilla oak. It's quite firm, with a fine-grained undercarriage beneath some penetrative dark berry/currant flavours, finishing with length and vibrant acidity.

| | | | |
| --- | --- | --- | --- |
| 2001 | 90 | 2009 | 2013+ |
| 2000 | 90 | 2008 | 2012+ |
| 1999 | 90 | 2004 | 2007 |
| 1998 | 93 | 2006 | 2010 |
| 1997 | 92 | 2005 | 2009+ |
| 1996 | 87 | 1998 | 2001 |
| 1995 | 92 | 2000 | 2003 |
| 1994 | 94 | 2002 | 2006 |
| 1993 | 90 | 1998 | 2003 |
| 1992 | 93 | 2000 | 2004 |
| 1991 | 93 | 1999 | 2003 |
| 1990 | 89 | 1998 | 2002 |

## CHARDONNAY

RANKING 4

**Yarra Valley**     $20–$29
**Current vintage: 2003**    **91**

Charming, delicate and compact chardonnay likely to develop richness and weight in the bottle. Its spicy, nutty aromas of lightly peachy fruit, oatmeal, vanilla, cloves and nutmeg herald a supple, even palate of tightly integrated peach/melon fruit with fine-grained dusty oak and soft acids. It finishes long, dry and savoury.

| | | | |
|---|---|---|---|
| 2003 | 91 | 2005 | 2008+ |
| 2002 | 86 | 2003 | 2004 |
| 2001 | 87 | 2002 | 2003 |
| 2000 | 90 | 2002 | 2005+ |
| 1999 | 92 | 2004 | 2007 |
| 1998 | 87 | 2000 | 2003 |
| 1997 | 84 | 1999 | 2002 |
| 1996 | 87 | 1998 | 2001 |

## PINOT NOIR

RANKING 5

**Yarra Valley**     $20–$29
**Current vintage: 2002**    **90**

Fresh, balanced young pinot with a delicate floral and lightly spicy perfume of dark cherries, plums and cedar/vanilla oak. Smooth and supple, its willowy palate of vibrant fruit reveals a genuine backbone of fine tannins, finishing with length of fruit and balance. Should develop well.

| | | | |
|---|---|---|---|
| 2002 | 90 | 2007 | 2010 |
| 2001 | 89 | 2003 | 2006 |
| 2000 | 86 | 2002 | 2005 |
| 1999 | 89 | 2001 | 2004 |
| 1998 | 87 | 2000 | 2003 |
| 1997 | 87 | 2002 | 2005 |
| 1996 | 87 | 1998 | 2001 |

## ROUSSANNE

RANKING 4

**Yarra Valley**     $20–$29
**Current vintage: 2003**    **90**

Elegant, lively and racy wine with a nutty and citrusy perfume of candied lemon rind, melon and musky spices. Its flowery varietal flavours are delivered along a vibrant, restrained and silky-smooth palate that finishes dusty and savoury, with refreshing acidity and nuances of mineral.

| | | | |
|---|---|---|---|
| 2003 | 90 | 2005 | 2008+ |
| 2002 | 90 | 2003 | 2004+ |
| 2000 | 86 | 2002 | 2005 |
| 1999 | 89 | 2001 | 2004 |
| 1998 | 87 | 1999 | 2000+ |

# Stanton & Killeen

Murray Valley Highway, Rutherglen Vic 3685. Tel: (02) 6032 9457. Fax: (02) 6032 8018.
website: www.stantonandkilleenwines.com.au Email: sk_wines@netc.net.au

Region: **Rutherglen** Winemaker: **Chris Killeen** Viticulturist: **Paul Geddes** Chief Executive: **Chris Killeen**

While I sometimes think Stanton & Killeen's flavoursome Rutherglen reds would be worthy of some more time in better oak, I enjoy their honesty and regional characters, especially with the Durif and Jack's Block Shiraz. The vibrant and briary 2002 Durif is the best under this label for some time, but the cooler 1999 season has marginally taken the edge off an otherwise very fine and savoury Vintage Port, creating a more supple and earlier-maturing edition of considerable charm.

## CABERNET BLEND

RANKING 5

**Rutherglen**     $20–$29
**Current vintage: 2003**    **87**

Smooth, earthy Rutherglen red with a spicy, floral aroma of blackcurrants, redcurrants and plums, with undertones of cherries and restrained cedar/vanilla oak. Its vibrant, juicy palate of cherry/plum flavours is slightly stewy, but offers pleasing softness and sweetness, framed by smooth tannins.

| | | | |
|---|---|---|---|
| 2003 | 87 | 2005 | 2008+ |
| 2002 | 80 | 2004 | 2007 |
| 2001 | 83 | 2003 | 2006 |
| 2000 | 82 | 2002 | 2005 |
| 1999 | 86 | 2004 | 2007 |
| 1998 | 86 | 2006 | 2010+ |
| 1996 | 87 | 2000 | 2003 |
| 1995 | 88 | 2000 | 2003 |
| 1992 | 92 | 2004 | 2012 |
| 1991 | 91 | 1999 | 2003 |
| 1990 | 88 | 2002 | 2010 |

## CABERNET SHIRAZ

RANKING 5

**Rutherglen**     $20–$29
**Current vintage: 2003**    **89**

A punchy regional red with a spicy, violet-like fragrance of cassis, plums, sweet vanilla oak and earthy influences. Its long, creamy palate offers minty, spicy flavours of plums and cassis, raspberries and redcurrants, framed by firm, but approachably fine tannins. Attractive balance and weight.

| | | | |
|---|---|---|---|
| 2003 | 89 | 2008 | 2011 |
| 2001 | 88 | 2006 | 2009+ |
| 1998 | 88 | 2006 | 2010 |
| 1997 | 90 | 2005 | 2009+ |
| 1996 | 90 | 2004 | 2008+ |
| 1995 | 88 | 2007 | 2015 |
| 1994 | 88 | 2006 | 2014 |
| 1992 | 91 | 2004 | 2012 |

# DURIF

RANKING 4

**Rutherglen** $20–$29
**Current vintage: 2002** 92

Elegant, ripe, polished and structured durif with a long future. Its sweet meaty fragrance of spicy plums, prunes and currants overlies nuances of mocha and violets, mint and menthol. Its long, elegant and balanced palate of sweet earthy, briary fruit is framed by fine, firm tannins. Finishes with lingering spicy fruits and lively acids.

| Year | Score | | |
|---|---|---|---|
| 2002 | 92 | 2014 | 2022 |
| 2000 | 92 | 2008 | 2012+ |
| 1999 | 90 | 2007 | 2011 |
| 1998 | 87 | 2010 | 2018 |
| 1997 | 89 | 2009 | 2017 |
| 1996 | 90 | 2008 | 2016 |
| 1995 | 90 | 2007 | 2015 |
| 1994 | 88 | 2006 | 2014 |
| 1992 | 92 | 2004 | 2012 |
| 1991 | 86 | 1999 | 2003 |
| 1990 | 93 | 2002 | 2010 |
| 1988 | 93 | 2000 | 2008 |
| 1987 | 88 | 1999 | 2004 |
| 1986 | 90 | 1998 | 2003 |

# JACK'S BLOCK SHIRAZ

RANKING 3

**Rutherglen** $30–$49
**Current vintage: 2000** 93

A real sleeper of a north-eastern shiraz; very closed but very concentrated. Underneath its dusty, earthy and meaty bouquet lie briary, vibrant berry fruit flavours of brightness and intensity. The palate is firm and fine, steeped in dark berry flavours, wrapped in tight tannins and will gradually open up.

| Year | Score | | |
|---|---|---|---|
| 2000 | 93 | 2012 | 2020 |
| 1998 | 94 | 2006 | 2010+ |
| 1997 | 93 | 2009 | 2017 |
| 1993 | 88 | 2001 | 2005+ |

# SHIRAZ

RANKING 5

**Rutherglen** $20–$29
**Current vintage: 2002** 87

A shorter-term, medium-weight shiraz with a sweet aroma of raspberries and plums, dusty older oak and leathery undertones. Smooth and supple, with up-front plum and currant-like fruit finishing with a modest grip, it should develop more fruit on the palate after a little more time in the bottle.

| Year | Score | | |
|---|---|---|---|
| 2002 | 87 | 2004 | 2007+ |
| 2001 | 82 | 2003 | 2006+ |
| 2000 | 86 | 2005 | 2008 |
| 1999 | 87 | 2004 | 2007 |
| 1996 | 90 | 2004 | 2008 |
| 1995 | 89 | 2007 | 2015 |
| 1993 | 91 | 2005 | 2013 |
| 1992 | 94 | 2004 | 2012 |
| 1991 | 88 | 1999 | 2003 |
| 1990 | 92 | 2002 | 2010 |
| 1988 | 85 | 1996 | 2000 |

# VINTAGE PORT

RANKING 2

**Rutherglen** $30–$49
**Current vintage: 1999** 93

Fine, elegant and Portuguese-influenced savoury vintage port style. Its meaty, spicy perfume of red-currants and plums, currants and raisins is lifted by fresh, clear spirit, while its smooth, savoury palate of lingering sweet and spicy currant-like fruit offers good, but not exceptional length. A lighter and earlier-maturing vintage.

| Year | Score | | |
|---|---|---|---|
| 1999 | 93 | 2007 | 2011+ |
| 1998 | 96 | 2010 | 2018+ |
| 1997 | 95 | 2009 | 2017 |
| 1996 | 95 | 2008 | 2016+ |
| 1995 | 95 | 2015 | 2025 |
| 1994 | 93 | 2006 | 2014 |
| 1993 | 94 | 2005 | 2013 |
| 1992 | 95 | 2004 | 2012 |
| 1991 | 94 | 2003 | 2011 |
| 1990 | 93 | 1998 | 2002 |
| 1989 | 90 | 1997 | 2001 |
| 1988 | 94 | 2000 | 2005 |
| 1987 | 88 | 1999 | 2004 |
| 1986 | 95 | 2006 | 2016 |

# Starvedog Lane

Ravenswood Lane, Hahndorf SA 5245. Tel: (08) 8388 1250. Fax: (08) 8388 7233.
Website: www.thelane.com.au  Email: helen@thelane.com.au
Region: **Adelaide Hills**  Winemaker: **Robert Mann**  Viticulturist: **John Edwards**
Chief Executive: **John Edwards**

With a well managed Adelaide Hills vineyard and the substantial winemaking resources of The Hardy Wine Company behind it, Starvedog Lane is maturing into a brand I respect greatly for its quality and value. Its Chardonnay has come to represent some of the best value in South Australia, the Sauvignon Blanc is amongst the best in the Adelaide Hills (Australia's premier region for 100% sauvignon blanc wines) and the 2001 Cabernet Sauvignon is smooth, restrained and intensely flavoured — the vineyard's finest effort yet.

## CABERNET SAUVIGNON

**Adelaide Hills** $20–$29
**Current vintage: 2001** 93

A firm, willowy, minty and slightly herbal cabernet with structure and balance. Its intense but slightly jammy aromas of small black and red berries are fragrant and floral, with a perfumed background of cedar/vanilla oak. Smooth, restrained and elegant, its translucent expression of tightly focused small berry fruit is tightly knit with firm, fine tannins and smart cedary oak.

| | | | |
|---|---|---|---|
| 2001 | 93 | 2009 | 2013+ |
| 2000 | 89 | 2008 | 2012 |
| 1999 | 87 | 2004 | 2007 |
| 1998 | 89 | 2010 | 2018 |

## CHARDONNAY

**Adelaide Hills** $20–$29
**Current vintage: 2003** 93

Stylish, balanced young chardonnay with a delicate, nutty aroma of peach and nectarine, grapefruit and melon supported by fresh creamy vanilla oak. Long, juicy and tangy, its vibrant expression of tropical fruit, apple and pear are tightly knit with sweet vanilla oak and punctuated by clean, refreshing acids.

| | | | |
|---|---|---|---|
| 2003 | 93 | 2005 | 2008+ |
| 2002 | 95 | 2004 | 2007+ |
| 2001 | 90 | 2003 | 2006+ |
| 2000 | 91 | 2002 | 2005+ |
| 1999 | 93 | 2001 | 2004+ |
| 1998 | 87 | 2000 | 2003 |

## SAUVIGNON BLANC

**Adelaide Hills** $12–$19
**Current vintage: 2003** 93

Pungent, sweaty varietal aromas of passionfruit, cassis and gooseberries, with a hint of smokiness. Rather herbal, but opens to reveal an intense core of musky fruit flavour, finishing long and chalky with just a hint of residual sugar.

| | | | |
|---|---|---|---|
| 2003 | 93 | 2003 | 2004+ |
| 2002 | 95 | 2003 | 2004+ |
| 2001 | 91 | 2002 | 2003 |
| 1999 | 90 | 2000 | 2001 |
| 1998 | 90 | 2000 | 2003 |

## SHIRAZ

**Adelaide Hills** $20–$29
**Current vintage: 2002** 88

Briary aromas of sweet small blackberries, red cherries, raspberries and sweet vanilla oak, with lightly meaty, floral and spicy complexity. Intensely focused flavours of small berries, redcurrants and plums saturate a taut and linear, but very concentrated palate structured around firm, bony tannins. A herbal tomato-stalk note does however underpin much of the wine, and its herbal undertones are likely to become more vegetal with time.

| | | | |
|---|---|---|---|
| 2002 | 88 | 2007 | 2010 |
| 2001 | 87 | 2006 | 2009 |
| 2000 | 80 | 2002 | 2005 |
| 1999 | 82 | 2001 | 2004+ |
| 1998 | 84 | 2003 | 2006 |
| 1997 | 87 | 2002 | 2005 |

# Stefano Lubiana

60 Rowbottoms Road, Granton Tas 7030. Tel: (03) 6263 7457. Fax: (03) 6263 7430.
Website: www.stefanolubiana.com  Email: wine@slw.com.au

Region: **Southern Tasmania** Winemaker: **Steve Lubiana** Chief Executive: **Steve Lubiana**

Stefano Lubiana has taken the opposite approach to many Tasmanian small winemakers by aiming for richness and palate structure in his wines — which are the steepest challenges for Tasmanian growers — before seeking to introduce a winemaker-driven element of complexity. The wonderfully vibrant and perfumed Primavera Pinot Noir is a more supple, fine and sappy expression of this variety, but underpinned by a genuine structure.

## CHARDONNAY

RANKING 3

| Southern Tasmania | $30–$49 | | 2002 | 85 | 2004 | 2007 |
| --- | --- | --- | --- | --- | --- | --- |
| **Current vintage: 2002** | **85** | | 2001 | 94 | 2006 | 2009 |
| | | | 2000 | 93 | 2005 | 2008 |
| | | | 1999 | 91 | 2004 | 2007 |
| | | | 1998 | 91 | 2000 | 2003 |

Nutty aromas of honeydew melon, tropical fruit, vanilla oak and creamy lees influences precede a forward, then lean and austere palate framed by greenish, metallic acids. The product of a cooler season, for drinking earlier than later.

## PINOT GRIGIO

RANKING 4

| Southern Tasmania | $20–$29 | | 2003 | 90 | 2005 | 2008 |
| --- | --- | --- | --- | --- | --- | --- |
| **Current vintage: 2003** | **90** | | 2002 | 83 | 2002 | 2003+ |
| | | | 2001 | 87 | 2002 | 2003+ |

Dusty, tight-knit and focused wine with a spicy, creamy aroma of dusty rose petals, citrus, stone-fruits and a pleasing nuttiness. Restrained but quite juicy, the smooth and elegant palate even becomes slightly silky before finishing with refreshing, racy acidity.

## PINOT NOIR

RANKING 5

| Southern Tasmania | $30–$49 | | 2002 | 87 | 2004 | 2007+ |
| --- | --- | --- | --- | --- | --- | --- |
| **Current vintage: 2002** | **87** | | 2001 | 92 | 2003 | 2006+ |
| | | | 2000 | 87 | 2002 | 2005 |
| | | | 1999 | 86 | 2001 | 2004 |
| | | | 1998 | 88 | 2000 | 2003 |

Lightly herbaceous pinot with some richness and Beaune-like elements of structure. Briary, slightly vegetal aromas of red cherries, plums and restrained oak precede a tight, moderately firm palate of undergrowth-like complexity. Fine and tight-knit, with a slightly sappy extract of tannin.

## PRIMAVERA PINOT NOIR

RANKING 3

| Southern Tasmania | $20–$29 | | 2003 | 94 | 2005 | 2008+ |
| --- | --- | --- | --- | --- | --- | --- |
| **Current vintage: 2003** | **94** | | 2002 | 93 | 2007 | 2010 |
| | | | 2001 | 89 | 2003 | 2006+ |

Pristine, stylish wine of wonderful varietal brightness, intensity, suppleness and charm. Its vibrant scent of rose petals, red and black cherries, plums and chocolate/vanilla oak is perfumed and penetrative, while its palate is dusty, silky-smooth and spotlessly pure, underpinned by tight-knit tannins. Presently round, fleshy and generous, with some nutty and earthy development, it is sure to build in colour, richness and texture in the bottle.

# Stonehaven

Riddoch Highway, Padthaway SA 5271. Tel: (08) 8765 6140. Fax: (08) 8765 6137.
Website: www.stonehavenvineyards.com.au  Email: info@stonehavenvineyards.com.au
Region: **Padthaway** Winemakers: **Suzanne Bell, Adrienne Cross** Viticulturist: **Graham Kaye**
Chief Executive: **David Woods**

The consistently bright and intense flavours of its Chardonnays and Viognier, which impress me more than its somewhat jammy and minty red wines, suggest that Stonehaven will ultimately end up with more of a white wine focus. Owned by The Hardy Wine Company, Stonehaven is the only large-scale winery in the Padthaway region. Its wines are entering the marketplace with considerable maturity.

## LIMESTONE COAST CABERNET MERLOT   RANKING 5

| Limestone Coast | $12–$19 | 2000 | 86 | 2002 | 2005 |
|---|---|---|---|---|---|
| Current vintage: 2000 | 86 | 1999 | 86 | 2004 | 2007 |
| | | 1998 | 88 | 2006 | 2010 |

Slightly greenish, minty blend with a fresh bouquet of blackcurrant, redcurrants, menthol, cedar/vanilla oak and lightly herbal complexity. Forward and lively, its minty expression of small berry fruits becomes a little hollow, before a rather green-edged finish.

## LIMESTONE COAST CHARDONNAY   RANKING 4

| Limestone Coast | $12–$19 | 2001 | 91 | 2003 | 2006 |
|---|---|---|---|---|---|
| Current vintage: 2001 | 91 | 2000 | 90 | 2002 | 2005 |
| | | 1999 | 89 | 2001 | 2004 |
| | | 1998 | 87 | 2000 | 2003 |

A lively young chardonnay with a punchy, vibrant earthy, chalky aroma of grapefruit and peaches, with nuances of melon and restrained vanilla oak. Juicy and forward, its intense palate of pineapple, melon and mango flavour culminates in a lingering, tightly knit finish of refreshing, citrusy acids.

## LIMESTONE COAST SHIRAZ   RANKING 4

| Limestone Coast | $12–$19 | 2000 | 90 | 2008 | 2012 |
|---|---|---|---|---|---|
| Current vintage: 2000 | 90 | 1999 | 87 | 2004 | 2007 |
| | | 1998 | 89 | 2003 | 2006+ |
| | | 1997 | 88 | 2002 | 2005 |
| | | 1996 | 91 | 2004 | 2008 |

Sumptuous, smooth and creamy shiraz whose lightly earthy, cooked aromas of jammy cassis and sweet gamey/vanilla oak precede an impressively flavoursome and focused palate of length and brightness. Framed by firm, soft tannins, its vibrant, spicy fruit and creamy oak finish with length and balance.

## LIMITED VINEYARD RELEASE CHARDONNAY   RANKING 4

| Padthaway | $20–$29 | 2001 | 91 | 2006 | 2009 |
|---|---|---|---|---|---|
| Current vintage: 2001 | 91 | 2000 | 92 | 2005 | 2008 |
| | | 1999 | 82 | 2001 | 2004 |

Fine, dry and elegant chardonnay with delicate floral aromas of grapefruit and melon, pineapple and spicy new clove/nutmeg oak. Reserved and tightly focused, its elegant, chalky and austere palate of lemony, peachy flavours culminates in a long and minerally finish.

## LIMITED VINEYARD RELEASE SHIRAZ

| Padthaway | $20–$29 |
|---|---|
| **Current vintage: 2000** | **87** |

Cooked, earthy aromas of treacle-like plums and jammy cassis are a little over-awed by roasted vanilla oak influences. Smoky and chocolatey, the palate presents some bright cassis, raspberry and plum flavours somewhat smothered by spicy new oak, finishing a little hollow and hard-edged.

| 2000 | 87 | 2002 | 2005+ |
|---|---|---|---|
| 1999 | 92 | 2007 | 2011 |
| 1998 | 89 | 2003 | 2006+ |
| 1997 | 89 | 2009 | 2017 |
| 1996 | 89 | 2008 | 2016 |

# Stoney Vineyard

105 Tea Tree Road, Campania Tas 7026. Tel: (03) 6260 4174. Fax: (03) 6260 4390.
Website: www.domaine-a.com.au  Email: althaus@domaine-a.com.au
Region: **Coal River Valley** Winemaker: **Peter Althaus** Viticulturist: **Peter Althaus** Chief Executive: **Peter Althaus**
Stoney Vineyard is the recently-expanded Coal River Valley vineyard whose best fruit is carefully metered into the Domaine A label, with the Stoney Vineyard name used as a pretty solid and interesting second brand. In researching this edition, I was particularly impressed by the Stoney Vineyard wines across all labels. The Sauvignon Blanc can be racy and vivacious, the Cabernet Sauvignon elegant and structured, and the Pinot Noir complex and textured.

## CABERNET SAUVIGNON

| Coal River Valley | $20–$29 |
|---|---|
| **Current vintage: 2001** | **91** |

Earthy, slightly cedary aromas of blackcurrants, plums and dark olives have plenty of depth and reveal nuances of dark olives, chocolate, undergrowth and briar. Firm and structured, it presents dark berry and plum fruit and cedar/vanilla oak along its smooth but moderately assertive palate, before a slightly drying and herbal finish.

| 2001 | 91 | 2006 | 2009+ |
|---|---|---|---|
| 2000 | 84 | 2005 | 2008 |
| 1998 | 80 | 2002 | 2003 |

## PINOT NOIR

| Coal River Valley | $20–$29 |
|---|---|
| **Current vintage: 2003** | **90** |

Vibrant floral and spicy aromas of maraschino cherries and raspberry confiture precede an expressive palate of juicy texture and vitality. Round and soft, framed by fine-grained but drying tannins, its lively kernel-like cherry/berry fruit finishes savoury and nutty, with a light meatiness.

| 2003 | 90 | 2005 | 2008 |
|---|---|---|---|
| 2001 | 90 | 2006 | 2009 |
| 1996 | 90 | 1998 | 2001+ |

## SAUVIGNON BLANC

| Coal River Valley | $12–$19 |
|---|---|
| **Current vintage: 2003** | **90** |

Pungent asparagus and tinned pineapple aromas of lemony, tropical and citrus fruit, with lightly sweaty nuances of apricots. Dry and savoury, rather Loire Valley-like in its shape and austerity, its creamy middle palate is intensely flavoured, nutty and smoky, just finishing without the real raciness it might have deserved.

| 2003 | 90 | 2004 | 2005+ |
|---|---|---|---|
| 2002 | 89 | 2003 | 2004+ |
| 2001 | 87 | 2002 | 2003+ |
| 2000 | 87 | 2002 | 2005+ |
| 1999 | 86 | 1998 | 1999+ |
| 1998 | 93 | 1999 | 2000+ |

# Stonier

2 Thompsons Lane, Merricks Vic 3916. Tel: (03) 5989 8300. Fax: (03) 5989 8709.
Website: www.stoniers.com.au  Email: stoniers@stoniers.com.au
Region: **Mornington Peninsula**  Winemaker: **Geraldine McFaul**  Viticulturist: **Stuart Marshall**
Chief Executive: **Peter Cowan**

Owned by Lion Nathan, Stonier divides its production between its premier Reserve label and its 'standard' brand that is sourced from various Mornington Peninsula properties. Its best wine is its tangy, citrusy Reserve Chardonnay, which has been astonishingly consistent in recent years. The Reserve Pinot Noir has slipped a little of late, flirting with wild and woolly flavours, but makes a spectacular return to form in 2003.

## CHARDONNAY

 RANKING **5**

| Mornington Peninsula | $20–$29 |
| Current vintage: 2003 | 87 |

Forward, tangy and citrusy aromas over lightly buttery and toasty oak precede a smooth and flavoursome, if angular palate of peach, nectarine and lemony flavour that finishes clean and spicy, but slightly lean and drying.

| | | | |
|---|---|---|---|
| 2003 | 87 | 2003 | 2004 |
| 2002 | 82 | 2003 | 2004 |
| 2001 | 87 | 2003 | 2006 |
| 2000 | 89 | 2002 | 2005 |
| 1999 | 89 | 2001 | 2004 |
| 1998 | 88 | 1999 | 2000 |
| 1997 | 88 | 1998 | 2001 |

## PINOT NOIR

RANKING **4**

| Mornington Peninsula | $30–$49 |
| Current vintage: 2003 | 90 |

Very pretty early-drinking pinot noir with surprising complexity. Its slightly confectionary perfume of cherries, plums and red berries precedes a sumptuous, ripe and juicy palate bursting with intense spicy cherry/plum fruit qualities over suggestions of mint and sweet vanilla oak. Love the mouthfeel and texture.

| | | | |
|---|---|---|---|
| 2003 | 90 | 2004 | 2005+ |
| 2002 | 88 | 2003 | 2004+ |
| 2001 | 88 | 2002 | 2003+ |
| 2000 | 91 | 2002 | 2005 |
| 1999 | 89 | 2001 | 2004 |
| 1998 | 88 | 1999 | 2000 |
| 1997 | 88 | 1999 | 2002 |
| 1996 | 91 | 2001 | 2004 |
| 1995 | 87 | 1997 | 2000 |

## RESERVE CHARDONNAY

RANKING **2**

| Mornington Peninsula | $30–$49 |
| Current vintage: 2002 | 93 |

Stylish, elegant and savoury chardonnay with a delicate perfume of honeysuckle, stonefruit and lemongrass, with undertones of sweetcorn and caramel. Smooth and silky, the palate is fine and fluffy, delivering fresh apple, melon and pear flavours before finishing with marginally herbaceous notes of green cashew and slightly metallic acids.

| | | | |
|---|---|---|---|
| 2002 | 93 | 2007 | 2010 |
| 2001 | 95 | 2006 | 2009 |
| 2000 | 95 | 2005 | 2008 |
| 1999 | 92 | 2001 | 2004 |
| 1998 | 95 | 2003 | 2006 |
| 1997 | 95 | 2002 | 2005 |
| 1996 | 92 | 1998 | 2001 |
| 1995 | 92 | 2003 | 2007 |
| 1994 | 93 | 1996 | 1999 |
| 1993 | 91 | 1998 | 2001 |

## RESERVE PINOT NOIR

RANKING **3**

| Mornington Peninsula | $30–$49 |
| Current vintage: 2001 | 84 |

Overworked, horsey pinot lacking in fruit length and drying out to a stark, metallic finish. There's some sweet rose garden and ripe cherry aroma, some forward confection-like fruit on the palate and some sweet vanilla/chocolate oak, but to all intents and purposes the wine's lack of fruit, austere finish and equine undertones suggest an excessive contribution courtesy the brettanomyces organism.

| | | | |
|---|---|---|---|
| 2001 | 84 | 2003 | 2006 |
| 2000 | 91 | 2002 | 2005 |
| 1999 | 93 | 2004 | 2007 |
| 1998 | 94 | 2003 | 2006 |
| 1997 | 95 | 2002 | 2005 |
| 1995 | 77 | 1997 | 2000 |
| 1994 | 93 | 1996 | 1999 |
| 1993 | 95 | 1998 | 2001 |
| 1992 | 93 | 1997 | 2000 |
| 1991 | 88 | 1993 | 1996 |

# Stringy Brae

Sawmill Road, Sevenhill SA 5453. Tel: (08) 8843 4313. Fax: (08) 8843 4319.
Website: www.stringybrae.com.au  Email: sales@stringybrae.com.au
Region: **Clare Valley** Winemaker: **Contract** Viticulturist: **Martin Rantanen** Chief Executive: **Donald Willson**

Stringy Brae is a small Clare Valley maker whose Rieslings are slightly more fatty and fractionally sweeter than those typical of the region, while its Shiraz is typically robust and briary.

## RIESLING

| | Clare Valley | $20–$29 |
| --- | --- | --- |
| | **Current vintage: 2003** | **89** |

| | | | |
| --- | --- | --- | --- |
| 2003 | 89 | 2008 | 2011 |
| 2002 | 91 | 2007 | 2010+ |
| 2001 | 90 | 2009 | 2013 |
| 2000 | 87 | 2002 | 2005+ |

Dusty mineral and leesy nuances lie beneath a floral perfume of lemon rind and honeysuckle. The palate begins round and juicy, with a creamy texture, but then becomes more austere and mineral. Finishes just slightly cloying, but is a fair attempt at a more complex and winemaker-influenced style.

## SHIRAZ

| | Clare Valley | $20–$29 |
| --- | --- | --- |
| | **Current vintage: 2001** | **88** |

| | | | |
| --- | --- | --- | --- |
| 2001 | 88 | 2003 | 2006+ |
| 2000 | 87 | 2002 | 2005+ |
| 1999 | 86 | 2001 | 2004+ |

Slightly thin and sappy to finish, but otherwise a good wine from the hot 2001 vintage. Its meaty white pepper fragrance of black and red berries, cloves and sweet cedar/vanilla oak precedes a generous, briary and lightly fleshy palate framed by smooth, fine-grained tannins.

# Suckfizzle

Lot 14 Kalkarrie Drive Augusta WA 6290. Tel: (08) 9758 0303. Fax: (08) 9758 0304.
Email: sfa@highway1.com.au
Region: **Margaret River** Winemaker: **Janice McDonald** Viticulturist: **Janice McDonald**
Chief Executive: **Janice McDonald**

Suckfizzle is a brand associated with a significant planting near Augusta, in the cooler, southerly reaches of the Margaret River region. Its white blend of Bordeaux varieties counters its significant oak-derived creaminess with wonderful length and racy austerity, while its Cabernet Sauvignon is rather herbaceous.

## SAUVIGNON BLANC SEMILLON

| | Margaret River | $30–$49 |
| --- | --- | --- |
| | **Current vintage: 2002** | **91** |

| | | | |
| --- | --- | --- | --- |
| 2002 | 91 | 2004 | 2007 |
| 2001 | 89 | 2002 | 2003+ |
| 1998 | 93 | 2000 | 2003 |
| 1997 | 95 | 1999 | 2002 |

Arresting aromas of capsicum and asparagus ably supported by assertive, roasted lemony/vanilla oak with underlying nuances of gooseberries and lychees. Long, smooth and seamless, coated with toasty oak and underpinned by quite a firm phenolic extract. Only a wine of this level of fruit intensity could gets away with such a significant degree of oakiness, and it does!

A B C D E F G H I J K L M N O P Q R **S** T U V W X Y Z

# Summerfield

5967 Stawell–Avoca Road, Moonambel Vic 3478. Tel: (03) 5467 2264. Fax: (03) 5467 2380.
Website: www.summerfieldwines.com  Email: info@summerfieldwines.com

Region: **Pyrenees** Winemakers: **Ian and Mark Summerfield** Viticulturist: **Ian Summerfield**
Chief Executive: **Ian Summerfield**

Summerfield is a small, mature and family-owned vineyard in the presently drought-ravaged Pyrenees area whose super-ripe Reserve Cabernet and Reserve Shiraz have not been able to avoid some of the stress associated with the region's severe climate. They are however packed with fruit and flavour, and will please those who enjoy such styles.

## RESERVE CABERNET SAUVIGNON

RANKING **5**

| Pyrenees | $30–$49 |
|---|---|
| **Current vintage: 2002** | **86** |

Floral, meaty and weedy aromas of stewed greenish fruit are suggestive of a long hang time to accumulate ripeness. Up-front and concentrated, its palate is similarly meaty and herbal, with a lingering and sappy finish of very extracted, under-ripe cold tea tannins.

| | | | |
|---|---|---|---|
| 2002 | 86 | 2007 | 2010 |
| 2001 | 86 | 2003 | 2006 |
| 2000 | 89 | 2005 | 2008+ |
| 1999 | 86 | 2004 | 2007 |

## RESERVE SHIRAZ

RANKING **5**

| Pyrenees | $30–$49 |
|---|---|
| **Current vintage: 2002** | **87** |

Pungent, deeply scented aromas of plums and black-berries with meaty, herbaceous undertones. Forward and substantial, impressively concentrated but lacking vitality and freshness, it finishes without its customary length and brightness.

| | | | |
|---|---|---|---|
| 2002 | 87 | 2004 | 2007+ |
| 2001 | 88 | 2003 | 2006 |
| 2000 | 88 | 2002 | 2005 |
| 1999 | 89 | 2004 | 2007 |

# Tahbilk

Off Goulburn Valley Highway, Tabilk Vic 3608. Tel: (03) 5794 2555. Fax: (03) 5794 2360.
Website: www.tahbilk.com.au  Email: admin@tahbilk.com.au

Region: **Nagambie Lakes** Winemakers: **Alister Purbrick, Neil Larson, Alan George** Viticulturist: **Ian Hendy**
Chief Executive: **Alister Purbrick**

Tahbilk is an historic vineyard and winery on the banks of the Goulburn River in central Victoria. Its whites are lively and refreshing, especially its tangy and citrusy Marsanne, while there is a substantial difference in quality between its 'reserve level' trio of reds and the less expensive and very old-fashioned Cabernet Sauvignon and Shiraz. Both Reserve reds and the 1860s Vineyard Shiraz are tending to offer more fruit sweetness and vitality than in previous years.

## 1860 VINES SHIRAZ (Formerly Claret)

RANKING **3**

| Nagambie Lakes | $50+ |
|---|---|
| **Current vintage: 1999** | **91** |

There's more sweetness of fruit and oak than many preceding vintages of this wine, although it does reveal some slightly under and over-ripe influences. There's a meaty, earthy, pruney aspect to its spicy and slightly herbal aromas, while its typically robust palate does offer some rather generous small black and red berry flavours. It's forward and concentrated, but as it moves down the palate reveals more prune/currant/raisin flavours augmented by sweet creamy/vanilla oak. It should develop plenty of character and complexity.

| | | | |
|---|---|---|---|
| 1999 | 91 | 2011 | 2019 |
| 1998 | 95 | 2010 | 2018+ |
| 1997 | 90 | 2009 | 2017+ |
| 1996 | 93 | 2008 | 2016+ |
| 1995 | 91 | 2007 | 2015 |
| 1994 | 90 | 2002 | 2006 |
| 1992 | 93 | 2012 | 2022 |
| 1991 | 90 | 2011 | 2021 |
| 1990 | 90 | 2010 | 2020 |
| 1989 | 82 | 2001 | 2011 |
| 1988 | 88 | 2000 | 2010 |
| 1987 | 92 | 2007 | 2017 |
| 1986 | 94 | 2006 | 2016 |

# CABERNET SAUVIGNON

RANKING **4**

**Nagambie Lakes** $12–$19
**Current vintage: 2001** 83

Evolving, shorter-term cabernet with a meaty, pruney aroma of baked red fruits, raisins and currants. Cooked and stewy, the palate is thin and lacks both freshness and length.

| | | | |
|---|---|---|---|
| 2001 | 83 | 2003 | 2006+ |
| 2000 | 90 | 2008 | 2012+ |
| 1999 | 88 | 2007 | 2011 |
| 1998 | 86 | 2006 | 2010 |
| 1997 | 86 | 2005 | 2009 |
| 1996 | 83 | 2001 | 2004 |
| 1995 | 92 | 2015 | 2025 |
| 1994 | 90 | 2006 | 2014 |
| 1993 | 91 | 2005 | 2013 |
| 1992 | 93 | 2004 | 2012 |
| 1991 | 93 | 2011 | 2021 |
| 1990 | 93 | 2010 | 2020 |
| 1989 | 84 | 1997 | 2001 |
| 1988 | 94 | 2000 | 2005 |
| 1987 | 88 | 1995 | 1999 |
| 1986 | 94 | 2006 | 2016 |
| 1985 | 94 | 2005 | 2015 |
| 1984 | 93 | 2004 | 2014 |
| 1983 | 93 | 2003 | 2013 |
| 1982 | 90 | 2002 | 2012 |

# CHARDONNAY

RANKING **5**

**Nagambie Lakes** $12–$19
**Current vintage: 2002** 89

Elegant, fleshy chardonnay whose delicate, nutty aromas of stonefruit bubblegum/vanilla oak reveal floral and spicy undertones. Sweet and juicy, its long, restrained palate might lack complexity but delivers appealing tropical and peach-like fruit before finishing long and soft with enduring flavours, lemony acids and restrained oak.

| | | | |
|---|---|---|---|
| 2002 | 89 | 2004 | 2007 |
| 2001 | 89 | 2003 | 2006+ |
| 2000 | 83 | 2003 | 2005 |
| 1999 | 81 | 2001 | 2004 |
| 1998 | 83 | 2000 | 2003 |
| 1997 | 85 | 1999 | 2002 |

# MARSANNE

RANKING **4**

**Nagambie Lakes** $12–19
**Current vintage: 2003** 92

A delightful example of this Victorian favourite, whose lightly nutty aromas of melon and citrus fruits precedes a lightly herbal, but smooth, generous and almost oily palate whose tangy, juicy fruit qualities build in the mouth towards a long, savoury, lemony finish. Truckloads of fruit and freshness.

| | | | |
|---|---|---|---|
| 2003 | 92 | 2011 | 2015 |
| 2002 | 91 | 2007 | 2010+ |
| 2001 | 87 | 2003 | 2006+ |
| 2000 | 88 | 2005 | 2008 |
| 1999 | 90 | 2004 | 2007 |
| 1998 | 88 | 2003 | 2006+ |
| 1997 | 90 | 2005 | 2009 |
| 1996 | 93 | 2004 | 2008 |
| 1995 | 90 | 2007 | 2015 |
| 1994 | 92 | 2006 | 2014 |
| 1993 | 87 | 1998 | 2001 |
| 1992 | 89 | 1997 | 2000+ |
| 1991 | 90 | 1999 | 2003 |

# RESERVE CABERNET SAUVIGNON

RANKING **3**

**Nagambie Lakes** $50+
**Current vintage: 1998** 93

Robust, profoundly structured and astringent red whose layers of fruit and flavour are only slowly coaxed from the glass. Its earthy aromas of sweet red and black berries, coffee grounds, cedar/chocolate oak and minty menthol complexity herald a firm, drying palate constructed about a firm rod of astringent tannins. It will take time to mellow, but there should be enough fruit remaining by the time it ultimately does.

| | | | |
|---|---|---|---|
| 1998 | 93 | 2010 | 2018+ |
| 1997 | 93 | 2009 | 2017+ |
| 1996 | 90 | 2008 | 2016+ |
| 1994 | 89 | 2014 | 2024 |
| 1993 | 88 | 2005 | 2013 |
| 1992 | 91 | 2012 | 2022 |

## RESERVE SHIRAZ

**Nagambie Lakes**    $50+
**Current vintage:1999**    92

Powerfully fruited and firmly structured shiraz with a meaty, gamey fragrance of small berries, red-currants and plums, backed by spicy nuances of cinnamon, clove and rosemary. Well-ripened and densely packed cassis, plum, prune and raisin-like flavours play along the entirety of the long, succulent, savoury and nutty palate, framed by creamy, but astringent tannins.

| 1999 | 92 | 2011 | 2019+ |
|---|---|---|---|
| 1998 | 95 | 2018 | 2028 |
| 1997 | 92 | 2009 | 2017 |
| 1996 | 90 | 2004 | 2008+ |
| 1994 | 90 | 2002 | 2006+ |

## RIESLING

RANKING 4

**Nagambie Lakes**    $12–$19
**Current vintage: 2003**    88

Early-drinking riesling with nuances of tinned tropical fruit beneath its slightly stressed aromas of apricot and orange rind. Fleshy, round and juicy, its generous apple, pear and stonefruit flavours culminate in a long, refreshing finish of clean acidity.

| 2003 | 88 | 2005 | 2008 |
|---|---|---|---|
| 2001 | 83 | 2003 | 2006 |
| 2000 | 90 | 2005 | 2008 |
| 1999 | 87 | 2001 | 2004 |
| 1998 | 82 | 2003 | 2006+ |
| 1997 | 93 | 2005 | 2009 |
| 1996 | 92 | 2004 | 2008 |
| 1995 | 90 | 2003 | 2007 |
| 1994 | 91 | 2002 | 2006 |
| 1993 | 90 | 2001 | 2005 |
| 1992 | 92 | 1997 | 2000 |

## SHIRAZ

RANKING 5

**Nagambie Lakes**    $12–$19
**Current vintage: 2001**    88

Firm and flavoursome shiraz whose lightly stewy and confectionary aromas of raspberries, cherries, plums and dusty, herbal, white pepper-like under-tones are supported by very light oak influences. Full to medium in weight, it's forward and spicy, slightly hollow but moderately long, finishing with lingering earthy blackberry/plum fruit and firm tannins.

| 2001 | 88 | 2009 | 2013 |
|---|---|---|---|
| 2000 | 89 | 2008 | 2012+ |
| 1999 | 87 | 2004 | 2007 |
| 1998 | 87 | 2006 | 2010+ |
| 1997 | 87 | 2005 | 2009 |
| 1996 | 82 | 2001 | 2004 |
| 1995 | 89 | 2007 | 2015 |
| 1994 | 90 | 2014 | 2024 |
| 1993 | 86 | 1998 | 2001 |
| 1992 | 93 | 2004 | 2012 |
| 1991 | 92 | 2011 | 2021 |
| 1990 | 89 | 2002 | 2010 |
| 1989 | 88 | 2001 | 2009 |
| 1988 | 93 | 2000 | 2008 |

# Tallarook

2 Delaney's Road, Warranwood Vic 3134. Tel: (03) 9876 7022. Fax: (03) 9876 7044.
Website: www.tallarook.com  Email: info@tallarook.com

Region: **Upper Goulburn** Winemaker: **Scott McCarthy** Viticulturist: **Kevin Burns**
General Manager: **Anthony Woollams**

Also planted to shiraz, marsanne and pinot noir, Tallarook's leading wine is handsomely its Chardonnay, which in 2000 produced an excellent, meaty and complex wine with lingering savoury and toasty qualities.

## CHARDONNAY

RANKING 5

**Upper Goulburn**    $20–$29
**Current vintage: 2001**    87

Lightly candied citrus and spicy aromas with under-lying buttery, vanilla oak precede a forward, developing palate that finishes a little stressed and dry with a nutty, smooth and creamy finish.

| 2001 | 87 | 2003 | 2006 |
|---|---|---|---|
| 2000 | 93 | 2002 | 2005+ |
| 1999 | 87 | 2001 | 2004 |
| 1998 | 89 | 2000 | 2003 |

# Taltarni

Taltarni Road, Moonambel Vic 3478. Tel: (03) 5459 7900. Fax: (03) 5467 2306.
Website: www.taltarni.com.au  Email: enquiries@taltarni.com.au
Region: **Pyrenees** Winemakers: **Leigh Clarnette, Loic le Calvez, Mark Laurence**
Viticulturist: **Michael Ciavarella** Chief Executive: **Peter Steer**

Taltarni has undergone several changes of personnel in recent years and is gradually re-emerging as a maker of a rounder, and more forward expression of red wine that should become easier to enjoy at a younger age without necessarily sacrificing any of the vineyard's historic cellaring potential. The company's new Cephas blend of shiraz and cabernet sauvignon made its debut with a smooth and silky 2000 vintage — a wine of tightness, elegance and piercingly intense flavours of small black and red berries..

## CABERNET MERLOT BLEND

RANKING **5**

| Pyrenees | $12–$19 |
|---|---|
| **Current vintage: 2001** | **89** |

Despite its rather dull minty nose of menthol, leather and some floral perfume, this is an elegant, fine and supple red blend with a surprisingly sweet and vibrant palate of cassis, redcurrant, plum and violet-like flavours supported by fine, bony tannins and fresh, lively acids. There's enough flavour, structure and firmness for short-term cellaring.

| | | | |
|---|---|---|---|
| 2001 | 89 | 2006 | 2009 |
| 2000 | 91 | 2005 | 2008 |
| 1999 | 82 | 2001 | 2004 |
| 1998 | 84 | 2000 | 2003 |
| 1997 | 82 | 2002 | 2005 |

## CABERNET SAUVIGNON

RANKING **4**

| Pyrenees | $30–$49 |
|---|---|
| **Current vintage: 2000** | **84** |

Reductive, mercaptan-like, closed, leathery, and dusty aromas of small berries and plums precede a smooth, tightly integrated palate of round, succulent red and black fruit and fine creamy caramel oak.

| | | | |
|---|---|---|---|
| 2000 | 84 | 2008 | 2012 |
| 1998 | 94 | 2006 | 2010+ |
| 1997 | 86 | 2002 | 2005+ |
| 1996 | 88 | 2004 | 2008 |
| 1995 | 89 | 2003 | 2007 |
| 1994 | 93 | 2006 | 2014+ |
| 1993 | 91 | 2005 | 2013 |
| 1992 | 93 | 2004 | 2012+ |
| 1991 | 91 | 2011 | 2021 |
| 1990 | 93 | 2002 | 2010+ |
| 1989 | 87 | 1997 | 2001 |
| 1988 | 94 | 2000 | 2008 |
| 1987 | 89 | 1999 | 2007 |
| 1986 | 89 | 1998 | 2006 |

## MERLOT

RANKING **4**

| Pyrenees | $30–$49 |
|---|---|
| **Current vintage: 1998** | **81** |

Rustic, horsey farmyard aromas with light cherry/berry fruit, before a reductive and meaty palate drying out with bandage-like influences and hard-edged metallic tannins.

| | | | |
|---|---|---|---|
| 1998 | 81 | 2003 | 2006 |
| 1996 | 90 | 2001 | 2004 |
| 1995 | 92 | 2003 | 2007 |
| 1994 | 93 | 2002 | 2006 |
| 1993 | 92 | 2001 | 2005 |
| 1992 | 89 | 2000 | 2004 |
| 1991 | 89 | 1999 | 2003 |

## RESERVE CABERNET SAUVIGNON

RANKING **2**

| Pyrenees | $50+ |
|---|---|
| **Current vintage: 1994** | **93** |

Simply a monstrously proportioned, powerfully concentrated and hugely extracted dense dry red, whose earthy dark berry and plum fruit, cedary and lightly smoky oak are thickly coated with lashings of firm, astringent tannins. It finishes long, dense and savoury, with a very light spike of volatility.

| | | | |
|---|---|---|---|
| 1994 | 93 | 2006 | 2014 |
| 1992 | 96 | 2012 | 2022 |
| 1988 | 94 | 2008 | 2018 |
| 1984 | 94 | 2004 | 2014 |
| 1979 | 97 | 1999 | 2009 |

## SAUVIGNON BLANC
RANKING 4

| Pyrenees | $12–$19 |
|---|---|
| Current vintage: 2003 | 87 |

Punchy, forward and honest sauvignon blanc with dusty, lemony aromas of passionfruit and bath-powder, before a generous, broad and slightly oily palate that just lacks real definition and finish.

| | | | |
|---|---|---|---|
| 2003 | 87 | 2004 | 2005 |
| 2002 | 91 | 2003 | 2004 |
| 2001 | 90 | 2001 | 2002 |
| 2000 | 90 | 2001 | 2002 |
| 1999 | 93 | 2000 | 2001+ |
| 1998 | 87 | 1999 | 2000 |
| 1997 | 86 | 1997 | 1998 |
| 1996 | 88 | 1998 | 2001 |

## SHIRAZ (Formerly French Syrah)
RANKING 3

| Pyrenees | $30–$49 |
|---|---|
| Current vintage: 2002 | 89 |

Firm, leathery and astringent shiraz whose fresh raspberry, cassis-like and cedary black pepper aromas reveal nuances of chocolate and licorice. Lean and linear, its robust palate gradually unfolds flavours of black and red berries, plums and sweet leather, finishing with suggestions of salty black olives and an astringent extract.

| | | | |
|---|---|---|---|
| 2002 | 89 | 2010 | 2014+ |
| 2001 | 90 | 2009 | 2013 |
| 2000 | 93 | 2008 | 2012+ |
| 1999 | 95 | 2007 | 2011 |
| 1998 | 95 | 2006 | 2010 |
| 1997 | 95 | 2005 | 2009+ |
| 1996 | 95 | 2004 | 2008 |
| 1995 | 87 | 2000 | 2003 |
| 1994 | 92 | 1999 | 2002 |
| 1993 | 94 | 2001 | 2005 |
| 1992 | 94 | 2004 | 2012 |
| 1991 | 93 | 2003 | 2011 |
| 1990 | 89 | 1998 | 2002+ |
| 1989 | 88 | 1997 | 2001 |
| 1988 | 94 | 2000 | 2008 |
| 1987 | 88 | 1995 | 1999 |
| 1986 | 94 | 1994 | 1998 |

# TarraWarra Estate

Healesville Road, Yarra Glen Vic 3775. Tel: (03) 5962 3311. Fax: (03) 5962 3887.
Website: www.tarrawarra.com.au  Email: enq@tarrawarra.com.au
Region: **Yarra Valley** Winemaker: **Clare Halloran** Viticulturist: **Michael Brocksopp**
Chief Executive: **Michael Matthews**

This dedicated and ambitious small winery operation in the Yarra Valley is owned by the Besen family. Its most impressive wine is its Chardonnay, a consistently classy, savoury and richly textured wine with a deep core of citrus and melon flavours. Less reliable is its Pinot Noir, which in years like 1998 can deliver a rare and hedonistic measure of intensity and opulence.

## CHARDONNAY
RANKING 3

| Yarra Valley | $30–$49 |
|---|---|
| Current vintage: 2002 | 94 |

Assertive cooler climate chardonnay with depth and firmness. It reveals a complex, floral bouquet of cumquat, peach and melon, with oatmeal-like and creamy, butterscotch influences. Its creamy richness borders on oiliness, but the palate is ultimately long, silky and savoury. The flavours tend to build in the mouth, finishing long and peachy with lingering nutty and bacony undertones.

| | | | |
|---|---|---|---|
| 2002 | 94 | 2007 | 2010 |
| 2001 | 92 | 2005 | 2008 |
| 2000 | 90 | 2002 | 2005 |
| 1999 | 90 | 2004 | 2007 |
| 1998 | 94 | 2006 | 2010 |
| 1997 | 95 | 2005 | 2009 |
| 1996 | 91 | 2001 | 2004 |
| 1995 | 91 | 2000 | 2003+ |
| 1994 | 88 | 1996 | 1999 |
| 1993 | 94 | 1998 | 2001+ |
| 1992 | 95 | 2000 | 2004 |
| 1991 | 94 | 1996 | 1999 |
| 1990 | 91 | 1995 | 1998 |

## PINOT NOIR

| | | | | | |
|---|---|---|---|---|---|
| **Yarra Valley** | | **$50+** | 2002 | 88 | 2004 | 2007 |

**Yarra Valley** $50+
**Current vintage: 2002** 88

Early-drinking pinot with a rose petal perfume of raspberries, cherries, strawberries and sweet vanilla oak. It's fine, fragile and delicate, with some forward small berry/cherry fruits and under-growth-like complexity that culminates in rather a sappy, greenish finish. Likely to become rather vegetal rather quickly.

| | | | |
|---|---|---|---|
| 2002 | 88 | 2004 | 2007 |
| 2001 | 89 | 2003 | 2006+ |
| 2000 | 83 | 2002 | 2005 |
| 1999 | 88 | 2001 | 2004 |
| 1998 | 95 | 2006 | 2010 |
| 1997 | 90 | 2002 | 2005 |
| 1996 | 95 | 2001 | 2004+ |
| 1995 | 93 | 2000 | 2003 |
| 1994 | 93 | 1999 | 2002 |
| 1993 | 89 | 1998 | 2001 |
| 1992 | 95 | 2000 | 2004 |
| 1991 | 88 | 1999 | 2003 |
| 1990 | 82 | 1998 | 2002 |

# Tatachilla

151 Main Road, McLaren Vale SA 5171. Tel: (08) 8323 8656. Fax: (08) 8323 9096.
Website: www.tatachillawinery.com.au Email: enquiries@tatachillawinery.com.au

Region: **McLaren Vale** Winemakers: **Justin McNamee** Viticulturist: **Kevin Fiddaman**
Chief Executive: **Peter Cowan**

Tatachilla is a successful Lion Nathan brand that was initially based in McLaren Vale, which is still the source of its best wines. Leaving aside its perfectly acceptable range of white wines, its reds are typically smooth and jammy, underpinned by sweet chocolate/vanilla oak and framed by soft tannins. The more expensive expressions, of which the Clarendon Vineyard Merlot is handsomely the finest, are made from more concentrated fruit and receive better oak.

## 1901 CABERNET SAUVIGNON

**McLaren Vale** $30–$49
**Current vintage: 2000** 82

Cooked, jammy and vegetal cabernet with a rustic, meaty and minty aroma of mulberries and black-berries. Up-front and confectionary, its palate is simple and eucalypt-like.

| | | | |
|---|---|---|---|
| 2000 | 82 | 2002 | 2005+ |
| 1999 | 89 | 2004 | 2007+ |
| 1998 | 91 | 2006 | 2010+ |

## CLARENDON VINEYARD MERLOT

**McLaren Vale** $30–$49
**Current vintage: 2000** 90

Generous, ripe and easy-drinking merlot with an appealingly fresh aroma of sweet raspberries, mul-berries and blackberries, given some assertive vanilla and creamy coconut oak. Smooth, soft and approachable, with a ripe, creamy palate of intense berry/plum fruit framed by soft tannins.

| | | | |
|---|---|---|---|
| 2000 | 90 | 2002 | 2005+ |
| 1999 | 87 | 2001 | 2004 |
| 1998 | 90 | 2003 | 2006 |
| 1997 | 87 | 2002 | 2005 |
| 1996 | 92 | 2001 | 2004+ |

## FOUNDATION SHIRAZ

**McLaren Vale** $30–$49
**Current vintage: 2000** 88

Rather jammy, vegetal red with under and over-ripe characteristics typical of this vintage. Minty, eucalypt-like aromas of stewed plums, blackberries and raspberries with polished, cedary and varnishy oak precede a soft, sappy but flavoursome palate whose sweet berry/plum fruit and cedary oak are framed by green-edged tannins.

| | | | |
|---|---|---|---|
| 2000 | 88 | 2002 | 2005+ |
| 1999 | 88 | 2001 | 2004+ |
| 1998 | 91 | 2006 | 2010 |
| 1997 | 89 | 1999 | 2002+ |
| 1996 | 89 | 1998 | 2001 |
| 1995 | 90 | 1997 | 2000 |

## KEYSTONE GRENACHE SHIRAZ

**McLaren Vale** $12–$19
**Current vintage: 2001** 87

A pretty, easy-drinking, soft and medium-weight red with genuine varietal qualities. It's spicy, floral and fragrant, and its confection-like presentation of raspberry, blueberry and maraschino cherry fruit is partnered by soft tannins and fresh acidity. Attractively spicy, with suggestions of licorice and cloves, it's just fractionally too cooked and jammy for higher points.

| 2001 | 87 | 2003 | 2006 |
|------|----|------|------|
| 2000 | 87 | 2001 | 2002+ |
| 1999 | 82 | 2000 | 2001 |
| 1998 | 86 | 2000 | 2003 |
| 1997 | 86 | 1999 | 2002+ |
| 1996 | 87 | 2001 | 2004 |

## McLAREN VALE CABERNET SAUVIGNON

**McLaren Vale** $20–$29
**Current vintage: 2001** 87

Minty, spicy aromas of cassis, plum and sweet chocolate/mocha/vanilla oak, with a brightly flavoured palate of ripe fruit, assertive oak and firm, well-integrated tannins. Sweet, fruity and oaky — a certain crowd-pleaser.

| 2001 | 87 | 2003 | 2006 |
|------|----|------|------|
| 2000 | 89 | 2002 | 2005+ |
| 1999 | 82 | 2001 | 2004 |
| 1998 | 91 | 2003 | 2006+ |
| 1997 | 89 | 1999 | 2002 |
| 1996 | 87 | 2001 | 2004 |
| 1995 | 87 | 2000 | 2003 |
| 1994 | 82 | 1996 | 1999 |

## McLAREN VALE CHARDONNAY

**McLaren Vale** $12–$19
**Current vintage: 2003** 86

Fast-developing and confectionary chardonnay with a simple bathpowdery aroma of citrus, melon and light vanilla oak and a juicy, soft and forward palate becoming quite broad.

| 2003 | 86 | 2004 | 2005 |
|------|----|------|------|
| 2002 | 87 | 2003 | 2004 |
| 2001 | 87 | 2002 | 2003 |
| 2000 | 86 | 2001 | 2002 |
| 1999 | 83 | 2000 | 2001 |
| 1998 | 88 | 2000 | 2003 |

## McLAREN VALE SHIRAZ

**McLaren Vale** $20–$29
**Current vintage: 2001** 88

Meaty, tarry aromas of dark berries and plums with slightly cooked undertones of prunes and currants, plus a varnishy oak background. Forward and richly flavoured, it tends towards a dead grape style, but does have enough fruit sweetness to enjoy over the short term.

| 2001 | 88 | 2003 | 2006 |
|------|----|------|------|
| 2000 | 81 | 2002 | 2005 |
| 1999 | 82 | 2001 | 2004 |
| 1998 | 90 | 2006 | 2010 |
| 1997 | 89 | 2002 | 2005 |
| 1996 | 90 | 2004 | 2008 |

## PADTHAWAY CABERNET SAUVIGNON

**Padthaway** $20–$29
**Current vintage: 2001** 80

Skinny, stewy and herbal red with a minty, eucalypt aroma of cassis, raspberries and light vanilla oak, plus a simple, cooked palate whose cassis/plum flavours thin out towards a green, dilute finish.

| 2001 | 80 | 2003 | 2006 |
|------|----|------|------|
| 2000 | 87 | 2002 | 2005 |
| 1999 | 84 | 2001 | 2004 |
| 1998 | 90 | 2003 | 2006 |

# Taylors

Taylors Road, Auburn SA 5451. Tel: (08) 8849 2008. Fax: (08) 8849 2240.
Website: www.taylorswines.com.au  Email: cdoor@taylorswines.com.au

Region: **Clare Valley** Winemakers: **Adam Eggins, Helen McCarthy** Viticulturists: **Ken Noack, Kate Strachan**
Chief Executive: **Mitchell Taylor**

Taylors is a comparatively large Clare Valley maker that has undertaken a lot of work in recent years to lift the standards of its popular range of varietal table wines. By and large it has succeeded in this, but by comparison its premier St Andrews range now looks rather over-ripe, clunky and over-priced.

## CABERNET SAUVIGNON

RANKING **4**

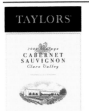

**Clare Valley** $12–$19
**Current vintage: 2003** 86

Intense aromas of blackberries, cassis, dark plums and cedar/vanilla oak reveal nuances of dried herbs and menthol. Full to medium in weight, it's smooth, creamy and very ripe, with a currant-like overcooked aspect to its sweet and chocolatey palate. Framed by firm, but approachable tannins, it finishes with some green, under-ripe edges.

| | | | |
|---|---|---|---|
| 2003 | 86 | 2005 | 2008 |
| 2002 | 88 | 2007 | 2010 |
| 2001 | 90 | 2009 | 2013 |
| 2000 | 88 | 2008 | 2012 |
| 1999 | 93 | 2004 | 2007+ |
| 1998 | 90 | 2003 | 2006 |
| 1997 | 81 | 1999 | 2002 |
| 1996 | 82 | 1998 | 2001 |
| 1995 | 86 | 1997 | 2000 |
| 1994 | 87 | 1999 | 2002 |
| 1993 | 81 | 2001 | 2005 |
| 1992 | 83 | 2000 | 2004 |

## CHARDONNAY

RANKING **5**

**Clare Valley** $12–$19
**Current vintage: 2002** 83

Slightly cooked and under-ripe, with light, resiny and floral aromas of cumquats, melon and sweet butter/vanilla oak and nutty undertones. Round and oily, its palate of green olives and cashews, citrus and herbal flavours finishes short and cloying.

| | | | |
|---|---|---|---|
| 2002 | 83 | 2003 | 2004+ |
| 2001 | 88 | 2003 | 2006 |
| 2000 | 83 | 2002 | 2005 |
| 1999 | 89 | 2001 | 2004 |
| 1998 | 81 | 1999 | 2000 |
| 1997 | 77 | 1998 | 1999 |
| 1996 | 88 | 2001 | 2004 |
| 1995 | 87 | 2000 | 2003 |
| 1994 | 82 | 1996 | 1999 |

## MERLOT

RANKING **5**

**Clare Valley** $12–$19
**Current vintage: 2003** 87

Honest, varietal merlot whose sweet aromas of cherries, plums, dark berries and sweet mocha/chocolate oak overlie nuances of mint and menthol. Forward and uncomplicated, its supple palate of lingering sweet fruit is well partnered by smooth vanilla oak.

| | | | |
|---|---|---|---|
| 2003 | 87 | 2005 | 2008 |
| 2002 | 89 | 2004 | 2007 |
| 2001 | 81 | 2002 | 2003+ |

## RIESLING

RANKING **4**

**Clare Valley** $12–$19
**Current vintage: 2003** 88

Dry, slatey riesling whose floral aromas of fresh citrus and pineapple reveal slightly herbal and soapy undertones. Forward and juicy, but lacking great length, it's up-front and attractive, finishing with invigorating fruit and clean acidity.

| | | | |
|---|---|---|---|
| 2003 | 88 | 2005 | 2008 |
| 2002 | 83 | 2003 | 2004 |
| 2001 | 93 | 2006 | 2009 |
| 2000 | 92 | 2005 | 2008 |
| 1999 | 86 | 2001 | 2004 |
| 1998 | 85 | 2000 | 2003 |
| 1997 | 85 | 1999 | 2002 |
| 1996 | 92 | 2004 | 2008 |
| 1994 | 93 | 2002 | 2006 |
| 1993 | 89 | 1995 | 1998 |

RANKING **5**

| Clare Valley | $12–$19 |
|---|---|
| **Current vintage: 2003** | **88** |

Vibrant, early-drinking shiraz with a peppery fragrance of raspberries, cherries, red plums and creamy coconut oak. Medium weight, it's supple and smooth, with pleasingly lively berry flavours and oak underpinned by light, powdery tannins.

| | | | |
|---|---|---|---|
| 2003 | 88 | 2005 | 2008 |
| 2002 | 89 | 2004 | 2007 |
| 2001 | 91 | 2003 | 2006+ |
| 2000 | 89 | 2002 | 2005+ |
| 1999 | 88 | 2001 | 2004 |
| 1998 | 90 | 2003 | 2006 |
| 1997 | 88 | 2002 | 2005 |
| 1996 | 87 | 2001 | 2004 |
| 1995 | 88 | 2000 | 2003 |
| 1994 | 87 | 1996 | 1999 |
| 1993 | 87 | 1998 | 2001 |

## ST ANDREWS CABERNET SAUVIGNON

RANKING **5**

| Clare Valley | $50+ |
|---|---|
| **Current vintage: 1999** | **90** |

A ripe, firm wine with strength and future. Fragrant, but slightly cooked cassis and plum fruit is given full treatment in cedary chocolate oak. Developing a firm, rich palate whose creamy texture is deeply flavoured, finishing firm and tight. Spicy, minty complexity gives distinct regional character.

| | | | |
|---|---|---|---|
| 1999 | 90 | 2007 | 2011 |
| 1998 | 87 | 2003 | 2006 |
| 1997 | 84 | 2002 | 2005 |

## ST ANDREWS SHIRAZ

RANKING **4**

| Clare Valley | $50+ |
|---|---|
| **Current vintage: 2000** | **87** |

Pruney, dark pepper aromas of smoked meats backed by nuances of mint, fennel and currants, before a dead grape-like palate lacking much vitality. Thick, heavily spiced flavours of prunes, currants and chocolate fruitcake are commanding, but lack charm. The finish is tinged with herbal, even salty influences.

| | | | |
|---|---|---|---|
| 2000 | 87 | 2005 | 2008+ |
| 1999 | 93 | 2007 | 2011 |
| 1998 | 90 | 2003 | 2006+ |
| 1997 | 89 | 2002 | 2005 |

# The Lane

Ravenswood Lane, Hahndorf SA 5245. Tel: (08) 8388 1250. Fax: (08) 8388 7233.
Website: www.thelane.com.au  Email: helen@thelane.com.au
Region: **Adelaide Hills**  Winemaker: **Robert Mann**  Viticulturist: **John Edwards**
Chief Executive: **John Edwards**

This brand recently had its name altered from Ravenswood Lane to 'The Lane'. It should perhaps be given more credit than it receives for its consistently classy and racy Sauvignon Blanc and its minerally Chardonnay. Its 2001 Reunion Shiraz is the first vintage of this wine with sufficient weight of fruit to complement the meaty, reductive and rustic characters deliberately introduced by winemaking artefact.

## BEGINNING CHARDONNAY

RANKING **4**

| Adelaide Hills | $30–$49 |
|---|---|
| **Current vintage: 2002** | **84** |

Green-edged and sappy, with grassy aromas of pineapple and tinned asparagus. Its simple, forward and hollow palate of under-ripe and green-edged fruit is lifted by simple toffee-like malo-lactic qualities, but just lacks sufficient ripeness.

| | | | |
|---|---|---|---|
| 2002 | 84 | 2004 | 2007 |
| 2001 | 90 | 2006 | 2009 |
| 2000 | 93 | 2002 | 2005 |
| 1999 | 88 | 2000 | 2001 |
| 1998 | 82 | 1999 | 2000 |

## GATHERING SAUVIGNON SEMILLON

RANKING **3**

| Adelaide Hills | $30–$49 | 2002 | 93 | 2003 | 2004+ |
|---|---|---|---|---|---|
| **Current vintage: 2002** | **93** | 2001 | 94 | 2003 | 2006 |
| | | 2000 | 75 | 2000 | 2001 |

Another fine Adelaide Hills sauvignon based-wine from 2002. It's especially aromatic and herbaceous, with intense aromas of tropical fruits, gooseberries, passionfruit and lychees, backed by a smidge of sweatiness. Long and juicy, the palate presents a ripe mouthfeel of tangy and penetrative tropical fruit punctuated by lingering grapefruit flavours and citrusy acids.

## REUNION SHIRAZ

RANKING **5**

| Adelaide Hills | $30–$49 | 2001 | 90 | 2006 | 2009+ |
|---|---|---|---|---|---|
| **Current vintage: 2001** | **90** | 2000 | 80 | 2002 | 2005 |
| | | 1999 | 87 | 2007 | 2011 |
| | | 1998 | 86 | 2000 | 2003+ |
| | | 1997 | 84 | 1999 | 2002 |
| | | 1996 | 88 | 1998 | 2001 |

Firm, astringent and reductive shiraz that could have been even better with a little aeration. Its earthy, spicy, herbal and white pepper aromas of sweet raspberries, dark cherries and blackberries are partnered with sweet vanilla/chocolate oak. Smooth and sumptuous, its berry flavours are very intense, but lifted by sweet chocolate and gamey French oak.

# Tim Adams

Warenda Road, Clare SA 5453. Tel: (08) 8842 2429. Fax: (08) 8842 3550.
Website: www.timadamswines.com.au  Email: tim@timadamswines.com.au
Region: **Clare Valley** Winemaker: **Tim Adams** Viticulturist: **Tim Adams**
Chief Executives: **Tim Adams, Pam Goldsack**

Very few wineries in Australia, large or small, offer the genuine quality, year after year, at such an affordable price as Tim Adams does. More admirably still, it's Tim Adam's ambition to maintain his present production levels, keep his prices where they are, and to improve quality as his new vineyards come on stream. Stylistically, his whites are fragrant, taut and trim, his reds deeply aromatic and concentrated, but quite restrained and linear. This company is dealing with the recent run of hot, dry Clare vintages as well as any other.

## CABERNET

RANKING **4**

| Clare Valley | $20–$29 | 2001 | 93 | 2009 | 2013+ |
|---|---|---|---|---|---|
| **Current vintage: 2001** | **93** | 2000 | 89 | 2005 | 2008+ |
| | | 1999 | 87 | 2004 | 2007 |
| | | 1998 | 93 | 2006 | 2010+ |
| | | 1997 | 89 | 2002 | 2005 |
| | | 1996 | 89 | 2004 | 2008 |
| | | 1995 | 89 | 2003 | 2007 |
| | | 1994 | 88 | 2002 | 2006 |
| | | 1993 | 90 | 2001 | 2005 |
| | | 1992 | 92 | 2000 | 2004 |
| | | 1991 | 90 | 2003 | 2011 |

Finely focused cabernet whose delicate, earthy and violet-like perfume of blackberries, cassis and plums overlies nuances of cedar/chocolate oak. Long and smooth, with briary small berry flavours, suggestions of forest floor and dusty, nutty vanilla oak framed by tight, firm tannins. Pleasing balance and integration.

## RIESLING

RANKING **3**

| Clare Valley | $20–$29 | 2004 | 92 | 2009 | 2012+ |
|---|---|---|---|---|---|
| **Current vintage: 2004** | **92** | 2003 | 94 | 2011 | 2015 |
| | | 2002 | 94 | 2010 | 2014+ |
| | | 2001 | 93 | 2009 | 2013 |
| | | 2000 | 92 | 2008 | 2012 |
| | | 1999 | 93 | 2007 | 2011 |
| | | 1998 | 92 | 2006 | 2010 |
| | | 1997 | 93 | 2005 | 2009 |
| | | 1996 | 91 | 2004 | 2008 |
| | | 1995 | 84 | 1997 | 2000 |
| | | 1994 | 93 | 2002 | 2006 |

Fragrant rose petal, lime and chalk aromas reveal light notes of mineral. Long, fine and generously flavoured, the palate is tight and austere, finishing with lively citrus fruit and tangy acidity.

# SEMILLON

RANKING **4**

| Clare Valley | | $12–$19 |
|---|---|---|
| **Current vintage: 2002** | | **90** |

Elegant, focused semillon with a delicate, nutty aroma of citrus and melon, lightly creamy but rather toasty vanilla oak over light grassy nuances. Given plenty of up-front oak treatment, the palate is creamy and fleshy, with lightly grassy honeydew melon fruit and toffee-like malolactic influences. A little too woody for a higher score.

| 2002 | 90 | 2004 | 2007+ |
|---|---|---|---|
| 2000 | 87 | 2002 | 2005 |
| 1999 | 82 | 2001 | 2004 |
| 1998 | 88 | 2003 | 2006 |
| 1997 | 94 | 2002 | 2005+ |
| 1996 | 92 | 2004 | 2008 |
| 1995 | 84 | 1997 | 2000 |
| 1994 | 94 | 2006 | 2014 |

# SHIRAZ

RANKING **3**

| Clare Valley | | $20–$29 |
|---|---|---|
| **Current vintage: 2002** | | **91** |

Elegant, smooth and polished Clare Valley shiraz whose peppery perfume of delicate small red and black berries and restrained vanilla oak reveals earthy nuances of cloves and nutmeg. Suggestions of mint, menthol and smoky vanilla oak permeate its restrained, but persistent palate of piercingly intense small fruit and fine, carefully measured tannic extract.

| 2002 | 91 | 2007 | 2010+ |
|---|---|---|---|
| 2001 | 94 | 2009 | 2013 |
| 2000 | 91 | 2005 | 2008+ |
| 1999 | 91 | 2004 | 2007 |
| 1998 | 93 | 2003 | 2006+ |
| 1997 | 92 | 2002 | 2005 |
| 1996 | 86 | 2001 | 2004 |
| 1995 | 91 | 2003 | 2007 |
| 1994 | 92 | 1999 | 2002 |
| 1993 | 90 | 1995 | 1998 |
| 1992 | 92 | 2000 | 2004 |

# THE ABERFELDY

RANKING **2**

| Clare Valley | | $30–$49 |
|---|---|---|
| **Current vintage: 2002** | | **88** |

Minty aromas of confiture-like cassis, redcurrants and dark plums reveal nuances of spice and dried herbs. Smooth, soft and luscious, it's principally a fruit-driven red whose rich, up-front flavours are also supported by sweet and lightly smoky oak. Lacking its customary depth and backbone, it finishes slightly sappy and green-edged.

| 2002 | 88 | 2007 | 2010+ |
|---|---|---|---|
| 2001 | 94 | 2009 | 2013+ |
| 2000 | 93 | 2008 | 2012 |
| 1999 | 96 | 2007 | 2011+ |
| 1998 | 97 | 2010 | 2018+ |
| 1997 | 95 | 2005 | 2009 |
| 1996 | 93 | 2008 | 2016 |
| 1995 | 93 | 2003 | 2007 |
| 1994 | 97 | 2006 | 2014+ |
| 1993 | 95 | 2005 | 2013 |
| 1992 | 94 | 2012 | 2022 |
| 1991 | 93 | 2003 | 2011 |
| 1990 | 89 | 1998 | 2002 |
| 1988 | 90 | 1996 | 2000+ |

# THE FERGUS GRENACHE

RANKING **3**

| Clare Valley | | $20–$29 |
|---|---|---|
| **Current vintage: 2002** | | **87** |

Meaty, spicy grenache with a slightly cooked, lightly oaked and jammy aroma of red berries, plums and cherries. Forward and generous, fractionally spirity, it presents a moderate length of slightly stressed and spicy fruit, finishing firm and leanish.

| 2002 | 87 | 2004 | 2007+ |
|---|---|---|---|
| 2001 | 91 | 2006 | 2009 |
| 2000 | 93 | 2005 | 2008 |
| 1999 | 94 | 2004 | 2007+ |
| 1998 | 93 | 2003 | 2006+ |
| 1997 | 92 | 2002 | 2005 |
| 1996 | 91 | 2001 | 2004 |
| 1995 | 93 | 2000 | 2003 |
| 1994 | 92 | 2002 | 2006 |
| 1993 | 93 | 1998 | 2001 |

# Tin Cows

Healesville Road, Yarra Glen Vic 3775. Tel: (03) 5962 3311. Fax: (03) 5962 3887.
Website: www.tincows.com.au  Email: enq@tincows.com.au

Region: **Yarra Valley** Winemaker: **Clare Halloran** Viticulturist: **Michael Brocksopp**
Chief Executive: **Michael Matthews**

Tin Cows is TarraWarra's second label, which once was known rather ingloriously as Tunnel Hill. Its juicy Chardonnay is its best wine, while it also releases a Pinot Noir, Shiraz and Merlot.

## CHARDONNAY

RANKING **5**

| | | | | |
|---|---|---|---|---|
| **Yarra Valley** | $12–$19 | 2002 | 86 | 2004 | 2007 |
| **Current vintage: 2002** | 86 | 2001 | 87 | 2003 | 2006 |
| | | 2000 | 83 | 2001 | 2002 |

Honest, flavoursome chardonnay whose lightly tropical, buttery aromas of juicy fruit and vanilla oak reveal undertones of sweetcorn and herbs. Round, forward and almost oily, with generous up-front melon and tropical fruit, it finishes slightly flabby.

# Torbreck

Lot 51 Roennfeldt Road, Marananga SA 5360. Tel: (08) 8562 4155. Fax: (08) 8562 4195.
Website: www.torbreck.com  Email: info@torbreck.com

Region: **Barossa Valley** Winemakers: **David Powell, Dan Standish** Viticulturist: **Michael Wilson**
Chief Executive: **David Powell**

Torbreck has burst onto the scene in Australia and the US on the back of several astonishingly good Barossa Valley wines, most of which were fashioned in a more rustic, complex and earthy, savoury style than anyone had ever experienced from this region. It has maintained exceptional consistency with its flagship labels of RunRig, The Factor and Descendant, and in The Struie Shiraz has created another wine of genuine excellence and individuality, this time with the inclusion of some Eden Valley fruit. The 2002 The Steading blend of grenache, mataro and shiraz is another highlight amongst many.

## CUVÉE JUVENILES

RANKING **4**

| | | | | |
|---|---|---|---|---|
| **Barossa Valley** | $30–$49 | 2003 | 89 | 2004 | 2005+ |
| **Current vintage: 2003** | 89 | 2002 | 90 | 2003 | 2004 |
| | | 2001 | 89 | 2001 | 2002 |
| | | 2000 | 90 | 2001 | 2002 |
| | | 1999 | 90 | 2001 | 2004+ |

Soft, smooth and slightly sweet, this early-drinking Barossa-made Rhône blend has a spicy, meaty fragrance of dark cherries, blueberries, cinnamon and cloves that reveals a hint of white pepper. Dark and meaty, slightly cooked and jammy, it presents typically spicy plum and small berry flavours.

## DESCENDANT SHIRAZ VIOGNIER

RANKING **2**

| | | | | |
|---|---|---|---|---|
| **Barossa Valley** | $50+ | 2002 | 96 | 2010 | 2014+ |
| **Current vintage: 2002** | 96 | 2001 | 94 | 2006 | 2009 |
| | | 2000 | 91 | 2002 | 2005 |
| | | 1999 | 95 | 2004 | 2007+ |
| | | 1998 | 92 | 2003 | 2006+ |

Its meaty, musky perfume of black pepper, black-berries, dark cherries and plums is lifted by nuances of ground coffee and licorice, violets and cassis, plus a subtle background of lightly smoky vanilla oak. Viognier lends a fragrant note of apricot blossom. Smooth, supple and silky, the palate simply bursts with jujube-like flavours of dark berries. Framed by tight-knit drying tannins, its length is truly remarkable, its balance exceptional. A magnificent expression of modern Barossa red that easily soaks up its 14.5% alcohol by volume without a hint of hot spirit or dehydrated fruit.

## MARSANNE VIOGNIER ROUSSANNE

| | | | |
|---|---|---|---|
| **Barossa Valley** | | $30–$49 | |
| **Current vintage: 2002** | | 91 | |

| 2002 | 91 | 2003 | 2004+ |
|---|---|---|---|
| 2001 | 80 | 2001 | 2001 |
| 2000 | 89 | 2001 | 2002 |

A complex, unctuous white blend with fragrant heady and lightly smoky aromas of apricots, honeysuckle, cinnamon and cloves over waxy nuances of dried flowers. Sumptuous and concentrated, its thick coating of stonefruit, citrus and grilled nut flavours borders on oily, but finishes with sufficiently fresh acidity. Savoury, slightly raw and phenolic, it's deliciously drinkable despite some technical imperfections.

## RUNRIG SHIRAZ VIOGNIER

| **Barossa Valley** | | $50+ | |
|---|---|---|---|
| **Current vintage: 2001** | | 94 | |

| 2001 | 94 | 2009 | 2013 |
|---|---|---|---|
| 1999 | 96 | 2007 | 2011 |
| 1998 | 97 | 2010 | 2018+ |
| 1997 | 93 | 2005 | 2009+ |
| 1996 | 95 | 2008 | 2016+ |

Sumptuous, concentrated and deeply spiced shiraz with meaty notes of treacle, licorice and currants. Clearly a hot year wine, it's both smooth and powerful, with a great depth and length of deeply ripened and slightly stewy raisin-like flavours. Viognier lends some attractive floral notes to its perfume, while the oak has a slightly varnishy aspect.

## THE FACTOR

| **Barossa Valley** | | $50+ | |
|---|---|---|---|
| **Current vintage: 2001** | | 91 | |

| 2001 | 91 | 2003 | 2006 |
|---|---|---|---|
| 2000 | 95 | 2005 | 2008+ |
| 1999 | 97 | 2007 | 2011+ |
| 1998 | 93 | 2006 | 2010+ |

A finely crafted wine made from a crop clearly carrying some measure of cooked or stressed fruit. Its wild and spicy aromas of intense jujube fruit and restrained oak suggest dark berries, cassis and plums, with underlying nuances of cloves and cinnamon, saltbush and seaweed. Long and smooth, with some dehydrated prune/bitumen flavours and salty edges, it does present some sumptuous plum and currant flavours. It finishes slightly raw and alcoholic, with a light saltiness.

## THE STEADING

| **Barossa Valley** | | $30–$49 | |
|---|---|---|---|
| **Current vintage: 2002** | | 95 | |

| 2002 | 95 | 2007 | 2010+ |
|---|---|---|---|
| 2001 | 90 | 2003 | 2006 |
| 2000 | 93 | 2005 | 2008 |
| 1999 | 95 | 2004 | 2007+ |
| 1998 | 87 | 2003 | 2006 |
| 1997 | 94 | 2002 | 2005+ |

An Australian wine with obvious Rhône Valley pretensions. Its spicy, meaty aromas of violets, blackberries, plums and undergrowth are laced with a perfume of cloves and cinnamon, with underlying suggestions of cured meats. Elegant and fine-grained despite its remarkable opulence and complexity, its juicy, fleshy palate of licorice-like red and black fruits culminates in a very long and savoury finish of lingering intensity. First-rate balance and integration.

# Tower Estate

cnr Halls and Broke Road, Pokolbin NSW 2320. Tel: (02) 4998 7989. Fax: (02) 4998 7919.
Website: www.towerestate.com  Email: sales@towerestate.com

Region: **Various** Winemaker: **Dan Dineen** Chief Executive: **Len Evans**

Tower Estate is fulfilling its promise of becoming something of a one-stop shop for some of the finest combinations of variety and region in Australia. The current releases are headed by a silky-smooth Barossa Shiraz from 2002, a minerally Clare Riesling from 2003 and a smooth and peachy Hunter Chardonnay from 2002.

## ADELAIDE HILLS SAUVIGNON BLANC  RANKING 5

| Adelaide Hills | $12–$19 |
|---|---|
| **Current vintage: 2003** | **87** |

Lacks its customary punch and intensity, with a delicate, herbal and slightly sweaty aroma of gooseberries and passionfruit. Up-front and confection-like, its palate then thins out towards a rather sappy and metallic finish.

| | | | |
|---|---|---|---|
| 2003 | 87 | 2003 | 2004+ |
| 2002 | 89 | 2002 | 2003 |
| 2001 | 81 | 2002 | 2003 |
| 2000 | 88 | 2000 | 2001 |
| 1999 | 94 | 2000 | 2001+ |

## BAROSSA SHIRAZ  RANKING 3

| Barossa Valley | $30–$49 |
|---|---|
| **Current vintage: 2002** | **94** |

A shiraz so immediately delicious and harmonious I sincerely doubt much will be left by the time it reaches its peak. Its perfume of violets and black pepper, cassis, dark cherries and ripe plums is lifted by some assertive, but balanced creamy mocha barrel ferment oak. Smooth and supple, its long, willowy palate bursts with pristine, penetrative small dark berries and red fruits, while creamy fine-grained oak and powdery tannins provide velvet-smooth support.

| | | | |
|---|---|---|---|
| 2002 | 94 | 2010 | 2014+ |
| 2001 | 92 | 2006 | 2009+ |
| 2000 | 93 | 2005 | 2008+ |
| 1999 | 94 | 2007 | 2011 |

## CLARE VALLEY RIESLING  RANKING 4

| Clare Valley | $20–$29 |
|---|---|
| **Current vintage: 2003** | **90** |

An intense aroma of lime juice, tropical fruits, slate and mineral precedes rather a juicy, broad and almost syrupy palate bursting with pristine citrus flavours. It finishes long, dry and mineral, but will mature relatively early.

| | | | |
|---|---|---|---|
| 2003 | 90 | 2005 | 2008+ |
| 2002 | 90 | 2007 | 2010 |
| 2001 | 89 | 2003 | 2006 |
| 2000 | 77 | 2001 | 2002 |
| 1999 | 91 | 2004 | 2007+ |

## COONAWARRA CABERNET SAUVIGNON  RANKING 5

| Coonawarra | $30–$49 |
|---|---|
| **Current vintage: 2001** | **87** |

A sweet oaky perfume of mocha and vanilla reveals nuances of violets, cassis and raspberries. Slightly overcooked, its moderately full palate presents some up-front fruit sweetness before becoming leaner and thinner towards its marginally metallic finish of under and over-ripe fruit.

| | | | |
|---|---|---|---|
| 2001 | 87 | 2006 | 2009 |
| 2000 | 85 | 2002 | 2005 |
| 1999 | 94 | 2007 | 2011+ |

## HUNTER VALLEY CHARDONNAY  RANKING 4

| Lower Hunter Valley | $20–$29 |
|---|---|
| **Current vintage: 2002** | **93** |

Generous, soft and round almost Californian-style chardonnay with a dusty, mealy aroma of melon, peach and cumquat backed by nutty, smoky and slightly reductive earthy undertones. Long, smooth and unctuous, its tightly integrated and assertively oaked palate delivers plenty of ripe, peachy flavour before a lingering, soft finish.

| | | | |
|---|---|---|---|
| 2002 | 93 | 2004 | 2007 |
| 2001 | 91 | 2006 | 2009 |
| 2000 | 91 | 2002 | 2005+ |
| 1999 | 90 | 2001 | 2004+ |

## HUNTER VALLEY SEMILLON RANKING

**Lower Hunter Valley** $20–$29
**Current vintage: 2004** 94

Delicate, pristine floral and lightly herbal aromas of honeydew melon precede a stylish, shapely palate that offers vastly more flesh and juiciness than its 11% alcohol by volume leads one to expect. Its generous, tangy expression of fresh apple, melon and lemony fruit finishes clean and refreshing, with lingering notes of minerals and citrusy acids.

| | | | |
|---|---|---|---|
| 2004 | 94 | 2012 | 2016 |
| 2003 | 91 | 2005 | 2008 |
| 2002 | 92 | 2004 | 2007+ |
| 2001 | 91 | 2003 | 2006+ |
| 2000 | 90 | 2005 | 2008 |
| 1999 | 93 | 2007 | 2011 |

## HUNTER VALLEY SHIRAZ RANKING

**Lower Hunter Valley** $30–$49
**Current vintage: 2002** 87

Lightly dusty and herbaceous, peppery and meaty aromas of berry fruit are backed by light cedar/vanilla oak. Tight, lean and green-edged, the palate reveals slightly under-ripe fruit characters lifted by smart new oak, finishing a little deficient in structure and length.

| | | | |
|---|---|---|---|
| 2002 | 87 | 2004 | 2007 |
| 2001 | 93 | 2009 | 2013+ |
| 2000 | 95 | 2008 | 2012 |
| 1999 | 93 | 2007 | 2011 |

# Trentham Estate

Sturt Highway, Trentham Cliffs NSW 2738. Tel: (03) 5024 8888. Fax: (03) 5024 8800.
Website: www.trenthamestate.com.au  Email: rebeccaw@trenthamestate.com.au
Region: **Murray River Valley** Winemaker: **Anthony Murphy** Viticulturist: **Pat Murphy**
Chief Executive: **Anthony Murphy**
Trentham Estate is expanding its range of fresh, lively and easy-drinking varietal table wines, especially in the area of Italian varietals and Viognier. Its wines are typically ripe, honest and open, and offer very reliable value for money.

## CABERNET SAUVIGNON MERLOT

**Murray River Valley** $12–$19
**Current vintage: 2001** 80

Tiring, stale and leathery, with ageing spicy fruit and rustic, farmyard influences drying out towards a thin, metallic finish.

| | | | |
|---|---|---|---|
| 2001 | 80 | 2002 | 2003 |
| 1999 | 83 | 2000 | 2001 |
| 1998 | 87 | 2000 | 2003 |
| 1997 | 82 | 1999 | 2002 |
| 1996 | 88 | 2001 | 2004 |
| 1995 | 82 | 1997 | 2000 |
| 1994 | 77 | 1995 | 1996 |
| 1993 | 88 | 1998 | 2001 |

## CHARDONNAY

**Murray River Valley** $12–$19
**Current vintage: 2003** 81

Fast-developing, oily and forward chardonnay with dusty and rather cooked aromas of peaches, pears and cream. Broad and citrusy, the palate finishes a little flat and lacking freshness.

| | | | |
|---|---|---|---|
| 2003 | 81 | 2003 | 2004 |
| 2002 | 86 | 2002 | 2003+ |
| 2001 | 86 | 2002 | 2003 |
| 2000 | 83 | 2000 | 2001 |

## MERLOT RANKING

**Murray River Valley** $12–$19
**Current vintage: 2001** 86

Pleasingly intense, early-drinking merlot whose light aromas of dark cherries and plums are backed by cedar/vanilla and chocolate oak influences with a hint of meatiness. Ripe and juicy, its jammy expression of dark cherry/plum flavours and sweet oak finish pleasingly soft and approachable.

| | | | |
|---|---|---|---|
| 2001 | 86 | 2003 | 2006 |
| 2000 | 87 | 2002 | 2005 |
| 1999 | 83 | 2000 | 2001 |
| 1998 | 90 | 2000 | 2003+ |
| 1997 | 85 | 1999 | 2002 |
| 1996 | 86 | 1998 | 2001 |
| 1995 | 87 | 1997 | 2000 |

## SHIRAZ

RANKING **5**

| Murray River Valley | $12–$19 | 2000 | 87 | 2002 | 2005 |
|---|---|---|---|---|---|
| Current vintage: 2000 | 87 | 1999 | 86 | 2001 | 2004 |
| | | 1998 | 82 | 2000 | 2003 |
| | | 1997 | 87 | 1999 | 2002 |
| | | 1996 | 93 | 2001 | 2004 |
| | | 1995 | 89 | 2000 | 2003 |

Rich, smooth and herbal shiraz with a pungent leathery and slightly sweaty and peppery bouquet of spicy redcurrants, plums and chocolatey oak. Soft and approachable, it offers a pleasing weight and intensity of flavour before a lightly herbal and sappy finish.

# Tuck's Ridge

37 Shoreham Rd, Red Hill South Vic 3937. Tel: (03) 5989 8660. Fax: (03) 5989 8579.
Email: trw@satlink.com.au
Region: **Mornington Peninsula** Winemaker: **Daniel Greene** Viticulturist: **Shane Strange**
Chief Executive: **Peter Hollick**
Tuck's Ridge is one of the largest makers on the Mornington Peninsula, where its best wines are typically made from the Burgundian varieties. Recent seasons have seen both Pinot Noir and Chardonnay become reliably smooth, polished and elegant wines in which vibrant fruit quality is impressively supported by restrained, tightly-integrated winemaking artefact. Each are relatively approachable and early-drinking styles.

## CHARDONNAY

RANKING **4**

| Mornington Peninsula | $30–$49 | 2002 | 92 | 2004 | 2007 |
|---|---|---|---|---|---|
| Current vintage: 2002 | 92 | 2001 | 91 | 2003 | 2006 |
| | | 2000 | 89 | 2002 | 2005 |
| | | 1999 | 85 | 2000 | 2001 |
| | | 1998 | 86 | 2000 | 2003 |
| | | 1997 | 90 | 1999 | 2002 |

Tangy, juicy chardonnay with a delicate and lightly herbal aroma of peach and pineapple, vanilla oak and spicy undertones. Smooth, soft and generous, its vibrant pear/pineapple flavours and creamy oak culminate in a focused and refreshing finish of clean, lively acidity.

## PINOT NOIR

RANKING **4**

| Mornington Peninsula | $30–$49 | 2002 | 89 | 2004 | 2007 |
|---|---|---|---|---|---|
| Current vintage: 2002 | 89 | 2001 | 90 | 2003 | 2006+ |
| | | 2000 | 90 | 2002 | 2005 |
| | | 1999 | 88 | 2001 | 2004 |
| | | 1998 | 87 | 2000 | 2003 |
| | | 1997 | 91 | 1999 | 2002 |
| | | 1996 | 87 | 1998 | 2001 |

A floral perfume of raspberry and cherry confection reveals hints of cinnamon, cloves and sweet vanilla oak. Smooth, supple and juicy, its sappy, easy-drinking palate is soft and gentle, offering charming, if jammy sweet fruit framed by fine tannins and refreshing acids. Elegant and harmonious.

# Turkey Flat

Bethany Road, Tanunda SA 5352. Tel: (08) 8563 2851. Fax: (08) 8563 3610.
Website: www.turkeyflat.com.au Email: turkeyflat@bigpond.com
Region: **Barossa Valley** Winemaker: **Peter Schell** Viticulturist: **Peter Schulz** Chief Executive: **Christie Schulz**
Turkey Flat boasts some of the oldest vineyards still in commercial production in Australia, which means about as old as any still being used for serious wine anywhere in the world. It enjoyed the cooler, but even 2002 season, creating a range of fine, supple, but deeply flavoured wines of both elegance and strength. The Butcher's Block blend offers excellent drinkability, character and value for money.

## BUTCHERS BLOCK

RANKING **4**

| Barossa Valley | $30–$49 | 2002 | 90 | 2004 | 2007 |
|---|---|---|---|---|---|
| Current vintage: 2002 | 90 | 2001 | 89 | 2003 | 2006 |
| | | 2000 | 89 | 2002 | 2005+ |
| | | 1999 | 90 | 2001 | 2004+ |
| | | 1998 | 88 | 2000 | 2003 |
| | | 1997 | 85 | 1998 | 1999 |

Meaty, spicy and savoury Barossa blend with an earthy aroma of dark plums, currants and polished leather. Round and generous, its juicy, fleshy palate of vibrant flavour sits atop a structure of firmish but essentially soft tannins. Ready to drink now, but will improve.

# CABERNET SAUVIGNON

**Barossa Valley** $30–$49
**Current vintage: 2002** 91

Elegant, fine-grained Barossa cabernet whose sweet perfume of briary dark berries, plums and violets overlies restrained vanilla oak and meaty suggestions of mint and menthol. Long, smooth and sumptuous, it's saturated with dark berries and plums before a slightly minty and fractionally herbal finish of cedary vanilla oak and fine-grained tannins.

| 2002 | 91 | 2010 | 2014+ |
|------|----|------|-------|
| 2001 | 85 | 2003 | 2006+ |
| 2000 | 89 | 2008 | 2012 |
| 1999 | 92 | 2004 | 2007 |
| 1998 | 90 | 2003 | 2006 |
| 1997 | 91 | 2002 | 2005 |
| 1996 | 88 | 2001 | 2004+ |

# GRENACHE

**Barossa Valley** $20–$29
**Current vintage: 2002** 89

Soft, juicy and very Australian grenache with a spicy and lightly herbal aroma of redcurrants, sweet plums, raspberries and blueberries with restrained vanilla oak. Smooth and spicy, its penetrative palate of berry/plum flavours is framed by soft, but moderately firm tannins, before a lingering finish of pleasing acidity.

| 2002 | 89 | 2007 | 2010+ |
|------|----|------|-------|
| 2001 | 88 | 2003 | 2006 |
| 2000 | 81 | 2002 | 2005 |
| 1999 | 90 | 2001 | 2004+ |
| 1998 | 87 | 2000 | 2003 |
| 1997 | 84 | 1998 | 1999 |
| 1996 | 89 | 2001 | 2004 |
| 1994 | 89 | 2002 | 2006 |

# SEMILLON MARSANNE BLEND

**Barossa Valley** $20–$29
**Current vintage: 2003** 84

A complex, savoury, honeyed and nutty wine whose delicate floral and wheatmeal complexity and generous, round palate of creamy citrus and melon fruit reveal pungent reductive influences that in all likelihood have been exacerbated by the screwcap used to seal this wine.

| 2003 | 84 | 2004 | 2005+ |
|------|----|------|-------|
| 2002 | 89 | 2003 | 2004+ |
| 2001 | 87 | 2002 | 2003 |
| 2000 | 90 | 2002 | 2005 |
| 1999 | 87 | 2001 | 2004 |
| 1998 | 82 | 1999 | 2000 |
| 1997 | 89 | 1999 | 2002+ |

# SHIRAZ

**Barossa Valley** $30–$49
**Current vintage: 2002** 94

Very stylish, elegant and concentrated shiraz with a perfume of fresh violets, white pepper, dark berries plus spicy, meaty complexity. Cool and minty, its velvet-like palate of pristine small dark and red berry flavours is harmoniously married with fine tannins and sweet vanilla oak. Very attractive poise and balance.

| 2002 | 94 | 2010 | 2014 |
|------|----|------|------|
| 2001 | 90 | 2006 | 2009 |
| 2000 | 90 | 2005 | 2008 |
| 1999 | 93 | 2007 | 2011 |
| 1998 | 95 | 2006 | 2010 |
| 1997 | 89 | 2002 | 2005 |
| 1996 | 94 | 2004 | 2008+ |
| 1993 | 89 | 2001 | 2005 |

# Tyrrell's

Broke Road, Pokolbin NSW 2320. Tel: (02) 4993 7000. Fax: (02) 4998 7723.
Website: www.tyrrells.com.au  Email: info@tyrrells.com.au

Region: **Lower Hunter Valley**  Winemakers: **Andrew Spinaze, Mark Richardson**
Viticulturists: **Cliff Currie, Rob Donoghue**  Chief Executive: **Bruce Tyrrell**

Tyrrell's considers itself to be a custodian of the traditional Hunter Valley wine styles of early-harvested, unwooded semillon and meaty, leathery shiraz of medium to full weight. In this it succeeds admirably, with a stable full of different semillons, each with different terroirs and stories to tell. Its reds are smooth and rustic, and still include the Vat 6 Pinot Noir, a rather incongruous phenomenon that can produce attractive meaty and earthy development with age. Its most consistent wine is however its superbly crafted Vat 47 Chardonnay, a wine made like no other in Australia, but with the proven ability to age with considerable grace and charm.

## BROKENBACK SHIRAZ     RANKING 5

| | | | | | | |
|---|---|---|---|---|---|---|
| **Lower Hunter Valley** | $20–$29 | 2002 | 89 | 2007 | 2010+ |
| **Current vintage: 2002** | 89 | 2001 | 87 | 2003 | 2006 |
| | | 2000 | 86 | 2002 | 2005 |
| Old-fashioned Hunter burgundy style whose | | 1999 | 89 | 2004 | 2007 |
| meaty, leathery aromas of cassis, plums and | | 1998 | 90 | 2006 | 2010 |
| cedar/vanilla oak precede a smooth, creamy | | 1997 | 85 | 1999 | 2002 |
| and fruit-driven palate. Its vibrant plummy fruit | | 1996 | 83 | 1998 | 2001 |
| and undertones of licorice and leather are gently | | 1995 | 89 | 2000 | 2003 |
| bound by soft tannins. | | 1994 | 90 | 2002 | 2006 |

## LOST BLOCK SEMILLON     RANKING 4

| | | | | | | |
|---|---|---|---|---|---|---|
| **Lower Hunter Valley** | $12–$19 | 2003 | 88 | 2005 | 2008+ |
| **Current vintage: 2003** | 88 | 2002 | 92 | 2007 | 2010+ |
| | | 2001 | 90 | 2003 | 2006 |
| An attractive, vibrant and zesty semillon whose | | 1999 | 89 | 2001 | 2004 |
| restrained dusty aromas of melon and lemon reveal | | 1998 | 94 | 2003 | 2006+ |
| lightly grassy nuances. Fresh and forward, its chalky | | 1997 | 90 | 2002 | 2005+ |
| bathpowder-like palate of lemon, melon and apple | | 1996 | 92 | 2004 | 2008 |
| flavour finishes with length and lively acidity. | | 1995 | 89 | 2000 | 2003+ |

## MOON MOUNTAIN CHARDONNAY     RANKING 4

| | | | | | | |
|---|---|---|---|---|---|---|
| **Lower Hunter Valley** | $20–$29 | 2003 | 75 | 2003 | 2004 |
| **Current vintage: 2003** | 75 | 2002 | 90 | 2004 | 2007 |
| | | 2000 | 90 | 2002 | 2005 |
| Smoky, bushfire-affected chardonnay whose | | 1998 | 85 | 1999 | 2000 |
| tobaccoey fruit is dominated by unpleasant | | 1997 | 82 | 1998 | 1999 |
| ashtray-like influences. | | 1996 | 90 | 1998 | 2001 |

## OLD WINERY CABERNET MERLOT

| | | | | | | |
|---|---|---|---|---|---|---|
| **Various** | $12–$19 | 2002 | 83 | 2004 | 2007 |
| **Current vintage: 2002** | 83 | 2001 | 88 | 2003 | 2006+ |
| | | 1999 | 81 | 2001 | 2004+ |
| Light, confectionary red with raspberry/plum flavours | | 1998 | 86 | 2000 | 2003 |
| over muddy, green-edged nuances, cedar and vanilla | | 1997 | 84 | 1999 | 2002 |
| oak. Medium to full in weight, lightly oaked and | | 1996 | 82 | 1998 | 2001 |
| wrapped in soft tannins, with a slightly thin and | | | | | |
| tinny finish. | | | | | |

# OLD WINERY SHIRAZ

**Various**      $12–$19
**Current vintage: 2001**      86

Early-drinking shiraz, with a spicy, leathery and lightly oaked aroma of red plums and berries. Smooth and soft, revealing a creamy expression of plums, prunes and redcurrants, it finishes with restrained tannins, but a little sappy and green-edged.

| | | | |
|---|---|---|---|
| 2001 | 86 | 2003 | 2006 |
| 2000 | 85 | 2002 | 2005 |
| 1998 | 88 | 2000 | 2003+ |
| 1997 | 83 | 1999 | 2002 |
| 1996 | 90 | 2001 | 2004 |
| 1995 | 89 | 1997 | 2000 |
| 1993 | 80 | 1995 | 1998 |

# RESERVE STEVENS SEMILLON

**Lower Hunter Valley**      $20–$29
**Current vintage: 1999**      93

Dusty and perfumed with scents of juicy citrus and melon, this is a taut and elegant semillon that should improve considerably with time in the bottle. Its juicy palate builds in the mouth, delivering intensely flavoured grassy melon and lemony flavours, before a lingering, chalky finish of citrusy acids. Likely to develop more length with cellaring.

| | | | |
|---|---|---|---|
| 1999 | 93 | 2007 | 2011+ |
| 1998 | 94 | 2006 | 2010+ |
| 1997 | 94 | 2005 | 2009 |
| 1996 | 86 | 2001 | 2004 |
| 1995 | 90 | 2003 | 2007+ |

# RESERVE STEVENS SHIRAZ

**Lower Hunter Valley**      $20–$29
**Current vintage: 2000**      89

Rustic, sweaty aromas of animal hide and meaty raspberries, cherries and plums precede a smooth, farmyard-like palate of earthy flavours. Old-fashioned and lightly metallic, it offers some forward richness, but dries out towards a slightly sappy finish. Cellar with caution.

| | | | |
|---|---|---|---|
| 2000 | 89 | 2005 | 2008+ |
| 1999 | 87 | 2001 | 2004+ |
| 1998 | 92 | 2006 | 2010+ |
| 1997 | 88 | 2002 | 2005 |
| 1996 | 84 | 1998 | 2001 |
| 1995 | 87 | 2000 | 2003 |

# VAT 1 SEMILLON

**Lower Hunter Valley**      $30–$49
**Current vintage: 1997**      96

Restrained, late-maturing Hunter semillon of surprising depth and texture given its meagre 10.4% alcohol. It reveals developed complex nutty aromas of toast, butter and honeysuckle, with under-lying scents of honeydew melon and tobacco leaf. Long and dry, with a remarkable depth of flavour and texture, it's toasty and persistent, with waxy complexity and a refreshing lemony finish.

| | | | |
|---|---|---|---|
| 1999 | 95 | 2011 | 2019 |
| 1998 | 92 | 2006 | 2010+ |
| 1997 | 96 | 2009 | 2017 |
| 1996 | 95 | 2004 | 2008 |
| 1995 | 95 | 2007 | 2015 |
| 1994 | 95 | 2006 | 2014 |
| 1993 | 95 | 2001 | 2005+ |
| 1992 | 95 | 2004 | 2012 |
| 1991 | 92 | 1999 | 2003 |
| 1990 | 88 | 1998 | 2002 |
| 1989 | 86 | 1991 | 1994 |
| 1988 | 88 | 1993 | 1996 |
| 1987 | 93 | 1995 | 1999 |
| 1986 | 95 | 1998 | 2008 |
| 1985 | 88 | 1993 | 1997 |
| 1984 | 93 | 1996 | 2004 |

# VAT 6 PINOT NOIR

**Lower Hunter Valley**      $30–$49
**Current vintage: 2000**      82

Horsey farmyard aromas of plums, cherries and red berries, with meaty bandage-like nuances. Forward and sinewy, drying out to a lean, herbal and slightly metallic finish.

| | | | |
|---|---|---|---|
| 2000 | 82 | 2002 | 2005 |
| 1999 | 88 | 2001 | 2004 |
| 1998 | 87 | 2003 | 2006 |
| 1997 | 92 | 2002 | 2005 |
| 1996 | 84 | 2001 | 2004 |
| 1994 | 90 | 1999 | 2002 |

## VAT 8 SHIRAZ CABERNET

RANKING **3**

**Lower Hunter Valley, Coonawarra** $30–$49
**Current vintage: 2000** 87

Herbal, slightly sappy blend whose sweet, slightly cooked and spicy shiraz and herbaceous cabernet aromas of small berries are supported by creamy vanilla oak. Smooth and creamy, its forward small berry fruit is framed by supple, fine-grained tannins, before a greenish, under-ripe finish lacking genuine length of fruit.

| | | | |
|---|---|---|---|
| 2000 | 87 | 2005 | 2008 |
| 1999 | 89 | 2004 | 2007+ |
| 1998 | 95 | 2006 | 2010 |
| 1997 | 92 | 2005 | 2009+ |
| 1996 | 91 | 2001 | 2004 |
| 1995 | 93 | 2003 | 2007 |
| 1994 | 92 | 2002 | 2006 |
| 1993 | 93 | 2001 | 2005 |
| 1992 | 93 | 1997 | 2000 |

## VAT 9 SHIRAZ

RANKING **4**

**Lower Hunter Valley** $30–$49
**Current vintage: 1999** 88

Meaty, earthy Hunter shiraz whose rustic, leathery aromas of plums, raspberries and dark cherries reveal reductive undertones. Full to medium weight, its generous, meaty and forward palate of developing fruit character is framed by slightly under-ripe tannin and finishes with lingering earthy, meaty flavours and greenish acids.

| | | | |
|---|---|---|---|
| 1999 | 88 | 2007 | 2011+ |
| 1998 | 94 | 2010 | 2018 |
| 1997 | 89 | 2002 | 2005+ |
| 1996 | 88 | 2004 | 2008 |
| 1995 | 80 | 1997 | 2000 |
| 1994 | 91 | 2002 | 2006+ |
| 1993 | 87 | 1998 | 2001 |
| 1992 | 93 | 1997 | 2000 |
| 1991 | 95 | 2003 | 2011 |

## VAT 47 CHARDONNAY

RANKING **2**

**Lower Hunter Valley** $30–$49
**Current vintage: 2002** 96

First-rate Hunter chardonnay. Its slightly earthy, dusty and smoky aromas of mangoes, peaches, melon and tobacco reveal nuances of oatmeal, creamy lees qualities and very restrained fine-grained oak. Smooth and voluptuous, it's more structured, complex and assertive than most young Vat 47s, revealing tightly integrated savoury, nutty and matchstick-like complexity interwoven with vibrant melon and stonefruit flavours. Long and refreshing, with a slightly mineral finish.

| | | | |
|---|---|---|---|
| 2002 | 96 | 2010 | 2014 |
| 2001 | 95 | 2009 | 2013 |
| 2000 | 96 | 2008 | 2012 |
| 1999 | 94 | 2001 | 2004+ |
| 1998 | 95 | 2006 | 2010+ |
| 1997 | 90 | 1999 | 2002+ |
| 1996 | 94 | 2001 | 2004+ |
| 1995 | 93 | 2003 | 2007+ |
| 1994 | 94 | 2002 | 2006+ |
| 1993 | 94 | 2001 | 2005 |
| 1992 | 93 | 2000 | 2004+ |
| 1991 | 84 | 1993 | 1996 |

# Vasse Felix

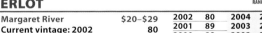

Cnr Caves Road, and Harmans Road, South Cowaramup WA 6284. Tel: (08) 9756 5000. Fax: (08) 9755 5425. Website: www.vassefelix.com.au Email: info@vassefelix.com.au

Region: **Margaret River** Winemakers: **Clive Otto, Will Shields** Viticulturist: **Julia Ryan**
Chief Executive: **Bob Baker**

Vasse Felix is one of the Margaret River region's leading wineries. Its white wines from 2002 and 2003 have performed exceptionally well, none better than the seamless and savoury 2003 Heytesbury Chardonnay. Other than the very stylish and deeply flavoured 2002 Shiraz, its current crop of reds fall below their recent standards, revealing significant leafy, greenish characters and sappy tannins.

## CABERNET MERLOT

RANKING **5**

**Margaret River** $20–$29
**Current vintage: 2002** 80

Rather herbaceous blend with snow pea-like aromas of raspberry and plum confection over nuances of cherries and menthol. Forward and weedy, its lean palate of under-ripe fruit finishes thin and sappy.

| | | | |
|---|---|---|---|
| 2002 | 80 | 2004 | 2007 |
| 2001 | 89 | 2003 | 2006 |
| 2000 | 88 | 2002 | 2005+ |
| 1999 | 82 | 2001 | 2004 |
| 1998 | 83 | 2000 | 2003 |
| 1997 | 88 | 2002 | 2005 |
| 1996 | 88 | 2001 | 2004 |
| 1995 | 87 | 2000 | 2003 |
| 1994 | 88 | 1996 | 1999 |
| 1993 | 87 | 1995 | 1998 |
| 1992 | 91 | 2000 | 2004 |
| 1991 | 89 | 1999 | 2003 |
| 1990 | 87 | 1995 | 1998 |

A
B
C
D
E
F
G
H
I
J
K
L
M
N
O
P
Q
R
S
T
U
V
W
X
Y
Z

## CABERNET SAUVIGNON

RANKING **3**

VASSE FELIX

*Margaret River*
*Cabernet Sauvignon*

750mL

| | | | |
|---|---|---|---|
| **Margaret River** | | **$30–$49** | |
| **Current vintage: 2002** | | **84** | |

Tomatoey aromas of weedy, stressed berry fruit and cedar/vanilla oak lack customary brightness and intensity. Smooth, supple and cedary, the palate presents some pleasing small berry flavours, but without the length to mask its austere, green finish.

| 2002 | 84 | 2004 | 2007 |
|---|---|---|---|
| 2001 | 90 | 2006 | 2009 |
| 2000 | 93 | 2008 | 2012 |
| 1999 | 93 | 2007 | 2011+ |
| 1998 | 96 | 2010 | 2018 |
| 1997 | 89 | 2002 | 2005+ |
| 1996 | 86 | 2001 | 2004+ |
| 1995 | 87 | 2003 | 2007 |
| 1994 | 93 | 2006 | 2014 |
| 1993 | 88 | 1995 | 1998 |
| 1991 | 93 | 2003 | 2011 |

## CHARDONNAY

RANKING **4**

VASSE FELIX
2003
Western Australia
CHARDONNAY
750mL

| | | | |
|---|---|---|---|
| **Margaret River** | | **$20–$29** | |
| **Current vintage: 2003** | | **89** | |

Fruity, tangy chardonnay with aromas of squashed cumquat, grapefruit and underlying herbal, tobaccoey influences. Creamy and almost brassy, its juicy palate of bright tropical and citrus flavours is long and tightly constrained by racy acidity. Well enough made; just lacks the depth and structure for a higher rating.

| 2003 | 89 | 2005 | 2008 |
|---|---|---|---|
| 2002 | 87 | 2004 | 2007 |
| 2001 | 92 | 2006 | 2009 |
| 2000 | 90 | 2002 | 2005+ |
| 1999 | 89 | 2001 | 2004 |
| 1998 | 80 | 1999 | 2000 |
| 1997 | 87 | 1999 | 2002 |
| 1996 | 88 | 1998 | 2001 |
| 1995 | 91 | 2000 | 2003 |

## HEYTESBURY (Cabernet blend)

RANKING **4**

VASSE FELIX

2002

HEYTESBURY

*Western Australia*

750mL

| | | | |
|---|---|---|---|
| **Margaret River** | | **$50+** | |
| **Current vintage: 2002** | | **87** | |

Dusty, herbal notes of capsicum over a light bouquet of blackberry and redcurrant fruit supported by lightly smoky cedar/vanilla oak. Its herbal fruit and smoky oak tend to counter each other on the palate, while its sappy tannins and acids leave a thin finish.

| 2002 | 87 | 2004 | 2007+ |
|---|---|---|---|
| 2001 | 91 | 2006 | 2009+ |
| 2000 | 90 | 2005 | 2008 |
| 1999 | 91 | 2004 | 2007 |
| 1998 | 89 | 2003 | 2006 |
| 1997 | 93 | 2005 | 2009 |
| 1996 | 89 | 2002 | 2008 |
| 1995 | 94 | 2003 | 2007+ |

## HEYTESBURY CHARDONNAY

RANKING **3**

VASSE FELIX
2001
HEYTESBURY
CHARDONNAY
750mL

| | | | |
|---|---|---|---|
| **Margaret River** | | **$30–$49** | |
| **Current vintage: 2003** | | **95** | |

Very stylish, structured and concentrated Margaret River chardonnay whose delicate perfume of peach, tinned pineapple and pear, apple and ruby grapefruit is interwoven with creamy lees and oak-derived influences. Vibrant, smooth and very elegant, its juicy core of bright fruit flavours is harmoniously knit with nutty, savoury oak and soft, but refreshing acids.

| 2003 | 95 | 2008 | 2011 |
|---|---|---|---|
| 2002 | 89 | 2004 | 2007 |
| 2001 | 95 | 2006 | 2009 |
| 2000 | 90 | 2002 | 2005 |
| 1999 | 90 | 2001 | 2004 |
| 1998 | 88 | 2000 | 2003+ |
| 1996 | 86 | 1997 | 1998 |

## SEMILLON

RANKING **4**

VASSE FELIX
2003
Margaret River
SEMILLON
750mL

| | | | |
|---|---|---|---|
| **Margaret River** | | **$20–$29** | |
| **Current vintage: 2002** | | **93** | |

Complex and fragrant, with dusty, herbal aromas of bright melon and lemon over underlying biscuit and oatmeal-like oak and creamy lees-derived influences. Long and creamy, with translucent, generous fruit qualities augmented by fractionally raw, but smoky, herbal and spicy new oak, the palate is neatly wrapped in zesty lemon acids.

| 2002 | 93 | 2004 | 2007 |
|---|---|---|---|
| 2001 | 89 | 2003 | 2006+ |
| 2000 | 90 | 2005 | 2008 |
| 1999 | 91 | 2004 | 2007 |
| 1998 | 86 | 2000 | 2003 |

## SHIRAZ

| Margaret River | $30–$49 |
|---|---|
| Current vintage: 2002 | 93 |

Very stylish, well-made wine with a musky perfume of violets, slightly meaty and over-cooked dark cherries, plums, raspberries and cassis. There's also a hint of tomato, which is also present on its long, firm and moderately concentrated palate. Revealing a generous depth of fruit, good integration and balance, it has elegance and fineness aplenty.

| 2002 | 93 | 2010 | 2014+ |
|---|---|---|---|
| 2001 | 93 | 2006 | 2009 |
| 2000 | 93 | 2008 | 2012 |
| 1999 | 93 | 2004 | 2007+ |
| 1998 | 82 | 2000 | 2003 |
| 1997 | 93 | 2005 | 2009 |
| 1996 | 90 | 2001 | 2004 |
| 1995 | 94 | 2000 | 2003 |
| 1994 | 93 | 2002 | 2006 |

# Virgin Hills

Salisbury Road, Lauriston Vic 3444. Tel: 1800 777 444. Fax: 1800 777 444.
Website: www.virginhills.com.au  Email: info@virginhills.com.au
Region: **Macedon Ranges**  Winemaker: **Josh Steele**  Viticulturist: **Neil Orton**  Chief Executive: **Michael Hope**
Virgin Hills is a marginal, mature and historically important small Victorian vineyard at Kyneton whose single eponymous wine, a blend of several red Bordeaux varieties and shiraz, has been rather thin and herbal in recent years. Under new ownership and management, it might return to its old quality.

## VIRGIN HILLS (Cabernet blend)

| Macedon Ranges | $30–$49 |
|---|---|
| Current vintage: 2000 | 78 |

Tinny, vegetal, green and soupy.

| 2000 | 78 | 2002 | 2005 |
|---|---|---|---|
| 1998 | 86 | 2003 | 2006 |
| 1997 | 80 | 2002 | 2005 |
| 1995 | 81 | 1997 | 2000 |
| 1994 | 91 | 2002 | 2006 |
| 1993 | 87 | 2001 | 2005 |
| 1992 | 90 | 2000 | 2004+ |
| 1991 | 94 | 2003 | 2011 |
| 1990 | 87 | 1998 | 2002+ |
| 1988 | 93 | 1996 | 2000 |
| 1987 | 89 | 1999 | 2004 |
| 1985 | 94 | 1993 | 1997 |

# Voyager Estate

Stevens Road, Margaret River WA 6285. Tel: (08) 9757 6354. Fax: (08) 9757 6494.
Website: www.voyagerestate.com.au  Email: wine@voyagerestate.com.au
Region: **Margaret River**  Winemaker: **Cliff Royle**  Viticulturist: **Steve James**  Chief Executive: **Michael Wright**
A spectacular Margaret River winery development, Voyager Estate has become one of the region's leading makers. It does well with most of the classic Margaret River varieties, although I am still to be convinced by its 'premier' and substantially more expensive Tom Price wines. Its exceptionally elegant and pristine 2002 Chardonnay is its best white ever released, and there's inside word that the 2003 reaches similar levels. The Rhôney 2001 Shiraz is complex and meaty, while the 2003 Sauvignon Blanc Semillon is racy and refreshing.

## CABERNET SAUVIGNON MERLOT

RANKING **3**

| Margaret River | $30–$49 |
|---|---|
| Current vintage: 2000 | 91 |

Elegant, rather stylish regional cabernet with a dusty, lightly herbal aroma of violets and black-berries, cassis and dark plums. There's a whiff of regional earthiness, plus some tight-knit cedary oak. Long, spotless and pristine, supple and earthy, it's smooth and easy drinking, with pleasing fine-grained tannins.

| 2000 | 91 | 2008 | 2012 |
|---|---|---|---|
| 1999 | 92 | 2011 | 2019 |
| 1998 | 96 | 2010 | 2018 |
| 1997 | 91 | 2005 | 2009 |
| 1996 | 95 | 2004 | 2008+ |
| 1995 | 95 | 2003 | 2007+ |
| 1994 | 94 | 2006 | 2014 |

## CHARDONNAY

RANKING 2

VOYAGER ESTATE
MARGARET RIVER

2002 | CHARDONNAY

PRODUCT OF AUSTRALIA 750 ML

**Margaret River**     $30–$49
**Current vintage: 2002**     **95**

Particularly stylish, tightly balanced and focused Margaret River chardonnay whose tangy citrus and pineapple aromas are backed by lightly charry oak and minerally lees-derived aspects. Long, bright and crystalline palate of excellent length and sculpted shape. There's some fluffy texture and lemon meringue-like flavour in the middle of the palate, which culminates in a tight, citrusy finish.

| | | | |
|---|---|---|---|
| 2002 | 95 | 2007 | 2010 |
| 2001 | 93 | 2006 | 2009 |
| 2000 | 93 | 2005 | 2008 |
| 1999 | 94 | 2001 | 2004 |
| 1998 | 88 | 2000 | 2003 |
| 1997 | 90 | **1999** | **2002** |
| 1996 | 91 | **1998** | **2001** |

## SAUVIGNON BLANC SEMILLON

RANKING 3

VOYAGER ESTATE
MARGARET RIVER

2003 | SAUVIGNON BLANC
SEMILLON

PRODUCT OF AUSTRALIA 750 ML

**Margaret River**     $20–$29
**Current vintage: 2003**     **93**

Vivacious, penetrative and herbal aromas of melon, passionfruit and tropical fruits, with a hint of soap and baby powder. Long, clean and mineral, with a crystal-clear expression of tangy, juicy citrus, melon and gooseberry flavours wrapped up in refreshing mineral acids.

| | | | |
|---|---|---|---|
| 2003 | 93 | 2004 | 2005+ |
| 2002 | 90 | 2004 | 2007 |
| 2001 | 87 | 2002 | 2003 |
| 2000 | 94 | 2005 | 2008 |
| 1999 | 95 | 2001 | 2004+ |
| 1996 | 95 | 2001 | 2004 |

## SEMILLON

RANKING 4

VOYAGER ESTATE
MARGARET RIVER

2001 | SEMILLON

PRODUCT OF AUSTRALIA 750 ML

**Margaret River**     $20–$29
**Current vintage: 2001**     **88**

Slightly over-oaked semillon whose citrusy, nutty, lightly herbal and nettle-like fruit aromas are over-shadowed by overt sweet, charred and vanilla oak influences. Long, tight and elegant, with lively melon flavours culminating in a drying, toasty finish and refreshing acidity.

| | | | |
|---|---|---|---|
| 2001 | 88 | 2003 | 2006 |
| 2000 | 91 | 2002 | 2005+ |
| 1999 | 90 | 2001 | 2004 |
| 1998 | 88 | 2000 | 2003 |
| 1997 | 92 | 2002 | 2005 |

## SHIRAZ

RANKING 3

VOYAGER ESTATE
MARGARET RIVER

2002 | SHIRAZ

PRODUCT OF AUSTRALIA 750 ML

**Margaret River**     $20–$29
**Current vintage: 2001**     **94**

Pungent, meaty and spicy aromas of raspberries and red cherries, mulberries and cassis are earthy and slightly reductive. Cedar/vanilla oak is scented and perfumed with white and black pepper, cloves and nutmeg. The robust, leathery palate reveals evolved, complex and meaty animal hide flavours, clearly made in a rustic, Rhône-like style of some conviction. Firm and smooth, it is framed with supple, fine tannins.

| | | | |
|---|---|---|---|
| 2001 | 94 | 2006 | 2009 |
| 2000 | 88 | 2005 | 2008 |
| 1999 | 92 | 2004 | 2007 |

## TOM PRICE CABERNET SAUVIGNON

RANKING 5

TOM PRICE

CABERNET SAUVIGNON 1995

VOYAGER ESTATE

PRODUCT OF AUSTRALIA 750ML

**Margaret River**     $50+
**Current vintage: 2000**     **87**

Green-edged leafy, capsicum and pea-like aromas with undertones of dusty, cedary and minty small red berries and menthol. Its assertive, but under-ripe tannins shroud its herbal fruit qualities and tight-knit cedar/vanilla oak, culminating in a grippy, but sappy finish.

| | | | |
|---|---|---|---|
| 1995 | 87 | 2003 | 2007 |
| 1994 | 89 | 2002 | 2006+ |
| 1992 | 89 | **1997** | **2000** |

## TOM PRICE WHITE BLEND

RANKING 4

TOM PRICE

| Margaret River | $30–$49 | 2000 | 90 | 2002 | 2005+ |
|---|---|---|---|---|---|
| Current vintage: 2000 | 90 | 1997 | 89 | 1999 | 2002 |
| | | 1996 | 93 | 2001 | 2004 |

Cut grass Margaret River semillon and lively, nutty vanilla oak aromas precede a juicy and lightly toasty palate of shape and elegance. Very herbal and supported by sweet vanilla oak, it's long and tangy, culminating in a lemony finish of mineral acids.

VOYAGER ESTATE

# Wandin Valley Estate

Wilderness Road, Lovedale, NSW 2320. Tel: (02) 4930 7317. Fax: (02) 4930 7814.
Website: www.wandinvalley.com.au  Email: wanval@ozemail.com.au
Region: **Lower Hunter Valley** Winemaker: **Sarah-Kate Wilson** Viticulturist: **Brian Hubbard**
Chief Executive: **James & Philippa Davern**
A small Hunter vineyard and winery, Wandin Valley Estate has produced some round and juicy Reserve Chardonnay, and some sumptuous, chocolatey and peppery Bridie's Shiraz.

## BRIDIE'S SHIRAZ

RANKING 4

WANDIN VALLEY
ESTATE

| Lower Hunter Valley | $20–$29 | 2001 | 83 | 2003 | 2006 |
|---|---|---|---|---|---|
| Current vintage: 2001 | 83 | 2000 | 90 | 2008 | 2012 |
| | | 1998 | 93 | 2006 | 2010+ |

Light, earthy and under-ripe red lacking its customary weight and richness. Its oaky palate finishes thin and green-edged.

# Wantirna Estate

10 Bushy Park Lane, Wantirna South Vic 3152. Tel: (03) 9801 2367. Fax: (03) 9887 0225
Region: **Yarra Valley** Winemakers: **Maryann Egan, Reg Egan** Viticulturist: **Reg Egan** Chief Executive: **Reg Egan**
Wantirna Estate's spotlessly crafted, elegant and fine-grained table wines typically reveal deeply scented perfumes of pristine fruit and fine-grained oak, before elegant, supple and seamless palates of intensity and integration. Despite their elegance and charm, as well as the near-fragility of some youthful Pinot Noir, they tend to cellar beautifully, reliant on their balance, fine-grained tannins and depth of fruit, to acquire richness and strength.

## AMELIA CABERNET SAUVIGNON MERLOT

RANKING 2

Wantirna Estate

Amelia Cabernet Sauvignon / Merlot

| Yarra Valley | $30–$49 | 2002 | 93 | 2010 | 2014+ |
|---|---|---|---|---|---|
| Current vintage: 2002 | 93 | 2001 | 95 | 2009 | 2013 |
| | | 2000 | 95 | 2008 | 2012+ |
| | | 1999 | 94 | 2007 | 2011+ |
| | | 1998 | 94 | 2006 | 2010 |
| | | 1997 | 96 | 2009 | 2017 |
| | | 1996 | 92 | 2004 | 2008 |
| | | 1995 | 94 | 2003 | 2007+ |

A firm and tightly structured blend with a lightly minty perfume of dark plums, small black and red berries, cedar/chocolate oak and underlying notes of dried herbs and forest floor. Its minty and sumptuous expression of vibrant blackcurrant, raspberries and sour cherries is both elegant, and fine-grained, but overlies a firm, slightly raw-edged extract.

## HANNAH CABERNET FRANC MERLOT

RANKING 2

Wantirna Estate

Hannah Cabernet Franc / Merlot

| Yarra Valley | $30–$49 | 2002 | 93 | 2007 | 2010+ |
|---|---|---|---|---|---|
| Current vintage: 2002 | 93 | 2001 | 95 | 2009 | 2013+ |
| | | 2000 | 95 | 2008 | 2012+ |
| | | 1999 | 95 | 2007 | 2011 |

Fine, supple and elegant claret style with a fragrant and slightly minty perfume of raspberries, blackberries and dark cherries over spicy, clove-like and fine-grained cedary oak. Smooth and stylish, long and vibrant, its pristine and intense flavours of red berries and plums are tightly knit with classy new oak and a surprisingly firm extract of silky tannins. A faint herbal edge is the only thing between this wine and a higher score.

## ISABELLA CHARDONNAY

**Yarra Valley** $30–$49
**Current vintage: 2003** 95

Elegant and tight-knit chardonnay with a delicate, spicy bouquet of peach, melon and pineapple fruit, nuances of wheatmeal and fine-grained clove/vanilla oak. Long and smooth, the palate has a seamless quality and babyfat-like texture, as its cumquat, peach and nectarine fruit and nutty, savoury oak finish dry and mineral, with slightly funky notes of lees-derived complexity.

| | | | |
|---|---|---|---|
| 2003 | 95 | 2008 | 2011 |
| 2002 | 96 | 2007 | 2010 |
| 2000 | 93 | 2005 | 2008 |
| 1999 | 90 | 2001 | 2004+ |
| 1998 | 95 | 2003 | 2006+ |
| 1997 | 93 | 2002 | 2005+ |
| 1996 | 96 | 2004 | 2008 |
| 1994 | 94 | 2002 | 2006 |

## LILY PINOT NOIR

RANKING 2

**Yarra Valley** $30–$49
**Current vintage: 2003** 94

Supple, willowy pinot with a spicy fragrance of rose petals, confection-like red cherries, plums and sweet vanilla oak. Its fine, juicy palate has a fleshiness and depth of pristine, penetrative varietal fruit tightly framed by fine-grained tannins and slightly chocolate-like vanilla oak. It finishes long and spicy, with a suggestion of fresh mint. Certain to build in the bottle.

| | | | |
|---|---|---|---|
| 2003 | 94 | 2008 | 2011 |
| 2002 | 95 | 2007 | 2010 |
| 2001 | 94 | 2006 | 2009 |
| 2000 | 95 | 2005 | 2008 |
| 1999 | 97 | 2004 | 2007+ |
| 1998 | 94 | 2003 | 2006 |
| 1997 | 95 | 2002 | 2005 |
| 1996 | 92 | 2001 | 2004+ |
| 1995 | 92 | 2000 | 2003 |

# Warrenmang

Mountain Creek Road, Moonambel Vic 3478. Tel: (03) 5467 2233. Fax: (03) 5467 2309.
Website: www.bazzani.com.au/warrenmang  Email: mail@pyreneeswines.com.au
Region: **Pyrenees** Winemaker: **Brett Duffin** Viticulturist: **Luigi Bazzani** Chief Executive: **Luigi Bazzani**

Warrenmang is presently part of a complex and very ambitious public offering also involving the nearby GlenKara Estate vineyard and the Massoni brands. Its reds offer the richness and flavour of Pyrenees fruit, but typically lack polish and finesse. The vineyard has also been affected by severe ongoing drought conditions.

## ESTATE SHIRAZ

RANKING 4

**Pyrenees** $20–$29
**Current vintage: 2002** 81

Spicy, meaty aromas of cooked plums and dark cherries with earthy undertones of cloves, cinnamon and pepper. Forward and then rather thin, its licorice-like flavours of slightly stressed blackcurrant and raspberry fruit do their best to handle some dirty, stale oak influences.

| | | | |
|---|---|---|---|
| 2002 | 81 | 2007 | 2010+ |
| 2001 | 89 | 2006 | 2009 |
| 2000 | 93 | 2012 | 2020 |
| 1999 | 92 | 2004 | 2007+ |
| 1998 | 81 | 2003 | 2006 |
| 1997 | 90 | 2002 | 2005+ |
| 1996 | 89 | 2004 | 2008 |
| 1995 | 80 | 2000 | 2003 |
| 1994 | 88 | 1999 | 2002 |
| 1993 | 90 | 2001 | 2005 |
| 1992 | 93 | 2004 | 2012 |

## GRAND PYRENEES

RANKING 5

**Pyrenees** $30–$49
**Current vintage: 2001** 89

Robust and generous, if rather blocky red with an earthy, menthol-like bouquet of spicy, slightly cooked plum and redcurrant-like fruit and vanilla oak. Assertive and firm, it opens up to reveal more berry sweetness and harmony, with lingering plum and currant-like fruit.

| | | | |
|---|---|---|---|
| 2001 | 89 | 2009 | 2013 |
| 2000 | 84 | 2005 | 2008+ |
| 1999 | 88 | 2007 | 2011+ |
| 1998 | 89 | 2006 | 2012 |
| 1997 | 86 | 2005 | 2009 |
| 1996 | 87 | 2004 | 2008 |
| 1995 | 87 | 2003 | 2007 |
| 1993 | 89 | 2001 | 2005 |
| 1992 | 88 | 2000 | 2004 |
| 1990 | 88 | 2002 | 2007 |
| 1989 | 82 | 1997 | 2003 |
| 1988 | 91 | 2000 | 2005 |

# Water Wheel

Raywood Road, Bridgewater-on-Loddon Vic 3516. Tel: (03) 5437 3060. Fax: (03) 5437 3082.
Website: www.waterwheelwine.com  Email: info@waterwheelwine.com
Region: **Bendigo**  Winemakers: **Peter Cumming, Bill Trevaskis**  Viticulturist: **Peter Cumming**
Chief Executive: **Peter Cumming**
Water Wheel is a very consumer-friendly operation of surprising scale given its relatively modest winemaking facility. Its typically ripe and forward varietal table wines are usually well-made, fresh and fruity, with generous length of palate flavour. The pick of the current crop is the spicy 2002 Shiraz.

## CABERNET SAUVIGNON

RANKING **5**

| Bendigo | $12–$19 |
|---|---|
| **Current vintage: 2002** | **87** |

Honest, if slightly cooked cabernet with a stewy aroma of plums, marzipan, sweet berries and liqueur cherries. Oak is also restrained on the firm, moderately full palate of spicy, currant-like fruit and rather coarse, drying tannins. There's good length, and the wine should develop well in the bottle.

| 2002 | 87 | 2007 | 2010 |
|---|---|---|---|
| 2001 | 88 | 2009 | 2013 |
| 2000 | 89 | 2008 | 2012 |
| 1999 | 87 | 2004 | 2007+ |
| 1998 | 91 | 2006 | 2010 |
| 1997 | 92 | 2002 | 2005+ |
| 1996 | 91 | 2001 | 2004 |
| 1995 | 90 | 2000 | 2003 |

## CHARDONNAY

RANKING **5**

| Bendigo | $12–$19 |
|---|---|
| **Current vintage: 2003** | **81** |

Slightly simple, confected and forward chardonnay with a sawdusty, cashew-like peachy aroma and a greenish palate that lacks its customary length and brightness.

| 2003 | 81 | 2003 | 2004+ |
|---|---|---|---|
| 2002 | 82 | 2002 | 2003 |
| 2001 | 87 | 2001 | 2002 |
| 2000 | 89 | 2000 | 2001 |
| 1999 | 89 | 2001 | 2004 |

## SHIRAZ

RANKING **4**

| Bendigo | $12–$19 |
|---|---|
| **Current vintage: 2002** | **92** |

Very balanced and harmonious central Victorian shiraz whose meaty, musky aromas of dark berries, plums and vanilla oak precede a smooth and surprisingly elegant palate. Lively, concentrated fresh berry fruits and licorice-like spiciness are framed by a fine cut of bony tannins, before a lingering savoury finish. If not for a slight rawness about its oak, I would have marked this wine higher.

| 2002 | 92 | 2007 | 2010 |
|---|---|---|---|
| 2001 | 87 | 2006 | 2009 |
| 2000 | 89 | 2005 | 2008+ |
| 1999 | 88 | 2004 | 2007 |
| 1998 | 94 | 2007 | 2010 |
| 1997 | 90 | 2005 | 2009+ |
| 1996 | 93 | 2004 | 2008 |
| 1995 | 89 | 2003 | 2007 |
| 1994 | 93 | 1999 | 2002+ |

# Wellington

Cnr Richmond & Denholms Roads, Cambridge Tas 7170. Tel: (03) 6248 5844. Fax: (03) 6248 5855.
Email: wellington@hoodwines.com
Region: **Southern Tasmania**  Winemaker: **Andrew Hood**  Chief Executive: **Andrew Hood**
Made by one of Tasmania's best winemakers in Andrew Hood, Wellington's wines are long and intensely flavoured, but fine and restrained. The whites are pleasingly crisp and acidic, exemplified by the steely and mineral 2003 Riesling, while the 2002 Pinot Noir is supple and charming.

## CHARDONNAY

RANKING **4**

| Southern Tasmania | $20–$29 |
|---|---|
| **Current vintage: 2002** | **88** |

Lightly floral, tropical and herbal aromas of peach and honeydew melon precede a juicy, lively and uncomplicated palate of nutty, lightly herbal primary fruit, culminating in a lightly green-edged mineral finish.

| 2002 | 88 | 2004 | 2007 |
|---|---|---|---|
| 2001 | 87 | 2003 | 2006 |
| 2000 | 91 | 2005 | 2008 |
| 1999 | 90 | 2004 | 2007 |
| 1998 | 90 | 2003 | 2006+ |
| 1997 | 87 | 2002 | 2005 |
| 1996 | 86 | 1998 | 2001 |
| 1995 | 89 | 2000 | 2003 |
| 1994 | 87 | 1996 | 1999 |

A B C D E F G H I J K L M N O P Q R S T U V W X Y Z

## ICED RIESLING

RANKING **4**

**Southern Tasmania $20–$29 (375 ml)**
**Current vintage: 2003**     **83**

Sweet, luscious and citrusy, this slightly contrived dessert wine has an estery, lemon tart aroma and a rather cloying palate of apple, pear and tinned pineapple flavour. It finishes a little raw and disjointed, with spicy citrusy undertones.

| 2003 | 83 | 2004 | 2005+ |
|---|---|---|---|
| 2000 | 93 | 2005 | 2008 |
| 1999 | 92 | 2004 | 2007 |
| 1998 | 83 | 1999 | 2000 |
| 1997 | 89 | 1999 | 2002 |

## PINOT NOIR

RANKING **4**

**Southern Tasmania**     **$20–$29**
**Current vintage: 2002**     **90**

Pristine aromas of rose petals, dark cherries and a hint of undergrowth precede a smooth, silky and willowy palate supported by pleasingly firm tannins and tightly integrated oak. There's just a hint of herbaceousness beneath its lively flavours of plums and red berries. Quite a charmer.

| 2002 | 90 | 2004 | 2007 |
|---|---|---|---|
| 2001 | 88 | 2003 | 2006 |
| 2000 | 89 | 2002 | 2005 |
| 1999 | 89 | 2001 | 2004 |
| 1998 | 92 | 2000 | 2003 |
| 1997 | 89 | 2002 | 2005 |
| 1994 | 90 | 1999 | 2002 |

## RIESLING

RANKING **3**

**Southern Tasmania**     **$20–$29**
**Current vintage: 2003**     **92**

Tangy, mineral riesling with an underlying chalkiness beneath its slightly estery aroma of fresh limes and tropical fruits. Juicy and forward, its palate then becomes long and steely, with a rich, round middle of intense green apple/pear flavours culminating in a long, lemony finish. Good definition and presence; should develop well.

| 2003 | 92 | 2008 | 2011 |
|---|---|---|---|
| 2000 | 91 | 2005 | 2008 |
| 1999 | 95 | 2007 | 2011 |
| 1998 | 89 | 2000 | 2003+ |
| 1997 | 89 | 2002 | 2005 |

# Wendouree

Wendouree Road, Clare SA 5453. Tel: (08) 8842 2896.

Region: **Clare Valley** Winemakers: **Tony & Lita Brady** Viticulturist: **I Cherchi**
Chief Executive: **Tony Brady**

I'm delighted to include Wendouree's wines in this edition, and offer sincere thanks to Craig Caulfied of Winewindow, who was instrumental in the recent vertical tastings that provided these ratings. The tastings blew apart a popular Wendouree myth — that you have to wait for decades for the wines to become ready to drink. Aside from the exceptional quality of many of the Shiraz and Shiraz Mataro wines we tasted from this iconic Clare Valley vineyard, I was totally taken aback by the balance, harmony and approachability of many of the wines.

## SHIRAZ

RANKING **2**

**Clare Valley**     **$50+**
**Current vintage: 2001**     **89**

An assertive, powerful shiraz with fragrant, meaty aromas of sweet berries, overtones of spicy prunes, currants and plums, plus a suggestion of black pepper. Richly structured, but lacking its customary core of vibrant fruit, it's perhaps a wine of shorter-term cellaring than usual from this vineyard.

| 2001 | 89 | 2009 | 2013+ |
|---|---|---|---|
| 2000 | 88 | 2008 | 2012 |
| 1999 | 96 | 2019 | 2029 |
| 1998 | 97 | 2018 | 2028+ |
| 1997 | 89 | 2009 | 2017+ |
| 1996 | 95 | 2008 | 2016+ |
| 1995 | 94 | 2015 | 2025 |
| 1994 | 91 | 2006 | 2014+ |
| 1993 | 86 | 2001 | 2005+ |
| 1992 | 91 | 2012 | 2022 |
| 1991 | 96 | 2021 | 2031 |
| 1990 | 90 | 2010 | 2020+ |
| 1989 | 93 | 2009 | 2019 |
| 1988 | 93 | 2008 | 2018 |
| 1987 | 88 | 1999 | 2007 |
| 1985 | 95 | 2005 | 2015 |
| 1983 | 89 | 2003 | 2013+ |

## SHIRAZ MATARO

| | | | |
|---|---|---|---|
| **Clare Valley** | | | **$50+** |
| **Current vintage: 2001** | | | **90** |

A smooth, polished and very concentrated red with a spicy, violet-like perfume of sweet plums, cassis and mint over smoky nuances of mocha. Very ripe, fractionally cooked and currant-like it's round and concentrated, lifted by smooth and polished tannins, but just ends a fractional flat at the finish.

| 2001 | 90 | 2021 | 2031 |
|---|---|---|---|
| 2000 | 87 | 2008 | 2012+ |
| 1999 | 95 | 2019 | 2029 |
| 1998 | 96 | 2018 | 2028+ |
| 1997 | 88 | 2009 | 2017 |
| 1996 | 94 | 2016 | 2026 |
| 1995 | 94 | 2005 | 2015+ |
| 1994 | 87 | 2004 | 2014 |
| 1991 | 95 | 2011 | 2021 |
| 1988 | 93 | 2000 | 2008+ |
| 1987 | 89 | 1999 | 2007 |
| 1977 | 94 | 1997 | 2007 |
| 1976 | 94 | 2006 | 2016 |
| 1975 | 89 | 1995 | 2005+ |

# Westend

1283 Brayne Road, Griffith NSW 2680. Tel: (02) 6964 1506. Fax: (02) 6962 1673.
Email: westend@webfront.net.au
Region: **Riverina** Winemakers: **William Calabria, Bryan Currie** Viticulturist: **Anthony Trimboli**
Chief Executive: **William Calabria**

Where there's a will, there's a way, which must surely come close to expressing Bill Calabria's very serious intent to create wines of stature and structure from Griffith-based vineyards. He's been doing it for long enough to prove it's no fluke, and his activities seriously put to question the attitude the Australian wine industry has long held towards the inland river regions and what they are capable of achieving. At a time when Australia is being regularly challenged to improve its bottom line in quality, Westend stands out like a beacon as a role model for other companies to follow. Anyone in any doubt should wrap their larynx around some 2002 Shiraz.

## 3 BRIDGES CABERNET SAUVIGNON

| | | | |
|---|---|---|---|
| **Riverina** | | | **$20–$29** |
| **Current vintage: 2002** | | | **88** |

Sweet violet and cassis aromas with mocha/cedary oak and minty undertones of eucalypt and dried herbs precede an oaky, forward and earthy palate of up-front jammy fruit. It's plummy, minty and vibrant, with a slightly hollow centre, and lacks the depth and structure for longer cellaring.

| 2002 | 88 | 2004 | 2007+ |
|---|---|---|---|
| 2001 | 91 | 2006 | 2009+ |
| 2000 | 87 | 2002 | 2005+ |
| 1999 | 89 | 2004 | 2007 |
| 1998 | 90 | 2003 | 2006+ |
| 1997 | 90 | 1999 | 2002+ |

## 3 BRIDGES CHARDONNAY

| | | | |
|---|---|---|---|
| **Riverina** | | | **$12–$19** |
| **Current vintage: 2003** | | | **87** |

Slightly cooked and mealy aromas of citrus fruit and buttery vanilla oak, before a generous, round and fruity palate of length and smoothness. Its nutty melon and citrus flavours finish soft and savoury, with refreshing acids.

| 2003 | 87 | 2004 | 2005+ |
|---|---|---|---|
| 2002 | 87 | 2003 | 2004 |
| 2001 | 84 | 2002 | 2002 |
| 2000 | 88 | 2001 | 2002+ |
| 1999 | 87 | 2000 | 2001 |
| 1998 | 87 | 1999 | 2000 |

## 3 BRIDGES DURIF

| | | | |
|---|---|---|---|
| **Riverina** | | | **$20–$29** |
| **Current vintage: 2003** | | | **89** |

A briary, spicy durif with an oaky, dark and spicy aromas of plums, dark currants with nutty undertones of raisins and prunes. Powerfully fruit, dark and concentrated, it drips with licorice-like flavours of dark fruit while creamy oak and smooth tannins do the rest.

| 2003 | 89 | 2005 | 2008 |
|---|---|---|---|
| 2002 | 93 | 2007 | 2010 |
| 2001 | 87 | 2003 | 2006+ |
| 2000 | 91 | 2005 | 2008+ |

## 3 BRIDGES RESERVE BOTRYTIS SEMILLON RANKING 5

**Riverina** $20–$29 (375 ml)
**Current vintage: 2003** 87

Buttery, toasty aromas of marmalade, apricot and melon are backed by slightly varnishy vanilla oak. Sweet and syrupy, the palate is luscious, forward and approachable, already showing some evolution. A low botrytis style, with juicy green melon flavours and clean, refreshing acidity.

| | | | |
|---|---|---|---|
| 2003 | 87 | 2005 | 2008 |
| 2002 | 89 | 2003 | 2004+ |
| 2001 | 88 | 2002 | 2003 |
| 1999 | 91 | 2001 | 2004+ |
| 1998 | 87 | 1999 | 2000 |
| 1997 | 94 | 1999 | 2002+ |
| 1996 | 90 | 1998 | 2001 |
| 1995 | 84 | 1996 | 1997 |

## 3 BRIDGES SHIRAZ RANKING 4

**Riverina** $20–$29
**Current vintage: 2002** 91

Sumptuous, chewy shiraz with a spicy and slightly minty fragrance of cassis, raspberries and dark plums, with overt chocolate/vanilla oak and underlying nuances of menthol. Richly fruited and assertively wooded, its handsomely structured palate steamrolls along, leaving a trail of lingering spicy dark fruits and sweet oak in its wake. Firm, but fine tannins frame this Riverland classic.

| | | | |
|---|---|---|---|
| 2002 | 91 | 2007 | 2010+ |
| 2001 | 90 | 2006 | 2009 |
| 2000 | 91 | 2005 | 2008+ |
| 1999 | 86 | 2001 | 2004 |

# Will Taylor

1B Victoria Avenue, Unley Park SA 5061. Tel: (08) 8271 6122. Fax: (08) 8271 6122.
Email: suzanne@willtaylor.com.au
Regions: **Various** Chief Executive: **Will Taylor**

Will Taylor is a virtual winery business that produces a range of table wines from Victoria, South Australia and New South Wales. The best of these are the two of the proven historic classics of Australian white wine: Clare Valley Riesling and Hunter Valley Semillon. The current releases are somewhat below usual par.

## CLARE VALLEY RIESLING RANKING 4

**Clare Valley** $12–$19
**Current vintage: 2003** 81

Rather broad and cooked, toasty and buttery, this very developed wine lacks its typical freshness and vitality, finishing hollow and hard-edged.

| | | | |
|---|---|---|---|
| 2003 | 81 | 2004 | 2005 |
| 2002 | 91 | 2007 | 2010+ |
| 2001 | 93 | 2009 | 2013+ |
| 2000 | 82 | 2001 | 2002 |
| 1999 | 88 | 2004 | 2007 |
| 1998 | 93 | 2003 | 2006 |

## HUNTER VALLEY SEMILLON RANKING 4

**Lower Hunter Valley** $12–$19
**Current vintage: 2003** 83

Its sweaty, reductive and rubbery aromas have probably been exacerbated by the screwtop seal. They precede a tangy melon/lemony palate that fades towards a lean and metallic finish.

| | | | |
|---|---|---|---|
| 2003 | 83 | 2004 | 2005+ |
| 2002 | 89 | 2004 | 2007+ |
| 2001 | 90 | 2006 | 2009+ |
| 2000 | 87 | 2001 | 2002 |
| 1999 | 90 | 2007 | 2011 |
| 1998 | 90 | 2003 | 2006 |

# Wilson Vineyard, The

Polish Hill Road, Sevenhill via Clare SA 5453. Tel: (08) 8843 4310.
Website: www.wilsonvineyard.com.au
Region: **Clare Valley** Winemakers: **Daniel Wilson, Dr John Wilson** Viticulturist: **Dr John Wilson**
Chief Executive: **Dr John Wilson**
The Wilson Vineyard is another of the Clare Valley's producers of classic Australian riesling. As the 2003 release illustrates, this vineyard's style is tight and fine, with a typically clean, clear palate, a fine chalky texture before a refreshing mineral finish. Its rather earthy and rustic variation on the Australian sparkling red wine theme is known as Hippocrene, which has released some very complex wines in previous years.

## GALLERY SERIES RIESLING

RANKING **4**

| | Clare Valley | $12–$19 |
|---|---|---|
| | **Current vintage: 2003** | **91** |

Closed, long-term riesling whose delicate and restrained lemon and lime juice aromas precede a taut, dry and austere palate offering a very reserved expression of pear and lime flavours. It finishes tight and savoury, with slate-like influences and lemony acids.

| 2003 | 91 | 2011 | 2015+ |
|---|---|---|---|
| 2002 | 89 | 2007 | 2010 |
| 2001 | 88 | 2006 | 2009 |
| 2000 | 91 | 2005 | 2008+ |
| 1999 | 94 | 2007 | 2011+ |
| 1998 | 95 | 2006 | 2010+ |
| 1997 | 87 | 2002 | 2005 |
| 1996 | 93 | 2004 | 2008 |
| 1995 | 94 | 2003 | 2007 |
| 1994 | 91 | 2002 | 2006 |
| 1993 | 90 | 1998 | 2001 |

## HIPPOCRENE

RANKING **5**

| | Clare Valley | $20–$29 |
|---|---|---|
| | **Current vintage: 1996** | **82** |

Tired, leathery and shaded fruit aromas precede a rustic, farmyard-like palate that has seen fresher days.

| 1996 | 82 | 1998 | 2001 |
|---|---|---|---|
| Bin 95 | 89 | 2000 | 2003+ |
| Bin 94 | 82 | 1996 | 1999 |
| Bin 93 | 80 | 1998 | 2001 |
| Bin 92 | 82 | 1997 | 2000 |
| Bin 91 | 92 | 1996 | 1999 |
| Bin 90 | 93 | 1998 | 2002 |

# Wirra Wirra

McMurtrie Road, McLaren Vale SA 5171. Tel: (08) 8323 8414. Fax: (08) 8323 8596.
Website: www.wirra.com.au Email: info@wirra.com.au
Region: **McLaren Vale, Various SA** Winemaker: **Samantha Connew** Viticulturist: **Tony Hoare**
Chief Executive: **Tim James**
Recent vintages have been tough to Wirra Wirra, one of McLaren Vale's best and most consistent producers. Given the professionalism of the viticultural and winemaking team under the experienced Tim James, I don't expect it will be long before the company bounces back to its usual form, as the 2001 RSW Shiraz suggests.

## CHARDONNAY

RANKING **5**

| | McLaren Vale | $20–$29 |
|---|---|---|
| | **Current vintage: 2002** | **86** |

Toasty, brassy chardonnay with toffee-like and bacony melon-like aromas and a broad, rather fat palate that lacks freshness and length. There's perhaps an excess of malolactic influence whose butterscotch characters overshadow the wine's stonefruit qualities.

| 2002 | 86 | 2004 | 2007 |
|---|---|---|---|
| 2000 | 81 | 2001 | 2002 |
| 1999 | 87 | 2001 | 2004 |
| 1998 | 88 | 2000 | 2003 |
| 1997 | 89 | 1999 | 2002 |

## CHURCH BLOCK

RANKING **5**

| | McLaren Vale, | |
|---|---|---|
| | **Limestone Coast** | $20–$29 |
| | **Current vintage: 2002** | **86** |

Elegant, flavoursome and early-drinking blend with a fresh aroma of cassis, blackberries and dark cherries balanced by light cedar/vanilla oak. Smooth and supple, its medium-weight palate offers vibrant dark berry flavours and creamy oak framed by soft tannins. Finishes clean, but slightly green.

| 2002 | 86 | 2003 | 2004+ |
|---|---|---|---|
| 2001 | 81 | 2002 | 2003+ |
| 2000 | 83 | 2002 | 2005 |
| 1999 | 92 | 2004 | 2007 |
| 1998 | 93 | 2003 | 2006+ |
| 1997 | 93 | 2002 | 2005+ |
| 1996 | 87 | 1998 | 2001 |
| 1995 | 88 | 2000 | 2003 |
| 1994 | 93 | 1999 | 2002 |
| 1993 | 91 | 1998 | 2001 |

## HAND PICKED RIESLING

RANKING 5

**Fleurieu Peninsula, Coonawarra, Grampians** $12–$19
**Current vintage: 2003** 86

Early-drinking riesling with a lightly herbaceous and tropical aroma of guava-like fruit before a juicy, rather full palate whose assertive, citrusy flavours finish with lively acids. A pleasant early-drinker.

| | | | |
|---|---|---|---|
| 2003 | 86 | 2004 | 2005 |
| 2002 | 82 | 2003 | 2004+ |
| 2001 | 87 | 2003 | 2006+ |
| 2000 | 82 | 2002 | 2005 |
| 1999 | 88 | 2001 | 2004+ |
| 1998 | 85 | 2003 | 2006 |
| 1997 | 86 | 1999 | 2002 |

## RSW SHIRAZ

RANKING 4

**McLaren Vale** $50+
**Current vintage: 2001** 91

Smooth, supple and harmoniously composed red with a perfume of ripe small cherries, plums and polished new vanilla, chocolate oak. Smooth and creamy, its smoky, earthy palate delivers pristine, bright flavours of small berry fruits tightly knit with cedary oak. Finishes long, with a fine, firm chassis of integrated tannins.

| | | | |
|---|---|---|---|
| 2001 | 91 | 2006 | 2009 |
| 2000 | 87 | 2002 | 2005+ |
| 1999 | 87 | 2004 | 2007 |
| 1998 | 94 | 2003 | 2006+ |
| 1997 | 90 | 2002 | 2005 |
| 1996 | 96 | 2004 | 2008 |
| 1995 | 92 | 2000 | 2003 |
| 1994 | 94 | 1999 | 2002 |
| 1993 | 91 | 1998 | 2001 |
| 1992 | 93 | 2000 | 2004 |

## SCRUBBY RISE WHITE

**Various South Australia** $12–$19
**Current vintage: 2003** 86

A distinctive spicy viognier perfume of apricot blossom overlies lightly herbal, lemony aromas, before a moderately full and generous, if slightly sweet and oily palate. Round, forward, slightly fat and lacking a little tightness, it finishes soft and easy.

| | | | |
|---|---|---|---|
| 2003 | 86 | 2004 | 2005 |
| 2002 | 87 | 2003 | 2004 |
| 2001 | 86 | 2001 | 2002 |
| 2000 | 80 | 2000 | 2001 |
| 1999 | 80 | 1999 | 2000 |
| 1998 | 87 | 2000 | 2003 |

## THE ANGELUS CABERNET SAUVIGNON

RANKING 4

**Adelaide, Coonawarra** $50+
**Current vintage: 2001** 87

Lightly herbal cabernet with an earthy aroma of leathery red berries, chocolate/vanilla oak and a leafy dustiness. Forward flavours of small red and black berries offset by creamy cedary oak precede a slightly thin and sappy finish.

| | | | |
|---|---|---|---|
| 2001 | 87 | 2006 | 2009 |
| 2000 | 90 | 2005 | 2008 |
| 1999 | 88 | 2004 | 2007 |
| 1998 | 95 | 2006 | 2010+ |
| 1997 | 86 | 2002 | 2005 |
| 1996 | 95 | 2004 | 2008+ |
| 1995 | 91 | 2003 | 2007 |
| 1994 | 88 | 1999 | 2002 |
| 1993 | 93 | 2001 | 2005 |
| 1992 | 93 | 2000 | 2004 |

# Wolf Blass

Sturt Highway, Nuriootpa SA 5355. Tel: (08) 8568 7303. Fax: (08) 8568 7380.
Website: www.wolfblass.com.au  Email: cellardoor@wolfblass.com.au

Regions: **Langhorne Creek, Barossa Valley, Various SA**
Winemakers: **John Glaetzer, Wendy Stuckey, Caroline Dunn, Chris Hatcher**
Viticulturist: **Vic Patrick** Chief Executive: **Jamie Odell**

All credit to Beringer Blass for gearing up the Wolf Blass label for some serious success. By reworking its hierarchy of labels into a clearly-defined collection of brands, Beringer has introduced new Grey Label, Gold Label and Red Label ranges, each of which has impressed me for quality. A genuine highlight is the 2002 Gold Label Chardonnay, while the 2002 Red Label Shiraz Cabernet is very impressive. I'm also very excited by the attention and effort being paid to the company's new flagship, the Platinum Label Shiraz, which in 2001 produced an absolute classic. Its new structure and quality should pay dividends for Wolf Blass, here and overseas.

## BLACK LABEL   RANKING 3

**Various, SA** $50+
**Current vintage: 2000** 92

Showing a little cut and polish, plus a lot of oak, this round, creamy and velvet-like red delivers ripe, if slightly baked fruit handsomely framed by smooth, fine-grained extract. Its confiture-like aromas of sweet blackberries and redcurrants, cinnamon, cloves and white pepper are given plenty of sweet vanilla/coconut oak, while its smooth and sumptuous palate is similarly composed, with deep flavours of ripe fruit and chocolate framed by fine-grained tannins. There's just a slight rawness about the oak treatment that holds back my score.

| | | | |
|---|---|---|---|
| 2000 | 92 | 2008 | 2012+ |
| 1999 | 95 | 2007 | 2011+ |
| 1998 | 93 | 2006 | 2010 |
| 1997 | 89 | 2005 | 2009 |
| 1996 | 93 | 2004 | 2008+ |
| 1995 | 90 | 2003 | 2007 |
| 1994 | 89 | 2000 | 2003 |
| 1993 | 93 | 2001 | 2005 |
| 1992 | 88 | 2000 | 2004 |
| 1991 | 95 | 2003 | 2011+ |
| 1990 | 94 | 2002 | 2010 |
| 1989 | 93 | 2001 | 2009 |
| 1988 | 94 | 1996 | 2000 |
| 1987 | 91 | 1995 | 1999 |
| 1986 | 94 | 1994 | 1998 |
| 1985 | 91 | 1993 | 1997 |
| 1984 | 93 | 1992 | 1996 |
| 1983 | 95 | 1995 | 2000 |
| 1982 | 90 | 1994 | 1999 |
| 1981 | 93 | 1993 | 1998 |
| 1980 | 94 | 1992 | 1997 |
| 1975 | 93 | 1995 | 2000 |

## BROWN LABEL SHIRAZ   RANKING 5

**Various, SA** $30–$49
**Current vintage: 2001** 88

A slightly schizophrenic red whose vibrant personality of pristine, jujube-like flavours of cassis and plums is slightly at odds with its cooked, meaty and pruney aspect which verges on the soupy and porty. The oak is very smoky and charry, with assertive vanillin characters, while its mouthfeel is smooth, jammy and creamy. Drink soon.

| | | | |
|---|---|---|---|
| 2001 | 88 | 2003 | 2006 |
| 2000 | 86 | 2002 | 2005 |
| 1999 | 88 | 2001 | 2004 |
| 1998 | 89 | 2006 | 2010 |
| 1997 | 88 | 2002 | 2005 |
| 1996 | 91 | 2004 | 2008 |
| 1995 | 87 | 2000 | 2003 |
| 1994 | 92 | 2002 | 2006 |
| 1993 | 89 | 1998 | 2001 |
| 1992 | 90 | 2000 | 2004 |
| 1990 | 92 | 1998 | 2002 |
| 1989 | 90 | 1997 | 2001 |
| 1988 | 93 | 1993 | 1996 |

## GOLD LABEL RIESLING   RANKING 3

**Clare Valley, Eden Valley** $12–$19
**Current vintage: 2003** 92

Intense aromas of musky, confectionary lime juice and lemon rind precede a forward, round and generous palate finishing with slatey, mineral acids. A little forward, broad and cooked for a higher rating.

| | | | |
|---|---|---|---|
| 2003 | 92 | 2005 | 2006 |
| 2002 | 94 | 2007 | 2010 |
| 2001 | 95 | 2006 | 2009+ |
| 2000 | 90 | 2002 | 2005 |
| 1999 | 90 | 2001 | 2004 |
| 1998 | 94 | 2003 | 2006 |
| 1997 | 91 | 2002 | 2005 |
| 1996 | 94 | 2004 | 2008 |
| 1995 | 87 | 1997 | 2000 |
| 1994 | 93 | 1999 | 2002 |

## GREY LABEL CABERNET SAUVIGNON

RANKING 4

**Various, SA** $30–$49
**Current vintage: 2002** 88

Very intense, minty eucalypt-like aromas of cassis and plums are backed by lightly smoky, cedar/vanilla oak. Long, fine and elegant, its searingly intense berry flavours are tightly knit with sweet oak and silky tannins. If it were not for a saltiness about this wine, which is not uncommon amongst modern Langhorne Creek reds, it would be marked much higher.

| | | | |
|---|---|---|---|
| 2002 | 88 | 2010 | 2014 |
| 2001 | 90 | 2006 | 2009 |
| 1999 | 87 | 2004 | 2007 |
| 1997 | 84 | 1999 | 2002 |
| 1996 | 90 | 2001 | 2004+ |
| 1995 | 93 | 2002 | 2007 |
| 1994 | 94 | 2002 | 2006 |
| 1993 | 89 | 2001 | 2005 |
| 1992 | 93 | 2000 | 2004 |
| 1991 | 94 | 1999 | 2003 |
| 1990 | 91 | 1995 | 1998 |

## PLATINUM LABEL SHIRAZ

RANKING 1

**Various, SA** $50+
**Current vintage: 2001** 97

The only problem about this outstanding Adelaide Hills shiraz is that despite its promise of exceptional longevity, it is so drinkable right now that I doubt much will ever be tasted near its peak. Laced with spicy, musky scents of violets and black pepper, cassis and raspberries blueberries and blackberries, it's supported by vanilla and bubblegum-like new oak aromas. A long, plush palate of unbelievably pure, pristine and vibrant dark berry and plum fruits is tightly integrated with new oak and supported by the finest of tannins. It might be the most expensive, but it's the best Wolf Blass wine ever released.

| | | | |
|---|---|---|---|
| 2001 | 97 | 2013 | 2021+ |
| 2000 | 95 | 2008 | 2012 |
| 1999 | 95 | 2011 | 2019+ |
| 1998 | 96 | 2010 | 2018+ |

## RED LABEL SHIRAZ CABERNET

RANKING 5

**South-Eastern Australia** $5–$11
**Current vintage: 2002** 89

Remarkable value for money. Fragrant, floral, peppery and spicy aromas of slightly jammy black-berries and cassis fit neatly with lightly smoky oak. Fine and elegant, the palate delivers fresh, earthy flavours of small black and red berries of spiciness and intensity, finishing long with a fine grip to tight tannins.

| | | | |
|---|---|---|---|
| 2002 | 89 | 2004 | 2007 |
| 2001 | 86 | 2003 | 2006 |
| 1999 | 82 | 2000 | 2001 |
| 1998 | 81 | 2002 | 2003 |
| 1997 | 87 | 1999 | 2002 |
| 1996 | 82 | 1997 | 1998 |

## VINTAGE PINOT NOIR CHARDONNAY

RANKING 4

**Southern Australia** $20–$29
**Current vintage: 1999** 83

Forward, short and a little thin, lacking its customary fruit and freshness, with a creamy, lemony scent of slightly sweaty and confectionary aromas.

| | | | |
|---|---|---|---|
| 1999 | 83 | 2001 | 2004 |
| 1997 | 92 | 2002 | 2005 |
| 1996 | 92 | 1998 | 2001+ |
| 1995 | 89 | 1997 | 2000 |

## YELLOW LABEL CABERNET SAUVIGNON

RANKING 5

**Southern Australia** $12–$19
**Current vintage: 2002** 88

Competent, generous and relatively stylish inland cabernet whose minty flavours of cassis, mulber-ries and dried herbs are neatly matched with creamy and lightly smoky chocolate oak. It's lively, vital and even polished, well made and tightly integrated.

| | | | |
|---|---|---|---|
| 2002 | 88 | 2005 | 2008+ |
| 2001 | 87 | 2003 | 2006 |
| 2000 | 88 | 2002 | 2005+ |
| 1998 | 89 | 2003 | 2006 |
| 1997 | 81 | 1999 | 2002 |
| 1996 | 88 | 1998 | 2001 |
| 1995 | 87 | 2000 | 2003 |
| 1994 | 82 | 1996 | 1999 |

## YELLOW LABEL RIESLING

RANKING 5

**Various, SA** $5–$11
**Current vintage: 2003** 82

Estery, yeasty aromas of developing toasty, buttery and citrusy aromas with underlying baby powder-like scents of lime juice. Forward and oily, its apricot/orange rind fruit overlies a chalky, slightly stressed palate.

| | | | |
|---|---|---|---|
| 2003 | 82 | 2003 | 2004 |
| 2002 | 83 | 2003 | 2004 |
| 2001 | 92 | 2005 | 2008 |
| 2000 | 87 | 2001 | 2002 |
| 1999 | 86 | 2000 | 2001 |
| 1998 | 92 | 2000 | 2003 |
| 1997 | 87 | 1999 | 2002 |
| 1996 | 87 | 1998 | 2001 |

# Woodstock

Douglas Gully Road, McLaren Flat SA 5171. Tel: (08) 8383 0156. Fax: (08) 8383 0437.
Website: www.woodstockwine.com.au Email: woodstock@woodstockwine.com.au

Regions: **McLaren Vale, Limestone Coast** Winemaker: **Scott Collett** Viticulturist: **Scott Collett**
Chief Executive: **Scott Collett**

Woodstock is a well-established small McLaren Vale maker whose flagship red, The Stocks Shiraz, has undergone
a very impressive make-over into a very contemporary style for the 2002 vintage. I'm keen to see if this development
will ultimately be applied to the winery's other smooth, but more rustic varietal reds. Drinking now, the 2000
Chardonnay is honest and charming.

## BOTRYTIS SWEET WHITE

RANKING **4**

| McLaren Vale | $20–$29 (375 ml) |
|---|---|
| **Current vintage: 1999** | **87** |

Early-drinking dessert wine whose prune juice and orange rind aromas precede a thick, syrupy palate that manages not to be excessively cloying despite its sweetness and lusciousness. Tangy and tropical, with lingering melon and citrusy flavours.

| | | | |
|---|---|---|---|
| 1999 | 87 | 2001 | 2004 |
| 97–98 | 81 | 2000 | 2003 |
| 1996 | 92 | 2001 | 2004 |
| 1995 | 93 | 2000 | 2003 |
| 1994 | 91 | 2002 | 2006 |
| 1993 | 90 | **1995** | **1998** |

## CABERNET SAUVIGNON

| McLaren Vale | $20–$29 |
|---|---|
| **Current vintage: 2001** | **86** |

Very ripe cabernet with a slightly cooked aroma of plums, prunes and currants over dusty, earthy influences. Forward and up-front, the palate of stewed plum and red berry flavours then dries out, becoming a little lean and hard towards its finish of powdery tannins.

| | | | |
|---|---|---|---|
| 2001 | 86 | 2006 | 2009 |
| 2000 | 81 | 2002 | 2005 |
| 1999 | 84 | 2001 | 2004+ |
| 1998 | 86 | 2003 | 2006 |
| 1997 | 89 | 2005 | 2009 |
| 1996 | 87 | 2001 | 2004 |
| 1995 | 87 | 2000 | 2003 |
| 1994 | 93 | 2002 | 2006 |
| 1993 | 91 | 2001 | 2005 |
| 1992 | 93 | 2004 | 2012 |
| 1991 | 95 | 2003 | 2011 |
| 1990 | 92 | 1998 | 2002 |

## CHARDONNAY

RANKING **5**

| McLaren Vale | $20–$29 |
|---|---|
| **Current vintage: 2000** | **89** |

Pleasing drink-now chardonnay developing some lightly smoky, floral aromas of toasty cumquat marmalade and hints of mineral. Round, soft and uncomplicated, its generous, toasty palate of buttery fruit finishes with just a hint of greenish sappiness.

| | | | |
|---|---|---|---|
| 2000 | 89 | 2002 | 2005 |
| 1999 | 87 | **2000** | **2001** |
| 1998 | 89 | 2003 | 2006 |
| 1997 | 87 | **1999** | **2002** |
| 1996 | 93 | 2001 | 2004 |

## SHIRAZ

RANKING **4**

| Limestone Coast, | |
|---|---|
| McLaren Vale | $20–$29 |
| **Current vintage: 2001** | **86** |

Plump, juicy shiraz with a musky, lightly sweaty aroma of cassis and plums over a liniment-like suggestion of mint and menthol. Its approachable palate of vibrant fruit and sweet chocolate oak is backed by a note of camphor, finishing soft and smooth.

| | | | |
|---|---|---|---|
| 2001 | 86 | 2003 | 2006+ |
| 2000 | 90 | 2005 | 2008 |
| 1999 | 83 | 2001 | 2004 |
| 1998 | 92 | 2006 | 2010 |
| 1997 | 90 | 2002 | 2005+ |
| 1996 | 92 | 2004 | 2008 |
| 1995 | 86 | 2000 | 2003 |
| 1994 | 88 | 1999 | 2002 |
| 1993 | 93 | 2001 | 2005 |

A
B
C
D
E
F
G
H
I
J
K
L
M
N
O
P
Q
R
S
T
U
V
**W**
X
Y
Z

## THE STOCKS

**McLaren Vale**      $30–$49
**Current vintage: 2002**     93

A polished, show pony-like shiraz whose meaty aroma of sweet plums, blackberries, cassis and blueberries overlies prune and currant-like nuances plus high-toned smoky, bacony new oak. Luscious, smooth and very ripe, its silky-fine and sumptuous palate just borders on over-ripeness, but is tightly shaped by fine, silky tannins and lively acids. A real change in style for this label.

| | | | |
|---|---|---|---|
| 2002 | 93 | 2007 | 2010+ |
| 2001 | 90 | 2003 | 2006+ |
| 2000 | 89 | 2002 | 2005+ |
| 1999 | 89 | 2001 | 2004+ |
| 1998 | 96 | 2010 | 2018 |
| 1997 | 87 | 1999 | 2002 |
| 1996 | 95 | 2004 | 2008 |
| 1995 | 92 | 2003 | 2007 |
| 1994 | 95 | 2002 | 2006 |
| 1993 | 93 | 2001 | 2005 |
| 1991 | 89 | 1999 | 2003 |

# Wyndham Estate

Dalwood Road, Dalwood NSW 2335. Tel: (02) 4938 3444. Fax: (02) 4938 3422.
Website: www.wyndhamestate.com.au

Region: **Various, Lower Hunter Valley** Winemaker: **Brett McKinnon** Viticulturist: **Stephen Guilbaud-Oulton**
Chief Executive: **Laurent Lacassgne**

While Wyndham Estate continues to release impressively flavoursome and polished wines under its re-invented Bin labels, the real quality story here lies in the 1998 edition of the Show Reserve Shiraz, a cracking good Hunter wine of elegance, complexity and exceptional balance.

## BIN 222 CHARDONNAY

**Various**      $12–$19
**Current vintage: 2003**     88

Vibrant, well-made and refreshing chardonnay whose peachy aromas of green cashews and citrus are supported by sweet, lightly dusty and toasty oak. Juicy, tangy and forward, it's fruit-driven and tightly balanced, with a refreshingly clean finish.

| | | | |
|---|---|---|---|
| 2003 | 88 | 2004 | 2005+ |
| 2002 | 89 | 2003 | 2004+ |
| 2001 | 88 | 2003 | 2006 |
| 2000 | 79 | 2001 | 2002 |

## BIN 555 SHIRAZ

**Various**      $12–$19
**Current vintage: 2001**     87

Good honest red with a spicy and lightly herbal aroma of raspberries, cherries and vanilla/chocolate oak before a slightly jammy, but smooth and easy-drinking palate. Its lively berry flavours, creamy oak, spicy cinnamon notes and earthy undertones finish with brightness and freshness.

| | | | |
|---|---|---|---|
| 2001 | 87 | 2003 | 2006 |
| 2000 | 82 | 2001 | 2002 |
| 1999 | 86 | 2001 | 2004+ |
| 1998 | 82 | 2000 | 2003 |
| 1997 | 88 | 1999 | 2002 |
| 1996 | 86 | 1998 | 2001 |
| 1995 | 86 | 2000 | 2003 |

## BIN 888 CABERNET MERLOT

**Various**      $12–$19
**Current vintage: 2001**     87

Elegant, fine and harmonious blend with an earthy, slightly muddy aroma of small berries and cedary oak. Smooth and supple, it's restrained but brightly flavoured, with vibrant cassis/raspberry fruit and cedar/vanilla oak finishing with appealing length, tightness and balance.

| | | | |
|---|---|---|---|
| 2001 | 87 | 2003 | 2006+ |
| 2000 | 81 | 2002 | 2005 |
| 1999 | 86 | 2001 | 2004 |
| 1998 | 80 | 2002 | 2003 |
| 1997 | 90 | 2002 | 2005+ |
| 1996 | 89 | 2001 | 2004 |
| 1995 | 86 | 2000 | 2003 |

## SHOW RESERVE SEMILLON

RANKING **4**

| Lower Hunter Valley | $20–$29 |
| Current vintage: 1997 | 88 |

Developing toasty, buttery aromas of lime and baby powder, with dusty, chalky undertones of lemon rind and confection. Its citrusy melon fruit has length and freshness; finishing with soft, clean acids.

| 1997 | 88 | 2005 | 2009 |
|------|----|------|------|
| 1996 | 90 | 2004 | 2009 |
| 1995 | 90 | 2003 | 2007+ |
| 1994 | 87 | 1999 | 2002 |

## SHOW RESERVE SHIRAZ

RANKING **5**

| Lower Hunter Valley | $30–$49 |
| Current vintage: 1998 | 95 |

Classic medium to full-bodied Hunter shiraz of magnificent depth, balance and longevity. Its sweet smoky leathery aromas of red berries and dark plums reveal complex and slightly funky, reductive notes of earth and cooked meat. It's silky-smooth and ripe, delivering deliciously vibrant and spicy dark plum and berry flavours against an earthy background of tightly integrated oak and fine-grained tannins. It finishes long, earthy and savoury.

| 1998 | 95 | 2010 | 2018+ |
|------|----|------|-------|
| 1997 | 88 | 2002 | 2005+ |
| 1996 | 87 | 2001 | 2004+ |
| 1995 | 87 | 2000 | 2003 |
| 1993 | 95 | 2001 | 2005+ |

# Wynns Coonawarra Estate

Memorial Drive, Coonawarra SA 5263. Tel: (08) 8736 3266. Fax: (08) 8736 3202.
Website: www.wynns.com.au

Region: **Coonawarra** Winemaker: **Sue Hodder** Viticulturist: **Alan Jenkins** Chief Executive: **John Ballard**

Southcorp, owners of the Wynns Coonawarra brand, are presently undertaking a major project to clean up and rejuvenate its Coonawarra vineyards, of which the Wynns label is the major recipient. Years of mechanical pruning have created very crowded and woody canopies leading to poor fruit exposure, irregular bunch size and increased risk of disease, which in the most severe cases are being redressed by entirely removing the existing canopy, and effectively starting again from single canes. The first vintage to really benefit from these renovations was 2003, which has produced some exceptional parcels of wine.

## CABERNET SAUVIGNON

RANKING **4**

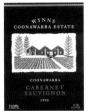

| Coonawarra | $20–$29 |
| Current vintage: 2001 | 90 |

Developing, slightly sweaty, tarry aromas of leather and chocolates, dark olives, plums and prunes with earthy undertones. Slightly cooked, robust palate of deep plum/cassis fruit framed by firm tannins and savoury oak. Older style, but quite advanced.

| 2001 | 90 | 2006 | 2009+ |
|------|----|------|-------|
| 2000 | 89 | 2005 | 2008 |
| 1999 | 89 | 2004 | 2007 |
| 1998 | 90 | 2006 | 2010 |
| 1997 | 88 | 2002 | 2005 |
| 1996 | 90 | 2004 | 2008 |
| 1995 | 90 | 2003 | 2007 |
| 1994 | 94 | 2006 | 2014 |
| 1993 | 93 | 2005 | 2013 |
| 1992 | 91 | 2000 | 2004 |
| 1991 | 95 | 2003 | 2011+ |
| 1990 | 95 | 2002 | 2010+ |

## CABERNET SHIRAZ MERLOT

| Coonawarra | $12–$19 |
| Current vintage: 2002 | 87 |

Lightly herbal, early-drinking blend with floral aromas of dried herbs, sweet blackcurrants and creamy vanilla oak. Smooth and supple, its slightly green-edged palate of medium to full weight offers lively, spicy plum, blackberry and cassis-like flavours supported by sweet oak and fine, soft tannins.

| 2002 | 87 | 2004 | 2007 |
|------|----|------|------|
| 2000 | 82 | 2002 | 2005 |
| 1999 | 82 | 2001 | 2004 |
| 1998 | 85 | 2000 | 2003 |
| 1997 | 83 | 1999 | 2002 |
| 1996 | 88 | 2004 | 2010 |
| 1995 | 90 | 2000 | 2003 |
| 1994 | 89 | 1999 | 2002 |

## CHARDONNAY

RANKING

| Coonawarra | $12–$19 |
|---|---|
| Current vintage: 2003 | 88 |

A soft, generous and rather restrained chardonnay with less oak than many today. Restrained nutty aromas of tropical fruit and oatmeal precede a smooth, creamy palate of richness and softness, whose melon and lemony fruit flavours culminate in a lingering finish of melon and apple.

| | | | |
|---|---|---|---|
| 2003 | 88 | 2005 | 2008 |
| 2002 | 84 | 2002 | 2004+ |
| 2001 | 88 | 2003 | 2006 |
| 2000 | 82 | 2001 | 2002 |
| 1999 | 87 | 2001 | 2004 |
| 1998 | 89 | 2000 | 2003 |
| 1997 | 88 | 1999 | 2002 |

## JOHN RIDDOCH CABERNET SAUVIGNON

RANKING

| Coonawarra | $50+ |
|---|---|
| Current vintage: 1999 | 95 |

Deep dark scents of plums, dark olives, mulberries and blackcurrants, with a dusty, earthy background of sweet leather, chocolate and cloves. Presently a little raw and angular, but destined to soften and integrate, its firm, drying and powdery palate reveals a plush core of intense dark fruit. More fruit sweetness than the comparatively subdued 1998 vintage.

| | | | |
|---|---|---|---|
| 1999 | 95 | 2019 | 2029 |
| 1998 | 95 | 2010 | 2018+ |
| 1997 | 89 | 2005 | 2009 |
| 1996 | 95 | 2016 | 2026 |
| 1994 | 95 | 2006 | 2014 |
| 1993 | 94 | 2001 | 2005 |
| 1992 | 93 | 2004 | 2012 |
| 1991 | 94 | 2003 | 2011 |
| 1990 | 96 | 2010 | 2020 |
| 1988 | 91 | 2000 | 2005 |
| 1987 | 93 | 1999 | 2004 |
| 1986 | 94 | 1998 | 2006 |
| 1985 | 90 | 1993 | 1997 |
| 1984 | 89 | 1992 | 1996 |
| 1982 | 96 | 1994 | 2002+ |

## MICHAEL SHIRAZ

RANKING

| Coonawarra | $50+ |
|---|---|
| Current vintage: 1999 | 89 |

Rather simple and jammy for this label; its dark, earthy aroma of dark plums and cassis is backed by licorice and treacle. Ripe and soft, its generous but uncomplicated fruit finishes savoury and firm, and the wine is permeated throughout by a greenish, sappy texture.

| | | | |
|---|---|---|---|
| 1999 | 89 | 2007 | 2011 |
| 1998 | 95 | 2010 | 2018 |
| 1997 | 87 | 2002 | 2005 |
| 1996 | 94 | 2008 | 2016 |
| 1994 | 96 | 2006 | 2014 |
| 1993 | 95 | 2005 | 2013 |
| 1991 | 95 | 2003 | 2011 |
| 1990 | 94 | 2002 | 2010 |
| 1955 | 97 | 1975 | 1985 |

## RIESLING

RANKING

| Coonawarra | $12–$19 |
|---|---|
| Current vintage: 2002 | 90 |

Delicate aromas of pear, apple and distinctive muscat-like spiciness precede a tangy, juicy palate whose generous and refreshing expression of oily lime/apple fruit finishes crisp and crunchy.

| | | | |
|---|---|---|---|
| 2002 | 90 | 2007 | 2010 |
| 2001 | 90 | 2006 | 2009 |
| 2000 | 90 | 2005 | 2008 |
| 1999 | 86 | 2001 | 2004 |
| 1998 | 90 | 2003 | 2006 |
| 1997 | 86 | 2002 | 2005 |
| 1996 | 90 | 2001 | 2004 |
| 1995 | 85 | 1997 | 2000 |
| 1994 | 91 | 1999 | 2002 |

## SHIRAZ

RANKING

| Coonawarra | $20–$29 |
|---|---|
| Current vintage: 2002 | 91 |

Supple, elegant Coonawarra shiraz with a musky, spicy floral perfume of intense blackcurrant, blackberry and plum. Smooth and silky, its sweet, supple expression of restrained dark berry fruit might lack real concentration and length, but presents delightfully peppery, spicy varietal qualities.

| | | | |
|---|---|---|---|
| 2002 | 91 | 2004 | 2007+ |
| 2001 | 86 | 2003 | 2006 |
| 2000 | 87 | 2002 | 2005 |
| 1999 | 89 | 2004 | 2007 |
| 1998 | 89 | 2003 | 2006 |
| 1997 | 88 | 2002 | 2005 |
| 1996 | 84 | 1998 | 2001 |
| 1995 | 89 | 2000 | 2003 |
| 1994 | 87 | 1996 | 1999 |
| 1993 | 88 | 1998 | 2001 |
| 1992 | 91 | 2000 | 2004 |
| 1991 | 89 | 1996 | 1999 |

# Xanadu

Boodjidup Road, Margaret River WA 6285. Tel: (08) 9757 2581. Fax: (08) 9757 3389.
Website: www.xanadunormans.com.au  Email: info@xanadunormans.com.au

Region: **Margaret River** Winemaker: **Jurg Muggli** Viticulturist: **Peter Gherardi** Chief Executive: **Sam Atkins**

At time of writing Xanadu is battling on a fiscal front, as well as dealing with the consequences of a serious fire that apparently damaged a substantial volume of its premier level stock. From a quality perspective, recent vintages haven't lived up to the company's potential or track record. One hopes that it is shortly able to fulfill the undoubted potential of its Margaret River vineyards.

## CABERNET MERLOT (Formerly Cabernet Sauvignon)

RANKING **5**

| Margaret River | $30–$49 |
|---|---|
| **Current vintage: 2002** | **89** |

Smooth, elegant and quite a complex blend whose earthy, muddy aromas of red berries, dark cherries and chocolate/vanilla oak precede a smooth, easy-drinking palate. Its sweet fruit, restrained oak and fine tannins comprise a generous, flavoursome and approachable regional red.

| | | | |
|---|---|---|---|
| 2002 | 88 | 2004 | 2007 |
| 2001 | 89 | 2006 | 2009+ |
| 2000 | 83 | 2002 | 2005 |
| 1999 | 89 | 2007 | 2011 |
| 1998 | 83 | 2003 | 2006 |
| 1997 | 87 | 2002 | 2005 |
| 1996 | 91 | 2004 | 2008 |
| 1995 | 94 | 2007 | 2014 |
| 1994 | 91 | 1999 | 2002 |
| 1993 | 94 | 2005 | 2013 |
| 1992 | 94 | 2000 | 2004 |
| 1991 | 91 | 2003 | 2011 |
| 1990 | 87 | 1992 | 1995 |
| 1989 | 88 | 1997 | 2001 |

## CHARDONNAY

RANKING **4**

| Margaret River | $20–$29 |
|---|---|
| **Current vintage: 2003** | **88** |

Complex, heavily worked wine with estery, spicy and slightly varnishy aromas of peach, melon, tropical fruits and oatmeal over assertive vanilla oak. Smooth and oaky, its concentrated palate is rich, buttery and creamy, with a lingering savoury finish of peach/apricot fruit. Oaky at present, but likely to settle down.

| | | | |
|---|---|---|---|
| 2003 | 88 | 2005 | 2008 |
| 2002 | 90 | 2004 | 2007 |
| 2001 | 88 | 2003 | 2006+ |
| 2000 | 93 | 2005 | 2008 |
| 1999 | 87 | 2001 | 2004 |
| 1998 | 92 | 2003 | 2006 |
| 1997 | 90 | 2002 | 2005 |
| 1996 | 94 | 2004 | 2008 |
| 1995 | 91 | 1997 | 2000 |
| 1994 | 94 | 2002 | 2006 |

## LAGAN ESTATE RESERVE

| Margaret River | $50+ |
|---|---|
| **Current vintage: 2000** | **82** |

Lean, green and oaky, with light, vegetal fruit lacking genuine ripeness.

| | | | |
|---|---|---|---|
| 2000 | 82 | 2005 | 2008 |
| 1999 | 83 | 2004 | 2007 |
| 1998 | 83 | 2000 | 2003+ |
| 1997 | 83 | 1999 | 2002 |
| 1996 | 87 | 2008 | 2016 |
| 1995 | 90 | 2003 | 2007+ |
| 1994 | 90 | 2006 | 2014 |
| 1993 | 93 | 2005 | 2013 |
| 1992 | 95 | 2004 | 2012 |
| 1991 | 95 | 2003 | 2011+ |
| 1990 | 94 | 2002 | 2010 |

## MERLOT

| Margaret River | $30–$49 |
|---|---|
| **Current vintage: 2002** | **86** |

A smoky, cedary and chocolatey red of moderately full weight with dark plum and cherry fruit, fine tannins and lively, assertive acidity. Earthy and savoury, rather lean and tight, it just lacks genuine flesh and structure.

| | | | |
|---|---|---|---|
| 2002 | 86 | 2004 | 2007+ |
| 2001 | 84 | 2003 | 2006+ |
| 2000 | 87 | 2005 | 2008 |
| 1999 | 81 | 2001 | 2004 |
| 1998 | 82 | 2000 | 2003 |
| 1997 | 75 | 1999 | 2002 |

## SECESSION WHITE BLEND

**Various, WA**      $12–$19
**Current vintage: 2003**      86

Lightly grassy, sweaty aromas of tropical fruits, gooseberries and melon precede a juicy but restrained palate whose juicy, grassy fruit finishes slightly short, but with clean, lemony acids.

| | | | |
|---|---|---|---|
| 2003 | 86 | 2003 | 2003 |
| 2002 | 89 | 2003 | 2004 |
| 2001 | 86 | 2002 | 2003 |
| 2000 | 87 | 2000 | 2001 |
| 1999 | 89 | 2000 | 2001+ |

## SEMILLON

RANKING 3

**Margaret River**      $20–$29
**Current vintage: 2003**      87

Heavily oaked, toasty and slightly brassy semillon whose herby, melon-like fruit is slightly subdued by creamy, toasty barrel ferment influences. Broad and charry, its generous, oaky palate of oily green melon flavours has roundness and texture, before a long, but charry finish.

| | | | |
|---|---|---|---|
| 2003 | 87 | 2005 | 2008 |
| 2002 | 94 | 2004 | 2007+ |
| 2001 | 92 | 2003 | 2006+ |
| 2000 | 89 | 2002 | 2005 |
| 1999 | 82 | 2001 | 2004 |
| 1998 | 93 | 2003 | 2006 |
| 1997 | 93 | 2002 | 2005 |
| 1996 | 94 | 2001 | 2004 |
| 1995 | 87 | 1996 | 1997 |

# Yalumba

Eden Valley Road, Angaston SA 5353. Tel: (08) 8561 3200. Fax: (08) 8561 3393.
Website: www.yalumba.com  Email: info@yalumba.com

Regions: **Barossa, Coonawarra** Winemakers: **Alan Hoey, Kevin Glastonbury, Louisa Rose, Natalie Fryar**
Viticulturist: **Robin Nettelbeck** Chief Executive: **Robert Hill Smith**

This large, historic and family-owned winery has added to the excellent riesling it makes under the Heggies Vineyard and Pewsey Vale labels with three excellent vintages of its Hand Picked Eden Valley Reserve Riesling, of which the 2001 wine is truly formidable. The latest 'D' sparkling wine is also very impressive. As a group, the most recent red releases reveal some herbal and cooked influences suggestive of raisined grapes left out hanging in the vineyard beyond the vine's ability to concentrate sugars through photosynthesis alone.

## BAROSSA CABERNET SHIRAZ

**Barossa Valley**      $12–$19
**Current vintage: 2001**      85

Floral, herbal and sweet, jammy aromas of raspberries, spicy cherries and vanilla oak with violet-like undertones, before a forward, juicy and fleshy palate whose confectionary-like berry fruits and vanilla/coconut oak are framed by slightly sappy tannins. Finishes a shade herbal.

| | | | |
|---|---|---|---|
| 2001 | 85 | 2003 | 2006 |
| 2000 | 87 | 2002 | 2005+ |
| 1999 | 82 | 2001 | 2004 |
| 1998 | 85 | 2000 | 2003 |

## BAROSSA SHIRAZ

 RANKING 5

**Barossa Valley**      $12–$19
**Current vintage: 2001**      87

Polished, assertive and regional shiraz with spicy, lightly minty aromas of violets, cassis, brambly small berries and menthol. Smooth and oaky, its creamy palate of intense small dark fruits and plums finishes with meaty, savoury characters.

| | | | |
|---|---|---|---|
| 2001 | 87 | 2003 | 2006 |
| 2000 | 87 | 2002 | 2005 |
| 1999 | 87 | 2001 | 2004+ |
| 1998 | 87 | 2000 | 2003 |
| 1997 | 90 | 2002 | 2005 |
| 1996 | 86 | 1998 | 2001 |
| 1995 | 89 | 1997 | 2000 |

# BAROSSA SHIRAZ VIOGNIER

RANKING **5**

**Barossa Valley** $30–$49
**Current vintage: 2002** 91

Smoky, oaky, perfumed and voluptuous northern Rhône blend slightly bullied by its modest dose of viognier, but delightful all the same. Its musky floral perfume of spicy dark berries, plums and sweet vanilla/chocolate oak precedes a plump, juicy and chocolatey palate saturated with vibrant cassis, plum and raspberry flavour that manages to finish with a fineness and tightness that borders on leanness. Framed by lightly drying and fine tannins, it has a future.

| | | | |
|---|---|---|---|
| 2002 | 91 | 2007 | 2010 |
| 2000 | 88 | 2002 | 2005 |
| 1999 | 88 | 2004 | 2007 |
| 1998 | 87 | 2000 | 2003+ |

# BUSH VINE GRENACHE

RANKING **5**

**Barossa Valley** $12–$19
**Current vintage: 2002** 89

Likely to develop delightful roundness and smoothness with time, this vibrant young red has a clove and cinnamon-like aroma of blueberries, raspberries and cherries, backed by dark plums and bubblegum-like oak. Underpinned by fine, firm tannins, its spicy small berry flavours are bright and lively.

| | | | |
|---|---|---|---|
| 2002 | 89 | 2004 | 2007+ |
| 2001 | 89 | 2003 | 2006+ |
| 2000 | 88 | 2002 | 2005 |
| 1999 | 86 | 2001 | 2004+ |
| 1998 | 89 | 2003 | 2006 |
| 1997 | 90 | 2002 | 2005 |
| 1996 | 87 | 1998 | 2001 |

# 'D' CUVÉE

RANKING **3**

**Tasmania, Victoria, South Australia** $30–$49
**Current vintage: 1999** 95

One of the best Australian sparkling wines around today, this complex and shapely offering from Yalumba has a complex, nutty and dusty bouquet of citrus fruit, cherries and sweet raspberries, with suggestions of creamy, bakery yeast. Smooth and creamy, with a crackly bead and racy acidity, it presents a long and refreshing palate with a lingering core of nutty, citrus, pear and apple flavours.

| | | | |
|---|---|---|---|
| 1999 | 95 | 2004 | 2007 |
| 1998 | 89 | 2003 | 2006 |
| 1997 | 90 | 1999 | 2002 |
| 1996 | 93 | 2001 | 2004 |
| 1995 | 90 | 2000 | 2003 |
| 1994 | 94 | 1999 | 2002 |

# EDEN VALLEY VIOGNIER

RANKING **5**

**Eden Valley** $12–$19
**Current vintage: 2003** 90

A measured, stylish viognier with a delicate nutty perfume of spicy floral notes. Juicy and up-front, it settles into a long, fine and elegant palate of restraint and freshness, finishing clean and dry with lemon and apricot flavours.

| | | | |
|---|---|---|---|
| 2003 | 90 | 2004 | 2005+ |
| 2002 | 89 | 2003 | 2004+ |
| 2001 | 88 | 2003 | 2006 |
| 2000 | 88 | 2001 | 2002 |
| 1999 | 86 | 2000 | 2001 |
| 1998 | 90 | 1999 | 2000 |

# HAND PICKED EDEN VALLEY RIESLING

RANKING **2**

**Eden Valley** $20–$29
**Current vintage: 2002** 94

Fragrant, flowery and lightly spicy aromas of lime juice, pears and apples. Forward, tangy palate of translucent riesling flavours, building towards a long, minerally finish of tightness and elegance.

| | | | |
|---|---|---|---|
| 2002 | 94 | 2007 | 2010 |
| 2001 | 95 | 2009 | 2013+ |
| 2000 | 94 | 2008 | 2012 |

# THE MENZIES CABERNET SAUVIGNON

RANKING **5**

**Coonawarra** $20–$29
**Current vintage: 2000** 86

Leafy, herbal aromas of mulberries and raspberry confiture, with cedary vanilla oak and undertones of dried herbs. Lean, tight and lacking real generosity, the palate offers some lightly cassis/mulberry fruit supported by cedar/vanilla oak and slightly raw, green-edged tannins.

| | | | |
|---|---|---|---|
| 2000 | 86 | 2005 | 2008 |
| 1999 | 89 | 2004 | 2007+ |
| 1998 | 88 | 2003 | 2006 |
| 1997 | 87 | 2002 | 2005 |
| 1996 | 94 | 2004 | 2008+ |
| 1995 | 89 | 2000 | 2003 |
| 1994 | 87 | 2006 | 2014 |
| 1993 | 89 | 2001 | 2005 |
| 1992 | 93 | 2002 | 2004 |

# THE OCTAVIUS SHIRAZ

RANKING **3**

| Barossa Valley | $50+ |
|---|---|
| **Current vintage: 2000** | **89** |

Typically oaky and concentrated, with pleasing richness and weight, this rather contrived red offers plenty of flavour but doesn't manage to conceal the under and over-ripe nature of its fruit. Sappy, green edges surround its slightly cooked flavours of plums and redcurrants, while its assertively charry vanilla/coconut oak and blocky tannins lack its customary refinement, complexity and integration.

| | | | |
|---|---|---|---|
| 2000 | 89 | 2008 | 2012 |
| 1999 | 93 | 2011 | 2019 |
| 1998 | 95 | 2006 | 2010 |
| 1997 | 87 | 2002 | 2005 |
| 1996 | 89 | 2004 | 2008 |
| 1995 | 93 | 2003 | 2007 |
| 1994 | 95 | 2002 | 2006+ |
| 1993 | 91 | 1998 | 2001 |
| 1992 | 95 | 2000 | 2004 |
| 1990 | 95 | 2002 | 2010 |

## THE RESERVE (Cabernet Sauvignon & Shiraz)

RANKING **5**

| Barossa Valley | $50+ |
|---|---|
| **Current vintage: 1998** | **86** |

Varnishy aromas of meaty, pruney and currant-like fruit with crushed bullant-like undertones. Suggestive of substantial hang-time, its strongly raisined fruit lacks vitality and freshness. Offering richness and generosity, it's framed by firm and drying tannins.

| | | | |
|---|---|---|---|
| 1998 | 86 | 2003 | 2006+ |
| 1996 | 87 | 2001 | 2004+ |
| 1992 | 87 | 2000 | 2004 |
| 1990 | 94 | 2002 | 2010+ |

## THE SIGNATURE (Cabernet Sauvignon & Shiraz)

RANKING **2**

| Barossa Valley | $30–$49 |
|---|---|
| **Current vintage: 2000** | **89** |

Tightly built, integrated but green-edged wine that just lacks the brightness and ripeness of fruit for a higher score. Its sweet menthol-like flavours of dark berries, currants and raisins are beefed up by mocha/chocolate oak. It's firm and generous, with a rather dusty, drying extract.

| | | | |
|---|---|---|---|
| 2000 | 89 | 2008 | 2012 |
| 1999 | 94 | 2011 | 2019 |
| 1998 | 95 | 2010 | 2018+ |
| 1997 | 89 | 2005 | 2009 |
| 1996 | 95 | 2008 | 2016 |
| 1995 | 90 | 2003 | 2007 |
| 1994 | 94 | 2006 | 2014 |
| 1993 | 93 | 2001 | 2005 |
| 1992 | 95 | 2004 | 2012 |
| 1991 | 94 | 2003 | 2011 |
| 1990 | 94 | 2002 | 2010 |
| 1989 | 93 | 1994 | 1997 |

## THE VIRGILIUS VIOGNIER

RANKING **4**

| Barossa Valley | $30–$49 |
|---|---|
| **Current vintage: 2002** | **90** |

Toasty, nutty mealy aromas of ripe, spicy clove and fennel-like viognier are perfumed, earthy, meaty and slightly reductive. Juicy, plump and concentrated, the palate is smooth and buttery, with powerful bacon/butterscotch barrel ferment and malolactic influences that marginally flatten its fruit. The oak is assertive, oily and charry. While the wine does finish with pleasing length and structure, it is too oaky for a higher score.

| | | | |
|---|---|---|---|
| 2002 | 90 | 2003 | 2004+ |
| 2001 | 91 | 2003 | 2006+ |
| 2000 | 87 | 2002 | 2005 |

## TRICENTENARY VINES GRENACHE

RANKING **5**

| Barossa Valley | $20–$29 |
|---|---|
| **Current vintage: 2001** | **87** |

Earthy, restrained and rustic grenache with an earthy, leathery expression of jammy and slightly stewed berry, plum and cherry fruit matured in older oak. Laced throughout by nuances of cloves and fennel, with more than a hint of the farm floor, it's moderately rich and long, with a slightly green-edged finish of metallic tannins.

| | | | |
|---|---|---|---|
| 2001 | 87 | 2003 | 2006+ |
| 2000 | 89 | 2005 | 2008 |
| 1999 | 86 | 2001 | 2004 |

# Yarra Burn

60 Settlement Road, Yarra Junction Vic 3797. Tel: (03) 5967 1428. Fax: (03) 5967 1146.
Website: www.yarraburn.com.au

Region: **Yarra Valley** Winemakers: **Mark O'Callaghan, Ed Carr (sparkling)** Viticulturist: **Ray Guerin**
Chief Executive: **David Woods**

Yarra Burn is The Hardy Wine Company's Yarra Valley brand, and it has access to some of the region's largest vineyards. Its Chardonnay has consistently been a well made and stylish wine, and its long-living Cabernet Sauvignon is usually deeply flavoured, balanced and elegant. This edition introduces the Bastard Hill Chardonnay, a sumptuous and superbly balanced wine named after its rather unfriendly slope at Hoddle's Creek.

## BASTARD HILL CHARDONNAY — RANKING 2

**Yarra Valley**      $30–$49
**Current vintage: 2000**      93

Slightly closed and withdrawn, this uncluttered and restrained chardonnay has a bright and toasty aroma of ripe melon, fig and tobacco with nutty, mealy undertones. Ripe and juicy, its initially concentrated fruit eases into a chalky, leesy palate whose lingering core of intense citrus/melon flavour slightly subdued by sweet buttery/vanilla oak.

| | | | |
|---|---|---|---|
| 2000 | 93 | 2005 | 2008 |
| 1999 | 95 | 2004 | 2007 |
| 1998 | 96 | 2003 | 2006 |
| 1997 | 90 | 2002 | 2004 |
| 1996 | 87 | **1997** | **1998** |
| 1994 | 91 | **1996** | **1999** |

## CABERNET SAUVIGNON — RANKING 3

**Yarra Valley**      $20–$29
**Current vintage: 2002**      89

Elegant, rather leafy cabernet with tightness and harmony. Its fragrant dusty vine leaf aromas of violets, cassis, plums, capsicum and cedar/vanilla oak precede a fine-grained mid-weight palate whose attractive length of intense small berry flavours is bound by loose-knit tannins.

| | | | |
|---|---|---|---|
| 2002 | 89 | 2007 | 2010+ |
| 2001 | 92 | 2009 | 2013+ |
| 2000 | 90 | 2008 | 2012 |
| 1999 | 95 | 2011 | 2019 |
| 1998 | 93 | 2006 | 2010 |
| 1997 | 89 | 2002 | 2005 |
| 1995 | 94 | 2003 | 2007 |
| 1994 | 89 | 1999 | 2002 |
| 1993 | 89 | **1998** | **2001** |
| 1992 | 94 | 2000 | 2004 |

## CHARDONNAY — RANKING 4

**Yarra Valley**      $20–$29
**Current vintage: 2003**      92

Clean, vibrant and fruit-driven chardonnay with a fresh, zesty aroma of peach and melon fruit with undertones of creamy, buttery oak and floral nuances. Tight, long and racy, its intensely flavoured palate of peach, melon and other tropical fruits finishes refreshingly clean and uncluttered.

| | | | |
|---|---|---|---|
| 2003 | 92 | 2005 | 2008+ |
| 2002 | 87 | 2003 | 2004+ |
| 2001 | 90 | 2003 | 2006+ |
| 2000 | 91 | 2005 | 2008 |
| 1999 | 91 | 2001 | 2004 |
| 1998 | 87 | **1999** | **2000** |
| 1997 | 93 | 2002 | 2005 |
| 1996 | 90 | 2001 | 2004 |

## PINOT NOIR — RANKING 5

**Yarra Valley**      $20–$29
**Current vintage: 2002**      87

A well-made wine with some firm, bony tannins and an earthy meaty red cherry fragrance, but with a green herbal thread beneath its aromas and palate. Competent, but just lacks genuine brightness and freshness.

| | | | |
|---|---|---|---|
| 2002 | 87 | 2004 | 2007 |
| 2001 | 89 | 2003 | 2006 |
| 2000 | 87 | 2002 | 2005 |
| 1999 | 82 | 2001 | 2004 |
| 1998 | 87 | 2003 | 2006 |
| 1997 | 92 | 2002 | 2005 |
| 1994 | 75 | 1999 | 2002 |

## SAUVIGNON BLANC SEMILLON — RANKING 5

**Yarra Valley**      $12–$19
**Current vintage: 2003**      87

Lightly grassy blend with a vibrant gooseberry and melon-like aroma before a forward, attractive and herby palate of moderate length and intensity.

| | | | |
|---|---|---|---|
| 2003 | 87 | 2004 | 2005 |
| 2002 | 87 | 2002 | 2003 |
| 2001 | 90 | 2002 | 2003 |
| 2000 | 88 | **2001** | **2002** |
| 1999 | 85 | 2000 | 2001 |

## SHIRAZ

RANKING **5**

| Yarra Valley | $20–$29 |
| --- | --- |
| **Current vintage: 2002** | **89** |

Honest, rustic shiraz with some Rhôney pretensions. Its meaty, spicy and musky aroma of animal
hide reveals lightly greenish berry/plum fruit and
cedar/vanilla oak. Slightly raw and green-edged,
its earthy palate of meaty blackberry and plum
flavour is rather reserved, but finishes with some
hard edges.

| 2002 | 89 | 2007 | 2010 |
| --- | --- | --- | --- |
| 2001 | 86 | 2003 | 2006+ |
| 2000 | 87 | 2003 | 2005+ |
| 1999 | 87 | 2001 | 2004+ |
| 1998 | 89 | 2003 | 2006+ |

## SPARKLING PINOT NOIR CHARDONNAY

RANKING **4**

| Yarra Valley | $20–$29 |
| --- | --- |
| **Current vintage: 2001** | **89** |

Well-made, very restrained and tangy, with a fresh,
delicate and creamy bouquet of lemony/melon
fruit with a light creamy yeastiness. A fine bead
permeates its elegant and refreshing palate of
pleasing length, freshness and vitality.

| 2001 | 89 | 2003 | 2006 |
| --- | --- | --- | --- |
| 2000 | 88 | 2002 | 2005 |
| 1999 | 88 | 2001 | 2004 |
| 1998 | 93 | 2000 | 2003 |
| 1997 | 95 | 1999 | 2002+ |
| 1996 | 85 | 1998 | 2001 |
| 1993 | 87 | 1995 | 2000 |

# Yarra Edge

Edward Road, Lilydale Vic 3140. Tel: (03) 9730 1107. Fax: (03) 9739 0135.
Website: www.yering.com  Email: info@yering.com
Region: **Yarra Valley** Winemaker: **Tom Carson** Viticulturist: **John Evans** Chief Executive: **Gordon Gebbie**
Yarra Edge is a well-sited and mature vineyard overlooking the Yarra River which is planted to chardonnay,
pinot noir and the red Bordeaux varieties. Today the property is leased by Yering Station, which has recently
added a Pinot Noir to its more established labels. Yarra Edge's Chardonnays have become amongst the most
impressive in the Yarra Valley, while the less consistent cabernet blend can present genuine style and finesse.

## SINGLE VINEYARD (Cabernet blend)

RANKING **4**

| Yarra Valley | $30–$49 |
| --- | --- |
| **Current vintage: 1999** | **83** |

Herbal, dusty and leafy aromas of bright berries,
cedar/vanilla oak with capsicum-like undertones. Sweet and forward, but then greenish and
slightly under-ripe, supported to some extent by
sweet vanilla oak.

| 1999 | 83 | 2001 | 2004+ |
| --- | --- | --- | --- |
| 1998 | 88 | 2003 | 2006 |
| 1997 | 94 | 2009 | 2017 |
| 1996 | 83 | 1998 | 2001 |
| 1995 | 93 | 2003 | 2007+ |
| 1994 | 95 | 2006 | 2014 |
| 1993 | 84 | 1998 | 2001 |
| 1992 | 94 | 2000 | 2004 |
| 1991 | 90 | 1999 | 2003 |
| 1990 | 93 | 1998 | 2002 |

## SINGLE VINEYARD CHARDONNAY

RANKING **2**

| Yarra Valley | $30–$49 |
| --- | --- |
| **Current vintage: 2001** | **94** |

A heavily worked Yarra Valley chardonnay of strength
and substance. Smoky, bacony and lightly cheesy
influences and vanilla oak underpin intense
melon and stonefruit aromas. Concentrated and
creamy, yet smooth and stylish, it delivers intense
ripe flavours harmoniously interwoven with
complex winemaking artefact, before finishing
with refreshing mineral acids.

| 2001 | 94 | 2006 | 2009 |
| --- | --- | --- | --- |
| 2000 | 94 | 2005 | 2008 |
| 1999 | 94 | 2004 | 2007 |
| 1998 | 91 | 2003 | 2006 |
| 1997 | 83 | 1999 | 2002 |
| 1996 | 89 | 1998 | 2001 |
| 1995 | 93 | 2000 | 2003 |

# Yarra Ridge

Glenview Road, Yarra Glen Vic 3775. Tel: (03) 9730 1022. Fax: (03) 9730 1131.
Website: www.yarraridge.com.au

Region: **Yarra Valley** Winemaker: **Matt Steel** Viticulturist: **Damien de Castella** Chief Executive: **Jamie Odell**

Unlike its St Huberts brand, whose wines will repay cellaring, Beringer Blass produces early-drinking, flavoursome and up-front wines of pleasing varietal characters under its Yarra Ridge label, whose winery is up for sale at time of writing.

## CHARDONNAY                                                              RANKING 5

| | | | | | |
|---|---|---|---|---|---|
| **Yarra Valley** | $20–$29 | 2003 | 87 | 2004 | 2005+ |
| **Current vintage: 2003** | **87** | 2001 | 90 | 2002 | 2003+ |
| | | 2000 | 87 | 2001 | 2002 |
| Pretty, delicate and shorter-term chardonnay | | 1999 | 86 | 1999 | 2000 |
| with a light, peachy and buttery aroma of fresh | | 1998 | 87 | 1999 | 2000 |
| melon and green olive fruit. Smooth and juicy, | | 1997 | 89 | 1998 | 1999 |
| its soft, buttery and very slightly varnishy palate | | | | | |
| finishes with soft acids and a lingering note of | | | | | |
| cumquat. | | | | | |

## MERLOT

| | | | | | |
|---|---|---|---|---|---|
| **Yarra Valley** | $20–$29 | 2001 | 86 | 2003 | 2006 |
| **Current vintage: 2001** | **86** | 2000 | 81 | 2001 | 2002 |
| | | 1999 | 79 | 2000 | 2001 |
| Cooked and slightly earthy merlot with meaty | | 1998 | 89 | 2000 | 2003 |
| aromas of stewed plums, cherries and sweet, | | 1997 | 89 | 1999 | 2002 |
| assertive vanilla/coconut oak. Smooth and soft, | | 1996 | 87 | 1998 | 2001 |
| round and plummy, it reveals some herbal and | | 1995 | 93 | 1997 | 2000 |
| currant-like edges over smooth toasty vanilla oak, | | 1994 | 89 | 1999 | 2002 |
| finishing a little grippy and greenish. | | 1993 | 82 | 1995 | 1998 |

## PINOT NOIR                                                              RANKING 5

| | | | | | |
|---|---|---|---|---|---|
| **Yarra Valley** | $20–$29 | 2002 | 88 | 2004 | 2007 |
| **Current vintage: 2002** | **88** | 2001 | 82 | 2003 | 2006 |
| | | 2000 | 89 | 2002 | 2005 |
| Juicy, vibrant young pinot with fresh aromas of | | 1999 | 85 | 2000 | 2001 |
| dark cherries, raspberries and sweet vanilla | | 1998 | 84 | 2000 | 2003 |
| /chocolate oak. Smooth and spicy, its attractive | | 1997 | 87 | 1999 | 2002 |
| flavours of dark plum and dark cherries overlie | | 1996 | 90 | 1998 | 2003 |
| lightly herbal nuances, but finish with pleasing | | 1995 | 91 | 2000 | 2003 |
| freshness and vitality. Drink young. | | 1994 | 93 | 1999 | 2002 |

# Yarra Yarra

239 Hunts Lane, Steels Creek Vic 3775. Tel: (03) 5965 2380. Fax: (03) 5965 2086.
Email: wine@yarrayarravineyard.com.au

Region: **Yarra Valley** Winemaker: **Ian Maclean** Viticulturist: **Ian Maclean** Chief Executives: **Ian & Anne Maclean**

Yarra Yarra is a small and dedicated maker of finely crafted Yarra Valley table wines from the Bordeaux varieties. Its premier red, The Yarra Yarra, is usually of considerable stature and finesse, while the Cabernets and tightly-oaked Sauvignon Semillon blend can closely resemble fine white Bordeaux.

## CABERNETS                                                              RANKING 3

| | | | | | |
|---|---|---|---|---|---|
| **Yarra Valley** | $30–$49 | 2000 | 93 | 2012 | 2020 |
| **Current vintage: 2000** | **93** | 1999 | 93 | 2007 | 2011 |
| | | 1998 | 90 | 2003 | 2006 |
| An elegant, silky wine of considerable finesse, with | | 1997 | 91 | 2005 | 2009+ |
| a minty, dusty and lightly herbal perfume of cassis, | | 1996 | 87 | 1998 | 2001+ |
| raspberries, red cherries and sweet, polished | | 1995 | 92 | 2003 | 2007+ |
| cedary oak. Pristine, smooth and penetrative, its | | 1994 | 93 | 2002 | 2006+ |
| fine-grained and tight-knit palate delivers layers | | 1993 | 90 | 2003 | 2007 |
| of red and black berry flavours entwined with cedary | | 1992 | 91 | 2003 | 2007 |
| oak and silky tannins. | | 1991 | 95 | 1999 | 2003+ |
| | | 1990 | 95 | 2002 | 2010+ |

## THE YARRA YARRA (Formerly Reserve Cabernet Sauvignon)

| Yarra Valley | $50+ | 2001 | 83 | 2013 | 2021 |
|---|---|---|---|---|---|
| **Current vintage: 2001** | **83** | 2000 | 96 | 2012 | 2020 |
| | | 1999 | 95 | 2007 | 2011+ |
| Meaty, very cooked and shrivelled characters of | | 1998 | 92 | 2003 | 2006 |
| prunes and currants overlie herbal and green-edged | | 1997 | 89 | 2002 | 2005+ |
| aromas, before an astringent, blocky palate | | 1995 | 95 | 2007 | 2015 |
| whose raisined flavours lack their usually freshness | | 1994 | 89 | 2002 | 2006+ |
| and vitality. | | 1993 | 89 | 1998 | 2001 |

## SAUVIGNON SEMILLON

| Yarra Valley | $30–$49 | 2001 | 88 | 2003 | 2006 |
|---|---|---|---|---|---|
| **Current vintage: 2001** | **88** | 2000 | 83 | 2002 | 2005 |
| | | 1999 | 95 | 2004 | 2007+ |
| Slightly over-oaked, this otherwise convincing white | | 1998 | 88 | 2003 | 2006 |
| Bordeaux look-alike has a lightly oxidised bouquet | | 1997 | 94 | 2002 | 2005 |
| of dried flowers, apples and pears before a soft, | | 1996 | 92 | 2001 | 2004 |
| generous palate of advancing and slightly | | 1995 | 95 | 2003 | 2007 |
| aldehydic flavour. There's undeniable fruit quality | | 1994 | 87 | 1999 | 2002 |
| and smoothness about this wine, which just looks | | 1993 | 86 | 1995 | 1998 |
| to me as if it needed a little more protection and | | | | | |
| less time in oak. | | | | | |

# Yarrabank

38 Melba Highway, Yering Vic 3775. Tel: (03) 9730 1107. Fax: (03) 9739 0135.
Website: www.yering.com  Email: info@yering.com
Region: **Various, Victoria** Winemakers: **Michael Parisot, Tom Carson** Viticulturist: **John Evans**
Chief Executives: **Doug Rathbone & Laurent Gillet**
From the small house of Devaux, Champagne winemaker Claude Thibaut collaborates with Tom Carson of Yering Station in the making of this blend from different Victorian cool climate regions. The exceptional 1999 vintage is a very classy, elegant and mineral wine.

## YARRABANK CUVÉE

| Various, Victoria | $30–$49 | 2000 | 90 | 2002 | 2005+ |
|---|---|---|---|---|---|
| **Current vintage: 1999** | **95** | 1999 | 95 | 2004 | 2007 |
| | | 1998 | 89 | 2000 | 2003+ |
| Nutty, lightly toasty, honey-like and biscuity | | 1997 | 88 | 2002 | 2005 |
| aromas of creamy yeast and citrusy fruit. Generous, | | 1996 | 89 | 2001 | 2004 |
| soft and open palate, supple and restrained, | | 1995 | 96 | 2003 | 2007 |
| with a bright core of vibrant raspberry and | | 1994 | 89 | 1996 | 1999+ |
| cherry fruit. Long and lingering, smooth and buttery, | | 1993 | 94 | 1998 | 2001+ |
| finishing with refreshing mineral acids. | | | | | |

# Yellowglen

White's Road, Smythesdale Vic 3351. Tel: (03) 5342 8617. Fax: (03) 5333 7102.
Website: www.yellowglen.com.au  Email: info@yellowglen.com.au
Region: **Bendigo** Winemaker: **Charles Hargrave** Chief Executive: **Jamie Odell**
Yellowglen is now home to a wide array of fashionably presented and priced 'Y' sparkling wines, but its reputation still rides to some extent on its premium vintage labels that have under-delivered in recent years.

## CUVÉE VICTORIA

| South Australia (?!) | $30–$49 | 1999 | 89 | 2001 | 2004 |
|---|---|---|---|---|---|
| **Current vintage: 1999** | **89** | 1997 | 89 | 1999 | 2002+ |
| | | 1996 | 93 | 2001 | 2004 |
| Smooth, fluffy sparkling wine with a delicate, nutty | | 1995 | 90 | 1997 | 2000 |
| bouquet of creamy leesy influences beneath light | | | | | |
| melon and citrus fruit. Its forward peach/nectarine | | | | | |
| flavours are fresh and clear, while it finishes with | | | | | |
| softness and freshness. Just lacks the length | | | | | |
| and tightness for a higher score. | | | | | |

## VINTAGE BRUT

RANKING **5**

**South-Eastern Australia** $12–$19
**Current vintage: 2000** 83

Toasty and forward, with up-front melon, apple and lemon sherbet flavours, its tobaccoey palate becomes rather hollow, lacking length and freshness.

| | | | |
|---|---|---|---|
| 2000 | 83 | 2002 | 2005 |
| 1999 | 87 | 2001 | 2004 |
| 1998 | 87 | 2000 | 2003 |
| 1997 | 88 | 1999 | 2002 |
| 1996 | 89 | 1998 | 2001 |

# Yering Station

38 Melba Highway, Yering Vic 3775. Tel: (03) 9730 0100. Fax: (03) 9739 0135.
Website: www.yering.com  Email: info@yering.com

Region: **Yarra Valley** Winemaker: **Tom Carson** Viticulturist: **John Evans** Chief Executive: **Gordon Gebbie**

Yering Station is one of the most impressive new facilities in the Yarra Valley and it has set its sights unquestionably high. The Reserve Chardonnay and Reserve Shiraz Viognier have quickly evolved into classic styles, while the 'standard' wines are finding more consistency and character. Tom Carson and his team are making some very fragrant and flavoursome wines from this Northern Rhône blend, and I doubt if they could ever offer better value for money than the pristine and perfumed Shiraz Viognier from 2002.

## CABERNET SAUVIGNON

RANKING **5**

**Yarra Valley** $20–$29
**Current vintage: 2001** 87

Elegant, slightly sappy cabernet with herbal, cedary aromas of cassis, mulberries and raspberries, with violet undertones. Medium to full weight, it's forward and lively, with a slightly thin middle palate.

| | | | |
|---|---|---|---|
| 2001 | 87 | 2003 | 2006+ |
| 2000 | 83 | 2002 | 2005 |
| 1999 | 89 | 2004 | 2007 |
| 1998 | 82 | 2000 | 2003 |

## CHARDONNAY

RANKING **5**

**Yarra Valley** $20–$29
**Current vintage: 2002** 87

Lightly floral, nutty and peachy/grapefruit aromas are backed by nutty and slightly reductive undertones. Elegant and juicy, it falls a little short, leaving a slightly drying finish of varnishy oak.

| | | | |
|---|---|---|---|
| 2002 | 87 | 2003 | 2004 |
| 2001 | 87 | 2003 | 2006 |
| 2000 | 84 | 2001 | 2002 |
| 1999 | 87 | 2000 | 2001 |
| 1998 | 93 | 2000 | 2003+ |
| 1997 | 90 | 1999 | 2002 |
| 1996 | 80 | 1997 | 1998 |

## E.D. ROSÉ (Pinot Noir)

RANKING **5**

**Yarra Valley** $20–$29
**Current vintage: 2003** 89

Crisp, dry and varietal, this rather chalky, slightly dusty rosé is long, clean and refreshing. It reveals slightly confected floral pinot aromas and juicy flavours of raspberries backed by nuances of forest floor. Uncomplicated, but fun.

| | | | |
|---|---|---|---|
| 2003 | 89 | 2003 | 2004+ |
| 2002 | 82 | 2002 | 2003 |
| 2001 | 83 | 2002 | 2003 |
| 2000 | 87 | 2000 | 2001 |

## PINOT NOIR

**Yarra Valley** $20–$29
**Current vintage: 2003** 86

Light, confectionary and herbal, with some lively berry/cherry fruit, but a little greenish and hollow.

| | | | |
|---|---|---|---|
| 2003 | 86 | 2004 | 2005 |
| 2002 | 86 | 2004 | 2007 |
| 2001 | 80 | 2002 | 2003 |
| 2000 | 88 | 2002 | 2005 |
| 1999 | 83 | 2000 | 2001 |
| 1998 | 89 | 2000 | 2003 |
| 1997 | 87 | 1998 | 1999 |
| 1996 | 88 | 1998 | 2001 |

## RESERVE CHARDONNAY

**Yarra Valley** $50+
**Current vintage: 2002** 95

Very delicate, perfumed, almost fragile expression of chardonnay destined to develop dramatically in the bottle. Its aromas of melon, grapefruit and light grainy oak are presently rather closed and floral, while its long, creamy palate of stonefruit and citrus, apple and pear, culminates in soft acids and lingering suggestions of quince and cumquat. Its flavours are bright and clear, while its slightly baby fat-like texture finishes with tightness and elegance. Excellent balance and harmony.

| | | | |
|---|---|---|---|
| 2002 | 95 | 2007 | 2010+ |
| 2001 | 95 | 2006 | 2009 |
| 1999 | 95 | 2004 | 2007+ |
| 1997 | 95 | 2002 | 2005 |

## RESERVE PINOT NOIR

**Yarra Valley** $50+
**Current vintage: 2002** 88

Lightly perfumed, fragrant and minty aromas of maraschino cherries, raspberries and plums over dusty nuances of cedary oak and earthy undertones. Lean and tight, but intensely flavoured, the firm and fine-grained palate offers texture and weight, but reveals an undercurrent of vegetal influences likely to evolve into tobaccoey complexity.

| | | | |
|---|---|---|---|
| 2002 | 88 | 2004 | 2007+ |
| 2000 | 90 | 2002 | 2005+ |
| 1998 | 87 | 2000 | 2003+ |
| 1997 | 93 | 2002 | 2005 |

## RESERVE SHIRAZ VIOGNIER

**Yarra Valley** $50+
**Current vintage: 2002** 96

Marvellously elegant, complex Rhône-influenced shiraz that simply flaunts its spotlessly pure, aromas of dark berries, flowers and musky spices. There's plenty of new oak in evidence, together with pungent, meaty complexity. Searingly intense, it's tightly focused and saturated with small berry flavours, while it finishes long and savoury with lingering earthy, meaty undertones. Superbly elegant and integrated.

| | | | |
|---|---|---|---|
| 2002 | 96 | 2014 | 2022 |
| 2001 | 93 | 2006 | 2009+ |
| 1998 | 90 | 2003 | 2006+ |
| 1997 | 95 | 2005 | 2009 |

## SHIRAZ VIOGNIER

**Yarra Valley** $20–$29
**Current vintage: 2002** 94

Perfumed, spicy aromas of cinnamon, apricot blossom, rose petals, black pepper and cloves over deep, dark and briary scents of redcurrants and blackberries with a meaty element beneath. Smooth and creamy, long and vibrant, its pristine, measured palate of pure dark berry flavours finishes with velvet-smooth tannins and lingering spicy fruits. A fine example of what the Yarra Valley might well be doing more of.

| | | | |
|---|---|---|---|
| 2002 | 94 | 2007 | 2010 |
| 2001 | 92 | 2003 | 2006+ |
| 2000 | 86 | 2002 | 2005 |
| 1999 | 81 | 2000 | 2001 |

# Yeringberg

Maroondah Highway, Yeringberg, Coldstream Vic 3770. Tel: (03) 9739 1453. Fax: (03) 9739 0048.

Region: **Yarra Valley** Winemaker: **Guill De Pury** Viticulturist: **David De Pury** Chief Executive: **Guill De Pury**

Yeringberg makes small volumes of fastidiously grown and produced wine in the cellars beneath its historic 19th century winery. The 2003 white wines are typically fine and flavoursome, the Marsanne Roussanne blend being the most punchy and forward for many vintages. Yeringberg's reds are supple and smooth, and depend on their fine balance with tight-knit tannins for their remarkable longevity.

## CHARDONNAY

RANKING **2**

**Yarra Valley** $30–$49
**Current vintage: 2003** 93

Shapely cool climate chardonnay whose delicate lemony fragrance of spicy apples, cashew nuts and dried flowers reveals a bubblegum-like nuance of barrel fermentation. Long and elegant, its powdery, nutty palate presents flavours of peaches and melons above suggestions of earthy complexity. Tightly integrated and dry, certain to build in the bottle.

| | | | |
|---|---|---|---|
| 2003 | 93 | 2008 | 2011 |
| 2002 | 94 | 2007 | 2010 |
| 2001 | 93 | 2006 | 2009+ |
| 2000 | 95 | 2005 | 2008+ |
| 1999 | 89 | 2004 | 2007 |
| 1998 | 95 | 2003 | 2006 |
| 1997 | 94 | 2005 | 2009 |
| 1996 | 94 | 2004 | 2008 |
| 1995 | 92 | 2003 | 2007 |

## MARSANNE ROUSSANNE

RANKING **3**

**Yarra Valley** $30–$49
**Current vintage: 2003** 94

Dusty, dry and savoury, this complex, nutty and chalky wine has a light lemony perfume of apples and cloves with tightly integrated fine-grained oak influences. There's length and tightness, with a fleshy middle of nutty stonefruit and citrus flavours. Quite assertive for this label, it does finish with customary length and restraint.

| | | | |
|---|---|---|---|
| 2003 | 94 | 2008 | 2011+ |
| 2002 | 90 | 2007 | 2010+ |
| 2001 | 93 | 2009 | 2013 |
| 2000 | 93 | 2008 | 2012 |
| 1999 | 93 | 2007 | 2011 |
| 1998 | 93 | 2003 | 2006 |
| 1997 | 94 | 2005 | 2009 |
| 1996 | 91 | 2004 | 2008 |
| 1995 | 88 | 2003 | 2007 |
| 1994 | 94 | 2002 | 2006 |

## PINOT NOIR

RANKING **3**

**Yarra Valley** $50+
**Current vintage: 2002** 94

A sweet perfume of slightly confected raspberry and red cherry fruit, vanilla/caramel oak and floral influences precedes a silky, fine-grained palate with a fleshy, juicy middle of appealing sappiness. Underneath lies a firm, fine-grained chassis of tight-knit bony tannins. With more than a passing resemblance to many modern Pommard reds, it's likely to gain weight and depth with age.

| | | | |
|---|---|---|---|
| 2002 | 94 | 2007 | 2010+ |
| 2001 | 90 | 2003 | 2006 |
| 2000 | 92 | 2005 | 2008 |
| 1999 | 89 | 2004 | 2007 |
| 1998 | 82 | 2000 | 2003 |
| 1997 | 96 | 2005 | 2009 |
| 1996 | 94 | 2004 | 2008 |
| 1995 | 90 | 2000 | 2003 |
| 1994 | 92 | 2002 | 2006 |
| 1993 | 91 | 1995 | 1998 |

## YERINGBERG CABERNET BLEND

RANKING **2**

**Yarra Valley** $50+
**Current vintage: 2002** 89

Compact, fine and elegant blend of moderate length and a pleasingly firm undercarriage of bony tannin. Sweet small berry aromas of dusty oak precede a tight-knit palate of forward raspberry, cherry, plum and mulberry flavours.

| | | | |
|---|---|---|---|
| 2002 | 89 | 2010 | 2014 |
| 2001 | 96 | 2013 | 2021 |
| 2000 | 94 | 2012 | 2020+ |
| 1999 | 92 | 2007 | 2011 |
| 1998 | 95 | 2010 | 2018 |
| 1997 | 95 | 2005 | 2009+ |
| 1996 | 93 | 2004 | 2008 |
| 1995 | 88 | 2003 | 2007 |
| 1994 | 94 | 2006 | 2014 |
| 1993 | 91 | 2001 | 2005 |
| 1992 | 95 | 2012 | 2022 |
| 1991 | 93 | 2003 | 2011 |
| 1990 | 95 | 2002 | 2010+ |
| 1989 | 86 | 1994 | 1997 |
| 1988 | 95 | 2000 | 2008+ |

# Zema Estate

Riddoch Highway, Coonawarra SA 5263. Tel: (08) 8736 3219. Fax: (08) 8736 3280.
Website: www.zema.com.au   Email: zemaestate@zema.com.au

Region: **Coonawarra** Winemaker: **Tom Simons** Viticulturist: **Nick Zema** Chief Executive: **Demetrio Zema**

Zema Estate is a small, family-owned winery whose growth in size and stature has been measured and even. This company now rates amongst the best in Coonawarra, and no Coonawarra vineyard is better managed than the 85 acres of hand-pruned land owned by the Zemas. They were amongst the first in the region to reject the popular forms of mechanical vineyard management that many accuse of diminishing its quality.

## CABERNET SAUVIGNON   RANKING

| Coonawarra | $20–$29 |
|---|---|
| **Current vintage: 2002** | **86** |

Herbal aromas of cassis, dark olives and cedary oak, with leafy capsicum-like undertones. Firm, grippy but slightly sappy, its slightly under and over-ripe fruit is smoothed over by creamy oak.

| | | | |
|---|---|---|---|
| 2002 | 86 | 2004 | 2007+ |
| 2001 | 91 | 2009 | 2013 |
| 2000 | 89 | 2002 | 2005+ |
| 1999 | 93 | 2007 | 2011 |
| 1998 | 94 | 2006 | 2010+ |
| 1997 | 89 | 2002 | 2005 |
| 1996 | 87 | 2001 | 2004 |
| 1995 | 90 | 2000 | 2003 |
| 1994 | 92 | 1999 | 2002 |
| 1993 | 91 | 2001 | 2005 |
| 1992 | 94 | 2000 | 2004 |
| 1991 | 92 | 1999 | 2003 |
| 1990 | 93 | 2002 | 2010 |

## CLUNY   RANKING

| Coonawarra | $12–$19 |
|---|---|
| **Current vintage: 2002** | **87** |

Slightly meaty, herbal and minty aromas of small berry fruits, with capsicum-like undertones. A lightly herbal thread runs beneath its sappy, supple and minty expression of red and black berries, before a dusty, herbal finish.

| | | | |
|---|---|---|---|
| 2002 | 87 | 2004 | 2007+ |
| 2001 | 87 | 2003 | 2006+ |
| 2000 | 82 | 2002 | 2005+ |
| 1999 | 91 | 2004 | 2007 |
| 1998 | 93 | 2006 | 2010 |
| 1997 | 87 | 2002 | 2005 |
| 1996 | 89 | 2001 | 2004 |
| 1995 | 88 | 2000 | 2003 |
| 1994 | 87 | 1999 | 2002 |

## FAMILY SELECTION CABERNET SAUVIGNON   RANKING

| Coonawarra | $30–$49 |
|---|---|
| **Current vintage: 2001** | **94** |

Delightfully intense, concentrated and natural Coonawarra cabernet with a fragrance of violets, mulberries, dark plums, black olives, cherries and sweet cedar/coffee/vanilla oak. Its plump, juicy palate stains the mouth with vibrant, intense flavours of small berries and plums, while polished cedar/vanilla oak and firm, fine tannins provide a comfortable frame and support.

| | | | |
|---|---|---|---|
| 2001 | 94 | 2013 | 2021 |
| 2000 | 88 | 2005 | 2008 |
| 1999 | 92 | 2007 | 2011 |
| 1996 | 94 | 2004 | 2008+ |
| 1994 | 91 | 2002 | 2006 |
| 1993 | 91 | 2001 | 2005 |
| 1992 | 89 | 2000 | 2004 |
| 1991 | 92 | 2003 | 2011 |
| 1990 | 89 | 1998 | 2002 |
| 1988 | 92 | 1996 | 2000 |

## SHIRAZ   RANKING

| Coonawarra | $20–$29 |
|---|---|
| **Current vintage: 2002** | **87** |

A spicy, white pepper fragrance of blackberries, plums, violets and light vanilla oak precedes a smooth, lively and lighter palate whose red and black berry flavours are framed by fine, but slightly sappy tannins. Finishes savoury, with some peppery complexity.

| | | | |
|---|---|---|---|
| 2002 | 87 | 2007 | 2010 |
| 2001 | 90 | 2006 | 2009 |
| 2000 | 89 | 2002 | 2005 |
| 1999 | 89 | 2004 | 2007 |
| 1998 | 95 | 2006 | 2010 |
| 1997 | 87 | 1999 | 2002 |
| 1996 | 88 | 2001 | 2004 |
| 1995 | 90 | 2003 | 2007 |
| 1994 | 88 | 1999 | 2002 |
| 1993 | 94 | 2001 | 2005 |
| 1992 | 89 | 1997 | 2000 |